Camellia
Nomenclature

Twenty-Ninth Revised Edition

2020

BRADFORD D. KING, Editor
RICHARD C. BUGGELN, Co-Editor
BETH M. STONE, Co-Editor

Adopted As The Official Nomenclature Book Of The
American Camellia Society

Contents

Edition Numbering Footnote

It should be noted that the 1981 (17th) Edition of CAMELLIA NOMENCLATURE was designated as the "Historical Edition." Commencing with the 1984 (18th) Edition, a large number of Species, Japonica, and Sasanqua cultivars were deleted to reduce both space and cost. Most, but not all, of the cultivars that were eliminated had been introduced prior to 1950 and, generally speaking, were no longer in "substantial commercial distribution".

The Southern California Camellia Society printed a SUPPLEMENT Edition in 1996 that listed all of the eliminated Species, Japonica, and Sasanqua that were referred to in the preceding paragraph. The combination of the 'SUPPLEMENT' and this Edition will include all of the cultivars that have been listed in CAMELLIA NOMENCLATURE books.

The color photographs in this publication have been
Provided by Bradford D. King

Cover Flower
'Island Sunset' - Red Coral Pink
Medium to large, semidouble.
U. S. 2006 – Nuccio's Nurseries

Introduction

This CAMELLIA NOMENCLATURE edition is a revised, descriptive list of cultivars (varieties) of various species and hybrids generally grown by the amateur camellia hobbyist in the English-speaking world and particularly in the United States of America. Cultivars originating in other countries are generally included only when they are introduced in the United States.

This book and the prior editions are based on a continuing research program by the Nomenclature Research Committee of The Southern California Camellia Society. This committee is composed of qualified people in this field from various camellia growing areas in the United States, and is a non-profit amateur effort. This reference has been adopted throughout the world as the best available source of nomenclature information and is generally used by amateur growers and camellia nurserymen.

The initial and continued purposes of this work are to decrease confusion and settle controversies surrounding the names of both old and new cultivars of camellias, and to present a short, concise nomenclature list for the elucidation and protection of the amateur grower generally.

In the preparation of this book, we have adopted the following procedures:

I.   Adopted and followed the International Code of Nomenclature with certain modifications which we believe necessary in a work published principally for use by the amateur camellia hobbyist.

A. FORMATION AND USE OF NAMES:
1.   Name should be a proper name or a word in common usage, and not a scientific name of Latin form.
2.   Each word of the name must begin with a capital letter, except when national custom requires otherwise.
3.   Single quotation marks are to be used to enclose a name.
4.   Name must be used only once and not for more than one species.
5.   Name preferably should consist of one or two words and should not consist of more than three words. Excessively long words or phrases cannot be used.
     (Example: 'Her Majesty Queen Elizabeth II')
6.   Name of sport should include name of parent as initial word where practicable, for example where a solid colored or variegated cultivar produces one sport consisting of a variegated or solid form and does not violate other rules, e.g., (1) below. However, when a cultivar produces various sports, a name not including the name of the parent is permissible, although reference should be made to the parent in a publication or registration, e.g., (2) below.
     (Example: (1) 'Herme Pink'; (2) 'Colonial Lady')
7.   Names containing an initial article must not be used unless required by linguistic custom.
     (Example: 'The Dove' is not permitted, while 'La Bella' is permitted.)
8.   Name containing initial abbreviation should not be used, except in abbreviations of forms of address.
     (Example: 'St. Andre' for 'Saint Andre')
9.   Name tending to suggest what is improper, indecent, or the like, cannot be used.
10. Although not mandatory, the use of the following names should be avoided:
     (a) Names containing forms of address liable to be confused as distinguished from forms of title.
         (Example: Miss, Mr., Mrs., but forms of title such as Dr., Judge, Capt., etc., are permissible.)
     (b) Name exaggerating the merits of a cultivar.
         (Example: 'Eleanor Martin Supreme')
     (c) Names likely to be confused.

3

(Example: 'Imperial'; 'Imperialis')
(d) Names resulting in a series of names with same initial word.
(Example: 'Pink Ball'; 'Pink Beauty'; 'White Ball'; 'White Beauty')

B. PRIORITY USE OF NAMES:

1. First validly published name has priority, except as hereinafter set forth in Paragraphs 2 and 3. Valid publication consists of listing of the name accompanied by a description sufficient to identify the cultivar in a dated (at least as to year), printed, or similarly duplicated publication which is distributed to the public, including horticultural books or magazines, nursery or trade catalogues, and publications of horticultural societies. Registration with an official registration authority without such valid publication does not give priority.

2. Where impossible to determine first validly published name, the best established and most widely known cultivar name is given priority.

3. Names generally established and in common use will take priority over a name first validly published. If a name has been in long use in the United States and research uncovers an older and first validly published but now obscure designation, we do not favor a change but elect to follow this rule and use the newly discovered name as a synonym to indicate the true situation.

C. CHANGE OF NAMES:

1. Name first validly published cannot be changed, except in the following cases:

(a) Where the same name is used for different species, the name may be changed if reference is made to disclose the former name in any listing or publication.

(b) Translation or transliteration is allowed where there are linguistic or other difficulties, except as to personal names. The first valid published translation or transliteration has priority in the particular language.

(c) Where a cultivar is introduced into another country, and its original name is commercially unacceptable due to the difficulty of pronunciation or when the original name or a translation would have a different connotation or implication, the name may be changed upon approval of the originator.

2. A name generally established or in common use should not be changed to comply with these rules.

II. List as synonyms all other names by which a cultivar may have been known in any given locality and which may have had any general usage. To avoid duplication the complete description of each cultivar is given only under the priority name, but all synonyms are listed after the priority name in parentheses. Cultivar names — synonyms or otherwise — are enclosed with single quotation marks. English translations also follow some of the priority names.

III. Separately named mutations or sports are included and are also listed as part of the description of the parent.

IV. Where an old cultivar has disappeared and its name has been given to a new and different cultivar, a brief description of the old cultivar is given when such facts become known.

V.   Follow, as far as possible, uniform rules as to color, size, form, type of growth, and blooming period in our description of cultivars, which rules are hereinafter set forth under "Classification and Description of Cultivars." Such rules are generally used in the United States.

VI. List source of each cultivar of Species, Japonica, Reticulata, and Non-Reticulata Hybrids in parentheses after the description of the cultivar.

There is also included in this book a list of the Species which are available in the United States.

The originators of the names of cultivars listed are from registrations, publications, and written requests by or on behalf of the originator. Any request for a listing must contain the name, form, size, color, and other description in accordance with the rules and regulations as set forth in the Introduction section of this CAMELLIA NOMENCLATURE.

In a work of this attempted size and scope, there always will be errors and omissions, as our judgment and knowledge cannot always be perfect. We hope and believe, however, that this effort to clarify and systematize this subject will be helpful to camellia amateurs and nurserymen alike, and will lead to greater universal interest in this our favorite flower. We especially invite comments and corrections, so that subsequent revisions may become as nearly perfect as possible.

Partial Originator/Source List

ORIGINATOR ALSO LISTED AT THE END OF MOST CULTIVAR DESCRIPTIONS

Ackerman, Dr. W. L., Ashton, MD
Alfter, Ted — Bakersfield, CA
Allan, Walter — Summerville, SC
Armstrong Nurseries — Ontario, CA
Arnesen, Edward B. — San Fernando, CA
Ashby, Mr. and Mrs. H. E. — Charleston, SC
Asper, Howard — Escondido, CA
Azalea Glen Nurseries — Loxley, AL

Baker, Rev. C. L. — Bay St. Louis, MS
Beasley, Dr. and Mrs. W. J. — Hartsville, SC
Berlese, Abbe — Paris, France
Boardman, Mr. and Mrs. A. P. — Augusta, GA
Bobbink and Atkins — Rutherford, NJ
Bolen Camellia Gardens — Lucedale, MS
Boutourlin — Florence, Italy
Bowman's Nursery — Pensacola, FL
Bradford's Wayside Nurseries —Ocean Springs, MS
Braewood Gardens and Nursery — Savannah, GA
Bray, W. F. — Pensacola, FL
Breschini, Caesar — San Jose, CA
Brock, Mr. and Mrs. P. H. — Tallahassee, FL
Brushfield, Keith — Sydney, NSW, Australia
Burgess, R. V. — Savannah, GA

Caledonia Nursery — Is. of Guernsey, England
Camellia Grove Nursery —St. Ives, Sydney, NSW, Australia
Camellia Hall — Sacramento, CA
Camelliana (Dr. John D. Lawson) — Antioch, CA
Carleton Reynard Way Nursery — San Diego, CA
Carlyon, G. — Tregrehan Camellia Nursery, Tregrehan, Cornwall, England
Carter's Camellia Gardens — Monterey Park, CA
Chandler, Alfred — Vauxhall, London, England (Chandler and Buckingham) (Chandler and Booth) (Chandler and Sons)
Charvet, Dan — Ft. Bragg, CA
Chiles, C. L. — Hattiesburg, MS
Chugai Nursery — Kobe, Japan
Clark, H. J. — New Lynn, Auckland, New Zealand
Clarke, Colonel R. S. — Borde Hill, Sussex, England
Clower, Mr. and Mrs. Thomas — Gulfport, MS
Cole, C. F. — Melbourne, Victoria, Australia
Coleman (S. D.) Nurseries — Fort Gaines, GA
Coolidge Rare Plant Gardens — Pasadena, CA
Councilman Camellia Acres — El Monte, CA

Da Silva, Joaquin Moreira — Oporto, Portugal
Davies, Victor — New Plymouth, New Zealand
Davis, D. W. — Seffner, FL

Davis Ornamental Nursery — Mobile, AL

Descanso Gardens — La Canada, CA
Doak, Dr. B. W. — Papatoetoe, N.Z.
Dodd, R. E. — Marshallville, GA
Domoto, Toichi — Hayward, CA
Doty and Doerner — Portland, OR
Durrant, Mr. and Mrs. Thomas — Rotorua, New Zealand.

Edinger, Mrs. Mary —Rosebud Farm, Hood, CA

Feathers, David L. — Lafayette, CA
Findlay, J – Whangarei, New Zealand
Fisher, Dr. Gilbert E. — Union Springs, AL
Florida Landscape and Nursery Co.
Flowerwood Nursery — Mobile, AL
Franchetti, Cesare — Florence, Italy
Fruitland Nurseries — Augusta, GA

Gentry, Ray — Jackson, MS
Gerbing Camellia Nursery — Fernandina, FL
Gilley, Paul — Grand Ridge, FL
Glen St. Mary Nursery — Glen St. Mary, FL
Goletto, Barney — Portland, OR
Gordy, C. M. & Lillian — Ocala, FL
Greenbrier Farms, Inc. — Norfolk, VA
Guichard Soeurs — Nantes, France
Guilfoyle, Michael — Double Bay, NSW, Australia

Habel, Dr. J. M., Jr. — Suffolk, VA
Hall, Houghton S., San Anselmo, CA
Hanger, Francis — Wisley, Exbury, England.
Harrison, W. H. — Marianna, FL
Harper, Mr. and Mrs. J. E. — Augusta, GA
Hartman, A. M. — San Fernando, CA
Haydon, Neville — Papakura, New Zealand
Haynie, J. M. — Theodore, AL
Hazlewood Bros. — Eppling, NSW, Australia
Hearn (Clarence S.) Nursery — Arcadia, CA
Henty, H. J., Balwyn, Victoria, Australia
Herrin, T. E., Sr. — Pensacola, FL
Hilsman, Dr. P. L. — Albany, GA
Holmes, Robert — Mt. Olive, NC
Homeyer, Dr. W. F., Jr. — Macon, GA
Howell, Vernon E. — Lucedale, MS
Hudson, Earl — Hemet, CA
Huested, Wm. P. — Glendale, CA
Hunter, Alexander — Somersby, Sydney, NSW, Australia
Huntington Botanical Gardens — San Marino, CA

Illges, John P. — Columbus, GA

James Rare Plant Nursery — Aptos, CA

Jannoch Nursery — Altadena, CA

Jenkins, H. E. — Glendale, CA
Jernigan, Marvin, Warner Robins, GA
Jones, Chas. S. — Flintridge, CA
Judice, Ernest A. — New Orleans, LA
Julington Nurseries, Inc. — Jacksonville, FL
Jury, L. E. — New Plymouth, New Zealand.

Katz, Mr. and Mrs. S. J. — Covington, LA
Kiyono Nurseries (now Semmes Nurseries) — Crichton, AL
Kramer Bros. Nursery — Upland, CA

Lechi, Count Bernardo — Brescia, Italy
Lee, Dr. W. G. — Macon, GA Lindo Nurseries — Chico, CA
Linton, G. C. — Somersby, NSW, Australia
Longview Nurseries — Crichton, AL
Loureiro, Jose Marques — Oporto, Portugal
Low & Co. — Clapton, England
Luzzati, Charles — Florence, Italy

Macarthur, Sir William — Camden Park, Sydney, NSW, Australia
Magnolia Plantation and Gardens — Charleston, SC
Maitland, Frank W. — 13159 Glenoaks Blvd., Sylmar, CA
Malbis Nursery — Daphne, AL
Mandarich, J. L., Menlo Park, CA
Marbury, S. L. — Wilmington, NC
Mariotti, Guido — Nervi, Italy
Marshall's Camellia Nursery — San Gabriel, CA
McCaskill Gardens — Pasadena, CA
McIlhenny, E. A. (Jungle Gardens) —Avery Island, LA
Mealing, Dr. and Mrs. H.G. —North Augusta, SC
Mercantelli, D. R. — Florence, Italy
Metcalf, Edwards — San Marino, CA
Middleton Gardens — Charleston, SC
Miellez — Lille, France

Novick, Harry — Woodland Hills, CA
Nuccio's Nurseries — Altadena, CA

Orton Plantation Nursery — Winnabow, NC
Overlook Nurseries — Crichton, AL

Parks, Dr. Clifford R. — Chapel Hill, NC
Paul, William — Chestnut, England
Peer, Mr. and Mrs. Ralph S. — Park Hill, Hollywood, CA
Piersons, T. E. — Hurstville, NSW, Australia
Piet, Meyer and Gaeta, Lee — Arcadia, CA
Pfingstl's Nursery — Montgomery, AL
Poe, W. L. — Birmingham, AL

Portland Camellia Nursery — Portland, OR
Pursel, Frank — Oakland, CA

Ragland, R. W. — Orange, CA
Reeves, Hubert — Pomona, CA
Rester, C. — Poplarville, MS
Rhodellia Nursery — West Linn, OR
Riverbank Camellia Nursery — Riverbank, CA
Rosa Camellia Nurseries — Tallahassee, FL
Royal Botanic Gardens — Melbourne, Victoria, Australia

Santarelli, M. — Florence, Italy
Satomi, Eikichi — Tokyo, Japan
Sebire, E. R. — Wandin North, Victoria, Australia
Seidel, T. J. — Dresden, Germany
Shackelford, Hugh — Albany, GA
Sheather, Silas — Parramatta, NSW, Australia
Shepherd & Co. — Rooty Hill, Sydney, NSW, Australia
Shepp's Shade Gardens — Pasadena, CA
Short, Harvey F. — La Mesa, CA
Siebold, Franz Von — Leydon, Germany
Smith, Hulyn, Valdosta, GA
Solomon, Judge Arthur W. — Savannah, GA
Star Nursery — Sierra Madre, CA
Stone, Mrs. H. S. — Baton Rouge, LA

Tait, Chas. S., Sr. — Brunswick, GA
Tammia Nursery (Ferol and Sam Zerkowksy) — Slidell, LA
Tea Gardens — Summerville, SC
Thomasville Nurseries — Thomasville, GA
Tick Tock Camellia Nursery — Thomasville, GA
Tuckfield, F. S. — Berwick, Victoria, Australia
Turnbull, Mrs. Hume — Melbourne, Victoria, Australia
Turner, Filo H. — Pensacola, FL

Veitch & Sons Nursery — Exeter, England
Verschaffelt, Alexandre — Ghent, Belgium

Waterhouse, E. G. — Gordon, Sydney, NSW, Australia
Waterhouse, Gordon — Kurrajong Heights, NSW, Australia
Weisner, John T. — Fernandina Beach, FL
Wells, Dr. Reeves F. — Panama City, FL
Wheeler's Central Georgia Nurseries — Macon, GA
Wilkinson, G. H. — Pensacola, FL
Williams, J. C. — Caerhays Castle Gardens, Cornwall, England
Wilson, Walter F., Jr. — Hammond, LA
Witman, Mr. and Mrs. M. J. — Macon, GA
Woodland Nursery — Pascagoula, MS
Wylam, William E. — Pasadena, CA

Yokohama Nursery Co. — Yokohama, Japan
Youtz, J. E. — Pasadena, CA

Classification and Description of Cultivars

The rules followed in the description of cultivars are hereinafter set forth and are based, to the extent that information is available, on flowers grown outdoors and not under protection, other than under trees or lath houses, or with special or chemical treatment such as gibberellic acid. However, in many cases the information received does not disclose the manner of growing and may be based on flowers grown under protection or with the use of chemical treatment. In such cases the color and form may vary from the predominant color and form of an outdoor grown flower, the size will generally be larger, and the blooming period earlier than with an outdoor grown flower.

1. COLOR:

The color description obtained from the originator, publications, reliable sources or our best judgment is used, but allowances should be made for differences of opinion and variations in color due to locality, type of soil, culture, and weather conditions.

2. SIZE:

The size of the flower is described as Miniature (2 1/2 inches or less); Small (over 2 1/2 inches to 3 inches); Medium (over 3 inches to 4 inches); Large (over 4 inches to 5 inches); and Very Large (over 5 inches). Sizes of flowers within a cultivar will vary due to locality, type of soil, culture, etc., and the sizes set forth herein are based upon normal outdoor growing without the use of chemical treatment.

As a general rule, and for all newly introduced cultivars, the indicated size of a cultivar is that which has been stated by the cultivar's originator in the application for registration, or if there has been no registration, in such other description which has been supplied. Where general (not local) growing experience indicates that the size classification obtained in the above manner is incorrect, a reclassification of size will be made. Experience has indicated that some cultivars vary in size due to location and growing conditions, and in such cases a variation of size is set forth as follows:

a) Some cultivars, particularly in the Miniature classification, increase in size as plants become established under normal culture and in such cases have been reclassified as Small. Some Medium and Large cultivars also have been reclassified in the same manner for the same reason.

(b) Some cultivars vary in size from Miniature to Small, or from Small to Medium, or from Medium to Large, or from Large to Very Large, and in such cases a variation of size is listed as a range of Miniature to Small, or a range of Small to Medium, or a range of Medium to Large, or a range of Large to Very Large.

A particular problem arises in entering and judging cultivars which vary in size in Camellia Shows which have divided classes and awards for different sizes of blooms. For example, an exhibited cultivar is Large in actual size, but is listed in this CAMELLIA NOMENCLATURE as Medium in size. It is suggested that as to cultivars that differ in size from that listed in this BOOK that Camellia Show Committees should decide for each show how such cultivars should be treated as to entering and judging. Please keep in mind that this Book is at best only a guideline for establishing size.

The Editor asks that he be informed of cultivars having blooming habits that differ from the classification shown herein, and the Nomenclature Research Committee will pursue such cases to determine if the variation is local or if it is sufficiently general in scope to warrant a change in classification—size or otherwise.

3. FORM*:

Based on practical experience and the ideas of Abbe Berlese in 1838, we have developed our own simplified form classification. We realize that neither this nor any other method of form classification can be perfect. The division and classification of flower forms is as follows:

CLASS I - SINGLE

One row of five to eight regular, irregular or loose petals with conspicuous stamens and with or without petaloids.

Examples: 'TAMA-NO-URA', 'TAMA ELECTRA' and 'YULETIDE'.

CLASS II - SEMIDOUBLE

Two or more rows of large regular, irregular or loose petals - nine or more. Very prominent stamens, sometimes with petaloids. The petals may overlap or be in rows. Sometimes blooms can have a concave center.
Examples: 'JULUIS NUCCIO', 'ROYAL VELVET', and 'WALTZ TIME'.

CLASS III - ANEMONE

One or more rows of large outer guard petals, lying flat or undulating; the center is a convex mass of intermingled petaloids and stamens. Often this is similar to a full peony form (see below) with guard petals.
Examples: 'ELEGANS SPLENDOR, 'MAN SIZE', and 'CHRIS BERGAMINI'

CLASS IV - PEONY FORM (INFORMAL DOUBLE)**

A deep rounded flower of the following sub-forms.

Loose Peony Form (Incomplete Informal Double)** - Loose petals which may be irregular with (1) intermingled stamens or (2) with intermingled petals, petaloids and stamens in center.
Examples: 'LADY LAURA, 'MAROON AND GOLD', and 'TIFFANY'.

Full Peony Form (Complete Informal Double)** - Convex mass of mixed irregular petals and petaloids with or without stamens showing.
Examples: 'DEBUTANTE','ELSIE JURY', and 'MARGARET DAVIS'.

CLASS V - ROSE FORM DOUBLE

Rows of imbricated or overlapping petals appearing as a rose bud in the early stage maturing to an open bud showing stamens in a concave center. This bloom form looks similar to a formal double in its early stages of development. Examples: 'GLEN 40', 'JUNIOR PROM', and 'SHISHI-GASHIRA'.

CLASS VI - FORMAL DOUBLE

Many rows of overlapping petals, never showing stamens. It usually has a center of tightly furled petals. There are four sub-forms (1) fully imbricated, (2) tiered, (3) spiral and (4) bud centered.
Examples: 'NUCCIO'S GEM', 'SEA FOAM', and 'VALENTINE DAY'.

* Pictures of flower form are on back cover
** Terms used in Australia, New Zealand and Europe

4. TYPE OF GROWTH:
We believe that many people have an interest in the type of growth, especially if a particular cultivar is intended for landscape purposes. Such descriptions have, therefore, been included whenever the necessary information has been available as to Species Japonica and Reticulata and Hybrids, but is not generally included as to other species.

5. BLOOMING PERIOD:
This is denoted by "E" (Early — Prior to Jan.1st); "M" (Mid-season — Jan.1st to Mar.1st); "L" (Late — Mar.1st and later). This information is included as to Species Japonica and Reticulata and Hybrids when available, but is not generally included as to other species. Such information, however, always must be considered as approximate, and based upon average conditions in the southern parts of the United States. The blooming period is affected by variable weather conditions, the amount of rainfall, the latitude, and variation in temperature in any given year.

Species Japonica

A. O. ELLISON - Rose Pink streaked Red. Large, single to semidouble. Open, upright growth. E-M. (Aus. 1945 - Hazlewood).

A. W. JESSEP - Ivory White. Large, semidouble inclined to be hose-in-hose form. Vigorous, slightly pendulous growth. M. (Aus. 1950 - Royal Botanical Gardens).

AARON'S RUBY - Metallic Red. Medium to large, semidouble to anemone form with petals intermixed with little flags and trumpet-shaped petaloids surrounding mass of Golden stamens. Vigorous, slender, slightly pendulous growth. E-L. (U.S. 1954 - Mrs. B. A. Ragusa, Lake Charles, LA).

AARON'S RUBY VARIEGATED - Metallic Red and White variation of 'Aaron's Ruby'.

ABBOT TURNER - Red with Red and White stamens. Large, peony form to anemone form. Vigorous, open growth. M. (U.S. 1951 - Mrs. A. D. Turner, Columbus, GA).

ABBOTSLEIGH - White. Very large, peony form. Open, spreading growth. M. (Aus. 1983 - C. Blumenthal, St. Ives, NSW).

ACCORDION - White. Large, rose form double. (U.S. 1955).

ACE HIGH - Bright Red. Miniature, formal double. Compact, upright growth. M-L. (Aus. 1982 - L. Hobbs, Doncaster East, Vic.).

ACE O' HEARTS - Deep Red. Medium to large, semidouble. Vigorous, compact, upright growth. M. (U.S. 1963 - Nuccio's).

ACS JUBILEE - Light Pink. Medium to large, formal double to rose form double. Average, dense, upright growth. E-M. (U.S. 1994 - Nuccio's).

ADA BIRD - White. Large, semidouble. Vigorous, compact growth. M. (U.S. 1967 - A. B. McDaniel, Eastman, GA).

ADA PIEPER - Coral Rose. Medium to large, semidouble. Vigorous, compact growth. M. (U.S. 1954 - McCaskill).

ADA WILSON - See 'Rosea Superba'.

ADAH PEARL - Pink. Medium, semidouble, with fluted center petals. Vigorous, upright growth. M. (U.S. 1940 - Youtz).

ADALYN - White shading to Pink at outer edges. Medium, formal double. Average, upright growth. E-L. (U.S. 1995 - F. Wilson, Leslie, GA).

ADAM GRANT - Bright Rose Pink with bright Yellow anthers. Very large, peony form. Average, upright growth. M-L. (U.S. 2010 - Marion Grant Hall, Dothan, AL).

ADELE CLAIRMONT - Light Pink. Medium, formal double. Vigorous, compact, upright growth. M. (U.S. 1961 - Mrs. J. Clairmont, Glendale, CA).

ADELE SALLY - Dark Red. Large to very large, semidouble to loose peony form. Average, open, upright growth. M. (U.S. 1968 - H. C. Wilson, Fresno, CA).

ADELINA PATTI - Pink shading to White at tips. Medium, single. Open, upright growth. M-L. (Japan to England [C. Waller] 1889).

ADELINA SARGENT - Pink with one or more Darker Pink stripes on each petal. Large, single to semidouble. Compact, upright growth. M. (Aus. 1982 - N. Sargent, Johnsonville, Vic.).

ADEYAKA - Bright Red. Small to medium, single. Vigorous, compact, upright growth. E-M. (U.S. 1981 - Parks).

ADMIRAL HALSEY - Deep Red marbled White. Medium, full peony to anemone form. (Variegated form of 'General Dwight Eisenhower'). (U.S. 1945 - Reeves).

ADMIRAL NIMITZ - See 'Kishu-Tsukasa'.

ADOLESCENT - White. Miniature, semidouble. Average, upright growth. M. (U.S. 1955).

ADOLPHE - See 'Adolphe Audusson'.

ADOLPHE AUDUSSON - ('Audrey Hopfer'; 'Adolphe'). Dark Red. Large, semidouble. Average, compact growth. M. (France 1877 - M. Audusson, Angers).

ADOLPHE AUDUSSON SPECIAL - A predominantly White 'Adolphe Audusson'. (Not consistent). (U.S. 1942 - Jenkins).

ADOLPHE AUDUSSON VARIEGATED - ('F. M. Uyematsu'). Dark Red spotted White variation of 'Adolphe Audusson'.

ADRIANNE'S BETTY - White veined and shaded Light Pink with petals edged Deeper Pink. Medium to large, semidouble to loose peony form. (Sport of Japonica 'Betty Sheffield Silver'). (U.S. 1982 - Mrs. A. B. Rhodes, Wilmington, NC).

ADVENT - Watermelon Red with Yellow stamens having Reddish cast at base and petaloids. Large, semidouble. Average, open, upright growth. E-M. (U.S. 1966 - G.A. Nelson, Florence, SC).

AGNES CELESTINE - White striped Pink. Medium, semidouble to peony form. M. (U.S. 1948 - McIlhenny).

AGNES FARMER - Pink. Medium, semidouble with irregular petals. Vigorous, compact, upright growth. M-L. (U.S. 1975 - Haynie).

AGNES OF THE OAKS - Pink marbled White. Large, semidouble with ruffled petals. Average, compact, upright growth. E-M. (U.S. 1949 - F. A. Godchaux, Abbeville, LA).

AGNES ROWELL - Red. Medium to large, semidouble with ruffled petals and occasional petaloids. Vigorous, compact, upright growth. M. (U.S. 1958 - M. E. Rowell, Fresno, CA).

AGNES ROWELL VARIEGATED - Red and White variation of 'Agnes Rowell'.

AILEEN - See 'Donckelarii'.

AITONIA (MAGNOLIA) - Light Rose Pink. Medium, semidouble with center of mixed petaloids and stamens. Vigorous, compact growth. M. (U.S. Late 1800's - Magnolia; not same as cultivar listed in old literature, which was a Single of Rose Pink).

AKA-DAIKAGURA - See 'Daikagura Red'.

AKAROA ROUGE - See 'Madame Picouline'.

AKASHI-GATA - See 'Lady Clare'.

AKATSUKI-NO-KAORI - Light Shell Pink. Large, semidouble with flared Pale Yellow stamens. See Higo.

AKEBONO - Light Pink. Medium, semidouble of cupped form. Average, compact growth. M. (Japan to U.S. [Domoto] 1917).

AL EWAN - Bright Red with Yellow anthers and Yellow filaments. Large to very large, semidouble. Average, upright growth. M. (U.S. 2009 - Albert Ewan, Charleston, SC).

ALABAMA DAWN - Red. Large, anemone form with Red and Red striped White center petaloids and fluffy outer petals. Vigorous, open, upright growth. M. (U.S. 1964 - R. W. Wilder, Fairhope, AL).

ALABAMA TIDE - Deep rich Red. Large, formal double to semidouble. Vigorous, upright growth. M-L. (U.S. 1979 - C. C. Crutcher, Theodore, AL).

ALABAMA'S LURLEEN - Blush Pink. Large, full peony form. Average growth. E-M. (U.S. 1968 - H. W. Steindorff, Greenville, AL).

ALABASTER - Cream White. Medium, semidouble. Vigorous growth. M-L. (U.S. 1957 - Julington).

ALAN DAVIS - Rose Pink. Medium, peony form. Average growth. E-M. (U.S. 1973 - N. M. Davis, Charlotte, NC).

ALARNI - White. Medium, single. Vigorous, compact, upright growth. M-L. (Aus. 1969 - A. Walker, Gordon, NSW).

ALASKA - White. Medium, semidouble with fluted petals. Vigorous, upright growth. M. (U.S. 1949 - Carleton).

ALASKAN BELLE - White. Large, semidouble with upright petals. Vigorous, compact, upright growth. (U.S. 1965 - G. S. Clarke, Savannah, GA).

ALBA FIMBRIATA - See 'Fimbriata'.

ALBA GIGANTEA - White with Yellow anthers and Yellow filaments. Very large, single with waxy, broad, thick, well shaped petals. M. (The biggest white single in existence). (Japan 1937 - Wada).

ALBA PLENA - White. Medium, formal double. Slow, bushy growth. E. (Variations of this cultivar include Japonicas 'Fimbriata'; 'Blush Plena'; 'Mrs. Hooper Connell'; 'Mattie R'). (China to England. [Capt. Connor] 1792).

ALBA PLENA IMPROVED - Contains more petals of heavier texture than the original. M. (Sport of Japonica 'Alba Plena'). (U.S. 1987 - Vi. Stone, Baton Rouge, LA).

ALBA QUEEN - White. Large, loose peony form. (U.S. 1950 - Goletto).

ALBA SPLENDENS - White. Medium, semidouble with wavy petals. Average, loose, upright growth. M. (U.S. Late 1800's - Magnolia).

ALBA SUPERBA - ('Nevius'; 'Northern'; 'Tonnie Leche'). White. Medium, semidouble. Vigorous, upright growth. M. (Europe to U.S. [Magnolia] 1840's).

ALBERT HORNE - Light Rose Pink striped Deep Rose Pink. Medium to large, semidouble with upright inner petals intermixed with petaloids. Average, compact, upright growth. M. (U.S. 1965 - A. S. Horne, Moncks Corner, SC).

ALBERTA LONG - White flecked Rose. Large, semidouble. Vigorous, spreading growth. E-M. (U.S. 1966 - Mrs. J. C. Long, Mt. Pleasant, SC).

ALBERTA MARIE - White center petals and Blush Pink outer petals. Medium, semidouble. Average growth. M. (U.S. 1965 - Dr. and Mrs. G. R. Johnson, Carthage, TX).

ALCYONE OSTBERG - Deep Pink, with Deeper Lavender Pink center. Large to very large, semidouble to loose peony form. Slow, open, upright growth. M-L. (U.S. 2005 - Gordy).

ALDA BOLL - Deep Rose Pink. Large, full peony form. Average, compact, upright growth. M. (U.S. 1989 - A. K. Boll, Jacksonville, FL).

ALEAN MILLER - Light Pink shading to Deeper Pink at edge. Medium, semidouble. Vigorous, compact, upright growth. M. (U.S. 1959 - McCaskill).

ALENA - Dark Red. Medium, anemone form. (Aus. 1953).

ALENE HOOD - Pink with Deeper Pink stripes and splashes, sporting Pink, Red and White. Large, anemone form. Average, upright growth. M-L. (U.S. 1974 - M. D. Hood, Texarkana, TX).

ALEXANDER BLACK - Dark Crimson. Medium, formal double. Upright, compact growth. (Aus. 1889 - Taylor and Sangster, Melbourne).

ALEXANDER NOWLIN - Red Spotted White. Medium, formal double. Average, compact, upright growth. M. (France to U.S. [Youtz] 1935).

ALEXINE WELCH - Red. Large, formal double. (U.S. 1959).

ALEXIS SMITH - Blush Pink edged Deeper Pink. Large, semidouble to loose peony form. Vigorous, compact, upright growth. M. (U.S. 1961 - Nuccio's).

ALFRED UPSON - Deep Pink. Medium, formal double. Average, dense, upright growth. M-L. (N.Z. 1991 - F. Upson, Kaponga).

ALICE - Pink. Medium, single. M. (Aus. 1947 - Melbourne Botanic Gdns., Melbourne).

ALICE ALLEN - Cameo Pink. Small, formal double. Slow, upright growth. E-M. (U.S. 1957 - Mrs. C. N. Durand, Denham Springs, LA).

ALICE BOON - Red heavily moiré Red and White. (Sport of Japonica 'Emperor of Russia'). (N.Z. 1973 - Mrs. A. Boon, Whakatane).

ALICE COCHRAN - White. Large, semidouble with White stamens. Vigorous, compact, upright growth. E-L. (U.S. 1962 - Mrs. C. T. Cochran, Summerville, SC).

ALICE CREIGHTON - Rose Pink with White borders at end of petals. Medium, formal double. Average, spreading open growth. (Japonica 'Tama Glitters' seedling). (U.S. 2003 - Walter Creighton, Semmes, AL).

ALICE HORNE - Deep Rose Pink with Deeper Pink veins. Very large, semidouble with intermixed stamens and trumpet formed petaloids. Average, open, upright growth. M. (U.S. 1965 - A.S. Horne, Moncks Corner, SC).

ALICE IN-THE PALACE - Bubble Gum Pink with Yellow anthers and White filaments. Large, semidouble to loose peony form. Vigorous, upright, spreading growth. M. (U.S. 2019 - Gordy).

ALICE JERNIGAN - Light Pink with Yellow anthers and White filaments. Medium, semidouble, usually with prominent Pink petaloids. Average, upright growth. M. (U.S. 2019 - Ed Jernigan, Greenville, AL).

ALICE MAREE - Deep Red. Large, loose peony form to rose form double. Average, upright growth. E-M. (U.S. 1967 - N. Cox, Georgetown, SC).

ALICE MORGAN - White marked and striped Carmine Red. Large, anemone form. Vigorous, upright growth. E-L. (Aus. 1987 - Mrs. A. Morgan, St. Ives, NSW).

ALICE MORRISON - Light Shell Pink. Medium, semidouble. Vigorous, compact, upright growth. M. (U.S. 1957 - R. E. Craig, San Gabriel, CA).

ALICE OF LINWOOD - White variegated Red and Pink. Medium, semidouble. Vigorous growth. M-L. (U.S. 1950 - Allan).

ALICE PARKES - White. Medium, rose form double. Average, spreading growth. M. (U.S. 1993 - E. Akin, Shreveport, LA).

ALICE SLACK - See 'Blood of China'.

ALICE STOKES - Light Pink. Medium, rose form double. Vigorous, upright growth. M. (U.S. 1949 - T. Dodd, Semmes, AL).

ALICE VALERIA - Bright Pink. Large, semidouble with Pink veined stamens. Average growth. M. (U.S. 1959 - Mrs. G. R. Crosby, Pavo, GA).

ALICE WOOD - Bright Red. Large, formal double. Vigorous, upright growth. E-M. (U.S. 1960 - Mrs. A. Wood, San Gabriel, CA).

ALISHA CARTER - Very Dark Red veined Black. Small to medium, peony form. Average, open growth. M-L. (N.Z. 1991 - T. Lennard, Te Puke).

ALISON CLARE - Rose Pink. Large, semidouble. Vigorous, open, upright growth. M. (Aus. 1968 - Dr. A. C. Burstal, Pymble, NSW).

ALISON LEIGH WOODROOF - Pale Pink shading to glowing Pink at edge. Small, semidouble. Vigorous, compact, upright growth. M. (U.S. 1955 - McCaskill).

ALL AMERICAN - Bright Red. Medium to large, full peony form. Vigorous, compact, upright growth. M. (U.S. 1973 - Alfter).

ALL AMERICAN VARIEGATED - Bright Red marbled White in various degrees up to ninety percent variation of 'All American'. (U.S. 1977 - Alfter).

ALLEN KLOMAN - White streaked Red. Miniature, semidouble to anemone form. Average, upright growth. L. (U.S. 1985 - Jernigan).

ALLEN SMITH VARIEGATED - Rose Red with mottled White variegation with Yellow anthers and White filaments. Medium, semidouble. Average, upright growth. E-L. (U.S. 2016 - Howell).

ALLENE GUNN - Blush Pink fading to Darker Pink on petal edges. Medium, loose peony form. Average, upright growth. M. (U.S. 1977 - C. V. Bozeman, Hattiesburg, MS).

ALLIE - Rose Pink with White overtones with Golden Yellow anthers and White filaments. Medium to large, semidouble to full peony. Vigorous, upright, open growth. E-M. (U.S. 2011 - Bill Howell, Wilmington, NC).

ALLIE BLUE - Blush to White shading to Pink margins. Medium, loose semidouble. Average, compact, upright growth. M. (U.S. 1964 - Habel).

ALLIE GORDY - Coral Pink. Medium, formal double. Vigorous, upright, dense growth. M. (U.S. 2012 - Gordy).

ALLIE HABEL - Shell Pink edged Deeper Pink. Medium to large, peony form. Average, compact growth. M. (U.S. 1965 - Habel).

ALLISON FAITH - Orchid Pink with soft Pink center petals. Medium, formal double. Upright, dense growth. M-L. (U.S. 1995 - Gordy).

ALMA HALECKI - White. Large, anemone form. Vigorous, upright growth. L. (U.S. 1977 - J. R. Halecki, Wilmington, NC).

ALMORINDA CARNEIRO - White. Small, full peony form. Average, upright growth. E. (U.S. 1959 - J. Carneiro, Los Angeles, CA).

ALOHA - See 'Arajishi'.

ALPINE GLOW - Red. Medium, semidouble. Average, compact, upright growth. M. (U.S. 1959 - Breschini).

ALPINE GLOW VARIEGATED - Red marbled White variation of 'Alpine Glow'.

ALTA GAVIN - White edged Deep Pink. Medium to large, semidouble to rose form double to formal double. Vigorous, compact growth. M-L. (U.S. 1962 - J. E. Gavin, Shreveport, LA).

ALTA RIMER - Very Dark Red with Burgundy hue. Medium, semidouble. Average, spreading growth. M. (U.S. 1970 - J. Rimer, Marion, SC).

ALTHEAFLORA - Dark Red. Medium, peony form. (England 1824 — Chandler).

ALTON LANG - Dark Pink. Large, semidouble. Average, upright growth. M. (U.S. 1977 - A. Lang, Bogalusa, LA).

ALYNE BROTHERS - White occasionally splotched Pink. Medium, full peony form. Average, upright growth. E-M. (Variations of this cultivar include Japonicas 'Ladell Brothers' and 'Linda Brothers'). (U.S. 1959 - S. L. Brothers, Madison, FL).

ALYSON POLLARD - Blush Pink with occasional small Rose streak. Medium, formal double. Average, open, spreading growth. E-M. (U.S. 1977 - D. Mayfield, Baton Rouge, LA).

AMABEL LANSDELL - Pink with Cream center. Large, semidouble. Average, open growth. M. (U.S. 1963 - Mrs. C. M. Meiere, Augusta, GA).

AMABILIS - ('Mrs. Francis Saunders'; 'White Poppy'). White. Medium, single of flat form with heavy cluster of stamens in center. Vigorous upright growth. M. (Not same as cultivar listed in old literature, which was a similar White single). (Japan 1893 - Yokohama).

AMABILIS BLUSH - Light Blush Pink. Medium, single with clusters of stamens in center. Vigorous growth. E-M. (U.S. late 1800's - Magnolia).

AMANDA ANN - Dark Red. Medium, formal double. Vigorous, upright, spreading growth. M-L. (U.S. 2014 - Steve and Gayle Lawrence).

AMAZING GRACES - Blush Pink shading to Deeper Pink at edge. Small, formal double with swirled inner petals. Average, open, upright growth. M. (U.S. 1979 - Stone).

AMELDIA - Dark Red flecked White. Medium, full peony form. E-M. (U.S. Late 1800's - Magnolia).

AMELIA THOMPSON - Rose Pink. Medium, peony form. Sturdy growth. M. (N.Z. 1953).

AMERICAN BEAUTY - Deep Pink marbled White. Medium, semidouble to rose form double. Average, compact, upright growth. M-L. (Europe to U.S. [Magnolia] 1840's).

AMERICAN GIRL - American Beauty Red. Large, rose form double. Average, compact growth. M. (U.S. 1954 - Fruitland).

AMICHAEL - Dark Red with beet root Purple shade toward edge. Medium, peony form. Vigorous growth. E. (U.S. 1953 - Clower).

AMIGO - Coral Rose. Small, anemone form with ring of stamens surrounding ring of petaloids. Vigorous, compact, upright growth. M. (U.S. 1962 - McCaskill).

AMY CONNOR - Red variegated White with Yellow anthers and White filaments. Medium to large, loose peony to rose form double. Average, spreading growth. E-M. (U.S. 2013 - Parker Connor, Edisto Island, SC).

AMY DOODLE - Light Pink center with Cream White edges with Yellow anthers and translucent White filaments. Large, semidouble to loose peony. Average, spreading, open growth. M-L. (U.S. 2013 - Gabriel C. Olsen, Pensacola, FL).

AMY MARYOTT - Rose Pink. Medium to large, semidouble form; crepe petals. Average growth. E-L. Fragrant. Very cold hardy. (U.S. 1999 - Dr. Arthur A. Maryott, Gaithersburg, MD).

AMY McCAY - Deep Pink, lighter at edges. Large, anemone form. Average, open, upright growth. E-M. (U.S. 1992 - Dr. L. Audioun, Biloxi, MS).

AMY STEPHENS - Deep Pink. Large, semidouble. Average, upright growth. L. (U.S. 1974 - G. T. Askew, Athens, GA).

AMY V. THOMAS - Red. Miniature to small, formal double. Vigorous, upright growth. M-L. (U.S. 1989 - L. A. Odom, Wilmington, NC).

ANACOSTIA - Medium Pink (RHS 55A) with Yellow antlers and Ivory filaments. Medium, semidouble. Average, upright growth. E-M. (Undetermined White flowered Japonica x Japonica 'Variety Z'). (U.S. 2010 - Sylvester "Skip" March, Washington, DC).

ANASTASIA - Warm Pink. Large, peony form. Average, compact, upright growth. L. (N.Z. 1989 - T. Steedman, Wanganui).

ANDRE LA SALLE - White with Blush Pink under petals. Medium, full peony form. Average, slender, open growth. E-L. (U.S. 1954 - Mrs. H. A. King, New Iberia, LA).

ANDREA SEBIRE - Pink, lighter toward center. Small, formal double. Compact, upright growth. M. (Aus. 1982 - Sebire).

ANDREW - Light Pink with Yellow anthers and Yellow filaments. Very large, semidouble to full peony; the petals are heavily veined. Slow, upright, dense growth. M-L. (U.S. 2013 - William Howell, Wilmington, NC).

ANDROMEDA - White streaked Carmine. Large, anemone form. (Aus. 1952 - Waterhouse).

ANEMONAEFLORA - ('Warratah'; 'Mrs. Sol Runyon'; 'Honeycomb').- Dark Crimson. Medium, anemone form. Vigorous, upright growth. M. (China to England [Kew Gardens] 1806).

ANEMONAEFLORA ALBA - ('Warratah White'; 'White Anemone'; 'Wroughtii'). White. Medium, anemone form. (England 1825 - Chandler).

AN-FLO-LEE - Dark Red. Large, full peony form to anemone form. Vigorous, upright growth. M. (U.S. 1949 - R. Lee, Pensacola, FL).

ANGEL - ('Candlelight'). White. Large, semidouble with fluted petals. Compact, upright growth. M. (U.S. 1953 - Councilman).

ANGEL KLOMAN - White to Cream. Large, formal double. Average, open growth. E-M. (U.S. 1984 - Homeyer).

ANGEL MARIE - Light Pink with Darker Pink stripes with Yellow anthers and White filaments. Medium, loose peony form. Average, upright, dense growth. M. (U.S. 2013 - James and Elaine Smelley, Moss Point, MS).

ANGEL'S BLUSH - ('Melissa Martini'). Pink. Miniature, semidouble. Average growth. M. (U.S. 1945 - Tom Dodd, Semmes, AL).

ANGELA GILMORE - White veined delicate Pink. Medium, formal double. Vigorous, compact growth. M. (U.S. 1952 - O. E. Hopfer, Oakland, CA).

ANGELA HELEN THOMAS - Snow White. Medium, anemone form. Vigorous, open, upright growth. M. (U.S. 1972 - B. V. Drinkard, Mobile, AL).

ANGELA LANSBURY - White. Medium, formal double with inner petals cupped inward. Average, spreading, upright growth. M-L. (U.S. 1995 - Homeyer).

ANGELIQUE - Ivory White. Miniature, formal double. Average, upright growth. M. (U.S. 1986 - Stone).

ANGIE CLEGG - Rose Pink with Creamy Silver sheen. Large, peony form. Average growth. E-M. (U.S. 1971 - G. R. Clegg, Tallahassee, FL).

ANITA - Light Pink striped Carmine. Medium, semidouble. Vigorous, upright, compact growth. M. (Variations of this cultivar include Japonicas 'Rio Rita': 'Anita's Blush'; 'White Anita'). (U.S. 1940 - Armstrong).

ANITA BENNETT - White. Large, semidouble. Average, upright growth. E-M. (U.S. 1987 - G. Johnson, Madison, FL).

ANITA ROCHE - Rose Pink, some veining on petals. Large to very large, semidouble form. Upright growth. M. (U.S. 1999 - Ken Hallstone Lafayette, CA).

ANITA'S BLUSH - White shading to Blush. Medium, semidouble. (Sport of Japonica 'Anita'). (U.S. 1949 - McCaskill).

ANITA'S TRIUMPH - Oriental Red streaked deeper. Medium, full peony form. Vigorous, compact, upright growth. M-L. (U.S. 1956 - Short).

ANN BLAIR BROWN - Light Pink with Darker Pink petaloids. Large, anemone form. Average, upright growth. M. (U.S. 1977 - Dodd).

ANN BLAIR BROWN VARIEGATED - Light Pink blotched White variation of 'Ann Blair Brown'. (U.S. 1977 - Dodd).

ANN CLAYTON - White shading to Pink. Miniature, formal double. Average growth. L. (U.S. 1980 - Habel).

ANN CURTIS - Light Pink. Medium to large, rose form double. Vigorous, upright, average growth. M. (U.S. 1983 - Mary McLeod, Monticello, FL).

ANN DODSON - Red with Gold anthers and Pinkish filaments. Medium to large, loose peony form. Average, upright, spreading growth. E-L. (U.S. 2018 - Bill Dodson, Birmingham, AL).

ANN FOWLER - Blush Pink. Large, anemone form. Average, compact growth. M. (U.S. 1954 - M. R. Murray, Fort Valley, GA).

ANN KELLEY - Deep Rose. Large, loose to full peony form. Compact growth. E. (U.S. 1965 - C. D. Cothran, Upland, CA).

ANN LAWTON - Pink. Large, semidouble with petaloids surrounding cluster of Yellow stamens. (U.S. 1959 - H L Lawton, Georgetown, SC).

ANN LEE - Rose Pink. Miniature, formal double. Average, upright growth. M. (U.S. 1991 - Dr. O. Lewis, Picayune, MS).

ANN MILLER - Light Salmon Pink. Medium, peony form. Vigorous, compact growth. M-L. (U.S. 1950 - Shepp).

ANN MORRISON - Light Pink shading darker to outer petals. Medium, rose form double. Slow, upright growth. M. (U.S. 1980 - C. V. Bozeman, Hattiesburg, MS).

ANN OLIVER - Light clear Pink. Large, loose peony form. Average, upright growth. M. (U.S. 1971 - Mrs. E. C. Oliver, Statesboro, GA).

ANN QUARLES - White. Large, semidouble with wavy petals. Average, open, upright growth. E-M. (U.S. 1961 - H. E. Quarles, Mobile, AL).

ANN REINHARD - Medium Red with Golden anthers and White filaments. Small, single. Average, upright growth. M. (U.S. 2018 - SACGC Botanical Garden, Savannah, GA).

ANN SOTHERN - Venetian Pink shading to porcelain White in center. Large, semidouble with upright petals among White stamens. Vigorous, compact, upright growth. E-M. (U.S. 1960 - Hudson).

ANN SWINTON - Deep Pink. Large, peony form. Average, spreading growth. E-M. (U.S. 1972 - Mrs. D. W. Ellis, Charleston, SC).

ANN WAHL - Blush Pink. Large, full peony form. Vigorous, upright growth. E-M. (U.S. 1958 - Mrs. E. F. Wahl, Thomasville, GA).

ANN WALTON - White. Large to very large, formal double. Average, upright growth. M-L. (U.S. 1999 - Jernigan).

ANN WILSON - Light Pink with darker veins. Medium, semidouble to peony form. M-L. (U.S. 1957 - Wilson's Nsy., Batesburg, SC).

ANNA BRUNEAU - Light Pink blotched White. Large, formal double. (Sport of Japonica 'Mathotiana Alba'). (Belgium 1856 - V. de Bischop, Ghent).

ANNA CELESTE - Clear Pale Pink with bright Golden Yellow anthers and White filaments. Large to very large, semidouble. Average, upright, open growth. M-L. (U.S. 2015 - Ann Schwarz Miller, Virginia Beach, VA).

ANNA HOWARD - Cerise Pink generally variegated with White. Medium, semidouble with irregular petals. Average, compact growth. M. (U.S. 1953 - T. E. Fletcher, Cordele, GA).

ANNA JANE - Soft Pink. Medium, rose form double. Average, open, upright growth. E-M. (U.S. 1959 - Mrs. D. Wirth, New Orleans, LA).

ANNA LOUISE - Red to Red variegated White. Large, semidouble with wavy edged petals. Average, compact growth. M-L. (U.S. 1975).

ANNA MARY STONE - Watermelon Pink. Large, semidouble with Deep Orange stamens. Vigorous, compact, upright growth. M. (U.S. 1961 - Mrs. A. M. Stommreich, Natchez, MS).

ANNA RAY - Rose Pink. Large, full peony form. Vigorous, compact growth. E-M. (U.S. 1962 - Mrs. H. Ray, Sr., Moultrie, GA).

ANNA RAY VARIEGATED - Rose Pink and White variation of 'Anna Ray'.

ANNA SMYRE - Pink. Large, semidouble with wavy, crinkled petals. Vigorous, compact, upright growth. M-L. (U.S. 1969 - E. J. Prevatt, Bonneau, SC).

ANNALEIGH'S STAR - Pink with Light Pink edge with Yellow anthers and Yellow filaments. Small to medium, loose peony; the stamens divide into a star shape. Average, upright, spreading growth. M-L. (U.S. 2015 - Marty and Diane Clark, Hampstead, NC).

ANNE ASKEW - Rose Pink. Large, semidouble with slightly fimbriated crepe petals. Average growth. E-M. (U.S. 1973 - J. T. Askew, Athens, GA).

ANNE E. SOLOMON - Blush Pink. Large, semidouble. Vigorous, open, upright growth. M. (U.S. 1960 - Solomon).

ANNE GRAMLING - Rose Red. Large, rose form double. Vigorous, open, upright growth. M. (U.S. 1978 - R. B. Gramling, Tallahassee, FL).

ANNE GRIFFIN - Rose Pink. Medium, peony form with irregular long and twisted petals curled toward center. Compact, upright growth. M. (U.S. 1957 - Wheeler).

ANNE JACKSON - Light Pink. Large, high centered semidouble to loose peony form. Average, compact, upright growth. M. (U.S. 1971 - Shackelford).

ANNE MARIE HOLMAN - White with occasional Pink or Red streaks. Medium, semidouble with occasional petaloids. Average, spreading growth. M. (Aus. 1969 - C. F. Walton, St. Ives, NSW).

ANNE POUND - Light Blush Pink. Large, semidouble with three rows of elongated petals with small, upright, elongated petals in center. Average, open, upright growth. E. (U.S. 1964 - Julington).

ANNE PRIDEAUX - Soft Pink inner petals and Darker Pink veined outer petals. Medium, peony form. Compact, upright growth. M. (Aus. 1982 - Mrs. A. Prideaux, Corinda, Qld.).

ANNE SHACKELFORD - Light Pink. Medium, semidouble with irregular, fluted petals. Vigorous, upright growth. M. (U.S. 1959 - Shackelford).

ANNE SMITH - Bright to Dark Red. Medium, semidouble. Compact, pendulous growth. M. (U.S. 1957 - Mrs. J. W. Mann, Valdosta, GA).

ANNE SYDENSTRICKER - Red blotched White. Medium, semidouble. M. (U.S. 1956 - Boardman).

ANNE VINCENT - White with Red to Pink border. Large, formal double with incurved petals. Average, upright growth. E-M. (U.S. 1978 - J. B. Adams, Lake Charles, LA).

ANNE WITMAN - Fire Red. Large, full peony form. Vigorous, spreading growth. M. (U.S. 1971 - Witman).

ANNELL MOORE VARIEGATED - Red variegated White with Yellow anthers and Pink filaments. Medium, semidouble. Average, upright, dense growth. E-L. (U.S. 2016 - Howell).

ANNETTE - Rose Pink. Large, semidouble with upright petals. (Aus. 1852 - Macarthur).

ANNETTE GEHRY - Light Lavender Pink shading to White at center. Medium to large, anemone form to loose peony form. Vigorous, compact, upright growth. E. (U.S. 1960 - Dr. E. L. Gehry, Orangeburg, SC).

ANNIE JONES - Pale Pink. Large, semidouble. Average, upright growth. E-L. (U.S. 1989 - A. Jones, Colquit, GA).

ANNIE L. BELL - White. Medium, semidouble. Vigorous, upright growth. M. (U.S. 1959 - Mrs. B. Airey, Wetumpka, AL).

ANNIE R. CANTEY - Purplish Pink. Large, full peony form. Average, spreading growth. M. (U.S. 1961 - S. O. Cantey, Marion, SC).

ANNIE TEE - Ruby Red. Large, loose peony form. Average, compact, upright growth. E-M. (U.S. 1966 - Mrs. A. T. Williams, Dothan, AL).

ANNIE WYLAM - Bright Pink shading to White in center. Medium, peony form with many slender petaloids. Average, open, upright growth. E-L. (U.S. 1959 - Wylam).

ANNIVERSARY - Bright Red. Medium, formal double. Vigorous, compact, upright growth. E-M. (U.S. 1958 - T. Eagleson, Port Arthur, TX).

ANTARCTIC STAR - White. Medium, anemone form. Average growth. M-L. (N.Z. 1981 - W. H. Peters, Tauranga).

AOI-SANGOSHÔ (BLUE CORAL REEF) - Deep Bluish Purple with White filaments and Yellow anthers. Miniature, single bloom. M. (Japan 1988 - Shigeyuki Iwatsubo, Tanegashima Island, Kagoshima Prefecture, Kyûshû).

APACHE - See 'Red Giant'.

APACHE CHIEF - Bright Rose Pink with undertone of Purple as it ages. Large, semidouble with some petaloids forming trumpets. Average, compact, upright growth. E-M. (U.S. 1965 - A. S. Horne, Moncks Corner, SC).

APACHE VARIEGATED - Deep Pink blotched White variation of 'Apache'.

APOLLO 14 - Deep Pink moiré White. Medium to large, formal double. Average, compact, upright growth. E. (U.S. 1971 - M. A. and N. Cox, Georgetown, SC).

APPLE QUEEN - White edged Blush Pink. Large, loose peony form with upright center petals. Vigorous, upright growth. M-L. (U.S. 1954 - Shackelford).

APRICOT MUFFIN - Light Pink. Medium, semidouble. Vigorous, upright growth. M. Fragrant. (U.S. 1998 - W. and M.A. Ray, Fresno, CA).

APRIL BLUES - Rose-Red; in cold weather can be Bluish Pink to Purple. Medium, formal double. Vigorous, upright, spreading growth. L. The plant is very cold hardy. (Japonica 'Bernice Body' x Japonica 'Kuro-tsubaki'). (U.S. 2014 - Camellia Forest, Chapel Hill, NC).

APRIL BLUSH - Shell Pink. Medium to large, semidouble. Relatively slow growth. M. Cold hardy to nearly 0°F. (U.S. 1995 - Parks).

APRIL DAWN - White with a few Deep Pink streaks. Small to medium, formal double. Vigorous, upright growth. M-L. Cold hardy. (U.S. 1993 - Parks).

APRIL DAWN BLUSH - Blush Pink with thin White edge on each petal. Small, formal double. Average open growth. M-L. (U.S. 2013 - Bob Black, Windsor, VA).

APRIL KISS - Pinkish Red. Small to medium, formal double. Slow to average, upright growth with heavy bud set. M. Cold hardy - Zone 6B. (Japonica 'Berenice Boddy' x Japonica 'Reg Ragland'). (U.S. 1995 - Parks).

APRIL LYNN POE - Peach Pink. Large, semidouble with wavy, crinkled petals. Vigorous, upright growth. M. (U.S. 1970 - Poe).

APRIL MELODY - Rose Red. Small, single. Strong growth. E. Very cold hardy. (U.S. 2008 - Parks).

APRIL PINK - Soft Pink. Large, formal double. Compact growth. M. Cold hardy to -9°. (U.S. 2008 - Parks).

APRIL REMEMBERED - Cream center to Pink shaded edges with Yellow anthers and Cream filaments. Medium to large, semidouble. Vigorous growth. E-L. Cold hardy to 0°F. (Japonica 'Berenice Boddy' x Japonica 'Dr. Tinsley'). (U.S. 1995 - Parks).

APRIL ROSE - Rose Red. Medium, formal double. L. Cold hardy. (U.S. 1993 - Parks).

APRIL SHOWERS - Clear Pink. Medium, anemone form with undulated outer guard petals and petaloids grown together at base. Average, upright growth. L. (U.S. 1957 - Marshall).

APRIL SNOW - White. Medium to large, rose form double. Slow, compact growth. L. Cold hardy. (U.S. 1993 - Parks).

APRIL TENILE - Light Blush Pink center deepens to a Pale Pink towards the outer petals with Gold Anthers and White filaments. Large, loose peony form with unpronounced stamens. Vigorous, upright, dense growth. M-L. (U.S. 2019 - Jill & Glenn Read, Lucedale, MS).

APRIL TRYST - Bright Red. Medium to large, anemone form. Average, upright growth. M. Cold hardy to nearly 0°F. (U.S. 1995 - Parks).

AQUARIUS - Pink. Medium, formal double. Slow, compact, upright growth. M-L. (U.S. 1971 - N. Rogers, Theodore, AL).

ARABIAN NIGHTS - Oriental Pink with shadings of Deeper Pink. Large, semidouble with ruffled petals. Vigorous, upright growth. M. (U.S. 1958 - McCaskill).

ARABIAN NIGHTS VARIEGATED - Oriental Pink blotched White variation of 'Arabian Nights'.

ARAJISHI - ('Aloha'; 'Beni-Arejishi'; 'Callie'). Dark Salmon Rose. Medium, full peony form. Vigorous, open, upright growth. E. (Japan 1891 - Yokohama).

ARAJISHI VARIEGATED - Dark Salmon Rose and White variation of 'Arajishi'.

ARCHIE LANIER - Pink shading Darker Pink. Large, semidouble. Average growth. M. (U.S. 1972 - V. L. Green, Ocala, FL).

ARCHIE'S ANGEL - Faint Pink. Miniature, formal double. Compact, upright growth. M-L. (U.S. 1975 - Gentry).

ARGENTINITA - ('Faithful'). Soft Pink spotted Rose Pink. Medium, semidouble. (Sport of Japonica 'Bidwell Variegated'). (U.S. 1942 - Coolidge).

ARIANA HALL - Pink tinted outer petal edges fading to Cream White. Large, semidouble with fluted petals. Average, upright growth. M-L. (U.S. 1973 - H. Hall).

ARIANA HALL SUPREME - Sweet Pea Pink outer petal edges fading to Cream White at center. Large, semidouble. Average, upright growth. M-L. (U.S. 1996 - H. Hall).

ARISTOCRAT - White. Medium to large, single with creped petals. Vigorous, upright growth. M. (U.S. 1955 - Short).

ARLENE IGNICO - Rose Pink. Medium, semidouble to loose peony form. Vigorous, compact growth. M. (U.S. 1950 - Wheeler).

ARLENE LEE SHEPP - Blended Pink and White to veined Pink bordered White. Medium, semidouble. (Sport of Japonica 'Olive Lee Shepp'). (U.S. 1950 - Shepp).

ARLENE MARSHALL - White. Large to very large, semidouble to anemone form. Vigorous, compact, upright growth. M. (U.S. 1954 - Marshall).

AROMA - Lavender Rose. Large, semidouble with White stamens. Vigorous, compact, upright growth. Pronounced fragrance similar to an Easter lily. (U.S. 1962 - Dr. W. C. Hava, Waveland, MS).

ARRABELLA - ('Donna Kaye').- Orange Red. Medium, semidouble with ruffled and notched petals. Vigorous, compact, upright growth. M-L. (U.S. 1949 - Edinger).

ART HOWARD - Rose Pink. Large, peony form. Vigorous, open, upright growth. M-L. (U.S. 1958 - F. Bergstrom, Pasadena, CA).

ART'S RUBY - Ruby Red. Small, semidouble with fluted petals. Open, upright growth with elongated leaves. M. (U.S. 2003 - Art Landry, Baton Rouge, LA).

ARTHUR BOLTON - Blush Pink. Medium, rose form double to formal double with reflexed, wavy petals. (Sport of Japonica 'Magnoliaeflora'). (Aus. 1967 - A. Bolton, Croydon, Vic.).

ARTHUR GAYLE - Dark Red. Very large, semidouble to anemone form. Vigorous, bushy, upright growth. M. (U.S. 1975 - Gentry).

ARTHUR WEISNER - Dark Red. Large, semidouble with large petals and petaloids among stamens and between petals. Average growth. E-M. (U.S. 1959 - Weisner).

ASAGAO - Pale Pink. Medium, single with flared Pale Yellow stamens. See Higo.

ASHLEY BLACK - Blush pink, flecked and occasionally streaked red, with a narrow white border at edge of petals. Miniature to small, formal double with 90 to 100 petals. Average, upright growth. M. (Sport of Japonica 'Grace Albritton'). (U.S. 2017 - Bob Black, Windsor, VA).

ASHLEY HALL - Mottled Rose over Pink, striped over all. Large, peony form. Vigorous, open, upright growth. E. (U.S. 2004 - Marion G. Hall, Dothan, AL).

ASHLEY HARDEE - Deep Rose with Purple cast. Large, peony form. Vigorous, open, upright growth. M. (U.S. 1961 - Mrs. V. Hardee, Madison, FL).

ASHLEY McCOMB - Pink. Large to very large, peony form. Average, spreading, upright growth. E-M. (U.S. 1989 - Tammia).

ASHLEY VARIEGATED - Deep Pink sometimes marked White. Large, semidouble. M. (U.S. 1953 - Simon's Nsy., Johns Island, SC).

ASHTON'S RED SUNSET - Red-Purple (RHS 58C) with Yellow anthers and Creamy White filaments. Medium, semidouble. Average, spreading, low, dense growth. E-M. (Japonica 'Frost Queen' x Japonica 'Variety Z'). (U.S. 2010 - Ackerman).

ASPASIA (UNITED STATES) - See 'Emperor of Russia Variegated'.

ASPASIA MACARTHUR - ('Paeoniaeflora'; 'Flore Celeste'). White to Cream White with a few Rose Red lines and dashes. Medium, full peony form. Slow, upright growth. E-M. (For other forms of this cultivar see Japonicas 'Camden Park'; 'Jean Clere'; 'Lady Loch'; 'Margaret Davis'; 'Otahuhu Beauty'; 'Strawberry Blonde'). (Aus. 1850 - Macarthur).

ASPASIA ROSEA - See 'Otahuhu Beauty'.

ASPASIA VARIEGATA - See 'Camden Park'.

ASTRO NOVA - White with Red stripes and spots with fimbriated petals. Large, semidouble to anemone form. Average, dense, upright growth. M. (U.S. 2002 - Ken Hallstone, Lafayette, CA).

ASTRONAUT - Rose Pink. Medium, single to semidouble. Vigorous, upright growth. M. (U.S. 1964 - Select Nsy., Brea, CA).

ATHELYNE - Red. Medium to large, semidouble with irregular petals. Average, compact growth. M. (U.S. 1957 - Bartlett's Nsy., Fort Valley, GA).

ATHELYNE VARIEGATED - Red blotched White variation of 'Athelyne'.

17

ATHENA - White marked Deep Rose. Medium, anemone form to loose peony form with slightly wavy outer petals. Average, upright growth. M-L. Fragrant. (U.S. 1957 - Julington).

ATKINS' GIFT - Pink. Large, formal double. Average, spreading growth. E-L. (U.S. 2004 - Camellia Heaven - John Grimm, Metairie, LA).

ATOMIC RED - Red. Medium, semidouble. Slow, open growth. M. (U.S. 1953 - Shackelford).

AUBREY HARRIS - Orange Pink to Red moiré White. Large, semidouble with some upright center petals. Slow, upright growth. M. (U.S. 1959 - Judice).

AUBURN MOONBRIGHT - White with Yellow anthers and Yellow filaments. Very large, semidouble. Average, upright growth. E. (Japonica 'Moonlight Bay' x Japonica 'Joshua Youtz'). (U.S. 2017 - Kenneth Rogers, Auburn, AL).

AUBURN WHITE - White. Large, semidouble with long, Yellow stamens. (Reported to be same as Japonica 'Mrs. Bertha A. Harms'). (U.S. 1900 - Auburn, WA).

AUDREY CALLANAN - Red. Medium, semidouble. Average, open, spreading growth. L. (Aus. 1968 - J. A. Richards, Hawthorne, Vic.).

AUDREY CHRISTINE - Pink (RHS color 55b); the veins in the basal petals tend to be slightly Red toward the edges. Medium to large, formal double; the center petals have some slight fimbriation. Average, upright growth. M-L. (Seedling of Japonica 'Adolphe Audusson'). (U.S. 2018 - Kenneth Rogers, Auburn, AL).

AUDREY CLAIRE - White. Large, formal double. Vigorous, upright growth. E-M. (U.S. 1990 - Mrs. M. Walker, Tallahassee, FL).

AUDREY HOPFER - See 'Adolphe Audusson'.

AUGUSTA EQUEN - Light Rose Pink. Large, formal double with petals diminishing in size toward center. Vigorous, upright growth. E-M. (A variation of this cultivar includes Japonica 'R. O. Rubel'). (U.S. 1955 - Longview).

AUGUSTA MORN - Carmine. Large, single with ruffled petals and Yellow anthers. Vigorous, compact, upright growth. M. (U.S. 1960 - O. J. Faircloth, Pensacola, FL).

AUGUSTA WILSON - ('Ashland Pink'; 'St. Elmo'). Soft Pink. Medium, full peony form. Vigorous, compact, upright growth. E-M. (U.S. 1937 - A. E. Wilson, Mobile, AL).

AUGUSTE DELFOSSE (BELGIUM) - Orange Red striped White. Large, formal double. M. (Belgium 1855 - E. Defresne, Liege).

AUGUSTO LEAL DE GOUVEIA PINTO - ('Portuguese Pink'; 'Jack McCaskill'; 'Augusto L'Gouveia Pinto'). Light Coral Pink sometimes flushed with Lavender and each petal bordered White. Large, semidouble to formal double. (Another variation of this cultivar includes Japonica 'Shepherdess'; sport of Japonica 'Grand Sultan'). (Portugal 1980 - Da Silva).

AUNT JETTY - ('Angelica'; 'Governor Mouton'). Oriental Red. Medium, semidouble to loose peony form. Vigorous, upright growth. M. Cold hardy. (U.S. 1811 - Originator unknown; 1990 - Registered by Tallahassee Camellia and Garden Club, FL).

AUNT MATIE - Pink inner petals and Rose outer petals. Medium, formal double. Vigorous, upright growth. M. (U.S. 1970 - T. Eagleson, Port Arthur, TX).

AUNTY LOLA - White. Medium, single. Average, upright growth. E-L. (N.Z. 1992 - B. Simmons, Blenheim).

AURORA BOREALIS - See 'Finlandia Variegated'.

AURORA ROSEA - See 'Finlandia Red'.

AUSTRALIS - Rose Red. Medium, peony form. Vigorous, compact, upright growth. M. (Aus. 1951 - Camellia Grove).

AUTUMN LANTERN - Rose Red. Medium, single. Upright growth. VE. (Japonica 'Berenice Boddy' x Japonica 'Dainty'). (U.S. 2004 - Camellia Forest Nursery, Chapel Hill, NC).

AUTUMN MIST - Pure White with Pink edges gradually fading to the center. Large, single. E-M. (U.S. 2008 - Parks).

AUTUMN PERFECTION - Clear Pink. Small, formal double. Vigorous, upright growth. E. (U.S. 2006 - Howell).

AUTUMN TWILIGHT - Lavender Pink. Large to very large, formal double form. Average, dense, upright growth. M. (U.S. 2005 - Gordy).

AVE MARIA - Silvery Pink. Small to medium, formal double. Slow, compact, upright growth. E-M. (U.S. 1956 - Breschini).

AVERY ISLAND - See 'Mathotiana Supreme Variegated'.

AVIS LOVE - Soft Coral Pink. Small, formal double. Average, spreading growth. M-L. (U.S. 2012 - Gordy).

AY-AY-AY! - Veined Deep Pink, Red stripes in background, some White on petal edges, and occasional White blotches. Medium, single to semidouble. Average, upright growth. E-L. (Sport of Japonica 'Oo-La-La!'). (U.S. 1995 - Nuccio's).

AYER MAID - White. Medium, semidouble. Average, spreading growth. M-L. (U.S. 1987 - C. M. Ayer, Madison, FL).

AZORA - Pink. Medium to large, single with flared stamens; some flowers are fully topped with White petaloids. See Higo.

AZTEC WARRIOR - Bright Red. Large, loose peony form to anemone form with large, somewhat twisted center petals surrounding smaller, curled, inner petals intermixed with petaloids and stamens. Average, open, upright growth. E-M. (U.S. 1965 - A. S. Horne, Moncks Corner, SC).

B. C. GOODMAN - Light Pink with Dark Pink stripes on some petals. Medium, full peony form. Vigorous, open growth. E. Distinct fragrance. (U.S. 1953 - B. C. Goodman, Pensacola, FL).

BABE HARRISON - Rose Pink. Medium, semidouble to peony form. Vigorous, open, upright growth. E-L. (U.S. 1954 - Turner).

BABETTE - White to Blush Pink. Large, multiform of all forms except single. Average growth. M. (U.S. 1975 - Tammia).

BABS ALSIP - White. Large, semidouble form; petals are fluted, usually five petals in top ring. Average growth. M. (U.S. 2004 - Gordon E. Eade, Pensacola, FL).

BABS BARNETTE - Light Peachy Pink. Small, formal double with curly petals. Average, upright growth. L. (U.S. 1996 - Elizabeth R. Scott, Aiken, SC).

BABY ANGEL - White. Miniature, semidouble. Average, upright growth. M-L. (U.S. 1968 - E. Pieri, San Gabriel, CA).

BABY BLUSH - Blush Pink. Miniature, formal double. (U.S. 1967 - K. K. Womack, Shreveport, Louisiana).

BABY DOLL - Light clear Pink. Miniature, tight centered anemone form. Average, dense, spreading growth. M-L. (U.S. 1992 - Nuccio's).

BABY PEARL - White washed and shaded Orchid Pink. Small, formal double. Average, bushy growth. M. (U.S. 1980 - Nuccio's).

BABY SARGENT - Dark Red. Miniature, full peony form, resembling 'Professor Charles S Sargent'. (U.S. 1949 - Pfingstl).

BABY SIS - White with a Pink stripe with Yellow stamens. Miniature, single with mass of petaloids in center. Slow, compact growth. M. (U.S. 1958 - Shackelford).

BABY SIS BLUSH - Blush Pink with a fine White edge on each petal. Miniature, single with mass of petaloids in center. Slow, compact growth. M. (Color sport of Japonica 'Baby Sis'). (U.S. 1980 - Don Bergamini, Martinez, CA).

BABY SIS BLUSH VARIEGATED - Light Blush Pink blotched White variation of 'Baby Sis Blush'. (U.S. - Don Bergamini, Martinez, CA).

BABY SIS PINK - Pink. (Sport of Japonica 'Baby Sis'). (U.S.1966 - Shackelford).

BADGEN'S BEAUTY - See 'Pink Pearl'.

BAIGENTS GIFT - Pink with Yellow stamens tipped White. Large, peony form. Average, compact, upright growth. E-M. (N.Z. 1985 - G. Baigent, Katikati).

BAISAN XUESHI (WHITE THREE SCHOLARS) - White with a rare Pink or Red mark. Medium, rose form double to formal double. Average, upright, very dense growth. M-L. (China 1981 - Wang and Yu).

BAKER - Pink. Large, semidouble to anemone form to peony form. M. (U.S. 1973 - Haynie).

BALI HA'I - White, sometimes marked Pink on one petal. Medium, semidouble with intermingled petaloids and stamens in center. Vigorous, compact, upright growth. M. (U.S. 1961 - McCaskill).

BALI HA'I DAWN - Soft Pink to Light Pink shading to White at edge. (Sport of Japonica 'Bali Ha'i'). (U.S. 1969 - McCaskill).

BALI HA'I PINK - Veined Pink. (Sport of Japonica 'Bali Ha'i'). (U.S. 1969 - McCaskill).

BALLERINA - Pink. Medium, semidouble with incurved petals. Bushy growth. M. (U.S. 1948 - Fruitland).

BALLERINA BELLE - White with Pink stripes with Yellow anthers and White filaments. Medium to large, single. Average, upright, spreading growth. E-L. (U.S. 2017 - Pat Johnson, Cairo, GA).

BALLET DANCER - Cream shading to Coral Pink at edge. Medium, full peony form with mixed petals and petaloids of full form. Average, compact, upright growth. E-L. (U.S. 1960 - Short).

BALUSTRADE - Scarlet Red. Small, single. Very narrow, upright growth. (Seeds from NW South Korea - Barry Yinger, et al - before 1986). (U.S. 2011 - Morris Arboretum, Philadelphia, PA).

BAMBINO - Coral Rose Pink. Small, peony form to anemone form. Vigorous, bushy, upright growth. M. (U.S. 1959 - McCaskill).

BANYO - Soft Rose Pink. Large, single. (Japan 1956 - Satomi, Kumamoto). See Higo.

BAR NONE - See 'Daitairin'.

BARBARA BEDAYN - Salmon Pink. Large, semidouble to anemone form. Slow, compact growth. M-L. (U.S. 1967 - Mrs. B. Bedayn, Orinda, CA).

BARBARA BEELAND REHDER - Light Blush Pink. Miniature, formal double. Average, upright growth. M-L. (U.S. 1996 - H. Rehder, Wilmington, NC).

BARBARA BOTTS - White with some Pink stripes. Large, semidouble. Average, upright growth. M-L. (U.S. 1995 - W. Wilson, Augusta, GA).

BARBARA CAROL - Rose Pink. Large, anemone form. Vigorous, compact, upright growth. M. (Aus. 1970 - Sebire).

BARBARA COLBERT - Clear Pink. Large, semidouble with wavy, crinkled petals. Vigorous, upright growth. E-M. (U.S. 1968 - Gerbing).

BARBARA COLBERT SILVER - White striped Pink. (Sport of Japonica 'Barbara Colbert'). (U.S. 1989 - A. K. Boll, Jacksonville, FL).

BARBARA GRACE - Purple with Deep Maroon center shading with Yellow anthers and Yellow filaments. Large, semidouble to rose form double to formal double; most often formal double. Average, upright growth. M. (U.S. 2013 - Howell).

BARBARA HARRISON - Pale Blush Pink. Large, anemone form. Average, spreading, upright growth. E-L. (U.S. 1990 - W. Harrison, Berkeley, CA).

BARBARA HOFF - Rose Red and White. Large, semidouble with loose petals. Vigorous, spreading growth. M. (U.S. 1958 - Fisher).

BARBARA MARY - Blush Pink. Large, peony form with delicate fragrance. E-M. (Aus. 1965 - Waterhouse).

BARBARA McBRIDE - Rose Pink. Large, rose form double with fimbriated petals. Average, open, upright growth. M. (U.S. 1974 - Homeyer).

BARBARA THOMPSON - Deep Pink. Small, formal double with inner rows of pointed petals and in the shape of a star. Average, compact growth. M. (U.S. 1957 - R. S. Mauldin, Hueytown, AL).

BARBARA WHALEY - Rose Pink striped Darker Pink. Medium, semidouble with petaloids intermixed with stamens. Average, upright growth. E-M. (U.S. 1957 - H. B. Whaley, Mobile, AL).

BARBARA WITTEN - Carmine. Large, peony form. Vigorous, slightly pendulous growth. M-L. (Aus. 1963 - Mrs. K. V. Rosenhain, Vic.).

BARBARA WOODROOF - Light Orchid Pink outer guard petals and Cream White center petaloids with an occasional Rose Pink petaloid. Medium to large, anemone form. (Sport of Japonica 'Elegans [Chandler] Variegated'). (U.S. 1957 - W E Woodroof, Sherman Oaks, CA).

BARBAREL - Neyron Rose petals with Crimson veining. Medium, formal double; center petals proportionally smaller, cupped and edges unrolled into a loose, budlike formation. M-L. (U.S. 1955).

BARBRA MITCHELL - White in center shading to Light Pink. Large, formal double. Average, upright growth. M-L. (U.S. 1995 - I. Mitchell, Melrose, FL).

BARKER COLLEGE - Pink with Deeper Pink stripes and slashes. Medium, semidouble. Bushy upright growth. M-L. (Aus. 2006 - Alan Truran).

BARNEY BARNARD - Deep Red with Gold anthers. Large, semidouble. Slow, upright growth. M-L. (U.S. 2018 - Laura Barnard, St. Elmo, AL).

BARNEY DIAMOND - Clear Pink. Large, semidouble with large, wavy, notched outer petals and intermixed crinkled and twisted petaloids and scattered stamens. Vigorous, open growth. M. (U.S. 1959 - S. Forbes, Savannah, GA).

BARNEY DIAMOND VARIEGATED - Clear Pink and White variation of 'Barney Diamond'. (U.S. 1960 - S. Forbes, Savannah, GA).

BARNEY WEEMS - Dark Red. Medium, anemone form. Vigorous, compact, upright growth. E-M. (U.S. 1975 - Wilson).

BARNSLEY PERFECTION - Blush Pink. Medium, formal double. Vigorous, spreading, upright growth. E-L. (U.S. 1968 - W. H. Barnsley, Apopka, FL).

BARONNE DE BLEICHROEDER (UNITED STATES) - ('Bleichroeder';'Otome Variegated'; 'Otome-Shibori'). Soft Pink streaked Crimson. Medium, rose form double. Slow, compact growth. M. (Variations of this cultivar include Japonicas 'Mother of Pearl'; Otome White'; 'Bleichroeder Pink'). (Japan 1891 to U.S. - Huntington Gardens 1917, under name of 'Otome-Shibori').

BARONNE DE BLEICHROEDER PINK - See 'Bleichroeder Pink'.

BART COLBERT - Deep Pink. Large, semidouble. Average, upright growth. M. (U.S. 1977 - R. E. May, Savannah, GA).

BART COLBERT VARIEGATED - Deep Pink variegated White variation of 'Bart Colbert'. (U.S. 1977 - R E May, Savannah, GA).

BASCOM HENDERSON - Red. Medium, full peony form. Slow, open growth. E-M. (U.S. 1955 - V. Hardee, Madison, FL).

BASTITA - See 'Herme Pink'.

BATCHELOR PINK - Purplish Pink with Purplish Pink petaloids and White stamens. Large, anemone form. Vigorous, compact growth. M. (U.S. 1962 - Dr. J. B. Anderson, Edgewater Park, MS).

BEA ROGERS - Alabaster White. Large, peony form. Average, upright growth. (U.S. 1971 - N. Rogers, Theodore, AL).

BEATRICE BISIACH - Carmine Red, splashed with White. Large to very large, semidouble form. Slow, spreading growth. E. (Italy 2001 - G. B. Bertolassi, Italy).

BEATRICE BURNS - Shaded Rose Pink. Large, semidouble with incurved petals. (Aus. 1951 - Dr. R. C. Merrillees, Melbourne).

BEATRICE HOOPER - White. Large, formal double to rose form double. Compact growth. M. (Aus. 1960 - G. Hooper, Bexley).

BEATRIX HOYT - Light Rose Pink. Large, semidouble. (U.S. 1955 - Miss B. Hoyt, Thomasville, GA).

BEAU BRUMMEL - Red heavily variegated White. Medium, peony form. Average growth. M. (U.S. 1957).

BEAU GESTE - Rich Red. Large, loose peony form. Average, upright growth. M-L. (U.S. 1972 - Haynie).

BEAU HARP - Red. Medium to large, peony form. Vigorous, upright growth. E-M. (U.S. 1949 - Wilkinson).

BEAU HARP VARIEGATED - See 'Dr. John D. Bell'.

BEAULIEU BELLE - White. Large, semidouble with upright center petals with slight Pink stripe. Average, compact, upright growth. M. (U.S. 1964 - G. S. Clarke, Savannah, GA).

BEAUTY OF HOLLAND - ('C. P. Morgan'; 'Doris Madalia'; 'Hermesport'; 'Princess Lucille'; 'Hikaru-Genji-Yokomoku'). Rose Pink spotted and blotched White. Medium, semidouble. (Sport of Japonica 'Herme'). (U.S. 1938 - Overlook).

BEAUVOIR - Red with Purple cast. Medium, semidouble with fluted petals. M. (U.S. 1945 - Clower).

BEBE WOODWARD - White with Yellow at the base of each petal. Medium to large, peony form to rose form double to formal double. Average, upright growth. E-L. Cold hardy. (U.S. 1995 - Elizabeth R. Scott, Aiken, SC).

BEBE'S BEST - Light Pink with Rose striping and bright Yellow anthers. Very large, loose peony form with crepe like petals in center of flower. Average, upright growth. E-L. (Sport of Japonica 'Adam Grant'). (U.S. 2012 - Marion Hall, Dothan, AL).

BECKET RED - Red. Large, semidouble. (U.S. 1959).

BECKY ANN - White. Large, anemone form. Average, open, upright growth. E. (U.S. 1962 - Bucks Nsy., Americus, GA).

BECKY VARNER - Deep Red changing to Purple with age. Large, full peony form. Slow, open, upright growth. M. (U.S. 1950 - Mrs. C. T. Springer, Union Springs, AL).

BELAIR - White. Very large, anemone form to peony form. Average, open, upright growth. E-M. (Aus. 1989 - D. Coe, Glenroy, Albury, NSW).

BELDEN PAGE - Cream White with White stamens. Medium, semidouble to rose form double. Average, open growth. L. (U.S. 1950 - R. J. Geimer, San Marino, CA).

BELINDA GAIL - Red with dark veining with Yellow anthers and White filaments. Medium, semidouble. Average, upright growth. M-L. (U.S. 2010 - Melvin Stallings, Chesapeake, VA).

BELLA JINHUA - ('Hongye Beila' and 'Jinhua Meinü' - Chinese names; 'Red Leaf Bella'). Dark Red with Black veining on the interior of the petals and lighter Red on the edges of the petals. Medium, formal double. Slow, bushy, upright growth; leaves are Burgundy Red for months before finally turning Light Green with Black streaks and flecks. E-M. (Leaf and bloom sport of Japonica 'Nuccio's Bella Rossa'). (China).

BELLA ROMANA - Light Pink striped and splashed Carmine. Medium, rose form double. Vigorous, bushy growth. M. (For a variation of this cultivar see Japonica 'La Bella'). (Italy 1863 - C. Lemaire. Rome).

BELLA ROMANA PINK - Solid Pink. Medium, rose form double. Vigorous, bushy growth. M. (Solid pink sport of Japonica 'Bella Romana'). (Europe 1987).

BELLA ROMANA RED - ('Cabrillo'). Rose Red. (Sport of Japonica 'Bella Romana'). (U.S. 1946).

BELLE NEIGE - White. Medium, semidouble of flat form with narrow petals. M. (Europe to U.S. [Magnolia] 1840's).

BELLE OF ORANGE - White. Large, full peony form. Vigorous, upright growth. M. (U.S. 1958 - Ragland).

BELLE OF THE BALL - Rosy Salmon. Large, semidouble to peony form. Vigorous, spreading growth. M. (U.S. 1965 - McCaskill).

BEN FRANKLIN - Crimson with Purple. Large, peony form. Average growth. M. (U.S. 1979 - H. B. Franklin, Tallahassee, FL).

BEN GEORGE - White striped Rose Pink. Very large, single to semidouble Higo style. Vigorous, upright growth. M. (U.S. 2007 - Hulyn Smith).

BEN LOMOND - Dark Red with White marked Red petaloids. Small, semidouble. Average, upright growth. M. (U.S. 1975 - H. Fish, Santa Cruz, CA).

BEN PARKER - China Rose. Medium, semidouble with petals and petaloids forming funnel-shaped trumpets with stamens in circle around trumpets. Slow, compact, upright growth. E-M. (U.S. 1955 - B. Parker, Foxworth, MS).

BEN PARKER VARIEGATED - China Rose and White variation of 'Ben Parker'.

BENI-AREJISHI - See 'Arajishi'.

BENI-BOTAN - See 'Herme Pink'.

BENI-DAIKAGURA - See 'Daikagura Red'.

BENITANCHO (RED HEAD CRANE) - Crimson with golden anthers and flesh filaments. Medium, single with 7-8 petals with about 140 flared stamens. M. (Sport of Japonica 'Tanchô'). (Japan 1977). See Higo.

BENJAMIN THOMPSON IV - Rose. Large, semidouble. Average, spreading growth. M-L. (U.S. 1988 - J. Aldrich, Brooklet, GA).

BENJO - Deep Salmon Red veined darker. Medium, loose peony form to semidouble. Average, compact growth. E-L. (U.S. 1979 - D. W. Townsend, Brookhaven, MS).

BENJY - Red. Large, semidouble. Average, upright growth. M. (U.S. 1958 - Mrs. H. K. Edwards, Columbia, SC).

BENTEN-KAGURA - Rose Pink splotched White. Medium to large, peony form. Slow, very compact growth; irregularly shaped Green leaf finely bordered Yellow. M. (Foliage Sport of Japonica 'Daikagura'). (Japan to U.S. - Nuccio's).

BENTEN-MRS. R. L. WHEELER - Pink. Medium, formal double. (U.S. - Camellia Forest, Chapel Hill, NC).

BERENICE BEAUTY - Pale Pink with Deeper Pink toward margin. Medium to large, semidouble to loose peony form. Vigorous, upright growth. E-M. (U.S. 1965 - Nuccio's).

BERENICE BODDY - Light Pink with Deep Pink under petals. Medium, semidouble. Vigorous, upright growth. M. Cold hardy. (For a variation of this cultivar see Japonica 'Kathryn Hall'). (U.S. 1946 - Descanso and Jones).

BERENICE PERFECTION - Pale Pink with Deeper Pink margin. Medium, formal double. Vigorous, columnar, upright growth. M. (U.S. 1965 - Nuccio's).

BERG'S BABY FORMAL - White striped Pink. Miniature, formal double with pointed petals. Slow, open, spreading growth. M. (N.Z. 1986 - Mrs. I. Berg, Whakatane).

BERNADETTE - Pink. Large, peony form. Average, open, upright growth. M-L. (U.S. 1988 - A. V. Ewan, Charleston, SC).

BERNARD WEISS - Delicate veined Pink shading to White toward edge. Large, semidouble with upright petals. Average, upright growth. M. (U.S. 1963 - A. C. Harris, Shreveport, LA).

BERNICE OWENS DEAL - Pastel Pink with Yellow anthers and White filaments. Small, semidouble. Vigorous, upright, open, loose growth. E-L. (Seedling of japonica 'Berenice Boddy'). (U.S. 2019 - E. W. & Gena Fredrickson, Wilmington, NC).

BERTA HAMILTON - Red. Medium, semidouble with fluted petals and Red stamens. Willowy growth. E-M. (U.S. 1955 - Tallahassee, FL).

BERTHA FAYE HOWELL - Bright Red. Large, semidouble with thick, wavy upright petals and Red stamens. Vigorous, upright growth. E-M. (U.S. 1959 - B. Howell, Mobile, AL).

BERTHA FAYE HOWELL VARIEGATED - Red blotched White variation of 'Bertha Faye Howell'.

BERTHA LEVI - Red to Pink. Large, flat semidouble. Vigorous, spreading growth. M. (U.S. 1965 - Ashby).

BERWICK - Deep Flesh Pink veined deeper. Medium, rose form double. Vigorous, upright growth. (Aus. 1968 - F. S. Tuckfield, Berwick, Vic.).

BERYL HEBITON - Blush Pink with narrow Pink stripes and dots. Large, peony form. E-M. (Aus. 1963 - W. Hebiton, Floriat Park).

BESSIE BATTLE - White with Golden stamens and White filaments. Medium, semidouble to loose peony form; the petals are wavy and notched at the end. Average, upright, spreading growth. M. (U.S. 1999 - Tom Dodd Nurseries, Semmes, AL).

BESSIE BOWMAN - Rose Pink to Rose Pink and White. Medium, semidouble with irregular petals to peony form. Average, spreading growth. M-L. (U.S. 1957 - Bowman).

BESSIE DICKSON - White. Medium, anemone form. Vigorous, compact, upright growth. E. Fragrant. (U.S. 1982 - Piet and Gaeta).

BESSIE HORTMAN - Dark Pink. Large, semidouble with heavy petals. Average, upright growth. L. (U.S. 1961 - C. Hortman, Columbus, GA).

BESSIE McARTHUR - Clear Pink. Medium, loose peony form. Vigorous, bushy growth. L. (U.S. 1943 - Gerbing).

BESSIE PERDUE WEAVER - Rose. Medium, semidouble. Average, compact growth. M. (U.S. 1953 - A. G. Weaver, Brewton, AL).

BESSIE SHEAROUSE - Light Rose Pink. Large to very large, semidouble with crepe upright center petals. Vigorous, compact growth. M. (U.S. 1967 - G. B. Shearouse, Jr., Thunderbolt, GA).

BESSIE STARING - Pink. Medium, full peony form. Average, pendulous growth. E. (U.S. 1954 - Mrs. S. Staring, Baton Rouge, LA).

BESSIE TIFT - Bright Pink with Gold anthers and Cream filaments. Medium, semidouble. Vigorous, upright, open growth. M-L. (U.S. 2015 - Gordy).

BETHLEHEM STAR - White with Gold anthers and White filaments. Large, semidouble to loose peony. Slow, upright, dense growth. M-L. (Seedling of Japonica 'Snow Lady'). (U.S. 2016 - Pat Johnson, Cairo, GA).

BETSY - Dark Pink with White marks. Miniature to small, semidouble. Average, upright growth. E-M. (U.S. 1983 - H. J. Martin, Sacramento, CA).

BETSY BLUSH - White, Blush Pink. (Sport of Japonica 'Betsy'). (U.S. 1997 - H. Martin, Sacramento, CA).

BETSY BOULWARE - White in center toned with soft Pink toward edge and in each petal. Medium to large, semidouble. Average, upright growth. M-L. (U.S. 1957 - Mrs. T. H. Symmes, St. Matthews, SC).

BETSY ROSS - See 'Mrs. Confer'.

BETTE ANNE - Light Lavender Pink. Medium, rose form double. Average, upright, dense growth. E-L. (U.S. 2009 - Richard Hooton, Pensacola, FL).

BETTIE KRAYOSKY - Rose Pink with Light Pink center. Medium to large, semidouble. Average, upright growth. E. (U.S. 1968 - Rester).

BETTIE WELLS - Salmon Red. Very large, loose peony form to rose form double. Vigorous, compact, upright growth. M-L. (U.S. 1984 - Alfter).

BETTY ARNOTT - White. Large, single. Average, pendulous growth. E. (Aus. 1963 - Mrs. G. S. Arnott, East Brighton).

BETTY BERWICK - Deep Red to Crimson. Medium, loose peony form. Vigorous, upright growth. M. (Aus. 1978 - Mrs. B. Berwick, Caringbah, NSW).

BETTY BURGESS - Blush Pink striped Cherry Red. Large, semidouble with upright petals. Average, open growth. M. (U.S. 1965 - Burgess).

BETTY BY GEORGE - Blush Pink, almost transparent, with very few Darker Pink marks. Medium to large, semidouble to loose peony form. (Sport of Japonica 'Betty Sheffield'). (U.S. 1982 - G. R. Clegg, Tallahassee, FL).

BETTY CROMLEY - Deep Salmon Red. Large, semidouble to peony form. Average, upright growth. M-L. (U.S. 1988 - J. Aldrich, Brooklet, GA).

BETTY CUTHBERT - Rose Pink. Large, formal double to rose form double with some petaloids. Average, spreading growth. E-M. (Aus. 1964 - Waterhouse).

BETTY DREWS - Pink. Miniature, formal double with cupped outer petals. Vigorous, upright growth. E. (U.S. 1981 - Rupert E. Drews, Charleston, SC).

BETTY FOY SANDERS - White with varying amounts of flecked, splotched, and spotted Rose Red marks or streaks. Medium, semidouble of flared trumpet shape. Average growth. E-M. (First Lady of Georgia Series). (U.S. 1965 - F. Smith, Statesboro, GA).

BETTY GABRIEL - White. Large, semidouble of cupped form with crinkled crepe petals. Vigorous, compact, upright growth. M. (U.S. 1977 - Dr. H. F. Gabriel, Oceanside, CA).

BETTY GOODWIN - Blush Pink or Blush Pink streaked White. Medium, semidouble. Vigorous, compact growth. M. (U.S. 1950 - Mrs. C. I. Goodwin, Sr., Orangeburg, SC).

BETTY GRANDY - White slightly Blushed Pink. Large, rose form double. Average, compact growth. M-L. (U.S. 1950 - Mrs. C. R. Grandy, Norfolk, VA).

BETTY LAVENDER BLUSH - Blush Lavender Pink with Golden anthers and Whitish filaments. Medium to large, semidouble to loose peony with slightly waved petals. Average, compact growth. M. (Sport of Japonica 'Betty Sheffield'). (U.S. 1967).

BETTY LOU - Red variegated White. Large, anemone form. Average, upright growth. E-M. (U.S. 1977 - H. Bailey, Plant City, FL).

BETTY LYON - Pink inner petals, incurved and small with darker outer edges, Dark Pink blotched Pale Pink, lightly cupped outer petals. Medium, formal double. Average, upright, open growth. M-L. (N.Z. 1999 - Betty Lyon).

BETTY M. LEE - Deep Red. Large, rose form double. Average, upright growth. M-L. (U.S. 1968 - S. Monroe, Waycross, GA).

BETTY MITCHELL - White. Medium, formal double. Average, upright growth. E-M. (U.S. 1984 - Mrs. H. Johnson, Madison, FL).

BETTY MORRIS - Deep Rose Pink with Purplish cast. Large, peony form with irregular petals. Average, compact growth. E-L. (U.S. 1950 - Mrs. R. Morris, Yemassee, SC).

BETTY NEILD - Blush Pink. Medium, anemone form. Average, compact growth. E-L. (U.S. 1954 - G. Pugh and E. F. Neild, Shreveport, LA).

BETTY PREGNALL - Deep Pink. Large, anemone form. Average, open, spreading growth. M. (U.S. 1969 - E. J. Prevatt, Bonneau, SC).

BETTY ROBINSON - Dark Red. Large, full peony form to anemone form. Vigorous, compact, upright growth. M. (U.S. 1957 - J. C. Robinson, La Cañada, CA).

BETTY SETTE - Pink. Medium, formal double. Average, dense, upright growth. L. Cold hardy to -10°F. (U.S. 1992 - Ackerman).

BETTY SHEFFIELD - White striped and blotched Red and Pink. Medium to large, semidouble to loose peony form with slightly waved petals. Average, compact growth. M. (Variations of this cultivar include Japonicas 'Funny Face Betty'; 'Lucky Seven'; 'Blond Betty'; 'Betty By George'; 'Elaine's Betty'). (U.S. 1949 - Mrs. A. B. Sheffield, Quitman, GA).

BETTY SHEFFIELD BLUSH - ('Wonder Child').- Light Pink with a few Deep Pink marks. (Sport of Japonica 'Betty Sheffield'). (U.S. 1958 - Thomasville).

BETTY SHEFFIELD BLUSH SUPREME - Blush Pink with wide edge of Deep Pink to Red. (Color sport of Japonica 'Betty Sheffield Supreme'). (U.S. 1962 - A. LeFebvre, Gulfport, MS and Thomasville).

BETTY SHEFFIELD CORAL - Coral Pink. (Sport of Japonica 'Betty Sheffield'). (U.S. 1964 - Thomasville).

BETTY SHEFFIELD DAWN - Dawn Pink. (Sport of Japonica 'Betty Sheffield'). (U.S. - Griffith's Nsy., Shreveport, LA).

BETTY SHEFFIELD DREAM - Pale Pink. (Sport of Japonica 'Betty Sheffield'). (U.S. - Griffith's Nsy., Shreveport, LA).

BETTY SHEFFIELD PINK - Deep Pink. (Sport of Japonica 'Betty Sheffield'). (U.S. 1957 - Thomasville).

BETTY SHEFFIELD PINK CHIFFON - Light Blush Pink with Orchid overcast. (Sport of Japonica 'Betty Sheffield'). (U.S. 1965 - M S Cannon, Dothan, AL).

BETTY SHEFFIELD PINK HEART - Blush Pink with Deep Pink center and White edge. (Sport of Japonica 'Betty Sheffield Silver'). (U.S. 1962 - Thomasville).

BETTY SHEFFIELD SILVER - Blush Pink bordered White with Silver sheen. (For another form of this cultivar see Japonica 'Adrianne's Betty' - Sport of Japonica 'Betty Sheffield Blush'). (U.S. 1960 - G. C. Comstock, Beaumont, TX).

BETTY SHEFFIELD SUPREME - White with Deep Pink to Red border on each petal. (Sport of Japonica 'Betty Sheffield'). (U.S. 1960 - Mrs. G. W. Alday, Thomasville, GA).

BETTY SHEFFIELD VARIEGATED - Deep Pink spotted White variation of 'Betty Sheffield Pink'. (U.S. 1958 - Thomasville).

BETTY SHEFFIELD WHITE - White. (Sport of Japonica 'Betty Sheffield'). (U.S. 1980 - Tammia).

BETTY SUE - White. Medium, semidouble. Average, upright growth. M. (U.S. 1978 - L. B. Wilson, Gulfport, MS).

BETTY THEISEN - Light Blush Pink shading deeper in center. Medium, semidouble with loose petals interspersed with stamens. Slow, bushy growth. M. (U.S. 1952 - Rosa).

BETTY'S BEAUTY - White with each petal edged Light Orchid. (Sport of Japonica 'Betty Sheffield Supreme'). (U.S. 1975 - F. Moore, West Covina, CA).

BETTY'S PINK ORGANDIE - Blush Pink. Medium to large, anemone form to peony form with rosettes around center cluster. M. (Sport of Japonica 'Betty Sheffield'). (U.S. 1980 - Tammia).

BEULAH ALPHIN - Red. Large, semidouble to peony form with loose petals. M. (U.S. 1964 - B. L. Alphin, Clinton, NC).

BEULAH B. BOBE - Pink. Large to very large, semidouble to rose form double. Upright spreading growth. M-L. (U.S. 2001 - Jernigan).

BEULAH BROWN BAXTER - Crimson Red. Large, single. Vigorous growth. M-L. (U.S. 1991 - L. and B. Baxter, Seneca, SC).

BEV PIET'S SMILE - Dark Red and White with Yellow anthers and Light Pink/White filaments. Medium to large, semidouble to peony form. Average, upright growth, M. (U.S. 2008 - Meyer Piet, Arcadia, CA).

BEV RITTER - Clear Light Pink. Medium, formal double. Vigorous, upright growth. M. (Sport of Japonica 'Show Time'). (U.S. 2010 - Charles Ritter, Melrose, FL).

BEVERLY PARKES-DAVIS - Deep Pink. Large, peony form. Slow, dense, bushy growth. M-L. (Aus. 1993 - Mrs. E. Parkes, E. Brighton, Vic.).

BICENTENARY JOY - White. Large, formal double with Cream center and fluted petals. Slow, upright growth. E-L. (Aus. 1987 - G. W. Hooper, Bexley North, NSW).

BIDWELL VARIEGATED - White striped Pink. Medium, semidouble. Vigorous, upright growth. M. (U.S. 1930 - Lindo).

BIENVENU AMI - Pink. Medium, formal double. Average, upright growth. M. (U.S. 1980 - Tammia).

BIENVILLE - White. Medium to large, formal double with incurved petal edges. Vigorous, compact growth. E-M. (U.S. 1961 - Overlook).

BIG BEAUTY - White blotched and dashed Pink. Large to very large, semidouble to loose peony form. Vigorous, upright growth. M-L. (Variations of this cultivar include Japonicas 'Mollie Moore Davis'; 'Tillie Wirth'; 'Sarah R'). (U.S. 1941 - McIlhenny).

BIG BEAUTY PINK - See 'Mollie Moore Davis'.

BIG DADDY - Deep Pink to Light Red with bright Gold anthers and Cream filaments. Medium to large, semidouble. Average, upright growth. M-L. (U.S. 2012 - Gordy).

BIG JACK - Pink to Deep Pink. Miniature, peony to formal double form; petals may be veined. Average, upright spreading growth. M. (U.S. 1999 - Bond Nursery Corp, Dallas, TX).

BIG TINY - Red. Medium, semidouble. Vigorous, open, upright growth. M. (U.S. 1961 - Feathers).

BILL ARANT - Pink. Large, semidouble to full peony form. Vigorous, upright growth. M. (U.S. 1965 - Dr. A. F. Burnside, Columbia, SC).

BILL BLOUNT - White with three Pink petals. Large, semidouble. Vigorous, upright growth. M. (U.S. 1965 - Ashby).

BILL BOLL - White. Large, anemone form to peony form. Average, upright growth. M. (U.S. 1990 - A. Boll, Jacksonville, FL).

BILL COLSEN - Dark Rose Pink. Large, semidouble. Vigorous, spreading growth. E-L. (U.S. 1992 - G. Gerbing, Millwood, GA).

BILL HAIRSTON - Red with Yellow anthers and White filaments. Large, semidouble. Average upright growth. M. (U.S. 2012 - Louise Poe Hairston, Birmingham, AL).

BILL J - Salmon Red. Large, semidouble to loose peony form. Average, open, upright growth. M. (U.S. 1956 - W. R. Johnson, Andalusia, AL).

BILL MURA - Light Rose Pink. Medium, semidouble with loose petals to loose peony form with occasional upright center petals. (U.S. 1960 - H. Mura, Augusta, GA).

BILL MURA VARIEGATED - Light Rose Pink and White variation of 'Bill Mura'.

BILL PEARCE - White with Cream center. Medium, formal double. Compact, upright growth. M-L. (Aus. 1985 - C. Elliot, Vista, S. Aus.).

BILL QUATTLEBAUM - Wine Red. Medium to large, anemone form with crepe effect on tips of center petaloids and small petals. Average, compact, upright growth. E-M. (U.S. 1966 - B. Quattlebaum, North Charleston, SC).

BILL QUATTLEBAUM VARIEGATED - Wine Red blotched White variation of 'Bill Quattlebaum'. (U.S. 1966 - B. Quattlebaum, North Charleston, SC).

BILL STEWART - Deep Rose Pink. Medium to large, semidouble with upright petals interspersed with stamens. Vigorous, upright growth. E-M. (U.S. 1957 - Mrs. W. G. Stewart, Moss Point, MS).

BILL STOUT - White lightly marked Rose Red. Small to medium, full peony form. Slow, upright growth. E. (U.S. 1981 - I. Meriwether, Pensacola, FL).

BILLIE McCASKILL - Shaded soft Pink. Medium, semidouble with deeply fimbriated petals. Average, compact, upright growth. M. (U.S. 1956 - McCaskill).

BILLIE McFARLAND - Rose Pink. Large, semidouble. Vigorous, compact, upright growth. M. (N.Z. 1963 - W. M. McFarland, Frankton Junction).

BILLIE ROUNTREE - White striped Red. Medium to large, loose peony form. Average, open, upright growth. M-L. (U.S. 1997 - C. Elliott, Swainsboro, GA).

BILLY GATES - Firey Red. Miniature, anemone form to peony form. Average, upright growth. M-L. (U.S. 1976 - Stone).

BIMBO - Rose Pink. Miniature, semidouble. M. (U.S. 1961 - Hartman).

BIRDIE ROGERS - Pink and White. Medium, peony form. (U.S. 1953 - Katz).

BIRTHDAY GIRL - Light Pink. Medium to large, single. Average, bushy, upright growth. E-M. (Aus. 1991 - L. Hobbs, Doncaster East, Vic.).

BISHONEN (BEAUTIFUL BOY) - Pink background with a peppering of Deeper Pink and Carmine stripes with Golden anthers. Large, semidouble. Spreading growth. M-L. (Sport of Higo Japonica 'Shintsukasa-nishiki'). (Japan 1969 - Ohta Nursery, Kumamoto). See Higo.

BLACK CHERRY - Dark Red shading Black on edges with Gold anthers and White filaments. Large, semidouble. Average, upright, spreading growth. M-L. (Seedling of Japonica 'Royal Velvet'). (U.S. 2016 - Pat Johnson, Cairo, GA).

BLACK DOMINO - Black Red with Dark Red stamens. Miniature, single. Slow, bushy growth. L. (U.S. 1961 - Short).

BLACK DRAGON - See 'Koku-Ryu'.

BLACK GOLD - Black Red. Small to medium, semidouble with wavy, crinkled petals. Average, compact growth. M. (U.S. 1982 - Gilley).

BLACK HEART - Black Red. Miniature to small, formal double with pointed petals. Average, compact growth with Mahogany Red new growth. M-L. (U.S. 1965 - Short).

BLACK MAGIC - Very Dark Glossy Red. Medium, semidouble to rose form double. Average, spreading, upright growth with unusual holly-like foliage. M-L. (U.S. 1992 - Nuccio's).

BLACK PEARL - Very Dark Red. Medium, full peony form. Slow, compact growth. M. (N.Z. 1973 - Mrs. M. E. Wilson, Bell Block, New Plymouth).

BLACK PRINCE - Black Red with Red stamens. Medium, semidouble. Vigorous, upright growth. L. (U.S. Late 1800's - Magnolia).

BLACK RED - Deep Red with Black trim with Yellow anthers and Pink filaments. Very large, semidouble. Average, upright growth. E-M. (U.S. 2013 - Howell).

BLACK TIE - Dark Red. Small, formal double resembling a rose bud. Average, open, upright growth. M. (U.S. 1968 - S. Walden, Albany, GA).

BLACK VELVET - Dark Red/Black with darker veining. Medium to large, rose form double to formal double. M-L. (N.Z. 1997 - J. and V. Bennet).

BLACKWATER - Dark Red. Miniature, semidouble with slightly conical shape. Slow growth. M-L. (N.Z. 1994 - G. Clapperton, Gisborne).

BLANCHE GRAHAM - Rose veined Darker Rose edged Silvery Blue. Medium to large, loose peony form with waved and curved outer petals standing high and apart around center grouped stamens. Average growth. M. (U.S. 1960 - Julington).

BLANCHE MAXWELL - White. Medium, formal double. (Sport of Japonica 'Pearl Maxwell'). (U.S. 1957 - Thomasville).

BLANCHE TRUESDALE - White. Large, semidouble to anemone form to peony form with White stamens. Average, spreading growth. M-L. (U.S. 1959 - Truesdale Nsy., West Columbia, SC).

BLAZE - Red. Medium, single. Vigorous, compact growth. M. (U.S. 1959 - Nuccio's).

BLAZE OF GLORY - Brilliant Red. Large, anemone form. Average, compact, upright growth. E-M. (U.S. 1965 - McCaskill).

BLEICHROEDER - See 'Baronne de Bleichroeder (United States)'.

BLEICHROEDER PINK - ('Baronne de Bleichroeder Pink'; 'Casablanca'; 'Huntington Pink'). Soft Pink. Medium, formal double to rose form double. M. (For another form of this cultivar see Japonica 'Sweetheart' - sport of Japonica 'Baronne de Bleichroeder [United States]'). (U.S. 1925 - Huntington).

BLEICHROEDER WHITE - See 'Otome White'.

BLOND BETTY - Peach Pink. Medium to large, semidouble to loose peony form. (Sport of Japonica 'Betty Sheffield'). (U.S. 1964 - Tammia).

BLOOD OF CHINA - ('Victor Emmanuel'; 'Alice Slack'). Deep Salmon Red. Medium, semidouble to loose peony form. Vigorous, compact growth. L. Cold hardy. (U.S. 1928 - Longview).

BLOOD OF CHINA VARIEGATED - Deep Salmon Red marked White variation of 'Blood of China.'(U.S. 1965 - H. W. Steindorff, Greenville, AL).

BLOOD OF CHRIST - See 'Mathotiana Alba'.

BLOODY MARY - Brilliant Red. Large, semidouble with loose, wavy petals to anemone form. Average, spreading growth. E-L. (U.S. 1976 - Stone).

BLOOMFIELD (MORRIS) - Scarlet Red. Small, single. Vigorous, fully branched to ground growth. (Seeds from NW South Korea - Barry Yinger, et al - before 1986). (U.S. 2011 - Morris Arboretum, Philadelphia, PA).

BLUE RIDGE SUNSET - Bright Lavender-Pink, Dark Lavender center. Medium to large, rose form double. Average, dense, upright growth. M. (U.S. 2005 - Gordy).

BLUSH ANNE - Bicolor Pink, darker outer, notched petals. Medium, semidouble form. Vigorous, dense growth. L. (U.S. 2005 - Lee County Historical Society, Bishopville, SC).

BLUSH EIDSON - Blush Pink. Large, peony form. (Sport of Japonica 'Frank Eidson'). (U.S. 1962 - Thomasville).

BLUSH HIBISCUS - White with Blush Pink at center. Medium, single to semidouble. Vigorous, upright, spreading growth. M. (U.S. 1940 - Overlook).

BLUSH PLENA - Blush Pink when first opens, fading to White after several days. Medium, formal double. (Sport of Japonica 'Alba Plena'). (U.S. 1957 - F. Honn, Arcadia, CA).

BLUSH TINSIE - Blush Pink. Miniature, anemone form. Vigorous, upright growth. E-M. (Sport of Japonica 'Tinsie'). (U.S. 1962).

BLUSH TRICOLOR - White Blushed Pink to Blush Pink. Medium, semidouble. (Sport of Japonica 'Tricolor (Siebold)'). (U.S. 1957 - Magnolia).

BLUSHING BEAUTY - White Blushed Pink. Medium, formal double. Vigorous, open, upright growth. M. (U.S. 1964 - Neal Cox, Georgetown, SC).

BLUSHING BRIDE - See 'Feasti'.

BO MORRIS - Rose Pink. Medium, semidouble. M. (U.S. 1955 - C. Morris, Greenville, SC).

BO PEEP - White. Medium, semidouble. Vigorous, upright growth. M. (U.S. 1959 - L. Stromeyer, San Gabriel, CA).

BOB HOPE - Black Red. Large, semidouble with irregular petals. Slow, compact growth. M. Cold hardy. (U.S. 1972 - Nuccio's).

BOB MEALING - Apple blossom Pink, quickly fading to White as flower ages. Medium, semidouble with occasional upright petals. Vigorous, upright growth. M-L. (U.S. 1962 - Mealing).

BOB'S TINSIE - Brilliant Red. Miniature to small, anemone form. Average, compact, upright growth. M. (U.S. 1962 - Nuccio's).

BOBBIE FAIN - Clear bright Red with Deep Red radial veining. Large, semidouble to anemone form. Average, upright growth. E-L. (U.S. 1988 - Homeyer).

BOBBIE FAIN VARIEGATED - Clear bright Red with Deep Red radial veining and White variation of 'Bobbie Fain'. (U.S. 1988 - Homeyer).

BOBBY GUILLOT - See 'Winifred Womack'.

BOBBY HUNTER - Salmon Rose Pink variegated White with Yellow anthers and White filaments. Medium to large, semidouble; distinctive crepe on petals; wide petals similar to 'Drama Girl'; stamens are less regular than the parent 'Katie'; overall size is smaller than 'Katie' even when treated. Vigorous, upright, dense growth. E-M. (Sport of Japonica 'Katie'). (U.S. 2016 - Thomas Sellers, Bolivia, NC).

BOBBYE DENNIS - Pale Blush Pink. Large, anemone form to peony form. Vigorous, open growth. M-L. (U.S. 1986 - Stone).

BO-BO - Rose Pink. Small, loose peony form. Vigorous, spreading growth. M. (U.S. 1975 - Novick).

BOGLISCO - Flesh Pink with veining of Pale Pink. Medium, formal double of 8-9 rows of petals. Average, upright, bushy growth. M. (Italy 1982 - Ghisleni).

BOKUHAN - See 'Tinsie'.

BOLEN'S PRIDE - See 'Vedrine'.

BOMBSHELL - Soft Rose Red with Gold anthers and Pale Pink filaments. Large, semidouble (sometimes with creped, ruffled petals). Average, upright growth. M-L. (U.S. 2015 - Gordy).

BON BON - White splotched Red. Miniature to small, peony form. Vigorous, upright growth. (U.S. 1961 - Domoto).

BON BON BLUSH - Deep Pink with each petal edged White. (Sport of Japonica 'Bon Bon'). (U.S. 1971 - McCaskill).

BON BON RED - Red. (Sport of Japonica 'Bon Bon'). (U.S. 1970 - Wilson).

BONNIE BELLE - Red. Miniature, bell shaped single with White, Yellow, and Red petaloids. Average growth. M. (N.Z. 1989 - Jury).

BONNIE TRIPPE - Light Pink center fading to Dark Pink edges with Yellow anthers and White filaments. Large, semidouble to anemone to loose peony to rose form double with fluted petals. Vigorous, upright growth. M. (U.S. 2018 - James Smelley, Moss Point, Mississippi).

BONSAI - Rose Red. Miniature, anemone form. Average, upright growth. M-L. (U.S. 1955).

BOOM-A-LOOM - Bright Pink with Pale Pink border shading into White. Medium to large, semidouble with crinkled and upright center petals. Vigorous, upright growth. E. (U.S. 1965 - G. C. LeCroy, Moncks Corner, SC).

BOROM'S GEM - Pink. Large to very large, rose form double. Vigorous, upright growth. M-L. (U.S. 1983 - S. T. Borom, Charleston, SC).

BOUTONNIERE - Dark Red with center petals streaked White. Miniature, rose form double. Slow, wide-spreading growth. M-L. (Europe to U.S. [Magnolia] 1940's).

BOWMAN'S WHITE - Cream White. Medium to large, peony form. Vigorous, upright growth. L. (U.S. 1957 - Bowman).

BOZZONI NOVA - Pink, lighter in the center. Miniature, formal double. (Italy 1855-Franchetti).

BRADFORD'S VARIEGATED - ('C. M. Hovey Variegated II'). Deep Red with White spots and margins. Medium, formal double. M. (Variation of Japonica 'C. M. Hovey'). (U.S. 1948 - Bradford).

BRADLEY FORD - Deep Coral Rose. Medium, semidouble. Average growth. M. (Aus. 1977 - A. Spragg, Sutherland, NSW).

BRANDI BARLOW - Flesh to Light Pink. Large, semidouble. Average, upright growth. M-L. (U.S. 1975 - Haynie).

BRASSENIE - Rose Red marbled White. Medium, rose form double. Slow, bushy growth. L. (France to U.S. [Fruitland] 1935).

BREAK O'DAY - Coral Pink. Large, peony form to anemone form. Vigorous, open, upright growth. E-L. (U.S. 1952 - Short).

BREATH OF SPRING - Dawn Pink. Medium, semidouble. Slow, compact, upright growth. E-M. (U.S. 1954 - Feathers).

BRENDA ANN HART - Rose Pink. Medium, formal double. Vigorous, upright growth. E-M. (U.S. 1978 - Tammia).

BRENDA BEACH - Blush Pink mottled with shades of Darker Pink. Large to very large, semidouble. Vigorous, upright growth. M-L. (U.S. 1996 - M. Beach, Mt. Pleasant, SC).

BRENDA GRIFFIN - Blush Pink. Large, semidouble with fluffy and some upright petals. M-L. (U.S. 1960 - F. Griffin, Sr., Columbia, SC).

BRENDA KAY - Deep Red. Miniature to small, formal double with incurved petals tipped Light Wine Red. Compact growth. M. (U.S. 1989 - L. C. Schaefer, Baton Rouge, LA).

BRENDA LEE WILLBERN - White with narrow Rose Red stripes. Large, peony form. Average, spreading growth. E-L. (U.S. 1993 - Dr. O. Lewis, Picayune, MS).

BRENDA TUCK - White. Large, rose form double. Average, spreading, upright growth. M-L. (U.S. 1964 - Dr. A. C. Tuck, Thomasville, GA).

BRESCHINI'S PRIDE - Pink border fading to Cream White in center. Large, semidouble. Average, open growth. M. (U.S. 1962 - Breschini).

BRIAN ANDERTON - Red Purple, shading from a mid Blue Red at the inner petal bases to much darker at tips; petals have prominent near black venation. Medium, anemone to peony form. Average growth. M-L. Light tea like fragrance. (N.Z. 2003 - C. J. Anderton).

BRIAN'S DAWN - Light Red with Darker Red stripes with Yellow anthers and White filaments. Medium, semidouble to anemone form. Average, upright growth. E. (U.S. 2012 - Brian S. Dick, Lakeland, FL).

BRIDAL PINK - Translucent Pink. Large, semidouble with fluted, lily like petals standing well apart. Average, compact, upright growth. M-L. (U.S. 1968 - Haynie).

BRIDAL VEIL - White. Large, single of flat form. Vigorous, open growth. M. (U.S. 1956 - Short).

BRIDE'S BLUSH - Blush White. Large, semidouble to anemone form. Average, upright, open growth. M-L. (Seedling of Japonica 'Snow Lady'). (U.S. 2016 - Pat Johnson, Cairo, GA).

BRIDE'S BOUQUET - White. Large, semidouble with fluted and notched petals. Average, open growth. M. (U.S. 1950 - Short).

BRIDESMAID - Blush White with each petal edged with a fine pencil outline of Orchid. Large, semidouble to loose peony form. (Sport of Japonica 'Margaret Wells'). (U.S. 1971 - R. Parshall, Sacramento, CA).

BRIGHT BOB - Bright Red, with faint Blackish veining. Medium to large, anemone form. Average, upright growth. E-L. (N.Z. 2005 - R. J. MacDonald, Waiuku).

BRIGHT BUOY - Scarlet Crimson. Medium, single. Bushy, spreading growth. E-L. (N.Z. 1975 - Jury).

BRIGHT SPRITE - Orange Red. Miniature, semidouble with loose, high, folded petals and center petaloids at times. Average, upright growth. E-M. (U.S. 1952 - Wylam).

BRILLIANT - ('Blackwell's Special'; 'Tutcheria'). Red. Medium, rose form double. Average, compact, upright growth. M. (Also a variegated form). (U.S. 1941 - Blackwell).

BRILLIANT REVIEW - Carmine Pink. Large, semidouble. Vigorous, upright growth. M-L. (U.S. 1953 - Short).

BROADUS TURNER - Light Rose Pink. Large, semidouble to anemone form. Vigorous, upright growth. E. (U.S. 1981 - J. R. Cantlou, Edgefield, SC).

BROADWATER - Deep Pink. Large, peony form. Vigorous, open, upright growth. E-M. (U.S. 1968 - L. B. Wilson, Jr., Gulfport, MS).

BROCKLING - Rose Pink with Lavender cast. Large, semidouble. Upright, willowy growth. M. (U.S. 1950 - Brock).

BRONWYN JAMES - Light Pink margined and shaded White. Miniature, semidouble to loose peony form. Average, open, upright growth. M. (Sport of Japonica 'Little Brad'). (N.Z. 1993 - T. Lennard, Te Puke).

BROOKE - Dark Rose Pink. Small to medium, formal double. Vigorous, dense, spreading growth. E-M. (U.S. 1990 - E. and J. Atkins, Shalimar, FL).

BROOKSIDE - Light Rose Pink shading deeper on outer petals. Very large, anemone form with upright center petaloids. Average, compact, upright growth. E-M. (U.S. 1965 - C. A. Coddington, Winter Park, FL).

BROOKSIE'S ROSEA - Highly variegated variation of 'Rosea Superba'. Large to very large, rose form double to formal double. (U.S. 1965 - Mrs. B. Anderson, Timmonsville, SC).

BROTHER ROSE - Orchid Pink. Large, rose form double. Average, compact, upright growth. M. (U.S. 1976 - Stone).

BROWN'S RED - Dark Red. Medium, peony form. Vigorous, compact, upright growth. M. (U.S. 1937 - Kiyono).

BROZZONI NOVA - Pink, lighter toward center. Miniature, formal double. (Italy 1855 - Franchetti).

BRUCE GREEN - Dark Wine Red. Large, semidouble. Vigorous, dense, bushy growth. E-M. (U.S. 2016 - Gordy).

BRUSHFIELD'S YELLOW - Antique White guard petals surround double center of lightly ruffled Pale Primrose Yellow petaloids. Medium, anemone form. Vigorous, compact, columnar growth. M-L. (See also Japonica 'Gwenneth Morey' which is similar but not identical). (Aus. 1968 - K. Brushfield).

BRYAN WRIGHT - Light Pink. Medium, semidouble to loose peony form. Average, compact, upright growth. M. (U.S. 1950 - Miss B. Hoyt, Thomasville, GA).

BRYANNA NICOLE - Vibrant Pink washed with Lighter Pink. Small, anemone form. Average, upright growth. M. (Japonica 'Tinker Bell' seedling). (U.S. 2006 - Don Bergamini, Martinez, CA).

BUCCANEER - Rose Red. Medium, semidouble with Pink stamens. Average, compact, upright growth. E-M. (U.S. 1959 - Weisner).

BUCK'S COOKEY - Dark Red. Large, semidouble. Average, upright growth. E-M. (U.S. 1962 - Buck's Nsy., Americus, GA).

BUCK'S DEW DROP - White. Medium, full peony form. Average, upright growth. E. (U.S. 1962 - Buck's Nsy., Americus, GA).

BUD MANCILL - Shell Pink striped Rose. Medium to large, formal double. Average, open, spreading growth. M-L. (U.S. 1970 - S. H. Mancill, Lafayette, LA).

BUDDIE BILLUPS - Red. Large, semidouble with stamens interspersed among petals. (U.S. 1961 – E. E. Puls, Hammond, LA).

BUDDY - Pink with Purplish cast. Small, semidouble with four inside petals coming to point at tips, with other petals round at tips. Slow, bushy growth. Fragrant. (U.S. 1951 - Azalea Glen).

BUDDY BENZ - Dark Red with Purple cast. Large to very large, anemone form. Average, open, upright growth. M. (U.S. 1970 - T. Eagleson, Port Arthur, TX).

BUDDY BOY - Deep Red. Large, peony form. Vigorous, upright growth. M. (U.S. 1946 - Mealing).

BUDDY PREGNALL - Pale Pink speckled and striped Deep Pink, and occasionally sports solid Pink. Large, semidouble. Vigorous, spreading growth. E-M. (U.S. 1971 - E. O. Kline, Charleston, SC).

BULL'S EYE - Dark Red with White or Light Pink center. Small to medium, formal double. Average, upright growth. M. (U.S. 1992 - Piet and Gaeta).

BURGUNDY AND GOLD - Burgundy Red with Gold Anthers and Yellow filaments. Medium, anemone form with numerous bright stamens. Average, upright, open growth. M-L. (U.S. 2008 - Gordy).

BURGUNDY BOY - Very Dark Red. Small to medium, semidouble. Slow, compact growth. M-L. (N.Z. 1985 - H. B. Cave, Wanganui).

BURGUNDY GEM - Dark Red. Miniature, anemone form to peony form. Average, upright growth. M. (N.Z. 1991 - Jury).

BURGUNDY ROSE - Burgundy. Medium, anemone form. Average, upright growth. M-L. (U.S. 2015 - Gordy).

BURNEYVILLE - Light Rose Pink. Medium, anemone form. Upright, compact growth. M-L. (U.S. 1951 - Riverbank).

BURNHAM BEECHES - Pink edged White. Large, peony form. (Sport of Japonica 'Countess of Orkney'). (Aus. 1952 - Waterhouse).

BURTIANE - Light Pink. Medium, single. Vigorous, compact, upright growth. M. (Aus. 1968 - I. D. Burt, Killara, NSW).

BUSCH GARDEN RED - See 'Rose Queen'.

BUSTER LEWIS - Deep Pink. Very large, semidouble. Average growth. M. (U.S. 1965 - C. E. Morgan, Greenville, SC).

BUSTER NEWMAN - Deep Red. Medium to large, loose peony form with folded petals. Average, upright growth. M. (U.S. 1957 - Beasley).

BUTCH BURTON - Light Pink with Yellow anthers and White filaments. Large, semidouble to loose peony form. Average, upright, open growth. E-L. (U.S. 2018 - Pat B. Johnson, Cairo, GA).

BUTCHIE - Rose Pink. Very large, anemone to peony form. Average, spreading, upright growth. M-L. (U.S. 1999 - W. T. Shepherd, N. Charleston, SC).

C. ALLEN FAVROT - Dark Red with Gold anthers and Pink filaments. Large, semidouble. Average, upright growth. M-L. (U.S. 2015 - Gordy).

C. C. CRUTCHER - Dark Red. Large, semidouble. Average, upright growth. M. (U.S. 1997 - Homeyer).

C. M. GORDY - Bright Pink with Gold anthers and Cream filaments. Large, semidouble with creped and ruffled petals. Vigorous, dense growth. E-M. (U.S. 2013 - Gordy).

C. M. HOVEY - ('Colonel Firey'; 'William S. Hastie [Mississippi]'; 'Duc de Devonshire'; 'Solaris'; 'Firey King'). Dark Red. Medium, formal double. Average, slender, upright growth. L. (U.S. 1853 - C. M. Hovey, Boston, MA).

C. M. HOVEY VARIEGATED I - See 'Scarlet O'Hara'.

C. M. HOVEY VARIEGATED II - See 'Bradford's Variegated'.

C. M. WILSON - ('Grace Burkard'; 'Lucille Ferrell'). Light Pink. Large to very large, anemone form. Cold hardy. (Sport of Japonica 'Elegans [Chandler] Variegated'). (Variations of this cultivar include Japonicas 'Shiro Chan'; 'Hawaii'; 'Elegans Splendor'). (U.S. 1949 - Mrs. A E Wilson, Pensacola, FL).

C. M. WILSON SPLENDOR - See 'Elegans Splendor'.

C. M. WILSON VARIEGATED - Light Pink shaded White variation of 'C M Wilson'.

C. N. MADSEN - See 'Mrs. Baldwin Wood'.

C. N. PORTER - Dark Red. Large, loose peony form. Vigorous, open, upright growth. M-L. (U.S. 1970 - C. N. Porter, Talladega Springs, AL).

C. P. MORGAN - See 'Beauty of Holland'.

C. R. POPE - Light Flesh Pink with interspersed Golden stamens. Medium to large, full peony form. Slow, upright growth. M-L. (U.S. 2019 - A 30+ year old Louisiana cultivar of unknown origin registered by Tommy Weeks, Conroe, TX).

C. RESTER - Red. Large to very large, semidouble. Vigorous, open, upright growth. E-M. (U.S. 1966 - Rester).

C. W. SWANN - Dark Red with Black-Red veining. Medium, semidouble. Slow, upright growth. E-L. (N.Z. 2005 - M. and L. Mangos, Tauranga).

CABERNET - Rich Burgundy Red. Small, formal double. Medium, bushy, upright growth. L. (U.S. 2009 - Nuccio's).

CABEZA DE VACA - Light Pink to light Pink and White. Medium, semidouble. (Sport of Japonica 'Quartette'). (U.S. 1946 - McIlhenny).

CABOOSE - White striped Rose Pink. Medium, semidouble with broad, wavy edged petals. Vigorous, compact, upright growth. L. (U.S. 1962 - Wheeler).

CABRILLO - See 'Bella Romana Red'.

CAJUN QUEEN - Pink. Large, anemone form.

CALDER'S TREASURE - Pink. Large, anemone form. (Aus. 1962 - J. Calder, Elsternwick).

CALICO QUEEN - White striped Rose Red. Medium, semidouble. Slow, compact growth. M. (U.S. 1956 - McCaskill).

CALIFORNIA - ('Durfee Road'). Light Rose Red. Large, semidouble with broad, thick petals. Average, bushy growth. M. (Japan to U.S. [H. Cate, Pico, CA] 1888).

CALIFORNIA DONCKELARII RED - See 'Monjisu Red'.

CALIFORNIA DONCKELARII VARIEGATED - See 'Monjisu'.

CALLIE - See 'Arajishi'.

CALLING CARD - White. Large, semidouble with fluted petals. Vigorous, compact, upright growth. M. (U.S. 1964 - Ashby).

CALVIN ENTREKIN - Deep Pink. Miniature, formal double. Average, spreading growth. E. (U.S. 1986 - C. Entrekin, Ocean Springs, MS).

CAMDEN PARK - ('Aspasia Variegata'). Rose Red blotched White. Medium, full peony form. (Sport of Japonica 'Aspasia Macarthur'). (Aus. 1952 - Macarthur).

CAMELLIA T - See 'Donckelarii'.

CAMELLIAN - See 'Pink Champagne'.

CAMEO GEM - Soft Light Pink. Small, full peony form. Vigorous, upright growth. M-L. (U.S. 1960 - Short).

CAMEO QUEEN - White. Large, semidouble with wavy, crinkled petals. Vigorous, upright growth. M. (U.S. 1981 - Shackelford).

CAMILLA INGRAM - Red with White variegation. Miniature to small, formal double. Vigorous, bushy, upright growth. M. (U.S. 1967 - McCaskill).

CAMILLE - Pink Rose. Large, formal double with heavy petal texture. Vigorous, upright growth. M. (U.S. 2006 - Hulyn Smith).

CAMILLE BRADFORD - Salmon Pink with two shades suffused. Medium, semidouble with fimbriated petals. Average, compact growth. M-L. (U.S. 1954 - Short).

CAMILLO GALLI - White and Red. Large, formal double. (U.S. 1957).

CAMPANELLA - Light Pink. Medium, single of campanulate form. (Aus. 1952 - Waterhouse).

CAMPARI - Pink striped and flecked Crimson. Medium, formal double. Vigorous, upright growth. M-L. (U.S. 1966 - Armstrong).

CAMPARI ROSE - Rose Red. (Sport of Japonica 'Campari'). (U.S. 1986 - Stone).

CAMPARI WHITE - White. (Sport of Japonica 'Campari'). (U.S. 1980 - B. Sansing, Pensacola, FL).

CAMPBELL ASHLEY - Dark Red. Medium, semidouble with loose, crepe petals. Vigorous, upright growth. L. (U.S. 1941 - Middleton).

CAMPBELL ASHLEY VARIEGATED - Dark Red and White variation of 'Campbell Ashley'.

CAMWOOD BRENDA - Purplish Red. Medium, full peony form. Average, upright, spreading growth. M. (U.S. 2018 - Camellia Heaven - John Grimm/Webb Hart, Bush, LA).

CAN CAN - Pale Pink with darker veining and darker petal edges. Medium, full peony form. (Sport of Japonica 'Lady Loch'). (Aus. 1961 - Camellia Grove).

CANARY - White. Small, anemone form with Yellow petaloids. M. (U.S. 1962 - Rogerson, Florence, SC).

CANDIDA ELEGANTISSIMA - See 'Nagasaki'.

CANDIDISSIMA - ('Louise Centurioni'; 'White Star'). White. Medium, formal double. Slow, compact growth. L. (Japan to England 1930 - Chandler).

CANDLELIGHT - See 'Angel'.

CANDY APPLE - Dark Red. Medium to large, semidouble to loose peony form. Average, dense, upright growth. M-L. (U.S. 1991 - Nuccio's).

CANDY CANE - White striped Red. Medium, formal double. Vigorous, compact, upright growth. M. (For a variation of this cultivar see Japonica 'Robin's Candy'). (U.S. 1963 - Nuccio's).

CANDY FLOSS - White striped Pink. Large, semidouble. Average, open, upright growth. E-L. (N.Z. 1982 - B. R. and T. G. Healy, Wanganui).

CANDY MINT - Pink heavily striped Red in petals and petaloids. Miniature to small, anemone form. Vigorous, compact, upright growth. M. (U.S. 1987 - Nuccio's).

CANDY STICK - White striped Dark Red. Medium, full peony form. Vigorous, compact, upright growth. M. (U.S. 1955 - Hudson).

CANDY STRIPE - White striped and flecked Red. Medium, single. Compact growth. M. Fragrant. (Aus. 1965 - Waterhouse).

CANTERBURY - Dark Red with Black veining. Medium to large, peony form. Vigorous, dense, upright growth. M-L. (N.Z. 1995 - Haydon).

CAP'N BROOKS - Rose Pink. Medium, formal double with incurved petals. E-L. (U.S. 1973 - Haynie).

CAPITOL CITY - Scarlet. Large, single with petaloids occasionally filling center. (Sport of Japonica 'Miss Sacramento'). (U.S. 1950 - Camellia Hall).

CAPPY DURDEN VARIEGATED - Dark Red and White. Large, semidouble. Vigorous, dense, upright growth. E-M. (U.S. 1990 - R. Gramling, Tallahassee, FL).

CAPRICCI - White with occasional Pink stripes, sometimes solid Pink or Rose stripes. Medium to large, peony form. Vigorous, upright growth. E-M. (U.S. 2001 - Gordy).

CAPRICCI BLUSH STRIPE - Light Pink with Dark Pink stripes. Medium to large, peony form. Vigorous, upright growth. E-M. (Sport of Japonica 'Capricci'). (U.S. 2006 - Gordy).

CAPT. DOUG SIMON - Black Red with Yellow anthers and Red filaments. Medium, semidouble to loose peony form with Red body and White tipped petaloids intermixed with stamens. Slow, dense growth. M-L. (Sport of Japonica 'Bob Hope'). (U.S. 2017 - Douglas Simon, Norfolk VA).

CAPTAIN BLOOD - Rose Red with Purplish cast. Medium, loose peony form with irregular and upright petals. Average, compact growth. M. (U.S. 1950 - McIlhenny).

CAPTAIN FOLK - Bright Rose-Red, some petals occasionally marked with White with Yellow anthers and White filaments. Large, loose semidouble, cup-shaped. Vigorous, upright growth. M-L. (U.S. 1945 - Flechtman, Superintendent of the Tea Gardens, Summerville, South Carolina).

CAPTAIN IKE DAVIS - Rose Red. Medium, loose peony form with large, ruffled petals. Vigorous, upright growth. M. (U.S. 1947 - Orton).

CAPTAIN JOHN SMITH - Rose Red sometimes spotted White. Medium, peony form. Average, compact growth. M. (U.S. 1953 - Wildwood Nsy., Walterboro, SC).

CAPTAIN JOHN SUTTER - See 'Kishu-Tsukasa'.

CAPTAIN MARTIN'S FAVORITE - Deep Pink splotched White. Medium, formal double to rose form double. Slow, compact, upright growth. M. (Europe to U.S. 1860's - Magnolia).

CAPTAIN PARKS - Rose-Pink. Small to medium, formal double; near imbricated. Upright, open-branched growth. M. (U.S. 1955).

CAPTAIN RICHARD ALEXANDER - Crimson and White. Large, semidouble. Slow, compact growth. M. (U.S. 1958 - Middleton).

CARA MIA - Pink shading to Blush Pink in center petals. Medium to large, semidouble with Golden stamens interspersed among petals. Vigorous, upright growth. E-M. (U.S. 1960 - Nuccio's).

CARA MIA VARIEGATED - Pink blotched White variation of 'Cara Mia'.

CARDINAL - Bright Red. Medium to large, full peony form. Vigorous, upright growth. M. (U.S. 1957 - Carter).

CARDINAL RICHELIEU - Rose Red. Medium, semidouble to loose peony form with irregular petals. Vigorous, compact, upright growth. M. (U.S. Late 1800's - Magnolia).

CARDINAL VARIEGATED - Bright Red and White variation of 'Cardinal'.

CARDINAL'S CAP - Cardinal Red. Miniature to small, anemone form. Average, compact, upright growth. M-L. (U.S. 1961 - Surina's Camellia Gardens, Sepulveda, CA).

CARDINIA - Blood Red. Medium, loose peony form. Vigorous, compact growth. M-L. (Aus. 1963 - F. S. Tuckfield, Berwick).

CARE FREE - Deep Salmon Rose Pink. Large, semidouble to loose peony form with large petals and petaloids interspersed with Golden stamens and upright petals. Average growth. E-M. (U.S. 1960 - G. Demetropolis, Mobile, AL).

CARILLON - White and Red. Large, single. M. (Aus. 1962 - Waterhouse).

CARL L. ALLEN, JR. - Rose Red, blotched White. Medium, anemone to peony form. Average, spreading growth. E-M. (U.S. 1999 - Henry B. Rehder, Wilmington, NC).

CARLA DOSSETT VARIEGATED - Medium Red variegated White with Yellow anthers and White filaments. Medium, semidouble. Slow, upright, spreading growth. L. (U.S. 2016 - Howell).

CARLTON LACOUR - Deep Dark Red with Yellow anthers. Medium to large, loose peony to full peony to formal double. Average, upright growth. M. (U.S. 2019 - Gordon Rabalais, Arnaudville, LA).

CARLTON LACOUR VARIEGATED - Deep Dark Red with White Blotches with Yellow anthers. Medium to large, loose peony to full peony to formal double. Average, upright growth. M. (U.S. 2019 - Gordon Rabalais, Arnaudville, LA).

CARLTON MARYOTT - Red. Medium to large, semidouble form. Average dense growth. M-L. Very cold hardy. (U.S. 1999 - Dr. Arthur A. Maryott, Gaithersburg, MD).

CARMEL - Blush Pink. Medium, formal double. Slow, upright growth. M. (U.S. 1968 - Camelliana).

CARMINE KING - Carmine. Medium, anemone form. (U.S. 1953 - McIlhenny).

CARNIVAL - Pink striped Red. Medium, semidouble with irregular petals to anemone form. Vigorous, compact, upright growth. M. (U.S. 1950 - R. Brown, Sacramento, CA).

CARNIVAL PRINCE - Deep Pink. Large to very large, semidouble. (Sport of Japonica 'Carnival Queen'). (U.S. 1971 - Nuccio's).

CARNIVAL PRINCESS - Light Pink edged White. Large to very large, semidouble. (Sport of Japonica 'Carnival Queen'). (U.S. 1971 - Nuccio's).

CARNIVAL QUEEN - White with occasional stripes of Rose Red and Pale Pink. Large to very large, semidouble with irregular petals to full peony form. Vigorous, bushy, upright growth. M. (Variations of this cultivar include Japonicas 'Carnival Prince'; 'Carnival Princess'). (U.S. 1969 - Nuccio's).

CAROL BETTES - Light Peach Pink. Medium, formal double with alternate rows of slightly curved, smallish, round petals. Average, compact, upright growth. M. (U.S. 1965 - Julington).

CAROL DICKERSON - Ivory White. Medium, formal double with tiered, incurved petals. Average, upright growth. M. (U.S. 1961 - Ragland).

CAROL HUMPHREY - Red. Medium to large, rose form double to formal double. Vigorous, dense, upright growth. M. (U.S. 1984 - Alfter).

CAROL LYNN - White striped Red. Large, semidouble with loose, slightly waved petals. Average growth. E-M. (U.S. 1959).

CAROL'S KATIE - Pink to Rose Pink with bright Yellow anthers and White to translucent filaments. Medium, semidouble. Average, dense and open growth. M-L. The flowers are fragrant. (U.S. 2013 - Carol Comber, Pensacola, FL).

CARO-LAN - Dark Pink with Lighter Pink in center. Medium, formal double with incurved petals, star shaped and stacked with heavy texture. Average, open growth. M-L. (U.S. 2006 - Harold Haeffele, Hampstead, NC).

CAROLE LOMBARD - See 'Souv. de Bahuaud Litou'.

CAROLINA BEAUTY - Light Shell Pink. Medium to large, semidouble with upright center petals. Vigorous growth. M. (U.S. 1959 - Holmes).

CAROLINA MOON - White. Large, rose form double to semidouble. Vigorous, compact, upright growth. M. (U.S. 1969 - Mealing).

CAROLINA SUNRISE - Deep Pink. Large, semidouble with wavy, crinkled petals. Vigorous, spreading, upright growth. M. (U.S. 1970 - Mrs. J. Luker, Savannah, GA).

CAROLINE BROWNE - Red. Large, loose peony form. Vigorous, spreading growth. M-L. (U.S. 1956 - S. M. Hutaff and R. Holmes, Fayetteville, NC).

CAROLINE BROWNE VARIEGATED - Red and White variation of 'Caroline Browne'.

CAROLINE LEONARD - Pink and White variegated. Medium to large, formal double. Average, spreading growth. E-M. (U.S. 1990 - G. Johnson, Madison, FL).

CAROLINE MORTON - Blush Pink. Large, semidouble of hose-in-hose form. Vigorous, upright growth. M. (Aus. 1970 - Mrs. L. R. Lucknow, Toorak, Vic.).

CAROLINE REHDER - White lightly striped Pink. Miniature, formal double. Average, upright growth. M-L. (U.S. 1975 - H. B. Rehder, Wilmington, NC).

CAROLINE SIMPSON - Pink streaked Deep Pink and broadly bordered White. Medium, semidouble. (Sport of Japonica 'Lady Vansittart'). (Aus. 1970 - Waterhouse).

CAROLYN - Light Salmon Pink with a few lighter veins and a few petaloids intermingled with White stamens. Large, semidouble. Slow, willowy growth. M. (U.S. 1957 - Mrs. L. McDaniel, McComb, MS).

CAROLYN BOURKE - Pink. Large, semidouble. Average, compact, upright growth. M-L. (Aus. 1973 - G. W. Hooper, Bexley North, NSW).

CAROLYN COLEMAN - Blush Pink with Orchid underside base petals. Medium, formal double. Average, compact growth. M. (U.S. 1968).

CAROLYN DICKSON - Deep Red. Medium to large, semidouble form with large cluster of stamens, petals at times ruffled. Average, upright growth. M-L. (U.S. 1999 - James Dickson III, N. Augusta, SC).

CAROLYN FELKEL - White with Pink and Pink petal edges. Large, rose form double. Vigorous, upright growth. L. (U.S. 1996 - B. Heniford, Fountain Inn, SC).

CAROLYN LUCE - Medium, peony form. (Sport of Japonica 'Eleanor Hagood'). (U.S. 1950 - E C Luce, Half Moon Bay, CA).

CAROLYN MAREE - Soft Pink. Medium, semidouble to formal double. Average, dense, spreading growth. E-M. (Aus. 1977 - Camellia Vale Nsy., Bexley North, NSW).

CAROLYN OYLER - Dark Pink with Red stripes and flecks with Yellow anthers and White filaments. Large, rose form double to semidouble. Vigorous, upright growth. E-L. (Seedling of Japonica 'Lady Laura'). (U.S. 2018 - James Smelley, Moss Point, Mississippi).

CAROLYN RABORN RANKIN - Deep Pink. Large, semidouble with upturned petal edges. Vigorous growth. M. (U.S. 1966 - Mrs. S. J. Raborn, Andalusia, AL).

CAROLYN TUTTLE - Rose Opal Pink. Medium, full peony form. Compact, upright growth. E-L. (U.S. 1954 - Tuttle Bros. Nsy., Pasadena, CA).

CAROLYN WILLIS - White striped Light Rose Pink, sporting Red, Pink, variegated and spotted or striped. Medium to large, semidouble to loose peony form with fluted petals and upright center petals. Average, open, upright growth. M. (U.S. 1957 - Wheeler).

CAROLYN WINIFRED - Pink. Large, formal double. Vigorous, compact, upright growth. M. (Aus. 1970 - Sebire).

CARR'S CIRCUS - Pink and White. Medium, semidouble to peony form with fluted petals. Vigorous, compact growth. M. (U.S. 1959 - R. C. Carr, Tulare, CA).

CARRIE LOU - Medium Blush Pink with Carmine and Pink stripes. Large, semi-double to peony form with distinct rabbit ears especially when treated. Average, upright, columnar growth. M-L. (U.S. 2011 - Julia A. Hilliard, Quitman, GA).

CARROLL GALE - Light Pink. Medium, rose form double. Vigorous, compact, upright growth. M. (U.S. 1958 - McCaskill).

CARROLL LENNARD - Dark Red. Medium, formal double. Slow, open, spreading growth. M. (N.Z. 1994 - T. Lennard, Te Puke).

CARROLL WALLER - Pale Pink. Large, peony form. Average growth. E-M. (U.S. 1999 - L. B. Wilson, Jr. and H. Schall, Jr., Gulfport, MS).

CARTER'S CARNIVAL - White striped Pink and Rose. Large, semidouble. Slow, upright growth. M-L. (For another form of this cultivar see Japonica 'Quaker Lady'). (U.S. 1957 - Carter).

CARTER'S SUNBURST - Pale Pink striped or marked Deeper Pink. Large to very large, semidouble to peony form to formal double. Average, spreading growth. E-L. (Variations of this cultivar include Japonicas 'Chow's Han-Ling' and 'Han-Ling Raspberry'). (U.S. 1959 - Carter).

CARTER'S SUNBURST BLUSH - Pale Pink striped Deeper Pink, bordered White. (Sport of Japonica 'Carter's Sunburst Pink'). (U.S. 1977 - Hulyn Smith).

CARTER'S SUNBURST PINK - Deep Pink. (Sport of Japonica 'Carter's Sunburst'). (U.S. 1964 - O. Locken, San Gabriel, CA).

CARTER'S SUNBURST PINK VARIEGATED - Deep Pink splotched White variation of 'Carter's Sunburst Pink'. (U.S. 1962 - Kramer).

CARTER'S SUNBURST SPECIAL - Medium Pink with Deeper Pink veining and an irregular White border with bright Yellow anthers and White filaments; the bloom is occasionally striped Dark Pink to Red. Large to very large, semidouble to loose peony to rose form double. Vigorous, upright growth. E-L. (Sport of Japonica 'Carter's Sunburst'). (U.S. 2014 - Tommy Alden, Byron, GA).

CARTER'S SUNBURST SWEETHEART - Blush Pink with very small Red spots and stripes. (Sport of Japonica 'Carter's Sunburst'). (U.S. 1982 - R L Wines, Ocala, FL).

CARTER'S SUNBURST VARIEGATED - Pale Pink striped or marked Deeper Pink and White variation of 'Carter's Sunburst'.

CARVAIN'S SILK MOIRE - Coral Rose Pink moiré White. Medium, semidouble with wavy, crinkled petals. Vigorous, compact, upright growth. M. (U.S. 1971 - J. L. Carvain, Fort Worth, TX).

CASABLANCA - See 'Bleichroeder Pink'.

CASILDA - Bright Flame Pink. Medium, single with Red stamens and with fluted, twisted petals of irregular length. Slow, compact growth. M. (Not same as cultivar listed in old literature, which was a formal double of White with Pink Blush at base of petals). (U.S. 1947 - McCaskill).

CATHERINE CATHCART - ('Leila'; 'Lord Darby'; 'San Antonio'). Pink mottled White. Medium, formal double. Slow, slender, upright growth. M-L. (Europe to U.S. [Magnolia] 1940's).

CATHERINE HALL - Light clear Pink. Large, anemone. Average, upright growth. E-M. (U.S. 2007 - Marion H. Hall, Dothan Alabama).

CATHERINE JANE - White. Miniature, formal double. Slow, upright growth. E-M. (N.Z. 1984 - J. Mortinson, Hamilton).

CATHERINE McCOWN - Light Pink. Medium, semidouble to anemone form. (Sport of Japonica 'Eleanor McCown'). (For a color variation of this cultivar see Japonica 'Margaret McCown'). (U.S. 1950 - Shepp).

CATHERINE STIMSON - Crimson. Large, semidouble. Vigorous, compact, upright growth. E-M. (Aus. 1964 - W. A. Stimson, Cheltenham).

CATHY BECHER - Deep Rose. Large, rose form double. (Aus. 1956 - Mrs. D M Andrew, NSW).

CATHY JONES - Salmon Pink at base fading to Light Pink at tips with Yellow anthers and White filaments. Medium, formal double. Vigorous, upright growth. M. (U.S. 2002 - Dr. Luther Baxter, Clemson, SC).

CAVALIER - Dark Pink to Light Red. Large, rose form double. Slow to average, upright growth. M-L. (U.S. 1969 - G. S. Watson, Albany, GA).

CAY McKENZIE - Light clear Pink. Large, anemone form. Vigorous, upright growth. M. (U.S. 1970 - L. Baggs, Macon, GA).

CDR DONALD OYLER - Light Pink with Yellow anthers and Pink filaments. Medium, rose form double. Vigorous, upright growth. E-L. (Seedling of Japonica 'Lady Laura'). (U.S. 2019 - Jim Smelley, Moss Point, MS).

CECIL BEARD - Red with high amount of White. Large, semidouble to peony form. Vigorous, dense, upright growth. M-L. (Japonica 'Ville de Nantes' x Japonica 'Granada'). (U.S. 1994 - Jernigan).

CECIL ROGERS - Pink. Large, formal double of tiered form. (U.S. 1965 - Habel).

CECILE - Soft Pink with Lavender cast. Medium, full peony form. Vigorous, upright growth. E-M. (U.S. 1966 - Maitland).

CECILE BRUNAZZI - Light Pink. Medium, semidouble to loose peony form with large outer petals and crepe, twisted, upright center petals. Open, upright growth. M. (U.S. 1957 - Wheeler).

CECILE BRUNAZZI VARIEGATED - Light Pink blotched White variation of 'Cecile Brunazzi'.

CELEBRITY - Blush White. Medium, semidouble with twisted petals and White stamens. Vigorous, open, upright growth. E-M. (U.S. 1959 - Weisner).

CELESTE G - Pale Pink to Rose on edges. Large, semidouble with ruffled petal edges and a few petaloids interspersed with stamens at times. Average, open, upright growth. M-L. (U.S. 1960 - Mrs. O. H. Wienges, St. Matthews, SC).

CELESTE OLIVIA - Deep Pink. Large to very large, formal double. Upright growth. E-M. (Aus. 1984 - T. J. Savige, Wirlinga, NSW).

CELESTINE - Rose Pink sometimes spotted White. Medium, formal double to rose form double. Average, compact growth. M. (U.S. 1868 - R. Buist, Philadelphia, PA).

33

CELINA DALY - Rose Pink. Large to very large, peony form. Average growth. M. (U.S. 1991 - O. Jacobson, Jacksonville Beach, FL).

CELINA VAUGHAN - White striped Red. Large, semidouble to rose form double with White stamens. Average, upright growth. M. (U.S. 1959 - J. A. Vaughan, Columbia, SC).

CELINA VAUGHAN RED - Red. Large, semidouble. (Sport of Japonica 'Celina Vaughan').

CENTENNIAL - Watermelon Pink. Large, semidouble with nearly round, crepe, fluffy petals. Vigorous, compact, columnar growth. M. (U.S. 1961 - Wilson).

CENTIFOLIA ALBA - White, sometimes striped Deep Rose Pink. Large, formal double with outer petals turned down. M. (For another form of this cultivar see Japonica 'Comtesse Woronzoff'). (Italy 1856 - Coutourlin).

CEREUS GARDENERS - Pale Pink shading to a Deeper Pink at the outer edges. Medium, formal double with outer petals standing and creating a cup form. Vigorous, upright growth. M-L. (U.S. 1995 - Elizabeth R. Scott, Aiken, SC).

CHALICE - See 'Hana-Fuki'.

CHALK PINK - Chalk Pink. Medium, semidouble. (Sport of Japonica 'Tricolor [Siebold]'). (U.S. 1965 - Mrs. L Rigsdill, Ruston, LA).

CHALLENGER - Light Pink. Medium, peony form. (U.S. 1944 - Magnolia).

CHAMELEON - Multi-color from Rose Red to Pink and variegations of White, sometimes speckled. Large, semidouble. (U.S. 1974 - Kramer).

CHAMPAGNE MUSIC - Deep Pink. Large, full peony form. Average, compact, upright growth. M-L. (U.S. 1973 - Mrs. J. Luker, Savannah, GA).

CHANDLER'S VICTORY - Coral Pink. Large, peony form. Upright growth. M. (Aus. 1947 - B. Chandler, Bayswater, W. Aus.).

CHANDLERI - Bright Red with occasional White blotches. Medium, semidouble to anemone form. Slow, compact growth. M. (Not same as 'Elegans [Chandler]'). (England 1825 - Chandler).

CHANDLERI ELEGANS - See 'Elegans (Chandler) Variegated'.

CHANDLERI ELEGANS IMPROVED - Rose Pink with center petaloids often spotted White. Large to very large, anemone form. Average, spreading growth; blossoms and leaves are larger than parent and growth is more vigorous. E-M. (U.S. 1985 - Nuccio's).

CHANDLERI ELEGANS PINK - See 'Elegans (Chandler)'.

CHAPEL BELLS - White. Medium to large, peony form. (U.S. 1965 - Tammia).

CHARISMA - Bright to Deep Red. Large, semidouble. Vigorous, compact, upright growth. M. (Aus. 1979 - A. Spragg, Sutherland, NSW).

CHARLENE ENOT - Very Dark Red. Medium, anemone form. Average, open growth. L. (U.S. 1950 - C. S. Robbins, Altadena, CA).

CHARLENE LEE - Pink. Medium, formal double. Vigorous, compact, upright growth. M. (U.S. 1975 - Haynie).

CHARLES A. NEWMAN - Dark Red veined deeper. Small, formal double. Compact, upright growth. M-L. (Aus. 1981 - C. A. Newman, Bayswater, W. Aus.).

CHARLES AUGUSTUS JONES - Edge of petals Light Pink, shading to pure White at center of flower. Medium, semidouble. Vigorous, upright growth. M-L. (U.S. 2005 - H. Finley Jones, Lake Charles, LA).

CHARLES F. HOLDEN - Bright Red. Medium, rose form double with sharply pointed petals. Slow, compact, upright growth. L. (U.S. 1958 - Feathers).

CHARLES F. O'MALLEY - Flesh Pink. Large, formal double. Average, compact, upright growth. M-L. (U.S. 1989 - M. O'Malley, Woodside, CA).

CHARLES HENTY - China Pink, veined deeper and shading to White edge. Large, semidouble to loose peony form. Vigorous, open, upright growth. M. (For a variation of this cultivar see Japonica 'Robert Henty'). (Aus. 1967 - Henty).

CHARLES KAHN - White with each petal bearing several bright Red streaks. Medium, loose peony form. Vigorous, willowy growth. E-M. (U.S. 1951 - J. L. Kahn, Pensacola, FL).

CHARLES MINARIK - White. Medium, single. Vigorous, upright growth. L. Cold hardy. (U.S. 1991 - C. and D. Minarik, West Harwich, MA).

CHARLES S. TAIT SR. - Light Pink variegated White. Medium, semidouble with rosette of petaloids. Average, compact growth. (U.S. 1956 - Tait).

CHARLES THOMAS - Rose Pink. Small, rose form double. Vigorous, dense growth. M. (U.S. 1998 - C. Elliott, Swainsboro, GA).

CHARLES TURNER - Dark Red. Large, semidouble. Vigorous, upright growth. M-L. (U.S. 1954 - Turner).

CHARLES ZERKOWSKY - Soft Pink flecked White. Large, peony form to rose form double. Average, upright growth. E-M. (U.S. 1982 - Tammia).

CHARLIE ADAMS - Bright Red with White variegation with Yellow anthers and Yellow filaments. Large, semidouble. Average, upright, open growth. M-L. (U.S. 2013 - Robert A. Stroud, Slidell, LA).

CHARLIE BETTES - White with Deep Yellow stamens. Large to very large, semidouble. Vigorous, compact growth. E. (U.S. 1960 - C. Bettes, Jacksonville, FL).

CHARLIE FORTE - Red. Large, semidouble with wide petals and Deep Pink stamens. Average, open, upright growth. E-M. (U.S. 1960 - Beasley).

CHARLIE MANSHIP - Bright Rose Pink. Large, semidouble with smaller, upright, center petals intermingled with stamens. Vigorous, open, upright growth. M. (U.S. 1964 - Beasley).

CHARLIE MASON - Deep Pink. Large, loose peony form. Vigorous, spreading growth. L. (U.S. 1980 - Habel).

CHARLIE V - Red and White with Yellow anthers. Medium, loose peony form. Vigorous, upright growth. M. (U.S. 2009 - Hal Vanis, Henderson, TX).

CHARLIE'S JEANNE - Medium Red with Yellow anthers and White filaments. Very large, semidouble. Average, upright, open growth. M-L. (U.S. 2018 - Pat Johnson, Cairo, GA).

CHARLINE PRESTON - Reddish Pink. Large, semidouble. Average, upright growth. M. (U.S. 1982 - L. C. Preston, Walnut Creek, CA).

CHARLOTTE BLOUNT - Strawberry Red. Large, semidouble to peony form. Average, upright growth. M. (U.S. 1981 - Homeyer).

CHARLOTTE BRADFORD - Phlox Pink variegated White in varied degrees. Medium, semidouble. (Sport of Japonica 'Mrs. Baldwin Wood'). (U.S. 1950 - Bradford).

CHARLOTTE HOAK - Porcelain White. Medium, single with irregular fluted petals and unique stamen formation. Vigorous, compact, upright growth. M. (U.S. 1955 - McCaskill).

CHARLOTTE HOLMAN - Faint Blush Pink with Deeper Pink flecks and dots. Medium, formal double. (U.S. 1955 - Allan).

CHARLOTTE JOHNSON - Black Red. Large, semidouble. Vigorous, compact, upright growth. M-L. (U.S. 1980 - Alfter).

CHARLOTTE JOHNSON VARIEGATED - Black Red and White variation of 'Charlotte Johnson'. (U.S. 1980 - Alfter).

CHARLOTTE WALKER - White. Medium, semidouble. Average, compact, upright growth. M. (U.S. 1962 - H. C. Wilson, Fresno, CA).

CHARMING BETTY - See 'Funny Face Betty'.

CHARTER - White. Large, anemone form. (U.S. 1950 - Mrs. R. Flournoy, Columbus, GA).

CHATHAM - Turkey Red. Large, semidouble to anemone form. Average growth. M. (U.S. 1964 - J. M. Jones, Savannah, GA).

CHEE-REE - Soft Pink. Large, loose peony form. Average growth. M. (U.S. 1972 - Joseph P. Carey, Denham Springs, LA).

CHEERFUL - ('Cheerfulness'; 'Lucida'; 'Hi-Otome'; 'Beni-Otome'). Rose Red. Medium, formal double to rose form double. Vigorous, compact, upright growth. M. (U.S. 1884 - S. Quin, McComb, MS).

CHEERFULNESS - See 'Cheerful'.

CHEERLEADER - Deep Rose Pink blotched White variation of 'Touchdown'. Large to very large, loose peony form. (U.S. 1965 - Nuccio's).

CHEP MORRISON - Dark Red. Medium, semidouble with irregular petals to peony form. Vigorous, compact growth. M. (U.S. 1955 - Clower).

CHERIE SHIRAH - Pink. Medium to large, formal double. Average, spreading growth. M. (U.S. 2005 - John W. Shirah, Lakeland, FL).

CHERRIES JUBILEE - Burgundy Red with Red and White petaloids intermingled with stamens. Medium, full semidouble to rose form double. Average, compact, upright growth. M. (U.S. 1983 - Nuccio's).

CHERRIES O'TOOLE - Cherry Red with Gold anthers and Translucent Pink filaments. Large, semidouble with petals flaring somewhat like a shoe horn. Average, upright growth, M-L. (Seedling of Japonica 'Royal Velvet'). (U.S. 2019 - Tommy Weeks, Conroe, TX).

CHERRY BLOSSOM - See 'Sakuraba-Tsubaki'. (Name also used for Sasanqua).

CHERRY BOUNCE - Dark Cherry Red. Large, rose form double with deep crepe petals. (Sport of Japonica 'Mathotiana Supreme'). (U.S. 1969 - G E Carver, Jr., Houston, TX).

CHERRY FROST - Red with Red and White petaloids. Miniature, anemone form. Average growth. M-L. (U.S. 1987 - D. Bergamini, Martinez, CA).

CHERYL DRINKARD - Rose on outer petals, shading lighter toward center. Large, formal double. Vigorous, compact, upright growth. E. (U.S. 1972 - B. V. Drinkard, Mobile, AL).

CHERYL HUNTER - Light Red with occasional Dark Red outer petal edges with Yellow anthers and Pink filaments. Very large, semidouble. Vigorous, upright, dense growth. E-L. (U.S. 2013 - Howell).

CHERYL HUNTER VARIEGATED - Deep Red with White moiré variegation with Yellow anthers and Red filaments. Very large, semidouble. Average, upright, open growth. M. (Virus variegated form of Japonica 'Cheryl Hunter'). (U.S. 2016 - Thomas Sellers, Bolivia, NC).

CHERYL THOMPSON - Dark Pink with Yellow anthers and Yellow filaments. Large, full peony to anemone. Average, dense growth. M. (U.S. 2015 - Gordy).

CHERYLL LYNN - Shell Pink. Medium to large, formal double. Vigorous, upright growth. M. (U.S. 1965 - H. H. Collier, Chowchilla, CA).

CHESTER D. BELLAMY - Camellia Pink. Large, rose form double to semidouble. Average, spreading, dense growth. E-L. (Chance Japonica seedling). (U.S. 2016 - Pat Johnson, Cairo, GA).

CHICHESTER - Rose Pink. Medium, peony form with twisted, curled, long narrow petals. Open, spreading growth. M. (U.S. 1948 - Clower).

CHICO - Light Pink flecked Rose. Medium, formal double. (U.S. 1935 - Linde).

CHIE TARUMOTO - Blush Pink. Medium, formal double. Average, upright growth. M-L. (U.S. 1977 - Homeyer).

CHIEF ARNOLD - Very Dark Red with Yellow anthers and Red and Yellow filaments. Large to very large, semidouble. Vigorous, upright growth. M. (Japonica 'Edna Campbell' x unknown pollen parent). (U.S. 2009 - Hulyn Smith).

CHIEF SLACK - White blotched and striped Red on one side of flower. Large, peony form. Average, open growth. M. (U.S. 1951 - G. J. Slack, Pensacola, FL).

CHIKUSHI-NO-HARU (SPRING IN CHIKUSHI) - Pale Pink with fine peppering of Pink dots large and round. Large, semidouble to peony form. E-M. (Japan 1970 - Murata Teruo, Fukuoka Prefecture).

CHILDE HAROLD - White. Large, semidouble to peony form with satin sheen on petals. (Portugal 1961).

CHINA DOLL - Blush White edged Coral. Medium to large, loose high-centered peony form with fluted petals. Average, compact growth. M. (U.S. 1958 - Shackelford).

CHINA MAID - Shell Pink. Medium, single of open trumpet form. Vigorous growth. M. (N.Z. 1955).

CHINESE LANTERNS - Blush Pink. Miniature, rose form double of buttercup form. Average, open growth. M. (U.S. 1972 - Witman).

CHIYODA-NISHIKI (MYRAID BROCADE) - ('Chitose-Nishiki'; 'Mallot Variegated'; 'Nana-Komachi'; 'Princess Bacahachie'; 'Princess Nagasakie'). Soft Pink marbled White and Rose Pink. Medium, semidouble. Vigorous, low, spreading growth. M. (Japan 1935 - Chugai).

CHO-CHO-SAN - ('Palmerston'). Light Pink. Medium, semidouble to anemone form. Average, compact growth. M. (Japan to U.S. (Domoto) 1936).

CHOJU-RAKU - Light Pink. Medium, cup-shaped single with flared White stamens. See Higo.

CHO-NO-HAGASANE - See 'Magnoliaeflora'.

CHO-NO-HANAGATA (BUTTERFLY FLOWER FORM) - ('Dorothea Blanche'; 'Heart's Desire'; 'Robinson 56'). Pink shaded White. Medium, semidouble to loose peony form. Average, upright, open growth. M. (Japan to U.S. [Star] 1930).

CHOW'S HAN-LING - White with Blush Pink center and occasional petals slightly striped Pink. Large to very large, semidouble to loose peony to formal double. (Sport of Japonica 'Carter's Sunburst'). (For a variation of this cultivar see Japonica 'Han-Ling Snow'). (U.S. 1971 - L E Chow, Bakersfield, CA).

CHOYO-NO-NISHIKI - (Brocade of Rising Sun). Pink striped Red. Medium, semidouble. Slow, compact growth. E. (Japan).

CHRIS - Light Pink blended Lighter Pink toward center. Large, peony form. Average, spreading growth. M. (U.S. 1964 - O. D. Edge, Columbus, GA).

CHRIS BERGAMINI - White, striped with varying shades of Pinks and Reds. Miniature to small, anemone form. Average, upright growth. M. (U.S. 1999 - Don Bergamini, Martinez, CA).

CHRIS BERGAMINI RED - Red, stripped with varying shades of Red. Miniature to small, anemone form. Average, upright growth. M. (Color sport of Japonica 'Chris Bergamini'). (U.S. 2001 - Don Bergamini, Martinez, CA).

CHRIS LEE - Bright Red heavily veined. Medium, anemone form. Average, upright growth. E-L. (U.S. 1992 - Dr. O. Lewis, Picayune, MS).

CHRISSIE - White. Medium, semidouble with pointed petals. Vigorous, bushy growth. M. (U.S. 1950 - Magnolia).

CHRISTELINE - Blush Pink with White anthers and White filaments. Medium, rose form double. Vigorous, dense, upright growth. E-L. (U.S. 2004 - Lionel Worthy, Gainesville, FL).

CHRISTIAN McSWEEN - Deep Pink. Large, semidouble with ruffled inner row of petals. Average, compact growth. M-L. (U.S. 1961 - Mrs. S. J. Raborn, Andalusia, AL).

CHRISTIAN PINK - Pale Pink to Deep Pink at petal edges. Large, anemone form. Average, dense, upright growth. M-L. (N.Z. 1996 - F. Melville).

CHRISTIAN TIMMONS - Dark Red. Large, peony form. Average, upright growth. M. (U.S. 1964 - Beasley).

CHRISTINE ANN - Pink. Medium, anemone form. Average growth. E-M. (N.Z. 1991 - M. Kennedy, Whangarei).

CHRISTINE COLLINS - Blush Pink with Yellow anthers and White filaments. Medium to large, semidouble to loose peony form. Slow, upright growth. L. (U.S. 2011 - James P. Taylor (deceased), Quitman, GA).

CHRISTINE DODD - Deep Pink outer petals with Light Pink to White inner petals. Very large, semidouble form; folded outer petals give bloom star shape. Average, upright spreading growth. M. (U.S. 1999 - Bond Nursery Corp., Dallas, TX).

CHRISTINE G. - Rose Red. Large, peony form. Average, spreading, upright growth. E-M. (U.S. 1980 - Gilley).

CHRISTINE LEE - Rose Pink. Medium, semidouble. Slow, spreading growth. M. (U.S. 1937 - Lee).

CHRISTINE MARIE - Light Pink. Small to medium, semidouble. (U.S. 1961 - M J Anthony, San Gabriel, CA).

CHRISTINE SCHREIBER - Bright Pink. Medium, formal double. M-L. (U.S. 1977 - H. A. Schreiber, Jr., Lafayette, CA).

CHRISTINE SMITH - Rose Pink. Large, semidouble to anemone form to peony form. Vigorous, compact, upright growth. M-L. (U.S. 1962 - Twin Pines Nsy., Theodore, AL).

CHRISTINE SMITH VARIEGATED - Rose Pink and White variation of 'Christine Smith'. (U.S. 1963 - C. O. Smith, Theodore, AL).

CHRISTMAS BEAUTY - Bright Red. Large, semidouble with fluted petals. Vigorous, upright growth. E. (U.S. 1958 - Howell).

CHRISTMAS BEAUTY VARIEGATED - Bright Red blotched White variation of 'Christmas Beauty'.

CHRISTMAS BELLS - Dark Red. Large, single. Average growth. E-M. (U.S. 1960 - J. C. Campbell, Natchez, MS).

CHRISTMAS CHEER - Rose Pink. Medium, single. E. (U.S. 1930 - Doty and Deemer).

CHRISTMAS PEONY - Turkey Red. Medium, anemone form. Loose, spreading growth. E. (U.S. 1955 - Riverbank).

CHRISTMAS STAR - White. Large, semidouble with outer petals producing a star formation and shorter, inner petals and intermingled petaloids and stamens in center. Average growth. M. (U.S. 1951 - Camelliana).

CHRISTOPHER SHUMAN - Light Red. Large, semidouble. Average, upright growth. M-L. (U.S. 1988 - J. Aldrich, Brooklet, GA).

CHUCK'S MAGIC - White with Red on outer edge of petals. Medium, full peony; the blooms are consistently smaller than the parent plant. Vigorous, upright, open growth. M. (Sport of Japonica 'Magic City'). (U.S. 2015 - Chuck Ritter, Melrose, FL).

CHÛJÔHAKU - Pure White with Yellow anthers and Yellow filaments. Large, single occasionally anemone. Slow, spreading growth. E-L. (Japan 1934 - Kansai District). See Higo.

CHÛJÔSHIRO - White. Medium, single. (Japan 1912). See Higo.

CHUNG CHO YANG - White with central portion Sulphur Yellow and flecked Pink. Medium, formal double. (Sport of Japonica 'Eighteen Scholars'). (U.S. [Peer] from Formosa/Taiwan 1954).

CHURSTON - Pale Pink minutely speckled and unevenly striped Carmine Rose. Large, single with slightly cupped, crimped and wavy petals. Vigorous, bushy growth. M. (Aus. 1963 - Mrs. J. R. Anderson, Toorak).

CILE STANALAND - White. Large, peony form. Average, spreading growth. M. (U.S. 1970 - C. R. Stanaland, Jr., Jacksonville, FL).

CILE WATFORD - White. Medium, rose form double. Vigorous, upright, dense growth. M. (U.S. 2009 - Homeyer).

CILIE SUTTON - White with Blush Pink tinges on outer edges of petals. Medium, single. Vigorous, upright, spreading growth. M. (Japonica 'Rebel Yell' x Japonica 'Omega'). (U.S. 2008 - CamelliaShop, Savannah, GA).

CINDERELLA - Predominantly White with streaks and blotches of Rose madder. Medium, semidouble with irregular and somewhat cupped petals, and with petal edges deeply lacinated and wrinkled. (Sport of Japonica 'Fred Sander'). (For a variation of this cultivar see Japonica 'Raspberry Ice'). (U.S. 1955 - Arnesen).

CINDY ANN - White dashed Pink. Large, semidouble with petals incurved. Vigorous, upright growth. E. (U.S. 1961 - Ashby).

CINDY B - White striped Rose. Very large, semidouble. Vigorous, open, upright growth. M. (U.S. 1965 - Herrin).

CIRCUIT RIDER - White in center shading to Pale Pink at edge. Medium, loose peony form. Average, upright growth. M-L. (U.S. 1972 - E. P. Akin, Shreveport, LA).

CIRCUS GIRL - Multicolor of every color combination from Red to Pink and variegations of White, Pink and Red. Large, semidouble. (U.S. 1958 - Shackelford).

CISSY PURVIS - Orchid Pink. Large, semidouble to anemone form. Average, upright growth. M. (U.S. 1979 - G. Stewart, Sacramento, CA).

CLAIR GOTHARD - Cherry Red. Medium, formal double. Vigorous, dense, upright growth. M. (U.S. 1992 - G. Comstock, Beaumont, TX).

CLAIRE LOUISE - Pink. Medium, anemone form. Upright, open growth. E-L. (N.Z. 2006 - Peter Matthews, Auckland).

CLAIRE RENEE - Dark Pink. Large to very large, anemone form. Vigorous growth. M. (U.S. 1959 - Shackelford).

CLAIRE RENEE VARIEGATED - Dark Pink blotched White variation of 'Claire Renee'.

CLAIRE THOMPSON - White slightly Blushed Pink, occasionally blotched Deep Pink. Large, semidouble to anemone form. Vigorous, compact growth. M. (U.S. 1950 - Dr. O. R. Thompson, Macon, GA).

CLARA ECHOLS MANN - Rose Pink with White variegated center petals. Medium, semidouble. Vigorous, upright growth. E-M. (U.S. 1967 - E. A. Mann, Danielsville, GA).

CLARA GREEN - Deep Rose Pink. Large, peony form to anemone form. Average, compact, upright growth. M. (U.S. 1952 - R. E. Green, Tallahassee, FL).

CLARA PIETER - Deep Red. Small to medium, anemone form. Vigorous, compact, upright growth. M. (U.S. 1986 - Piet and Gaeta).

CLARE O'BRIEN - Pink. Medium, semidouble. (Sport of Japonica 'Dearie Mealing'). (U.S. 1953 - Bartlett's Nsy., Fort Valley, GA).

CLARE TOMLINSON - Pink with strong Lavender cast with Yellow anthers and White filaments. Large to very large, semidouble to loose peony form. Average, upright, open growth. M-L. (U.S. 2013 - Richard Dodd, Marshallville, GA).

CLARENCE HEARN - Deep Rose Red. Large, anemone form. Average, compact, upright growth. E-M. (U.S. 1966 - Mrs. J. M. Hearn, Arcadia, CA).

CLARENCE O. NEIGHBORS - Rose Pink with margin of petals Blue as flower ages. Large, full peony form. Average, compact growth. M-L. (U.S. 1963 - H. L. Neighbors, Alexander City, AL).

CLARISE CARLETON - Red. Large to very large, semidouble. Vigorous, upright growth. M. (U.S. 1955 - Carleton).

CLARISE CARLETON VARIEGATED - Red blotched White variation of 'Clarise Carlton'.

CLARISSA - Pale Pink striped Rose. Large, single. M. (Aus. 1957 - Turnbull).

CLARITAS ALBA - White. Medium, semidouble. Loose, upright growth. M-L. (U.S. Late 1800's - Magnolia).

CLARK HUBBS - Brilliant Dark Red. Large, full to loose peony form with fimbriated petals. Vigorous, compact, upright growth. M. (U.S. 1960 - M. E. Rowell, Fresno, CA).

CLARK HUBBS VARIEGATED - Dark Red and White variation of 'Clark Hubbs'.

CLASSIC PINK - Pale Pink. Medium, formal double. L. Cold hardy. (U.S. - Parks).

CLAUDIA LEA - Delicate Pink. Small, single. Vigorous, upright growth. M. (U.S. 1939 - Dr. H. M. Wilds, Augusta, GA).

CLAUDIA PHELPS - ('Coral Duchess'; 'Tillie Rice'). Delicate Pink shading to White toward edge and sometimes splashed White. Large, semidouble. (Sport of Japonica 'Duchess of Sutherland'). (U.S. 1948 - Fruitland).

CLAUDIA VANIS - Hot Pink. Large, rose form double; petals may be crinkled or lightly streaked Lighter Pink. Vigorous, dense, upright growth. M. (U.S. 1999 - Bond Nursery Corp., Dallas, TX).

CLAYTON CLASSIC - Pink outer petals shading to Paler Pink in the center. Large, formal double. Vigorous, upright growth. E-M. (U.S. 1995 - Mandarich).

CLEO AKINS - Dark Red. Large, semidouble with five separate sections of stamens. Average, upright growth. M-L. (U.S. 1988 - J. Aldrich, Brooklet, GA).

CLEO GLIDDON ARRAS - Deep Rose. Medium, formal double with incurved petals. Average, spreading growth. E-M. (U.S. 2008 - Frances Arras Ashcraft, Mobile, AL).

CLEO WITTIE - See 'Vedrine'.

CLEVE JAMES - Deep Rose. Large to very large, peony form. Vigorous, compact, upright growth. M. (U.S. 1974 - Homeyer).

CLIFF HARRIS - White and Salmon Rose Pink. Medium to large, semidouble to loose peony form. (Variegated form of Japonica 'Her Majesty Queen Elizabeth II'). (U.S. 1959 - Longview).

CLIFFORD WENDELL SEBRING - Pinkish Red with Yellow anthers and Pale Yellow filaments. Medium to large, semidouble. Average, upright, spreading growth. M-L. (U.S. 2019 - E. W. & Gena Fredrickson, Wilmington, NC).

CLIVEANA - Clear Pink. Medium, anemone form. Vigorous, compact growth. L. (Not the same as the old cultivar, which is spelled 'Cliviana' and is Cherry Red). (U.S. 1939 - Gerbing).

CLOISONNÉ - Soft Pink with opaque heavy petals delicately outlined White. Medium to large, semidouble. Vigorous, upright growth. M-L. (U.S. 1988 - McCaskill).

CLORINE BOWEN - Light Pink striped and dashed Darker Pink. Miniature, formal double. M. (U.S. 1973 - Haynie).

CLOUD NINE - Pale Flesh Pink. Large to very large, anemone form. Average growth. M. (N.Z. 1991 - N. Turner, Feilding).

CLOWER RED - China Rose. Large, full peony form. Slow, compact, upright growth. M. (U.S. 1951 - Clower).

CLOWER WHITE - White with Golden anthers. Medium, loose peony form. Vigorous, open growth. M. (Japonica 'Gloire de Nantes' x Japonica 'Nobilissima'). (U.S. 1949 - Clower).

CLOWN - Rose Red, clear Red, Dark Red and White in fine stripes. Medium, full peony form. Average growth. M. (U.S. 1960 - Julington).

CLOWN RED - Red with Yellow stamens. Medium, Full peony form. Average growth rate. M. (Sport of Japonica 'Clown'). (U.S. 1968 - Tammia Nurseries).

CLYDE LESTER - Red. Small, semidouble. Average, upright growth. L. (U.S. 1995 - W. Wilson, Augusta, GA).

COACH MATHIS - Rose pink, commonly variegated White with Yellow anthers and White filaments. Medium to large, full peony to anemone form. Average, spreading growth. E-L. (U.S. 2019 - Clayton Mathis, Douglas, GA).

COED - Blush Pink. Medium to large, formal double to rose form double. Vigorous, compact, upright growth. E-M. (U.S. 1962 - Nuccio's).

COLLARETTE - Rose Pink. Large, anemone form with overlapping guard petals surrounding ruff of folded petals and petaloids which surround elaborate center of petaloids. (U.S. 1959 - T. K. Willett, Lafayette, LA).

COLLETII - ('Colletii Maculata'; 'Girard Debaillon'; 'Purpliana'; 'Genevieve de Barbier'). Red blotched White, varying from nearly solid Red to nearly pure White. Small to medium, full peony form. Slow, bushy growth. E-M. (Belgium 1843 - M. Makoy, Liege).

COLONEL FIREY - See 'C. M. Hovey'.

COLONEL L. E. EDWARDS - Carmine Red. Large, loose peony form. Vigorous, upright growth. M-L. (U.S. 1961 - L. H. Knock, Frederick, MD).

COLONEL REB - Red. Large to very large, semidouble with stamens and Purple tipped petaloids to anemone form to peony form with twisted petaloids separating stamens into five separate groups. Vigorous, spreading growth. E-M. (U.S. 1965 - L. B. Wilson Jr., Gulfport, MS).

COLONIAL DAME - ('Gertrude Murray'; 'Goldlocks'). White, occasionally Blushed Pink. Large, semidouble to peony form to formal double. Open, slender, upright growth. M. (U.S. 1955 - Tick Tock).

COLONIAL LADY - ('Crystal Lake'; 'Striped'; 'White Jordan's Pride'). White with Rose Red stripes and flecks. Medium, semidouble. Fragrant. (Sport of Japonica 'Herme'). (For other forms of this cultivar see 'Orchid Pink'; 'Spring Sonnet'). (U.S. 1938 - McCaskill).

COME ABOARD - Deep Rose. Large, semidouble. Average, spreading growth. E-M. (U.S. 1968 - E. Cooley, Slidell, LA).

COMMANDER MULROY - Blush to White edged Pink with Pink bud center. Medium, formal double. Average, compact, upright growth. M. (U.S. 1961 - T. C. Patin, Hammond, LA).

COMMANDING GENERAL FREDRICKSON - Red with Yellow anthers and White filaments. Small, semidouble. Average, upright, dense growth. E-L. (U.S. 2013 - Gena Owens Fredrickson, Wilmington, NC).

COMPTON'S BROW - Pink or White. Medium, single. (England 1953).

COMTE DE NESSELRODE - Deep Pink striped and splotched Red. Medium, semidouble to loose peony form. Average, upright growth. M-L. (Possibly not same as cultivar listed in old literature, which was Rose Pink tipped and edged White). (Germany [Seidel] to U.S. [McIlhenny] 1937).

COMTESSE DE FLERS - Peach Pink shading to White. Large, semidouble with wavy crinkled petals. Average growth. E-L. (U.S. 1973 - H. W. Turner, Ridgeland, SC).

COMTESSE WORONZOFF - Soft Pink veined Carmine. Large, formal double. (Sport of Japonica 'Centifolia Alba'). (For another form of this cultivar see Japonica 'Lavendel'). (Italy 1858).

CONFEDERATE - Soft Phlox Pink. Large, rose form double. Average, compact growth. E-M. (U.S. 1953 - Fisher).

CONFETTI - White splotched Red. Miniature to small, formal double to anemone form. Vigorous, bushy, upright growth. M. (U.S. 1971 - McCaskill).

CONFETTI BLUSH - Pink with occasional Red stripe and edged White. (Sport of Japonica 'Confetti'). (U.S. 1971 - McCaskill).

CONFETTI RED - Red. (Sport of Japonica 'Confetti'). (U.S. 1971 - McCaskill).

CONQUISTADOR - Coral Rose. Large, semidouble with fluted petals intermixed with stamens. Vigorous, upright, compact growth. M-L. (U.S. 1959 - Nuccio's).

CONQUISTADOR VARIEGATED - Coral Rose and White variation of 'Conquistador'.

CONRAD HILTON - ('White High Hat'). White. Medium to large, peony form. (Sport of Japonica 'High Hat'). (U.S. 1955 - F. R. Honn, Arcadia, CA).

CONSTANCE - Rose Pink. Large, semidouble. Vigorous, bushy growth. M. (Aus. 1938 - Hunter).

CONSTANCY - Turkey Red. Medium, peony form. Loose, upright growth. M. (U.S. 1955).

CONTE BOUTURLIN - Bright salmon Red, with a Purple tint at the edges and in the center. Medium, formal double; imbricated. Open, upright growth. M-L. (Italy 1825 - Carlo Luzzati).

COOPER POWERS - Soft Shell Pink. Large, semidouble with slightly curved center petals and petaloids interspersed with stamens. Average, compact growth. M. (U.S. 1958 - Mrs. C. Powers, Quitman, GA).

COQUETTI - See 'Glen 40'. ('Coquetti' is reported as priority name for this cultivar but, as 'Glen 40' has been in such common use in the U.S., we do not believe a change is necessary or warranted. Also not same as cultivar listed in old literature, which was an anemone form of Deep Salmon Pink often streaked White).

CORA NELSON - White. Medium, formal double to rose form double. Average, upright growth. E-M. (U.S. 1957 - C. M. Nelson, Pearl River, LA).

CORA V. CAMP - Pink with Peppermint stripes of Deeper Pink. Large, semidouble. Vigorous, compact, upright growth. E-L. (U.S. 1961 - Mrs. J. M. Hagood, Charleston, SC).

CORAL CHALICE - Coral. Medium to large, formal double. Spreading growth. M. (Aus. 1981 - T. J. Savige, Wirlinga, NSW).

CORAL DUCHESS - See 'Claudia Phelps'.

CORAL GLOW - Coral Watermelon Pink. Large, semidouble. Average, compact growth. M. (U.S. 1952 - J. Lodge, Pasadena, CA).

CORAL MIST - White veined and splotched clear Pink. Medium, loose peony form with dense collar of petaloids and stamens between ruffled petals. Vigorous, compact, upright growth. M. (U.S. 1959 - Shackelford).

CORAL MIST BLUSH - Blush Pink. (Sport of Japonica 'Coral Mist'). (U.S. 1964).

CORAL PINK LOTUS - Coral Pink with Darker Pink veins. Very large, semidouble. Average, spreading growth. M. (U.S. 1955 - Shepp).

CORAL PINK LOTUS VARIEGATED - Coral Pink blotched White variation of 'Coral Pink Lotus'.

CORAL QUEEN - Light Pink shading to Coral Pink at edge. Medium to large, semidouble with upright petals. Vigorous, compact, upright growth. M-L. (U.S. 1963 - Nuccio's).

CORAL REEFS - Coral to Salmon Red. Large, full peony form to formal double. Average, upright growth. M-L. (U.S. 1957 - Short).

CORALIE BLAND MILER - Blush Pink. Large, semidouble with wavy, crinkled petals. Average, upright growth. M. (U.S. 1975 - Mrs. G. G. Miler, Summerville, SC).

CORNELIA WALDEN - Light Pink. Large, anemone form. Average, upright growth. M. (U.S. 1970 - S. C. Walden, Jr., Albany, GA).

CORNELIA WHITE - White. Medium, formal double. M. (U.S. 1953 - Florida L and N Co.).

CORONATION - White. Very large, semidouble. Vigorous, open, spreading growth. M. (U.S. 1954 - McCaskill).

CORPORAL PUGG JOHNSON - Dark Red. Medium, single. Average growth. E. (U.S. 1967 - J. L. Soloman, Augusta, GA).

CORROBOREE - White striped Crimson. Medium, semidouble. M. (Aus. 1962 - Waterhouse).

CORSAGE - Pink. Medium, formal double. Average, compact growth. E-M. (U.S. 1961 - Wilson).

COTTONTAIL - White. Miniature, full peony form. Average, compact, upright growth. M. (U.S. 1965 - McCaskill).

COUNTESS OF ORKNEY - Cream White striped Rose Pink. Large, peony form. Slow, compact growth. M. (Variations of this cultivar include Japonicas 'Burnham Beeches' and 'Countess of Orkney Rosea'). (England 1847 - Nicholson).

COUNTESS OF ORKNEY (UNITED STATES) - ('Americana'; 'Maid of Orleans').- White streaked Rose. Medium, formal double to rose form double. Slow, compact growth. (U.S. 1848).

COUNTESS OF ORKNEY ROSEA - Rose Pink. Large, peony form. (Sport of Japonica 'Countess of Orkney').

COUNTRY DOCTOR - Deep Metallic Pink with Deeper Pink veins. Large, semidouble with crepe petals and curled, upright inner petals. Vigorous, upright growth. E-M. (U.S. 1957 - F. Hamiter, Shreveport, LA).

COUNTRY DOCTOR VARIEGATED - Deep metallic Pink and White variation of 'Country Doctor'.

COURAGEOUS - Red. Large, anemone form with petaloids flecked White. Slow growth. M. (U.S. 1965 - J. F. Marscher, Beaufort, SC).

COURT YARD WHITE - White. Medium, semidouble. (U.S. 1956 - Tait).

COURTESAN - Bright Red with Darker Red stripes to Light Pink margined White. Medium, semidouble of bell shape. Average, compact, upright growth. M. (Aus. 1971 - Tuckfield).

COURTESAN ROUGE - Deep Red. (Sport of Japonica 'Courtesan'). (Aus. 1971 - Tuckfield).

COURTNEY - Blush Pink. Medium, formal double. Average growth. M-L. (U.S. 1984 - C. C. Crutcher, Theodore, AL).

COURTNEY DOSSETT - White. Miniature, formal double; the petals are pointed, shape is irregular, never a perfectly round bloom. Average, upright, spreading growth. L. (U.S. 2016 - Howell).

COURTNEY HALL - White. Medium, formal double with reverse petals that curl inward. Average, upright growth. M-L. (U.S. 1996 - Marion Hall, Dothan AL).

COVENTRY - White. Large, semidouble with loose, wavy petals and six clusters of stamens intermingled with petaloids. Average, open growth. M-L. (U.S. 1970 - Haynie).

COVER GIRL - Clear Pink. Medium, formal double with irregular petals. Average, compact, upright growth. M-L. (U.S. 1965 - Nuccio's).

COVINA - Rose Red. Small to medium, semidouble to rose form double. Vigorous, bushy growth. M. (U.S. 1888 - Dr. Burdick, Glendora, CA).

CRADLE SONG - Pale Blush Pink. Medium, formal double to rose form double. Vigorous, compact, upright growth. M. (U.S. 1971 - V. Shuey, Temple City, CA).

CRANE'S FEATHER - White. Very large, anemone form. Slow, open growth. M. (N.Z. 1967 - Mrs. T. Durrant, Tirau).

CRAZY SUE - Red to Pink to White blotched Red or Pink and various other combinations of Red and/or Pink and/or White. Medium, peony form. Vigorous, dense, upright growth. E-M. (U.S. 1995 - W. Smith, Gainesville, FL).

CREAM PUFF - Chalky White. Medium, peony form. Average, compact growth. M-L. Cold hardy to -5°F. (U.S. 1986 - Ackerman).

CREPE ROSETTE - Deep Pink veined Red with White margined petals. Medium, semidouble with twisted outer petals intermingled with stamens. Average, compact growth. E-L. (U.S. 1941 - Middleton).

CRIMSON BUOY - Crimson. Medium, single. Average, open growth. M-L. (N.Z. 1981 - Jury).

CRIMSON FANTASY - Crimson Red. Large, rose form double. Vigorous, upright growth. M. (U.S. 1992 - H. Hall).

CRIMSON GLORY - Crimson. Medium, semidouble with petaloids and Red stamens. Slow, open growth. M-L. (U.S. 1959 - B. F. McKenzie, Columbia, MS).

CRIMSON RUFFLE - Crimson. Large, semidouble with ruffled petals. Vigorous, compact, upright growth. M-L. (U.S. 1956 - Short).

CRISTY - Soft pastel Pink. Medium, formal double. Slow, bushy growth. M. (Aus. 1989 - A. Savage, Mt. Pleasant, W. Aus.).

CROWNED PRINCE - Cream White. Medium, semidouble to loose peony form with crown of Yellow stamens. Average growth. M. (U.S. 1959 - Holmes).

CROWNING GLORY - White tipped Lavender Pink. Miniature, anemone form. Average, compact, upright growth. E-L. (U.S. 1977 - Feathers).

CRUSADER - See 'Prince of Orange'

CRUSHED STRAWBERRY - Red, Pink and White. Medium, formal double. (U.S. 1953 - Riverbank).

CRUSSELLE - Bright Red. Medium, loose peony form with upright petals. Average, upright growth. L. (Similar to Japonica 'Blood of China'). (U.S. 1957 - T. A. Crusselle, Atlanta, GA).

CRYSTAL LAKE - See 'Colonial Lady'.

CUCAMONGA - Vermillion Red. Medium to large, rose form double. Bushy growth. M-L. Fragrant. (Sport of Japonica 'Kramer's Supreme'). (U.S. 1980 - Kramer).

CUP OF BEAUTY (UNITED STATES) - Rose Red. Medium, rose form double to semidouble of cupped form. M. (Europe to U.S. [Magnolia] 1940's).

CURLY LADY - Red. Medium, semidouble to peony; twisted branches and leaves. M. (Sport of Japonica 'Lady Campbell'). (Netherlands 2008 - Van Vliet New Plants).

CUTEY PIE - Rose Pink. Miniature, semidouble. Slow, upright growth. M-L. (U.S. 1975 - Novick).

CUTIE BUTTONS - White with Yellow anthers and White filaments. Small, full peony to anemone. Average, upright growth. E-M. (U.S. 2016 - John Rumbach, Jacksonville, FL).

CYNTHIA - White. Small, semidouble. Average, upright growth. M. (U.S. 1957 - D. W. Davis).

CYNTHIA HOOGLAND - Deep Red. Large, loose peony form with upright petals. Vigorous, compact growth. L. (U.S. 1959 - Woodland).

CZARINA - See 'Emperor of Russia Variegated'.

D. E. HUGER - Red. Large, semidouble. Average growth. M. (U.S. 1950 - Middleton).

D. HERZILIA DE FREITAS MAGALHAES - See 'Dona Herzilia de Freitas Magalhães'.

D'IBERVILLE - White suffused and lined Pink. Small, formal double. (U.S. 1950 - McIlhenny).

DAD'S PINK - Candy striped half Pink or solid Pink. Medium, formal double. Vigorous, compact growth. M. (Color sport of Japonica 'Romany'). (U.S. 2011 - Ray Watson, Sanford, NC).

DADDY MAC - White with flecks and streaks of Dark Red, Coral Pink and Light Red to medium Pink mixed in an irregular pattern throughout the bloom; Light Yellow anthers and Yellow filaments. Large, peony to anemone form. Slow, spreading, open growth. E-M. (U.S. 2009 - John M. Davy, Pace, FL).

DAHLIAFLORA - Raspberry Red with darker veining. Medium, semidouble to peony form to anemone form with center petaloids pointed and swirled as in a dahlia. Vigorous, compact growth. M. (U.S. 1953 - T. H. Seavey, Alhambra, CA).

DAHLOHNEGA - Canary Yellow. Small to medium, formal double. Slow, open, upright growth. M. (U.S. 1986. Homeyer).

DAI HASSU - See 'Daitairin'.

DAIJÔKAN (LARGE CASTLE CROWN) - ('Daijôhkan', 'Daijyôkan'). White with Gold anthers and light Yellow filaments. Large to very large, semidouble. L. (Japan 1964 - Castle of Nagoya).

DAIKAGURA - ('Idaten-Shibori'; 'Kiyosu'; 'Daikagura [Ward]'). Bright Rose Pink splotched White. Medium to large, peony form. Slow, compact growth. E. (For variations of this cultivar see below and Japonicas 'Benten-Kagura' and 'High Hat'). (Japan 1891 - Yokohama).

DAIKAGURA (WARD) - See 'Daikagura'.

DAIKAGURA PINK - See 'Daikagura Red'.

DAIKAGURA RED - ('Beni-Daikagura'; 'Pink Kagura'; 'Shangri-La'; 'Aka-Daikagura'; 'Pink Daikagura'). Deep Pink to Rose Red. (Sport of Japonica 'Daikagura'). (Japan 1936 - Chugai).

DAINTRIE SIEVERS - Clear Pink. Medium, loose peony form. L. (Aus. 1964 - Brushfield).

DAINTY (CALIFORNIA) - Blush White striped Red with fringed petals. Medium, semidouble. (Sport of Japonica 'Tricolor [Siebold]'). (U.S. 1953 - Carter).

DAINTY (SOUTH) - Soft Pink. Medium, single of bell form. (U.S. 1950 - Pfingstl).

DAINTY MAIDEN - Pink. Medium, semidouble to peony form. Pendulous growth. M. (Aus. 1952 - Waterhouse).

DAISY BANKS - White. Medium, semidouble. Vigorous, spreading growth. M-L. (U.S. 1943 - Gerbing).

DAISY EAGLESON - Light Pink and White having 50 petals. Miniature, rose form double. Vigorous, upright, dense growth. E-M. (Grafted Japonica seedling onto Sasanqua 'Maiden's Blush' under stock). (U.S. 1961 - Tom Eagleson, Port Arthur, TX).

DAITAIRIN - ('Pink Fimbriata'; 'Golden Temple'; 'Dai-Hassu'; 'Bar None'; 'Hatsu-Zakura'; 'Osaka-zuki'). Light Rose Pink. Large, single with mass of petaloids in center. Vigorous, upright growth. E. (Japan 1941 - K. Wada, Nagoya).

DAKOTA VARIEGATED - Variegated Red and White. Medium, peony form. Average, open, upright growth. M-L. (U.S. 2004 - William Smith, Gainesville, FL).

DALE FITZGERALD - Rose Pink. Large, peony form. Vigorous, upright growth. E-M. (U.S. 2007 - Jerry Conrad, Erinon Camellias, Plymouth, FL).

DALLAS PRATT - Pink. Large, anemone form. Average, spreading growth. E-L. (U.S. 1971 - Mrs. W. E. Laughlin, Aiken, SC).

DAN GRANT - Pale Pink veined Darker Pink and spotted and streaked White. Large, semidouble with small, upright center petals intermixed with stamens. Vigorous, spreading growth. E-L. (U.S. 1965 - T. A. Grant, Savannah, GA).

DAN GRAVES - Oriental Red. Medium to large, semidouble with large, thick, fluted, upright petals. Vigorous, upright growth. M. (U.S. 1963 - Mrs. D. W. Graves, Bogalusa, LA).

DAN GRAVES VARIEGATED - Oriental Red and White variation of 'Dan Graves'.

DAN STEWART - Rose. Large, full peony form. Average, compact, upright growth. M. (U.S. 1967 - D. Stewart, Minden, LA).

DANATTA MERRYDAY - Rose Pink. Medium, rose form double to formal double. Average, upright, spreading growth. M-L. (U.S. 2017 - Danatta Merryday, Tallahassee, FL).

DANTE - See 'Kagiri'. (Not the same cultivar as listed in old literature which was a White with a few delicate Pink stripes).

DANTE'S INFERNO - Scarlet. Medium, peony form. Slow, compact growth. M. (U.S. 1951 - J. L. Kahn, Pensacola, FL).

DANZADOR - Blush Pink with dots and dashes of Pink. Medium, semidouble of flat form with flared petals. Slow, compact growth. M-L. (U.S. 1956 - S. W. Miller, El Cajon, CA).

DAPHNE DU MAURIER - Metallic Red. Medium, semidouble to anemone form. Open, upright growth. (England: 1972 - Carlyon).

DAPHNE T. - White. Medium, semidouble. Average, open, spreading growth. M. (U.S. 1997 - C. Elliott, Swainsboro, GA).

DARBY - Burgundy. Medium, anemone. Average, upright growth. M-L. (U.S. 2017 - William & Linda Nichols. Cottonwood, AL).

DARK OF NIGHT - Dark Red with Yellow Anthers and Pink filaments. Medium, semidouble. Average, upright growth. M-L. (Japonica 'Tinsie' x Japonica 'Fuyajo'). (U.S. 2009 - Jim Moon, Portland, OR).

DARK OF THE MOON - Maroon. Medium, full peony form. Vigorous, upright growth. M. (U.S. 1955 - Short).

DARK SECRET - Very Dark Red. Small to medium, semidouble with fringed petals. Vigorous, compact growth. M-L. (U.S. 1953 - Short).

DARLEEN GRACE - Cream White with a touch of Pink on the outer petals with Gold anthers and Cream filaments; it sometimes blooms Blush Pink with Darker Pink late in the season. Medium, semidouble to loose peony. Average, upright growth. M-L. (U.S. 2013 - Gordy).

DARLING PINK - Rose Pink with frosty White in center. Large, formal double. M. (U.S. 1950 - Malbis).

DAUTEL'S SUPREME - Reported in three forms: a darker and heavier 'Mathotiana Supreme'; pompon center of petaloids; and two rows of very large petals with large cluster of bright Yellow stamens. Large to very large, rose form double to formal double. (Sport of Japonica 'Mathotiana'). (U.S. 1961 - Dautel's Nsy., Lake Charles, LA).

DAVE BULL - Soft Pink with some Darker Pink streaks. Miniature, anemone form. Average, dense, upright growth. L. (N.Z. 1992 - D. Bull, Auckland).

DAVE C. STROTHER - Blush Peach Pink. Medium, semidouble to anemone form. Vigorous, upright growth. M-L. (U.S. 1950 - Katz).

DAVID HONOUR NELSON - White occasionally marked or striped Rose Red. Large, semidouble. Average, spreading growth. L. (U.S. 1969 - G. A. Nelson, Florence, SC).

DAVID RATCLIFF - Bright Red. Large, loose peony form. Average, upright growth. E-M. (U.S. 1995 - J. Ratcliff, Tifton, GA).

DAVID RATCLIFF VARIEGATED - Bright Red and White variation of 'David Ratcliff'. (U.S. 1995 - J. Ratcliff, Tifton, GA).

DAVID STUART - White. Large, semidouble of flat form. Vigorous, upright growth. M-L. (U.S. 1955 - Feathers).

DAVID SURINA - Light Red. Medium to large, formal double. Average, compact, upright growth. M-L. (U.S. 1966 - Surina's Camellia Gdns., Sepulveda, CA).

DAVID WILSON - White. Large, peony form. Average, upright growth. M-L. (U.S. 1989 - W. Wilson, Augusta, GA).

DAVID WIRTH - Wine Red. Large, semidouble to loose peony form with heavy, erect, twisted petals. Slow, compact, upright growth. E. (U.S. 1955 - Judice).

DAVID WIRTH VARIEGATED - Wine Red blotched White variation of 'David Wirth'.

DAWN LYNN - Deep Pink with Gold anthers and Yellow filaments. Medium, anemone form. M-L. (U.S. 1994 - Gordy).

DAWN'S EARLY LIGHT - Light Orchid Pink with Deeper Pink intermixed. Medium to large, full peony form, occasional rose form double to formal double. Vigorous, upright growth. E-L. (U.S. 1985 - Nuccio's).

DAWN'S OWN - Pink. Small to medium, anemone form. Average, dense growth. M-L. (Aus. 1995 - K. Brown, Mitcham, Vic.).

DAWSON PINK - Dark Pink. Medium, semidouble of tiered form. Average, pendulous growth. M. (U.S. 1955 - Bowman).

DAYBREAK - ('Flesh Pink Peony'). Light Pink. Medium, full peony form. Vigorous, bushy growth. L. (U.S. Late 1800's - Magnolia).

DAZZLE - Pink. Large, semidouble with upright center petals interspersed with groups of stamens. Average, open, upright growth. M-L. (U.S. 1964 - G. C. Clark, Savannah, GA).

DE SOTO - Pink with many petaloids blotched White. Medium, peony form with large pompon center. (U.S. 1955 - McIlhenny).

DEACON DODD - See 'Kumasaka Variegated'.

DEANE'S DARLING - Garnet Red with Red petaloids with imbricated, incurved outside petals. Small to medium, anemone form. Slow, dense, upright growth. M-L. (U.S. 2003 - Deane Burch, Citrus Heights, CA).

DEANNA J. - Rose Pink center to Blush Pink at outer edges. Large, peony form to rose form double. Average, spreading growth. E-L. (U.S. 1997 - O. Jacobson, Jacksonville Beach, FL).

DEAR JENNY - White. Large, semidouble. Vigorous, compact growth. E-M. (U.S. 1959 - C. W. Hand, Pelman, GA).

DEAREST - See 'Finlandia'.

DEARIE MEALING - White marked Pink. Medium, semidouble of flat form. Slow growth. M. (For a variation of this cultivar see Japonica 'Clare O'Brien'). (U.S. 1941 - Magnolia).

DEBBIE STUTTS - Deep Salmon Rose Pink. Large, semidouble with White petaloids. (U.S. 1959 - L W Ruffin, Ellisville, MS).

DEBORAH ANN - Delicate Rose Pink striped Deep Rose Pink. Large, semidouble. Average, compact, upright growth. M. (U.S. 1956 - Mrs. F. W. Hamel, Yazoo City, MS).

DEBUTANTE - ('Sara C. Hastie'). Light Pink. Medium, full peony form. Vigorous, upright growth. E-M. Cold hardy. (For a variation of this cultivar see Japonica 'Gladys Marie'). (U.S. Early 1900's - Magnolia).

DEBUTANTE BLUSH - Blush Pink. Medium, full peony form. (Sport of Japonica 'Debutante'). (U.S. 1972 - Dr. R. K. Womack, Shreveport, LA).

DEBUTANTE-BENTEN - Light Pink. Small to medium, peony form. Vigorous, upright growth. E-M. (Leaf sport of Japonica 'Debutante'). (U.S. 2002 - Nuccio's).

DEE DAVIS - Rose Pink. Medium, rose form double. Vigorous, open, upright growth. M. (U.S. 1976 - Dr. J. Davis, Tuscaloosa, AL).

DEE DAVIS VARIEGATED - Rose Pink blotched White variation of 'Dee Davis'. (U.S. 1976 - Dr. J. Davis, Tuscaloosa, AL).

DEE DOT - Pale Pink to Deeper Pink on edge, sometimes striped Red. Medium, formal double. Average, upright growth. M-L. (U.S. 1981 - E. P. Akin, Shreveport, LA).

DEEDY - Light Rose Pink with some White stripes in center petals. Large, semidouble to peony form. Vigorous, open, upright growth. (U.S. 1964 - G. C. Lecroy, Moncks Corner, SC).

DEEN DAY SMITH - White. Large to very large, rose form double to peony form with long, fluted, and notched petals. Average, spreading, upright growth. M. (U.S. 1989 - Homeyer).

DEEP DRIFT - White. Large, semidouble of flat form with evenly notched petals. Vigorous, upright growth. M-L. (U.S. 1956 - Short).

DEEP PINK CLOUDS - Silver Pink. Large, loose peony form. (Sport of Japonica 'Pink Clouds'). (U.S. 1957 - Fisher).

DEEP PURPLE DREAM - Deep Purple Red with Yellow anthers and Yellow filaments. Medium, semidouble to rose form double to peony form. Vigorous, upright, dense growth. E-M. (U.S. 2008 - John L. Spencer, Lakeland, FL).

DEEP SECRET - Cardinal Red veined Darker Red. Medium to large, semidouble. Average, upright growth. M. (N.Z. 1991 - Jury).

DEEP SOUTH - Dark Rose Red. Medium to large, semidouble to loose peony form. Average, compact, upright growth. M. (U.S. 1950 - Short).

DEL RIO - Light Rose and Crimson candy striped. Medium, peony form with large petaloids. M. (Aus. 1960 - G. Hooper, Bexley).

DELECTISSIMA - White with a wide Pink stripe. Medium, single. Vigorous, spreading growth. E-M. (Not the same cultivar listed in old literature, which was a rose form double of White striped Rose Pink). (U.S. Early 1900's - Magnolia).

DELIGHT - See 'Mrs. Josephine M. Hearn'.

DELIGHTFUL - White. Large, single with fluted petals. Vigorous, upright growth. E-M. (Aus. 1988 - C. Carroll, West Pymble, NSW).

DELLIE McCAW - Pink. Medium, formal double. Average, spreading growth. E-L. (U.S. 1975 - J. M. Almand, Warner Robins, GA).

DELORES THOMPSON - Light Pink. Small, rose form double to formal double. Average, spreading growth. M. (U.S. 1988 - J. Aldrich, Brooklet, GA).

DELPHINE JOHNSON - Pale Pink with Maroon stripes. Medium, formal double form; star shaped petals. Average, dense, upright growth. M-L. (U.S. 1999 - Elizabeth R. Scott, Aiken, SC).

DELTA KING - Light Red. Large, semidouble with irregular, folded, frilled petals with intermixed stamens and petaloids in center. (U.S. 1961 - Camelliana).

DELTA QUEEN - Blush with occasional Pink streak. Large, formal double. L. (U.S. 1968 - Camelliana).

DEMI-TASSE - Peach blossom Pink. Small to medium, semidouble of hose-in-hose form with row of petaloids between petals. Vigorous, compact, upright growth. M. (U.S. 1962 - McCaskill).

DENEEN FENDIG - White suffused with irregular markings of Light Pink margined White. Large, semidouble. (Sport of Japonica 'Gladys Fendig'). (U.S. 1956 - A. Fendig, Sea Island, GA).

DENNIS VAUGHN - Deep Velvet Red. Large, formal double with curled inner petals. Average, spreading growth. E-M. (U.S. 1982 - M. McLeod, Monticello, FL).

DERA MAY - White with blotch of Red on one or two center petals. Medium, semidouble to loose peony form. Vigorous, bushy growth. M. (U.S. 1959).

DERBYANA - ('Tasse de Beau'; 'Zachary Taylor').— Red to Purplish Red. Medium to large, semidouble to anemone form. Vigorous, compact, upright growth. M-L. (France 1838 - Berlese).

DESCANSO BLUSH - White overlaid with Blush Pink. Medium, loose peony form. Compact growth. E-M. (U.S. 1957 - Descanso).

DESCANSO YULETIDE - White irregularly striped Maroon. Large, semidouble. Average, upright growth. E-M. (U.S. 1959 - Descanso).

DESCANSO'S SURPRISE - White. Medium, anemone form. Average, upright growth. E. (U.S. 1949 - Descanso).

DESERT SUNSET - Bright Coral Pink with bright Gold anthers and Cream filaments. Large, semidouble; the flower has retic-like characteristics and will sometime have rabbit ears in cooler weather. Vigorous, upright, dense growth. M. (U.S. 2013 - Gordy).

DESERTION - Pale Pink. Medium, rose form double. M-L. (U.S. 1950 - Pfingstl).

DESIRE - Pale Pink edged Deep Pink. Medium, formal double. Vigorous, compact, upright growth. M. (U.S. 1977 - Feathers).

DESSA THOMPSON - Cream White. Medium, full peony form. Compact, upright growth. E-L. (U.S. 1948 - McCaskill).

DESTINY - White streaked Deep Pink. Large, semidouble. (Sport of Japonica 'Lady Clare'). (Japan to U.S. [Domoto] 1955).

DIAN HARTMAN - White with slight fleck of Reddish Pink to Red. Medium, semidouble with irregular petals to anemone form. Average, upright growth. M-L. (For another form of this cultivar see Japonica 'Dian's Fancy'). (U.S. 1957 - Hartman).

DIAN'S FANCY - Pink. Medium, semidouble. (Sport of Japonica 'Dian Hartman'). (U.S. 1960 - Hartman).

DIANA MOON - Soft Mauve Pink splotched White. Large, semidouble. Upright growth. M-L. (U.S. 1960 - F. Griffin, Sr., Columbia, SC).

DIANE KRAUEL - Light Pink center to Dark Pink on outer edges. Medium to large, semidouble. Slow, upright growth. E-M. (U.S. 1997 - R. Hendrick, Shreveport, LA).

DIANNE DICKSON REYNOLDS - Rose Red. Large, formal double. Vigorous, upright growth. M. (U.S. 2019 - Gordy).

DICK DODD - Cherry Red. Large, rose form double. Average, dense, upright growth. M. (U.S. 1998 - R. Dodd, Marshallville, GA).

DICK HARDISON - Red edged Black Red. Medium to large, formal double with incurved petals. Average, dense growth. E-L. (U.S. 1997 - D. Hardison, Tallahassee, FL).

DICK RANKIN - Crimson Red shaded Blue. Medium to large, semidouble to peony form with loose petals. Vigorous, upright growth. M-L. (U.S. 1959 - Clower).

DICKIE THOMAS - Pink striped Carmine. Medium, semidouble. Average, open growth. M. (U.S. 1956 - Miss E. W. Boorman, Temple City, CA).

DIDDY MEALING - Cream White with Yellow cast in throat, and an occasional Pink stripe. Medium, rose form double to formal double. Average, slightly pendulous growth. M. (For another variation of this cultivar see Japonica 'Pink Diddy'). (U.S. 1948 - Mealing).

DIDDY MEALING PEONY - White with occasional Pink stripe. Medium, peony form. (Sport of Japonica 'Diddy Mealing'). (U.S. 1973 - Mealing).

DIDDY'S PINK ORGANDIE - Dawn Pink at base blending to Light Pink toward edge of petals and edged White. Medium, rose form double to formal double. (Sport of Japonica 'Diddy Mealing'). (U.S. 1953 - Mealing).

DIMPLE DARLING - Blush Pink. Large, semidouble with White stamens. Vigorous, open, upright growth. M. (U.S. 1961 - Weisner).

DIMPLES - Reddish Pink. Miniature, anemone form. Average, compact growth. M. (U.S. 1955 - Wylam).

DISNEYLAND - Rose Pink with center petaloids moired White. Very large, semidouble to anemone form. Vigorous, compact growth. M. (U.S. 1960 - Nuccio's).

DIVA - Deep rich Red with Deep Red veining. Large, semidouble. Average to slow, dense growth. M-L. (N.Z. 1999 - Haydon).

DIXIE BEGGS - Red with some inner petals marked Rose Pink. Medium, semidouble. Average, dense, upright growth. M-L. (U.S. 1992 - W. Stout, Pensacola, FL).

DIXIE BELLE - Light Pink shading to White, Blush Pink to Deeper Pink on outer petals. Large, anemone form. Average, spreading growth. E-M. (U.S. 1980 - Mrs. H. Johnson, Madison, FL).

DIXIE KNIGHT - Deep Red. Medium, loose peony form with irregular petals. Vigorous, upright growth. M-L. (U.S. 1955 - Wheeler).

DIXIE KNIGHT SUPREME - Variegated variation of 'Dixie Knight' - Deep Red heavily moired White. (U.S. 1961 - Wheeler).

DIXIE KNIGHT VARIEGATED - Deep Red streaked White variation of 'Dixie Knight'.

DIXIE MAID - Light Pink. Small, formal double. Average, open growth. M-L. (U.S. 1976 - Haynie).

DIXIE RED - Wine or Mahogany Red. Small, anemone form. Slow, upright growth. M-L. (U.S. 1962 - Wheeler).

DIXIE RED VARIEGATED - Wine or Mahogany Red blotched White variation of 'Dixie Red'.

DIXIERAMA - Rose Pink. Large, loose peony form with petals crinkled toward center. Average, compact growth. E-M. (U.S. 1960 - Overlook).

DO POZO - Rose (RHSCC 54B-55B) with darker veins (55A), petals bordered White, and a few may have White stripes. Medium, full peony form. Average, shrubby and slightly open growth. M. (Spain 1986 - Maciñeira Nursery, Galicia).

DOC GLAUSIER - Blush Pink with Dark Pink and Red stripes. Small, anemone to full peony form. Average-slow, upright, columnar growth. M-L. (U.S. 1970 - C. E. Glausier, Quitman, GA).

DODY'S DELIGHT - Pale Pink with Darker Pink speckles and stripes. Very large, semidouble form. Vigorous, upright growth. M. (Japonica sport of unnamed parentage). (U.S. 2004 - Tom Gilfoy. LaCañada, CA).

DOIRON'S LEGACY - White with Pink petal edges, Medium to large, full peony. Average, bushy growth. M. (U.S. 2019 - Francis J. Doiron, Baton Rouge, LA).

DOLLY - Soft Pink center shading to Deeper Pink edge. Medium, semidouble. Average, open, upright growth. E-M. (Aus. 1989 - K. Abbott, Rossmoyne, W. Aus.).

DOLLY BOWEN - ('Moss Point Red'). Red. Large, loose peony form. Open growth. M. (U.S. 1959).

DOLLY DYER - Scarlet. Miniature, anemone form. Vigorous, upright growth. E-M. (Aus. 1973 - G. W. Hooper, Bexley North, NSW).

DOLLY HUSSEY - Bright Rose Pink. Medium, single with eight slightly cupped petals around distinctive central mass of petaloids. (N.Z. 1961 - Mrs. J. Hussey, Wanganui).

DOLLY O'DRISCOLL - Shell Pink shading to White center. Large, formal double. Average growth. M-L. (N.Z. 1982 - T. Lennard, Te Puke).

DOLLY PARLER - Rose Pink. Large, anemone form. Average, upright growth. M. (U.S. 1977 - A. R. Parler, Elloree, SC).

DOLLY VARDEN - Light Pink with darker Pink splashes with Gold anthers and White filaments. Large, semidouble. E. (U.S. early 2000's - Al Taylor, Fresno, California).

DOLORES JACKSON - White. Large to very large, loose peony form. Vigorous, open, upright growth. M. (U.S. 1981 - Alfter).

DOLORES OATES - Ice Pink to darker shading. Large, anemone form. Average growth. E-L. (U.S. 1973 - J. T. Oates, Daphne, AL).

45

DOMINIC DiTOMASSO - Deep Cherry Red. Medium to large, loose peony to semidouble form. Average, upright, bushy growth. E-L. (Japonica 'Edna Campbell' seedling). (U.S. 2005 - Hulyn Smith).

DOMOTO'S PETITE - Pink. Miniature, anemone form. Average growth. M-L. (U.S. 1997 - Domoto).

DON PEDRO - White with rare stripes of soft Pink. Medium, formal double. (Portugal 1851 - De Jonghe).

DON WILSON - Pink veined deeper. Medium, formal double. Upright growth. E-M. (Aus. 1981 - Camellia Vale Nsy., Bexley North, NSW).

DONA HERZÍLIA DE FREITAS MAGALHÃES - Mauve Pink to deep Purple. Medium, semidouble to anemone form. M. (Portugal 1925 - da Silva).

DONA JULIA - Light Salmon Pink to Dark Rose. Large, anemone form. Vigorous, upright growth. M. (For another variation of this cultivar see Japonica 'Vaughn Drinkard'). (U.S. 1959 - Longview).

DONCKELARII - Red marbled White in varying degrees. Medium to large, semidouble. Slow, bushy growth. M. Cold hardy. (For a variation of this cultivar see Japonica 'Ville de Nantes'; there are many named strains of this cultivar e.g., Japonicas 'Tea Garden', 'Middleton No. 15', 'Cantelou', 'English', 'Camellia T', 'Tallahassee', 'Mary Robertson', 'Winnie Davis' and 'Aileen'. However, it would appear that there is only one 'Donckelarii' which varies in degree of variegation). (China to Belgium [Siebold] 1834).

DONCKELARII RED - See 'Eugene Bolen'.

DON-MAC - Dark Red. Medium to large, semidouble to loose peony form with curled and crepe petals surrounding large mass of White stamens. Average, upright growth. E-L. (U.S. 1956 - Mrs. S. W. Donohoo - Pensacola, FL).

DON-MAC VARIEGATED - Dark Red and White variation of 'Don-Mac'.

DONNA BUONO - Silvery Pink. Large, rose form double with upright petals folding over and a few White stamens. Average, upright growth. (U.S. 1961 - Tammia).

DONNA CLARA - Camellia Rose. Medium, loose peony form with ring of large petaloids above and around group of stamens. Vigorous, pendulous growth. (U.S. 1950 - R. H. Roberts, Biloxi, MS).

DONNA DERRICK - Soft Pink with Deeper Pink veins. Large, formal double. Average, upright growth. M. (U.S. 1970 - S. E. Derrick, Columbia, SC).

DONNA LYN - Bright Red. Medium, semidouble. Vigorous, open growth. M-L. (U.S. 1979 - Gilley).

DONNA NEWTON - White. Large, loose peony form. Average, compact, upright growth. M. (U.S. 1979 - Mrs. D. Newton, Dawson, GA).

DONNAN'S DREAM - White washed and shaded Orchid Pink. Medium to large, formal double. Average, compact, upright growth. E-L. (For a variation of this cultivar see Japonica 'Jerry Donnan'). (U.S. 1984 - Nuccio's).

DONNYBROOK - White. Large, semidouble with pointed and turned up petal tips. (U.S. 1955).

DORA DEE WALKER - Dark Red blotched White with Yellow stamens. Large to very large, full peony form to semidouble with occasional fimbriated petals. Average, spreading growth. M-L. (U.S. 1967 - W. M. Walker, Spartanburg, SC).

DOREEN - Crimson. Medium to large, single of tulip form with long Yellow stamens. (U.S. 1957 - H. H. Harms, Portland, OR).

DORIAN - Soft Pink with faint Salmon Pink tone. Medium, semidouble with curved and twisted petals and center of intermixed small petals, petaloids and stamens. Vigorous, spreading growth. M. (Aus. 1960 - Henty).

DORIS ELLIS - Pale Blush Pink with Darker Pink outer petals and Coral Rose center. Medium, formal double. Vigorous, upright growth. E. (U.S. 1969 - J. W. Ellis, Jacksonville, FL).

DORIS ELLIS PINK - Pale Pink. Medium, rose form double with incurved, swirled petals. (Sport of Japonica 'Doris Ellis'). (U.S. 1978 - R. B. Gramling, Tallahassee, FL).

DORIS FREEMAN - Pink marbled and blotched White. Large, semidouble to peony form. Compact, upright growth. M. (U.S. 1956 - W. H. Barnsley, Apopka, FL).

DORIS HIRST - White. Large, semidouble to anemone form. Vigorous, compact, upright growth. M. (Aus. 1961 - W. Neville, Castle Hill).

DORIS MADALIA - See 'Beauty of Holland'.

DORIS NADEAU - Deep Pink. Large, formal double. (U.S. 1953).

DORIS STONE - Deep Red. Large to very large, semidouble form; petals turn toward stem. Vigorous, spreading growth. E-L. Very cold hardy. (U.S. 2000 - Elizabeth R. Scott, Aiken, SC).

DOROTHY ASHLEY - Light Rose Pink. Large, semidouble. Vigorous, upright growth. M. (U.S. 1959 - Middleton).

DOROTHY B. DECUERS - Rose Pink with Yellow to Orange anthers and Ivory filaments. Medium to large, semidouble to rose form double. Average, upright growth. (Sport of Japonica 'Happy Birthday'). (U.S. 2008 - John W. Shirah, Lakeland, FL).

DOROTHY BROWN - Soft Pink shading to Deeper Pink at edge. Large, peony form. Average growth. E-M. (U.S. 1968 - L. B. Wilson, Jr., Gulfport, MS).

DOROTHY CHESTER - White. Large, peony form. Vigorous, spreading, upright growth. E-M. (U.S. 1979 - G. C. Chester, Augusta, GA).

DOROTHY COPELAND - White. Medium to large, semidouble with long, fluted, wavy petals. Average, upright growth. M. (U.S. 1971 - C. X. Copeland, Jackson, MS).

DOROTHY CULVER - White. Large, peony form. Vigorous, upright growth. M. (U.S. 1978 - Gilley).

DOROTHY HENRY - Rose Pink. Medium, formal double. Average, upright growth. M-L. (U.S. 1988 - J. Aldrich, Brooklet, GA).

DOROTHY HILLS - Blush Pink shading to Darker Pink border. Medium, formal double. Vigorous, compact, upright growth. M. (U.S. 1976 - Tammia).

DOROTHY HOOPER - Red. Medium, anemone form. Vigorous, spreading, upright growth. E-M. (U.S. 1984 - G. B. Hooper, Modesto, CA).

DOROTHY JESSEP - Pink. Medium, semidouble. M. (Aus. 1952 - Royal Botanic Gardens).

DOROTHY JOCELYN - Deep Pink. Large, formal double. Average, open, spreading growth. M-L. (N.Z. 1993 - T. Lennard, Te Puke).

DOROTHY L. CHATTIN - Pink. Medium, formal double. Slow, spreading growth. (U.S. 2008 - Shirah's Camellia Nursery, Lakeland, FL).

DOROTHY MAC - White. Medium, anemone form. Vigorous, bushy growth. M. (U.S. 1948 - Mrs. S. McPherson, Glendale, CA).

DOROTHY MARBUTT - White striped Pink. Medium, semidouble. Vigorous growth. E-M. (U.S. 1959 - McDonald, Augusta, GA).

DOROTHY MEREDITH KERNAGHAN - Blush Pink. Medium, rose form double. Vigorous, compact, upright growth. M-L. (U.S. 1980 - G. C. Chester, Augusta, GA).

DOROTHY MINARIK - Rose Pink. Medium, single. Vigorous, compact, upright growth. L. Cold hardy. (U.S. 1991 - C. and D. Minarik, West Harwich, MA).

DOROTHY MURPHY - Off White to very Light Pink. Medium, semidouble. Average, open, upright growth. E-L. (Aus. 1977 - A. Spragg, Sutherland, NSW).

DOROTHY PARKER - See 'Emmett Pfingstl'.

DOROTHY PEET - Blush Pink center shading to Light Pink. Large, semidouble. Average growth. E-M. (U.S. 1959 - Feathers).

DOROTHY ROSE - Rose Pink. Medium, rose form double. Vigorous, compact, upright growth. E-M. (U.S. 1956 - T. Eagleson, Port Arthur, TX).

DOROTHY SCHMITT - Deep Red. Miniature, formal double with star shaped center. Average, open, spreading growth. M. (U.S. 1978 - C. G. Schmitt, Mobile, AL).

DOROTHY SMITH - Pink and Red. Medium, peony form. E. (Aus. 1962 - Mr. Smith, Wollongbar).

DOROTHY SPENGLER - White. Large, rose form double. Average growth. L. (U.S. 1968 - Mrs. J. J. Spengler, Durham, NC).

DOROTHY STRONG - Pink and White. Large, formal double with high center. (U.S. 1957 - Gerbing).

DOROTHY TILLETT - White. Miniature to small, formal double. Average, upright growth. M. (U.S. 1980 - Tammia).

DOROTHY ZERKOWSKY - White to Blush Pink with some Pink spots and sporting Light Pink. Large, peony form. Average, open, upright growth. M. (U.S. 1973 - Tammia).

DOROTHY'S FOLLY - Deep Rose, few White stripes. Medium, anemone form. Vigorous, dense, upright growth. E-M. Very cold hardy. (U.S. 1998 - Dorothy F. Minarik, W. Harwich, MA).

DORRIE CHANDLER - Rose Pink. Medium, peony form. Average, open, upright growth. E-M. (Aus. 1967 - E. V. R. Chandler, East St. Kilda, Vic.).

DOT CADY - Light Pink with White center. Medium, formal double. Average, spreading growth. M-L. (U.S. 1981 - E. A. Akin, Shreveport, LA).

DOTTIE LYNCH - Phlox Pink with a few White spots. Large, loose peony form with irregular petals. Upright growth. M. (U.S. 1961 - Fisher).

DOUBLE PINK POMPON - Deep Rose Pink lightly veined Rose. Large, peony form. (U.S. 1953 - McIlhenny).

DOUG HAVILAND - Rose Pink with darker veining. Medium, single. Slow, spreading growth. M. (Aus. 1999 - Alan Truran, Hornsby, NSW).

DOUGLAS DEAN HALL - Deep Rose Pink to Red with Yellow anthers. Small, rose form double to formal double. Average growth. E-M. (U.S. 1987 - Ackerman).

DOUGLAS MAYFIELD - White. Medium, anemone form. Vigorous growth. E-M. (U.S. 1986 - Stone).

DOUGLAS POTTER - Deep Rose. Large, full peony form. Vigorous, open, upright growth. E-M. (U.S. 1977 - D. Mayfield, Baton Rouge, LA).

DOVE OF PEACE - White. Medium, formal double. Vigorous, upright growth. M. (U.S. 1965 - McCaskill).

DOVIE FIFIELD - Blush Pink speckled Pink. Large, peony form with slightly sunken groups of petaloids. Average, bushy growth. M. (U.S. 1960 - H. C. Petteway, Lakeland, FL).

DR. AGNEW HILSMAN - White suffused Blush Pink streaked, striped, blotched and dotted Rose Pink and Turkey Red, and sporting solid Red, and Rose Pink striped Turkey Red. Medium, semidouble to peony form. Vigorous, compact, upright growth. E-M. (U.S. 1956 - Hilsman).

DR. ARCHIE SASSER - Light Red. Medium, anemone form. (U.S. 1957 - Mark S. Cannon, Dothan, AL).

DR. BILL HARRISON - Deep Rose Pink to Coral Pink to Deep Blush Pink. Large, semidouble with upright, whirled petals intermingled with stamens. Vigorous, upright growth. M. (U.S. 1960 - Harrison).

DR. BLISS SHAFER - Pale Pink striped Rose, sporting Pink, Pink and White, and Blush. Large, peony form. Average, upright growth. M. (U.S. 1970 - S. H. Mancill, Lafayette, LA).

DR. BOB - Rose. Miniature, formal double. Slow, compact, upright growth. M. (U.S. 1952 - Dr. E. J. Petitjean, Opelousas, LA).

DR. BURNSIDE - Dark Red. Medium to large, semidouble to peony form. Average, upright growth. M. (U.S. 1962 - Dr. A. F. Burnside, Sr., Columbia, SC).

DR. BURNSIDE VARIEGATED - Dark Red blotched White variation of 'Dr Burnside'.

DR. CAMPBELL - See 'Jacksoni'.

DR. CARL BEARD - Red and White. Large, semidouble. Average, dense, upright growth. M-L. (U.S. 1996 - Jernigan).

DR. CHARLES PETTEWAY - Rose Pink. Medium, rose form double. Average growth. M. (U.S. 1964 - H. C. Petteway, Lakeland, FL).

DR. CHARLES PETTEWAY VARIEGATED - Rose Pink and White variation of 'Dr Charles Petteway'. (U.S. 1964 - H. C. Petteway, Lakeland, FL).

DR. CHARLES THOMPSON - Light Pink striped Red. Medium to large, semidouble. Vigorous, compact, upright growth. M. (U.S. 1975 - Haynie).

DR. CY. ECHOLS - Deep Rose Pink and White. Large, semidouble. Vigorous growth. M. (U.S. 1986 - Gilley).

DR. DAN ELLIS - Deep Pink. Large, peony form with deeply veined petals. Average, compact, upright growth. E-M. (For a variation of this cultivar see Japonica 'Kitty Ellis'). (U.S. 1972 - Mrs. D. W. Ellis, Charleston, SC).

DR. DAN J. - Rose Red with Orange Red satin sheen. Very large, semidouble to rose form double. Average, spreading growth. E-M. (U.S. 1991 - O. Jacobson, Jacksonville Beach, FL).

DR. DAVID SLOAN - White. Medium, formal double. Vigorous, open growth. M. (U.S. 1981 - Marbury).

DR. DONALD KOONCE - Dark Red. Large, anemone form. Average, compact growth. M. (U.S. 1961 - Marbury).

DR. ED - White. Large, semidouble with wavy, crinkled petals. Average, upright growth. M-L. (U.S. 1977 - W. Garoni, Greenville, SC).

DR. EDWARD PORUBSKY - Pink. Very large, peony form. Vigorous, upright growth. M. (U.S. 2001 - Hulyn Smith).

DR. FAY SHAW - Deep Pink. Large, semidouble with wavy, crinkled petals. Vigorous, compact growth. M-L. (U.S. 1968 - Gerbing).

DR. FIRTH - Pink to Lavender Pink. Large, peony form. (U.S. 1957 - L W Ruffin, Ellisville, MS).

DR. FRANK POOLE - Ivory White. Medium, semidouble to loose peony form with irregular petals. (U.S. 1957 - Fisher).

DR. FRANK WILSON - Raspberry Red. Small, formal double with incurved petals. Average, upright, dense growth. E-M. (Japonica 'Edna Campbell' x unknown pollen parent). (U.S. 2013 - Hulyn Smith).

DR. FRED LEE - White with Pink stripes or spots. Large, semidouble with crinkled petals. Vigorous, compact, upright growth. M. (U.S. 1975 - Haynie).

DR. GARY CARROLL - Dark Red. Medium, semidouble to peony form. Average, upright growth. M. (U.S. 1980 - Tammia).

DR. GEECHEE - Bright Red. Very large, semidouble with twisted, upright and folded center petals. Vigorous, spreading, upright growth. M. (U.S. 1968 - Burgess).

DR. GEORGE BUNCH - See 'Sarah R'.

DR. GUY BETHEA - Dark waxy Red. Medium, semidouble with irregular petals. Vigorous, upright growth. M. (U.S. 1967 - Dr. G. Bethea, Hattiesburg, MS).

DR. H. G. MEALING - Blood Red. Large, semidouble. Vigorous, open growth. L. (U.S. 1946 - Allan).

DR. H. G. MEALING VARIEGATED - Blood Red blotched White variation of 'Dr H G Mealing'.

DR. HAGOOD - Dark Purplish Red. Medium, formal double. Slow, upright growth. L. (U.S. 1955 - J. Smith, Mullins, SC).

DR. HENRY B. HARVEY - Soft Rose Red. Small, formal double with center petals incurved, swirled, and sharply pointed at tips. Vigorous, dense, upright growth. E-M. (U.S. 1995 - H. V. Stone, Baton Rouge LA).

DR. HOWARD HOUSE - Rose Pink. Large, semidouble to loose peony form. Vigorous, spreading growth. M. (U.S. 1965 - Dr. J. B. Tarver, San Marino, CA).

DR. HUFFMAN - Pink. Large, semidouble to anemone form. Vigorous, compact, upright growth. M. (U.S. 1965 - Marbury).

DR. HUGO - White. Large, semidouble with wavy crepe outer petals and upright center petals. Average, upright growth. M. (U.S. 1973 - J. Luker, Savannah, GA).

DR. J. C. RAULSTON - Bright Red to Red Orange. Very large, anemone form, halo of stamens around center petaloids. Vigorous, dense, upright growth. M-L. (U.S. 1998 - Bond Nursery Corp., Dallas, TX).

DR. J. M. HOWELL - White. Large, rose form double. Vigorous, upright growth. E-M. (U.S. 1986 - Dr. O. V. Lewis, Picayune, MS).

DR. J. V. KNAPP - Deep Red. Medium, semidouble with loose petals. Average, upright growth. M. (U.S. 1956 - R. W. Vincent, Zellwood, FL).

DR. JAMES BROWN - Rose Red. Large, loose to full peony form to anemone form to rose form double. Vigorous, compact, upright growth. E-M. (U.S. 1971 - Tammia).

DR. JAMES BROWN VARIEGATED - Rose Red heavily variegated White variation of 'Dr James Brown'. (U.S. 1971 - Tammia).

DR. JOHN - Dark Red. Small, peony form. Vigorous, compact, upright growth. E. (U.S. 1955 - Feathers).

DR. JOHN D. BELL - Variegated variation of 'Beau Harp' - Dark Red heavily variegated White. (U.S. 1950 - Wilkinson).

DR. JOHN VAUGHN - Bright Rose lighter in center. Large, formal double. Vigorous, spreading growth. E-M. (U.S. 1971 - Judge H. C. Petteway, Auburndale, FL).

DR. JUDGE - Pale Blush Pink with Darker Pink at edges and reverse side of petals. Medium, semidouble. Average, upright growth. M-L. (U.S. 1995 - W. Smith, Gainesville, FL).

DR. KARL HORN - White. Medium, formal double. Average, upright, open growth. M. (U.S. 2013 - Howell).

DR. KING - Light Red. Large, semidouble. Upright, bushy growth. M-L. (Aus. 1945 - Camellia Grove).

DR. LEWIS SHELTON, JR. - Deep Red. Large, semidouble to rose form double. Vigorous, upright growth. M. (U.S. 1973 - Dr. L. Shelton, Jr., Jacksonville, FL).

DR. LILYAN HANCHEY - Very Pale Blush Pink. Medium, formal double. Average, open, upright growth. M. (U.S. 1976 - Stone).

DR. M. WOLFE - White with many Red stripes and dots. Medium, semidouble. (U.S. 1957 - Baker).

DR. MACGRUDER - Light Rose Pink. Medium to large, peony form. (U.S. 1959 - G M Wheeler, Birmingham, AL).

DR. MacLEOD - Red. Large, semidouble. (U.S. 1955 - Fresno, CA).

DR. MARY BURCH - White with Yellow anthers and White filaments. Large, semidouble to loose peony. Vigorous, upright, dense growth. E-M. (U.S. 2018 - Randolph Maphis - Tallahassee, FL).

DR. MAX - Red blotched White. Medium, single. Compact, upright growth. M. (Japan to U.S. 1940 - Camellia Hall).

DR. NICKY SHUMAN - White. Large, anemone form. Average, spreading growth. M-L. (U.S. 1988 - J. Aldrich, Brooklet, GA).

DR. O. V. LEWIS - Dark Red. Large, anemone form. Vigorous, upright growth. E-M. (U.S. 1985 - Dr. O. V. Lewis, Picayune, MS).

DR. OLIN OWEN - Oriental Red. Large, semidouble. Average, dense, upright growth. M-L. (U.S. 1991 - Dr. O. Owen - Charlotte, NC).

DR. PAUL SANDERS - Deep Pink. Large, semidouble with swirled and fluted petals. Vigorous, compact, upright growth. M. (U.S. 1959 - Miss F. Sanders, Charleston, SC).

DR. PAUL SANDERS VARIEGATED - Deep Pink and White variation of 'Dr Paul Sanders'.

DR. PERCY JENKINS - Pale Pink shading Deeper Pink on outer petal edges. Large, semidouble. Bushy, upright growth. (Aus. 2006 - Mrs. Mary Elizabeth Jenkins, Vic.).

DR. QUATTLEBAUM - Turkey or Oriental Red. Medium to large, semidouble. Average, upright growth. M-L. (U.S. 1960 - Coleman).

DR. RALPH GLADEN - White streaked Crimson. Medium, formal double of tiered form. Average, compact, pendulous growth. M. (U.S. 1951 - Councilman).

DR. RICHARD HARDISON - Turkey Red with Golden anthers and White filaments. Large, semidouble. Vigorous, spreading growth. E-M. (U.S. 2015 - Randolph Maphis, Tallahassee, FL).

DR. ROBERT E. SCHWARTZ - Metallic Red. Medium to large, anemone to loose peony form. (Sport of Japonica 'Vedrine'). (U.S. 1957 - M Baldwin, Hattiesburg, MS).

DR. ROBERT PIGFORD - Rose Pink. Large, peony form. Average, open growth. M. (U.S. 1965 - W. H. Powell, Garner, NC).

DR. SALK - Deep Pink shading to Light Lavender vein on outer margin. Medium, anemone form to full peony form. Average, compact, upright growth. M-L. (U.S. 1956 - Woodland).

DR. SALK VARIEGATED - Deep Pink blotched White variation of 'Dr Salk'.

DR. SHEPHERD - See 'Te Deum'.

DR. STAFFORD - Vivid Pink. Large, semidouble, with wavy crinkled petals. Average, upright growth. E-L. (U.S. 1978 - Mrs. M. J. Hein, Lecompte, LA).

DR. THEODOR BELLMANN - Pale Pink. Large, semidouble of hose-in-hose form. Spreading, open growth. M-L. (Aus. 1981 - T. J. Savige, Wirlinga, NSW).

DR. TINSLEY - Very Pale Pink at base shading to Deeper Pink at edge with reverse side Flesh Pink. Medium, semidouble. Compact, upright growth. M. Cold hardy. (U.S. 1949 - Mrs. G. J. Tinsley, Hammond, LA).

DR. TINSLEY SUPREME - Has double the number of rows of petals of original. (Sport of Japonica 'Dr. Tinsley'). (U.S. 1962 - Gerbing).

DR. W. G. LEE - Dark Red. Medium, semidouble of round form. Average, spreading growth. M-L. (U.S. 1947 - Lee).

DR. W. H. McINTOSH - Rose Red tinged Purple on petal edges. Medium, semidouble. Vigorous, open, pendulous growth. E-M. (U.S. 1954 - Chiles).

DR. W. L. BARTON - Light Pink. Medium to large, semidouble with loose, crepe petals to compact incurved petals. Vigorous, upright growth. L. (U.S. 1977 - Dodd).

DR. WELCH - Dark Red. Large, full peony form. (U.S. 1957).

DR. WILDS - White. Medium, semidouble. M. (U.S. 1948 - Fruitland).

DR. WILLIAM BEASLEY - White. Medium, rose form double with upright petals surrounding intermingled petaloids and stamens. Average, open, upright growth. M. (U.S. 1964 - Beasley).

DR. WILLIAM BECKMAN - Rose Red with darker veining. Large, semidouble with large and rounded petals and upright center petals. Vigorous, compact, upright growth. (U.S. 1968 - H. W. Johnson, Mt. Pleasant, SC).

DRAGON EYE - Dark Red. Miniature, anemone form. Slow growth. M. (U.S. 1964 - Dr. L. E. Chow, Bakersfield, CA).

DRAGON LADY - Clear Pink with Pink and White petaloids. Medium, semidouble to loose peony form with twisted outer petals. Average, bushy, pendulous growth. M-L. (U.S. 1952 - Coucilman).

DRAMA GIRL - Deep Salmon Rose Pink. Very large, semidouble. Vigorous, open, pendulous growth. M. (For variations of this cultivar see below and Japonica 'Estella D'Ancona'). (U.S. 1950 - E. W. Miller, Escondido, CA).

DRAMA GIRL DREAM - Petaloids in center. (Sport of Japonica 'Drama Girl').

DRAMA GIRL TISON - Pink petals with a White margin. Very large, semidouble. Vigorous, upright, open growth. E-M. (Sport of Japonica 'Drama Girl'). (U.S. 2008 - Dr. Frank A. Wilson III, Leslie GA).

DRAMA GIRL VARIEGATED - Deep Salmon Rose Pink blotched White variation of 'Drama Girl'.

DREAM AWHILE - Light Lavender Pink. Medium to large, semidouble with upright petals. Average, bushy growth. M. (U.S. 1960 - Short).

DREAM SPINNER - Pale Pink to Deep Pink on edge. Medium, single with fine fimbriated petals. Slow, compact, upright growth. M-L. (N.Z. 1989 - Mrs. K. A. Campbell, Wanganui).

DREAM TIME - Blush Pink shaded Light Orchid. Large, semidouble. Average, upright growth. M. (U.S. - 1973).

DREAMY - Red with half variegated White. Large, semidouble to rose form double. Average, spreading, upright growth. M. (U.S. 1980 - Alfter).

DRESS PARADE - Red. Medium, semidouble to loose peony form. Average, spreading growth. M. (U.S. 1975 - Novick).

DRIFTWOOD - See 'Margaret McCown'.

DRUMLEA - Crimson. Large, semidouble. Vigorous, upright growth. M. (N.Z. 1962 - Mrs. W. M. McFarland, Frankton Junction).

DRYADE - ('Iride'). Rose Pink shading to Light Pink at center. Miniature, formal double. Compact, upright growth. M. (Italy 1849 - Negri).

DRYADE VARIEGATED - Rose Pink and blotched White variation of 'Dryade'.

DUBONNET - Dark Wine Red with darker veining. Medium, semidouble to peony form. Vigorous, upright growth. M. (U.S. 1952 - Malbis).

DUBONNET VARIEGATED - Dark Wine Red and White variation of 'Dubonnet'.

DUC DE BRABANT - White tinged delicate Pink and striped Carmine. Medium, semidouble to peony form. M. (Belgium 1851 - Moens, Antwerp).

DUC DE DEVONSHIRE - See 'C. M. Hovey'. (Not the cultivar listed in old literature, which is listed immediately below).

DUC DE DEVONSHIRE (ENGLAND) - Bright Cherry Red. Large, formal double. (England to Belgium [Verschaffelt] 1851).

DUCHESS OF COVINGTON - White, flecked and moired Pink. Large, semidouble. (Sport of Japonica 'Duchess of Sutherland'). (U.S. 1953 - Katz).

DUCHESS OF SUTHERLAND - White, sometimes with Pink stripe on one petal. Large, semidouble of flat form, sometimes with curled inner petals. Vigorous, spreading, upright growth. M-L. (For other forms of this cultivar see Japonicas 'Ruth Royer'; 'Claudia Phelps'; 'Duchess of Covington'). (U.S. Late 1800's, Magnolia).

DUCHESS OF SUTHERLAND PINK - Solid Pink. (Sport of Japonica 'Duchess of Sutherland').

DUCHESS OF WINDSOR - White. Medium, loose peony form. Low, bushy growth. E. (U.S. 1942 - Magnolia).

DUCHESS OF YORK - See 'Lady Loch'.

DUCHESSE DE ROHAN - ('Preston Rose'). Salmon Pink. Medium, peony form. Vigorous, upright growth. M-L. (England 1874 - Caledonia).

DUCHESSE DECAZES - ('Hime'; 'Opelousas Peony'; 'Duchesse De Cases'; 'Juanita'; 'Mrs. Conrad Wall Jr.'). Flesh Pink veined Pink and edged White. Medium, full peony form. Vigorous, compact, upright growth. M. (France 1908 - Guichard).

DUDLEY BOUDREAUX - White. Medium, semidouble to loose peony form. Vigorous, dense, upright growth. M. (U.S. 2003 - Hyman R. Norsworthy, Beaumont, TX).

DUKE OF BURGUNDY - Deep Pink fading to White around edge. Large, semidouble. Compact growth. M. (U.S. 1944 - Magnolia).

DUKE OF WELLINGTON - Red. Large, semidouble with loose petals intermixed with stamens. (Europe to U.S. [Magnolia] 1848).

DUKE OF WINDSOR - Pink. Large, formal double. (Sport of Japonica 'Mathotiana Alba'). (Probably same as Japonica 'Mathotiana Rosea'). (U.S. 1955 - Magnolia).

DUKE OF YORK - See 'Otahuhu Beauty'.

DURRANT'S DILEMMA - Red with White stripe in center of many petals. Medium, formal double with spiral petals. Slow, bushy growth. M. (N.Z. 1969 - Mrs. T. Durrant, Tirau).

DUSTY - Dusty Rose Pink. Large, formal double. Vigorous, upright growth. M-L. (U.S. 1986 - E. F. Achterberg, Citrus Heights, CA).

DUSTY WELLBORN - White with Pink flecks with Gold anthers and White filaments. Medium, semidouble to rose form double; the flower is fimbriated. Average, upright, spreading growth. E-M. (U.S. 2017 - Hulyn Smith).

E. A. McILHENNY - See 'Kishu-Tsukasa'.

E. G. WELLER - White with Lemon tint in center. Miniature to small, peony form to formal double. Compact, upright growth. M. (Aus. 1983 - E. G. Weller, Bisbane, Qld.).

EARL KLINE - Red. Large, semidouble with swirled, fluted, velvety textured petals. Vigorous, open, upright growth. M. (U.S. 1959 - Shady Acres Nsy., Charleston, SC).

EARL SMITH - Red. Large to very large, semidouble with fluted petals. Average, open, upright growth. M. (U.S. 1997 - L. Smith, Beaufort, SC).

EARLY AUTUMN - Lavender Rose with center petals edged Deep Lavender. Medium, formal double form. Average, upright growth. E-M. (U.S. 2001 - Gordy).

EARLY BIRD - Pink. Medium, semidouble. Average, upright growth. E. (U.S. 1962 - Wheeler).

EARLY BIRD VARIEGATED - Pink blotched White variation of 'Early Bird'.

EARLY DAWN - Dark Pink to Light Purple. Medium, formal double. Average, upright growth. E. (U.S. 1964 - G. Sheffield, Silsbee, TX).

EARLY WOODVILLE RED - Early blooming, Large, peony form. (Sport of Japonica 'Woodville Red').

EASTER BASKET - Bright Pink with White edges on each petal, occasional Dark Pink stripes with Yellow anthers and White filaments. Small to medium, single to anemone; the blooms occasionally have petaloids. Average, upright, spreading growth. E-L. (U.S. 2017 - Don Bergamini, Martinez, CA).

EASTER MORN - Baby Pink. Very large, semidouble with irregular petals to full peony form. Average, upright growth. M-L. (U.S. 1965 - Dr. C. C. Wright, Sacramento, CA).

EASTER PARADE - Blush Pink. Medium, formal double. (U.S. 1964 - Shackelford).

EASTERN SUN - White. Medium, rose form double to full peony form with Lemon-tinted petaloids. Slow, bushy growth. M. (U.S. 1945 - Gerbing).

ECCLEFIELD - White. Large to very large, semidouble to anemone form. Vigorous, compact, upright growth. M. (U.S. 1959 - Domoto).

ECKIE JOHNSON - Pink. Medium to large, rose form double. Average, upright growth. E-L. (U.S. 1989 - Dr. A. Johnson, New Orleans, LA).

ECLATANTE - Soft Pink. Medium to large, semidouble. Compact growth. M. (U.S. 1953 - G. Willis, Thomasville, GA).

ECSTASY (CALIFORNIA) - See 'Madame. Hovey'.

ED ALSIP - Light Pink, Pinkness decreases to Blush at center. Small to medium, formal double form. Average, upright growth. M. (U.S. 2005 - Gordon Eade, Pensacola, FL).

ED ANDERSON - See 'Tomorrow'.

ED COMBATALADE - Red. Medium, formal double. Average, upright growth. M-L. (U.S. 1977 - Kramer).

ED JERNIGAN - Pink with White blotches with Yellow anthers and Pink filaments. Medium, semidouble. Average, upright growth. M. (U.S. 2019 - Ed Jernigan, Greenville, AL).

ED POWERS - Deep Rose variegated with White in a moiré pattern with Yellow anthers and White filaments. Large, rose form double. Average, open growth. E-L. (U.S. 2006 - Ed Powers, Wilmington, NC).

EDDIE GILLEY - Dark Red. Large, semidouble with wavy, crinkled petals. Average, upright growth. M. (U.S. 1974 - Gilley).

EDELWEISS - White. Large, loose peony form. Vigorous, semi-pendulous, upright growth. E-M. (U.S. 1956 - Breschini).

EDGEWOOD - Soft Rose Pink. Large, semidouble with notched petals. Average, upright growth. M. (U.S. 1967 - J. N. Sewell, Jacksonville, FL).

EDITH CHURCHILL - White. Medium, loose peony form. Slow, bushy growth. M. (U.S. 1940 - Gerbing).

EDITH COOK FISHER - Soft delicate Pink. Large, formal double. Vigorous, compact, upright growth. M. (U.S. 1961 - Fisher).

EDITH HALL - Rose Pink. Large, rose form double to peony form. Vigorous, spreading growth. E-M. (U.S. 1979 - Mrs. A. Grant, Dothan, AL).

EDITH HALL VARIEGATED - Rose Pink and White variation of 'Edith Hall'.

EDITH LINTON - Pink shading to Silvery Pink. Medium, semidouble to peony form,. (Sport of Japonica 'Jean Lyne'). (Aus. 1941 - Linton).

EDMUND B. - Rose veined deeper. Large, semidouble with White stamens. Vigorous, compact, upright growth. M. (U.S. 1959 - Breschini).

EDMUND HARDING - Pink. Large, semidouble with waved, crinkled petals. Average, open, upright growth. M. (U.S. 1970 - Marbury).

EDNA BASS - Deep Red. Very large, semidouble to peony form. Average, open, upright growth. E. (U.S. 1992 - Homeyer).

EDNA CAMPBELL - Dark Mahogany Red. Medium, semidouble with long, slender petals. Average, compact growth. E-L. (U.S. 1954 - Brock).

EDNA CATO - Deep Pink. Medium, formal double. (U.S. 1957).

EDNA DEADWYLER - White splashed Red. Large, anemone form. Average, spreading growth. M. (U.S. 1964 - V. A. Boudolf, Charleston, SC).

EDNA MARTIN - Red overlaid with Mauve. Large, anemone form to peony form. Average growth. M. (N.Z. 1985 - Mrs. J. Bennett, Whakatane).

EDNA PARKES - Rose veined Carmine. Medium, anemone form. Vigorous, upright growth. M-L. (Aus. 1961 - Mrs. E. Parkes, East Bentleigh).

EDONISHIKI - See 'Lady Vansittart'.

EDWARD BILLING - See 'Lady Loch'.

EDWARD DOUGLAS WHITE - Rose Pink lined and veined Rose Red tipped White. Medium, rose form double. (U.S. 1953 - McIlhenny).

EDWARD LOFVING - Light Pink edged Deeper Pink and gradually fading at center with petaloids having a distinct Yellow cast. Medium to large, semidouble, some flowers having cup-shaped petaloids forming tuft in center. M. (U.S. 1950 - Mealing).

EDWARD MARSH - Light Pink, peppered and striped Carmine. Large, peony form to anemone form. Upright growth. M. (Aus. 1956 - A. L. Stewart, Melbourne).

EDWIN H. FOLK - Bright Red. Large, semidouble with loose petals. Vigorous, upright growth. M-L. (U.S. 1948 - Tea Gardens).

EDWIN H. FOLK VARIEGATED - Bright Red spotted White form of 'Edwin H. Folk'.

EDWIN S. NORTHRUP - Cream White. Large, peony form with notched petals. Vigorous, spreading growth. M. (U.S. 1950 - Wilkinson).

EGAO - Light Pink. Large, single with circular White stamens. (Not to be confused with Vernalis 'Egao' - a separate variety). See Higo.

EIGHTEEN SCHOLARS - White background sporting eighteen different flowers in combinations of White, Pink and Red. Medium, formal double. (For another form of this cultivar see 'Chung Cho Yang'). (U.S. [Peer] from Formosa/Taiwan 1955).

EILEEN WEIDMAN - Medium Pink with Yellow anthers and White filaments. Large, anemone to full peony form. Average, upright, dense growth. M. (U.S. 2019 - Gordy).

EL DIABLO ROJO - French Raspberry. Large, loose peony to semidouble form with waxy, thin, crepe textured, irregular petals. Average, upright growth. E-L. (Japonica 'Don-Mac' x Japonica 'Guilio Nuccio'). (U.S. 2016 - Fred and Sandra Jones, Moultrie, GA).

EL MATADOR - Dark Red. Large, semidouble with upright petals. Compact, upright growth. M. (U.S. 1962 - Camelliana).

EL ROJO - Bright Deep Red. Medium, rose form double to formal double. Average, upright growth. M. (U.S. 1972 - Wilson).

ELAINE SMELLEY - Light Pink edged White. Medium, formal double. Average, compact, upright growth. M-L. (U.S. 1978 - Belle Fontaine Nsy., Theodore, AL).

ELAINE'S BETTY - Pale Peach Pink center with occasional Rose Red stripes and spots shading to Deeper Pink at petal edges. Medium, peony form to rose form double with highly ruffled petals. Vigorous, open, upright growth; foliage is creped and serrated. M. (Sport of Japonica 'Betty Sheffield'). (U.S. 1996 - J. and E. Smelley, Moss Point, MS).

ELAINE'S BETTY BLUSH - Deep Pink in the center, shading to Peachy Pink, with Blush Pink edges with Gold anthers and Pale Yellow filaments. Medium to large, loose peony to rose form double. Vigorous, upright, spreading growth; bloom is much more robust than most 'Elaine's Betty' sports. M. (Color sport of Japonica 'Elaine's Betty'). (U.S. 2018 - Gordon Rabalais, Arnaudville, LA).

ELAINE'S BETTY PINK - Medium Pink center shading to Deeper Pink at petal edges. Medium, peony form to rose form double with highly ruffled petals. Vigorous, open upright growth; foliage is creped and serrated. M. (Sport of Japonica 'Elaine's Betty'). (U.S. 2010 - James and Elaine Smelley, Moss Point, MS).

ELAINE'S BETTY RED - Deep Rose to Red center shading to Deeper Red at petal edges. Medium, peony form to rose form double with highly ruffled petals. Vigorous, open, upright growth; foliage is creped and serrated. M. (Sport of Japonica 'Elaine's Betty'). (U.S. 2010 - James and Elaine Smelley, Moss Point, MS).

ELAINE'S BETTY WHITE - Glossy White with Pink streaks with Gold anthers and Pale Yellow filaments. Medium, loose peony to rose form double; the tips of the petals are green at the bud stage which open very ruffled and fimbriated. Average, upright, spreading growth. M. (Color and form sport of Japonica 'Elaine's Betty'). (U.S. 2018 - Gordon Rabalais, Arnaudville, LA).

ELBERT BOTTS - Pink. Medium, star shaped rose form double. Average, upright growth. M-L. (U.S. 1995 - W. Wilson, Augusta, GA).

ELEANOR FINLEY - Red at center of flower, edge of petals Violet shading into Pink. Medium to large, semidouble form. Average, upright growth. E-M. (U.S. 2005 - H. Finley Jones, Lake Charles, LA).

ELEANOR FRANCHETTI - White striped Rose Pink. Medium, full peony form. (Italy 1881 - Franchetti).

ELEANOR FRANCHETTI PINK - Solid Pink form of 'Eleanor Franchetti'.

ELEANOR GRANT - Delicate Rose. Large, semidouble to loose peony form with large, slightly ruffled and waved petals. Vigorous, upright growth. E-M. (U.S. 1958 - Mrs. A. Grant, Dothan, AL).

ELEANOR GRANT VARIEGATED - Delicate Rose blotched White variation of 'Eleanor Grant'.

ELEANOR GREENWAY - Blush streaked and flecked Deep Pink. Large, semidouble. Vigorous, compact, upright growth. M. (U.S. 1959 - Mrs. C. H. Maryott, Augusta, GA).

ELEANOR GREENWAY PINK - Light Pink with Golden anthers and White filaments. Large, semidouble. Vigorous, compact, upright growth. M. (Sport of Japonica 'Eleanor Greenway'). (U.S. 2019 - Paul Greenway, Martinez, GA).

ELEANOR HAGOOD - Pale Pink. Medium, formal double. Vigorous, upright growth. L. Cold hardy. (For a variation of this cultivar see Japonica 'Carolyn Luce'). (U.S. early 1900's - Magnolia).

ELEANOR HAGOOD VARIEGATED - Pale Pink and White variation of 'Eleanor Hagood'.

ELEANOR HOLTZMAN - White washed and shaded Orchid Pink. Medium, semidouble with Higo-like stamens. Vigorous, upright growth. E-L. (U.S. 1981 - J. Holtzman, Crow's Landing, CA).

ELEANOR K - Pink. Medium to large, formal double. Average, upright growth. M. (U.S. 1964 - Ashby).

ELEANOR MARTIN - Red. Medium to large, semidouble with wide, concave petals. Vigorous, open, upright growth. M-L. (U.S. 1964 - Breschini).

ELEANOR MARTIN SUPREME - Red heavily variegated White variation of 'Eleanor Martin'. (U.S. 1964 - Breschini).

ELEANOR McCOWN - White streaked Red and Pink. Medium, semidouble to anemone form. Vigorous, loose, upright growth. M. (For a variation of this cultivar see Japonica 'Catherine McCown'). (U.S. 1942 - Shepp).

ELEANOR McCRADY - Bright Pink. Very large, semidouble with loose petals. Vigorous, upright growth. M. (U.S. Early 1900's - Magnolia).

ELEANOR McCRADY VARIEGATED - Bright Pink and White form of 'Eleanor McCrady'.

ELEANOR McDOWELL - Rose Pink. Large, semidouble of pine cone form. Compact, upright growth. M-L. (U.S. 1950 - Tea Gardens).

ELEANOR MERTSON - Dark Red. Large, semidouble with flared stamens. Average, upright growth. M-L. (U.S. 1982 - Magnolia).

ELEANOR NICHOLS - Pinkish White spotted and lined Pink. Small, formal double. Vigorous growth. L. (U.S. 1953 - Dr. W. E. Nichols, Pasadena, CA).

ELEANOR OF FAIROAKS - ('Vedrine Variegated'). Deep Ruby Red marbled White. (Variegated variation of Japonica 'Vedrine'). (U.S. [LA]. From Italy 1906).

ELEANOR WALTZ - White. Medium, formal double with swirled notched petals. Average, open, upright growth. L. (U.S. 1980 - E. E. Waltz, Perry Hall, MD).

ELEANOR WILDS - Light Pink with petals faintly margined palest Pink. Medium, semidouble. Slow, compact growth. M. (U.S. 1940 - Dr. R. H. Wilds, Aiken, SC).

ELEGANS (CHANDLER) - ('Chandleri Elegans Pink'; 'Francine'). Rose Pink with center petaloids often spotted White. Large to very large, anemone form. Slow, spreading growth. E-M. Cold hardy. (England: 1831 - Chandler).

ELEGANS (CHANDLER) VARIEGATED - ('Chandleri Elegans'; 'Pride of the Emperor's Garden'). Rose Pink and White variation of 'Elegans (Chandler)'. (For variations of this cultivar see Japonicas 'Barbara Woodroof'; 'C M Wilson').

ELEGANS CHAMPAGNE - White with Cream center petaloids with Pink occasionally at base of petals. Large to very large, anemone form. (Sport of Japonica 'Elegans Splendor'). (U.S. 1975 - Nuccio's).

ELEGANS IMPROVED - Rose Pink with center petaloids often spotted White. Large to very large, anemone form. Slow, spreading growth. E-M. (Sport of Japonica 'Elegans' with larger leaves and flowers). (U.S. 2010).

ELEGANS MINIATA - Light Lavender Pink to nearly White. Medium, anemone form of 'Elegans (Chandler)' form. Slow growth.

ELEGANS SPLENDOR - ('C. M. Wilson Splendor'). Light Pink edged White with deep petal serrations. Large to very large, anemone form; foliage and type of flower similar to 'Elegans Supreme'. (Sport of Japonica 'C M Wilson'). (U.S. 1969 - Paul Gaines Nsy., San Dimas, CA).

ELEGANS SUPREME - Rose Pink with very deep petal serrations. Large to very large, anemone form. (Sport of Japonica 'Elegans [Chandler]'). (For a variation of this cultivar see Japonica 'Happy Memories'). (U.S. 1960 - W. F. Bray, Pensacola, FL).

ELENA LORENZO - Rose Red. Large, semidouble. Vigorous, compact, upright growth. M. (U.S. 1967 - Dr. M. B. Wine, Thomasville, GA).

ELENA NOBILE - ('Napa Red'). Flame Red. Medium, rose form double. Slow, upright growth. L. (Italy 1881 - Franchetti).

ELFIN CHARM - Oriental Red. Miniature, formal double. Average, compact, upright growth. L. (U.S. 1960 - Short).

ELISABETH - ('Montironi'; 'Trois Marie'; 'Elizabeth'; 'Teutonia White'; 'Victoria and Albert'). White, sometimes striped light Pink. Medium, formal double. Vigorous, upright, spreading growth. L. (For another form of this cultivar, see Japonica 'Milady'). (Belgium [Vershaffelt] from Italy 1851).

ELISABETH HOLMES, JUNIOR - Pale Pink. Large, semidouble. Vigorous, compact, upright growth. M. (U.S. 1958 - Holmes).

ELISABETH SIZEMORE - White. Large, round semidouble with large, smooth, thick petals. Average, spreading, upright growth. E-M. (U.S. 1969 - D. English, Jr., Dawson, GA).

ELISE ALDRICH - White. Large, formal double with spiral, cupped petals. Average, spreading growth. M-L. (U.S. 1988 - J. Aldrich, Brooklet, GA).

ELISKA-DEON - Dark Red. Large, peony form. E-M. (U.S. 1957 - Mrs. V. D. Myers, McComb, MS).

ELIZABETH ACREE - White shading to Pink at outer petal edges. Medium to large, formal double. Average, upright growth. M-L. (U.S. 1996 - T. Dodd Nurseries, Semmes, AL).

ELIZABETH ANN - White with petals edged Pink. Large to very large, peony to formal double form. Vigorous, bushy, upright growth. M-L. (U.S. 1999 - Bond Nursery Corp., Dallas, TX).

ELIZABETH ANN LINHUBER - Dark Red veined Dark Purple and center petaloids streaked White. Large, anemone form. E-M. (U.S. 1969 - J. C. Reuther, New Orleans, LA).

ELIZABETH ARDEN - Soft Pink and White striped Rose Pink and sporting solid Pink. Medium, formal double to semidouble. Vigorous, upright growth. M. (U.S. Early 1900's - Magnolia).

ELIZABETH BAY - Rose mottled White. Medium, peony form. M. (Aus. 1962 - Elizabeth Bay, Sydney).

ELIZABETH CARROLL - White. Large, semidouble. Vigorous, upright growth. E. (U.S. 1958 - Casadaban Nsy., Abita Springs, LA).

ELIZABETH COOPER - White. Medium, formal double with swirled petals. Average, upright growth. M. (U.S. 1977 - Tammia).

ELIZABETH COUNCILMAN - Brilliant Red. Large, semidouble with fluted petals. Average, spreading growth. M-L. (U.S. 1961 - Councilman).

ELIZABETH DELL - White with a few Red dashes. Large, semidouble. Average, open, upright growth. M. (U.S. 1964 - Julington).

ELIZABETH DOWD - White with small dashes of Pink on some petals. Large, rose form double. Vigorous, open, upright growth. M. (U.S. 1960 - Ashby).

ELIZABETH DOWD MYSTIQUE - White to Pale Pink with Darker Pink water markings with Yellow anthers and White filaments; base of the petals is White, edges of the petal is White with water marking in the center. Medium, semidouble to rose form double. Average, upright, open growth; the leaves are very uniquely colored medium Green with random markings of soft Lime Green, resembling markings done by an artist's brush; at times there are three shades of Green on some leaves. M-L. (Sport of Japonica 'Elizabeth Dowd Silver'). (U.S. 2013 - James and Elaine Smelley, Moss Point, MS).

ELIZABETH DOWD ROSE - Solid Rose Pink. (Sport of Japonica 'Elizabeth Dowd'). (U.S. 1975 - Wilson).

ELIZABETH DOWD SILVER - Blush Pink bordered White. Large, rose form double. (Sport of Japonica 'Elizabeth Dowd'). (U.S. 1973 - Wilson).

ELIZABETH DOWD STRIPE - White with numerous Red and Pink stripes. (Sport of Japonica 'Elizabeth Dowd'). (U.S. 1975 - Wilson).

ELIZABETH FLEMING - Pink. Medium, semidouble. Average, bushy growth. M. (U.S. 1944 - Boardman).

ELIZABETH GIBBS - Rose Red. Medium, full peony form. Vigorous, open growth. E. (U.S. 1955 - Mrs. E. P. Seay, Charleston, SC).

ELIZABETH GLUNT - Rose Pink variegated White with Rose Pink stripes. Miniature, formal double with incurved petals. Average, upright growth. M. (U.S. 1997 - C. Elliott, Swainsboro, GA).

ELIZABETH GORTON - White. Medium, semidouble with inner petals turning upward and outer petals ruffled and slightly turned down. Average, compact growth. M. (U.S. 1953 - Jenkins).

ELIZABETH HARRIS - Burgundy Red with Yellow anthers and White filaments. Medium, anemone to full peony form. Average, upright, dense growth. E-M. (First Lady of Georgia Series). (U.S. 2018 - Gordy).

ELIZABETH HAWKINS - Bright Red. Small, anemone form. (England: 1972 - Carlyon).

ELIZABETH HICKLIN - Soft Pink shading to Lighter Pink at ruffled edge of petals. Large, rose form double with light stamens and a few crinkled petaloids. Compact, upright growth. (U.S. 1961 - Mrs. E W Hicklin, Columbia, SC).

ELIZABETH HILL - Rose Pink splotched White, sporting Rose Pink. Small, anemone form. Slow, spreading growth. E-L. (U.S. 1963 - W. F. Hutcheson, Texarkana, TX).

ELIZABETH HOLMES - Light Pink with Deeper Pink markings. Medium, semidouble of cupped form opening with bud center. Compact growth. L. (U.S. 1956 - Magnolia).

ELIZABETH HYATT HAYNIE - Clear bright Rose with Blue undertones. Large, semidouble with upright, folded petals. Average, open, upright growth. M-L. (U.S. 1967 - Haynie).

ELIZABETH JOHNSTON - See 'Lady Loch'.

ELIZABETH LE BEY - Light Rose Pink. Large, loose to full peony form with large petals and large, erect petaloids. Vigorous, pendulous growth. E-L. (U.S. 1948 - Wilkinson).

ELIZABETH LE BEY BLUSH - Light Pink margined White. (Sport of Japonica 'Elizabeth Le Bey'). (U.S. 1966 - Mrs. W M Harrison, Pensacola, FL).

ELIZABETH LE BEY VARIEGATED - Light Rose Pink and White variation of 'Elizabeth Le Bey'.

ELIZABETH M. TARVER - Creamy White. Large, semidouble to loose peony form with long, Blond stamens and ruffled and twisted petaloids. Vigorous, compact growth. M. (U.S. 1960 - Dr. J. B. Tarver, San Marino, CA).

ELIZABETH NEDRA MATHIS - Dark Red with Yellow anthers and Red filaments. Large, semidouble. Vigorous, upright, dense growth. M. (U.S. 2009 - Homeyer).

ELIZABETH PAYNE - Red marbled White. Large, anemone form to loose peony form. M. (Portugal 1960 - Da Silva).

ELIZABETH STANTON - Rose Pink spotted White on larger petals. Medium, formal double. (Sport of Japonica 'Feasti'). (U.S. 1953 - H. B. Stanton, Savannah, GA).

ELIZABETH TARRANT - Rose Pink. Very large, anemone form. Vigorous, upright growth. M. (U.S. 1998 - Rupert E. Drews, Charleston, SC).

ELIZABETH WEAVER - Coral Pink. Medium to large, formal double. Average, open, upright growth. E-M. (U.S. 1975 - Homeyer).

ELIZABETH WEEMS - Rose Pink. Large, semidouble. Average growth. E-M. (U.S. 1967 - C. A. Owens, Aiken, SC).

ELLA DRAYTON (MAGNOLIA GARDENS) - Pink fading to lighter Pink in center. Small, formal double. (Europe to U.S. [Magnolia] 1840's).

ELLA GAYLE HAMLIN - Vivid Pink. Very large, peony form. Average, upright, dense, spreading growth. E-M. (U.S. 1989 - Tammia).

ELLA JANE METCALF - White with a few Pink stripes. Medium, formal double. M-L. (U.S. 1976 - Gentry).

ELLA JOE - Clear Pink. Medium, formal double. Upright, average growth. M. (U.S. 2006 - Dick Hardison, Tallahassee, FL).

ELLA WARD PARSONS - White shaded Orchid Pink. Medium, formal double to rose form double. (U.S. 1968 - Habel).

ELLA WEEKS - Light Pink with Deeper Pink margin. Large, semidouble. Average, spreading growth. M. (U.S. 1989 - Elizabeth R. Scott, Aiken, SC).

ELLA WOOD - White, frequently striped or blotched Pink. Medium, semidouble to peony form with five groups of stamens forming a star. Vigorous, open, upright growth. E-M. (U.S. 1952 - H. D. Ponton, Lake Charles, LA).

ELLA WOOD PINK - Pink. (Sport of Japonica 'Ella Wood').

ELLEN DANIEL - Blush Pink with Red stripes. Miniature to small, formal double to peony form. Average, upright growth. M. (U.S. 1971 - Tammia).

ELLEN DANIEL RED - Bright Red. Miniature to small, formal double to peony form. Average, upright growth. M. (Color sport of Japonica 'Ellen Daniel'). (U.S. 1980's).

ELLEN DANIEL RED VARIEGATED - Bright Red with vivid White mottling. Miniature to small, formal double to peony form. Average, upright growth. M. (Virus variegated form of Japonica 'Ellen Daniel Red'). (U.S. 1980's).

ELLEN DOUBLEDAY - Flesh Pink marked deep Pink. Medium, formal double to rose form double. Vigorous, slender growth. M. (U.S. 1946 - Magnolia).

ELLEN GOFF - Bright Pink. Large, semidouble to peony form of thick form with upright petals. Average, open growth. M. (U.S. 1960 - M. Goff, West Columbia, SC).

ELLEN GOFF VARIEGATED - Bright Pink blotched White variation of 'Ellen Goff'.

ELLEN SAMPSON - Rose Carmine Pink. Large, semidouble with two rows of large, wavy petals set apart and surrounding central Gold tipped stamens. Vigorous, compact growth. M-L. (N.Z. 1938 - Mrs. Haines, Wellington).

ELOVINE CARPENDER - Deep Pink. Medium, anemone form to full peony form. Vigorous, compact, upright growth. E-M. (U.S. 1974 - C. C. Carpender, Wilmington, NC).

ELSIE RUTH MARSHALL - Light Pink to Light Purplish Pink. Large, rose form double to loose peony form. Vigorous, compact, upright growth. M-L. (U.S. 1965 - Marshall).

ELVIGE - Blush to White. Large, rose form double. Vigorous, spreading, upright growth. M. (U.S. 1976 - Belle Fontaine Nsy., Theodore, AL).

EM HYER - Dark Red with Purplish cast at petal edges. Large, rose form double. Vigorous, open growth. M. (U.S. 1954 - Turner).

EMBERGLOW - Bluish Rose fading to Magenta. Small to medium, semidouble to formal double. Slow, upright growth. M-L. (Japonica 'Edna Campbell Variegated' x unknown pollen parent). (U.S. 2012 - Gordy).

EMERSON WALTZ - Pale Peach Pink. Large, semidouble with upright, notched petals. Vigorous, open, upright growth. L. (U.S. 1987 - Ackerman).

EMIL'S JANE - Rose Red. Miniature, anemone form. Vigorous, dense, upright growth. E-M. (U.S. 1996 - E. Carroll, Albuquerque, NM).

EMILIE BLUSH - Light Pink. Large, semidouble. Average, compact, upright growth. E-M. (U.S. 1954 - Miss E. Raggio, Scott, LA).

EMILIE ENGLISH - Clear Pink. Small, rose form double to formal double. Average, spreading growth. M. (U.S. 2016 - Gordy).

EMILY BROWN - See 'Hishi-Karaito'.

EMILY MATHIS - White with Cream center. Large, semidouble with notched, twisted, upright petals and bunched stamens. Average, upright growth. E-M. (U.S. 1963 - Dr. W. F. Mathis, Moultrie, GA).

EMILY WILSON - Light Pink. Medium, semidouble to loose peony form. Vigorous, compact, upright growth. M. (U.S. 1953 - A. T. Wilson, Batesburg, SC).

EMJAMBA - Red with Yellow anthers and White filaments. Medium, single. Average, upright growth. M. (U.S. 2004 - William Brierly, Mobile, AL).

EMMA - Light Pink. Medium, rose form double to loose peony form. Slow, spreading growth. M. (Germany 1911 - Seidel).

EMMA ALIA - Radiant Deep Rose Pink center petals darken to a slightly Deeper Pink at the petal edges. Large, formal double. Vigorous, upright, dense growth. M-L. (U.S. 2019 - Jill & Glenn Read, Lucedale, MS).

EMMA GRACE - Scarlet. Very large, rose form double. Vigorous, spreading growth. E. (Aus. 1977 - Mrs. E. M. Peterson, Kilsyth, Vic.).

EMMA J. MITCHELL - White. Very large, rose form double to formal double. Vigorous, dense, upright growth. M-L. (U.S. 2003 - Paul W. Haskee, Woodacre, CA).

EMMA JEAN CROCKER - White. Small to medium, rose form double to peony form. Average growth. M-L. (U.S. 1989 - E. C. Hart, Odessa, FL).

EMMA WATKINS - ('Tylertown Pink'). Pink. Large, rose form double. (Sport of Japonica 'Moore's Majestic'). (U.S. 1948 - Mrs. W. R. Watkins, McComb, MS).

EMMA WILSON - Light Pink. Medium, semidouble. Average, upright growth. M. (U.S. 1980 - W. A. Wilson, Augusta, GA).

56

EMMALENE - Light Rose Pink. Large, semidouble with wavy, crinkled petals. Vigorous, upright growth. M. (U.S. 1977 - Gilley).

EMMETT BARNES - White. Large, semidouble with ruffled and twisted petals and stamens intermixed. Vigorous, compact growth. E. (U.S. 1949 - F. F. Baker, Macon, GA).

EMMETT PFINGSTL - ('Joseph Pfingstl Variegated'; 'Dorothy Parker'). Dark Red and White variation of 'Joseph Pfingstl'. Medium to large, semidouble to loose peony form. (U.S. 1950 - Pfingstl).

EMMY BALCHEN - White. Medium, semidouble to anemone form. Vigorous, compact, upright growth. M. (U.S. [Star] 1946).

EMMY ROOS - Pink. Large, peony form. Vigorous, upright growth. M-L. (Aus. 1963 - Mrs. E. Roos, Lane Cove).

EMORY PREVATT - Deep Purplish Pink. Large, full peony form. Average, spreading growth. M. (U.S. 1972 - Mrs. D. R. Ellis, Charleston, SC).

EMPEROR FREDERICK WILHELM - See 'Gigantea'.

EMPEROR OF RUSSIA - ('Stevens Plant'). Scarlet. Medium, peony form. Slow, compact growth. M. (For another form of this cultivar see Japonica 'Alice Boon'). (Belgium 1856 - Van de Geert).

EMPEROR OF RUSSIA VARIEGATED - ('Aspasia [United States]'; 'Czarina'; 'Great Eastern [New Zealand]'). Scarlet spotted White variation of 'Emperor of Russia'.

EMPEROR WILHELM - See 'Gigantea'.

EMPRESS - See 'Lady Clare'.

EMPRESS LOUISE - Deep Pink. Medium, semidouble. L. (U.S. 1953 - Greenbrier).

EMPRESS VARIEGATED - See 'Oniji'.

ENA'S JOY - Pink to wide White border. Large, peony form. Vigorous, open, upright growth. E-L. (Aus. 1993 - G. Oke, Bomaderry, NSW).

ENCHANTED EVENING - Deep Lavender with bright Gold anthers and Pink filaments. Medium, anemone; the blooms have many tightly clustered petaloids mingled with bright Gold stamens. Average, open growth. M. (Japonica 'Edna Campbell' seedling). (U.S. 2013 - Gordy).

ENCORE - Blood Red. Large, semidouble with leathery textured petals and one or two smaller center petals. (U.S. 1961 - Mrs. J. P. Moon, Lake Charles, LA).

ENGLISH KUHNE DREWS - Rose Pink and White variegated with Pink anthers, White filaments. Medium, anemone form. Slow, upright growth. E-M. (U.S. 2003 - Rupert E. Drews, Charleston, SC).

ENRICO BETTONI - ('Elata'; 'Haley's Monarch'; 'Red Walker'; 'Hite Pink'; 'June'; 'Lateriatus'; 'Macey Taylor'; 'Maurice Hurst'; 'Venus'). Clear Pink. Medium to large, semidouble. Vigorous, upright growth. (Not the cultivar described in old literature, which was an anemone form of Cherry Red sometimes striped White). (Europe to U.S. [Magnolia] 1848).

EOLINE NELSON - Strawberry Pink striped Red. Medium, semidouble. Average growth. L. (U.S. 1963 - G. A. Nelson, Florence, SC).

ERIC WILSON - Rose Pink. Large to very large, semidouble. Average, upright growth. M. (U.S. 1989 - W. A. Wilson, Augusta, GA).

ERICA - Light Pink. Miniature to small, formal double. Average, upright growth. E-M. (U.S. 2001 - Julia Leisenring, Aiken, SC).

ERICA McMINN - Blush Pink fading to Silver Pink. Small, formal double. Vigorous, compact, upright growth. M. (Aus. 1965 - N. R. McMinn, Vic.).

ERICA SIEVERS - Deep Rose. Large, semidouble with large, heavily veined petals. M-L. (Aus. 1959 - Brushfield).

ERIKA MERRYN - Light Salmon Pink with iridescent sheen. Large, semidouble. Vigorous, open, upright growth. E-M. (Aus. 1993 - R. Keightley, Wattle Park, S. Aus.).

ERIN FARMER - White washed and shaded Orchid Pink. Large, semidouble to loose peony form with twisted, curled petals. Vigorous, upright growth. M. (U.S. 1962 - Ashby).

ERIN FARMER PINK - Orchid Pink with Gold anthers. Large, semidouble to loose peony form with twisted, curled petals. Vigorous, upright growth. M. (Color sport of Japonica 'Erin Farmer'). (U.S. 2019 - Tommy Weeks, Conroe, TX).

ERLE STANLEY GARDNER - Salmon Rose with Blue cast. Large, anemone form. Vigorous, open, upright growth. E. (U.S. 1964 - B. V. Drinkard, Mobile, AL).

ERNEST F. BEALE, SR. - Deep Coral Pink; White to light, very fine edge on or around the Pink petals. Medium to large, semidouble form. Average, spreading growth. E-M. (U.S. 2003 - Melissa Beale and John B. Talley, Wilmington, NC).

ERNEST GILL - White suffused with Pale Blush Pink in bud. Large, semidouble. Average, upright growth. M. (Aus. 1967 - V. A. and V. R. Lambette, East Brighton, Vic.).

ERNEST GILLEY - Bright Pink. Large, semidouble with wavy, crinkled petals. Average, upright growth. M. (U.S. 1982 - Gilley).

ERNEST J. PALMER - Pink to Red. Large, rose form double with White stamens. Slow, compact growth. E-M. (U.S. 1962 - Mrs. E. J. Palmer, Savannah, GA).

ERNESTINE BOWMAN - Salmon Pink and White. Medium, semidouble with fluted petals. Vigorous growth. E. (U.S. 1958 - Fisher).

ERNESTINE LAW - Deep Lavender Pink. Medium, semidouble to loose peony form. Average, upright growth. M. Cold hardy. (U.S. 1998 - Elizabeth R. Scott, Aiken, SC).

ESME HINTON - Rose Pink. Large, semidouble to rose form double. Vigorous, compact, upright growth. M. (Aus. 1969 - Henty).

ESSIE M. ROLLINSON - White. Large, formal double with upright, pointed petals. Compact, upright growth. E-L. (U.S. 1960 - Gerbing).

ESTELLA D'ANCONA - Rose Red with Yellow anthers. Very large, peony form. (Sport of Japonica 'Drama Girl'). (U.S. 1967 - W M Levi, Sumter, SC).

ESTHER ANN - Light Red variegated White. Large, formal double. Average, upright growth. E-M. (U.S. 1977 - Gilley).

ESTHER HENTY - Soft Pink. Large, loose peony form. Vigorous growth. (Aus. 1956 - Mrs. Henty, Melbourne).

ESTHER MOAD - Light Rose. Medium, full peony form. Open, upright growth. M-L. (U.S. 1951 - Riverbank).

ESTHER MOAD VARIEGATED - Light Rose and White variation of 'Esther Moad'.

ESTHER SMITH - White and Pink. Medium, full peony form. Average growth. M. (U.S. 1989 - J. C. Smith, Weirsdale, FL).

ESTHER SMITH PINK - Light Pink. Medium, full peony form. Average, upright growth. M. (Color sport of Japonica 'Esther Smith'). (U.S. 2019 - John Bigger. North Augusta, SC).

ESTHER TERRELL - Crimson to Deep Rose Pink. Medium, formal double. (U.S. 1953 - R E Greene, Tallahassee, FL).

ESTHER'S TOMORROW - Light Pink variegated White and occasional Darker Pink with Yellow anthers and Yellow filaments. Medium to large, full peony form. Average, spreading, open growth. M. (Sport of Japonica 'Leanne's Tomorrow'). (U.S. 2013 - Esther Lawrence, Tallahassee, FL).

ETHA PRICKETT - Deep Pink. Small, formal double. Slow, upright growth. (U.S. 2006 - Ertha Prickett Carson, Augusta, GA).

ETHEL DAVIS - Clear Pink. Medium to large, loose peony form. Vigorous, upright growth. M. (U.S. 1947 - Davis).

ETHEL DAVIS VARIEGATED - ('Rebecca Jones'). Clear Pink and White form of 'Ethel Davis'.

ETHEL McGEE - Light Pink. Large, peony form to anemone form. Vigorous, upright growth. M. (U.S. 1960 - Ashby).

ETHEL P. ARTHUS - Red. Large, semidouble. Average, upright growth. E. (U.S. 1960 - Judice).

ETHEL POSEY - Rose Red. Very large, semidouble with petals standing apart. (U.S. 1957 - C. D. Posey, Arabi, GA).

ETHEL RHYNE - White edged Pink. Medium, formal double. Average, upright growth. M-L. (U.S. 1987 - Marshall Rhyne, Belmont, NC).

ETHEL RIVERS - Dark Red. Large, semidouble to peony form. Vigorous, open, upright growth. E-M. (U.S. 1955 - Shady Acres Nsy., Charleston, SC).

ETHEL ROSS - Pale Pink. Large, peony form with large petaloids. Vigorous, upright growth. M-L. (Aus. 1963 - Henty).

ETHEL WEBER - See 'King Lear'.

ETHEL-NOOK-SCIVICQUE - Soft Pink. Small, full peony form. Upright columnar growth. M. (U.S. 1985 - J. L. Scivicque, Denham Springs, LA).

ETHELYN HARMON - Pale Pink in varying shades. Large, peony form. Average, upright growth. M. (U.S. 1982 - L. C. Preston, Walnut Creek, CA).

ETHYL RHYNE - White edged Pink. Medium, formal double. Average, upright growth. M-L. (U.S. 1987 - M. Rhyne, Belmont, NC).

ETIENNE DE BORE - See 'Lady Mackinnon'.

ETOILE FONTAINE - Silver Pink. Medium, formal double. Vigorous, upright growth. E-M. (U.S. 2016 - Malinda Bergin, Savannah, GA).

EUGANEA - White. Large, peony form. Vigorous, compact, upright growth. E. (Aus. 1958 - G. Waterhouse).

EUGENE BOLEN - ('Donckelarii Red'). Solid Red form of 'Donckelarii'. Large, semidouble. (U.S. 1945 - Bolen).

EUGENE LIZE - ('Lady Jane Grey'; 'Annie McDonald'). Light Rose Pink marbled and splashed White. Medium, semidouble to loose peony form. Slow, compact growth. M-L. (France 1908 - Guichard).

EUGENIA HOWELL - Deep Pink to Red splotched and flecked White. Very large, loose peony form. (Sport of Japonica 'Mathotiana Variegated'). (U.S. 1958 - V. T. Howell, Semmes, AL).

EUGENIE DE MASSENA - Light Pink veined deeper Pink edged White. (Sport of Japonica 'Don Pedro'). (England 1877 - W. Bull).

EULALIA SALLY - See 'Lady de Saumarez'.

EUNICE BUCKLEY - Rose Pink. Medium to large, semidouble of flat form. Vigorous, compact, upright growth. M. (U.S. 1955 - Wheeler).

EUREKA VARIEGATED - ('Peppermint Stick'). White lined Rose. Medium, rose form double. Vigorous, bushy growth. M-L. (Japan to U.S. [Star] 1930).

EVA DOWLING - Bright Pink. Large, peony form to anemone form. Average, open, upright growth. E-M. (U.S. 1960 - Beasley).

EVA GRACE - Rose Red. Medium, rose form double. Vigorous, compact growth. M-L. (U.S. 1960 - Miss E. G. Sutton, Minden, LA).

EVA ROSS - Ivory White streaked and splotched Cherry Red with Yellow anthers and Cream filaments. Medium, semidouble. Vigorous, spreading growth. M. (Japonica 'Magnoliaeflora' x Japonica 'Ville de Nantes'). (U.S. 1999 - Frank Galloway, Bolivia, NC).

EVALAND - Watermelon Red with veining. Large, semidouble. Average, upright growth. M. (U.S. 1960 - F. C. Landman, Gulfport, MS).

EVAN DAVIS - Rose Red. Large, semidouble with fluffy petals to loose peony form. Average, bushy growth. M-L. (U.S. 1956 - Davis).

EVAN WARRINER - Medium Pink center with Darker Pink edged petals and White petaloids and Medium Pink rabbit ears with Yellow anthers and Yellow filaments. Large to very large, anemone form to semidouble. Vigorous, upright, spreading growth. M. (U.S. 2018 - Tom Warriner, Birmingham, AL).

EVANGELIA KALAFATAS - Pink. Large, formal double. Average, upright growth. E-M. (Aus. 1989 - K. Abbott, Rossmoyne, W. Aus.).

EVANGELINE - Rose Pink shading to Pale Pink at center. Miniature, rose form double. Average, open growth. M-L. (U.S. 1957 - C. Rose, Temple City, CA).

EVELINA - White. Large, loose peony form with large petals. Average, spreading, open growth. M-L. (U.S. 1959 - Wilson).

EVELYN CHACE - Blush Pink. Medium to large, rose form double. Vigorous, open, upright growth. M. (U.S. 1969 - W. I. McGill, Adams Run, SC).

EVELYN FULTON - Soft Pink and White. Medium, loose peony form. Average, compact, upright growth. M. (U.S. 1959 - Fisher).

EVELYN HENDERSON - Blush Pink. Medium, semidouble with scalloped and fluted petals. Vigorous, upright growth. M. (U.S. 1961 - Mrs. J. Clairmont, Glendale, CA).

EVELYN JERNIGAN - White. Medium, loose peony form with upright petals. Average, compact growth. M. (U.S. 1953 - Mrs. E. Jernigan, Brewton, AL).

EVELYN POE - White with a few Pink splashes. Medium to large, full peony form. Average, spreading, upright growth. M. (U.S. 1968 - Poe).

EVELYN POE BLUSH - Blush, darker at center gradually shading to lighter color with two or three Pink markings. (Sport of Japonica 'Evelyn Poe'). (U.S. 1970 - Poe).

EVELYN POE PINK - Pink. (Sport of Japonica 'Evelyn Poe'). (U.S. 1969 - Poe).

EVELYN RAMIREZ - Rose Red. Very large, semidouble to anemone form to loose peony form. Vigorous, upright growth. M-L. (U.S. 1981 - Alfter).

EVENSONG - Medium Pink. Medium, formal double. Average, upright growth. E-M. (U.S. 2013 - Gordy).

EVENTIDE - Soft to Rose Pink veined Deeper Pink. Large to very large, semidouble. Vigorous, upright growth. M-L. (U.S. 1987 - I. J. Mitchell, Melrose, FL).

EVETTA MOYER - Light Pink. Large, loose peony form. Vigorous, upright growth. M. (U.S. 1961 - Mr. Moyer, Johnston, SC).

EXTRAVAGANZA - White vividly and profusely marked and striped Light Red. Large to very large, anemone form. Average, compact, upright growth. M. (U.S. 1960 - Short).

EXTRAVAGANZA PINK - Deep Pink. (Sport of Japonica 'Extravaganza').

EYES OF MARCH - Deep Pink with Red veining. Small, single. Vigorous, dense, spreading growth. L. Cold hardy. (U.S. 1996 - Stephenson's Nsy., Willow Spring, NC).

EZO - (Northern Folk).- Pink. Large, single. See Higo.

EZO-NISHIKI - Variegated form of 'Ezo'. See Higo.

F. G. NO. 2 - See 'Iwane'.

F. M. UYEMATSU - See 'Adolphe Audusson Variegated'.

FAINT WHISPER - Delicate Shell Pink. Medium to large, semidouble with Golden stamens mixed through petals. Average, compact, upright growth. M-L. (U.S. 1962 - Short).

FAIR DODD - Bright Red. Large, semidouble. Average, upright growth. M-L. (U.S. 1977 - Dodd).

FAIREST DAY - White. Medium to large, single of flat form. Average, compact growth. M-L. (U.S. 1955 - Short).

FAIRHOPE JUBILEE - White streaked Pink. Large, peony form. Average, upright growth. M. (U.S. 1964 - R. W. Wilder, Fairhope, AL).

FAIRY FOUNTAIN - White. Small, single with column of White petaloids. Open, spreading growth. M. (U.S. 1959 - Wylam).

FAIRY GARDEN - White. Miniature, single of cone shape. M. (U.S. 1962 - Short).

FAITH - Rose Pink. Large, semidouble with irregular petals to anemone form with slightly variegated White petaloids. Vigorous, sturdy, upright growth. M. (U.S. 1956 - Mrs. R. H. Brodie, Biloxi, MS).

FAITH HOPE LOVE - Red with Yellow anthers and Cream filaments. Large, semidouble. Vigorous, upright, dense growth. M-L. (Seedling of Japonica 'Bob Hope'). (U.S. 2016 - Pat Johnson, Cairo, GA).

FAITH VARIEGATED - Rose Pink and White variation of 'Faith'.

FAN HENRY - Salmon Pink margined White. Medium to large, semidouble with irregular petals to full peony form. Vigorous, upright growth. M. (U.S. 1958 - Chiles).

FANCY FREE - White at base shading out through Pale Pink to Deeper Rosy Pink. Medium, semidouble to rose form double with notched petals. Vigorous, compact growth. M. (U.S. 1960 - McCaskill).

FANDANGO - White and Pink with bright Red stripes. Large, peony form. Vigorous, bushy, upright growth. M. (U.S. 1969 - McCaskill).

FANDANGO RED - Red. (Sport of Japonica 'Fandango'). (U.S. 1971 - McCaskill).

FANNIE LOUGHRIDGE - Red. Large, anemone form to loose peony form with upright center petals. Vigorous, upright growth. M. (U.S. 1959 - Mrs. F. Loughridge, Pascagoula, MS).

FANNIE LOUGHRIDGE VARIEGATED - Red blotched White variation of 'Fannie Loughridge'.

FANNY DAVENPORT - See 'Gigantea'.

FANTASIA - Red mottled White form of 'Jarvis Red'. Small, semidouble. (U.S. 1949 - Armstrong).

FANTASY (CALIFORNIA) - White or Shell Pink or Pink and White. Medium, semidouble. Vigorous, upright growth. M. (U.S. 1935 - McCaskill).

FASHION NOTE - Light Blush Pink. Large, semidouble with fluted petals to peony form with incurved center petaloids. Average, open growth. M. (U.S. 1953 - Short).

FASHIONATA - Apricot Pink. Large, semidouble with curled and crepe outer petals and occasional cluster of petaloids. Vigorous, open, upright growth. M. (Reported to be sport of Japonica 'Faith'). (U.S. 1964 - F. D. Everette, Mobile, AL).

FAWN - Creamy Pink shaded Deeper Pink. Miniature, semidouble with twisted petals in center. Vigorous, bushy, upright growth. M. (U.S. 1973 - McCaskill).

FAYE WHEELER - Light Pink. Medium, semidouble to loose peony form with long, irregular petals and upright center petals. Vigorous, compact growth. M. (U.S. 1956 - Wheeler).

FEASTI - ('Blushing Bride'). White dashed Pink. Medium, formal double. Vigorous, angular, upright growth. M. (Variations of this cultivar include 'Sharon Raye Pearson'; 'Elizabeth Stanton'). (U.S. 1841 - S. Feast, Baltimore, MD).

FEATHERY TOUCH - White with faint Blush at center and on back of petals and highly ruffled petals. Medium, semidouble. (Sport of Japonica 'Frizzle White'). (U.S. 1971 - C. R. Butler, Mobile, AL).

FEDERATION - Deep Pink at edge of petals, shading to White at base of petals. Large, loose peony form. Average, bushy, upright growth. M. (Aus. 2003 - Camellias Victoria Inc., Mount Waverley, Vic.).

FENSAN XUESHI (PINK THREE SCHOLARS) - Pink with occasional Red tick. Medium, formal double, star-shaped with incurved petal edges. Average, upright, very dense growth. M-L. (Sport of Japonica 'Baisan Xueshi'). (China 1981 - Wang and Yu).

FERNANDINA - Velvety Red. Medium, loose peony form. Slow, spreading growth. M. (U.S. 1943 - Gerbing).

FEROL ILENE - White. Medium, formal double. Average, compact, upright growth. M. (U.S. 1971 - Tammia).

FEROL ZERKOWSKY - Blush Pink. Large to very large, semidouble to peony form. Average, spreading growth. M. (U.S. 1987 - Tammia).

FERRIS WHEEL - White with multiple Red and Pink streaks in various lengths throughout the flower with Yellow anthers and White filaments; at times there may be Pink shading on the petals. Large to very large, semidouble to loose peony with an occasional anemone flower. Average, upright growth. E-M. (U.S. 2016 - Nuccio's).

FESTIVAL - Blush Pink. Medium to large, formal double. Vigorous, compact, upright growth. M. (U.S. 1970 - Kramer).

FIERY FURNACE - Fire Red. Medium to large, full peony form. Vigorous, compact, upright growth. M-L. (U.S. 1960 - Short).

FIESTA - Light Coral Red. Large, semidouble to peony form. Bushy, pendulous growth. M-L. (U.S. 1956 - Marshall).

FIESTA VARIEGATED - Light Coral Red blotched White variation of 'Fiesta'.

FIFTH AVENUE - White. Medium to large, full peony form. Average, compact growth. M. (U.S. 1967 - Shackelford).

FIFTY FIRST BATTALION - Light Crimson Red. Medium to large, semidouble. Vigorous, dense, upright growth. E-L. (Aus. 1991 - K. Abbott, Rossmoyne, W. Aus.).

FILO JUNIOR - Light Pink. Medium, full peony form. Open, pendulous growth. M. (U.S. 1954 - Turner).

FIMBRIATA - ('Alba Fimbriata'; 'Fimbriata Alba'). White fringed petals. Medium, formal double. (Sport of Japonica 'Alba Plena'). (China to England [Chandler] 1816).

FIMBRIATA ALBA - See 'Fimbriata'.

FIMBRIATA SUPERBA - See 'Fred Sander'.

FIMBRIATA SUPERBA VARIEGATED - See 'Fred Sander Variegated'.

FINLANDIA - ('Dearest'; 'Nellie White'). White. Medium, semidouble with swirled and fluted petals. Average, compact growth. E-M. (For other forms of this cultivar see below and 'King Lear'; 'Monte Carlo'; 'Sunset Oaks'). (Japan to U.S. [Covina, CA]. 1910).

FINLANDIA BLUSH - ('Marie Griffin'). Blush Pink form of 'Finlandia'. (U.S. 1952 - Shepp).

FINLANDIA RED - ('Finlandia Rosea'; 'Aurora Rosea'; 'Pert'). Salmon Red form of 'Finlandia'.

FINLANDIA ROSEA - See 'Finlandia Red'.

FINLANDIA ROSEA VARIEGATED - See 'King Lear'.

FINLANDIA VARIEGATED - ('Margaret Jack'; 'Aurora Borealis'; 'Speckles'). Variegated variation of 'Finlandia' - White streaked Crimson. (Japan to U.S. - CA, 1910).

FIONA CAPP - White. Large, single. Average, dense, spreading growth. E-M. (Aus. 1971 - R. Wilkins, Rosanna, Vic.).

FIRCONE - Blood Red. Miniature, semidouble similar to a fir cone. Vigorous, bushy growth. M. (U.S. 1950 - Rhodellia).

FIRCONE VARIEGATED - Blood Red and White variation of 'Fircone'.

FIRE DANCE - Deep Red. Medium, semidouble with narrow petals. Vigorous, compact, upright growth. M. (U.S. 1979 - Nuccio's).

FIRE DANCE VARIEGATED - Deep Red and White variation of 'Firedance'. (U.S. 1993 - Nuccio's).

FIRE FALLS - Glowing Crimson. Medium to large, full peony form. Vigorous, open, upright growth. E-L. (U.S. 1955 - Short).

FIREBIRD - Satin Red. Large, anemone form to full peony form to semidouble with large, broad, twisted petals and large, erect, irregular petaloids. Average, open growth. E-M. (U.S. 1961 - M. E. Rowell, Fresno, CA).

FIREBIRD VARIEGATED - Satin Red blotched White variation of 'Firebird'.

FIREBRAND - Scarlet. Medium, semidouble with large petals. Vigorous, upright growth. M. (Europe to U.S. [Magnolia] 1840's).

FIREBRAND VARIEGATED - Scarlet blotched White form of 'Firebrand'.

FIRECRACKER - Red hot Red. Medium, semidouble. Vigorous, compact growth. M. (U.S. 1955 - McCaskill).

FIREGOLD - See 'Te Deum'.

FIRELIGHT - Deep Red. Large, single with bunched Pink anthers. Vigorous, compact, upright growth. E-M. (Aus. 1969 - H. P. Matthews, East Brighton, Vic.).

FIREY KING - See 'C. M. Hovey'.

FIRST LADY - White. Large, semidouble with heavy textured petals, Yellow stamens and some petaloids. Vigorous, upright growth. M. (U.S. 1964 - J. L. Sparkman, Jacksonville, FL).

FIRST LADY BETTYJEAN - Rose Pink. Medium, formal double. Vigorous, upright growth. M-L. (U.S. 2016 - Tsubaki Camellias, Savannah, GA).

FIRST LOVE - Deep Rose Pink. Medium, semidouble. Vigorous, compact growth. M. (U.S. 1950 - F. T. Bergstrom, Pasadena, CA).

FIRST PROM - White with Blush undertone. Medium, formal double. Vigorous, compact, upright growth. M-L. (U.S. 1963 - Marshall).

FIRSTBORN - Bright Red. Medium, semidouble with petals standing apart. Open, upright growth. M. (U.S. 1959 - R. H. Smelser, Lake Charles, LA).

FIVE STAR GENERAL - Dark Red. Medium, loose peony form. Vigorous, upright growth. M. (U.S. 1958 - Shackelford).

FLAME - Deep Flame Red. Medium to large, semidouble. Vigorous, upright, compact growth. M. Cold hardy. (Japan to U.S. [Domoto] 1917).

FLAME (AUSTRALIA) - See 'Moshio'.

FLAME VARIEGATED - Deep Flame Red spotted White variation of 'Flame'.

FLAMING STAR - Bright flame Pink with Yellow stamens and White filaments. Large, single with wavy petals of irregular length that are twisted and fluted. Slow, sturdy, compact growth attaining pyramidal shape. (U.S. 1950 - McCaskill Gardens, East Pasadena, CA).

FLAMINGO - Pale Pink. Medium, semidouble with petaloids sometimes mixed with stamens. Vigorous, upright growth. M. (U.S. 1948 - Rosa).

FLASHDANCE - White with Red and Pink stripes. Large, anemone form to peony form. Average, open, upright growth. E-M. (Aus. 1989 - D. Coe, Glenroy, Albury, NSW).

FLETCHER PEARSON CROWN - Rose Pink. Medium, anemone form. Average growth. E-M. (U.S. 1959 - Mrs. A. A. Geiger, Atlanta, GA).

FLICKER - Crimson. Large, semidouble. Slow, compact growth. M-L. (U.S. 1951 - Hearn).

FLIP - White or Pink spotted Red. Medium, formal double. Average, upright growth. L. (U.S. 1980 - Habel).

FLO-ADRIAN - White. Medium, formal double. Compact growth. M-L. (U.S. 1976 - C. V. Bozeman, Hattiesburg, MS).

FLORA COOPER - Pink. Small to medium, formal double occasionally rose form double. Average, open, upright growth. M-L. (U.S. 1998 - W. Stout, Pensacola, FL).

FLORA ELLEN - White. Large, semidouble. Vigorous, open, pendulous growth. E-M. (U.S. 1952 - A. J. Parsons, Norfolk, VA).

61

FLORA EYSTER - White. Large, anemone form. Average, upright growth. M. (U.S. 1986 - Tammia).

FLORA HOLLINGSWORTH - Light Pink. Medium, full peony form. Average, open growth. M. (U.S. 1957 - Magnolia).

FLORABEL - Rose Pink. Large, formal double. Average, spreading growth. M-L. (U.S. 1953 - Armstrong).

FLORADORA GIRL - Light Blush Pink. Large, semidouble with wavy petals and trumpet of White stamens in center. Vigorous, open, upright growth. M. (U.S. 1961 - J. M. Hull, Mobile, AL).

FLORE CELESTE - See 'Aspasia Macarthur'.

FLORENCE COKER ROGERS - Pure White. Medium, formal double. E-M. (U.S. 1930's - Kalmia Gardens, Hartsville, SC).

FLORENCE DANIEL - Soft Pink. Miniature, anemone form. Slow, compact, upright growth. M. (U.S. 1947 - McCaskill).

FLORENCE HOLLIS - China White with White filaments. Medium, semidouble. Vigorous, upright growth. M-L. (U.S. 1949 - J. L. Hand, Pelman, GA).

FLORENCE HUDSON - Blush Pink. Medium, anemone form. Vigorous, spreading growth. M. (U.S. 1956 - Hudson).

FLORENCE JANE - Blush Pink to White. Large, peony form. Vigorous, spreading growth. M-L. (Aus. 1973 - F. S. Spencer, Cheltenham, Vic.).

FLORENCE KIRBY - Dark Pink. Large to very large, formal double. M. (U.S. 1973 - Wilson).

FLORENCE STRATTON - White with some petals solid Pink. Medium to large, formal double to rose form double with cupped inner petals. Vigorous, bushy growth. L. (For another form of this cultivar see 'Sieur De Bienville'). (U.S. 1941 - McIlhenny).

FLORENCE STRATTON BLUSH - Blush Pink with some petals solid Pink. (Sport of Japonica 'Florence Stratton'). (U.S. 1981 - J. K. Blanchard, Wallace, NC).

FLORENCE WOOD - Deep Pink. Medium, full peony form. Average growth. E-M. (U.S. 1967 - C. D. Norwood, Thomasville, GA).

FLORENCE'S DEBUTANTE - Rose Pink bordered with a Darker Rose Pink with Yellow anthers and White filaments. Medium, semidouble to full peony form. Vigorous, spreading growth. E-L. (Japonica 'Debutante' x Japonica 'Mathotiana Supreme'). (U.S. 2013 - Florence Crowder, Denham Springs, LA).

FLOSSIE GOODSON - Clear Pink. Large, semidouble to loose peony form. Average, upright growth. M. (U.S. 1977 - C. Bozeman, Hattiesburg, MS).

FLOSSIE SMITH - Light Red. Medium, peony form. Average, open, upright growth. M. (U.S. 1964 - Smith's Nsy., Theodore, AL).

FLOWER SONG - Salmon Rose Pink. Medium, formal double shaped like a dahlia. Average, compact, upright growth. E-M. (U.S. 1955 - Short).

FLOWERWOOD - ('Mathotiana Fimbriata'). Large, fimbriated. (Sport of Japonica 'Mathotiana'). (U.S. 1951 Domoto).

FLOWERWOOD VARIEGATED - Crimson spotted White variation of 'Flowerwood'.

FLOY JOHNSTON - Dark Red. Medium, semidouble. Compact, upright growth. E-M. (U.S. 1957 - Mrs. A. S. Behling, St. George, SC).

FLOYD A. ROWE - Peppermint. Large, peony form. Vigorous, upright growth. E-M. (U.S. 1975 - F. A. Rowe, Waverly, GA).

FLOYD MAGEE - White. Large, peony form to anemone form. Average, upright growth. M. (U.S. 1977 - R. S. Magee, Bogalusa, LA).

FLEURETTE - Rose Red. Miniature, formal double. Slow, bushy growth. M. (U.S. 1945 - McCaskill).

FLUFF - Cream White blended with soft Pink. Medium, full peony form. Vigorous, compact, upright growth. M. (U.S. 1954 - Short).

FLYING SAUCER - Bright Red. Medium, semidouble with three rows of wavy petals and stamens in center. Vigorous, compact, upright growth. M. (U.S. 1959 - Ashby).

FLYNN SANS - Soft Pink shading Deeper Pink at edge. Miniature, semidouble with folded petals. Average growth. M. (U.S. 1963 - Metcalf).

FOREST FIRE - Turkey Red. Large, semidouble with stamens among petaloids and upright petals. Average, upright growth. M. (U.S. 1967 - J. R. Moore, Hampton, VA).

FOREST GREEN - Red. Small to medium, formal double to rose form double. Vigorous, compact, upright growth with Dark Green foliage. M-L. (U.S. 1954 - Short).

FORMALITY - Red. Large, formal double. Average, spreading growth. E-M. (U.S. 1960 - Dr. R. K. Womack, Shreveport, LA).

FORTUNE TELLER - Light Pink. Large, loose peony form with upright petals and intermingled petaloids and stamens. Average, compact, upright growth. M-L. (U.S. 1962 - Short).

FRAGRANCE - Light Rose. Medium, peony form. Average, compact growth. Fragrant. (U.S. 1955 - Mrs. H. C. Murphy, Moultrie, GA).

FRAGRANT - Red. Large, full peony form. Spicy fragrance. (U.S. 1955).

FRAGRANT BOUTONNIERE - Bright Red. Medium, peony form. Average, upright growth. M. Fragrant. (N.Z. 1991 - J. Finlay).

FRAGRANT FRILL - White, Blush or Pink. Large, anemone form. Compact growth. M. Fragrant. (U.S. 1960 - E. Luce, Half Moon Bay, CA).

FRAGRANT GIRL - Shell Pink. Medium, formal double. Vigorous, upright growth. M-L. Fragrant. (U.S. 1992 - H. Hall).

FRAGRANT JONQUIL - White. Medium, anemone form resembling a jonquil. Vigorous, open growth. M. Fragrant. (U.S. 1953 - Short).

FRAGRANT STAR - White. Large, semidouble with long, narrow, upright center petals. Average, upright growth. M. Fragrant. (U.S. 1956 - B. D. Colombo, Martinez, CA).

FRAGRANT STRIPED - See 'Colonial Lady'.

FRAN BLACKWELL - Bright Rose Red. Large, semidouble. Vigorous, compact, upright growth. E-M. (Aus. 1983 - Mrs. E. M. Gulan, Arcadia, NSW).

FRAN BOUDOLF - Light Pink to Darker Pink petal edges. Miniature, formal double. Average, open, upright growth. E-M. (U.S. 1998 - E. Atkins, Shalimar, FL).

FRAN HOMEYER - Pearl Pink. Large, formal double. Average, spreading growth. E-M. (U.S. 1974 - Homeyer).

FRAN MATHIS - Champagne Pink. Medium to large, semidouble with eight rows of petals ruffled toward center. Vigorous, upright growth. E-M. (U.S. 1961 - Dr. W. F. Mathis, Moultrie, GA).

FRAN MATHIS VARIEGATED - Champagne Pink and White variation of 'Fran Mathis'. (U.S. 1965 - Dr. W. F. Mathis, Moultrie, GA).

FRANCES - White. Small, semidouble. Compact, pendulous growth. M. (U.S. 1950 - Miss H. Brandon, Thomasville, GA).

FRANCES B. HOMER - Blush Pink. Large to very large, peony form. Average, spreading, upright growth. M. (U.S. 1978 - Homeyer).

FRANCES B. MUCKENFUSS - Light Pink shading Dark Pink on petal tips. Small to medium, peony form. Average, dense, upright growth. M-L. (U.S. 1999 - A. A. Muckenfuss Jr., Summerville, SC).

FRANCES BLACK - Pink to Pink and White. Large, rose form double. Average, spreading growth. E. (U.S. 1980 - Tammia).

FRANCES BOSWELL - Pink shading lighter. Large, rose form double. Average, upright growth. M. (U.S. 1973 - M. B. Boswell, Ocala, FL).

FRANCES BUTLER - Deep Coral Rose. Medium, semidouble of tulip form with notched petals. Average, compact growth. M. (U.S. 1958 - Ragland).

FRANCES COUNCIL - White. Miniature to small, formal double. Average, upright growth. E-M. (U.S. 1971 - Tammia).

FRANCES GARONI - Soft Rose Pink. Medium to large, loose peony form with twisted, fluted petals. Average, slightly pendulous growth. M-L. (U.S. 1957 - W. Garoni, Greenville, SC).

FRANCES GARONI SUPREME - Soft Rose Pink blotched White with Golden anthers and Creamy Yellow filaments. Medium to large, loose peony form with twisted, fluted petals. Average, slightly pendulous growth. M-L. (Virus variegated form of Japonica 'Frances Garoni). (U.S. 1963).

FRANCES HILL - Light Pink. Large, loose peony form. M. (Aus. 1962 - Mrs. F. Hill, Warrawee).

FRANCES HOWELL - Light Red. Large, loose peony form. Vigorous, upright growth. E. (U.S. 1964 - B. W. Howell, Thomasville, GA).

FRANCES KRYGER - Rose Pink. Medium, formal double. Vigorous, compact, upright growth. E-M. (U.S. 1969 - L. Kryger, Pasadena, CA).

FRANCES LEONARD - Shell to Coral Pink. Medium, formal double. Vigorous, open growth. L. (U.S. 1954 - Turner).

FRANCES LUNSFORD - White. Large, semidouble. Vigorous, spreading, upright growth. M-L. (U.S. 1989 - Jernigan).

FRANCES M. SOLOMON - Soft Rose Pink. Large, semidouble. (Sport of Japonica 'Frau Geheimrat Oldevig'). (U.S. 1959 - Solomon).

FRANCES McLANAHAN - Light Pink. Medium, semidouble. (Sport of Japonica 'Lady Vansittart'). (U.S. 1953 - D. C. Strother, Fort Valley, GA).

FRANCES PENTON - Soft Pink. Medium, semidouble. Average, open, spreading growth. E-M. (U.S. 1969 - Marbury).

FRANCES SESSIONS HICKS - White. Large, semidouble of fairly flat form with prominent stamens to full peony form. Average growth. M. (U.S. 1962 - R. D. Hicks, Troutville, VA).

FRANCES WHEATON - Dark Crimson shading lighter toward center. Large, anemone form. Vigorous, upright growth. M-L. (U.S. 1959 - H. H. Wheaton, Fresno, CA).

FRANCESKA LAWSON - Blush White. Very large, rose form double. Average, open, upright growth. M-L. (U.S. 1968 - Camelliana).

FRANCINE - See 'Elegans (Chandler)'.

FRANCIS EUGENE PHILLIPS - Soft Pink, bordered White. Large to very large, peony form. Vigorous, upright growth; very unusual holly-like foliage with heavy serrations. M-L. (U.S. - 1999, Gene Phillips, Gene's Nursery, Savannah, GA).

FRANCIS ROONEY - Pink. Medium, semidouble to peony form. Vigorous, upright growth. E-L. (U.S. 1954 - Turner).

FRANCOIS WIOT - ('Lady of The Lake [New Zealand]'). Crimson. Large, anemone form with Golden variegated foliage. (Belgium 1868).

FRANK BAKER - White. Medium, semidouble with irregular petals. Average, open growth. E-M. (U.S. 1950 - F. F. Baker, Jr., Macon, GA).

FRANK BISBEE - White. Large, peony form to formal double. Average growth. E-M. (U.S. 1961 - F. Bisbee, Jacksonville, FL).

FRANK BROWNLEE - Deep Red. Large, semidouble. Average, upright growth. L. (U.S. 1965 - Mrs. R. F. Brownlee, Anderson, SC).

FRANK EIDSON - White splashed Pink and Red. Large, peony form. E. (For other forms of this cultivar see 'Blush Eidson', 'Rose Eidson'). (U.S. 1953 - F. V. Eidson, Thomasville, GA).

FRANK FOOTE - Deep Pink. Large, semidouble with crepe and ruffled outer petals, fimbriated inner petals and a few petaloids among the stamens. (U.S. 1959 - Mrs. H. S. Hagerty, Hattiesburg, MS).

FRANK GIBSON - White with mass of White petaloids edged Yellow. Medium, anemone form. Vigorous, open, upright growth. E-M. (U.S. 1951 - Mrs. F. L. Gibson, Thomasville, GA).

FRANK ROBINSON - Red. Large, semidouble. Compact, upright growth. M-L. (U.S. 1950 - Mrs. F. Robinson, Anderson, SC).

FRANK WILLIAMS JR. - Orange Red. Large, semidouble with fluted petals. Vigorous, upright growth. M. (Similar to 'Red Wonder'). (U.S. 1952 - F. Williams, Beverly Hills, CA).

FRANKIE WINN - Pastel Pink. Large, full peony form. Vigorous, upright growth. M-L. (U.S. 1978 - Mrs. J. Luker, Savannah, GA).

FRANKIE WINN VARIEGATED - Pastel Pink, blotched White variation of 'Frankie Winn'. (U.S. - 2000, W. C. Sutton, Savannah, GA).

FRAU GEHEIMRAT OLDEVIG - ('Mme. Chiang Kai Shek'; 'Thomas Plant'). Deep Pink, sometimes mottled White. Medium, semidouble. Slow, compact growth. M. (For a variation of this cultivar see 'Frances M Solomon'). (Germany 1911 - Seidel).

FRAU MINNA SEIDEL - See 'Pink Perfection'. ('Frau Minna Seidel' is reported as priority name for this cultivar but as 'Pink Perfection' [U.S. 1890's - Domoto] has been in such common use in the U.S. we do not believe a change is necessary or warranted). (Germany 1893 - Seidel).

FRECKLES - White with Pink dots and flecks. Miniature, formal double. Average, upright growth. M. (U.S. 1997 - Feathers).

FRED GERALD - Red and White. Large, loose peony form with serrated petals. Slow, compact, upright growth. M-L. (U.S. 1968 - K. G. Durio, Jr., Opelousas, LA).

FRED MAYO - Bright Red. Medium, formal double with rose bud center. Vigorous, upright, dense growth. M-L. (U.S. 2007 - Fred Mayo, Fayetteville, NC).

FRED SANDER - ('Fimbriata Superba'). Crimson with curled, fimbriated petals. Medium, semidouble. (Sport of Japonica 'Tricolor [Siebold]'). (For another form of this cultivar see 'Cinderella'). (Belgium 1913 - F. Sander, Brussels).

FRED SANDER VARIEGATED - ('Fimbriata Superba Variegated'). Crimson and White variation of 'Fred Sander'.

FRED SMITH - Light Pink. Medium, semidouble. Vigorous, upright growth. M. (U.S. 1957 - W. Smith, Statesboro, GA).

FRED'S CHOICE - Pink. Miniature, semidouble. Upright growth. M. (U.S. 1960's - F. Hamilton, Santa Maria, CA).

FREDA HOWELL VARIEGATED - Deep Pink variegated White with Yellow anthers and White filaments. Medium, semidouble. Average, upright, spreading growth. M-L. (U.S. 2016 - Howell).

FREDERICK BECK - Brick Red. Large, single with six petals and Dark Yellow stamens. Vigorous, upright growth. M-L. (U.S. 1953 - F. Beck, Shreveport, LA).

FRIENDSHIP - White. Large, tiered semidouble. Vigorous growth. M-L. (U.S. 1960 - Feathers).

FRITZ TAYLOR - White graduating to Deep Pink on outer petals. Medium, formal double with small, cupped petals. Slow, upright growth. L. (U.S. 1955 - Mrs. A. M. Nickerson, Norfolk, VA).

FRIZZLE WHITE - ('Susan Carter'). White. Large, semidouble with wavy, crinkled petals. Vigorous, spreading growth. M. (A form sport of this cultivar is 'Feathery Touch'). (U.S. 1935 - Overlook).

FROST QUEEN - White. Large, semidouble. Average, upright growth. E-L. Cold hardy to -5°F. (U.S. 1971 - U.S. Dept. of Agr., Glenn Dale, MD).

FROSTY MORN - White. Large, anemone form. Average, open growth. M-L. (U.S. 1950 - Short).

FUJI - White changing to Soft Pink. Large, single with flared Pale Yellow stamens. See Higo.

FUJI-NO-MINE - White. Medium, single. See Higo.

FUJI-NO-YUKI - (Snow on Mt. Fujiyama). White. Medium, single. See 'Higo'.

FUKUTSUZUMI (FORTUNE'S HAND DRUM) - Dark Red petals mottled White with Yellow anthers and Red filaments. Small, single. Medium, somewhat open growth. M. (A variegated form of Japonica 'Kuro-wabisuke'). (Japan 1971 - Andoh).

FULL HOUSE - White occasionally streaked or splotched Pink. Large, rose form double, often showing tuft of small petaloids in center. Willowy growth. M. (U.S. 1960 - Ashby).

FUNNY FACE BETTY - ('Charming Betty'). Pale Pink that turns Darker Pink and then Pale Pink again. Medium to large, semidouble to loose peony form. (Sport of Japonica 'Betty Sheffield'). (U.S. 1961 - Tammia).

FUYAJO - ('Pupurea'). Black Red. Small, single. (Japan 1935 - Chugai).

G. W. ELLIS - Rose Pink flecked White. Large, formal double to rose form double. Average, compact growth. M-L. (Similar to 'Rosea Superba'). (U.S. 1945 - Huested).

GABBIE LAVER - Light Red. Medium, anemone form. Compact growth. E-M. (Aus. 1983 - R. Hawkes, Woodside, SAAC).

GABRIEL LEWIS - Light Pink with Gold anthers. Large, rose form double to semidouble. Average, upright growth. E-L. (Seedling of Japonica 'Marie Bracey'). (U.S. 2016 - Pat Johnson, Cairo, GA).

GABRIEL'S BLUSH - Blushing White. Large, formal double to rose form double. Average, upright, open growth. E-L. (Seedling of Japonica 'Snow Lady'). (U.S. 2016 - Pat Johnson, Cairo, GA).

GAIETY - See 'Gigantea'. (Not the cultivar listed in old literature, which was an anemone form of White striped Pink).

GAIL - Deep Pink. Medium, semidouble with upright petals. Average, spreading growth. E. (U.S. 1959 - Wells).

GAIL EVANS - Blush Pink. Large, semidouble with inner folded petals and Blonde stamens. Vigorous, upright, open growth. M. (U.S. 1959 - Ragland).

GAIL HOOKS - Crimson. Medium, formal double. Average, dense growth. L. (U.S. 2006 - Senator George Hooks, Americus, GA).

GAIL PHELAN - Deep Rose Pink. Medium, semidouble. Average, dense, upright growth. L. Cold hardy. (U.S. 1995 - Dr. C. Minarik, West Harwich, MA).

GALILEE - Pink. Medium, semidouble with loose, upright petals. Vigorous, compact, slender growth. M. (U.S. 1943 - Fruitland).

GALILEE VARIEGATED - Pink and White form of 'Galilee'.

GALLANT ARRAY - Rich Dark Red. Medium to large, loose peony form. Vigorous, compact growth. M-L. (U.S. 1958 - Short).

GALLIC MOODS - Varicolored changing from White to Pink to Red. Large, semidouble. Vigorous, upright growth. M. (U.S. 1973 - Witman).

GARDENIA (BRADFORD) - White. Miniature, full peony form. Compact, upright growth. M. (U.S. 1935 - Bradford).

GARNETT AVANT - White. Medium, formal double. Average, spreading, dense growth. E-M. (U.S. 2017 - Randolph Maphis, Tallahassee, FL).

GARY'S RED - Turkey Red edged Purple. Medium, semidouble with Golden anthers and bright Red filaments. Average, open, upright growth. E-M. (U.S. 1966 - Stone).

GARY'S RED VARIEGATED - Turkey Red and White variation of 'Gary's Red'. (U.S. 1970).

GATE OF HEAVEN - Pink with White radiating from center. Medium, semidouble. M. (U.S. 1952 - Baker).

GAUNTLETTII - See 'Lotus'. ('Gauntletti' is reported as priority name for this cultivar over 'Sode-Gakushi', but as 'Lotus' has been in such common use in the U.S. we do not believe a change is necessary or warranted).

GAY ANN STEWART - Crimson with Purple cast on petal tips. Large, semidouble with upright, folded inner petals. Average, upright growth. E-M. (U.S. 1975 - Haynie).

GAY BOY - See 'Kumasaka Variegated'.

GAY CHIEFTAIN - Vivid Red and White. Large, semidouble with upright petals. Vigorous, open growth. M-L. (U.S. 1960 - Short).

GAY CHIEFTAIN RED - Vivid Red. (Sport of Japonica 'Gay Chieftain'). (U.S. 1965 - Short).

GAY MARMEE - Pale Pink. Medium, semidouble with open petal rows of flat, hose-in-hose form. Bushy, spreading growth. M. (Aus. 1963 - Mr. Sayce, Melbourne).

GAYLE BEARDON - Vibrant Red with Golden anthers and Golden filaments. Large, semidouble to loose peony to anemone; there is some petal fimbriation. Vigorous, upright, spreading growth. M-L. (U.S. 2014 - Vi and Hank Stone, Baton Rouge, LA).

GAYLE GIBSON - Light Pink dashed and striped Darker Pink. Small, anemone form. Average, bushy growth. M. (U.S. 1973 - Haynie).

GAYLE GIBSON PINK - Solid Light Pink. Small, anemone form. Average, bushy growth. M. (Color sport of Japonica 'Gayle Gibson'). (U.S. 2019 - Tommy Weeks, Conroe, TX).

GAYLE WALDEN - Light Pink. Medium, peony form to anemone form. Vigorous, upright growth. M. (U.S. 1954 - S. Walden, Jr., Albany, GA).

GAYNELL - Bright clear Pink. Large, anemone form. Average, open growth. E-M. (U.S. 1966 - Bray).

GEE HOMEYER - Glowing Pink veined Dark Red. Medium, formal double. Vigorous, open, upright growth. M. (U.S. 1972 - Homeyer).

GEISHA GIRL - Light Pink with Darker Pink stripes and blotches. Large, semidouble. Average, open, upright growth. M. (U.S. 1959 - L. W. Strohmeyer, San Gabriel, CA).

GE-JUAN WILKES - Pink. Large, semidouble with slightly ruffled petals. Average, upright growth. E-L. (U.S. 1980 - Mrs. H. Johnson, Madison, FL).

GENA OWENS FREDRICKSON - Light Pink in center to Dark Pink at edges with Yellow anthers and White filaments. Medium, semidouble to loose peony form. Average, upright growth. M. (U.S. 2012 - Edward W. Fredrickson, Wilmington, NC).

GENE PLOOF - Bright Pink. Medium, loose peony form. Average, open growth. M. (U.S. 1964 - Julington).

GENERAL CLAIRE L. CHENNAULT - Purplish Pink edged Reddish Purple and dotted and flecked White. Large, formal double with cupped petal edges. (U.S. 1953 - McIlhenny).

GENERAL DOUGLAS MacARTHUR II - Rose Pink veined Red with Red petaloids grading to White at edges. Large, semidouble of cupped form. (U.S. 1950 - McIlhenny).

GENERAL DWIGHT EISENHOWER - Deep Red. Medium, full peony form to anemone form. Vigorous, compact, upright growth. M. (For another form of this cultivar, see 'Admiral Halsey'). (U.S. 1946 - Reeves).

GENERAL GEORGE PATTON - ('Pink Purity'). Bright Pink. Medium, rose form double. Vigorous, upright, open growth. M-L. (U.S. 1946 - Coolidge).

GENERAL GEORGE PATTON VARIEGATED - Bright Pink blotched White variation of 'General George Patton'.

GENERAL LECLERC - Dark Red. Large, semidouble to loose peony form with irregular petals. Average, compact growth. M. (France 1950 - Guichard).

GENERAL LECLERC VARIEGATED - Dark Red and White variation of 'General Leclerc'.

GENERAL MARK CLARK - Dark Pink. Large, semidouble to peony form. Vigorous, upright growth. M. (U.S. 1959).

GENERAL MOULTRIE - Red. Medium, peony form. Vigorous, open, upright growth. M-L. (U.S. 1950 - Garden Hill Nsy., Summerville, SC).

GENOLDEN BLUSH - Blush Pink. Medium, peony form. Average growth. M. (U.S. 1984 - R. H. Enfinger, Cantonment, FL).

GEOFF HAMILTON - Pale Pink edged White. Medium, formal double. (Sport of Japonica 'Yirgella'). (Aus. 1981 - Dr. R M Withers, Hawthorn, Vic.).

GEORGE ANSEL NELSON - Hibiscus Red. Large, semidouble with petaloids interspersed with stamens. Average growth. M. (U.S. 1966 - G. A. Nelson, Florence, SC).

GEORGE B. BARRETT - White. Medium, semidouble with large, fluted outer petals to full peony form. Average, compact growth. E-M. (Plant Patent No. 866). (U.S. 1948 - Mrs. G. Barrett, Augusta, GA).

GEORGE BROCKMAN - Rose Red veined deeper. Miniature, formal double. Vigorous, upright growth. M. (U.S. 1978 - Gentry).

GEORGE CLEGG - Rose Pink. Large, semidouble. Vigorous, upright growth. E-M. (U.S. 1980 - G. R. Clegg, Tallahassee, FL).

GEORGE COUNTS - White. Large, semidouble. Vigorous, upright growth. M. (U.S. 1969 - Roadside Nsy., Savannah, GA).

GEORGE LUMSDEN - Light Pink with Whiter center with Yellow anthers and White filaments. Small, loose peony to rose form double. Average, dense growth. M-L. (U.S. 2016 - Hulyn Smith).

GEORGE O. ANDERSON - Pink. Large, rose form double to semidouble with petaloids streaked Pinkish White. Average, open growth. M-L. (U.S. 1959 - Dr. J. B. Anderson, Edgewater Park, MS).

GEORGE PRIEST - Red and White. Large, semidouble. Vigorous, spreading, upright growth. M. (U.S. 1984 - Alfter).

GEORGE SHEPHERD - Satiny Rose. Large, semidouble with ruffled petal edges. Slow, open, upright growth. M. (Similar to 'Tomorrow'). (U.S. 1961 - G. W. Shepherd, Orlando, FL).

GEORGE STEWART - Red with Deeper Red veining. Large, semidouble. Vigorous, compact, upright growth. M. (U.S. 1979 - G. Stewart, Sacramento, CA).

GEORGIA BELLE - Rose Pink. Medium, loose peony form. Vigorous, upright growth. E-M. (U.S. 1962 - Wheeler).

GEORGIA BELLE VARIEGATED - Rose Pink blotched White variation of 'Georgia Belle'.

GEORGIA ELLEN - Rose. Large, semidouble with irregular outer petals and upright center petals inter-mingled with stamens. Average, upright growth. M. (U.S. 1966 - D. Matthews, Tifton, GA).

GEORGIA FIRE - Dark Red with Yellow anthers and Yellow filaments. Medium, rose form double. Vigorous, upright growth. M-L. (U.S. 2009 - Hulyn Smith).

GEORGIA NATIONAL FAIR - Red with a large amount of White. Large to very large, semidouble to tight peony form. Vigorous, dense, upright growth. E-L. (U.S. 1995 - Rupert E. Drews, Charleston, SC).

GEORGIA NATIONAL FAIR BLUSH - Blush Pink with a large amount of White with Yellow anthers and Yellow filaments. Large to very large, semidouble to full peony form. Vigorous, upright, dense growth. E-L. (Sport of Japonica 'Georgia National Fair'). (U.S. 2009 - Hulyn Smith).

GEORGIA ROUSE - Vivid Pink. Medium to large, full peony form. Vigorous, spreading growth. E-M. (U.S. 1964 - A. H. Rouse, Gulfport, MS).

GEORGIA SUNSET - Deep Rose. Medium to large, anemone form with group of small petals interspersed with stamens and petaloids and some upright petals. Vigorous, compact, upright growth. M. (U.S. 1966 - Mrs. J. Luker, Savannah, GA).

GEORGIE VAN DE KAMP - White occasionally striped Pink. Medium to large, semidouble to anemone form. Compact, upright growth. M-L. (U.S. 1983 - Gentry).

GERALDINE PEMBER - Bright Rose Red. Large, anemone form. Vigorous, upright growth. M. (U.S. 1992 - R. Ehrhart, Walnut Creek, CA).

GERTRUDE CIRLOT - Wine Red. Large, full peony form. Average growth. E. (U.S. 1968 - J. M. Cirlot, Moss Point, MS).

GERTRUDE MURRAY - See 'Colonial Dame'.

GERVAISE SMELSER - Flesh Pink. Large, semidouble. M-L. (Portugal 1960 - Da Silva).

GHENTRY J. - White and Blush White. Large, rose form double with twisted and curled petals. Average growth. E-M. (U.S. 1989 - O. L. Jacobson, Jacksonville Beach, FL).

GIBSON GIRL - White striped Red. Medium, semidouble. Vigorous, compact, upright growth. M. (For a variation of this cultivar see 'John Clairmont'). (U.S. 1947 - Descanso).

GIGANTEA - ('Emperor Wilhelm'; 'Emperor Frederick Wilhelm'; 'Magnolia King'; 'Mary Bell Glennan'; 'Fanny Davenport'; 'Kilvintoniana'; 'Monstruoso Rubra'; 'Jolly Roger'; 'Gaiety'). Red marbled White. Large to very large, semidouble to anemone form to peony form. Vigorous, open growth. M. (For a variation of this cultivar see 'Jacksoni'). (Europe to U.S. [Magnolia] 1840's).

GIGANTEA ALBA - White. Large, single. Vigorous, upright growth. M. (Japan to U.S. [McIlhenny] 1942).

GIGANTEA RED - See 'Jacksoni'.

GILBEAU PINK - Light Pink. Medium, peony form. Vigorous, loose, upright growth. M. (N.Z. 1904).

GILBERT FISHER - Light Rose Red, sometimes spotted White. Large, semidouble with large petaloids. Vigorous, sturdy, upright growth. M. (U.S. 1950 - Malbis).

GILLETTE'S FLUFFY RED - China Rose. Large, anemone form. M. (U.S. 1955).

GILLETTE'S FLUFFY WHITE - See 'Palmer Gillette'.

GILLEYS-34 - Coral Rose. Large, loose peony form. Vigorous, open, upright growth. E-M. (U.S. 1976 - Gilley).

GINETTE WALTERS - White splashed Pink. Large, peony form to rose form double. Vigorous, compact, upright growth. M. (U.S. 1984 - Tammia).

GINGA - White, slightly striped Pink. Medium, single. See Higo.

GINGER - Ivory White. Miniature, full peony form. Average, upright growth. M-L. (U.S. 1958 - Hartman).

GINNY ANDERSON - Light Rose Pink. Large, peony form. Average growth. M. (U.S. 1982 - Gilley).

GINNY ELLSWORTH - Flesh Pink occasionally striped Deeper Pink. Large, formal double to rose form double. M-L. (U.S. 1952 - Fisher).

GIN'YÔ-TSUBAKI (**SILVER LEAF CAMELLIA**) - Peach red with yellow anthers and white filaments. Small, single. E-M. (Japan 1979 - Shu Ôta, Izu Ohshima).

GLADYS DARLING - Rose Red spotted White. Large, semidouble with upright center petals. Average upright growth. E-M. (U.S. 1972 - J. H. Morton, Waycross, GA).

GLADYS FENDIG - Deep Pink. Large, semidouble. (For a variation of this cultivar see 'Rosalie Deneen Fendig'). (U.S. 1956 - Tait).

GLADYS GLAUSIER - Light Pink. Large, semidouble. Average growth. E-M. (U.S. 1966 - C. E. Glausier, Quitman, GA).

GLADYS MARIE - Deep Rose Pink to Red. Medium, full peony form. Vigorous, upright growth. E-M. (Sport of Japonica 'Debutante'). (U.S. 1965 - R. Hobson, Tampa, FL).

GLADYS MENARD - Pink. Large, semidouble with some upright petals and White stamens. Average, spreading growth. M. (U.S. 1962 - Judice).

GLADYS PINKERTON - Dark Red. Large, semidouble to full peony form. Vigorous, open, upright growth. M. (U.S. 1965 - J. Pinkerton, Columbia, SC).

GLADYS WANNAMAKER - Pale Pink. Medium, semidouble. Vigorous, compact, upright growth. M. (U.S. 1957 - Ashby).

GLADYS WILMOT - White flushed Pink, light at center deepening to margins. Small, semidouble. Average, spreading, upright growth. E-M. (U.S. 1962 - R. J. Wilmot, Gainesville, FL).

GLAMOUR GIRL - Veined Pink marked Deep Pink. Medium, full peony form. (Sport of Japonica 'Strawberry Blonde'). (U.S. 1955 - Carter).

GLEN 40 - Deep Red. Medium, formal double to rose form double. Slow, compact, upright growth. M-L. Cold hardy. (U.S. 1942 - Azalea Glen Nsy., Loxley, AL).

GLEN 40 VARIEGATED - ('Thunderbolt'). Deep Red Blotched White variation of 'Glen 40'.

GLEN ARDEN - Carmine to Rhodonite Red. Small, single. Dwarf, open growth. L. (U.S. 1971 - U.S. National Arboretum, Washington, DC).

GLEN BLACKWELL JOHNSON - Pink and White with Red stripes varying in width. Large, semidouble with ruffled, upright petals. Average, open, upright growth. E-M. (U.S. 1978 - Mrs. H. Johnson, Madison, FL).

GLEN STANLEY - Dark Red. Large, peony form. Average, upright growth. M-L. (U.S. 1969 - H. W. Steindorff, Greenville, AL).

GLENN ALLAN - Deep Rose Red. Medium, semidouble. Slow, compact growth. M. (U.S. 1945 - Allan).

GLENN ALLAN VARIEGATED - Deep Rose Red spotted White form of 'Glenn Allan'.

GLENN HANCHEY - White. Medium, formal double. Average, open growth. E-L. (U.S. 1989 - Stone).

GLENN-ELLA - Coral Pink petals shading to White at base. Medium to large, loose peony form. Average, upright growth. E-L. (N.Z. 1990 - A. Gamlin, Manaia).

GLENNIS GOODRICH - Red. Large, semidouble with thick petals. Vigorous, open, upright growth. M. (U.S. 1967 - Mrs. G. M. Goodrich, Houston, TX).

GLENWOOD - Red heavily variegated White in center. Medium, full peony form. Vigorous, upright growth. E-M. (U.S. 1965 - J. U. Smith, Columbia, SC).

GLOIRE DE NANTES - ('Rose Glory'; 'Autumn Rose'). Rose Pink. Medium, semidouble. Average, compact, upright growth. E. (France 1895 - Guichard).

GLORIA - See 'Kagira'.

GLORIA DE FATIMA - Light Pink. Large, formal double. M. (Portugal 1960 - Da Silva).

GLORIA NAN - Clear Pink. Medium, peony form. Vigorous, spreading growth. M-L. (U.S. 1979 - Gilley).

GLORIA STUART - White. Large, semidouble with fluted petals. Vigorous, upright growth. E. (U.S. 1961 - A. P. Barry and O. G. Thomas, Macon, GA).

GLORY - Nopal Red. Medium to large, semidouble with large petaloids. Vigorous, upright growth. L. (U.S. 1950 - Mrs. W. W. Harmon, Birmingham, AL).

GLORY B - Bright Pink with Gold anthers and White filaments. Medium, semidouble. Average, upright growth. M-L. (U.S. 2017 - Gordy).

GOGGY - Light Pink to Shell Pink, almost White with translucent petals. Medium, formal double. Vigorous, upright growth. M. (U.S. 1979 - R. Bond, Dallas, TX).

GOLD DUST - Golden Red. Medium, semidouble to peony form. Vigorous, open growth. M. (U.S. 1955 - Azalea Glen).

GOLD TONE - White. Large, formal double to semidouble to anemone form with many bright Yellow stamens and petaloids having a distinct Yellow cast. Average, upright growth. M. (U.S. 1961 - Wilson).

GOLDEN DOME - White with heavy Golden stamens. Very large, semidouble. Average, upright growth. M-L. (U.S. 1981 - Mrs. M. O'Malley, Woodside, CA).

GOLDEN EMBERS - Turkey Red. Medium, single. Average, upright growth. M. (Aus. 1967 - A. Lang, Wahroonga, NSW).

GOLDEN GATE - White outer guard petals and Golden-Yellow center petaloids. Large, anemone form. Vigorous, open, upright growth. M-L. (U.S. 1976 - H. Hall).

GOLDEN TEMPLE - See 'Daitairin'.

GOLDILOCKS - See 'Colonial Dame'.

GOLDWATER - Red. Large, semidouble to anemone form. Average, upright growth. M-L. (U.S. 1963 - Wheeler).

GOLDWATER VARIEGATED - Red blotched White variation of 'Goldwater'.

GONE AGAIN - White with few Pink dashes and stripes. Medium, formal double. Bushy, upright growth. M-L. (U.S. 1974 - Haynie).

GONE AGAIN BLUSH - Blush Pink. (Sport of Japonica 'Gone Again'). (U.S. 1975 - Haynie).

GONE AGAIN PINK - Dark Pink. (Sport of Japonica 'Gone Again'). (U.S. 1977 - Haynie).

GONE AGAIN SILVER - Light Pink bordered White. (Sport of Japonica 'Gone Again'). (U.S. 1978 - Haynie).

GORDY'S PRETTY LADY - Clear Pink with soft Yellow stamens. Large to very large, semidouble to loose peony form. Average, open and upright growth. E-L. (Previously invalidly named Japonica 'Pretty Lady'). (U.S. 2005 - Gordy).

GORGEOUS - Cardinal Red. Large, semidouble to anemone form. (U.S. 1954 - Mrs. B E Kemp, Jr., Amite, LA).

GOSHO-GURUMA - ('Rhodellia King'). Deep Red. Medium, peony form. Slow, compact, upright growth. M. (For a variation of this cultivar see 'Kara-Ito'). (Japan to U.S. [Domoto] 1935).

GOSHO-ZAKURA - Light Cherry Pink Whitish to base. Medium, single with circular Pale Yellow stamens. See Higo.

GOVERNOR EARL WARREN - Rose Pink. Medium to large, rose form double to loose peony form. Vigorous, open, upright growth. M. (U.S. 1949 - J. Edwards, Palo Alto, CA).

GOVERNOR EARL WARREN VARIEGATED - Rose Pink and White form of 'Governor Earl Warren'.

GOVERNOR HUGH WHITE - Magenta Red. Medium, semidouble to loose peony form. Vigorous, open, upright growth. E. (U.S. 1954 - Clower).

GOVERNOR KENNON - Rose Pink. Medium, semidouble to anemone form with notched, outer guard petals. Vigorous, compact growth. E-M. (U.S. 1953 - Turner).

GOVERNOR LESTER MADDOX - Deep Pink with heavy veining. Large, semidouble to formal double. M. (U.S. 1973 - W. Stewart, Savannah, GA).

GOVERNOR MOUTON - ('Aunt Jetty'; 'Angelica'). Oriental Red, sometimes splotched White. Medium, semidouble to loose peony form. Vigorous, upright growth. M. Cold hardy. (U.S. Early 1900's - Lafayette, LA [Lost label]).

GOVERNOR RICHARD W. LECHE - Deep Rose Pink lightly lined Rose. Large, semidouble of cupped form with long, narrow petals. Vigorous, slender growth. L. (U.S. 1944 - McIlhenny).

GOVERNOR RICHARDS - Deep Red. Medium, semidouble. Average, spreading growth. E-L. (U.S. 1981 - Welsh Nsy., Tallahassee, FL).

GOVERNOR ROBERT HOLMES - Coral Pink. Large, semidouble with loose, wavy petals. Vigorous growth. M. (U.S. 1958 - Fisher).

GOVERNOR WILLIAM BRADFORD - Deep Orange Red blotched White variation of 'Prince of Orange'. Large, loose to full peony form to anemone form. (U.S. 1950 - Bradford).

GRACE - Rose Pink. Medium, formal double. Average, upright growth. M-L. (U.S. 1983 - S. T. Borom, Charleston, SC).

GRACE ALBRITTON - Light Pink deeper at edge to White with Pink center and border. Miniature to small, formal double. Average, upright growth. M. (U.S. 1970 - A. D. Albritton, Tallahassee, FL).

GRACE ALBRITTON BLUSH - Blush Pink. (Sport of Japonica 'Grace Albritton'). (U.S. 1980 - Gentry).

GRACE ALBRITTON FLAIR - White with a few flakes of Pink. (Sport of Japonica 'Grace Albritton'). (U.S. 1980 - Gentry).

GRACE ALBRITTON PINK - Pink. (Sport of Japonica 'Grace Albritton'). (U.S. 1981 - Gentry).

GRACE ALBRITTON RED - Red. (Sport of Japonica 'Grace Albritton'). (U.S. 1997 - D. Simon, Norfolk, VA).

GRACE ALBRITTON STARFIRE - Light Pink shading to Darker Pink at center and flecked Red. (Sport of Japonica 'Grace Albritton). (U.S. 1980 - C. X. Copeland, Jackson, MS).

GRACE ALBRITTON WHITE - White. (Sport of Japonica 'Grace Albritton'). (U.S. 1980 - Gentry).

GRACE ANGLIN - Soft Pink. Large, semidouble. Average growth. M. (U.S. 1969 - W. M. Anglin, Bogalusa, LA).

GRACE BUNTON - Deep Rose Pink edging to Cream White at base with underside slightly deeper. Medium, semidouble. Vigorous, compact, upright growth. M. (U.S. 1950 - W. J. Robinson and C. J. Hayes, Norfolk, VA).

GRACE BURKHARD - See 'C. M. Wilson'.

GRACE CHOW - Delicate Pink striped and flecked Red. Medium to large, semidouble. Average growth. E-L. (U.S. 1989 - L. E. Chow, Bakersfield, CA).

GRACE GERDEL - Pink. Large, anemone form. Vigorous, open, upright growth. L. (U.S. 1979 - R. W. Gerdel, Roseville, CA).

GRACE GORDON - White with occasional Pink stripe. Small, formal double. Vigorous, upright growth. M-L. (China to U.S. [Piet] 1978).

GRACE MARIE - White heavily dashed and flecked Light Red. Small, formal double with round petals. Average, upright growth. M. (U.S. 1960 - Julington).

GRACE WARD - Coral Rose. Large, peony form. Average growth. M. (U.S. 1988 - J. B. McFerrin, Gainesville, FL).

GRACE'S SWEET PEA - White with Pink under petals. Miniature to small, formal double. (Sport of Japonica 'Grace Albritton'). (U.S. 1982 - Gentry).

GRACELAND - Light Pink edged Deeper Pink. Medium, rose form double. Average, compact growth. M. (U.S. 1981 - Feathers).

GRAN SULTANO - See 'Grand Sultan'.

GRANADA - Vivid Red. Large to very large, semidouble to full peony form. Vigorous, upright growth. M. (U.S. 1968 - Peer).

GRAND FINALE - White. Large to very large, semidouble with irregular, fan-shaped petals fluted at edges and spray of stamens in center. Vigorous, upright growth. M. (U.S. 1957 - Short).

GRAND MARSHAL - Rich Deep Red. Medium to large, peony form to anemone form. Vigorous, upright growth. M. (U.S. 1988 - Nuccio's).

GRAND MARSHAL VARIEGATED - Rich Deep Red and White variation of 'Grand Marshal'. (U.S. 1993 - Nuccio's).

GRAND PRIX - Brilliant Red. Very large, semidouble with irregular petals. Vigorous, upright growth. M. (U.S. 1968 - Nuccio's).

GRAND SLAM - Brilliant Dark Red. Large to very large, semidouble to anemone form. Vigorous, open, upright growth. M. (U.S. 1962 - Nuccio's).

GRAND SLAM VARIEGATED - Dark Red blotched White variation of 'Grand Slam'.

GRAND SULTAN - ('Gran Sultano'). Dark Red. Large, semidouble to formal double. Slow, open growth. M-L. (For a variation of this cultivar see 'Augusto L'Gouveia Pinto'). (Probably same as 'Te Deum'). (Italy to Belgium [Verschaffelt] 1849).

GRANDEUR - Coral Rose. Large to very large, semidouble with large, separated, upright petals. Vigorous, compact, upright growth. M. (U.S. 1963 - Nuccio's).

GRANDIFLORA ROSEA - ('Louise Maclay'; 'Tea Garden 113'). Deep Pink. Large, semidouble with crinkled petals. Slow, upright growth. M-L. (Europe to U.S. [Tea Gardens] 1890).

GRANDIFLORA ROSEA VARIEGATED - ('Louise Maclay Variegated').- Deep Pink and White form of 'Grandiflora Rosea'.

GRANDMA'S GARDEN - Dark Purple Pink with some variegation of central petals with Yellow anthers and Whitish filaments. Large, semidouble to loose peony form. Average, upright, open growth. M-L. (Seedling of Japonica 'Snow Lady'). (U.S. 2016 - Pat Johnson, Cairo, GA).

GRANITE DELLS - Pink. Medium, semidouble to peony form. Average, compact growth. M-L. (U.S. 1956 - Short).

GRANT BLACK - Light Pink. Small, formal double. Average, spreading growth. M. (U.S. 1979 - Tammia).

GRANT CAMPBELL - Medium Red with Yellow anthers and Pink filaments. Medium, semidouble. Average, upright growth. M. (U.S. 2019 - Tommy Weeks, Conroe, TX).

GRANT CAMPBELL VARIEGATED - Medium Red and White variation of 'Grant Campbell'. (U.S. 2019 - Tommy Weeks, Conroe, TX).

GRANTHAM'S FRAGRANT - White. Large, semidouble with notched and fluted petals. Average, upright growth. E-M. Fragrant. (U.S. 1961 - T. T. Grantham, Gulfport, MS).

GRAPE SODA - Lavender to Lavender Red. Small to medium, single. Vigorous, open, upright growth. M. (U.S. 1988 - Nuccio's).

GREAT DAY - Rose Red. Large, semidouble with folded, twisted petals. Vigorous, compact, upright growth. M. (U.S. 1967 - J. R. Moore, Hampton, VA).

GREAT EASTERN - Rose Red. Medium to large, semidouble with irregular petals. Vigorous, bushy growth. M. (Aus. 1873 - J. Harris).

GREAT EASTERN (NEW ZEALAND) - See 'Emperor of Russia Variegated'.

GREENSBORO RED - Light Red. Medium, semidouble. Vigorous, compact, upright growth. L. (U.S. 1960 - Lindley Nsy., Greensboro, NC).

GREGORY CONWAY - White. Medium, formal double. Average, compact, upright growth. M-L. (U.S. 1968 - Mrs. W. Hathorn, Monroe, LA).

GREGORY HOFF - Pale Silver Pink with Peach Pink tones in bud center. Large, formal double. Average, spreading growth. M-L. (U.S. 1968 - W. Mann, Statesboro, GA).

GREYSEN JAMES SEATON - White with Gold anthers and Yellow filaments. Small to medium, single. Average, upright growth. E-L. (U.S. 2017 - Edward W. Fredrickson, Wilmington, NC).

GROVER C. CHESTER - Pink. Large, semidouble to peony form. Vigorous, spreading, upright growth. M-L. (U.S. 1980 - G. C. Chester, Augusta, GA).

GROVER MEADERS - Bright Red. Large to very large, semidouble to anemone form to peony form. Vigorous, upright growth. M-L. (U.S. 1969 - G. A. Meaders, Macon, GA).

GRUENWALD RED - See 'Woodville Red'.

GUEST OF HONOR - Salmon Pink. Large to very large, semidouble to loose peony form. Vigorous, compact, upright growth. M. (U.S. 1955 - Short).

GUEST OF HONOR VARIEGATED - Salmon Pink blotched White variation of 'Guest of Honor'.

GUEST STAR - Pink shading to White. Medium, formal double. Average, compact growth. M-L. (U.S. 1974 - J. R. Moore, Hampton, VA).

GUILIO NUCCIO - Coral Rose Pink. Large to very large, semidouble with irregular petals. Vigorous, upright growth. M. (U.S. 1956 - Nuccio's).

GUILIO NUCCIO FIMBRIATED - Coral Rose Pink. Medium to large, semidouble with notched and fimbriated petals. (Sport of Japonica 'Guilio Nuccio'). (U.S. 1963 - Tammia).

GUILIO NUCCIO PINK - Light Rose Pink. Large, semidouble. (Sport of Japonica 'Guilio Nuccio'). (U.S. 1973 - Dr. M B Wine, Thomasville, GA).

GUILIO NUCCIO VARIEGATED - Coral Rose Pink and White variation of 'Guilio Nuccio'. (For a variation of this cultivar see 'McVey's Guilio Nuccio').

GULF PARK - White splashed Red. Large, semidouble with wide crinkled petals. Slow, open, spreading growth. E-M. (U.S. 1951 - Clower).

GULFPORT PURPLE - Crimson madder with Purple flecks. Medium, peony form to anemone form. Vigorous, compact, upright growth. E. (U.S. 1950 - Clower).

GUNGAH - White. Medium, anemone form. Slow, compact growth. E-M. (Aus. 1992 - A. and J. Wilson, Monterey, NSW).

GUNSMOKE - Red. Large, semidouble with coarse textured petals twisted at end. Average, upright growth. M. (U.S. 1961 - Burgess).

GUNSMOKE VARIEGATED - Red blotched White variation of 'Gunsmoke'.

GUS MENARD - White with Canary Yellow petaloids. Large, anemone form with center petals divided by petaloids. Average, upright growth. M. (U.S. 1962 - Judice).

GUSTAV GERBING - Rose. Medium to large, semidouble with Pink stamens. Average, compact, upright growth. M. (U.S. 1961 - Weisner).

GUY LENNARD - Red. Small to medium, formal double with spiraled petals. Average growth. M-L. (N.Z. 1982 - T. Lennard, Te Puke).

GUY MERRY - White. Medium, semidouble. M-L. (U.S. 1959 - Mayo's Nsy., Augusta, GA).

GWENNETH MOREY - White outer petals and Deep Cream to Pale Primrose Yellow petaloids. Medium, anemone form. Average, upright growth. M-L. See also 'Brushfield's Yellow' which is similar but not identical. (Aus. 1965 - Dr. B. R. Morey, Carlingford).

GWYNNE WALKER - Red. Large, single with five large petals and White stamens. Slow, compact growth. E-M. (U.S. 1961 - Mrs. M. H. Walker, Lafayette, LA).

GYPSY - Dark Red. Medium, rose form double. Vigorous, compact, upright growth. L. (U.S. ,1940 - Doty and Doerner).

GYPSY ROSE - Bright Red. Medium, formal double with fimbriated petals. Vigorous, upright growth. M-L. (Aus. 1979 - Sebire).

GYPSY VARIEGATED - Dark Red and White form of 'Gypsy'.

H. A. DOWNING - ('Helen of Troy'; 'Lady Mulberry'; 'Lauren Bacall'). Rose Red veined Blood Red. Medium, semidouble. Vigorous, bushy growth. M-L. (Europe to U.S. [Magnolia] 1848).

H. A. DOWNING VARIEGATED - ('Mardi Gras'). Rose Red marbled White form of 'H A Downing'.

H. C. SCOTT - Deep Pink striped Red. Medium, formal double. Average, compact growth. L. (U.S. 1986 - Elizabeth R. Scott, Aiken, SC).

HAGLER - Deep Red and White. Large, anemone form of variable form. (U.S. 1961 - Mrs. Hagler, Augusta, GA).

HAGOROMO - Crimson. Medium, single. See Higo.

HAGOROMO - See 'Magnoliaeflora'. ('Hagoromo' is reported as priority name for this cultivar but as 'Magnoliaeflora' [Japan to Italy 1886] has been in such common use in the U.S. we do not believe a change is necessary or warranted). (Japan 1695).

HAHN SUPREME - Bright veined Pink. Very large, semidouble with irregular petals and interspersed petaloids and stamens. Vigorous, upright growth. M. (U.S. 1970 - Nuccio's).

HAKU-RAKUTEN - ('Refugee'). White. Medium to large, semidouble to loose peony form with curved and fluted petals. Vigorous, upright growth. M. (Name of Famous Poet in Old China). (Japan to U.S. [Domoto] 1929).

HAKU-TAKA - White. Large, single with flared White stamens. See Higo.

HAKU-TSURU - (White Crane; White Stork). White. Medium, single to semidouble with large, rounded, crinkled petals. Vigorous, upright growth. M. (Japan 1934 - Chugai).

HALCYON - See 'Nellie McGrath'.

HALLELUJAH - White. Very large, semidouble. Vigorous, compact, upright growth. M-L. (U.S. 1986 - Piet and Gaeta).

HALLIE - Light Orchid Pink shading lighter at edge. Medium to large, semidouble with mixed petaloids in center to anemone form. Average, compact growth. M. (U.S. 1974 - W. E. Woodroof, Sherman Oaks, CA).

HALLIE BLAND - Light Rose Pink. Large, peony form. Vigorous, compact, upright growth. E-M. (U.S. 1966 - H. C. Bland, Sumter, SC).

HALLMARK - White. Large, semidouble with crinkled petals. Vigorous, upright growth. E-M. (U.S. 1958 - Ashby).

HAMILTON BLAND - Light Rose Pink. Very large, peony form. Vigorous, open, upright growth. E-M. (U.S. 1963 - H. C. Bland, Sumter, SC).

HANA-FUKI - ('Chalice'; 'Mrs. Howard Asper'). Soft Pink, sometimes blotched White. Medium to large, semidouble of cupped form. Average, compact growth. M. (Japan to U.S. [Star] 1930).

HANA-FUKI VARIEGATED - Soft Pink blotched White variation of 'Hana-Fuki'.

HANA-NO-SATO (FLOWER VILLAGE) - Crimson with Gold anthers and Red filaments. Large, semidouble with 3-4 rows of petals with fluted and ruffled margins, standing apart and a center cylinder of about 50 stamens. M. (Japan 1975 - San-in Camellian Club, Matsu'e City, Shimane Prefecture).

HANK'S CHOICE - Pale Blush with prominent Red splotches and stripes. Large, semidouble. Vigorous, open, spreading growth. M. (U.S. 2007 - V. Stone, Baton Rouge, LA).

HAN-LING RASPBERRY - Raspberry on White. Large to very large, semidouble to peony form to formal double. (Sport of Japonica 'Carter's Sunburst'). (U.S. 1977 - L E Chow, Bakersfield, CA).

HAN-LING SNOW - Pure White. Large to very large, semidouble to peony form to formal double. (Sport of Japonica 'Chow's Han-Ling'). (U.S. 1977 - L E Chow, Bakersfield, CA).

HANNAM'S DREAM - Glowing Red. Medium, semidouble. Average, open, upright growth. M-L. (N.Z. 1994 - A. and R. Hannam, Putaruru).

HAPPY AMY FENSKA - Pink in various shades. Small, rose form double to formal double with spiraled or stacked petals. Average growth. M-L. (U.S. 1986 - Piet and Gaeta).

HAPPY BIRTHDAY - Light Pink striped Deeper Pink. Large, peony form; petals are fluted and ruffled. Vigorous, upright growth. E-M. (U.S. 1979 - L. G. McDowell, Lakeland, FL).

HAPPY HARLEQUIN - Strawberry Pink veined with rose stripes toning deeper at center with a narrow irregular margin. Medium to large, semidouble. Vigorous, upright, open growth. E-M. (U.S. 2006 - Nuccio's).

HAPPY HIGO - Red. Large to very large, single to semidouble with flared Yellow stamens. Vigorous, open, upright growth. M. (U.S. 1992 - Nuccio's). See Higo.

HAPPY HOLIDAYS - Light Pink. Medium, formal double. Average, compact, upright growth. E-M. (U.S. 1984 - Nuccio's).

HAPPY MEMORIES - Soft Pink edged White with one outer petal having a Red streak and Ivory to Blush petaloids. Medium, anemone form. (Sport of Japonica 'Elegans Supreme'). (U.S. 1981 - Stone).

HAPPY TALK - Soft Coral Red with Gold anthers and Cream filaments. Medium, semidouble to rose form double. Average, upright growth. (Japonica 'Happy Times' seedling). (U.S. 2013 - Gordy).

HAPPY TIMES - Soft Red and White. Small to medium, semidouble form. Average, open, upright growth. M-L. (U.S. 2005 - Gordy).

HARBOR LIGHTS - Red with White frosting on petaloids. Medium to large, anemone form. Average, upright growth. E-M. Very cold hardy. (U.S. 1980's - Mark Cannon, Dothan, AL).

HARDY BEAUTY - Pinkish Red. Large, semidouble. Average, compact growth. M. (Belgium 1958 - Brussels).

HARMONIUS - See 'Herme Pink'.

HAROLD L. SMITH - Pink to Lavender. Large, peony form. Average, compact growth. E-M. (U.S. 1964 - Smith's Nsy., Theodore, AL).

HARRIET BEECHER SHEATHER - ('Mrs. H. B. Sheather'). Rosy Salmon. Medium, formal double. Vigorous, spreading growth. M. (Aus. 1873 - Sheather).

HARRIET BISBEE - Blush Pink. Medium, formal double with incurved petals. Vigorous, open, upright growth. E-M. (U.S. 1966 - F. D. Bisbee, Jacksonville, FL).

HARRIET DURRANT - Rose Pink. Large, semi double to peony form with wavy and upright inner petals. Slow, spreading growth. M. (N.Z. 1963 - Mrs. J. D. Crisp, Tiran).

HARRIET I. LAUB - See 'Purity'.

HARRIET KNAPP - Rose variegated White. Large, peony form. Average, upright growth. E-M. (U.S. 1967 - A. D. Albritton, Tallahassee, FL).

HARRIETT MOUGHON - Red variegated White. Large, formal double. Average, spreading growth. M-L. (U.S. 1968 - G. W. Moughon, Birmingham, AL).

HARRISON JONES - Light Salmon Pink, usually variegated with White pin stripes and White sometimes suffused with Pink. Large, anemone form with very large outer petals. Vigorous, upright growth. M. (U.S. 1955 - Longview).

HARRISON JONES PINK - Salmon Pink. (Sport of Japonica 'Harrison Jones').

HARRY BETTES - White. Large, anemone form to full peony form and occasional formal double to semidouble. Vigorous, compact, upright growth. E-M. (U.S. 1977 - Tammia).

HARRY CAVE - Deep Scarlet Red. Medium, semidouble. Slow, compact growth. E-M. (N.Z. 1989 - H. and V. Cave, Wanganui).

HARRY D. WILSON - Purplish Rose. Large, anemone form. Vigorous, upright growth. M. (U.S. 1953 - Mrs. B. E. Kemp, Jr., Amite, LA).

HARTIGAN DOUBLE RED - Bright Red. Medium, rose form double to peony form. (U.S. 1955 - Greenbrier).

HARU-NO-UTENA - White spotted or striped Rose. Medium, semidouble. Slow, bushy growth. M-L. (Japan).

HARVEST MOON - Red. Large, semidouble with notched outer petals and interspersed Pale Red stamens and petaloids in center. Vigorous, upright growth. E-M. (U.S. 1963 - Ragland).

HARVEST TIME - Blush Pink. Large, anemone form. Vigorous, upright growth. E-M. (U.S. 1962 - Marshall).

HARVEY SHORT'S FINALE - White. Very large, semidouble. Vigorous, upright growth. M-L. (U.S. 1980 - Short).

HARVEY TAYLOR - Brilliant Red. Large, anemone form to peony form. Average, spreading growth. E-M. (U.S. 1982 - Taylor's Nsy., Lecompte, LA).

HASAWACA - Rose Pink. Large, anemone form. Average, upright growth. M. (U.S. 1978 - W. R. Morris, Vidalia, GA).

HATCHETT - Pink and White. Medium, peony form with loose petals. (U.S. 1950 - Pfingstl).

HATSU-WARAI (BABY'S FIRST SMILE) - Light Pink with darker Pink base. Medium, single. See Higo.

HATSU-ZAKURA - See 'Daitairin'.

HAWAII - Pale Pink. Medium to large, peony form with fimbriated petals. (Sport of Japonica 'C M Wilson'). (Variations of this cultivar include Japonicas 'Hawaiian Bride' and 'Kona'). (U.S. 1961 - Hamilton and Clark Nsy., Upland, CA).

HAWAIIAN BRIDE - White. Very large, peony form with fimbriated petals. Average, upright growth. M-L. (Sport of Japonica 'Hawaii'). (N.Z. 1992 - T. and L. Armstrong, Christchurch).

HAYNSWORTH PINK - See 'Solomon's Pink'.

HAYWARD CURLEE - Rose Red. Large, peony to rose form double. Average, open growth. M-L. (U.S. 1999 - Miles A. Beach, Mt. Pleasant, SC).

HAZEL E. HERRIN - Old Rose. Medium to large, semidouble with loose, wide petals and large petaloids. Average, open growth. M. (U.S. 1949 - Herrin).

HAZEL E. HERRIN VARIEGATED - Old Rose blotched White form of 'Hazel E Herrin'.

HEAD TABLE - Strawberry Red. Large, anemone form. Average, upright growth. E-M. (U.S. 1967 - N. Cox, Georgetown, SC).

HEART O'GOLD - Orange Red. Medium, single with mass of Golden stamens. Average, open growth. M-L. (U.S. 1950 - Short).

HEAVEN SCENT - Rose Red. Medium, peony form. Vigorous, compact growth. E-M. Fragrant. (U.S. 1951 - Mrs. M. Verfurth, Southgate, CA).

HEAVENLY - Cream White. Large, peony form to rose form double. Average, compact, upright growth. L. (U.S. 1953 - Councilman).

HEAVENLY DAZE - Pale Pink with Blush White tones. Large, anemone form with crinkled center petaloids varying from Pale Pink to Blush Pink in center. Average, open growth. E-L. (U.S. 1966 - C. W. Lattin, Lauderdale, MS).

HEAVENLY FRAGRANCE - Pale Pink. Medium, peony form. Average, upright growth. M. Fragrant. (U.S. 1957).

HELEN BEACH - Pink with Rose Red splotches variegated White (Moired). Medium, loose peony to rose form double. Average, open growth. M. (Sport of Japonica 'Mary Edna Curlee'). (U.S. 2004 - Miles A. Beach, Mt. Pleasant, SC).

HELEN BOEHM - Blush Pink. Large, peony form to anemone form. Average, upright growth. M. (U.S. 1977 - Homeyer).

HELEN BOWER - Rose Red with Purple shading. Large, rose form double to formal double. M-L. (Sport [chimera] of 'Dr. Knapp' grafted on 'Mathotiana Variegated'). (Similar to 'Mathotiana' or 'Rosea Superba'). (U.S. 1964 - T. O. Bower, Mobile, AL).

HELEN BOWER VARIEGATED - Rose Red with Purple shading and White blotched or moired variation of 'Helen Bower'.

HELEN BRIGGS - Pink marked and shaded Lighter Pink toward center. Medium, semidouble with irregular petals and inner petals and petaloids interspersed with stamens. Average, upright growth. M. (U.S. 1961 - R. F. Dickson, Pasadena, CA).

HELEN BUTLER - White to Pink on edge. Medium, semidouble. Average, compact, upright growth. M-L. (U.S. 1975 - Haynie).

HELEN BUZARD - Blush Pink. Medium, single. Vigorous, open, upright growth. M. (U.S. 1957 - McCaskill).

HELEN CALCUTT - White striped Pink and Carmine. Large, single to semidouble with cylinder of stamens and occasional petaloid in center. Upright, open growth. M. (Sports Carmine and Pink edged White with occasional Carmine stripe). (Aus. 1960 - Brushfield).

HELEN CHRISTIAN - Delicate Pink. Large, rose form double. Vigorous, compact, upright growth. M-L. (U.S. 1960 - O. D. Edge, Columbus, GA).

HELEN COVINGTON - Pink. Very large, semidouble. Average, upright growth. E. (U.S. 1964 - Dr. A. Mazyck, Dothan, AL).

HELEN DIAMOND - Blush Pink. Large, semidouble with large petals and irregular cluster of stamens. Vigorous, upright growth. M. (U.S. 1959 - Braewood).

HELEN DORN - White. Medium, semidouble. Vigorous, upright growth. M. (U.S. 1957).

HELEN FORBES - Rose Pink. Large, rose form double. Vigorous, compact, upright growth. M. (Aus. 1969 - Henty).

HELEN G - Pink. Large, anemone form. Average growth. M. (U.S. 1982 - Gilley).

HELEN GLENN - Red. Medium to large, semidouble. Average, spreading growth. E-M. (U.S. 1970 - H. Hintermister, Gainesville, FL).

HELEN JENE - Red. Large to very large, rose form double. Average, upright growth. E-M. (U.S. 1977 - H. Bailey, Plant City, FL).

HELEN K - Delicate Pink at base, gradually darker towards edge and edged Pale Lavender. Medium, peony form. Vigorous, compact growth. E-M. (U.S. 1951 - J. L. Kahn, Pensacola, FL).

HELEN MADDEN - Deep Pink. Large, rose form double. Vigorous growth. M. (U.S. 1959 - J. A. Vaughan, Columbia. SC).

HELEN METSON - Rose Pink. Large, semidouble. Average, dense, spreading growth. E-L. (N.Z. 1972 - D. G. O'Toole, Ohope).

HELEN PLENN - Fluorescent Red. Medium, semidouble with long, slender petals. Average, spreading growth. E-M. (U.S. 1968 - Mrs. J. H. Hinterminster IV, Gainesville, FL).

HELEN RAINER - Rose to Coral Pink. Large, anemone form. Average, compact, upright growth. E-M. (U.S. 1966 - J. P. Rainer, Tifton, GA).

HELEN SHARP - Deep Red. Medium, semidouble. M-L. (Portugal 1959 - Da Silva).

HELEN SHARPE - Pink highlighted White. Large to very large, semidouble to anemone form to peony form. Average, compact, upright growth. M. (U.S. 1984 - Tammia).

HELEN SHERMAN - Bright Rose Pink. Large, anemone form with six rows of small, slightly ruffled, outer petals. Average, open growth. M. (U.S. 1964 - Julington).

HELEN VAN AKEN - Light Pink with Lavender shade as flower ages. Large, loose peony form. Average, open, upright growth. M-L. (U.S. 1969 - Haynie).

HELEN'S BALLERINA - Pale Shell Pink. Large, formal double. Vigorous, open, upright growth. L. (U.S. 1987 - Mrs. H. Hill, Arlington, VA).

HELENE CARLIN - Rose to Light Pink. Large, semidouble with large, outer petals and large burst of Golden stamens surrounded by a circle of small, upright, notched inner petals of Lighter Pink. Average, upright growth. M. (U.S. 1961 - B. A. Carlin, Mobile, AL).

HELENE ROUX - Coral Pink. Large, semidouble with wavy crinkled petals. Average, compact growth. M. (U.S. 1973 - Witman).

HEMALATA - Bright Cerise. Large, peony form. Vigorous, slightly pendulous growth. E-M. (Aus. 1964 - A. Nightingale, Emerald).

HENINGHAM SMITH - White. Medium, rose form double. Vigorous, spreading growth. M. (U.S. 1942 - Middleton).

HENNY DREWS - Pale Pink and White. Medium, peony form. Average, upright growth. E-M. (U.S. 2006 - Rupert E. Drews, Charleston, SC).

HENRI BRY - See 'Woodville Red'.

HENRIETTA L. BRADFORD - White. Medium to large, semidouble with wavy, upright petals and White stamens with Golden anthers. Vigorous, compact, upright growth. M. (U.S. 1961 - J. W. Bradford, San Diego, CA).

HENRIETTA M. ALLAN - Clear Pink with lighter center. Medium, formal double to rose form double. Vigorous, compact growth. L. (U.S. 1945 - Allan).

HENRIETTA McDEARMON - Red. Large to very large, semidouble. Average, compact growth. E. (U.S. 1968 - Camelliana).

HENRY BARNETT - See 'Uncle Sam'.

HENRY E. HUNTINGTON - Rich Light Pink. Large to very large, semidouble. Vigorous, dense, upright growth. E-M. (U.S. 1994 - Nuccio's).

HENRY E. HUNTINGTON VARIEGATED - Rich Light Pink and White variegated form of 'Henry E Huntington'. (U.S. 2013 - Nuccio's).

HENRY J. HENTY - China Pink. Large, loose peony form with large row of wavy and crimped outer petals. Average, bushy, upright growth. M. (Aus. 1967 - Henty).

HENRY LUNSFORD - Bright Red. Large to very large, semidouble to peony form. Vigorous, upright growth. M-L. (U.S. 1989 - Jernigan).

HENRY MIDDLETON - Dark Red. Medium, semidouble. Average, upright growth. E-L. (U.S. 1941 - Middleton).

HENRY MIDDLETON VARIEGATED - Dark Red and White to predominately White form of 'Henry Middleton'.

HENRY PARRISH - Dark Red. Medium, loose peony to semidouble and rarely formal double. Vigorous, upright, dense growth. M. (U.S. 2007 - Hulyn Smith).

HENRY PRICE - Deep Crimson. Large, formal double. M. (Aus. 1965 - Waterhouse).

HENRY TURNBULL - White. Large, single to semidouble. E. (Aus. 1950 - Turnbull).

HENRY VIII - Deep Rose-Pink (also has variegated form) with Yellow anthers and White filaments. Medium, semidouble to full peony; petaloids and stamens within lower petals are also common. Vigorous, upright growth. E. (U.S. 1938-1939 - G. Gerbing, Fernandina, FL).

HER MAJESTY QUEEN ELIZABETH II - Salmon Rose Pink. Medium to large, semidouble to loose peony form with wavy, ruffled petals. Vigorous, compact growth. M. (For a variation of this cultivar see 'Cliff Harris'). (U.S. 1955 - Longview).

HERBERT EARL GATCH - White with Red streaks and flecks. Large, formal double to rose form double. Vigorous, upright growth. M-L. (Japonica 'Lady Laura' seedling). (U.S. 2013 - Jerry Conrad Plymouth, FL).

HERCULES - Red. Large, semidouble. Average, compact growth. M. (U.S. 1961 - Shackelford).

HERMAN JOHNSON - Blush Pink with Red spot on one petal. Large, semidouble. Average, spreading growth. E-M. (For a variation of this cultivar see 'Mom Johnson'). (U.S. 1979 - Mrs. H. Johnson, Madison, FL).

HERMAN'S PRIDE - Red. Large, full peony form. Average growth. E-M. (U.S. 1977 - Mrs. H. Johnson, Madison, FL).

HERME - ('Hikaru-Genji'; 'Jordan's Pride'; 'Souv. D' Henri Guichard'). Pink petals with irregular White border and streaked Deep Pink. Medium, semidouble. Vigorous, upright growth. M. Cold hardy. (Variations of this cultivar include 'Beauty of Holland'; 'Colonial Lady'; 'The Mikado'; 'Look-Away'; 'Quaintance'; 'Orchid Pink'; 'Spring Sonnet'). (Japan to U.S. 1875 - Sacramento, CA).

HERME PINK - ('Batista'; 'Beni-Botan'; 'Harmonius'; 'Herme Red'; 'Hikaru-Genji-Aka'; 'Majestic'; 'Pink Herme'; 'Pink Jordan's Pride'; 'Powell's Pink'; 'Radiant Glow'; 'Red Herme'; 'Red Jordan's Pride'; 'Rosy Dawn'; 'Wings'). Rose Red. (Sport of Japonica 'Herme'). (Japan to U.S. [Star] 1930).

HERME RED - See 'Herme Pink'.

HERME WHITE - White variation of 'Herme'.

HERMESPORT - See 'Beauty of Holland'.

HETTIE LOVE WINE - Light Pink. Large, semidouble with wavy, crinkled petals. Vigorous, spreading, upright growth. M. (U.S. 1981 - Dr. M. B. Wine, Thomasville, GA).

HIBISCUS - ('Cherokee'). Rose Pink. Medium, single. Vigorous, upright, spreading growth. M. (U.S. Late 1800's - Magnolia).

HIDDEN TREASURE - White with occasional Rose streak. Small, anemone form. Slow, spreading growth. M-L. (U.S. 1959 - Wylam).

HIGH HAT - Light Pink. Medium to large, peony form. (Sport of Japonica 'Daikagura'). (For a variation of this cultivar see 'Conrad Hilton'). (U.S. 1945 - Coolidge).

HIGH HILLS - White. Medium to large, full peony form. Average, compact growth. M. (U.S. 1953 - Short).

HIGH JINKS - White blotched Red. Medium to large, full peony form. (Sport of Japonica 'Helenor'). (Aus. 1945).

HIGH NOON - Red. Large, semidouble with large, crinkled petals dividing bright Yellow stamens into five separate groups. Average, compact, upright growth. M. Fragrant. (U.S. 1965 - L. B. Wilson, Jr., Gulfport, MS).

HIGH SOCIETY - Clear Pink. Medium, peony form with high center. Vigorous growth. M. (U.S. 1958 - Shackelford).

HIGH SOCIETY VARIEGATED - Clear Pink and White variation of 'High Society'.

HIGH TIME - Carmine Rose. Large, peony form. Vigorous, upright growth. M-L. (U.S. 1987 - H. Hall).

HIGH WIDE 'N HANDSOME - Luminous Pink shading to Pink tones in heart of flower. Large, semidouble with very large, fluted, separated and erect petals and White stamens. Vigorous, upright growth. M. (U.S. 1960 - McCaskill).

HIGO - Name used as general name for special garden form of Camellia Japonica, developed in Kumamoto, Japan, located in district formerly called Higo Province; form is generally single (a few cultivars are slightly semidouble), with thick, round, broad petals and prominent stamens of White, soft Pink and Pale Yellow which are generally flared (a few cultivars having circular or tubular stamens), standing out independently from the base. Some cultivars have stamens topped with petaloids. Cultivars are listed by name with description as to color, size and form with reference to Higo. (Japan 1800's - Kumamoto).

HIGO-OZEKI - Crimson with spreading Gold anthers and White filaments. Very large, single. (Japan - Kumamoto Prefecture).

HI-JINX - Pink. Medium, semidouble to peony form. Vigorous, open growth. M-L. (U.S. 1955 - Mrs. J. W. Anderson, Rock Hill, SC).

HI-JINX VARIEGATED - Pink blotched White variation of 'Hi-Jinx'.

HIKARU-GENJI - See 'Herme'. ('Hikaru-Genji' is reported as priority name for this cultivar but as 'Herme' [Germany 1893 - Seidel] has been in such common use in the U.S. we do not believe a change is necessary or warranted). (Japan 1879 - Yokohama).

HIKARU-GENJI-AKA - See 'Herme Pink'.

HIKARU-GENJI-YOKOMOKU - See 'Beauty of Holland'.

HILDA JAMIESON - Deep Pink shading to White at base. Large, semidouble with ruffled petals. Vigorous, upright growth. M-L. (Aus. 1977 - Miss H. B. Jamieson, Wahroonga, NSW).

HILL - White spotted Pink, sporting to solid Pink. Medium, semidouble. (U.S. 1953).

HIME-SHIRA-YUKI - White. Miniature, semidouble. Compact growth. M-L. (Japan to U.S. 1981 - Nuccio's).

HI-NO-HAKAMA - Scarlet. Large, single with flared White stamens. See Higo.

HI-NO-MARU - Red with flared soft Pink stamens. Medium to large, single with wavy petals. See Higo.

HI-NO-TSUKASA - (Lord of Scarlet). Scarlet. Large, single. See Higo.

HIODOSHI - Scarlet. Medium to large, single with flared White stamens. See Higo.

HIROSHIMA F. N. - Pink. Large, semidouble with group of petaloids in center. E-M. (U.S. 1953 - Fruitland).

HIS MAJESTY - Deep Rose Red. Medium, semidouble with loose petals. Vigorous, upright growth. M. (Europe to U.S. [Magnolia] 1840's).

HISHI-KARAITO - ('Emily Brown'; 'Pink Lace'; 'Lacy Pink'). Delicate Pink. Small, semidouble with mixed petaloids and stamens. Average, compact growth. M-L. (Japan 1934 - Chugai).

HIT PARADE - Pink. Large, semidouble with upright petals. Vigorous, compact growth. M. (U.S. 1961 - Nuccio's).

HOLIDAY - Pink streaked Deeper Pink. Medium, formal double. (U.S. 1955 - Feathers).

HOLLIFOLIA - Deep Pink. Medium, semidouble. Vigorous growth. M. (U.S. 1942).

HOLLIS C. BOARDMAN - Pink. Medium, semidouble. L. (U.S. 1948 - Boardman).

HOLLY BLADES - Shell Pink. Medium, formal double. Vigorous, upright growth. M. (U.S. 1975 - Dr. G. R. Johnson, Carthage, TX).

HOLLY BLUFF'S PRIDE - Deep Pink. Large, peony form. Vigorous, spreading growth. M. (U.S. 1959 - J. F. Crump, Bay St. Louis, MS).

HOLLY BRIGHT - Glossy Salmon Red. Large, semidouble with crepe petals. Average, compact, upright growth; unique crinkled holly-like foliage. M. (U.S. 1985 - Nuccio's).

HOLLY LEAF - Cardinal Red. Medium, single with five twisted petals which have incurving edges with slight serrations. Vigorous, compact growth with foliage which resembles English holly. E. (U.S. 1954 - Feathers).

HOLLY MAC - Red. Medium, semidouble with loose petals. Vigorous, upright growth. M. (U.S. 1959 - Mayo's Nsy., Augusta, GA).

HOLLYHOCK - See 'Kumasaka'.

HOLY WHITE - White with Yellow anthers and Light Cream filaments. Large, semidouble. Average, upright, open growth. M-L. (Seedling of Japonica 'Snow Lady'). (U.S. 2019 - Pat Johnson, Cairo, GA).

HOMER FRITCHIE - White spotted Pink. Miniature, tiered formal double. Vigorous, compact, upright growth. M. (U.S. 1975 - Tammia).

HON-AMI - See 'Kamo-Hon-Ami'.

HONEY BEE - Red to Red and White. Medium, formal double to loose peony form. Average, compact growth. M-L. (U.S. 1970 - Alfter).

HONEY BUNCH - Blush Pink. Medium, formal double. Average, upright growth. M. (U.S. 1968 - W. Stewart, Savannah, GA).

HONEY CHILE - Deep Red. Large, semidouble with upright petals interspersed with White petaloids, and narrow, twisted petaloids interspersed with crown of stamens in center. (U.S. 1959 - W. D. Pleasant, Beaumont, TX).

HONEYGLOW - Deep Honey color to Ivory center petals and faint Blush under petals. Medium, formal double with incurved center petals resembling six pointed star. Vigorous, open, upright growth. M-L. (U.S. 1974 - Stone).

HONGLUZHEN (RED SHOWING TREASURE) - Deep Scarlet. Large, semidouble to loose peony form. Vigorous, upright growth. M-L. (Sport of Japonica 'Hualuzhen'). (China 1993 - Jiyin Gao, Fujian Province).

HONGYE BEILA - See 'Bella Jinhua'

HOOPER CONNELL - See 'Mrs. Hooper Connell'.

HOPE GRIFFIN - Ivory White. Large to very large, semidouble to anemone form with rabbit ears and stamens. Average, upright growth. M-L. (Sport of Japonica 'Nuccio's Pink Lace'). (U.S. 1999 - G. Griffin, Nashville, TN).

HOPKIN'S PINK - Soft Pink with occasional streak, spot or petal of Red. Miniature, peony form. Vigorous, compact growth. M-L. (U.S. 1959 - Hopkins, Anderson, CA).

HOPKIN'S PINK DAWN - Soft Pink to Light Pink shading to White at edge. (Sport of Japonica 'Hopkin's Pink'). (U.S. 1969 - McCaskill).

HOPKIN'S RED - Red. (Sport of Japonica 'Hopkin's Pink'). (U.S. 1969 - C. A. Boynton, Lodi, CA).

HOPKIN'S ROSE PINK - Rose Pink. (Sport of Japonica 'Hopkin's Pink'). (U.S. 1966 - McCaskill).

HOPKIN'S WHITE - White. Medium, single. (U.S. 1953 - Lindo).

HORKAN - ('Mille Beaux'; 'Variabilis'; 'Missima'; 'Pearl Marginata'; 'Dan McCarthy'). White striped Red, Pink and Rose and in solid colors. Medium, variform. Vigorous, angular growth. L. (Not the same variety as Japonica 'Rena Campbell' - 2014). (England from Orient 1816).

HORRY FROST - Red and White. Small, formal double. E-M. (U.S. 1942 - Magnolia).

HOT LIPS - Dark Red. Medium, semidouble form. Average, upright growth. M. (U.S. 2004 - Doug Simon, Norfolk, VA).

HOTSHOT - Deep Dark Red. Miniature, formal double. Slow, upright growth. M-L. (U.S. 1997 - Domoto).

HOULTONWOOD - Dark Pink with occasional Darker Pink stripes with Yellow anthers and White filaments. Medium, semidouble. Average, bushy growth. M. (U.S. 2019 - Morris Marlborough, Hammond, LA).

HOUSE OF GOLD - Red. Medium, full peony form. Vigorous, upright growth. M. (U.S. 1952 - Baker).

HOUSE PARTY - Pink. Large, peony form. Average, upright growth. M. (U.S. 1964 - Shackelford).

HUBERT OSTEEN - Red. Large, semidouble to anemone form. Vigorous, upright growth. E-M. (U.S. 1950 - H. G. Osteen, Sumter, SC).

HUBY COOPER - Bright Red. Large, peony form. Average, spreading growth. M-L. (Reported similar to 'Dixie Knight Variegated'). (U.S. 1971 - H. Cooper, Springfield, SC).

HUGH KENNEDY - Light Crimson. Medium, semidouble with slightly crinkled petals. (Sport of Japonica 'The Czar'). (Aus. 1953 - Mrs. E G Kennedy, Melbourne).

HUGO JAHNZ - Dark Rose Red. Medium to large, single. Vigorous, upright growth. M. (U.S. 1955 - Mrs. T. W. Salisbury, Summerville, SC).

HUNTINGTON PINK - See 'Bleichoreder Pink'.

HUSSAR - Pink. Large, semidouble. Loose, upright growth. M. (U.S. Early 1900's - Magnolia).

HYACINTH B. THURMAN - Vibrant Pink. Large, semidouble with irregular petals. Vigorous, open growth. M. (U.S. 1967 - J. E. Thurman, Covington, LA).

I BELIEVE - Frosted watermelon Red. Large, semidouble to loose peony form with wavy, fluted petals. Upright growth. M. (Reported to be similar to 'Mena Ladnier'). (U.S. 1959 - K. C. Ellsworth, Myrtle Beach, SC).

ICE QUEEN - White. Large, semidouble. Compact growth. M. (Aus. 1965).

ICED FRAGRANCE - White. Large, semidouble to peony form. Slow, dense, upright growth. E-L. Fragrant. (Aus. 1990 - Mildorrie Camellias, Jasper's Brush, NSW).

ICELAND - White. Large, semidouble with oval petals standing apart. Average, compact growth. M-L. (U.S. 1965 - Julington).

IDA KING - Blush. Large, semidouble with stamens intermingled with petaloids. Vigorous, spreading growth. M. (U.S. 1969 - E. J. Prevatt, Bonneau, SC).

IDA MAY JOHNSTON - White striped Pink. Large, semidouble to loose peony form. M. (U.S. 1961 - J. W. Bradford, San Diego, CA).

IDA WEISNER - White. Large, semidouble with tight cluster of stamens in center. Vigorous, open, pendulous growth. E-M. (U.S. 1965 - Weisner).

IDA'S BLUSH - Soft Pink at petal edges shading to Cream at center. Small, rose form double. Average, upright growth. M. (U.S. 1997 - E. and B. Achterberg, Citrus Heights, CA).

IDALIA - White with Pale Pink halo through center of each petal. Large, rose form double. Average, upright growth. E. (U.S. 1971 - J. Moon, Lake Charles, LA).

IDATEN-SHIBORI - See 'Daikagura'.

IGLOO - White. Large, full peony form. Average, upright growth. M. (U.S. 1965 - Breschini).

ILA RESTER - Light Pink. Large, semidouble with wavy, crinkled petals. Average, upright, spreading growth. E-M. (U.S. 1968 - Rester).

ILAM SATIN - Red. Very large, anemone form to peony form. Slow, compact growth. M. (N.Z. 1975 - Mrs. A. M. Coker, Christchurch).

ILLUSTRIOUS - Brilliant Rose Pink. Medium to large, semidouble with broad, round, crinkled petals. Slow, compact growth. M. (U.S. 1950 - Short).

IMAGINATION - Pure White. Medium to large, semidouble form with deeply fluted petals, and a waxy sheen. Vigorous, open, upright growth. M-L. (U.S. 2005 - Gordy).

IMA-KUMAGAI - Bright Crimson. Medium, single. See Higo.

IMBRICATA RUBRA PLENA - See 'Prince Eugene Napoleon'.

IMP - Dark Pink. Small to medium, formal double. Average, open, upright growth. M. (U.S. 1973 - Tammia).

IMPERATOR (AMERICAN) - Scarlet with Yellow anthers and Whitish filaments. Small to medium, semidouble. Vigorous, bushy growth. E. (U.S. 1945).

IMPERATOR (FRANCE) - ('Big Daddy'). Dark Red. Large, full peony form. Average, open, upright growth. M. (France 1908 - Guichard).

IMPERIAL SPLENDOUR - Deep Red. Large, semidouble to peony form with Golden stamens. Spreading, bushy growth. M-L. (Aus. 1980 - T. J. Savige, Wirlinga, NSW).

IMURA - White. Medium to large, semidouble. Vigorous, open, willowy growth. M. (Reported to be same as 'Miyakodori'). (U.S. 1939 - Overlook).

IN THE PINK - Rose Pink. Medium, formal double to rose form double. Vigorous, compact, upright growth. M-L. (U.S. 1971 - Kramer).

IN THE PINK VARIEGATED - White striped Pink variation of 'In the Pink'. (U.S. 1977 - Kramer).

IN THE PINK VARIEGATED (WEEKS) - Rose Pink variegated White. Medium, rose form double to formal double. Vigorous, compact, upright growth. M-L. (Virus variegated form of Japonica 'In the Pink'; not to be confused with 'In the Pink Variegated' - Pink with White stripes). (U.S. 2019 - Tommy Weeks, Conroe, TX).

IN THE PURPLE - Dark to Purplish Red with darker veining. Medium, peony form. Average growth. M-L. (N.Z. 1982 - Miss J. Farmer, Palmerston North).

IN THE RED - Rose Red. (Sport of Japonica 'In The Pink'). (U.S. 1975 - Kramer).

INCONSTANT BEAUTY - See 'Mathotiana Alba'.

INDIA - Dawn Pink. Large, semidouble with loose, semi-upright petals. (U.S. 1956 - B L Kersey. Blythe Is., GA).

INDIA KRUGER - See 'Lady de Saumarez'.

INDIAN CHIEF - Red. Large, full peony form. Vigorous, upright growth. E-M. (U.S. 1958 - Shackelford).

INDIAN CHIEF VARIEGATED - Red blotched White variation of 'Indian Chief'.

INDIAN SUMMER - Deep Rose Red. Large to very large, full peony form. Vigorous, upright growth. E-L. (U.S. 1955 - McCaskill).

INDIAN SUMMER VARIEGATED - Deep Rose Red blotched White variation of 'Indian Summer'.

INDISCREET - White penciled Red with Red petaloids to Cream White penciled Pink with Pink petaloids to solid Red. Medium, peony form. Slow, compact, upright growth. E-M. (U.S. 1949 - S. W. Miller, El Cajon, CA).

INEZ MOLL - Deep Salmon Pink with Rose undertone. Large, anemone form to loose peony form with large, rounded petals and intermixed smaller, curved petals and low Golden stamens. Vigorous, open growth. E-M. (U.S. 1957 - Julington).

INTRIGUE - Deep Red. Large, varies from single to full peony form. Vigorous, upright growth. M-L. (U.S. 1964 - G. C. Lecroy, Moncks Corner, SC).

INVICTUS - Dull Red. Medium, full peony form. M. (U.S. 1953 - Fruitland).

IRENE - Pink with White mixed with Red stripes. Small, formal double. Average, spreading growth. M-L. (U.S. 1983 - A. Gonos, Fresno, CA).

IRENE COKER - White, lightly striped Pink, occasionally solid Pink. Medium, rose form double. Average, compact growth. E-M. (U.S. 1955 - B. F. Coker, Pensacola, FL).

IRENE COKER PINK - Pink. (Sport of Japonica 'Irene Coker').

IRENE RED - Red. Small, formal double. Average growth. (Sport of Japonica 'Irene').

IRENE RESTER - Currant Red. Large, semidouble to anemone to peony form. Vigorous, upright growth. E-M. (U.S. 1956 - Rester).

IRENE RESTER VARIEGATED - Currant Red blotched White variation of 'Irene Rester'.

IRENE'S PRIDE - Light Pink in three shades. Large, peony form. Vigorous, upright growth. M. (U.S. 1977 - G. R. Blanton, Summerville, SC).

IRIS - White with a few pink strips. Medium, formal double. Upright growth. M. (Aus. 1848 - Baptiste & Son Nursery, Sydney).

IRISH MIST - Cherry Red. Large to very large, anemone form. Vigorous, upright growth. (U.S. 1982 - Mrs. M O'Malley, Woodside, CA).

IRMA JUDICE - Rose Pink. Medium, semidouble to anemone form. Slow, upright, compact growth. E. (U.S. 1955 - Judice).

IRRATIONAL EXUBERANCE - White (typically 50-80%) with extensive Red veining at center with Yellow anthers and Flesh colored filaments. Medium to large, rose form double. Slow, spreading growth. M. (Japonica 'Tama-no-ura' seedling). (U.S. 2014 - Bobby Green, Green Nurseries, Fairhope, AL).

IRVING CORBETT - Light Pink. Large, semidouble with upright, twisted, curled petals. Average, open, upright growth. M. (U.S. 1964 - Marbury).

ISABEL - White. Medium, formal double. M-L. (For other forms of this cultivar see 'Yirgella' and 'Geoff Hamilton'). (Aus. 1868 - Macarthur).

ISABEL HERMANN - Dark antique Red. Medium, peony form. Average, upright growth. M-L. (U.S. 1959 - B. J. Hermann, Mobile, AL).

ISABEL LEWIS - Light Pink. Large to very large, rose form double to loose peony. Average, upright, open growth. E-M. (Seedling of Japonica 'Marie Bracey'). (U.S. 2016 - Pat Johnson, Cairo, GA).

ISLAND ECHO - See 'Red Wonder'.

ISLAND OF FIRE - Red. Large, semidouble. Average, open, upright growth. M. (U.S. 1965 - Novick).

ISLE OF CAPRI - Light Pink. Large, loose peony form. Vigorous, upright growth. M. (U.S. 1959 - Shackelford).

ITCH - White with Yellow anthers and White filaments. Large, semidouble. Average, upright growth. E-M. (U.S. 2009 - William Brierly, Mobile, AL).

IVEY MAE - Light Pink. Large, peony form. Average, compact growth. M. (U.S. 1957).

IVORY TOWER - White. Large, formal double with high center to peony form. Average, compact growth. M. (U.S. 1966 - Shackelford).

IWANE - ('Iwane-Shibori'; 'F. G. #2'). Rose Red mottled White. Medium, semidouble. Slow, compact growth. M. (Japan 1891 - Yokohama).

IWANE-SHIBORI - See 'Iwane'.

IZA HOUSER - White. Large, semidouble. Vigorous, compact growth. M. (U.S. 1956 - M. R. Murray, Fort Valley, GA).

J BIRD VARIEGATED - Dark Red with White variegation. Large, peony form. Average, open, upright growth. E-L. (Formerly called JAY BIRD). (U.S. 1999 - Jay Ellis Jr., Keystone Hts., FL).

J-WINGS - Medium Red. Large, formal double. Average, spreading, open growth. M-L. (U.S. 2019 - Pat Johnson, Cairo, GA).

J. BISHOP ALEXANDER II - Rose Pink. Large, loose peony form. Vigorous, upright growth. M. (U.S. 1953 - Mealing).

J. J. JOYNER - Bright Red. Medium, semidouble with prominent Yellow stamens. Compact, upright growth. E-M. (U.S. 1959 - D. W. Davis).

J. J. PRINGLE SMITH - Bright Red to Rose Pink. Large, semidouble. Slow, compact growth. M-L. (U.S. 1941 - Middleton).

J. J. PRINGLE SMITH VARIEGATED - Bright Red and White form of 'J J Pringle Smith'.

J. J. WHITFIELD - Dark Red. Medium, loose to full peony form. Vigorous, upright growth. E-M. (U.S. 1950 - Magnolia).

J. J. WHITFIELD VARIEGATED - Dark Red blotched White variation of 'J J Whitfield'.

J. L. SCIVICQUE - Brilliant Red. Large, loose peony form, intermingled stamens. Average growth. M. (U.S. 19886 - J. L. Scivicque, Denham Springs, LA).

J. M. HAYNIE - Rose Pink. Large, semidouble. Vigorous, compact, upright growth. M. (U.S. 1977 - Haynie).

J. MORGAN SPROTT - Deep Cherry Red. Large, semidouble with loose irregular petals. Average, upright growth. L. (U.S. 1973 - J. M. Sprott, Elloree, SC).

J. R. ROSA - Pink. Medium, semidouble. (U.S. 1950 - Rosa).

J. STEWART HOWARD - Bright Red. Large, semidouble with large, crinkled, iridescent petals. Vigorous, compact, upright growth. E-M. (U.S. 1983 - R. Bond, Dallas, TX).

J. STEWART HOWARD VARIEGATED - Bright Red blotched or moired White variation of 'J Stewart Howard'. (U.S. 1983 - R. Bond, Dallas, TX).

JACK BURSON - Pink. Large, semidouble with fimbriated petals. Vigorous, upright growth. E. (U.S. 1961 - Mrs. J. Burson, Long Beach, MS).

JACK FROST - White. Large, semidouble with frosted appearance on upper surface of petals. M-L. (U.S. 1957 - Bowman).

JACK GLENN - Red. Large, peony form. Vigorous, upright growth. E-M. (U.S. 1977 - Gilley).

JACK I. CROCKER - White with Dark Pink stripes and flecks. Small, semidouble form with rabbit ears. Vigorous, upright growth. M. (U.S. 2001 - Eileen C. Hart, Odessa, FL).

JACK McCASKILL - See 'Augusto L' Gouveia Pinto'.

JACK OF HEARTS - Red. Medium, anemone form to formal double. Slow, compact growth. M-L. (U.S. 1955 - Bradford).

JACK WILSON - Strawberry Red. Large, peony form. Average growth. M-L. (U.S. 1978 - A. T. Wilson Jr., Batesburg, SC).

JACK WILSON VARIEGATED - Strawberry Red blotched White variation of 'Jack Wilson'. (U.S. 1978 - A. T. Wilson Jr., Batesburg, SC).

JACKIE D. - Dark Red. Small, formal double. Slow, dense, upright growth. M-L. (U.S. 1995 - W. Smith, Gainesville, FL).

JACKIE GILES - White. Large, peony form with irregular petals and interspersed stamens of hemispherical form. (U.S. 1957 - H. G. McCord, Augusta, GA).

JACKIE MANN - White. Large to very large, formal double. M. (U.S. 1973 - Haynie).

JACKIE NUGENT - Dark rich Red. Very large, semidouble. Average, upright growth. M. (U.S. 1990 - C. Nugent, New Orleans, LA).

JACKS - Rose Pink. Medium, formal double to rose form double. Average, compact growth. M-L. (U.S.).

JACK'S PRIDE - Red blotched White. Large, formal double; the bloom consists of 28-30 petals. Vigorous, upright, open growth. M. (U.S. 2019 - Jack Wint, Destin, FL).

JACKSONI - ('Gigantea Red'; 'Dr. Campbell'). Solid Red form of 'Gigantea'. Large, semidouble to anemone form to peony form. (Not the cultivar described in old literature, which was a formal double of Red striped White). (France [Guichard] to U.S. [McIlhenny] 1937).

JACOB'S HOLLY - White with occasional Red stripes. Large to very large, peony form. Vigorous, upright growth; very unusual holly-like foliage with heavy serrations. M-L. (Sport of Japonica 'Francis Eugene Phillips'). (U.S. 2008 - CamelliaShop, Savannah, GA).

JACQUELINE - Dark Red. Large, anemone form to full peony form. Average, compact, upright growth. E-M. (U.S. 1965 - A. Vasquez, San Gabriel, CA).

JADE SNOW - White. Large to very large, anemone form. Slow, upright growth. E. (U.S. 1968 - Camelliana).

JAKE'S BUDDY - Wine Red. Medium to large, anemone form to peony form. Average, compact, upright growth. E-M. (U.S. 1984 - O. L. Jacobson, Jacksonville Beach, FL).

JAMAR - Blush. Medium to large, semidouble form. Average, open, upright growth. M-L. (U.S. 2004 - Howard Smith, Gainesville, FL).

JAMES ALLAN - Fire Red. Large, single to semidouble to anemone form to peony form. Average, open growth. M. (U.S. 1942 - Allan).

JAMES ALLAN VARIEGATED - Red and White form of 'James Allan'.

JAMES HORNE - Soft Pink. Medium, semidouble with irregular petals to full peony form. Compact, upright growth. M-L. (U.S. 1958 - Tick Tock).

JAMES HYDE PORTER - White striped Pink. Medium, loose peony form. Average, spreading growth. E-M. (U.S. 1942 - Lee).

JAMES LAMEY III - Medium Red with Yellow anthers and White filaments. Large to very large, semidouble. Average, upright, dense growth. M. (U.S. 2013 - Howell).

JAMES LEONARD - White with occasional blotches of Rose Pink. Medium, anemone form. Vigorous, upright growth. M. (U.S. 1954 - Turner).

JAN J. - Rose Pink. Very large, peony form. Average, upright growth. E-M. (U.S. 1989 - O. L. Jacobson, Jacksonville, FL).

JAN'S CHANCE - Bright Pink. Very large, anemone form to peony form. Slow, bushy growth. E-L. (Aus. 1991 - R. Garling, Mt. Waverly, Vic.).

JANE - Light Pink with flakes of Red. Small, formal double with incurved petals. Vigorous, upright growth. M. (U.S. 1975 - Haynie).

JANE BLACKWELL - White. Medium, semidouble with fluted petals. M. (U.S. 1959 - Gerbing).

JANE COMER - Blush Pink. Miniature, semidouble. Average, upright growth. E-M. (U.S. 1982 - Mrs. H. Johnson, Madison, FL).

JANE EAGLESON - Deep Red. Miniature, formal double. Average, upright growth. E-M. (U.S. 1973 - T. Eagleson, Port Arthur, TX).

JANE GRIFFIN - Shell Pink. Small, formal double. Average, upright growth. M. (U.S. 1985 - J. and G. Griffin, Nashville, TN).

JANE HARRELL - White. Medium, full peony form. Compact growth. M. (U.S. 1958 - E. H. Harrell, Thomasville, GA).

JANE HOOD - Rose Red. Medium, formal double with tiered, cupped petals. Vigorous growth. M-L. (U.S. 1960 - Mrs. J. Hood, San Marino, CA).

JANE LAWTON - Pink. Large to very large, semidouble. Average, open growth. M. (U.S. 1986 - O. T. McIntosh, Savannah, GA).

JANE MOON - Iridescent Pink. Medium, semidouble with creped petals. Vigorous, compact, upright growth. M. (U.S. 1959 - Fisher).

JANE MURTAGH - Mauve Pink. Very large, peony form. Upright growth. M. (N.Z. 1980 - A. P. Gamlin, Masaia).

JANE POLIZZI - Dark Pink. Small, deep formal double. Average, upright growth. L. (U.S. 1979 - Tammia).

JANE STARKS - Pink. Medium, formal double with incurved petals. Average, upright growth. M. (U.S. 1963 - R. E. Higginbotham, Texarkana, AR).

JANE STRUBY - Deep Pink. Medium to large, anemone form. Vigorous, compact, upright growth. M. (U.S. 1964 - B. Struby, Macon, GA).

JANE WHITNEY - Old Rose. Large, peony form to rose form double to formal double. Average, open, upright growth. E-M. (U.S. 1973 - Tammia).

JANEEN ELIZABETH - White to Blush Pink with irregular Red stripes and flecks. Small, formal double to rose form double. Average, upright growth. M-L. (Japonica 'Tinker Bell' seedling). (U.S. 2004 - Don Bergamini, Martinez, CA).

JANET K - Rose to Pink variegated White. Small, formal double with six tiers of petals. Vigorous, upright growth. M. (U.S. 1977 - T. E. Lundy, Pensacola, FL).

JANET WATERHOUSE - White. Large, semidouble with compact center of stamens and anthers. (Aus. 1952 - Waterhouse).

JANETTE HABAS - White. Large, full peony form to anemone form. Average, compact, upright growth. M. (U.S. 1975 - Tammia).

JANEY MAYER - White with Pink pencil stripe at point of several petals. Medium, formal double. Vigorous, compact, upright growth. M. (U.S. 1960 - Solomon).

JANIE DOVER - Rose Pink to Lighter Pink center. Miniature to small, formal double with spiraled petals. Average, dense, upright growth. M. (U.S. 1988 - Mrs. H. Stone, Baton Rouge, LA).

JANIE LEE OTT - Crimson. Medium, full peony form. Vigorous, compact, upright growth. M. (U.S. 1956 - E. C. Wolfe, Branchville, SC).

JANIE PEARL - Blush to White center. Small, formal double. Vigorous, compact, upright growth. M-L. (U.S. 1975 - Haynie).

JANIE SANS - Light Pink. Small, semidouble. (Sport of Japonica 'Mama Sans'). (U.S. 1957 - Metcalf).

JANIE WOOD - Rose Red veined deeper. Medium, semidouble with wavy, crinkled petals. Average, spreading growth. M. (U.S. 1970 - J. B. Wood, Florence, SC).

JANIS SMITH - Rose Pink. Large, semidouble to rose form double. Average, compact, upright growth. M-L. (U.S. 1971 - Twin Pines Nsy., Theodore, AL).

JARED - Pink mottled White. Miniature to small, formal double. Average, compact growth. M-L. (U.S. 1989 - Kramer).

JARVIS RED - Turkey Red. Small to medium, semidouble with tufted center of smaller petals. Vigorous, wide, spreading growth. M. Cold hardy. (For another form of this cultivar, see 'Fantasia'). (Japan to U.S. [Kiyono] 1911).

JASON MALBIS - Red and White. Medium, semidouble. (U.S. 1952 - Malbis).

JASTIL - Deep Rose Pink, edged with a slight touch of Purple. Large, loose peony form. M-L. (Aus. 2002 - Mrs. Helen Simon, Wahroonga, NSW).

JAY ELLIS - Dark Red. Large to very large, semidouble. Vigorous, spreading growth. E-L. (U.S. 1999 - Jay Ellis Jr., Keystone Hts., FL).

JAYLYLE - Rose Pink. Medium, anemone form with Yellow tipped White stamens. Average, spreading growth. E-M. (U.S. 1960 - Wells).

JEAN BARDOW - Rose Pink. Miniature, anemone form. Average, upright growth. M-L. (U.S. 1955 - Councilman).

JEAN CLERE - Red with narrow band of White around edge. Medium, full peony form. (Sport of Japonica 'Aspasia Macarthur'). (N.Z. 1969 - R. H. Clere, Hawera).

JEAN EVANS - Pink. Medium, semidouble. Average, spreading, upright growth. M-L. (Aus. 1996 - C. Newman).

JEAN FEATHERS - Pale Pink to Deep Pink edges. Medium, semidouble. Vigorous, spreading growth. M. (U.S. 1980 - Feathers).

JEAN KERNAGHAN - White interspersed with Pink. Medium, loose peony form. Average, compact, upright growth. M-L. (U.S. 1980 - G. C. Chester, Augusta, GA).

JEAN LIVINGSTONE - China Rose. Large, semidouble with occasional petaloids. Average, open, upright growth. M. (N.Z. 1963 - Mrs. W. M. McFarland, Frankton Junction).

JEAN LYNE - White striped and flecked Carmine. Medium, semidouble to peony form. Average, compact growth. M. (Variations of this cultivar include 'Edith Linton'; 'Nancy Bird'). (Aus. 1941 - Hunter).

JEAN MARIE - Blush Pink. Medium, formal double. Average, spreading, upright growth. L. (U.S. 1960 - E. C. Perry, Santa Clara, CA).

JEAN MILHET - White with White stamens. Medium, rose form double. (U.S. 1950 - McIlhenny).

JEAN NORTON - Salmon Pink. Medium to large, semidouble. (Sport of Japonica 'Robert Norton'). (U.S. 1945 - Overlook).

JEAN PACE - White marked and striped Red. Large, semidouble. Vigorous, compact, upright growth. M-L. (U.S. 1962 - Shackelford).

JEAN SMITH - Pink. Large, peony form with irregular petals and upright center petals surrounding interspersed stamens and petaloids. Average, upright growth. M-L. (U.S. 1964 - J. U. Smith, Columbia, SC).

JEAN'S UNSURPASSABLE - Pale Pink with flecks of Deeper Pink. Large, semidouble to anemone form. Vigorous, compact, upright growth. M-L. (U.S. 1970 - G. W. Moughon, Birmingham, AL).

JEANETTE BATLEY - White. Large, semidouble to peony form. Average, upright growth. L. (Aus. 1967 - R. Windeyer, Lindfield, NSW).

JEANETTE COUSIN - Bright Pink. Large to very large, semidouble. Vigorous, compact, upright growth. M. (Aus. 1970 - R. T. C. Cousin, Pakenham, East Vic.).

JEANETTE LANE - Lavender Pink. Medium, formal double to rose form double. Average, compact growth. M-L. (U.S. 1952 - Mrs. J. Lane, North Hollywood, CA).

JEANNE KERR - See 'Kumasaka'.

JEANNE LEWIS - Deep to Rose Pink with Silver sheen. Large, anemone form. Vigorous, spreading growth. E-M. (U.S. 1985 - Dr. O. V. Lewis, Picayune, MS).

JEFFREY HOOD - Deep Pink. Large to very large, semidouble with irregular petals to anemone form with large petals. Vigorous, open growth. E-M. (U.S. 1969 - M. D. Hood, Texarkana, AR).

JEFFREY WEBSTER - White with a few Red flecks and stripes. Medium, semidouble to loose peony form. Average, upright growth. M. (U.S. 1989 - Elizabeth R. Scott, Aiken, SC).

JENELI - Light Pink. Large, semidouble with very long, tufted petaloids in center. Vigorous, pendulous growth. M. (U.S. 1963 - Wilson).

JENKS DOWLING - Deep Rose Red. Large, semidouble with loose petals to anemone form. Vigorous, upright growth. E-M. (U.S. 1960 - Beasley).

JENNIE J. LEWIS - Dark Red. Large, formal double to rose form double. Average, upright, spreading growth. E-L. (Seedling of Japonica 'Holly Bright'). (U.S. 2016 - Pat Johnson, Cairo, GA).

JENNIE MILLS - Silver Pink with overtones of Lavender and Silver margined petals. Medium, semidouble with three tiers of petals and compact column of White stamens. Vigorous, compact, upright growth. M. (U.S. 1958 - Ragland).

JENNIFER MURRAY - White. Large, semidouble. Weeping growth. M. (N.Z. 1962 - Mrs. W. M. McFarland, Frankton Junction).

JENNIFER TURNBULL - Shell Pink, Paler towards center. Medium, single. Vigorous growth. M. (Aus. 1959 - Turnbull).

JENNIFER WRIGHT - Flesh Pink. Large, semidouble. M. (U.S. 1973 - Haynie).

JENNY D. - Pink. Medium, formal double. Average, open, upright growth. E-L. (U.S. 1995 - W. Smith, Gainesville, FL).

JENNY JONES - White. Medium to large, semidouble. Average, bushy growth. M. (U.S. 1942 - Jones).

JENNY LIND - White with a few faint Pink streaks. Medium, formal double. Upright growth. M. (For another form of this cultivar, see 'Mme. Louis Van Houtte'). (U.S. 1854 - W. McKenzie, Philadelphia, PA).

JERRY CONRAD - Rose-Red with Yellow anthers and Cream filaments. Large, semidouble to loose peony. Vigorous, upright growth. M. (Japonica 'Moonlight Bay' seedling). (U.S. 2014 - Jerry Conrad, Mt. Plymouth, FL).

JERRY DONNAN - Pale to Light Pink. Medium to large, formal double with ruffled petals. Average, dense, upright growth. E-L. (Sport of Japonica 'Donnan's Dream'). (U.S. 1990 - A. Gonos and B. Donnan, CA).

JERRY HILL - Rose Pink. Medium, formal double. Average, dense, upright growth. L. Cold hardy to -10°F. (U.S. 1996 - Ackerman).

JERRY SWINT - Dark Red. Large, semidouble. Average growth. M-L. (U.S. 1972 - F. Smith, Statesboro, GA).

JERRY WILSON - White striped and blotched Pink. Large, formal double. Average, compact, upright growth. E-M. (U.S. 1965 - Wilson).

JERRY WILSON PINK - Pink. (Sport of Japonica 'Jerry Wilson'). (U.S. 1965 - Wilson).

JESSAMOND - Pink. Small, formal double with loose petals. Average, open, upright growth. M. (U.S. 1984 - Mrs. H. Johnson, Madison, FL).

JESSICA - Bright Red. Medium, semidouble. Vigorous, upright growth. M. (U.S. 1939 - Mrs. Kite, Nichols, AL).

JESSICA BEACH - Pink with Yellow anthers and White filaments. Medium, semidouble to full peony to rose form double. Vigorous, upright growth. M. (Japonica 'Angel's Blush' seedling). (U.S. 2013 - Miles A Beach, Mt. Pleasant, SC).

JESSICA VARIEGATED - ('Dorothy M.'). Bright Red blotched White form of 'Jessica'.

JESSIE BRYSON - Rose Pink to Red. Medium, loose peony form. (U.S. 1950 - J. H. Bryson, Dothan, AL).

JESSIE BURGESS - Rose with Silver cast. Large, semidouble. Average, upright growth. E. (U.S. 1960 - Burgess).

JESSIE CONNER - Rose shading to Cream White in center. Small to medium, formal double with water lily cupped petals. M. (U.S. 1976 - G. Yates, Charlotte, NC).

JESSIE GALE - Glossy Red. Medium, single. Average, compact, upright growth. M. (U.S. 1958 - McCaskill).

JESSIE KATZ - Watermelon Pink. Large, semidouble with crepe and wavy petals. (Sport of Japonica 'Troubadour'). (U.S. 1948 - Magnolia).

JESSIE MURPH - Red with Pink stamens, sometimes showing Creamy petaloids. Large, semidouble. (U.S. 1955 - Mrs. J. Murph, Marshallville, GA).

JET AROUND - Dark Red with Black edges with Gold anthers and Red filaments. Large, semidouble. Average, upright, open growth. M-L. (Seedling of Japonica 'Royal Velvet'). (U.S. 2019 - Pat Johnson, Cairo, GA).

JEUNE FILLE - White. Medium, semidouble. E. (Aus. 1962 - H. K. C. Dettman, Wahroonga).

JEWEL BAILEY - Blush Pink deep stripe with Rose splotches. Large, peony form. Vigorous, spreading growth. M. (U.S. 1972 - Burgess).

JEWEL BOWDEN - White with Pink throat. Medium, semidouble. (Sport of Japonica 'Tricolor [Siebold]'). (U.S. 1957 - Mrs. J. A. Bowden, Shreveport, LA).

JEZEBEL - Red. Large, semidouble. Vigorous, upright growth. M. (U.S. 1974 - D. C. Strother, Fort Valley, GA).

JIL FREEMAN - Rose. Very large, semidouble. Vigorous, upright growth. E-M. (U.S. 1966 - G. E. Freeman, Claxton, GA).

JILLIAN VARGA - Dark Red. Medium, semidouble to anemone form. Average, upright growth. M-L. (Aus. 1999 - Augustin Varga, Daw Park, S. Aus.).

JIM ALFTER - Bright Red and White. Large to very large, rose form double. Vigorous, upright growth. (U.S. 1981 - Alfter).

JIM CHAVAUX - Light Pink with Yellow anthers and White filaments. Large, semidouble to loose peony form. Average, upright, open growth. E-M. (Seedling of Japonica 'Steve Blount'). (U.S. 2018 - Pat Johnson, Cairo, GA).

JIM FINLAY'S FRAGRANT - Light Red. Medium, peony form. Average growth. E-L. Fragrant. (N.Z. 1994 - J. Finlay).

JIM GOLDMAN - Light Pink. Medium, semidouble. Upright growth. M. (U.S. 1948 - Harper).

JIM HABEL - Rose and White with Pink filaments. Large, anemone to loose peony form with petaloids center. Average, upright growth. M-L. (U.S. 2003 - Douglas Simon, Norfolk, VA).

JIM McCORMACK - Pink (RHS 62A) at margins, fading to Pale Pink (RHS 62D) in the center with Yellow anthers and Creamy White filaments. Medium, semidouble. Vigorous, upright, dense growth. E-M. (U.S. 2009 - Ackerman).

JIM McHENRY - Red. Large, semidouble with fluted petals. Average, upright, open growth. M. (U.S. 1959 - Ragland).

JIM SMITH - Rose Red with Gold anthers and Cream filaments. Large, semidouble. Average, upright growth. M-L. (U.S. 2015 - Gordy).

JIMBO - White with Yellow shading near the center. Small, formal double. Average, upright growth. M-L. (U.S. 2001 - Marion G. Hall, Dothan, AL).

JIMMY CARTER - Light pink edged white with red stripes with yellow anthers and white filaments. Medium, rose form double. Average, upright, open growth. M-L. (U.S. 2018 - Gordy).

JIMMY GILLEY - Dark Red variegated White. Medium to large, semidouble with wavy, crinkled petals. Average, upright growth. M. (U.S. 1979 - Gilley).

JIMMY STREET - Red. Large, semidouble. Slow, upright growth. M-L. (U.S. 1964 - W. P. Richardson, Chapel Hill, NC).

JINGLE BELLS - Red. Small, anemone form. (Sport of Japonica 'Tinker Bell'). (U.S. 1959 - Nuccio's).

JINHUA MEINÜ - See 'Bella Jinhua'

JITSU-GETSU-SEI - Red splotched White. Medium, single with crepe petals and flared soft Pink stamens. See Higo.

JO ANNA WILSON - Bright Scarlet. Small, rose form double with irregular and ruffled petals and center petaloids. Vigorous, bushy growth. M-L. (U.S. 1988 - J. T. Wilson, Shreveport. LA).

JO CINDA - Rose Pink. Miniature to small, formal double. Upright growth. M-L. (U.S. 1987 - I. V. Mitchell, Melrose, FL).

JO LEIGH LEWIS - Soft Pink. Very large, rose form double. Average, spreading growth. E-M. (U.S. 1986 - Dr. O. V. Lewis, Picayune, MS).

JO VINCENT - White marked Pink to solid Pink. Medium, full peony form. Average, compact growth. M. (U.S. 1949 - Tea Gardens).

JOAN HOLDEN - Blush Rose with Deeper Rose striping speckles with Yellow anthers and Creamy Yellow stamens. Large, hose-in-hose semidouble. Average, upright, open growth. E-M. (U.S. 2002 - Alfred M. Holden, Baton Rouge, LA).

JOAN WATSON - Deep Pink. Medium, peony form. Average, compact, upright growth. M. (U.S. 1965 - Monticello Nsy. Co., Monticello, FL).

JOE PYRON - Rich Deep Red. Medium to large, semidouble with fimbriated ruffled petals and some twisted, upright petals. Average, compact growth. M. (U.S. 1968 - Burgess).

JOE RESTER - Light Pink. Large, semidouble with wavy, crinkled petals. Average, compact, upright growth. M. (U.S. 1968 - Rester).

JOE RUBENSTEIN - Dark Red. Large, semidouble to peony form. Average, upright growth. M. (U.S. 1980 - Tammia).

JOELLEN CHRISTINE - Pink with White and Pink petaloids with Yellow anthers and White filaments. Small, anemone form with cupped-shaped petals. Average, upright growth. M-L. (Japonica 'Tinker Bell' seedling). (U.S. 2004 - Don Bergamini, Martinez, CA).

JOHANNA BUTLER - Bright Red. Medium, semidouble to loose peony form. Average growth. L. (U.S. 1967 - Miss K. Butler, Ruston, LA).

JOHANNA HOWERTON REHDER - Light Pink, Dark Pink edges. Medium, semidouble. Vigorous, upright growth. E-L. (U.S. 1999 - H. B. Rehder Sr., Wilmington, NC).

JOHANNA TAYLOR - White with an occasional Pink stripe or two with Yellow anthers and Yellow filaments. Medium, semidouble. Average, upright growth. M. (U.S. 2010 - Donald Taylor, New Bern, NC).

JOHN CLAIRMONT - Pink. Medium, semidouble. (Sport of Japonica 'Gibson Girl'). (U.S. 1956 - Dr. J. Clairmont, Glendale, CA).

JOHN CULVERHOUSE - American Beauty Red. Large, peony form with slightly curled and twisted petals. M. (U.S. 1965 - Witman).

JOHN E. THURMAN - White, Blush toward center. Medium, peony form. Average, upright growth. E-M. (U.S. 1988 - J. E. Thurman, Covington, LA).

JOHN EDWARDS - Dark Red with Gold stamens. Large, semidouble. Average, upright, spreading growth. M-L. (U.S. 2006 - John K. Edwards, Jr., Pensacola, FL).

JOHN HARVARD - Purple Red. Small, rose form double. (U.S. Late 1800's - Magnolia).

JOHN HOLLIMAN - Dark Pink. Medium, anemone form. Average, dense, spreading growth. E-M. (U.S. 1992 - J. Holliman, Thomaston, GA).

JOHN ILLGES - Bright Red. Medium, single of flat form. Average, loose, upright growth. M. (Europe to U.S. [Magnolia] 1840's).

JOHN L. SHIRAH - White, with a slight Blush. Medium to large, formal double form. Vigorous, spreading growth. E-M. (U.S. 2005 - John W. Shirah, Lakeland, FL).

JOHN RUMBACH - Dark Red with Yellow anthers and White filaments. Large, semidouble to loose peony form. Average, spreading, dense growth. M. (U.S. 2013 - John Rumbach, Jacksonville, FL).

JOHN SHIRAH JR. - White with Light Pink flecks with Yellow anthers and Ivory filaments. Very large, semidouble. Vigorous, upright growth. E-M. (Sport of Japonica 'Happy Birthday'). (U.S. 2008 - John W. Shirah, Lakeland, FL).

JOHN SWAN - White. Medium, semidouble. M. (Aus. 1962 - Hunter).

JOHN WILLIAMS - Rose and White. Large, single. (U.S. 1946 - Riverbank).

JOHNNY ALDRICH - Deep Purplish Pink shading darker at margin. Large, loose peony form. Average, upright growth. M. (U.S. 1995 - J. Aldrich, Brooklet, GA).

JOHNNY BERGIN - Deep Rose and White. Medium, anemone form. Average, compact, upright growth. M-L. (U.S. 1979 - J. Bergin, Valparaiso, FL).

JOHNNY LAMEY, III - Medium Red with Yellow anthers and White filaments. Large to very large, semidouble with stamens spreading out into five parts. Average, upright, dense growth. M. (U.S. 2013 - Howell).

JOHNNY REB - Light Blush Pink, some petals with soft Pink streaks and specks. Large, semidouble to anemone form. Average, open, upright growth. M-L. (U.S. 1969 - Haynie).

JOHNNY REB PINK - Soft Pink. (Sport of Japonica 'Johnny Reb'). (U.S. 1972 - Haynie).

JOHNNY'S FOLLY - White striped Red. Small, anemone form. Average, spreading, open growth. M. (U.S. 1957 - J. E. Robinson, La Cañada, CA).

JOHNSON VAN CATHERINE - Deep Rose Pink with White dapples at outside of petals with Yellow anthers and White filaments. Medium, semidouble; the petaloids divert the stamens. Vigorous, upright growth. M-L. (U.S. 2014 - Catherine Johnson, Perry, GA).

JOLLY ROGER - See 'Gigantea'.

JOLYNN RESTER - Red. Large to very large, semidouble with large, crinkled and irregular petals. Vigorous, upright growth. E-M. (U.S. 1966 - Rester).

JONATHAN - Deep Pink. Large, semidouble to peony form. Vigorous, upright growth. M. (U.S. 1968 - Dr. J. Cone, Thomasville, GA).

JONATHAN LOUIS GRIMM - Red. Medium to large, formal double. Average, bushy growth. M. (U.S. 2019 - Bobby Green, Green Nurseries, Fairhope, AL).

JONATHAN WILSON - White. Medium, rose form double to formal double. Average, spreading growth. L. (U.S. 1991 - W. Wilson, Augusta, GA).

JONEL - Rose Pink. Small to medium, formal double. Average, upright growth. M. (U.S. 2009 - John Rumbach, Jacksonville, FL).

JONI SANS - White. Miniature, semidouble with occasional petaloids in center. Average, upright growth. M-L. (U.S. 1959 - Metcalf).

JORDAN'S PRIDE - See 'Herme'.

JOSEPH HOLLAND - Pink. Medium, rose form double with small, rounded petals. Vigorous, loose, upright growth. M. (Europe to U.S. [Magnolia] 1840's).

JOSEPH PFINGSTL - Dark Red. Medium to large, semidouble with irregular petals to loose peony form with wavy outer petals and fluted center petals. Vigorous, sturdy growth. E-M. (For a variation of this cultivar see 'Emmett Pfingstl'). (U.S. 1948 - Pfingstl).

JOSEPH PFINGSTL VARIEGATED - See 'Emmett Pfingstl'.

JOSEPHINE CARUSO - Oriental Red, moired or mottled White; heavily variegated. Medium, semidouble form. Average, spreading growth. M-L. (U.S. 2002 - Silvio W. Caruso, Clinton, NC).

JOSEPHINE DUELL - Soft Pink. Medium, semidouble. Average, upright growth. M. (U.S. 1941 - Middleton).

JOSEPHINE LOUISE NEWCOMB - White with White stamens. Medium, semidouble with loose petals and center petals interspersed with stamens. (U.S. 1946 - McIlhenny).

JOSH SPROTT - Light Pink. Miniature, formal double. Average growth. M. (U.S. 1977 - Tammia).

JOSHUA DURR - Rose Red. Large, peony form. Vigorous, open, upright growth. M-L. (U.S. 1981 - T. E. Lundy, Pensacola, FL).

JOSHUA E. YOUTZ - ('White Daikagura').- White. Large, peony form to formal double. Slow, compact growth. E. (Japan to U.S. 1915 - Star).

JOSHUA FENSKA - Dark Red. Small, formal double with spiral petals. Vigorous growth. E-L. (U.S. 1983 - Piet and Gaeta).

JOSIE BOND - Light Blush Pink with Cream center. Medium, formal double form. Average, dense, upright growth. M-L. (U.S. 1999 - Bond Nursery Corp., Dallas, TX).

JOSIE HALL - Deep Rose edged Purple. Large, semidouble. Slow, spreading growth. M. (U.S. 1957 - Mrs. L. Harvard, Dothan, AL).

JOY KENDRICK - White to Blush Pink with Light Pink stripes. Large, formal double. Average, spreading, upright growth. M. (U.S. 1985 - Tammia).

JOY MOONEY - Shell Pink. Medium, peony form. Vigorous, upright growth. M. (N.Z. 1989 - J. Mooney, Taradale).

JOYCE BUTLER - Rose Red. Medium, loose peony form with irregular and upright petals. Upright growth. M. (U.S. 1959 - Mrs. H. H. Butler, Columbia, MS).

JOYCE STILL - Rose Pink. Large, semidouble. (U.S. 1961 - W. I. McGill, Adams Run, SC).

JOYNER'S JOY - Dark Rose outer petals and Rose to Light Pink inner petals and petaloids. Large, full peony form. Average, open, upright growth. E. (U.S. 1961 - A. Joyner, Goldsboro, NC).

JUANITA HUTCHESON - Rose Pink and White. Large to very large, peony form to anemone form. Average, upright growth. E-L. (Reported to be same as 'Tomorrow Variegated'). (U.S. 1972 - W. F. Hutcheson, Texarkana, TX).

JUANITA SMITH - White shading to narrow edge of Blush Rose. Medium, semidouble with fluffy, notched, upright petals. Vigorous, spreading, upright growth. E-M. (U.S. 1959 - Mrs. J. Smith, Franklinton, LA).

JUDGE MARVIN MANN - ('Riptide'). Rose Pink. Large, loose peony form with turned and twisted petals. Average, open, upright growth. M. (U.S. 1958 - Ashby).

JUDGE MARVIN MANN VARIEGATED - Rose Pink blotched White variation of 'Judge Marvin Mann'.

JUDGE RICHARD HILL - Rose Red. Large, semidouble to formal double. Vigorous, upright growth. M. (U.S. 1975 - Tammia).

JUDGE RICHARD HILL VARIEGATED - Rose Red blotched White variation of 'Judge Richard Hill'. (U.S. 1975 - Tammia).

JUDGE SOLOMON - Rose Pink. Medium to large, full peony form. Vigorous, compact growth. M. (U.S. 1956 - Nuccio's).

JUDGE STOUT - Very Light Pink inner petals with outer petals edged Dark Pink. Medium to large, semidouble. Vigorous, dense, upright growth. M. (U.S. 1997 - W. Stout, Pensacola, FL).

JUDGE TALBOT - Light Red. Large, formal double. Vigorous, upright growth. E-M. (U.S. 1959 - Wilson).

JUDGE THOMAS PORTER - Rose Pink. Medium to large, semidouble with stamens in three distinct groups intermixed with petaloids. Average, spreading growth. E-M. (U.S. 1961 - Mrs. J. P. Moon, Lake Charles, LA).

JUDGE W. T. RAGLAND - Rich Red. Large, semidouble with undulant, upright petals and White stamens tipped with Golden anthers. Average, upright growth. M. (U.S. 1961 - Ragland).

JUDITH SPROULE - White marked Red. Medium, semidouble. Slow, open growth. E-M. (U.S. 1959 - J. F. Delage, Beaumont, TX).

JUDY CAMBLIN - Frosted Pink. Medium, formal double with rows of larger petals cupped around a broad center of smaller petals. Vigorous, compact growth. L. (U.S. 1956 - Julington).

JUDY M. STRAUS - Bright Pink with Yellow anthers and Yellow filaments. Miniature, semidouble. Vigorous, upright, spreading growth. E. (U.S. 1983 - Temple S. Cleive, Sacramento, CA).

JUDY MATTHEWS - Blush Pink. Medium to large, loose peony form with fluffy petals and fluted, twisted, center petals. Average, upright growth. M. (U.S. 1961 - G. M. Wheeler, Birmingham, AL).

JUDY O'GRADY - White, delicately striped Rose Pink. Large, semidouble. Vigorous, compact, upright growth. M. (U.S. 1954 - McCaskill).

JULIA BROCK - Rose Pink with Lavender tint. Medium, semidouble. E-L. (U.S. 1952 - Brock).

JULIA C. TAYLOR - Stark White. Large, rose form double with Yellow stamens when fully open. M-L. (U.S. 1956 - James P. Taylor, Quitman, GA. Propagated by Mark Crawford, Valdosta, GA).

JULIA DIAL - White. Large, semidouble to anemone form. Average, compact, upright growth. M. (U.S. 1948 - R. V. Dial, Madison, FL).

JULIA DRAYTON - See 'Mathotiana'.

JULIA DRAYTON VARIEGATED - See 'Mathotiana Variegated'.

JULIA FRANCE - Light Pink. Large, semidouble with fluted petals to rose form double to formal double. Vigorous, upright growth with large foliage. M. (U.S. 1958 - Ashby).

JULIA STAFFORD - White. Medium, formal double with erect petals. Average, compact growth. M-L. (U.S. 1954 - Feathers).

JULIA WILSON - Soft Pink. Medium to large, semidouble with loose petals. (U.S. 1961 - W. A. Wilson, Augusta, GA).

JULIA'S FAVORITE - Cream White marked Pink to Blush Pink. Medium to large, peony form. Average, bushy growth. E-L. (U.S. 1955 - Short).

JULIA'S WISH - White with occasional Pink fleck. Large, peony form. Vigorous, compact growth. M-L. (Aus. 1964 - J. Waine, Warrawee).

JULIANA REGINA - White. Very large, anemone form. Average growth. M. (N.Z. 1983 - O. F. Over de Linden, Papakura).

JULIANNE AGEE - White. Large, anemone form with ruffled edges on petals and petaloids. Slow, upright growth. E-M. (U.S. 1987 - K. E. and M. Agee, Nacogdoches, TX).

JULIE BLUSH - Soft Pink. Large, anemone. (Sport of Japonica 'Julie Nixon'). (U.S. 1979 - Kramer).

JULIE MARIE - White. Large, full peony form with upright center petals. Average, compact growth. E-L. (U.S. 1965 - L. W. Strohmeyer, San Gabriel, CA).

JULIE NIXON - White. Large, anemone. (Sport of Japonica 'Pat Nixon'). (For another form of this cultivar see 'Julie Blush'; formerly named Japonica 'Julie'). (U.S. 1974 - Kramer).

JULIETTE GORDON LOW - Pale Blush Pink. Large, semidouble with fluted petals. Average, compact, upright growth. M. (U.S. 1965 - W. H. Fleetwood, Savannah, GA).

JULIUS NUCCIO - Brilliant Dark Red. Large to very large, irregular semidouble. Vigorous upright growth, M-L. (U.S. 2014 - Nuccio's).

JUNE ATKINS - Pink and White. Medium, formal double. Average growth. M-L. (U.S. 1983 - E. L. Atkins, Shalimar, FL).

JUNE BUCHANAN - Pale Pink. Medium to large, peony form. Average, upright growth. E-L. (N.Z. 1990 - H. Buchanan, Palmerston North).

JUNE MacKAYE - White. Medium, formal double. Average, open, upright growth. M. (U.S. 1982 - Homeyer).

JUNE McCASKILL - Clear Pink. Medium, semidouble with trumpet center. Vigorous, compact, upright growth. M. (U.S. 1954 - McCaskill).

JUNE STEWART - Orange Rose Red. Medium, peony form with loose petals. Average, compact growth. M-L. (U.S. 1965 - Breschini).

JUNE STEWART SUPREME - Orange Rose Red highly variegated White form of 'June Stewart'. (U.S. 1964 - Breschini).

85

JUNELLA HARDISON - Deep Pink. Very large, semidouble to anemone form to peony form. Average, dense, upright growth. E-M. (U.S. 1994 - D. Hardison, Tallahassee, FL).

JUNIE LANCASTER - Light Red. Medium to large, anemone form. Vigorous, upright growth. E. (U.S. 1997 - Habel).

JUNIOR MISS - Blush to Pink on edge. Medium, semidouble. Vigorous, compact, upright growth. M. (U.S. 1971 - C. Crutcher Jr., Mobile, AL).

JUNIOR PROM - White to faint Blush Pink. Large, rose form double; occasionally loose peony form. Vigorous, dense, upright growth. E-M. (U.S. 1996 - Nuccio's).

JUST DARLING - Shell Pink. Miniature, formal double. Vigorous, upright growth. M. (U.S. 1976 - Dr. W. F. Mathis, Moultrie, GA).

JUST SUE - ('Maureen Ostler'). Light Pink edged bright Rose. Medium, full peony form. (Sport of Japonica 'Margaret Davis'). (Aus. 1971 - R. H. Hall, Tea Tree Gully, S. Australia).

JUSTINE CARROLL - Light bright Pink. Medium, formal double. Average, upright growth. E-M. (U.S. 1982 - E. Carroll, Conroe, TX).

K. OHARA - White. Medium to large, semidouble with wavy and upright petals. Average, upright growth. M-L. (Japan 1996 - Kinji Ohara, Tateyama City).

K. SAWADA - ('Silver Moon'; 'Mrs. Albert Dekker'). White. Large, formal double to rose form double. Vigorous, semi-upright growth. M. (U.S. 1940 - Overlook).

KAGIRI - ('Dante'; 'Pine Cone White'; 'Gloria'). White. Medium, semidouble of pine cone form with high center. Slow, bushy growth. L. (Japan 1891 - Yokohama).

KAGO TSURUBE - Rose Pink. Medium, single with flared soft Pink stamens. See Higo.

KAGOSHIMA - See 'Matsukasa'.

KAKI - Light Pink. Medium, formal double. Upright growth. M. (U.S. 1961 - Rogerson's Garden Nsy., Florence, SC).

KAKUREISO - Dark wine Red edged White. Small to medium, single. Average, compact, upright growth. E-M. (Japan to U.S. 1978 - Nuccio's).

KALARENA - Watermelon Red tipped Purple. Large, formal double with incurved petals. Slow, upright growth. M-L. (U.S. 1953 - J. H. Brown, Spartanburg, SC).

KALEIDOSCOPE - Very Light Pink with many Dark Red stripes with Gold anthers and White filaments. Medium, single. Average, upright, bushy growth. M. (U.S. 2019 - Nuccio's).

KALGOORLIE STORM - Red. Large, formal double. Vigorous, dense, upright growth. E. (Aus. 1992 - K. Abbott, Rossmoyne, W. Aus.).

KALLISTA - See 'Mrs. H. Boyce Rosea'.

KAMMER'S LEGACY - Red blotched White with Yellow anthers and Pink filaments. Large, peony form consisting of 25 petals and 300 petaloids. Average, bushy, dense growth. M. (U.S. 2019 - Bob and Peggy Kammer, Fort Walton Beach, FL).

KAMO-HON-AMI - ('Hon-Ami'; 'Sotan'). White. Large, single. E-M. (Similar to 'Amabilis'). (Japan 1935 - Chugai).

KARA-ITO - Red. Medium, single to semidouble to anemone form. (Sport of Japonica 'Gosho-Guruma'). (Japan to U.S. 1930 - Star).

KARA-NISHIKI - Light Pink dotted White. Medium, semidouble. (Japan to U.S. 1930 - Star).

KAREN ALBRITTON - White with Pink and Rose streaks and stripes. Medium, semidouble to loose peony form. Slow, upright growth. M-L. (U.S. 1998 - C. Elliott, Swainsboro, GA).

KAREN GILLEY - Dark Red. Large, semidouble with flared stamens. Average, upright growth. M. (U.S. 1983 - Gilley).

KAREN HENSON - Vibrant Rose. Small, formal double. Average, compact, upright growth. M. (U.S. 1979 - T. Eagleson, Port Arthur, TX).

KAREN PIET - Very Dark Red. Medium, formal double with incurved petals. Vigorous, compact, upright growth. M. (U.S. 1986 - Piet and Gaeta).

KASU-GANO - Pink dotted White. Large, semidouble. (Japan to U.S. [Star] 1930).

KATE CARGILL - Soft Pink. Medium, semidouble to loose peony form with irregular petals. Upright growth. M. (U.S. 1958 - Chiles).

KATE HARDIE - Pearl White to Blush Pink. Medium, formal double with cupped center petals, occasionally with six pointed star center. Average, open, upright growth. E-M. (U.S. 1989 - Homeyer).

KATE SHEPARD - White. Large to very large, anemone form. Average, upright growth. E-L. (N.Z. 1991 - A. Gamlin, Manaia).

KATE SMITH - See 'Mathotiana Supreme Variegated'.

KATE THRASH - Rose Pink. Medium, full peony form. Vigorous, open growth. E-M. (U.S. 1956 - Mrs. W. E. Roughton, Thomasville, GA).

KATE THRASH VARIEGATED - Rose Pink and White variation of 'Kate Thrash'. (U.S. 1962 - Mrs. I. H. McCormick, Thomasville, GA).

KATHERINE ALLAN - Delicate Pink. Medium, semidouble with loose petals to anemone form. Vigorous, open, pendulous growth. M. (U.S. 1950 - Allan).

KATHERINE CHISHOLM - Pink. Large, semidouble with wavy, crinkled petals. Average, upright growth. E-M. (U.S. 1978 - F. A. Chisholm, Savannah, GA).

KATHERINE HART - White. Large, peony form. (U.S. 1953).

KATHERINE MARYOTT - Pink. Large, rose form double. Average, upright growth. L. (U.S. 1959 - Mrs. C. H. Maryott, Augusta, GA).

KATHERINE MEALING - Cardinal Red. Large, peony form. Average, upright growth. M. (U.S. 1964 - Mealing).

KATHERINE NUCCIO - Rose Red. Medium, formal double to rose form double. Vigorous, compact growth. M. (U.S. 1950 - Nuccio's).

KATHIE BROWN - Deep Pink. Large, peony form to anemone form. Vigorous, spreading, upright growth. M-L. (U.S. 1978 - D. K. Walker, Charleston, SC).

KATHLEEN - Pink. Medium, semidouble. (U.S. 1955 - Mrs. C. Bradley, Milwaukie, OR).

KATHNSTU CLARK - Red, plus Pink and Cream petaloids in the center. Small, anemone form. Vigorous, upright growth. (Aus.2003-Patrick Clark, Pymble, NSW).

KATHRYN BEVIS - Clear Pink with Darker Pink to Carmine Rose outer petals and Light Pink at center. Medium to large, peony form. Average, upright growth. E-M. (U.S. 1998 - J. Hogsette, Gainesville, FL).

KATHRYN FLUGGE - Pink. Large, semidouble. Vigorous, upright growth. E-M. (Aus. 1999 - Keith Abbot, Rossmoyne, W. Aus.).

KATHRYN FUNARI - Deep veined Pink. Large, formal double. Average growth. E. (U.S. 1975 - A. Funari, Santa Clara, CA).

KATHRYN HALL - Sweet pea Pink with Deeper Pink at the center. Medium to large, rose form double. (Sport of Japonica 'Berenice Boddy'). (U.S. 1969 - B. Hall, Jackson, MS).

KATHRYN JONES - White. Small, peony form with two rows of large, outer petals surrounding smaller petals, which surround one row of erect, large petals encircling stamens in center. Vigorous, compact growth. M. (U.S. 1955 - Longview).

KATHRYN LAND - Red with White anthers and Golden filaments. Large, semidouble with heavy petal texture. M. (U.S. 1998 - Hulyn Smith).

KATHRYN MARBURY - Blush. Medium, formal double. Average, upright growth. M-L. (U.S. 1964 - Marbury).

KATHRYN SNOW - Off-White edged Pink. Medium, semidouble with semi-upright center petals. Average growth. M-L. (U.S. 1965 - Marbury).

KATHRYN SPOONER - White. Large, full peony form without guard petals. Vigorous, spreading, upright growth. E-L. (U.S. 1994 - R. Gramling, Tallahassee, FL).

KATHY MANN - Deep Rose Pink. Medium, formal double. Average, upright growth. E-M. (U.S. 1960 - Julington).

KATHY PRATT - Light Pink fading to White on outer petals and blotched Deeper Pink. Large, semidouble to loose peony form. Vigorous, spreading growth. M. (U.S. 1968 - N. Pratt, Sacramento, CA).

KATHY SMYRE - Pink. Large, rose form double. Average, compact, upright growth. M. (U.S. 1969 - E. J. Prevatt, Bonneau, SC).

KATIE - Salmon Rose Pink. Very large, semidouble. Vigorous, compact, upright growth. E-M. (U.S. 1979 - Nuccio's).

KATIE GETZEN - Pink in bud, fading to White with Deep Pink on tips of petals. Medium, rose form double. M. (U.S. 1950 - Mealing).

KATIE KELLY - Pink center petals fading to White at edge. Miniature, formal double with spiral petals. Average, spreading growth. L. (U.S. 1983 - Miss K. Kelly, Graham, NC).

KATIE NORTHCUTT - Light Pink variegated White with Yellow anthers and Yellow filaments. Very large, semidouble to peony form. Vigorous, upright growth. E-M. (U.S. 2010 - Ed Northcutt, Tallahassee, FL).

KATIE VARIEGATED - Salmon Rose Pink evenly blotched White variation of 'Katie'. (U.S. 1985 - Nuccio's).

KATIE WOOTTON - White to Blush Pink. Very large, semidouble form; inner petals are crinkled, notched and folded. Vigorous, upright growth. E. (U.S. 2000 - H. Harms, Savannah, GA).

KATSUYA NOMURA - Pink with White trim with Golden anthers and White filaments. Small to medium, single to semidouble. Vigorous, upright growth with semi-weeping habit. E-M. (Seedling of Japonica 'Tama-no-ura'). (U.S. 2012 - Green Nurseries, Fairhope, AL).

KAY ACKER - Soft Blush Pink. Medium, formal double with long, pointed center petals of star formation. Average, spreading growth. M-L. (U.S. 1969 - Marbury).

KAY BERRIDGE - Mingled Red and White. Small, formal double. Average, upright growth. M. (U.S. 1979 - Gilley).

KAY BERRIDGE RED - Dark Red. Small, formal double. Slow, upright, dense growth. M. (Sport of Japonica 'Kay Berridge'). (U.S. 2013 - Howard and Mary Rhodes, Tallahassee, FL).

KAY TRUESDALE - Light Lavender Pink. Large, formal double to rose form double with wide, slightly veined petals. Vigorous, upright growth. E-M. (U.S. 1962 - E. V. Truesdale, West Columbia, SC).

KAYEL - Rose Pink with light serrations. Medium, formal double. (Sport of Japonica 'William Bull'). (Aus. 1970 - R. Loughlin, Hawthorndene, S. Aus.).

KEEPSAKE - Coral Rose. Medium, formal double. Average, compact, upright growth. M-L. (U.S. 1950 - Short).

KELLY GAYE - Bright Pink. Medium to large, formal double. Average, compact growth. M-L. (N.Z. 1985 - A. Webster, Te Puke).

KELLY'S RED - Bright Red. Small, semidouble. Sturdy, upright growth. M. (U.S. 1955 - W. Kelly, Pasadena, CA).

KEN BLANCHARD - Brilliant Red turning darker. Large, semidouble. Average, upright growth. M-L. (U.S. 1989 - J. K. Blanchard, Wallace, NC).

KENNY - ('Kenny Glen'). Deep Rose Pink blotched White. Large, semidouble to peony form. Slow, compact growth. L. (France 1908 - Guichard).

KENNY GLEN - See 'Kenny'.

KENNY HOWARD - Rose Pink. Small to medium, formal double with swirled or stacked petals. Vigorous, spreading growth. M. (U.S. 1994 - K. Howard, Auburn, AL).

KERLEREC - Cameo Pink. Medium, semidouble to anemone form. Average, compact growth. E-M. (U.S. 1949 - McIlhenny).

KERRYLAND - Pink. Large to very large, semidouble with curled and crinkled petals. Average, upright growth. M. (U.S. 1968 - Novick).

KERWIN - White. Large, semidouble with a few unusual petaloids in center. Vigorous, compact, upright growth. M. (U.S. 1960 - A. C. Thompson, Rosemead, CA).

KEVIN MURPHY - Faint Pink, darker at edges. Small, formal double. Average, upright growth. M. (U.S. 1982 - Mrs. M. Bozeman, Thunderbolt, GA).

KEWPIE DOLL - Chalky Light Pink. Miniature, anemone form with high petaloid center. Vigorous, bushy, upright growth. M. (U.S. 1971 - McCaskill).

KIANDRA - Cream White. Medium to large, semidouble to loose peony form. (Sport of Japonica 'Kosciusko'). (Aus. 1967 - J. R. Williams, Turramurra, NSW).

KICK OFF - Pale Pink marked Deep Pink. Large to very large, loose peony form. Vigorous, compact, upright growth. E-M. (For a variation of this cultivar see 'Touchdown'). (U.S. 1962 - Nuccio's).

KIFUKURIN BENIKARATO (YELLOW BORDERED RED ANEMONE) - Red. Miniature to small, anemone form flower with a tight, tufted center and five outer petals. Compact, upright growth with variegated Yellowish Green on mid-green leaves. M-L. (Sport of Japonica 'Benikarako'). (Replaces KIFUKURIN-BENTEN). (Japan 1859 - Kantô area).

KI-KARAKO - White with stamens tipped with Creamy petaloids. Medium, single. See Higo.

KIKU-TOJI - Deep Red blotched White. Small, formal double. Vigorous, bushy growth. E. (Japan 1895 - Yokohama).

KIKU-TOJI POINTED - Pointed petals. (Sport of Japonica 'Kiku-Toji').

KIKU-TOJI RED - Solid Red variation of 'Kiku-Toji'.

KILLARA - Pink. Medium, peony form. M. (Aus. 1962 - Linton).

KILVINTONIANA - See 'Gigantea'.

KIM MacGOWAN - White. Large, rose form double to formal double. Average, compact, upright growth. M. (U.S. 1980 - Mandarich).

KIMBERLEY - ('Crimson Cup'). Carmine with Red stamens. Medium, single of cupped form. Vigorous, compact, upright growth. M. (For another form of this cultivar, see 'Sylvia'). (England from Orient 1923).

KIMBERLEY JUNIOR - Dark Red. Miniature, full peony form. (U.S. 1958 - Hudson).

KIMBERLY PIET - Light Pink center petals and Dark Pink outer petals and rosebud center. Small to medium, formal double. Vigorous growth. M. (U.S. 1983 - Piet and Gaeta).

KIMI YAMAMOTO - Very Pale Pink. Medium, semidouble with broad, wavy edged petals. Average, compact, upright growth. M. (U.S. 1965 - McCaskill).

KING COTTON - White. Large, anemone form. Average, compact growth. E. (U.S. 1953 - Shackelford).

KING LEAR - ('Finlandia Rosea Variegated'; 'Ethel Weber'). Cherry Red marbled White. Medium, semidouble. (Variegated variation of 'Finlandia'). (Japan to 1939 - Rhodellia).

KING SIZE - ('Red Elephant'). Dark Red. Large, loose peony form. Vigorous, upright growth. M. (U.S. 1954 - Shackelford).

KING SIZE VARIEGATED - Dark Red blotched White variation of 'King Size'.

KING SOLOMON - Pink. Large, formal double. Vigorous, compact, upright growth. M. (U.S. 1966 - Shackelford).

KING'S CUP - White with a Maroon center with Yellow anthers and White filaments. Medium, semidouble. Vigorous, spreading, dense growth. M. (Japonica 'Tama Peacock' x Japonica 'San Dimas'). (U.S. 2019 - Bradford King, Arcadia, CA).

KING'S RANSOM - Pale Pink to Deeper Pink as flower ages. Medium, loose peony form with broad, wavy petals. Vigorous, compact, upright growth. M. (U.S. 1960 - Magnolia).

KING'S RUBY - Ruby Red. Large, loose peony form. Vigorous, upright growth. M. (U.S. 1964 - Armstrong).

KINGYO-TSUBAKI - See 'Pink Mermaid'

KIRSI - Light Red. Large, semidouble. Slow, compact growth. M-L. (Aus. 1969 - C. F. Walton, St. Ives, NSW).

KIRSTEN - Soft Pink becoming Paler at center of bloom. Large, formal double with pointed petals. M-L. (N.Z. 1997 - R. Young).

KIRSTI LEIGH - White. Large, loose peony form. Average, spreading, upright growth. E-M. (U.S. 2005 - Sally H. and Stephen A. Erickson, Kiln, MS).

KISHU-TSUKASA - ('Admiral Nimitz'; 'Captain John Sutter'; 'E. A. McIlhenny'). Deep Rose Pink and White. Medium, formal double. Vigorous, compact, upright growth. M-L. (Japan 1937 - Chugai).

KITTY - White with Pink border. Miniature to small, formal double. Bushy growth. L. (U.S. 1955 - Azalea Glen).

KITTY BAWDEN - White with Golden tipped anthers. Very large, anemone form to peony form. Slow, dense growth. E-M. (Aus. 1989 - K. Abbott, Rossmoyne, W. Aus.).

KITTY BERRY - Light Peach Pink. Medium, loose peony form. Average, compact, upright growth. M. (U.S. 1956 - Wheeler).

KITTY BERRY VARIEGATED - Light Peach Pink blotched White variation of 'Kitty Berry'.

KITTY ELLIS - White, splotched and marbled Deep Pink. Large, peony form. (Sport of Japonica 'Dr. Dan Ellis'). (U.S. 1972 - Mrs. D. W. Ellis, Charleston, SC).

KITTY'S FAVORITE VARIEGATED - Pink mottled White. Medium to large, formal double. Average, open, upright growth. L. (U.S. 1997 - Ackerman).

KIYOSU - See 'Daikagura'.

KNIGHT'S FERRY - Rose. Medium, semidouble with crinkly, heart-shaped petals. Vigorous, open growth. M-L. (U.S. 1951 - Riverbank).

KOBAI - Red. Medium to large, single with flared soft Pink stamens. See Higo.

KOKU-RYU (BLACK DRAGON) - ('Black Dragon'; 'Carol Compton'). Dark Red. Medium, semidouble with irregular petals to loose peony form with loose petals. Average, compact growth. M-L. (Japan to U.S. [Star] 1930).

KOLLOCK - See 'Woodville Red'.

KONA - White to unusual Greenish White. Medium to large, peony form. (Sport of Japonica 'Hawaii'). (For a variation of this cultivar see 'Maui'). (U.S. 1969 - Hamilton and Clark Nsy., Upland, CA).

KONA BENTEN - White sometimes tinged Green. Small to medium, anemone form with fimbriated petals. Slow growth. L. (N.Z. 1990 - Haydon).

KON-WABISUKE - Blackish Dark Red with Golden anthers and Pink filaments. Small, single cup shaped. M-L. (Japan 1937 - Hyôgo Prefecture).

KOREAN FIRE - Red. Small to medium, single. Compact growth with handsome foliage. E. Cold hardy. (Korea 1984 - Barry Yinger, Lewisberry, PA).

KOREAN SNOW - Pure White with Golden anthers and Yellow filaments. Medium, single. Upright, open growth. E. Cold hardy. (Seeds from NW South Korea - Barry Yinger, et al - before 1986). (U.S. - Camellia Forest, Chapel Hill, NC).

KOSCIUSKO - White. Medium to large, semidouble to loose peony form with upright center petals and intermixed stamens. Upright, compact growth. M. (For a variation of this cultivar see 'Kiandra'). (Aus. 1957 - Camellia Grove Nsy.).

KOSHI-NO-YOSO'OI (NIIGATA ADORNMENT) - Blush Orchid Pink. Small to medium, formal double with small, rounded, shallow notched petals arranged in tiered or star shape. Upright, sturdy growth. E-M. (Japan 1970 - Mitsuroku Makino, Fuchû Town, Niigata Prefecture).

KOSHO-NO-REIJIN - Dark Peach colored whorls on a Milk-White background with Yellow anthers and White filaments. Medium, rose form double. Strong, spreading growth. M. (Japan 1979 - Hideyo Katô, Niigata Prefecture).

KRAMER'S BEAUTY - Vibrant Red. Medium to large, full peony form. Vigorous, compact, upright growth. M. Fragrant. (U.S. 1980 - Kramer).

KRAMER'S DELIGHT - Rose Pink. Large, full peony form. Vigorous, compact, upright growth. M. Fragrant. (U.S. 1980 - Kramer).

KRAMER'S SUPREME - Turkey Red. Large to very large, full peony form. Vigorous, compact, upright growth. M. Fragrant. (For a variation of this cultivar see 'Cucamonga'). (U.S. 1957 - Kramer).

KRAMER'S SUPREME VARIEGATED - Turkey Red blotched White variation of 'Kramer's Supreme'. Fragrant.

KREENA - Brilliant Red. Large, single. (U.S. 1953 - Smythe Nsy., Ross, CA).

KRISTEN LYNN - White with Yellow anthers and White filaments. Large to very large, semidouble to loose peony form. Vigorous, upright, dense growth. M. (Seedling of Japonica 'Gus Menard). (U.S. 2019 – Jim Smelley, Moss Point, MS).

KRISTIN WOODROOF - Clear veined Pink. Large, semidouble with fluted, upright center petals. Average, compact growth. E-M. (U.S. 1964 - W. E. Woodroof, Sherman Oaks, CA).

KRISTY PIET - White with occasional Pink specks and streaks. Miniature, formal double. Vigorous, compact, upright growth. M. (U.S. 1986 - Piet and Gaeta).

KUBAL KAIN - Ruby Red. Medium to large, loose peony form. Average, compact growth. M. (U.S. 1965 - Shackelford).

KUBAL KAIN SUPREME - Variegated variation of 'Kubal Kain' - Ruby Red moiré White. (U.S. 1967 - Shackelford).

KUJAKU-TSUBAKI - Red mottled White. Small, single with slender, tubular petals. Average, semi-cascading growth. M-L. (Japan to U.S. 1977 - Nuccio's).

KUMAGAI - Dark Red. Large, single with flared White stamens which in most flowers are fully capped with Pink and White petaloids. See Higo.

KUMAGAI (NAGOYA) - Same as parent except reported that stamens in all flowers are fully capped with petaloids. (Sport of Japonica 'Kumagai').

KUMASAKA - ('Lady Marion'; 'Jeanne Kerr'; 'Maiden'; 'Sherbrooke'; 'Kumasaka-Beni'; 'Hollyhock'). Rose Pink. Medium, rose form double to peony form. Vigorous, compact growth. M-L. Cold hardy. (Japan 1896 - Tokyo Nsy.).

KUMASAKA VARIEGATED - ('Deacon Dodd'; 'Gay Boy'). Rose Pink blotched White variation of 'Kumasaka'.

KUMASAKA WHITE - White. (Sport of Japonica 'Kumasaka'). (U.S. 1959 - Hudson).

KUMASAKA-BENI - See 'Kumasaka'.

KUNI-NO-HIKARI - Rose Red. Medium, single with flared soft Pink stamens. See Higo.

KURO DELIGHT - Maroon Red. Medium to large, semidouble form. Average, spreading growth with unique foliage. M-L. Cold hardy to - 10°F. (U.S. 1999 - Ackerman).

KURO-TSUBAKI - Black Red with Red stamens. Small, semidouble. Average, compact growth. M-L. (Japan 1896 - Tokyo Nsy.).

KURRAJONG - Cream White. Medium, formal double with pointed petals. Vigorous growth. M-L. (Aus. 1959 - Waterhouse).

KUTE KATE - Bright Red. Small, formal double to peony form. Average, upright, open growth. E-M. (Japonica 'Edna Campbell' x unknown pollen parent). (U.S. 2009 - John L. Spencer, Lakeland, FL).

KYLE - Bright Red with Yellow anthers and Yellow filaments. Very large, semidouble. Average, upright growth. E-M. (U.S. 2013 - Howell).

KYLE VARIEGATED - Bright Red and White variegated form of 'Kyle'. (U.S. 2013 - Howell).

KYLE WHITE - White with Yellow anthers and White filaments. Medium, semidouble to rose form double; the edges of each petal have a notch in the center. Average, upright, open growth. M-L. (U.S. 2013 - Barbara Kyle, New Iberia, LA).

KYO-KANOKO - Red. Medium, semidouble to peony form. Average, bushy growth. M. (Japan to U.S. 1930 - Star).

KYO-KANOKO SURPRISE - Light Pink throat with tips of petals ringed with White. (Sport of Japonica 'Kyo-Kanoko'). (U.S. 1964 - J M Jones, Savannah, GA).

KYO-KANOKO VARIEGATED - ('Kyo-Ko'). Red and White variation of 'Kyo-Kanoko'.

KYO-KO - See 'Kyo-Kanoko Variegated'.

KYO-NISHIKI - (Brocade of Kyoto). White streaked and spotted Pink. Medium, single. See 'Higo'.

L. T. DEES - Red. Large, formal double. Average, upright growth. M-L. (U.S. 1983 - C. V. Bozeman, Hattiesburg, MS).

L. T. DEES VARIEGATED - Red blotched White variation of 'L T Dees'. (U.S. 1983 - C. V. Bozeman, Hattiesburg, MS).

L'AVENIRE - See 'Lallarook'. (L'Avenire is reported as priority name for this cultivar but as 'Lallarook' [France 1893 - Guichard] has been in such common use in the U.S. we do not believe a change is necessary or warranted). (Italy 1854 - Corsi, Florence).

LA BELLA - Rose splashed White. Medium, rose form double. (Sport of Japonica 'Bella Romana'). (U.S. 1945 - J. S. Tormey, Temple City, CA).

LA BELLE FRANCE - Pink edged White. Medium, semidouble. Average, compact growth. M-L. (U.S. 1983 - Feathers).

LA ESPERANZA - Red. Medium, formal double. Vigorous, open, upright growth. M-L. (U.S. 1959 - Miss E. Spears, Charleston, SC).

LA GRACIOLA - See 'Odoratissima'.

LA PEPPERMINT - White striped Carmine to pale Pink striped Carmine. Medium, rose form double. Bushy, upright growth. E-M. (For another form of this cultivar, see 'Brilliant [South]'.

LA SANDRA - Deep Rose variegated White. Medium to large, peony form. Average, upright growth. M. (U.S. 1979 - Gilley).

LA SORELLA - Red, White and Pink. Medium, rose form double. (U.S. 1945 - Malbis).

LACY PINK - See 'Hishi-Karaito'.

LADELL BROTHERS - Rose Pink. Medium, full peony form. (Sport of Japonica 'Alyne Brothers'). (U.S. 1965 - S L Brothers, Gainesville, FL).

LADINER'S RED - See 'Prince Eugene Napoleon'.

LADY ANN - White. Large, semidouble to peony form with fimbriated petals. M. (U.S. 1976 - M. Talia, Santa Clara, CA).

LADY BIRD - White splashed and streaked Rose Red. Large, full peony form. Vigorous, compact growth. M. (U.S. 1950 - H. C. Wilson, Fresno, CA).

LADY CHARLOTTE - Clear pale Pink. Medium, semidouble. Vigorous, compact, upright growth. M. (U.S. 1941 - Magnolia).

LADY CHARLOTTE VARIEGATED - Pale Pink and White form of 'Lady Charlotte'.

LADY CLARE - ('Empress'; 'Akashi-Gata'; 'Nellie Bly'). Deep Pink. Large, semidouble. Vigorous, bushy growth. E-M. Cold hardy. (Variations of this cultivar include 'Oniji'; 'Destiny'; 'Linda Laughlin'; 'Mrs. Leroy Epps'). (Japan to England 1887 - Caledonia).

LADY CLARE VARIEGATED - See 'Oniji'.

LADY DE SAUMAREZ - ('Pride of Rosebud Farm'; 'Tricolor [Siebold] Folki'; 'Eulalia Sally'; 'Pride of Portland'; 'India Kruger'). Bright Red spotted White. Medium, semidouble. (Variation of Japonica 'Tricolor [Siebold]'). (England 1920 - Caledonia).

LADY DE VERE - Shell Pink. Medium, semidouble. Loose, upright growth. M. (U.S. Early 1900's - Magnolia).

LADY EDINGER - White striped Pink. Medium, semidouble to peony form. M. (U.S. 1953 - Edinger).

LADY ERMA - Soft Pink. Medium, formal double to peony form with scalloped edged petals. E-M. (U.S. 1953 - M. Munger, Fresno, CA).

LADY ESTELLE PEEL - Dark Pink shaded to Pale Pink. Very large, semidouble with ruffled petals inter-mingled with petaloids and stamens. Average growth. M. (U.S. 1985 - V. E. Majette, Pensacola, FL).

LADY ETHEL HILL - Fuschia Pink. Large, single with petals having velvet sheen and standing slightly apart. Vigorous, spreading, upright growth. M. (U.S. 1962 - D. English, Jr., Dawson, GA).

LADY EVA - Light Pink flushing to Lighter Pink at edge. Large, semidouble to loose peony form. Vigorous, spreading, upright growth. M-L. (U.S. 1974 - Jernigan).

LADY EVA MAY - Hot Pink with bright Yellow anthers and bright Yellow filaments. Large, full peony. Average, upright and open growth. M. (U.S. 2015 - Thomas Sellers, Bolivia, NC).

LADY EVA MAY VARIEGATED - Red with White variegation with Yellow anthers and Yellow filaments. Very large, semidouble. Vigorous, upright, open growth. M-L (Virus variegated form of Japonica 'Lady Eva May') (U.S. 2016 - Thomas Sellers, Bolivia, NC).

LADY FAIR - Light Pink. Very large, semidouble with large, heavy, and some crepe petals. Average, upright growth. E-M. (U.S. 1965 - Mrs. C. T. Brown, Guyton, GA).

LADY FERNANDA - Pink with some shading. Medium, rose form double. Upright, dense growth. M. (U.S. 2006 - Magnolia).

LADY FRANCIS - See 'Souv. de Bahuaud Litou'.

LADY FRASER - Pale Pink striped Rose. Medium, peony form. Average, compact, upright growth. M-L. (U.S. 1981 - F. Ledbetter, St. Simons Island, GA).

LADY HELEN - See 'Helen Hunt'.

LADY HOPE - Light Pink flaked White. Medium, formal double. (Sport of Japonica 'Prince Frederick William'). (Aus. 1944 - Camellia Grove, Nsy.).

LADY HUME'S BLUSH - ('Buff'). White blushed Pink. Small, formal double. Slow, loose, spreading growth. E. (China to England 1806).

LADY IDA PEARL - White. Large, formal double. Vigorous, spreading dense growth. M-L. (U.S. 2013 - Thomas Sellers, Bolivia, NC).

LADY IN PINK - Bright Rose Pink. Large, semidouble with ruffled petals. Average, upright growth. E-M. (U.S. 1981 - Gilley).

LADY IN RED - Reddest Red. Very large, semidouble with waxy sheen on petals. Vigorous, compact, upright growth. M. (U.S. 1959 - McCaskill).

LADY IN RED VARIEGATED - Reddest Red and White variation of 'Lady in Red'.

LADY KAY - Red blotched White. Medium to large, loose to full peony form, sometimes fimbriated. (Sport of Japonica 'Ville de Nantes'). (U.S. 1949 - A. Cordoza, Palo Alto, CA).

LADY KAY RED - Solid Red form of 'Lady Kay'.

LADY LAURA - Pink variegated Rose. Medium to large, peony form to rose form double to formal double. Average, open, upright growth. M. (U.S. 1972 - T. E. Lundy, Pensacola, FL).

LADY LAURA RED - Red. (Sport of Japonica 'Lady Laura'). (U.S. 1983 - J. Ferry, Fort Walton Beach, FL).

LADY LOCH - ('Pink Lady'; 'Edward Billing'; 'Duchess of York'; 'Elizabeth Johnston'). Light Pink sometimes veined Deeper Pink and edged White. Medium, full peony form. (Sport of Japonica 'Aspasia Macarthur'). (For another variation of this cultivar see 'Can Can'). (Aus. 1898 - Cremorne Nsy., Melbourne).

LADY LUCILLE - White. Large, semidouble to full peony form. Average, bushy, upright growth. L. (U.S. 1949 - Madsen, Ocean Springs, MS).

LADY MACKINNON - ('Tricolor Folki', 'Pride of Portland', 'Pride of Rosebud Farm'; 'Eulalia Sally'; 'India Kruger;, 'Quartet Mottled'; 'Etienne de Bore'; 'Hopkins Variegated'). Rich Crimson blotched White with Golden anthers and White filaments. Medium, semidouble slightly cupped form. Vigorous, compact, upright growth. M. (Virus variegated form of Japonica 'Lady de Saumarez'). (Japan to England 1891 - Gerald Waller).

LADY MACON - Pink. Large, semidouble to peony form to anemone form. Average, compact growth. M-L. (U.S. 1960 - Wheeler).

LADY MACON VARIEGATED - Pink blotched White variation of 'Lady Macon'.

LADY MARION - See 'Kumasaka'.

LADY MARY CROMARTIE - ('La Reine I'). Deep Rose Pink. Large, semidouble to loose peony form. Vigorous, compact, upright growth. M-L. (Europe to U.S. [Magnolia] 1840's).

LADY MARY CROMARTIE VARIEGATED - ('La Reine Variegated I'; 'Forever Amber'). Deep Pink splotched White form of 'Lady Mary Cromartie'.

LADY McCAMLEY - Deep Pink with White margin on each petal. Medium, single with fluted petals. Vigorous, bushy growth. E. (Aus. 1995 - F. McCamley, Blakehurst, NSW).

LADY OF THE LAKE - White. Medium, semidouble with irregular, fluted petals. Vigorous, open, spreading growth. M. (U.S. Early 1900's. - Magnolia).

LADY OF THE LAKE (NEW ZEALAND) - See 'Francois Wiot'.

LADY PIELMEIER - Light Rose Pink. Medium, peony form. Vigorous, compact growth. M-L. (U.S. 1951 - Mrs. E. R. Pielmeier, San Marino, CA).

LADY SADIE - White. Medium, semidouble with fluted petals. Vigorous, compact, upright growth. M. (U.S. 1945 - Jenkins).

LADY ST. CLAIR - ('Pink Shell'). Light Pink. Medium, formal double with high center to semidouble. Vigorous, upright growth. M. (Aus. 1879 - S. Purchase, Parramatta).

LADY SUMEREZ - Red. Small, peony form of pom-pon type. Bushy growth. M. (U.S. 1953 - Lindo).

LADY SUSAN - Deep Rose Pink. Large, semidouble. Vigorous, compact, upright growth. M. (U.S. 1965 - Shady Acres Nsy., Charleston, SC).

LADY VANSITTART - ('Lady Vansittart Variegated'; 'Edonishiki'). White striped Rose Pink. Medium, semidouble with broad, wavy edged petals. Slow, bushy growth with holly-like foliage. M-L. Cold hardy. (Variations of this cultivar include 'Caroline Simpson'; 'Frances McLanahan'; 'Yours Truly'). (Japan to England 1887 - Caledonia).

LADY VANSITTART BLUSH - Pale Blush Pink. (Sport of Japonica 'Lady Vansittart'). (U.S. 1959 - H. B. Rehder, Wilmington, NC).

LADY VANSITTART PINK - See 'Lady Vansittart Red'.

LADY VANSITTART RED - ('Lady Vansittart Pink'). Deep Pink to Red. Cold hardy. (Sport of Japonica 'Lady Vansittart'). (England 1887 - Caledonia).

LADY VANSITTART SHELL - See 'Yours Truly'.

LADY VANSITTART VARIEGATED - See 'Lady Vansittart'.

LADY VELMA - Deep Rose Pink. Large, semidouble with irregular petals to loose peony form with upright and folded petals. Vigorous, compact growth. M. (U.S. 1962 - D. W. Davis).

LADY VELMA VARIEGATED - Deep Rose Pink blotched White variation of 'Lady Velma'.

LADY WINNEKE - Red. Small, peony form. Open, upright growth. E-M. (Aus. 1981 - L. Hobbs, Doncaster East, Vic.).

LAFCADIO HEARN - Red veined Purple Red with White stamens. Medium, rose form double with irregular groups of inner petals interspersed with stamens. (U.S. 1946 - McIlhenny).

LAFE ALEWINE - Deep Pink. Large, formal double with waxy petals. Average growth. E-M. (U.S. 1962 - A. L. Alewine, Waycross, GA).

LALLAROOK - ('Laurel Leaf'; 'L'Avenire'). Pink marbled White. Medium to large, formal double, sometimes with incurved petal edges. Slow, compact growth with foliage resembling that of a laurel. M-L. (France from Italy 1893 - Guichard).

LAMAR WILKES - Dark Rose Pink. Large, peony form. Average, upright growth. M. (U.S. 1985 - Mrs. H. Johnson, Madison, FL).

LAMONT GLASS - White. Large, semidouble. Average growth. M. (U.S. 1962 - H. W. Steindorff, Greenville, AL).

LANDON WATERS - White with flecks and spots of Red. Medium, formal double. Upright, average growth. (U.S. 2006 - Don Bergamini, Martinez, CA).

LANDRETHII - Rose Pink. Small, formal double. Vigorous, bushy growth. M. (U.S. 1832 - D. Landreth, Philadelphia, PA).

LANDSCAPE BEAUTY - Light Pink. Large, semidouble. Vigorous, narrow, upright growth. M. (U.S. 1958 - Shackelford).

LANE MOSS HAGAAD - Coral with White blotches. Large, peony form. Average, upright, dense growth. M. (U.S. 2006 - no further information available).

LASANDRA - Deep Rose variegated White with Bright Yellow anthers and light filaments. Large, peony form. Average, upright, average growth. M. (Japonica 'Tiffany' seedling). (U.S. 1980 - Gilley).

LASSIE - Light Red. Large, anemone form. Vigorous, upright growth. E-M. (U.S. 1977 - Gilley).

LATE WHITE EMPRESS - See 'Overlook White'.

LATIFOLIA - Soft Rose Red. Medium, semidouble. Vigorous, bushy growth. M. (Belgium 1884).

LATIFOLIA VARIEGATED - ('Fanny Bolis'). Soft Rose Red blotched White form of 'Latifolia'.

LAURA CAMP - Pink. Large to very large, semidouble with stamens among central petaloids. Average, compact, upright growth. E-M. (U.S. 1954 - Shackelford).

LAURA CLAIRE - Soft Pink, fading to Cream in center; center petals sometimes incurved, of a Deep Lavender Pink. Small to medium, formal double. Average, open and upright growth. M. (U.S. 2005 - Gordy).

LAURA COOPER - Pale Pink striped Deeper Pink. Medium, formal double. Average, dense, upright growth. M. (U.S. 1993 - W. Stout, Pensacola, FL).

LAURA DASHER - See 'Rosea Superba'.

LAURA E. GREGGS - Light Pink striped Deeper Pink. Large, formal double. Average, upright growth. E-M. (U.S. 1980 - Gilley).

LAURA GORDY - Soft Pink with Gold anthers and Cream filaments. Medium, semidouble to rose form double. Average, spreading growth. M. (U.S. 2013 - Gordy).

LAURA LINKER - White with Yellow anthers and Yellow filaments. Medium, loose peony. Average, upright, open growth. M-L. (U.S. 2017 - Thomas Sellers, Bolivia, NC).

LAURA LOVELY - Pink. Large, peony form with high center. (U.S. 1959 - Feathers).

LAURA NEILL - Rose Red to Red. Very large, semidouble. Vigorous, open, upright growth. E-M. (U.S. 1979 - D. V. Neill, Gulfport, MS).

LAURA SCHAFER - ('White Angel'). White. Large, semidouble of chalice form. Slow, compact growth. M-L. (U.S. 1954 - Mrs. L. Schafer, W. Aus.).

LAURA STOKES - Deep Red with Purplish cast and White flecks. Medium, peony form. Average, upright growth. M. (U.S. 1999 - Richard A. Stokes, Minneola, FL).

LAURA WALKER - Bright Red. Large, semidouble to anemone form. Vigorous, compact, upright growth. E-M. (U.S. 1956 - Mrs. L. Walker, Marshallville, GA).

LAURA WALKER VARIEGATED - Bright Red marked White variation of 'Laura Walker'.

LAURA'S BEAUTY - Red and White striped. Medium to large, semidouble to peony form. Average, upright, open growth. E-L. (U.S. 2011 - N. C. Barnard, St. Elmo, AL).

LAUREL LEAF - See 'Lallarook'.

LAUREN HALL - Tiffany Pink. Medium, formal double. Average, upright growth. M-L. (U.S. 1996 - Marion Hall, Dothan, AL).

LAUREN TUDOR - Pink with small Red flecks. Very large, peony form. Vigorous, upright growth. E-M. (U.S. 1999 - Hulyn Smith).

LAUREN TUDOR PINK - Solid Pink with Gold anthers and Gold filaments. Very large, peony form. Vigorous, upright growth. E-M. (Sport of Japonica 'Lauren Tudor'). (U.S. 2004 - Hulyn Smith).

LAUREN TUDOR VARIEGATED - Pink with small Red flecks and White variegation. Very large, peony form. Vigorous, upright growth. E-M. (U.S. 2007 - Buck and Tyler Mizzell, Santee, SC).

LAURENTINE NOLAN - White. Large, full peony form to anemone form to rose form double. Average, upright growth. E-M. (U.S. 1976 - J. W. Nolan, Waveland, MS).

LAURIE - Rose Pink. Small, formal double. Average, dense, upright growth. M. (U.S. 1998 - C. Elliott, Swainsboro, GA).

LAURIE BRAY - Soft Pink. Medium to large, semidouble with spaced and ruffled petals. Upright growth. M. (Aus. 1955 - Linton).

LAVADA BAILEY - Deep Pink. Large to very large, peony form. Average, upright growth. M. (U.S. 1977 - H. Bailey, Plant City, FL).

LAVENDEL - Purple. (Sport of Japonica 'Comtesse Woronzoff'). (Aus. 1962).

LAVERNE NORRIS - Pink variegated White. Medium to large, semidouble. Average, dense, spreading, upright growth. M-L. (U.S. 1998 - Jernigan).

LAVERNE RAGLAND - Brilliant Red. Medium, formal double. Average, compact, upright growth. M. (U.S. 1968 - Ragland).

LAVINIA LANE ROUNTREE - White. Large, loose peony form. Average, spreading growth. E-L. (U.S. 1997 - J. Peacock, Twin City, GA).

LAWRENCE HAINES - Dark Red. Medium, full peony form. Vigorous, upright growth. M. (U.S. 1943 - Gerbing).

LAWRENCE WALKER - Red. Medium to large, loose peony form to anemone form. Vigorous, compact, upright growth. M-L. (U.S. 1946 - Tea Gardens).

LAWRENCE WALKER VARIEGATED - Red spotted White form of 'Lawrence Walker'.

LAWSON BONNER - Deep Pink. Large, semidouble. Vigorous, upright growth. M. (U.S. 1963 - J. F. Brown, Jr., Macon, GA).

LAZETTA - Brick Red. Large, anemone form. Compact, upright growth. M-L. (U.S. 1951 - Riverbank).

LE LYS - White. Small, loose peony form. (France, Botanical Gdn., Nantes to U.S. 1971 - U.S. Dept. of Agriculture, Glenn Dale, MD).

LEADING LADY - Salmon Pink. Medium to large, semidouble with elongated petals. Average, compact growth. M-L. (U.S. 1955 - Short).

LEADING LADY VARIEGATED - Salmon Pink and White variation of 'Leading Lady.'

LEAH BAGGS - Light Pink, veined Dark Pink and edged White. Large, semidouble to peony form to rose form double. Average growth. E-M. (U.S. 1986 - L. D. Baggs, Sr., Macon, GA).

LEAH HOMEYER - Rose Pink. Large, loose peony form. Vigorous, spreading, upright growth. M. (U.S. 1974 - Homeyer).

LEANNAH LOUISE - White with Pink stripes with Yellow anthers and White filaments. Medium, single to semidouble. Slow, open growth. M-L. (U.S. 2013 - Lyman F. Holland, Jr., Mobile, AL).

LEANNE'S TOMORROW - See 'Tomorrow, Leanne's'.

LEANORA P. MARSCHER - Light Pink. Large, peony form. Average, upright growth. M. (U.S. 1965 - J. F. Marscher, Beaufort, SC).

LEDA - White dotted and striped Pink. Large, anemone form with wide, numerous petals. (Belgium from Italy 1848 - Alexandre Verschaffelt).

LEDA ALBA - White. Medium to large, formal double - imbricated. (Sport of Japonica 'Leda'). (Belgium from Italy 1848 - Alexandre Verschaffelt).

LEDA ROSEA - Pink. (Sport of Japonica 'Leda'). (Aus. 1963 - Hazelwood).

LEE BABY - Light Pink, deeper in center. Medium, rose form double. Average, upright growth. M-L. (U.S. 1975 - Mealing).

LEE EAGLESON - Clear bright Pink. Medium, semidouble. Average, upright growth. M. (U.S. 1973 - T. Eagleson, Port Arthur, TX).

LEE POE - Pink fading to Lighter Pink in center. Large, anemone form. Average growth. M. (U.S. 1980 - L. P. Hairston, Birmingham, AL).

LEE RYAN - Delicate Pink. Medium, formal double. Vigorous, upright growth. M. (U.S. 1974 - O. L. Ryan, Greenville, AL).

LEE WELLS - Rose Red. Medium, semidouble with two or more rows of petals, inner petals curved and twisted and mass of Golden stamens. Average, spreading growth. E-M. (U.S. 1961 - Wells).

LEE WILKES - Red. Large, single of bell shape. Vigorous, upright growth. E-M. (U.S. 1979 - Mrs. H. Johnson, Madison, FL).

LEE WILKINS - Red variegated White with Yellow anthers and White filaments. Large, semidouble. Average, spreading, dense growth. M. (U.S. 2013 - Howell).

LEIGH - Blush marked Deeper Pink. Medium, formal double. Average, upright growth. M-L. (U.S. 1987 - J. Aldrich, Brooklet, GA).

LEILA BELL - Light Pink to Darker Pink at edge. Large, semidouble. Vigorous, upright growth. E-M. (U.S. 1982 - J. Lynch, Franklington, LA).

LEILA GIBSON - White. Large, peony form. Vigorous growth. M. (U.S. 1983 - L. M. Gibson, Madison, FL).

LELA ASHLEY - Light Pink with one or two Dark Pink stripes. Miniature, formal double cup form. Slow, dense, upright growth. E-M. Cold hardy. (U.S. 1999 - Elizabeth R. Scott, Aiken, SC).

LELA LAURENTS - Dark Red. Miniature, formal double. Vigorous, open, upright growth. E. (U.S. 1973 - T. Eagleson, Port Arthur, TX).

LELIA MARYOTT - Rose Pink to shell Pink. Large, peony to rose form double. Average, upright growth. M-L. Cold hardy. (U.S. 1999 - Dr. Arthur A. Maryott, Gatherburg, MD).

LELLAH CALLISON - White. Large to very large, semidouble with wavy, crinkled petals to full peony form. Vigorous, spreading, open growth. M-L. (U.S. 1963 - J. J. Callison, Portland, OR).

LEMON DROP - White with Lemon center. Miniature, anemone form to rose form double to formal double. Average, dense, upright growth. M. (U.S. 1981 - Nuccio's).

LEMON GLOW - Creamy Yellow. Small to medium, formal double. Slow, upright, compact growth. M. (Sport of Japonica 'Dahlohnega'). (U.S. 2009 - Cam Too Camellia Nursery, Greensboro, NC).

LEMON HONEY - Lemon Yellow against Cream White. Medium, formal double. Average, upright growth. M. (N.Z. 1972 - D. G. O'Toole, Ohope).

LEN HOBBS - Vivid Red. Medium to large, single with notched, fimbriated, and curled petals. Average, open growth. E-L. (Aus. 1994 - L. Hobbs, Doncaster East, Vic.).

LEN JACOBS - Pale Pink to Darker Pink at edge. Large, peony form. Compact, upright growth. M-L. (Aus. 1985 - L. Jacobs, Wattle Park, S. Aus.).

LEN'S GIFT - Light Pink. Large, informal double. Fast, upright growth. E-M. (Aus. 2006 - Len Hobbs, Vic.).

LENA JACKSON - Blush Pink. Medium, rose form double to semidouble. Average, bushy growth. M. (U.S. 1949 - Ingleside Nsy., Baconton, GA).

LENA-BETH - Deep Pink with Orange cast. Large, peony form. M. (U.S. 1957 - Mrs. L. McDaniel, McComb, MS).

LENORA TAYLOR - Pink striped Red. Small, peony form. Average, compact, upright growth. E-M. (U.S. 1974 - H. V. Taylor, Lecompte, LA).

LEON BENSON - Pink. Large, anemone form to peony form with rosettes surrounding center petals. Vigorous, compact, upright growth. M. (U.S. 1978 - Tammia).

LEONA RISH - Pale Pink. Medium, peony form. Average, upright growth. E-M. (U.S. 1998 - W. Rish, Winnsboro, SC).

LEONA WILLSEY - White. Large, semidouble with scallop petals. Average, open growth. E-M. (U.S. 1966 - S. A. Willsey, Lockhart, FL).

LEONE SUMMERSON - White. Large to very large, anemone form. Average, spreading growth. M. (U.S. 1995 - Piet and Gaeta).

LEONIE COWAN - Coral Pink shading to almost White in center. Large, semidouble. Average, open, upright growth. M. (N.Z. 1973 - Mrs. I. Berg, Whakatane).

LEONORA NOVICK - White. Large to very large, loose peony form. Average, upright growth. E-M. (U.S. 1968 - Novick).

LEONORA WEIL - Deep Pink with Blush in throat and Rose stripes. Medium, semidouble to rose form double. (Sport of Japonica 'Mrs. Baldwin Wood'). (U.S. 1960 - N. Weil, Jr., Jacksonville, FL).

LERLIND - White. Medium, rose form double to formal double. Average growth. E-L. (U.S. 1974 - Stone).

LES MARBURY - Pink and White striped Red. Small, formal double. Vigorous, dense, upright growth. M. (U.S. 1991 - Habel).

LES MARBURY BLUSH - Blush Pink bleeding out to a White border. Small, formal double. Vigorous, dense, upright growth. M. (Sport of Japonica 'Les Marbury'). (U.S. 2013 - Bob Black, Windsor, VA).

LES MARBURY RED - Red. Small, formal double. (Sport of Japonica 'Les Marbury'). (U.S. 1997 - Habel).

LES RICHARD - Deep Cardinal Red. Large, cup-shaped semidouble of tiered form. Compact, upright growth. M. (U.S. 1965 - Witman).

LESLIE HOWARD - Pink mottled White. Medium, semidouble. Vigorous, bushy growth. M. (U.S. Mid-1900's - Mrs. J. S. Howard, Salembury, NC).

LESLIE R. - Light Pink. Large, semidouble to anemone form with large petals. E-M. (U.S. 1959 - L. Richards, Mobile, AL).

LESLIE WILKES - Rose. Large, semidouble. Average growth. E-M. (U.S. 1977 - Mrs. H. Johnson, Madison, FL).

LES-TAY-HOME - White and Red. Miniature, full peony form. Average, upright growth. E-M. (U.S. 1961 - Dr. J. L. Taylor, Theodore, AL).

LETITIA SCHRADER - Dark Red. Medium to large, medallion shaped peony to anemone form with small center petals graduating to long, guard petals. Average, compact growth. M. (U.S. 1948 - Rosa).

LETITIA SCHRADER VARIEGATED - Dark Red shaded White form of 'Letitia Schrader'.

LETTIE MARINDA - Deep Rose veined Deeper Rose. Large, full peony form. Average, compact growth. E. (U.S. 1957 - Burgess).

LEUCANTHA - ('Wakanoura White'; 'Tricolor [Siebold] White'; 'Shiro-Wakanoura'; 'Wakanoura-Shiro'). White variation of 'Tricolor [Siebold]'. Cold hardy. (Not cultivar listed in old literature, which was a Deep Crimson spotted White). (U.S. 1937 - McIlhenny).

LEVERTON'S - Scarlet mottled White. Large, semidouble to peony form. (Sport of Japonica 'Odoratissima'). (Aus. 1953 - Camellia Grove).

LEVIATHAN - ('Maranui'; 'Maranui Pink'). Scarlet. Large, peony form. Vigorous growth. (Aus. 1862 - Shepherd).

LEWELLYN - Red tipped Carmine. Medium, semidouble with loose petals to rose form double. (U.S. 1937 - Domoto).

LEWELLYN VARIEGATED - See 'Sweeti Vera'.

LEWIS RED PEONY - See 'Vedrine'.

LIB SCOTT - Pale Pink with different size Red stripes. Large to very large, semidouble to peony form. Average, dense, spreading growth. E. Cold hardy. (U.S. 1998 - Elizabeth R. Scott, Aiken, SC).

LIBERTY - Coral Pink. Medium, semidouble to loose peony form. Compact growth. M. (U.S. 1959 - Gerbing).

LIBERTY BELL - White. Medium, peony form. Vigorous, semi-upright growth. E-L. (U.S. 1940 - Overlook).

LIBERTY VARIEGATED - ('Rangerette'). Coral Pink blotched White variation of 'Liberty'.

LIDDY JENKINS - Deep Rose. Large, rose form double with spoon-like overlapping petals. Average, compact growth. M. (U.S. 1973 - Witman).

LIEUTENANT BENNIE FOLSOM - Rose Pink. Large, semidouble with crinkled petals and three very large petaloids. Average, open, upright growth. M. (U.S. 1962 - J. B. Folsom, Sumter, SC).

LIEUTENANT VICTOR JOHNSON - Bright Red. Medium, formal double. (U.S. 1955 - Riverbank).

LIEUTENANT WILLIAM HEARN - Strawberry Red shaded lighter in center. Large, semidouble to peony form. Average, open, upright growth. M-L. (U.S. 1951 - Hearn).

LIKE SARGENT - Deep Red. Large, full peony form. Average, spreading, open growth. M. (U.S. 2013 - Howell).

LIL RED DEVIL - Red. Small, single. (U.S. 1953 - Fruitland).

LIL SCHAEFER - Pale Blush with Rose to Carmine stripes. Medium, formal double to rose form double. Average, open, spreading growth. M. (U.S. 1979 - Stone).

LIL STELLA - Rosy Red. Medium, semidouble with wavy, crinkled outer petals. Average, upright growth. M. (U.S. 1976 - Stone).

LIL SYMONDS - Deep Red. Large, semidouble to rose form double; petals fimbriated. Average, dense, upright growth. M-L. Cold hardy. (U.S. 2001 - Elizabeth R. Scott, Aiken, SC).

LIL TIFF - Light Pink with White to Light Pink petaloids. Miniature, anemone form. Average spreading, open growth. M-L. (U.S. 1978 - P. A. Menard, Slidell, LA).

LILA FRETWELL - Deep Pink shading to White in center. Medium, semidouble. Average growth. E-M. (U.S. 1965 - Mrs. R. F. Brownlee, Anderson, SC).

LILA LEE - Snow White. Medium, peony form. Vigorous, compact, upright growth. E-M. (Plant Patent No. 891). (U.S. 1947 - Armstrong).

LILA MOORE - Red. Medium, semidouble with loose petals to peony form. (U.S. 1955 - J M Moore, Charleston, SC).

LILA ROSA - Clear Pink. Medium, peony form. Vigorous, compact growth. E-L. (U.S. 1948 - Rosa).

LILA S. ROBERTS - Light Pink with Darker Pink stripes and flecks with Yellow anthers and White filaments. Medium, rose form double to formal double. Average, upright and dense growth. M. (U.S. 2014 - Lawrence and Lila Roberts, Tallahassee, FL).

LILEMAC - White. Miniature, formal double. Average growth. L. (U.S. 1976 - A. B. McIver, Jr., Shreveport, LA).

LILIAN BURGESS - White striped and splashed Deep Pink. Medium, peony form. Vigorous, open, upright growth. (Aus. 1965 - Mrs. P L Waring, Brisbane).

LILIANE WELLS - White, sometimes with Blush throat and Pink stripes. Very large, anemone form. Average, spreading, upright growth. E-M. (U.S. 1963 - H. Wilson, Fresno, CA).

LILLA FLETCHER INMAN - White to Blush with several petals striped Pink. Large, rose form double to anemone form. Average, upright growth. E-M. (U.S. 1967 - Mrs. C. Inman, Quincy, FL).

LILLI BREWSTER - White. Large, anemone form. Slow, open, low spreading growth. L. (U.S. 1954 - Mrs. L. Marioneux, Shreveport, LA).

LILLIAN GORDY - Brilliant Pink with Yellow anthers and White filaments. Very large, full peony to anemone. Vigorous, upright, dense growth. E-M. (U.S. 2016 - Gordy).

LILLIAN JERNIGAN - White splotched and striped Pink and Red with Yellow anthers and Cream filaments. Large, semidouble. Average, upright, spreading, dense growth. E. (U.S. 1986 - Ed Jernigan, Greenville, AL).

LILLIAN MANN - Dark Red. Large, loose to full peony form. Average, compact, upright growth. M. (U.S. 1964 - W. H. Veo, Orlando, FL).

LILLIAN'S CHERRY PIE - Very Dark Red with Golden anthers and White filaments. Medium, loose peony to semidouble; the bloom is very shiny like cherry pie. Average, upright, dense growth. M. (U.S. 2016 - Gordy).

LILLIAN'S SHINING STAR - Light Clear Pink with Yellow anthers and White filaments. Large, loose peony to full peony; bloom is star shaped with petaloids present in full peony form. Vigorous, upright growth. E-M. (Seedling of Japonica 'Whoopee'). (U.S. 2019 - Gordy).

LILLIE G. MEALING - Rose Pink with darker veins. Large, loose to full peony form. Average, open growth. M. (U.S. 1969 - Mealing).

LILLIE ROBINSON - Blush Pink. Medium, anemone form to full peony form. Average, compact growth. M. (U.S. 1957 - Julington).

LILLIE S. ADAMS - Rose Pink to Light Rose Pink. Medium to large, semidouble to peony form with loose, undulating petals and occasional, intermixed stamens. Vigorous, compact, upright growth. M. (U.S. 1964 - N. J. Adams, Albany, GA).

LILLY RAMSEY - Deep Red. Medium to large, anemone form. Upright growth. M. (U.S. 1949 - T. R. Ramsey, Bainbridge, GA).

LILLYE ROSEMAN - Soft Pink washed White with White center bud. Small, formal double. Slow, open growth. E-L. (U.S. 1989 - Stone).

LILY BARRON SLAY - Rose Red. Medium, rose form double. E-M. (U.S. 1960 - Tammia).

LILY GRACE - Soft Pink with Yellow anthers and Cream filaments. Small, anemone form. Average, upright growth. M. (U.S. 2012 - Gordy).

LILY LANGTRY - White streaked Pink. Medium, full peony form. Vigorous, upright growth. M. (U.S. Early 1900's - Magnolia).

LILY PONS - White. Medium, single to semidouble with very long, narrow, delicate, trough-like petals surrounding a cluster of long stamens that have a Pale Greenish cast at base. Average growth. M. (U.S. 1955 - Goletto).

LILY SCHLAUDECKER - Pink. Large, semidouble to peony form. Vigorous, bushy growth. M. (U.S. 1975 - Mrs. L. Schlaudecker, Amite, LA).

LINDA ABBOTT - Blush Pink variegated Pink, Red and White. Large, loose peony form with numerous center petaloids. Vigorous, upright growth. E-M. (U.S. 1961 - E. Abbott, Monticello, FL).

LINDA B. BROWNE - Light and Medium Pink with Yellow anthers and Cream filaments. Large, semidouble to loose peony form. Average, upright, dense growth. E-L. (Seedling of Japonica 'Lady Macon'). (U.S. 2018 - Pat Johnson, Cairo, GA).

LINDA BROTHERS - Shell Pink. Medium, full peony form. (Sport of Japonica 'Alyne Brothers'). (U.S. 1965 - S L Brothers, Gainesville, FL).

LINDA BROTHERS BLUSH - Shell Pink bordered White with occasional Rose Pink petals. (Sport of Japonica 'Linda Brothers'). (U.S. 1984 - J. Terry, Fort Walton Beach, FL).

LINDA BRUCE - White. Large, peony form. Open, upright growth. M. (Aus. 1983 - Mrs. J. S. Drake, Warrawee, NSW).

LINDA HENSON - White with few Pink streaks. Medium to large, formal double. Vigorous, open, upright growth. E-M. (U.S. 1973 - T. Eagleson, Port Arthur, TX).

LINDA LAUGHLIN - Pale Pink flecked Rose. Large, semidouble. (Sport of Japonica 'Lady Clare'). (U.S. 1958 - Mrs. W. Laughlin, Aiken, SC).

LINDA LEARY - Pink veined. Medium to large, semidouble. Vigorous, upright growth. (U.S. 1975 - Haynie).

LINDA MARGARET - Bright Pink. Medium, formal double. Vigorous, spreading growth. E. (U.S. 1957 - Wilson).

LINDA MARIE ROGERS - Chalk White with occasional Red or Pink stripe and short, Pale, Yellow stamens. Medium, semidouble. Compact, upright growth. M-L. (U.S. 1957 - F. Griffin, Sr., Columbia, SC).

LINDA MARIE ROGERS PINK - Pink. Sport of Japonica 'Linda Marie Rogers').

LINDA MARIE ROGERS RED - Red. (Sport of Japonica 'Linda Marie Rogers').

LINDA ROBERTS - Watermelon Pink to Strawberry Red. Medium, loose semidouble to peony form with small rosettes over entire flower. Slow, open growth. M. (U.S. 1951 - W. W. Osborn, Savannah, GA).

LINDA ROBERTS VARIEGATED - Red and White variation of 'Linda Roberts'.

LINDA RUTH DAVIS - White with occasional Rose stripe. Large, semidouble with twisted petals interspersed with Golden stamens and petaloids. (U.S. 1956 - R. Davis, Mobile, AL).

LINDA'S BLUSH - Light Blush Pink. Medium, semidouble. M. (U.S. 1960 - Poole's Nsy., Lecompte, LA).

LINDEN HILL - Pale Pink with some Red stripes. Small, formal double with pointed petals. Average, dense, upright growth. L. (U.S. 1997 - H. Hill, Arlington, VA).

LINDSAY NEILL - Dark Red marbled White. Medium to large, semidouble to loose peony form with twisted petals. Average, compact growth. M. (England to U.S. [Columbus, GA] 1840).

LINDSEY - Bright Pink with numerous Darker Pink stripes and flecks. Medium, formal double. Vigorous, upright growth. E-M. (Seedling of 'Marie Bracey'). (U.S. 2008 - CamelliaShop, Savannah, GA).

LIPSTICK - Dark Red with White petaloids bordered Red. Miniature, anemone form. Average, compact, upright growth. M. (U.S. 1981 - Nuccio's).

LISA ADAMS - Rose Red. Large, semidouble. Average, compact, upright growth. M-L. (U.S. 1966 - B. F. Marshall, Mobile, AL).

LISA ADELE SHUMAN - Shaded Rose Pink. Medium, formal double. Spreading growth. M-L. (U.S. 1988 - J. Aldrich, Brooklet, GA).

LISA BUONO - Blush with Pink center shading to Light Pink with Dark Pink edge. Small, semidouble to anemone form to formal double. Average, upright growth. E-M. (U.S. 1973 - Tammia).

LISA BURTON - White with Yellow anthers and White filaments. Medium, semidouble to rose form double. Average, upright, open growth. M-L. Chance seedling (Japonica). (U.S. 2016 - Pat Johnson, Cairo, GA).

LISA CASHION - Rose Pink. Small, formal double. Average, compact, upright growth. L. (U.S. 1974 - W. R. Cashion, Florence, SC).

LISA MAIBACH - White to Pink in last two rows of petals. Medium, formal double. Average, upright growth. E-L. (U.S. 1968 - E. Wile, Shreveport, LA).

LISA RHODY - Dark Pink. Large, rose form double. Average, upright growth. E-M. (U.S. 1989 - Tammia).

LITTLE 'UN - Rose. Miniature, semidouble. Slow, compact growth. L. (U.S. 1959 - Wylam).

LITTLE AGGIE - Strong to Light Purplish Pink. Miniature to small, single with all stamens being uniform petaloids. Slow, spreading to weeping growth. M-L. (U.S. 1976 - M. E. Rowell, Fresno, CA).

LITTLE BABE - Dark Red. Small, rose form double to formal double. Vigorous, compact growth. E-L. (U.S. 1974 - W. M. Harrison, Pensacola, FL).

LITTLE BABE VARIEGATED - Red and White blotched variation of 'Little Babe'.

LITTLE BIT - Red flecked White to solid Red. Small, peony form. Average, upright growth. M. (U.S. 1958 - Camelliana).

LITTLE BO PEEP - Pale Pink. Miniature to small, formal double. Vigorous, open, upright growth. M. (U.S. 1981 - Nuccio's).

LITTLE BRAD - White. Small, semidouble. Average, spreading, upright growth. M. (For a variation of this cultivar see 'Bronwyn James'). (U.S. 1963 - Dr. L. E. Chow, Bakersfield, CA).

LITTLE CHEEPER - Rose Pink. Small, formal double. Average, open growth. M. (U.S. 1975 - Haynie).

LITTLE CUTIE - Light Pink. Medium, formal double. Vigorous, compact, upright growth. M-L. (U.S. 1981 - Alfter).

LITTLE DAVID - Rose Red spotted White. Miniature, formal double. Open growth. M. (U.S. 1958).

LITTLE DIXIE - Shell Pink. Miniature, formal double. Bushy growth. E-M. (U.S. 1976 - Haynie).

LITTLE GINGER - Pink at edge fading to White in center. Small, formal double. Average, upright growth. L. (U.S. 1977 - Habel).

LITTLE GLEN - Soft Pink, veined on outer edges, Creamy center. Miniature, peony form. Compact, upright growth. M. (N.Z. 1980 - A. Gamlin, Manaia).

LITTLE HOOPER - White. Small, anemone form. Average, upright growth. E. (U.S. 1993 - I. Mitchell, Melrose, FL).

LITTLE JON - Red. Large, semidouble. Average growth. E-M. (U.S. 1960 - J. C. Campbell, Natchez, MS).

LITTLE JOY - Rose Pink. Medium, anemone form. Average, spreading, upright growth. M-L. (Aus. 1992 - D. Haviland, Asquith, NSW).

LITTLE KATIE - Red with Yellow anthers and White filaments. Small to medium, semidouble. Average, spreading, dense growth. E-M. (Japonica 'Tama-no-ura' x Japonica 'San Dimas'). (U.S. 2019 - Bradford King, Arcadia, CA).

LITTLE LADY - White. Medium, formal double. Average, upright growth. M. (U.S. 1964 - S. M. Mixson, Gainesville, FL).

LITTLE LIZ - White with Yellow anthers and Cream filaments. Small, semidouble. Average, spreading, open growth. M. (Japonica 'Elizabeth Boardman' seedling). (U.S. 2000 - Louise Hairston, Birmingham, AL).

LITTLE MAN - White, shading to Pink. Small, formal double to rose form double. Vigorous, upright growth. M. (U.S. 1953 - Shackelford).

LITTLE MASTERPIECE - White. Small, formal double to rose form double. Vigorous, upright growth. E-L. (U.S. 1987 - E. F. Achterberg, Citrus Heights, CA).

LITTLE MICHAEL - Soft Pink with Creamy White petaloids. Miniature to small, anemone form. Average, compact, upright growth. M. (U.S. 1981 - F. Moore, West Covina, CA).

LITTLE POPPY - Soft Pink with center of Creamy petaloids. Miniature, anemone form. Vigorous, bushy, upright growth. M. (U.S. 1973 - McCaskill).

LITTLE RED RIDINGHOOD - Crimson. Miniature to small, formal double to peony form. Vigorous, compact, upright growth. M-L. (U.S. 1965 - McCaskill).

LITTLE RUBY - Rich Red. Miniature, loose peony form to semidouble. Compact growth. M. (U.S. 1976 - Haynie).

LITTLE SITTART - Red to White and Red. Miniature to small, semidouble. Compact, upright growth. M. (U.S. 1962 - Wheeler).

LITTLE SLAM - Rich Red. Miniature, full peony form. Average, compact, upright growth. E-M. (U.S. 1969 - Nuccio's).

LITTLE SLAM PINK - Bright Pink. (Sport of Japonica 'Little Slam'). (U.S. 1988 - M Vallery, Forest Hill, LA).

LITTLE SLAM VARIEGATED - Red and White blotched variation of 'Little Slam'.

LITTLE SUSIE - Blush Pink. Small, formal double. Average, upright growth. M-L. (U.S. 1972 - Mrs. J. Luker, Savannah, GA).

LITTLE TOO - White with Red spots and streaks. Miniature, semidouble. Average, spreading, upright growth. M-L. (U.S. 1966 - Ashby).

LIZ BEEBE - Soft Pink with irregular shading of Deeper Pink. Medium, semidouble. Vigorous, bushy growth. M. (U.S. 1958 - McCaskill).

LIZ CARTER - Ruby Red with Black veining. Small to medium, semidouble. Average growth. M-L. (N.Z. 1989 - T. Lennard, Te Puke).

LOIS COKER - White. Small to medium, formal double. Vigorous, compact, upright growth. M. (U.S. 1979 - Mrs. R. R. Coker, Hartsville, SC).

LOIS HILL - ('Elizabeth Colville'). Light Pink veined deeper Pink and edged White. Medium, semidouble. Average, compact growth. (Sport of 'Tricolor California'). (U.S. 1942 - Mrs. Hill, Pasadena, CA).

LOIS NORVELL - Dark Red with Red at base of stamens. Medium, semidouble with prominent, short, circular stamens. Compact, upright growth. M. (U.S. 1953 - Wheeler).

LOIS NORVELL VARIEGATED - Dark Red and White variation of 'Lois Norvell'.

LOLA - Ivory White. Medium, loose peony form. Vigorous, upright growth. M. (U.S. 1962 - D. W. Davis).

LOLA BARNES - Shrimp Pink. Large, semidouble. Average, spreading growth. M. (U.S. 1966 - Julington).

LOLITA - Red moiré White or Light Pink. Large, semidouble to peony form. Vigorous, upright growth. M. (U.S. 1962 - W. M. Harrison, Pensacola, FL).

LONGWOOD CENTENNIAL - Pink with Yellow anthers and light pink filaments. Miniature, single. Average, upright, dense growth. E. Exceptionally cold hardy. (Seed from Sochong Island, South Korea). (U.S. 2006 - Longwood Gardens, Kennett Square, PA).

LONGWOOD VALENTINE - Pink with Yellow anthers and light pink filaments. Miniature, single with six petals. Average, upright growth. E-M. Exceptionally cold hardy. (Seed from Sochong Island, South Korea). (U.S. 2006 - Longwood Gardens, Kennett Square, PA)..

LONJAN - See 'Nagasaki'.

LOOK AGAIN - Light to Blush Pink with iridescent Darker Pink on outer petals. Medium, anemone form. Average, compact, upright growth. E-L. (U.S. 1977 - M. Talia, Santa Clara, CA).

LOOK-AWAY - Deep Rose Pink in throat with wide border of White. Medium, semidouble. (Sport of Japonica 'Herme'). (For a variation of this cultivar see 'White Surprise'). (U.S. 1948 - Mealing).

LORA DALE JOHNSON - Light Silver Pink. Large, semidouble, sometimes with full cluster of petaloids in center. Vigorous, upright growth. M. (U.S. 1952 - O. H. Johnson, Hattiesburg, MS).

LORELEI - Rose Pink to Crimson. Medium, peony form to anemone form with crimped edged petals. Vigorous, compact growth. M-L. (U.S. 1948 - Armstrong).

LOREN LITTLETON - Rose Pink. Large, anemone form. Vigorous, spreading, upright growth. M-L. (U.S. 1967 - Mrs. R. J. Scruggs, Hakira, GA).

LORI BURTON - Flesh Pink. Medium, formal double with incurved petals. M. (U.S. 1973 - Haynie).

LORI CLEVENGER - Dark Pink with streaks and flecks of Dark Coral Pink. Small to medium, peony form. Average, upright, spreading, open growth. E-M. (U.S. 2009 - John M. Davy, Pace, FL).

LORI SMITH - Light Pink. Miniature, formal double; the bloom is always circular. Vigorous, upright, dense growth. E-L. (U.S. 2016 - Howell).

LORI WEEKS - Very Light Pink with Dark Pink streaks radiating along petals. Medium, formal double to rose form double with cupped imbricated petals. Average, upright growth. M. (U.S. 2019 - Tommy Weeks, Conroe, TX).

LORRAINE CROSS - Deep Fire Red. Large, peony form with curled and twisted petals divided to expose bunches of stamens. Average, spreading growth. M. (U.S. 1972 - Witman).

LOTTIE'S LAVENDER - Lavender to Reddish Lavender. Large, formal double to peony form. Slow, compact growth. M. (U.S. 1955).

LOTUS - ('Sode-Gakushi'; 'Gauntletti'). White. Very large, semidouble of water lily form. Vigorous, upright growth. M. (Japan to U.S. 1909 - Baldwin Park, CA).

LOU AKIN - Pink. Medium, loose peony form. Average growth. E-M. (U.S. 1993 - E. Akin, Shreveport, LA).

LOU POWERS - Medium Pink variegated White with Yellow anthers and White filaments. Large, semidouble. M-L. (Sport of Japonica 'Betty Burgess'). (U.S. 2006 - Ed Powers, Wilmington, NC).

LOUIS LAW - Rose Pink. Large, anemone form. Average, spreading, upright growth. E-M. (U.S. 1966 - L. F. Law, Brunswick, GA).

LOUISA PENN - Deep Rose. Large, anemone form to peony form. M-L. (U.S. 1959).

LOUISA WILSON - Blush White. Large, semidouble with White stamens. Average, open, upright growth. M. (U.S. 1961 - D. L. Wilson, Macon, GA).

LOUISE BEASLEY - Deep Rose Red. Large, semidouble with loose petals and Yellow stamens in six sections intermingled with upright, twisted and fluted petaloids and petals. Average, open, upright growth. M. (U.S. 1960 - Beasley).

LOUISE DOVELL - Rose Pink. Large, semidouble with partially interspersed stamens. Average, upright growth. M. (U.S. 1967 - J. N. Sewell, Jacksonville, FL).

LOUISE DOVELL VARIEGATED - Rose Pink with high amount of White variation of 'Louise Dovell'.

LOUISE ENGLISH - Bright Red. Medium, anemone form with velvety sheen. Average, open, upright growth. M. (U.S. 1964 - D. English, Jr., Dawson, GA).

LOUISE FITZGERALD - Creamy Pink with lighter outer markings with Creamy Golden anthers and Creamy Golden filaments. Large to very large, semidouble. Rapid, upright, spreading growth. E-M. (Sport of Japonica 'Sweetie Pie'). (U.S. 2007 - Jerry Conrad, Plymouth, FL).

LOUISE HAIRSTON - Clear Pink with undertones of Coral. Large, semidouble with seven rows of petals and five or six rows of petaloids mixed with stamens. Upright growth. M. (U.S. 1966 - Poe).

LOUISE HAIRSTON VARIEGATED - Clear Pink blotched White variation of 'Louise Hairston'.

LOUISE HOWELL - Pale Blush with bright Pink overtones. Medium, anemone form. Average, upright growth. E-M. (U.S. 1994 - Dr. O. Lewis, Picayune, MS).

LOUISE SOMERVELL - White striped Pink. Medium, semidouble. Vigorous, upright growth. M. (U.S. 1973 - Mrs. A. Waldon, Ocala, FL).

LOUISE VAN DUSEN - Pink with Yellow anthers and White filaments. Medium, anemone form. Average, dense growth. M-L. (U.S. 2008 - Don Bergamini, Martinez, CA).

LOUISE WEICK - Fire Red. Medium, semidouble with large, cluster of petaloids. Vigorous, compact, upright growth. M. (U.S. 1946 - Magnolia).

LOUISE WHITING - Blush. Large, full semidouble to peony form. Average, compact growth. M. (U.S. 1979 - Shackelford).

LOUISE-ONETTA - White. Medium, semidouble to loose peony form with irregular petals. Vigorous growth. M. (U.S. 1937 - B. Kirby, Newman, GA).

LOUISIANA PURCHASE - Magenta Red. Medium, semidouble to loose peony form. Vigorous, compact growth. E-M. (U.S. 1953 - Clower).

LOVE BOAT - Light Pink to White margined vivid Pink. Medium, semidouble to full peony form. Average, compact, upright growth. M. (U.S. 1981 - Feathers).

LOVE LETTERS - Pink. Medium, anemone form to peony form with a series of five rosettes of stamens and petaloids spaced equally around bloom. Vigorous, upright growth. E-M. (U.S. 1957 - Ashby).

LOVELIGHT - White. Large, semidouble with heavy petals. Vigorous, upright growth. M. (U.S. 1960 - Short).

LOVER BOY - Rose Red. Very large, semidouble with crinkled petals. Vigorous, open, upright growth. M. (U.S. 1977 - Belle Fontaine Nsy., Theodore, AL).

LOYCE WOODLE - Light Rose Pink shading to Light Silver Pink at edge with Deep Rose Pink on back of petals. Large, peony form. Vigorous, compact, upright growth. E-L. (U.S. 1964 - A. D. Woodle, Jr., Savannah, GA).

LU ANN CROWLEY - Deep Pink speckled Red. Large, formal double. Average, spreading growth. M. (U.S. 1988 - J. Aldrich, Brooklet, GA).

LUANA'S ANGEL - Pale Pink outer petals with Pink center petaloids. Large, anemone form. Compact, upright growth. L. (Aus. 1980 - F. N. Spencer, Cheltenham, Vic.).

LUCIE LANHAM - Light Pink. Large, semidouble to anemone form. Slow, spreading growth. M-L. (U.S. 1957 - Ashby).

LUCIE SCHWOERER - Rose. Large, anemone form to peony form. Average, compact growth. M-L. (U.S. 1959 - J. L. Schwoerer, Oakland, CA).

LUCILE DICKSON - Deep Rose. Medium, semidouble form that approaches rose form; center petals have vegetative veins with outer edge of each petal rolled upward. Average, dense, upright growth. M-L. (U.S. 2005 - James D. Dickson, North Augusta, SC).

LUCILLE DAVIS - White. Large, anemone form. Average, upright growth. M. (U.S. 1965 - D. W. Davis).

LUCILLE FERRELL - See 'C. M. Wilson'.

LUCILLE FLANAGAN - Deep Rose. Medium, semidouble with trumpet of petaloids. Average growth. M. (U.S. 1949 - Mrs. A. J. Tennant, Houston, TX).

LUCILLE JACKSON HARRIS - White with Blush tint, some outer petals partly Light Pink. Large to very large, semidouble to anemone form. Average, open, upright growth. M-L. (U.S. 1969 - Haynie).

LUCILLE JERNIGAN - White. Medium to large, loose peony form to anemone form. Vigorous, upright growth. M-L. (U.S. 1989 - Jernigan).

LUCILLE MORRIS - Red. Medium, semidouble with irregular petals. L. (U.S. 1955 - C. Morris, Greenville, SC).

LUCILLE SMITH - White striped Red. Large, anemone form. Average, upright growth. M. (U.S. 1971 - F. Smith, Statesboro, GA).

LUCKY SEVEN - Red. Medium to large, semidouble to loose peony form. (Sport of Japonica 'Betty Sheffield').

LUCKY THIRTEEN - Bright Red. Large, peony form to anemone form. Vigorous, upright growth. M-L. (U.S. 1958 - Ashby).

LUCY ELLEN McCURDIE - Deep Rose Pink tinged Purple. Large, loose peony form with large, curled petaloids. Vigorous growth. M. (U.S. 1957 - C. H. Welch, Hattiesburg, MS).

LUCY HESTER - Silver Pink. Large to very large, semidouble of 'Lotus' form. Vigorous, upright growth. M. (U.S. 1959 - K. O. Hester, Laguna Hills, CA).

LUCY HESTER VARIEGATED - Silver Pink and White variation of 'Lucy Hester'.

LUCY O - White with Yellow anthers and Light Yellow filaments. Large, semidouble. Average, upright spreading, open growth. E-M. (U.S. 2011 - Lindsey Odom, Wilmington, NC).

LUCY ROONEY - Creamy White, peppered and streaked Tyron Pink. Medium, peony form. Slow, open growth. M. (U.S. 1954 - Turner).

LUCY SHIRAH - Pink with variegation. Medium to large, formal double. Vigorous, upright growth. E-M. (U.S. 2005 - John W. Shirah, Lakeland, FL).

LUCY STEWART - White. Large to very large, loose peony form. Vigorous, upright growth. M. (U.S. 1971 - Haynie).

LUCY TURNER - White to Cream White with occasional, small, Pink stripes. Large, full peony form. Average, compact growth. M. (U.S. 1954 - Turner).

LUISA ANN LEE - Pale Pink with Darker Pink markings with bright Yellow anthers and White filaments. Medium, semidouble to full peony form. Average, upright growth. M-L. (Sport of Japonica 'Alyne Brothers'). (U.S. 2012 - M. S. "Mack" McKinnon, Murrells Inlet, SC).

LUKE HILL - White. Medium, formal double. Average, upright, dense growth. M-L. (U.S. 2016 - Gordy).

LULU BELLE - White. Large, semidouble to loose peony form. Vigorous, upright growth. E. (U.S. 1969 - H. E. Dryden, San Marino, CA).

LUMINOSA - Red with luminous sheen. Medium, single. (U.S. 1953 - Fruitland).

LUNDY'S LEGACY - Coral Red with Blush Pink fringe with Gold anthers and Cream filaments. Medium to large, peony form. Average, upright growth. M-L. (U.S. 2009 - T. E. Lundy Pensacola, FL).

LURIE'S FAVORITE - Soft Lavender Pink. Medium, semidouble with crinkled petals. Vigorous, compact, upright growth. M. (U.S. 1935 - Overlook).

LURLEEN WALLACE - Rose Pink. Large, rose form double. Average, upright growth. M-L. (U.S. 1971 - C. C. Crutcher, Jr., Mobile, AL).

LUSCIOUS LADY - Dark Red. Large, peony form with heavy textured petals. Average growth. E-M. (Reported to be sport of Japonica 'Mathotiana'). (U.S. 1961 - Harrison).

LYDIA ADAMS - Soft Pink. Large, loose peony form. Vigorous, upright growth. E-L. (U.S. 1961 - B. F. Marshall, Mobile, AL).

LYNDA'S OWN - Pink. Small to medium, anemone form with notched petals. Average, dense growth. M-L. (Aus. 1995 - K. Brown, Mitcham, Vic.).

LYNN HAIRSTON - Light Pink in center shading to Dark Pink to Red at edges with White anthers and White filaments. Medium, formal double. Average, upright, open growth. M. (U.S. 2012 - Louise Poe Hairston, Birmingham, AL).

LYNN MARIE - Blush veined Rose Pink. Medium, full peony form. Average, compact, upright growth. M-L. (U.S. 1959 - H. Larson, Orange, CA).

LYNNE WOODROOF - Light Peach Pink. Medium, full peony form. Average, compact, upright growth. M. (U.S. 1956 - Ragland).

M. J. VARIEGATED - Red and White. Very large, semidouble to peony form. Vigorous, dense, spreading, upright growth. M-L. (U.S. 1995 - Jernigan).

M. L. SPENCER - Light Pink with Lavender shading. Small to medium, formal double. Average, upright growth. E. (U.S. 2005 - John L. Spencer, Lakeland, FL).

MABEL BLACKWELL - White shading to soft Pink on margins of petals. Medium, full peony form. Vigorous, upright growth. M. (U.S. 1959 - Gerbing).

MABEL BRYAN - White spotted or striped Red. Large, semidouble with irregular and occasionally fimbriated petals to formal double. Vigorous, upright growth. M. (U.S. 1968 - S. T. Bryan, Mt. View, CA).

MABEL BRYAN STRAWBERRY - Red and Pink stripes on Light Pink field veined Deeper Pink, lighter at edges. Large, semidouble. (Sport of Japonica 'Mabel Bryan'). (U.S. 1995 - Nuccio's).

MABEL MORSE MARSHALL - Dark Red. Large, semidouble with Red stamens tipped White. Average, open, upright growth. M. (U.S. 1961 - B. F. Marshall, Mobile, AL).

MABLE BARNSLEY - Rose Pink. Large, anemone form. Average, spreading, upright growth. M. (U.S. 1968 - W. H. Barnsley, Apopka, FL).

MACYE JUSTICE - Velvet Red with variegated Rose petaloids and Yellow stamens. Large, anemone form. Average, compact, upright growth. M. (U.S. 1963 - Justice Nsy., Fitzgerald, GA).

MADAME CHARLES BLARD - White. Medium, peony form. Average, upright growth. M. (France 1920 - Guichard).

MADAME DE MAINTENON - Light Pink with a few White blotches with Yellow anthers and White filaments. Large, semidouble; there are four rows of petals with center petals forming a cup with several groups of stamens. Average, loose, upright growth. M. (Europe to U.S. [Magnolia] 1840's).

MADAME DE STREKALOFF - Pale pink striped white. Medium, formal double to peony form. Average, loose, upright growth. M. (Italy 1855 - Cesare Franchetti, Florence).

MADAME HAAS - Light Red with more deeply colored veins with a floral center marked Light Pink. Medium, formal double. Vigorous, upright growth. M. (France 1879 - E. Haas).

MADAME HAHN - Bright Pink. Medium, semidouble. Vigorous, upright growth. M. (Japan to U.S. [Star] 1915).

MADAME HAHN VARIEGATED - See 'Sierra Spring'.

MADAME HOVEY - ('Ecstacy [California]'). Clear Pink. Medium, formal double. Vigorous, compact growth. M. (U.S. 1940 - Doty and Doerner).

MADAME JANNOCH - Light Red. Medium, semidouble. Vigorous, compact, upright growth. E. (U.S. 1942 — Jannoch).

MADAME LEBOIS - ('Carl Rosenquist'; 'Rosedale's Beauty').- Red. Medium, rose form double. Vigorous, compact, upright growth. E-L. (For another form of this cultivar, see 'Admiration'). (France 1854 - Miellez).

MADAME MARGUERITE CALUSAUT - White, striped pink. Large, semidouble. Average, upright growth. E-M. (U.S. 1948 - Magnolia Plantation & Gardens, Charleston, SC).

MADAME PICOULINE - Cherry Red. Medium, peony form. Average, upright growth. (Synonym for Japonica 'Akaroa Rouge'). (Belgium, about 1850 - M Francotte, Sr., Liege).

MADELIN NADEAU - Crimson. Large, semidouble of variable form. Average, spreading, upright growth. M. (U.S. 1967 - H. Cawood, Americus, GA).

MADELINE BAYORS - Light Pink. Large, semidouble with irregular petals. E-M. (U.S. 1959).

MADELINE ROBERTS - Deep Rose Red. Large, anemone form. Vigorous, upright growth. E-M. (U.S. 1965 - Mrs. C. H. Roberts, Adel, GA).

MADGE MILLER - ('Chandleri Alba'; 'White Chandleri'). White. Medium, anemone form. Average, upright growth. M. (U.S. 1938 - H. K. Miller, Monticello, FL).

MADGE ROUSE - Clear Light Pink. Large, anemone form to peony form to rose form double. Vigorous, dense, upright growth. E-M. (U.S. 1995 - R. D. Rouse, Auburn, AL).

MADISON'S HOLLY - Pink. Large to very large, peony form. Vigorous, upright growth; very unusual holly-like foliage with heavy serration. M-L. (Sport of Japonica 'Francis Eugene Phillips'). (U.S. 2008 - CamelliaShop, Savannah, GA).

MA-DOT-CHA - Pink marbled and blotched White. Large, full peony form. Vigorous, upright growth. E-M. (Reported same as 'Doris Freeman'). (U.S. 1956 - M. S. Cannon, Dothan, AL).

MAE ROBICHAUX - Silvery Pink. Large, semidouble to peony form. Average, upright growth. M. (U.S. 1986 - Tammia).

MAGALHAES VARIEGATED - Red marbled and striped White. (Variegated variation of Japonica 'D. Herzilia De Freitas Magalhaes'). (Aus. 1987 - G. Woltaston, Deleruere, S. Aus.).

MAGIC CITY - Fire Red variegated White. Medium, peony form. Vigorous, open, upright growth. M. (U.S. 1965 - Dr. R. T. Cale, Hueytown, AL).

MAGIC MOMENTS - Soft Peach Pink. Medium to large, semidouble with tiered center petals. Average, compact growth. M. (U.S. 1960 - Short).

MAGIC TOUCH - Soft Pink with Light Gold anthers and Pink filaments. Large, semidouble. Average, upright growth. M. (U.S. 2013 - Gordy).

MAGNOLIA BLUSH - White center shading to Blush Red on outer edge. Large, semidouble. Slow growth. M. (Aus. 1989 - M. Schultz, Edwardstown, S. Aus.).

MAGNOLIA KING - See 'Gigantea'.

MAGNOLIA PIXIE - Vibrant Pink with Yellow anthers and White filaments. Small, semidouble. Average, upright, open growth. M. (U.S. 2006 - Magnolia).

MAGNOLIA QUEEN - ('Priscilla Brooks'). White striped Red. Large, semidouble with irregular petals. Average, bushy growth. L. (U.S. Early 1900's - Magnolia).

MAGNOLIAEFLORA - ('Hagoromo'; 'Rose of Dawn'; 'Cho-No-Hagasane'). Blush Pink. Medium, semidouble. Average, compact growth. M. (Variations of this cultivar include 'Arthur Bolton' and 'Rudy's Magnoliaeflora'). (Japan to Italy 1886).

MAHOGANY GLOW - Dark Red. Small to medium, semidouble with smaller petals toward center and Red foliage. L. (U.S. 1953 - Short).

MAHOROBA (EXCELLENT COUNTRY) - Deep Pink bordered White. Medium to large, formal double, imbricated petals. Vigorous, upright growth. M-L. (Japonica 'Benihagoromo' x Japonica 'Etenraku'). (Japan 2007 - Soshin Harai).

MAID OF HONOR - Shell Pink. Medium, full peony form. Average, bushy growth. M-L. (U.S. 1954 - Short).

MAID OF THE MIST - White. Large, anemone form. Slow, compact growth. E. (U.S. 1953 - Shackelford).

MAIDEN - See 'Kumasaka'.

MAIDEN LANE - Light Pink. Medium, semidouble with long, narrow, overlapping petals lighter at base, producing pine cone effect. Vigorous, compact, upright growth. M-L. (U.S. 1960 - Camelliana).

MAIDEN OF GREAT PROMISE - Pink. Medium to large, peony. Compact growth. L. The plant is very cold hardy. (U.S. 2008 - Ohio).

MAIDEN'S BLUSH - Flesh Pink veined deeper Pink. Medium, formal double with incurved petals. M. (Japan to U.S. [Overlook] Early 1900's).

MAIZURU - Light Pink edged White with occasional Red stripe. Medium, single with flared Pale Yellow stamens. See Higo.

MAJESTIC - See 'Herme Pink'.

MAJESTIC QUEEN - Light Pink. Very large, semidouble to loose peony form. Average, compact, upright growth. E-M. (U.S. 1988 - Nuccio's).

MAJESTIC SNOW - White. Medium to large, formal double. Average, upright growth. E-M. (U.S. 1988 - Nuccio's).

MAJOR GENERAL PENDER - Pinkish Purple with Yellow anthers and White filaments. Medium, semidouble. Average, upright, open growth. M. (U.S. 2017 - Edward W. Fredrickson, Wilmington, NC).

MAJOR'S SAWTOOTH - Red with White blotches. Large to very large, semidouble. Average, upright growth. M. (U.S. 1994 - B. Livingston, Prattville, AL).

MAJORETTE - Rose Pink with petals veined slightly darker and slight border of White. Medium, formal double. Vigorous, upright growth. M-L. (U.S. 1959 - Hartman).

MALCOLM ROPER - Reddish Pink. Large, formal double. Average, upright growth. M. (U.S. 1982 - L. C. Preston, Walnut Creek, CA).

MALISSA DUGGAN - Pink. Large, formal double. Average, compact growth. M. (U.S. 1966 - S. Walden, Albany, GA).

MAM'SELLE - Light Lavender Pink. Large, semidouble of cup form. Vigorous, spreading growth. M. (U.S. 1957 - McCaskill).

MAMA BABY - White washed Light Pink to Rose Pink on petal edges. Medium, loose peony form. Average, dense, upright growth. M-L. (U.S. 1995 - A. Fendig and J. Ledbetter, St. Simons Island, GA).

MAMA DOT - Blush Pink. Medium, semidouble. Slow, dense, upright growth. E-L. (U.S. 1998 - C. Elliott, Swainsboro, GA).

MAMA SANS - White striped Pink. Small, semidouble. Average, open, upright growth. M-L. (For a variation of this cultivar see 'Janie Sans'). (U.S. 1955 - Metcalf).

MAMIE - White with two or three Light Pink petals. Medium, semidouble. M. (U.S. 1955 - C. Thomas, San Dimas, CA).

MAMIE BREWER - White with White stamens. Large, semidouble. (U.S. 1957 - Mrs. R. W. Brewer, McComb, MS).

MAMIE LOU - Light Pink edged White. Medium, semidouble. (Sport of Japonica 'Mamie'). (U.S. 1983 - Mrs. L Rowe, Upland, CA).

MAN SIZE - White. Miniature to small, anemone form. Average, open, upright growth. M. (U.S. 1961 - Wilson).

MANA CHAFFIN - Bright Rose Pink outer petals fading to Light Pink center. Medium, formal double with incurved and swirled petals. Average, upright growth. E-M. (U.S. 1994 - Dr. O. Lewis, Picayune, MS).

MAÑANA - Dark Red. Medium, semidouble to peony form. Vigorous, sturdy growth. E-M. (U.S. 1950 - R. C. Carr, Tulare, CA).

MANDALAY - Rose Red. Medium to large, peony form showing distinct, separate anemone form flower in center. Vigorous, compact, upright growth. M. (U.S. 1954 - Short).

MANDIE SHUMAN - Pink edged White streaked Deep Pink. Large, anemone form. Average, upright growth. M-L. (U.S. 1987 - J.Aldrich, Brooklet, GA).

MANDY LANE - Pink. Medium to large, formal double with incurved petals. Average, open, upright growth. M. (U.S. 1995 - E. Atkins, Shalimar, FL).

MANGETSU - White. Medium, single with flared Pale Yellow stamens. See Higo.

MANUROA ROAD - Deep Blood Red. Large, formal double. Average, dense growth with Dark Green foliage. M-L. (N.Z. 2001 - Haydon).

MANZAI-RAKU - Rose Pink, streaked and moired White and edged White. Large, single. See Higo.

MARANUI - See 'Leviathan (Australia)'.

MARANUI PINK - See 'Leviathan (Australia)'.

MARASCHINO - Bright Red. Medium, formal double. Average, compact, upright growth. L. (U.S. 1941 - Doty and Doemer).

MARBLE HALLS - White, Pink, Rose and variegated. Small, formal double to rose form double. Vigorous, bushy growth. M-L. (U.S. 1956 - Short).

MARC ELEVEN - Cherry Red. Large, semidouble with wavy, upright petals. Vigorous, spreading, upright growth. M-L. (U.S. 1969 - Mandarich).

MARCEL VALOIS - Ruby Red. Small, semidouble with wavy, upright petals and White stamens. Average, upright growth. E-M. (U.S. 1961 - T. C. Patin, Hammond, LA).

MARCELLA HOVEY - Light Pink veined and splotched Deep Red. Large, formal double. Vigorous, compact, upright growth. M. (U.S. 1963 - J. D. O'Conner, Red Bluff, CA).

MARCHIONESS OF EXETER - ('Marquis d' Exeter'). Pink to Rose Pink. Medium to large, full peony form. Vigorous, open, spreading growth. E-M. (England 1874 - Caledonia).

MARCHIONESS OF EXETER VARIEGATED - Light Pink blotched White form of 'Marchioness of Exeter'.

MARCHIONESS OF SALISBURY - Dark Red marked White. Small, full peony form. Slow, bushy growth. M. (England to U.S. [Magnolia] late 1800's).

MARCIA McVEY - Light Pink center petals to Deep Pink outer petals. Large, formal double. Vigorous, spreading growth. E-M. (U.S. 1970 - C. T. McVey, Glendora, CA).

MARGARET - Rose Pink. Large, peony form with stamens in several clusters among petals. Upright growth. E. (U.S. 1953 - Clower).

MARGARET ALWYN - Rose Pink. Large, peony form. M. (Aus. 1957 - Dr. C. R. Merrillees, Melbourne).

MARGARET BURSTAL - Flesh Pink. Large, anemone form. M. (Aus. 1967 - Dr. J. R. Burstal, Pymble, NSW).

MARGARET CROZIER - Delicate Rose Pink. Large, peony form. Pendulous growth. E. (Aus. 1957 - Cole).

MARGARET CRUTCHER - Bright Red. Large, anemone form. Average, spreading growth. M. (U.S. 1976 - C. C. Crutcher, Theodore, AL).

MARGARET D. O'CONNOR - Deep Pink. Very large, semidouble with wavy, crepe petals. Vigorous, upright growth. M. (U.S. 1962 - G. Hovey, Red Bluff, CA).

MARGARET DAVIS - White to Cream White with a few Rose Red lines and dashed and edged bright Vermillion. Medium, full peony form. (Sport of Japonica 'Aspasia MacArthur'). (Variations of this cultivar include 'Just Sue' and 'Maureen Ostler'). (Aus. 1961 - A M Davis, Cammeray).

MARGARET DAVIS ASHLEY - Same as parent except heavier dashes of Vermillion from outer edges toward center. (Sport of Japonica 'Margaret Davis'). (U.S. 1983 - G. King, Monroe, LA).

MARGARET DAVIS PICOTEE - White with intermittent dashes of Carmine Pink around edge of each petal. (Sport of Japonica 'Margaret Davis'). (U.S. 1982 - W E Woodroof, Sherman Oaks, CA).

MARGARET ELLEN - Salmon Pink. Large, formal double. Vigorous growth. E-M. (Aus. 1957 - Mrs. M. Thompson, Sydney).

MARGARET FERRIS - White with few Pink stripes. Medium, semidouble. Average, open, upright growth. E-M. (U.S. 1968 - B. G. Ferris, Orlando, FL).

MARGARET HEARN - Red. Small, peony form. Vigorous, bushy growth. M. (U.S. 1934 - Hearn).

MARGARET HIGDON - ('Elizabeth Grandy'). Rose Red, sometimes showing White margined petals. Medium, semidouble. Vigorous, compact, upright growth. M. (U.S. Early 1900's - Magnolia).

MARGARET JACK - See 'Finlandia Variegated'.

MARGARET JOHNSON - White. Large, formal double. Average, spreading, upright growth. E-L. (U.S. 1972 - F. D. Bisbee, Jacksonville, FL).

MARGARET K. CUTTER - Rose Opal. Medium, single. Upright growth. E. (U.S. 1951 - R. K. Cutter, Berkeley, CA).

MARGARET LAWRENCE - See 'Vedrine'.

MARGARET LESHER - Purplish Red. Medium, rose form double. Average, upright growth. E-M. (U.S. 1992 - R. Ehrhart, Walnut Creek, CA).

MARGARET McCOWN - ('Driftwood'). Light Pink and White. Medium, semidouble to anemone form. (Variegated variation of Japonica 'Catherine McCown'). (U.S. 1957 - Shepp).

MARGARET McLENDON - Rose Pink. Large, semidouble of flat form. (U.S. 1957 - Coleman).

MARGARET NOONAN - Light Rose Pink striped and splashed Darker Rose Pink. Medium, peony form. Vigorous, open, upright growth. M. (U.S. 1950 - W. S. Duncan, Pensacola, FL).

MARGARET RATCLIFFE - Blush Pink. Medium, semidouble. Vigorous, open, upright growth. M. (U.S. 1956 - Tait).

MARGARET SANDUSKY - See 'Rosea Superba'.

MARGARET SHORT - Deep Lavender Pink. Large, semidouble with irregular, upright, fluted petals around center of Blonde stamens. Average, compact growth. M. (U.S. 1958 - Short).

MARGARET SHORT VARIEGATED - Deep Lavender Pink blotched White variation of 'Margaret Short'.

MARGARET WALKER - White striped Pink. Medium, semidouble to rose form double with loose petaloids and stamens in center. Average, upright growth. M-L. (Europe to U.S. [Tea Gardens] 1890).

MARGARET WEEMS - Light Peach Pink. Medium, semidouble with irregular petals. Vigorous, bushy growth. (U.S. 1975 - Haynie).

MARGARET WELLS - Deep Rose shading to Purple at edge. Medium, semidouble to loose peony form with heavy textured petals. Average, upright growth. E-M. (For a variation of this cultivar see 'Bridesmaid'). (U.S. 1960 - Wells).

MARGARET WELLS DELIGHT - Deep Rose and White. (Variegated variation of Japonica 'Margaret Wells'). (U.S. 1965 - Azalea Road Nsy., Mobile, AL).

MARGARET WILLIAMS - Purple. Small, formal double. Vigorous, compact, upright growth. M. (U.S. 1988 - J. H. Williams, Tampa, FL).

MARGARET'S JOY - White with Pale Peach Pink center and under petals. Medium to large, formal double. Vigorous growth. E-M. (U.S. 1987 - M. and W. Harmsen, Claremont, CA).

MARGARETE HERTRICH - White. Medium, formal double with numerous smaller petals. Vigorous, compact, upright growth. M. (U.S. 1944 - Huntington).

MARGERY ADAMS - Cream to Lavender Pink at edge. Medium, formal double. Vigorous, compact, upright growth. L. (U.S. 1974 - Dr. C. Adams, Charlotte, NC).

MARGHERITA COLEONI - ('General Douglas MacArthur'; 'Campbelli'; 'Red Queen'; 'Tokayama [South]'). Dark Red. Medium, rose form double to formal double. Vigorous, upright growth. L. (In certain old publications this cultivar is spelled 'Margharita Caleonie'). (Belgium [Verschaffelt] from Italy 1859).

MARGHERITA COLEONI VARIEGATED - ('Azuma-Shibori'; 'Mary Hare'; 'Princess Bachinachi'; 'Berkeley Square'). Deep Red blotched White form of 'Margherita Coleoni'.

MARGIE - White. Large, formal double. E-M. (U.S. 1968 - Orinda Nsy., Bridgeville, DE).

MARGIE B. - White. Large, semidouble to loose peony form with fluted petals and Green stamens. Average, compact, upright growth. E-M. (U.S. 1959 - L. A. Brantley, Savannah, GA).

MARGIE DEE FISHER - Soft Pink lightly variegated White. Large, semidouble with loose petals. Vigorous, upright growth. M. (U.S. 1954 - Fisher).

MARGO-ANNE LOE - White with broken Pink stripes and Red spotted White. Small, formal double. Vigorous, compact, upright growth. M. (U.S. 1988 - Tammia).

MARGO-LYN - Purplish Red to Rose Pink. Medium, semidouble. Average, open growth. M-L. (Aus. 1968 - G. W. Hooper, Bexley North, NSW).

MARGUERITA - See 'Nagasaki'.

MARGUERITE CANNON - Clear Pink. Large, semidouble with many large fluted petals. Slow, open growth. M-L. (U.S. 1960 - Ashby).

MARGUERITE CANNON VARIEGATED - Clear Pink blotched White variation of 'Marguerite Cannon'.

MARGUERITE CARBON - Rose Red. Medium, formal double. Spreading growth. M-L. (U.S. from Italy 1955 - Peer).

MARGUERITE ENID - White to Blush Pink. Large, semidouble. Vigorous, compact, upright growth. E-M. (Aus. 1977 - M. Stephenson, Castle Hill, NSW).

MARGUERITE GOUILLON - ('Duc D'Orleans'; 'General Lamorciere'). Delicate Pink slightly striped and flecked deeper Pink. Medium, full peony form. Vigorous, bushy growth. M. (France 1850 - Drouard).

MARGUERITE SEARS - Light Pink toward center gradually deepening to Coral Pink at margin. Large, semidouble with irregular petals to loose peony form. Vigorous, compact growth. M. (U.S. 1969 - Mrs. G. Sears, Moultrie, GA).

MARGUERITE TOURJE - Pink margined White. Large, semidouble to anemone form. Sport of Japonica 'Masquerade'). (U.S. 1955 - Nuccio's).

MARGUERITE TURNER - Cream White lightly striped and flecked Pink. Large, semidouble to peony form with alternating clusters of stamens, petals and large petaloids. Vigorous, compact growth. E-M. (U.S. 1954 - Turner).

MARGUERITE VEO - Deep Rose. Large, full peony form. Average, open, upright growth. E-M. (U.S. 1962 - W. H. Veo, Orlando, FL).

MARGUERYTE SHARP - White. Medium, anemone form. Average, compact, upright growth. M. (U.S. 1980 - Tammia).

MARIA MORREN - ('Climax'; 'Ella Drayton'; 'Festiva').- Rose Pink veined Carmine. Medium, formal double with smaller center petals. Vigorous, upright growth. M-L. (Belgium 1847 - H. Haquin, Ghent).

MARIAN FAIRCLOTH - Light Pink with Dark Pink stripes. Large, peony form. Average, spreading growth. E-M. (U.S. 1970 - O. J. Faircloth, Pensacola, FL).

MARIAN HARRISON - Cerise Pink. Large, anemone form to peony form. Average, open, upright growth. M. (U.S. 1961 - Harrison).

MARIAN MITCHELL - Scarlet Red with Yellow anthers and White filaments. Large, semidouble. Slow, upright growth. L. (U.S. - 1942 - Magnolia Plantation & Gardens, Charleston, SC).

MARIANA - ('Red Waratah'). Dark Crimson. Medium, anemone form. Compact, bushy growth. M. (Aus. 1874 - MacArthur).

MARIANN - Red. Medium to large, full peony form to anemone form. Average, upright growth. E-M. (U.S. 1984 - A. W. Garner, Glendale, CA).

MARIANNA GAETA - See 'Marianna Gaete'.

MARIANNA GAETE - ('Barbara Lodge'; 'Marianna Gaeta'). Bright Pink with lighter center. Medium, rose form double to formal double. Vigorous, spreading growth. L. (Italy 1881 - Gaete, Florence).

MARIANNE O. MARSCHER - Red. Large, rose form double to loose peony form. Average, upright growth. M. (U.S. 1965 - J. F. Marscher, Beaufort, SC).

MARIANNE RANKIN - Dark Red. Large, semidouble with irregular petals to peony form. Average growth. M. (U.S. 1960 - Clower).

MARIANNE'S BLUSH - Rose Pink. Medium, semidouble. Average, upright growth. E-L. (U.S. 1969 - D. English, Jr., Dawson, GA).

MARIE - White. Medium, semidouble. Slow, spreading growth. M-L. (U.S. 1983 - A. Gonos, Fresno, CA).

MARIE BARNES - Red with Yellow anthers and White filaments. Large, semidouble. Average, upright, dense growth. M-L. (First Lady of Georgia Series). (U.S. 2018 - Gordy).

MARIE BRACEY - ('Spellbound'; 'October Delight'). Coral Rose. Large, semidouble to loose peony form with slightly curved and a few upright petals. Average, compact, upright growth. E-M. Cold hardy. (U.S. 1953 - Mrs. H. T. Brice, Valdosta, GA).

MARIE BRACEY VARIEGATED - Coral Rose and White variation of 'Marie Bracey'. (U.S. 1962 - Thomasville).

MARIE CAMP - Light Pink. Medium to large, formal double. Average, compact growth. M. (U.S. 1971 - Shackelford).

MARIE CRAWFORD - Soft Pink with Gold anthers and Cream filaments. Medium, semidouble to loose peony form. Average, spreading growth. E-M. (Japonica 'Laverne Norris' x unknown pollen parent). (U.S. 2010 - Gordy).

MARIE CROCKETT - Rich Red. Large, formal double. Vigorous, spreading growth. E-M. (U.S. 1968 - M. G. Crockett, Valdosta, GA).

MARIE GOODLETT - White. Medium to large, anemone form. Average, upright growth. E. Cold hardy. (U.S. 1999 - Elizabeth R. Scott, Aiken, SC).

MARIE GRIFFIN - See 'Finlandia Blush'.

MARIE HALL - Light Rose base to Darker Rose center. Medium, formal double. Average, open growth. E-M. (U.S. 1995 - O. Jacobson, Jacksonville Beach, FL).

MARIE MACKALL - Light Pink, petals blending to Deep Pink toward edges. Large, rose form double to semidouble. Upright growth. M. (U.S. 1980 - Kramer).

MARIE MACKALL VARIEGATED - Light Pink mottled White variation of 'Marie Mackall'. (U.S. 1982 - Kramer).

MARIE McHENRY - White. Large, semidouble with irregular petals and White stamens. Average, open, upright growth. E-M. (U.S. 1959 - Ragland).

MARIE RAVEN - Soft Pink. Large, full peony form to anemone form with crimped, wavy and fluted guard petals. Upright, compact growth. M. (Aus. 1960 - R. J. Raven, Tecoma).

MARIE SHACKELFORD - White. Medium, formal double to rose form double. Average, compact growth. E. (U.S. 1959 - Shackelford).

MARIE WOOD - White. Medium, semidouble. Vigorous, compact growth. E-M. (U.S. 1950 - W. T. Wood, Macon, GA).

MARILEA - White marked Red with Rose tinted petals near base fading towards edge. Large, semidouble to loose peony form. Compact, upright growth. M. (U.S. 1957 - Dr. L. U. Graves, Tallahassee, FL).

MARILEE GRAY - Peach Pink. Medium, formal double. Low, compact growth. M-L. (U.S. 1989 - Kramer).

MARILEE GRAY VARIEGATED - Peach Pink and White variation of 'Marilee Gray'. (U.S. 1989 - Kramer).

MARILYN McELVEEN - Rose Red. Large, semidouble with irregular petals to anemone form. Average growth. E-M. (U.S. 1969 - W. M. Anglin, Bogalusa, LA).

MARILYN NICKEL - White striped Rose Pink. Large, semidouble. Vigorous, spreading growth. M. (U.S. 1955 - G. Nickel, Arcadia, CA).

MARIO BERGAMINI - Red. Large to very large, semidouble to anemone form. Average, upright growth. M. (U.S. 1996 - Mandarich).

MARION DARSOW - Dark Red. Small, formal double. Average, upright growth. M. (Aus. 1955 - Linton).

MARION HALL - Rosy Red and White with Yellow anthers. Large, peony form. Vigorous, upright, dense growth. E-M. (U.S. 2006 Marion Hall, Dothan, Al).

MARION HATCHER - Currant Red veined Dark Red. Medium, formal double. Average, spreading, upright growth. M-L. (U.S. 1979 - Homeyer).

MARION MITCHELL - Scarlet. Medium, semidouble, sometimes with fragile petaloids intermixed with stamens. Average, compact, upright growth. M. (U.S. Early 1900's - Magnolia).

MARION MITCHELL VARIEGATED - Scarlet Red and White form of 'Marion Mitchell'.

MARISSA MOORE VARIEGATED - Deep Pink variegated White. Medium, formal double; the bloom has petaloids in the center and is very circular. Average, upright, spreading growth. M-L. (U.S. 2016 - Howell).

MARJORIE HUCKABEE - Light Pink. Medium, semidouble with irregular petals to peony form. Vigorous, upright growth. M. (U.S. 1956 - Wheeler).

MARJORIE HUCKABEE VARIEGATED - Light Pink blotched White variation of 'Marjorie Huckabee'.

MARJORIE MAGNIFICENT - Light Pink. Medium, semidouble to anemone form. Average, compact growth. E-M. (U.S. 1949 - Wilkinson).

MARJORIE NAN - Deep Red. Large, semidouble with curved petals. M. (U.S. 1965 - Wells).

MARJORIE TOWNSEND - White. Large, semidouble with irregular petals. Average, compact, upright growth. M. (U.S. 1953 - Huntington).

MARJORIE'S DOUBLE - Deep Pink, lighter in center. Large, formal double. Vigorous, compact, upright growth. L. (N.Z. 1984 - E. W. E. Butcher, Hamilton).

MARK ALAN - Wine Red. Large, semidouble to loose peony form with smallish petals. Average, compact, upright growth. E-M. (For a variation of this cultivar see 'My Nancy'). (U.S. 1958 - Ashby).

MARK ALAN VARIEGATED - Wine Red blotched and marbled White variation of 'Mark Alan'.

MARK CHASON - Dark Red with Orange cast. Large, semidouble with wavy, crinkled petals. Vigorous, upright growth. M. (U.S. 1977 - Gilley).

MARK CULVER - Fiery Red. Large, semidouble to peony form. Average, open, upright growth. M-L. (U.S. 1963 - Wilson).

MARK CULVER VARIEGATED - Fiery Red blotched White variation of 'Mark Culver'.

MARK J. - Rose Pink. Very large, semidouble to peony form. Average, upright growth. E-M. (U.S. 1989 - O. L. Jacobson, Jacksonville Beach, FL).

MARK STEWART - Red. Large, semidouble. Vigorous, compact, upright growth. M. (U.S. 1975 - Haynie).

MARKY COOPER - Pink outer petals shading to White in center. Large, rose form double. Vigorous, upright growth. M-L. (U.S. 1988 - J. W. Cooper, Jr., Kentfield, CA).

MARLENA BOZEMAN - Dark Red. Medium, semidouble. Average, upright growth. M. (U.S. 1994 - C. Bozeman, Hattiesburg, MS).

MARLENE - Light Pink. Large, semidouble. Vigorous, willowy growth. E-M. (U.S. 1956 - Ashby).

MARLIBSU - Pink with White streak down each petal. Large, rose form double. Vigorous, compact, upright growth. M. (U.S. 1966 - Thomasville, GA).

MAROON AND GOLD - Maroon. Small to medium, loose peony form with Golden stamens. Vigorous, upright growth. M-L. (U.S. 1961 - Nuccio's).

MARQUIS D'EXETER - See 'Marchioness of Exeter'.

MARQUIS DE LAFAYETTE - Rose Red. Large, semidouble to anemone form. Average, open, upright growth. E. (U.S. 1982 - J. K. Blanchard, Wallace, NC).

MARQUIS DE MONTCALM - Rose Pink. Medium, semidouble of pine cone form with petals becoming narrower near center and finally becoming petaloids. Slow, bushy growth. M. (U.S. Late 1800's - Magnolia).

MARQUIS DE MONTCALM VARIEGATED - Rose Pink and White form of 'Marquis de Montcalm'.

MARS - Crimson. Large, semidouble. (England 1911 - Paul).

MARSHMALLOW - Pink with White petaloids with Pale Pink bases. Miniature, anemone form. Average growth. M-L. (N.Z. 2000 - Haydon).

MARTHA ALICE BROWN - Blush Pink. Large, semidouble. Vigorous, upright growth. M-L. (U.S. 1978 - M. L. Gardins, Cochran, TX).

MARTHA ANN - Pink and White. Large, semidouble with irregular petals. M. (U.S. 1955).

MARTHA ANNE - Blush Pink to White edged Coral. Medium, semidouble to peony form. Vigorous, upright growth. M. (U.S. 1981 - Shackelford).

MARTHA BEATTY - Slightly Deeper Pink than Blush Pink. Medium, semidouble with notched petals. Average, open, upright growth. M. (U.S. 1995 - Homeyer).

MARTHA BRICE - Light Lavender Pink. Medium, semidouble to anemone form. Average, spreading growth. M. (U.S. 1940 - Mrs. M. E. Brice, Quitman, GA).

MARTHA BRINSON - Red. Large, semidouble with fluted, trumpet, upright petals. Vigorous, compact growth. M-L. (U.S. 1958 - W. G. Brinson, Norfolk, VA).

MARTHA BROOKS - Pale Pink, lightly veined, fading to soft White at edges. Medium to large, semidouble to anemone form. Average, upright, open growth. M-L. (U.S. 1998 - Bond Nursery Corp., Dallas, TX).

MARTHA FLOYD - White. Large, semidouble. Average, upright growth. M. (U.S. 1988 - J. Aldrich, Brooklet, GA).

MARTHA ISRAEL - White. Medium, rose form double to formal double of star shape. Average, upright growth. E-M. (U.S. 1977 - Tammia).

MARTHA MURRAY - Soft Pink. Medium, peony form. Average, compact growth. M. (U.S. 1954 - M. R. Murray, Fort Valley, GA).

MARTHA NORWOOD - Dark Red. Large, semidouble. Average growth. E-M. (U.S. 1965 - C. D. Norwood, Thomasville, GA).

MARTHA PROPPE - Deep Salmon Pink. Medium, single. Average, compact growth. M. (U.S. 1953 - Mrs. M. Proppe, Portland, OR).

MARTHA SANDERS - Salmon Pink. Medium, semidouble. (U.S. 1957 - Mrs. C. O. Maxwell, Reno, GA).

JAPONICA

M-M

107

MARTHA SMITH - Light Pink to Deeper Pink on outer petals. Miniature, formal double. Average, dense, upright growth. E-M. (U.S. 1990 - Mrs. Elizabeth R. Scott, Aiken, SC).

MARTHA TUCK - White. Large, semidouble with fluted petals. Average, compact, upright growth. E. (U.S. 1959 - Dr. M. B. Wine, Thomasville, GA).

MARTHA WRIGHT - Pink. Medium, semidouble. Average, upright growth. M. (U.S. 1942 - Miss B. Hoyt, Thomasville, GA).

MARTIE DETERMAN - Light Orchid Pink. Large to very large, semidouble. Average growth. E-L. (U.S. 1996 - H. Hall).

MARTIN - Rich Red. Medium to large, peony form. Average, spreading growth. E-L. (N.Z. 1986 - E. W. E. Butcher, Hamilton).

MARTIN ROBERTS - See 'Woodville Red'.

MARTY A. KEMP - Delicate Pink with Deeper Pink stripes. Small, formal double. Average, spreading, open growth. M-L. (Seedling of Japonica 'Snow Lady'). (U.S. 2019 - Pat Johnson, Cairo, GA).

MAR-VEL MURRAY - Pink. Medium, peony form. Average growth. M. (U.S. 1953 - F. K. Murray, San Marino, CA).

MARVIN JERNIGAN - Red and White. Large, semidouble to peony form. Vigorous, dense, spreading, upright growth. M-L. (U.S. 1995 - Jernigan).

MARY A. GREER - Red. Medium, peony form. Average, compact growth. M-L. (U.S. 1959 - Carleton).

MARY ADGER - Pink. Large, semidouble, with swirled and fluted petals. Average, spreading growth. M. (U.S. 1962 - B. A. Carlin, Mobile, AL).

MARY AGNES PATIN - China Rose. Large, rose form double with some upright, fimbriated petals and occasional cluster of petaloids. Vigorous, open, upright growth. E. (U.S. 1961 - T. C. Patin, Hammond, LA).

MARY AGNES PATIN VARIEGATED - China Rose blotched White variation of 'Mary Agnes Patin'.

MARY ALICE - Deep Red blotched White. Medium, semidouble. Vigorous, spreading growth. M. (Sport of Japonica 'Marlena Bozeman'). (U.S. 2003 - Lyman C. Fillingame, Lumberton, MS).

MARY ALICE COX - White. Medium to large, formal double with slightly cupped petal ends. Average, upright growth. E-M. (U.S. 1966 - T. N. Cox, Georgetown, SC).

MARY ALLEN SARGENT - Cherry Red with Light Yellow anthers, Small to medium, anemone form. Compact growth. E. Cold hardy. (Seedling of Japonica 'Edna Campbell'). (U.S. 2018 - Green Nurseries- Bobby Green - Fairhope, AL).

MARY ANDERSON - Red. Large, semidouble with White stamens. Vigorous, compact growth. M. (U.S. 1960 - G. Roberts, Savannah, GA).

MARY ANN HOOKS - White. Miniature, full peony form. Average, open, upright growth. E-M. (U.S. 2004 - George Hooks, Americus, GA).

MARY ANN LAWRENCE - Bright Red with Yellow anthers and White filaments; there is a vivid contrast of Red petals and Yellow anthers. Large, semidouble. Average, spreading, dense growth. M-L. (Japonica 'Royal Velvet' seedling). (U.S. 2013 - Steve and Gayle Lawrence, Tallahassee, FL).

MARY ANNE HOUSER - Rose. Large, loose peony form with irregular center of stamens and smaller petals twisted and intermixed. Average, compact, upright growth. M. (U.S. 1954 - Wheeler).

MARY ANNE HOUSER VARIEGATED - Rose and White variation of 'Mary Anne Houser'.

MARY B KING - Pale Pink. Very large, semidouble form with center petaloids. Average, open, upright growth. M-L. (U.S. 2000 - John King Jr., Thomasville, GA).

MARY BATES - Deep Rose. Medium, formal double. Average, open, upright growth. M. (U.S. 1968 - R. E. Bates, Sr., Waycross, GA).

MARY BELL GLENNAN - See 'Gigantea'.

MARY BETH - White dashed Pink. Medium, semidouble to loose peony form. M. (U.S. 1973 - Haynie).

MARY BETH BUSBEE - Hot pink with Yellow anthers and White filaments. Large, full peony to loose peony form. Average, spreading, open growth. E-M. (Seedling of Japonica 'Scarlet Glory'). (First Lady of Georgia Series). (U.S. 2018 - Gordy).

MARY BETHEA - Red shading to Purple at edge. Medium, semidouble. Slow, open growth. M-L. (U.S. 1950 - Clower).

MARY BOYCE - Dark Pink. Large, loose peony form. Vigorous, compact, upright growth. M. (U.S. 1975 - Haynie).

MARY BUTLER - Pale Pink. Large, full peony form. Average, compact growth. M. (U.S. 1957 - H. N. Butler, Albany, GA).

MARY CANTEY - Blush Pink. Medium, formal double. Slow, compact growth. M-L. (U.S. 1961 - J. S. Cantey, Marion, SC).

MARY CHARLOTTE - Light Pink. Medium, anemone form. Vigorous, compact, upright growth. M. (U.S. 1947 - Jones).

MARY COMPTON - White with Deep Pink markings and occasionally solid Pink. Large, semidouble with three alternate rows of slightly wavy heart shaped petals standing apart and high stamens. Average, upright growth. L. (U.S. 1960 - Julington).

MARY CORLEY - Light Pink with few Deeper Pink stripes. Medium to large, semidouble. Average, upright growth. E-M. (U.S. 2004 - Tom E. Corley, Auburn, AL).

MARY COSTA - White. Large, loose anemone form with fluted, undulated guard petals, and long strap-like petaloids. Average, compact, upright growth. E-M. (U.S. 1971 - Feathers).

MARY COWAN - Pink. Miniature, rose form double. Slow, upright growth. M-L. (U.S. 1983 - E. D. Cowan, Ruston, LA).

MARY DILLARD - Light Rose base to Deep Lavender inner petals. Large, formal double. Average, dense growth. E-M. (U.S. 1995 - O. Jacobson, Jacksonville Beach, FL).

MARY DUDLEY - Pink. Small, formal double with incurved petals. E-M. (U.S. 1959).

MARY EDNA CURLEE - Blush Pink splotched with Rose Pink and Dark Red highlights. Medium, peony form. Average, upright growth. M. (U.S. 1996 - M. Beach, Mt. Pleasant, SC).

MARY EDNA CURLEE RED - Dark Red with muted Darker Red stripes on petal edges. Medium, loose peony form. Average, upright growth. M. (Sport of Japonica 'Mary Edna Curlee'). (U.S. 2019 - Tommy Weeks, Conroe, TX).

MARY ELIZABETH BALLARD - Pink fading to White in center. Medium, formal double with some incurved petals. Average, upright growth. M. (U.S. 1983 - Gentry).

MARY EMMA MOTES - White. Large, semidouble to loose peony form. Average growth. M. (U.S. 1989 - Homeyer).

MARY FERRONI - Deep Pink. Large, semidouble. Average growth. M. (U.S. 1964 - Mrs. F. Newton, Folsom, LA).

MARY FISCHER - Blush Pink to Deeper Pink outer petals. Large, irregular semidouble to loose peony form. Bushy growth. M. (U.S. 1980 - Kramer).

MARY GRAMLING - Red and White. Large, rose form double. Average, dense, upright growth. E-M. (U.S. 1990 - R. Gramling, Tallahassee, FL).

MARY GRANT HALL - White with Pink edges. Large, peony form. Upright growth. M. (U.S. 2006 - Marion Hall, Dothan, AL).

MARY HALE - Rose Pink. Medium, rose form double. (U.S. 1957 - Baker).

MARY J. WHEELER - Orchid Pink to Light Pink to White at base of petals. Medium, loose peony form with wavy petals and twisted upright center petals. Average, upright growth. M. (U.S. 1957 - Wheeler).

MARY J. WHEELER VARIEGATED - Orchid Pink blotched White variation of 'Mary J Wheeler'.

MARY JANE - Red. Large, loose peony form. Vigorous, bushy growth. M. (U.S. 1949 - Malbis).

MARY JANE LEU - Rose Pink shading to Light Pink and streaked White. Miniature, formal double with incurved outer petals. Average, dense, upright growth. M-L. (U.S. 1995 - H. Leu, Orlando, FL).

MARY JO - Soft Salmon Pink. Large, peony form. Vigorous, open, upright growth. E-L. (U.S. 1957 - Hearn).

MARY JO GHEEMS - White. Large, semidouble to loose peony form. Average growth. M. (U.S. 1967 - L. B. Wilson, Jr., Gulfport, MS).

MARY JO MORGAN - Deep Rose veined Deeper Rose. Large, semidouble with full ring of stamens. Vigorous growth. (U.S. 1957 - C. H. Welch, Hattiesburg, MS).

MARY K - Pink blotched White. Large, peony form. (U.S. 1955).

MARY KNOCK - Bright Pink. Medium, formal double to rose form double. Vigorous, compact, upright growth. M-L. (U.S. 1957 - L. H. Knock, Frederick, MD).

MARY LATANE - Rose Pink. Large to very large, loose semidouble to peony form, with fimbriated petals. Average, upright growth. E. (U.S. 2003 - Robbie S. Snell, Mt. Hermon, LA).

MARY LEE - White. Large, semidouble. Average, compact growth. M-L. (U.S. 1952 - Mrs. J. H. Gary, Norfolk, VA).

MARY LIBBY - White striped Pink. Large, semidouble with White stamens. Vigorous, open, upright growth. E-M. (U.S. 1955 - Weisner).

MARY LIGON - Light Pink. Large, semidouble. Average, upright growth. M. (U.S. 1964 - S. E. Ligon, Abbeville, SC).

MARY LILLA DUMAS - White to Chartreuse. Large to very large, semidouble to loose peony form. Vigorous, upright growth. M. (U.S. 1984 - Homeyer).

MARY LOUISE CANTELOU - Blush Pink shading darker toward edge. Large, semidouble. Vigorous, upright growth. M-L. (U.S. 1977 - Dodd).

MARY LOVE - White. Large to very large, semidouble with loose petals. M. (U.S. 1973 - Haynie).

MARY LU - Blush Pink. Medium, formal double. Average, open, upright growth. E-M. (U.S. 1963 - Windy Hill Nsy., Jacksonville, FL).

MARY LUCAS - Red variegated White. Large, semidouble with irregular petals. Average growth. M. (Similar to 'Nagasaki'). (U.S. 1957 - Lucas, Hattiesburg, MS).

MARY LUDINGTON - Pink and White. Medium, semidouble. Average, upright growth. M. (U.S. 1960 - Marbury).

MARY LUDINGTON PINK - Pink. (Sport of Japonica 'Mary Ludington').

MARY LUNSFORD - Bright Pink. Medium, formal double with rounded petals and pointed rosebud center. Slow, spreading growth. M-L. (U.S. 1964 - Julington).

MARY MARGARET - Rose Red. Large, anemone form with some White petaloids. Vigorous, upright growth. M. (U.S. 1956 - Hudson).

MARY McKINNON - Rose Pink. Large to very large, semidouble with White anthers. Average, spreading growth. E-M. (U.S. 1965 - Mrs. L. T. McKinnon, Brunswick, GA).

MARY MERRITT - Dark Red with Pink filaments. Medium, semidouble. Vigorous, upright growth. M. (U.S. 1954 - Turner).

MARY MOUGHON - Glowing Red. Large, semidouble to loose peony form. Average, upright, spreading growth. M-L. (U.S. 1964 - G. W. Moughon, Birmingham, AL).

MARY MYRICK - Light Blush Pink. Medium, semidouble. Average, upright growth. M. (U.S. 1975 - Emanuel Kronstadt, Savannah, GA).

MARY NOBLE - White. Large, peony form. Average, spreading growth. E-M. (U.S. 1970 - F. R. Bisbee, Jacksonville, FL).

MARY NOEL GREEN - Bright Red. Large, loose anemone form with four alternate rows of slightly wavy, large, round petals and several rows of petals graduating in size toward center. Average, compact growth. M. (U.S. 1965 - Julington).

MARY PAIGE - Soft, Light Pink slightly shaded. Medium to large, formal double. Sturdy, compact, upright growth. M-L. (U.S. 1964 - H. L. Paige, Lafayette, CA).

MARY PERDUE - Red. Medium, formal double to rose form double with slightly incurved petals. Average, upright, open growth. M-L. (First Lady of Georgia Series). (U.S. 2018 - Gordy).

MARY R. SOLOMON - White splotched Red. Medium, semidouble. Average, spreading growth. M. (U.S. 1970 - J. L. Solomon, Augusta, GA).

MARY ROBERTSON - See 'Donckelarii'.

MARY ROBINSON - Pink. Small, formal double. Slow growth. M. (U.S. 1972 - E. D. Robinson, St. Pauls, NC).

MARY RUTH SMITH - Deep Pink with Deeper Red veining. Large, formal double. Average, dense, spreading growth. M-L. (U.S. 1995 - W. Smith, Gainesville, FL).

MARY SEBRING FREDRICKSON - Medium Pink with Yellow anthers and White filaments. Small, semidouble. Average, upright, dense growth. E-L. (U.S. 2013 - Edward W. Fredrickson, Wilmington, NC).

MARY SEIBELS - Pink. Medium to large, loose peony form. Average, compact growth. M. (U.S. 1952 - M. Ball, Summerville, SC).

MARY STEWART DENNIS - Translucent Soft Pink. Large to very large, loose peony form. Vigorous, spreading and upright growth. M. (U.S. 2005 - Gordon Rabalais, Arnaudville, LA).

MARY TAYLOR - Faint Blush Pink shading White with a few Pink splotches. Large, full peony form. (U.S. 1965 - Mrs. J. Leslie Taylor, Theodore, AL).

MARY TAYLOR PINK - Blush Pink. (Sport of Japonica 'Mary Taylor'). (U.S. 1972 - Mrs. J. Leslie Taylor, Theodore, AL).

MARY THOMAS - White with Green petaloids. Medium, peony form. Vigorous, upright growth. L. (U.S. 1952 - C. W. Thomas, San Dimas, CA).

MARY TREACEY - Deep Pink. Large, semidouble. Vigorous, pendulous growth. M-L. (Aus. 1963 - J. W. Treacey, Kew).

MARY WEIS - Dark Red. Large, loose peony form. Average, compact growth. M. (U.S. 1953).

MARYLAND - Deep Cerise. Large, semidouble with White stamens and occasional petaloids. Average, upright growth. M. (U.S. 1959 - Breschini).

MARYLAND VARIEGATED - Deep Cerise marked and splotched White variation of 'Maryland'.

MARYON CAPERS - Rose Pink. Medium, formal double. Average, compact growth. E-M. (U.S. 1961 - Q. C. Roberts, Ocean Springs, MS).

MASQUERADE - White striped Pink on one or more petals. Large, semidouble to anemone form with lacy petaloids in center. Average, compact growth. M. (For a variation of this cultivar see 'Marguerite Tourje'). (U.S. 1953 - Nuccio's).

MASTERPIECE - White, opening from a Blush bud. Large, formal double with a high center to rose formal double. Vigorous, open, upright growth; large foliage. M. (U.S. 1950 - Short).

MASTERPIECE PINK - Pink. (Sport of Japonica 'Masterpiece'). (U.S. 1962 - Mrs. J. P. Moon, Lake Charles, LA).

MATADOR - Dark Red. Large, semidouble to loose peony form. Vigorous, open, upright growth. M-L. (U.S. 1967 - Nuccio's).

MATHOTIANA - ('Julia Drayton'; 'Mathotiana Rubra'; 'Purple Dawn'; 'Purple Emperor'; 'Purple Prince'; 'William S. Hastie'). Crimson, sometimes with Purple cast. Large to very large, rose form double to formal double. Vigorous, compact, upright growth. M-L. Cold hardy. (Variations of this cultivar include 'Flowerwood'; 'Sultana'; 'Red Wonder'; 'Rosea Superba'). (Not same as cultivar listed in old literature, which was a very large Red formal double). (Europe to U.S. - [Magnolia] 1840's).

MATHOTIANA ALBA - ('Blood of Christ'; 'Inconstant Beauty'). White, sometimes tinged Pink. Large, formal double. Vigorous, upright growth. L. (Variations of this cultivar include 'Anna Bruneau'; 'Mathotiana Rosea'; 'Souv. de Bahuaud Litou'; 'Duke of Windsor'). (Belgium 1858 - M Mathot, Ghent).

MATHOTIANA FIMBRIATA - See 'Flowerwood'.

MATHOTIANA ROSEA - ('Pink Beauty;' 'Laura Polka'; 'Warwick'). Clear Pink. Large, formal double. (Sport of Japonica 'Mathotiana Alba'). (England 1875 - Veitch).

MATHOTIANA RUBRA - See 'Mathotiana.

MATHOTIANA SPECIAL - A variegated 'Mathotiana' with fewer and larger White spots. Large to very large, rose form double to formal double. (U.S. 1961 - R. Lang, Atlanta, GA).

MATHOTIANA SUPREME - ('Mima-Mac'). Very large, semidouble with loose, irregular petals interspersed with stamens. (Sport of Japonica 'Mathotiana'). (For other forms of this cultivar see 'Cherry Bounce' and 'Sue Ann Mouton'). (U.S. 1951 - Flowerwood).

MATHOTIANA SUPREME VARIEGATED - ('Avery Island'; 'Kate Smith'). Scarlet blotched White variations of 'Mathotiana Supreme'.

MATHOTIANA VARIEGATED - ('Julia Drayton Variegated';' Paulina'). Scarlet blotched White variation of 'Mathotiana'. Large to very large, rose form double to formal double. (For a variation of this cultivar see 'Eugenia Howell').

MATILDA BRADFORD - Dark Red. Medium, peony with numerous petaloids. Average, dense, spreading growth. M-L. (U.S. 2003 - J. A. Peninger, Shreveport, LA).

MATILIJA POPPY - White. Large to very large, semidouble with crinkled petals. Vigorous, compact, dense growth. M-L. (U.S. 1991 - Nuccio's).

MATOSI - Soft Pink marbled White. Medium, formal double. Average, compact, upright growth. M. (For another form of this cultivar, see 'Sacco Rosea'). (Japan).

MATSUKASA - ('Kagoshima'; 'Pine Cone'). Rose Pink marked White. Medium, semidouble of pine cone formation with high center and wavy petals. Slow, bushy growth. L. (Japan to U.S. 1932 - Domoto).

MATTERHORN - White. Medium to large, formal double. Average, upright growth. M. (U.S. 1997 - Feathers).

MATTHEW COOPER - Soft Blush Pink with minute misty Deep Pink specks. Small, formal double. Average, upright growth. M. (U.S. 1981 - Stone).

MATTIE COLE - Rose Carmine. Large, single. Spreading, upright growth. M. (Aus. 1955 - Cole).

MATTIE GRAYSON - Red. Large, rose form double to peony form with four to five upright petals around center. Average, upright growth. M. (U.S. 1960 - Rester).

MATTIE O'REILLY - Coral Rose Pink. Large, semidouble to full peony form. Slow, compact, upright growth. E-L. (U.S. 1947 - McCaskill).

MATTIE R - Medium, with incurved petals. (Sport of Japonica 'Alba Plena'). (U.S. 1961 - J L Gautier, Jr., Moss Point, MS).

MAUDE FOOTE - Clear Pink. Large, semidouble, sometimes with intermixed petaloids and stamens. Vigorous growth. M. (U.S. 1957 - Mrs. F. W. Foote, Hattiesburg, MS).

MAUDE FOOTE VARIEGATED - Clear Pink and White variation of 'Maude Foote'.

MAUDE HAINES - Phlox Pink. Large, semidouble with occasional petaloids. Dense, spreading growth. M. (N.Z. 1962 - Mrs. M. Haines, Wellington).

MAUDIE CLARINDA - Light Red. Medium, formal double. Average, upright growth. E-M. (U.S. 2019 - Gordy).

MAUI - White. Large, heavy anemone form with rippled guard petals. Average, bushy growth. M. (Sport of Japonica 'Kona'). (U.S. 1975 - Nuccio's).

MAUREEN ELIZABETH - White with imbricated petals. Large, formal double. Average, upright growth. M. (Aus. 2006 - M. H. Schultz, Edwardston, S. Aus.).

MAUREEN OSTLER - See 'Just Sue'.

MAURY PINK - Pale Pink. Medium, semidouble. (U.S. 1953 - Greenbrier).

MAVERICK - See 'Tomorrow Variegated'.

MAVIS EDNA - White. Medium, semidouble. Slow, compact, dense growth. M-L. (Aus. 1993 - D. O'Reilly, Ainslie, Australian Capital Territory).

MAVIS GWALTNEY - Deep Pink. Very large, semidouble with loose, wide petals, sometimes with petaloids. Average, upright growth. E-M. (U.S. 1968 - Mrs. A. T. Williams, Dothan, AL).

MAVIS MERSON - Cardinal Red. Very large, semidouble. Average, spreading growth. (N.Z. 1967 - Mrs. T. B. Merson).

MAVOURNEEN - Very Pale Pink merging Cream and changing to Pale Lime Green in center. Large, rose form double. Average growth. M. (N.Z. 1972 - D. G. O'Toole, Ohope).

MAX COTTON - Red. Medium, formal double. Compact growth. M. (Aus. 1962 - E. G. Waterhouse).

MAX GOODLEY - Light Pink. Medium to large, semidouble with irregular petals. Vigorous, open, upright growth. M-L. (U.S. 1954 - Illges).

MAX HOLLIMAN - Deep Bluish Red with darker veining. Medium to large, peony form. Vigorous, dense, upright growth. M-L. (U.S. 1994 - J. Holliman, Thomaston, GA).

MAX SWISHER - Red. Medium, semidouble. (U.S. 1956 - Gerbing).

MAXINE - Faint Pink striped Darker Pink. Medium, formal double. Pendulous growth. M-L. (U.S. 1975 - Haynie).

MAY A'VARD - Light Pink. Large, semidouble. Average, open, upright growth. M-L. (Aus. 1967 - Mrs. M. A'Vard, Emerald, Vic.).

MAY INGRAM - Orchid Pink. Medium, formal double. Vigorous, upright growth. E. (U.S. 1959 - Nuccio's).

MAYBELL PAULIN - Blush Pink. Medium, rose form double. M-L. (Portugal 1959 - Da Silva).

MAYBELLE RAGLAND - Soft Pink with Silver overtones. Large, semidouble to loose peony form with wavy, rounded, notched outer petals and folded, upright center petals and White stamens. Average, open, upright growth. M. (U.S. 1959 - Ragland).

MAYER ISRAEL - Blush to Light Pink flecked Darker Pink. Large, formal double, sometimes with incurved, swirled petals. Average, upright growth. E-M. (U.S. 1977 - Tammia).

MAYFLOWER - Deep Rose shading to White center petaloids. Medium, rose form double. Vigorous, upright growth. M-L. (U.S. 1958 - Novick).

MAYLENE WONG - Crimson. Large, loose peony form to anemone form. Vigorous, compact, upright growth. M-L. (U.S. 1954 - H. C. Wilson, Fresno, CA).

MAYLENE WONG VARIEGATED - Crimson blotched White variation of 'Maylene Wong'.

MAYTIME - Pale Pink edged White. Large, formal double. Average, upright growth. L. (U.S. 1959 - F. Wittsche, Sacramento, CA).

McQUISTON - Camellia Rose, central segments showing slightly White variegation with Yellow anthers and White filaments. Medium, loose peony form. Upright, open-branched growth. M. (U.S. 1945).

McVEY'S GUILIO NUCCIO - A heavily variegated 'Guilio Nuccio'. Large to very large, semidouble.

MEDALLION - Rose Pink shading to Paler Pink in center with light stripe in center of each petal. Medium, formal double with incurved petals. L. (U.S. 1955 - M. Ruster, Pasadena, CA).

MEHL'S RED - See 'Vedrine'.

MEI-LING - Deep Red. Large, semidouble to loose peony form. Vigorous, upright growth. M. (U.S. 1955 - Nuccio's).

MEL'S MINIATURE - Darkest Red with White speckles. Miniature, anemone form. Vigorous, dense growth. M. (U.S. 1995 - Piet and Gaeta).

MELANIE ANNE POE - White to Light Pink with one to two Red petals with medium Yellow anthers and Cream filaments. Very large, anemone form. Average, spreading growth. M-L. (U.S. 2009 - W. Lee Poe, Jr., Aiken, SC).

MELANIE CHAVAUX - White with occasional Pink stripe. Small, formal double. Average, upright, open growth. M-L. (Seedling of Japonica 'Betty Sheffield Blush'). (U.S. 2016 - Pat Johnson, Cairo, GA).

MELANIE'S FAVORITE - White in the center shading to Pale Pink with Deeper Pink stripes with Yellow anthers and White filaments. Large, semidouble to loose peony form. Average, upright, open growth. M-L. (U.S. 2018 - Pat Johnson, Cairo, GA).

MELINDA HACKETT - Pink. Medium to large, anemone form to full peony form. Average growth. E-M. (U.S. 1966 - Mrs. W. Laughlin, Aiken, SC).

MELINDA LOU - Dusky Pink. Medium, full peony form. Average, compact growth. M. (U.S. 1953).

MELINDA WILLIAMS - Dark Red. Large, semidouble to anemone form. Vigorous, upright growth. M. (U.S. 1948 - F. Williams, Beverly Hills, CA).

MELISSA - Blush Pink. Miniature, semidouble. (U.S. 1961 - E Vallot, Youngsville, LA).

MELISSA ANNE - White. Large to very large, loose to full peony form with clusters of Light Yellow interspersed stamens. Vigorous, dense growth. E-L. (U.S. 1995 - Dr. L. Audioun, Biloxi, MS).

MELISSA BEALE TALLEY - Medium Pink with Yellow anthers and White filaments. Large, semidouble. Average, upright, open growth. M. (U.S. 2010 - John Talley, Wilmington, NC).

MELISSA HARDISON - Pink and White. Large to very large, anemone form to peony form. Average, spreading growth. M. (U.S. 1997 - D. Hardison, Tallahassee, FL).

MELODY LANE - Blushed Pink striped Red. Large, semidouble. Average, compact growth. M. (U.S. 1951 - E. W. Miller, Escondido, CA).

MELODY LANE SPECIAL - Pink. (Sport of Japonica 'Melody Lane'). (U.S. 1956 - Fisher).

MELODY SHEPHERD - Bright Rose Red. Large, semidouble, anemone form to peony form with irregular petals. Vigorous, compact, upright growth. E-L. (U.S. 1972 - W. T. Shepherd, North Charleston, SC).

MELODY SHEPHERD VARIEGATED - Bright Rose Red and White variation of 'Melody Shepherd'. (U.S. 1977 - W. T. Shepherd, North Charleston, SC).

MEMENTO - Coral Rose. Miniature, anemone form. Vigorous, upright growth. M. (U.S. 1959 - Short).

MEMPHIS BELLE - Red heavily variegated White. Medium to large, semidouble. M. (Note: Previously listed incorrectly as 'Memphis Bell'). (U.S. 1965 - Wilkes Nsy., Moultrie, GA).

MEN'S MINI - Deep Red with Silver sheen. Miniature, semidouble to anemone form. Average, upright growth. M-L. (U.S. 1971 - A. H. Walters, Laurel, MS).

MENA - Red striped and blotched White. Medium, anemone form to peony form. Low, spreading growth. E. (U.S. 1959 - H. Mura, Augusta, GA).

MENIA WHEAT - Red. Large, semidouble with three very large, wavy petals around outer edge of stamens forming trumpet-like center. Average, upright growth. M. (U.S. 1960 - Rester).

MERCURY - Deep Rose Pink to Scarlet. Large, semidouble, sometimes with upright center petals. Average, compact growth. M. (England 1911 - Paul).

MERCURY SUPREME - Form similar to 'Donckelarii'. (Sport of Japonica 'Mercury'). (U.S. 1961).

MERCURY VARIEGATED - Scarlet and White variation of 'Mercury'.

MEREDITH - Pale Pink to Crimson on outer petals. Large, semidouble. Average, compact growth. L. (U.S. 1980 - Mrs. W. W. Hentz, Harwood, MD).

MEREDITH KAY SHUMAN - Pink marked Deep Pink. Large, semidouble to peony form. Average, upright growth. M-L. (U.S. 1988 - J. Aldrich, Brooklet, GA).

MEREDITH LAKE - ('Della Robbia'). White with pale Lilac overtone. Medium, semidouble. Vigorous, bushy growth. M. (Japan to U.S. [Huntington] 1918).

MERIAM LEWIS - Pink. Large, semidouble with upright petals. Average, upright growth. E-M. (U.S. 1965 - F. C. Lewis Nsy., Norfolk, VA).

MERIAM LEWIS VARIEGATED - Pink and White variation of 'Meriam Lewis'. (U.S. 1965 - F. C. Lewis Nsy., Norfolk, VA).

MERLE GRAY - Blush Pink. Large, full peony form. Vigorous, compact growth. M. (U.S. 1953 - Miss M. Gray, Burton, SC).

MERRI BRANTLEY - Pale delicate Pink shading to White at the center with Gold anthers and White filaments. Large, semidouble. Average, upright, open growth. M-L. (Seedling of Japonica 'Beatrix Hoyt'). (U.S. 2019 - Pat Johnson, Cairo, GA).

MERRILLEES - White. Large, peony form with very large, ruffled outer petals and low center of twisted petaloids. M. (Aus. 1957 - Waterhouse).

MERRY CHRISTMAS - Brilliant Red to Red bordered White. Medium, single to semidouble. Average, upright growth. E-M. (U.S. 1991 - Nuccio's).

MERRY MEN - Shell Pink. Medium to large, semidouble with three rows of very large petals. Vigorous, spreading growth. M-L. (U.S. 1958 - Fruitland).

MESSUGAH - Dark Red. Medium, hose-in-hose to semidouble. Average, upright growth. M. (U.S. 1990 - V. Stone, Baton Rouge, LA).

METCALF RED - Brilliant Red. Medium to large, semidouble. Vigorous growth. E. (U.S. 1953 - Clower).

MEXICALI ROSE - Brilliant Red. Large, semidouble. Average, compact, upright growth. M. (U.S. 1964 - L. W. Strohmeyer, San Gabriel, CA).

MICHAEL JACKSON - White. Very large, semidouble with rippled petals and compact stamens. Vigorous, compact growth. M-L. (U.S. 1961 - M. P. Jackson, Florence, SC).

MICHAEL JOHNSON - White striped Pink. Large, semidouble. M. (U.S. 1953 - Brock).

MICHAEL SPRY - Pink. Large, single. Slow, open, upright growth. E-L. (Aus. 1989 - W. Spry, The Basin, Vic.).

MICHAEL WITMAN - White. Large, semidouble with frilled and fluted petals. Average growth. M. (U.S. 1971 - Witman).

MICHAEL'S JOY - Wine Red with near Black veining, giving the flower a Deep Wine Red appearance. Small, semidouble. Average, dense growth. M-L. (N.Z. 2000 - Haydon).

MICHELLE COOPER - Rose Red. Medium, loose semidouble. Open, upright growth. M. (U.S. 2001 - V. Stone, Baton Rouge, LA).

MICHELLE HOWELL - Maroon and White with Yellow anthers and Yellow filaments. Large, semidouble. Average, upright, dense growth. M. (U.S. 2013 - Howell).

MICHELLE S. VARIEGATED - Rose Pink and White Miniature, semidouble, occasionally formal double. Slow, dense growth. M-L. (U.S. 2004 - Doug Simon, Norfolk, VA).

MIDDLE GEORGIA - Dark Red. Medium to large, formal double. Average, dense, upright growth. E-L. (U.S. 1992 - Homeyer).

MIDDY PETTEWAY - Rose Pink. Medium, formal double. Vigorous, compact, upright growth. E-L. (U.S. 1964 - H. C. Petteway, Lakeland, FL).

MIDGET WHEELER - Flesh Pink dotted and dashed Rose Pink. Miniature, formal double. Average, upright growth. M-L. (U.S. 1974 - G. M. Wheeler, Shelby, AL).

MIDNIGHT - Black Red. Medium, semidouble to anemone form. Vigorous, compact, upright growth. M. (U.S. 1963 - Nuccio's).

113

MIDNIGHT MAGIC - Very Dark Red with center petaloids marked White in varying degrees. Medium to large, full peony form. Vigorous, compact, upright growth. L. (U.S. 1985 - Nuccio's).

MIDNIGHT SERENADE - Brilliant Darkest Red. Medium to large, single. Average, bushy, upright growth. M-L. (U.S. 1973 - Nuccio's).

MIDNIGHT VARIEGATED - Black Red marked White variation of 'Midnight'. (Aus. 1983 - A. F. Savage, Mt. Pleasant, W. Aus.).

MIGNON FAVROT - Soft Pink. Medium, formal double. Average, upright, dense growth. M. (U.S. 2015 - Gordy).

MIKASA-NO-TSUKI - Deep pink, veined Deeper Pink with clear White edge with Golden anthers and White filaments. Large, campanulate single, five petals. (Sport of Japonica 'Tafuku-benten). (Japan Early 1940's - Chûbu Area).

MIKE PRATCH - Rose Red. Large, semidouble. Vigorous, compact growth. M. (U.S. 1972 - Nuccio's).

MIKE WITMAN - Coral Pink. Large, peony form with curled and wavy petals. Average, upright growth. M. (U.S. 1968 - Witman).

MIKE WITMAN VARIEGATED - Coral Pink and White variation of 'Mike Witman'. (U.S. 1972).

MIKENJAKU - See 'Nagasaki'. ('Mikenjaku' is reported as priority name for this cultivar but as 'Nagasaki' [Japan to England 1889 - G. Waller] has been in such common use in the U.S. we do not believe a change is necessary or warranted). (Japan 1879 - Ito).

MIKES DELIGHT - Light Crimson at center, deeper color on edge of petals. Medium, semidouble. Average, bushy, upright growth. E-M. (Aus. 1999 - Kevin J. Coase, Tamborine Mt, Qld.).

MIKEY B - Dark Red. Miniature, formal double. Average, compact growth. M. (U.S. 1986 - J. Holtzman, Crows Landing, CA).

MIKUNI-NO-HOMARE - Veined Pink bordered White. Medium to large, single with flared Pale Yellow stamens. See Higo.

MIKUNI-NO-HOMARE RED - Red. (Sport of Japonica 'Mikuni-No-Homare'). See Higo.

MILDRED ELLIMAN - White. Medium to large, formal double. Vigorous growth. M. (U.S. 1957 - Magnolia).

MILDRED GILMORE - Deep Red. Medium, single. Vigorous, upright growth. M-L. (U.S. 1977 - W. L. Gilmore, Conroe, TX).

MILDRED LEE MELDER - Red. Large, semidouble. Average, upright growth. M. (U.S. 1954 - Poole Bros. Nsy., Forest Hill, LA).

MILDRED STOLTZ - Red. Small, single. Vigorous, compact, upright growth. M. (U.S. 1965 - Miss O. Fogt, Macon, GA).

MILES HARDY - White. Large, rose form double. Open, upright growth. E-M. (U.S. 1950 - Clower).

MILINDA - White shading to Orchid at edge. Medium, formal double. Vigorous, compact, upright growth. M. (U.S. 1977 - Piet).

MIMA-MAE - See 'Mathotiana Supreme'.

MINE-NO-YUKI - Light Pink splashed Deeper Pink. Medium to large, single with circular soft Pink stamens. (Not to be confused with Sasanqua 'Mine-no-yuki' - a separate cultivar). See Higo.

MINI ALBA - White. Miniature, peony form. Average, compact, upright growth. M-L. (U.S. 1981 - T. E. Lundy, Pensacola, FL).

MINI FACES - White with Rose and Carmine stripes and specks. Miniature, semidouble. Average, spreading growth. M. (U.S. 1997 - D. Mayfield, Baton Rouge, LA).

MINI FACES BLUSH - Blush Pink. (Sport of Japonica 'Mini Faces'). (U.S. 1999 - A. Landry, Baton Rouge, LA).

MINI PEP - Rose Pink to Off-White streaked Rose to White spotted Rose. Miniature, formal double. Slow, spreading, upright growth. E. (U.S. 1988 - T. Eagleson, Beaumont, TX).

MINI PINK - Light Pink. Miniature, semidouble with wavy, crinkled petals to anemone form with Creamy petaloids. Vigorous, spreading growth. M. (U.S. 1970 - D. C. Strother, Fort Valley, GA).

MINIFLORA - Delicate two-toned Pink. Small, semidouble. Slow, compact growth. M-L. (U.S. 1983 - Feathers).

MINNA HELMS - Rose. Large, loose peony form with some incurved, wavy petals and occasional petaloids. Vigorous, upright growth. M. (U.S. 1956 - C. G. Carter, Jacksonville, FL).

MINNIE BEASLEY SMITH - White striped and blotched Red. Large, peony form. Vigorous, dense, upright growth. E-M. (U.S. 1997 - L. Smith, Beaufort, SC).

MINNIE BODEKER - Bright Red. Large, semidouble with heavy textured petals intermixed with stamens. Vigorous, upright growth. E-M. (U.S. 1964 - Miss M. Bodeker, Augusta, GA).

MINNIE ELIZABETH - Red. Medium, semidouble with small petaloids. Vigorous, open, upright growth. M-L. (U.S. 1950 - Mrs. W. W. Harman, Birmingham, AL).

MINNIE MADDERN FISKE - Light Pink. Medium, semidouble with broad, round outer petals and irregularly frilled inner petals. Average, compact growth. M. (U.S. 1946 - McIlhenny).

MINNIE RUTH - Rose Pink. Medium, formal double. Average, compact, upright growth. E-L. (U.S. 1977 - Gilley).

MINNIE TURNER - Rose Pink. Large, semidouble. Vigorous, pendulous growth. E-M. (U.S. 1955 - Weisner).

114

MINOR LEAGUE - Rose Pink. Miniature, full peony form. Average, upright growth. M. (U.S. 1975 - B. F. Seale, Sr., Birmingham, AL).

MINUTE - Light Pink. Miniature, formal double. Compact, upright growth. M. (U.S. 1962 - Wheeler).

MIRACLE MADGE - White with occasional splotches of Pink. Large, anemone form. (U.S. 1959 - Ms. P. Kennon, Bogalusa, LA).

MIRIAM STEVENSON - Soft Blush Pink. Medium, semidouble to loose peony form. Average to vigorous, upright growth. M. (U.S. 1954 - Wheeler).

MIRIAM STEVENSON VARIEGATED - Soft Blush Pink and White variation of 'Miriam Stevenson'.

MIRROR OF JUSTICE - White to Pink marked Darker Pink. Medium, semidouble to anemone form. M. (U.S. 1954 - Baker).

MISS AIKEN - Light Pink. Medium to large, semidouble. Average growth. E-M. (U.S. 1975 - G. M. Owens, Aiken, SC).

MISS AMERICA - Rose Pink. Large, semidouble, sometimes with intermixed stamens and petaloids. Vigorous, upright growth. M. (U.S. 1957 - Davis).

MISS ANAHEIM - Soft Pink. Medium to large, semidouble to loose peony form. Vigorous, compact, upright growth. M. (U.S. 1961 - McCaskill).

MISS ANNETTE - Deep Pink. Large, semidouble with upright petals. Upright, spreading growth. M. (U.S. 1961 - McIlhenny).

MISS BAKERSFIELD - Bright Red. Large, loose to full peony form. Vigorous, compact, upright growth. M-L. (U.S. 1982 - Alfter).

MISS BAKERSFIELD VARIEGATED - Bright Red and White variation of 'Miss Bakersfield'. (U.S. 1982 - Alfter).

MISS BESSIE BEVILLE - Rose to Phlox Pink. Medium, formal double. Average, spreading growth. E-L. (U.S. 1979 - Homeyer).

MISS BETTY - White streaked Blush Pink and Crimson. Large, semidouble to anemone form. Average, compact, pendulous growth. M. (U.S. 1952 - Councilman).

MISS BETTY PINK - Blush Pink. (Sport of Japonica 'Miss Betty').

MISS BETTY RED - Crimson. (Sport of Japonica 'Miss Betty').

MISS BILOXI - White. Medium, rose form double to peony form. Average, compact growth. M. (U.S. 1957 - R. H. Brodie, Biloxi, MS).

MISS CHARLESTON - Deep Red. Medium to large, semidouble with high center to formal double. Average, upright growth. M-L. (U.S. 1961 - W. I. McGill, Adams Run, SC).

MISS CHARLESTON VARIEGATED - Deep Red blotched White variation of 'Miss Charleston'.

MISS CLEMSON - Cherry Red. Small, formal double. Average growth. L. (U.S. 1970 - W. C. Bowen, Clemson, SC).

MISS DOT - Pink. Large, peony form. (U.S. 1957 - Davis).

MISS ETHEL - Soft Pink and White Blush. Medium to large, rose form double. Vigorous, spreading, open and upright growth. E-M. (U.S. 2004 - Sen. George Hooks, Americus, GA).

MISS FAYETTEVILLE - Pink. Large, peony form. Average, upright growth. M. (U.S. 1991 - Habel).

MISS FORT WALTON BEACH - Rose Pink. Medium, peony form to rose form double. Average, upright growth. M. Cold hardy. (U.S. 1993 - Ed and June Atkins, Shalimar, FL).

MISS FRANKIE - Soft Pink. Medium to large, peony form. Vigorous, upright growth. M. (U.S. 1957 - Nuccio's).

MISS GEORGIA - Light Pink edged White. Small to medium, single with five petals and two petaloids. Vigorous, compact growth. M. (U.S. 1953 - Shackelford).

MISS GLADYS - Pale Pink. Large, rose form double with petals cupping upward. Upright growth. M. (U.S. 2006 - Gladys Weinspach, Ocala, Fl).

MISS HENNI - Dark Rose to Violet. Small, rose form double. Slow, upright growth. M-L. (U.S. 2006 - John Grimm, Metarie, LA).

MISS HOLLYWOOD - Light Pink speckled and with occasional narrow stripes of Darker Pink. Medium, formal double. Average, compact growth. E. (U.S. 1957 - Carter).

MISS IDAH - Blush Pink. Medium, semidouble. Average, upright growth. M. (U.S. 1984 - Mrs. H. Johnson, Madison, FL).

MISS IRENE - Pink. Small, formal double. Vigorous, upright growth. E-L. (U.S. 2016 - Howell).

MISS LAKELAND - Pink with Red stripes. Miniature, rose form double to formal double. Vigorous, upright growth. E-M. (U.S. 2005 - John W. Shirah, Lakeland, FL).

MISS LEILA - White variegated Rose. Large, semidouble. Average, compact growth. M. (U.S. 1981 - Mrs. N. Johnson, Madison, FL).

MISS LILLIAN - Creamy White with petals bordered Pink; blooms sometimes are Pale Pink with Darker Pink on petal borders. Small to medium, formal double. Vigorous, upright growth. M. (U.S. 2001 - Gordy).

MISS LILLIAS - Pink. Small, semidouble with wavy, crepe petals. Average, open, upright growth. M-L. (U.S. 1974 - D. C. Strother, Fort Valley, GA).

MISS LU-ANN - Coral Red and White. Large, semidouble with wavy, crinkled petals. Average, open, upright growth. M. (U.S. 1969 - D. J. Videll, Memphis, TN).

MISS LUCY - Light Pink flecked Rose. Medium, formal double. Average growth. M-L. (U.S. 1976 - T. E. Lundy, Pensacola, FL).

MISS LYLA - White marked Pink. Large, semidouble to rose form double with swirled, fluted petals and crepe center petals and White stamens. Slow, open, spreading growth. L. (U.S. 1961 - Solomon).

MISS MANDIE - Deep Red. Large, semidouble to full peony form. Average, compact, upright growth. M-L. (U.S. 1967 - T. N. Cox, Georgetown, SC).

MISS MANDIE SUPREME - Variegated variation of 'Miss Mandie' - Red heavily variegated White. (U.S. 1968 - T. N. Cox, Georgetown, SC).

MISS MARGARET - Bright Pink. Medium, formal double. Average, upright, open growth. M. (U.S. 2017 - Thomas Sellers, Bolivia, NC).

MISS MARY - Blush Pink. Medium, semidouble to peony form. Vigorous, compact, upright growth. M. (U.S. 1960 - McIlhenny).

MISS MIDDLETON - Pink. Medium, semidouble. Average, compact growth. M. (U.S. 1955 - Middleton).

MISS MUFFET - Rose Red. Small, anemone form. Vigorous, compact, upright growth. E-L. (U.S. 1962 - Mrs. B. Lindsley, San Diego, CA).

MISS OLGA - Deep Red shading to Purple. Small, semidouble. Average growth. E-M. (U.S. 1968 - J. R. Anderson, Apopka, FL).

MISS OLLIE - White. Small, semidouble with long, compact stamens. Vigorous, spreading growth. E-L. (U.S. 1976 - W. F. Freshwater, Fort Valley, GA).

MISS ORLANDO - Blush Pink. Medium, formal double with incurved petals. Average, open, upright growth. (U.S. 1963 - W. H. Veo, Orlando, FL).

MISS OZARK - White with Pink and Red stripes, Medium, formal double. Average, bushy growth. M. (U.S. 2019 - Provenance Unknown - from Walter S. (Hody) Garden, Hammond, LA).

MISS OZARK PINK - Light Pink, Medium, formal double. Average, bushy growth. M. (Pink Sport of Japonica 'Miss Ozark'). (U.S. 2019 - Camellia Heaven - John Grimm, Bush, LA).

MISS PASADENA - Clear Pink. Medium, anemone form. Vigorous, bushy growth. M. (Japan to U.S. [Star] 1915).

MISS SACRAMENTO - Scarlet. Large, single with rounded, velvety petals. M. (For a variation of this cultivar see 'Capitol City'). (Japan - U.S. 1940's - Sacramento, CA).

MISS SHORT - Pink with darker stripes and a White border. Large, semidouble. Average, dense, upright growth. E-M. (U.S. 1998 - C. Elliott, Swainsboro, GA).

MISS UNIVERSE - White. Medium to large, peony form. Vigorous, upright growth. M-L. (U.S. 1960 - Kramer).

MISSION DOLORES - Deep Pink. Large, formal double. Average, compact, upright growth. L. (U.S. 1968 - Camelliana).

MISSISSIPPI BEAUTY - White blotched and striped Pink. Large, semidouble to anemone form. Slow, upright growth. E-M. (U.S. 1956 - Chiles).

MISSISSIPPI BEAUTY RED - Red. (Sport of Japonica 'Mississippi Beauty').

MISSISSIPPI BEAUTY WHITE - White. (Sport of Japonica 'Mississippi Beauty').

MISTER GEORGE - Rose Pink. Large, semidouble with wavy, crinkled petals. Vigorous, spreading, upright growth. E-L. (U.S. 1973 - Mrs. W. McEachern, Wilmington, NC).

MISTER SAM - Soft Shell Pink. Large, rose form double. Vigorous, upright growth. E-M. (U.S. 1964 - Thomasville).

MISTER TIM - Dark Red with Yellow anthers and White filaments. Medium, semidouble. Average, upright growth. L. (U.S. 2009 - Webb Hart, Carriere, MS).

MISTER WILLIAM - Rose. Large, semidouble. Vigorous, compact, upright growth. M-L. (U.S. 1969 - D. F. Miller, Augusta, GA).

MISTY MORN - Pale Pink at edge fading to White toward base. Small to medium, formal double. Average growth. M-L. (N.Z. 1982 - Mr. and Mrs. W. H. Peters, Tauranga).

MISTY SUNRISE - White shading to Deep Red on outer edge. Medium, peony form. Average, compact, upright growth. M. (N.Z. 1970 - B. J. Rayner, Stratford).

MITISSA - White. Medium, loose peony form. Vigorous, compact, upright growth. E-M. (U.S. 1953 - Fisher).

MITT CARTER - White in center shading to Blush Pink over all. Medium, single. Average, upright growth. E-M. (U.S. 1985 - Mrs. H. Johnson, Madison, FL).

MITZI - Blush through soft Pink, Deep Pink to Rose Pink occasionally marked Dark Red. Medium, semidouble. E-M. (U.S. 1961 - Camelliana).

MIYA - ('Edith Nichols'). Light Pink. Medium, semidouble with irregular, fluted, narrow petals and interspersed petaloids sometimes tipped Green. Average, compact, upright growth. M-L. (Japan to U.S. [Star] 1930).

MIYAKO-DORI (SEAGULL) - ('Magnoliaeflora Alba'; ' Snowdrift'). White with Pale Yellow anthers and White filaments. Medium, hose-in-hose semidouble with long, channeled petals. Slow, upright growth. M-L. (Japan - Kantô Region).

MIYAKO-DORI-NAGOYA (NAGOYA GULL) - White with a shade of Yellow at base. Large, formal double. L. (Japan 1968 - Aichi Prefecture).

MIYAKO-NO-HARU - Pink. Medium to large, single with flared Pale Yellow stamens. See Higo.

MIYAKO-NO-NISHIKI - (Brocade of City). White, occasionally streaked light Pink or Rose Pink. Large, semidouble. Slow, bushy growth. E-M. (Japan 1939 - T. Sakata).

MME. CHIANG KAI-SHEK - See 'Frau Geheimrat Oldevig'.

MOCKINGBIRD BLUSH - Blush Pink. Medium to large, rose form double to formal double. Vigorous, compact, upright growth. E-M. (Japonica 'Magnoliaeflora' ['Hagoromo'] seedling). (U.S. 2009 - Bobby Green, Green Nurseries, Fairhope, AL).

MODERN ART - Red heavily variegated with stripes and spots of other shades of Red. Large, anemone form. M. (N.Z. 1973 - Mrs. I. Berg, Whakatane).

MODESTO - Light Rose Pink. Medium, anemone form. Vigorous, upright growth. M-L. (U.S. 1951 - Riverbank, CA).

MOLLIE MOORE DAVIS - ('Big Beauty Pink'). Deep Rose Pink. Large to very large, semidouble to loose peony form. (Sport of Japonica 'Big Beauty'). (U.S. 1946 - McIlhenny).

MOLLIE O. ODOM - Red. Medium, peony form. Slow, average growth. M-L. (U.S. 1990 - L. Odom, Wilmington, NC).

MOLLY - Light Pink variegated White with Yellow anthers and Light Yellow filaments. Very large, semidouble. Average, upright, open growth. M-L. (U.S. 2013 - Bill Howell, Wilmington, NC).

MOLLY HAMILTON - White, random Coral stripes, vertical on petal. Medium to large, semidouble. Vigorous, open upright growth. M-L. Cold hardy. (U.S. 2001 - Mabel M. Hamilton, Georgetown, SC).

MOM JOHNSON - Rose Pink. Large, rose form double with rabbit ears. Vigorous, upright growth. E. (Sport of Japonica 'Herman Johnson'). (U.S. 1993 - Glen Johnson, Madison, FL).

MOMIJI-GARI - Scarlet. Large, single with flared White stamens. See Higo.

MOMOIRO BOKUHAN - Dark Rose outer petals with Rose petaloids fringed with White with Light Yellow stamens. Miniature to small, anemone. Very slow, dense growth. E-M. Very cold hardy. (Japan 1960 - Kansai area).

MOMOJI-NO-HIGURASHI (AN EVENING IN MO-MOJI) - Deep Pink petals with Crimson and White streaks with Yellow anthers and Creamy filaments. Medium, semidouble. Medium, upright growth. E-L. (Japan 1971 - Minoru Satô, Aichi Prefecture).

MONA FREEMAN - White. Medium, semidouble. Vigorous, compact, upright growth. M. (U.S. 1949 - McCaskill).

MONA HARVEY - White. Large, formal double. Average, upright growth. M-L. (N.Z. 1994 - V. and R. Bieleski, Manukau).

MONA LISA - White. Large, peony form. Average, upright growth. M. (U.S. 1975 - Shackelford).

MONA MONIQUE - Soft Pink to a soft Pink shading to Fuchsia Pink at edge of petals and on under petals. Medium, formal double to rose form double to peony form. Vigorous, upright growth. M. (Japan to U.S. 1954 - Peer).

MONARCH - ('Pauline Lapleau'). Deep Pink, sometimes spotted White. Large, full peony form. Average, compact growth. M. (England 1852 - Hally, London).

MONDAY'S CHILD - Deep Pink with bright Gold anthers and Pink filaments. Large, anemone form. Average, upright growth. M-L. (U.S. 2013 - Gordy).

MONICA - White with Pink and Rose Pink stripes. Miniature, formal double. Slow, upright growth. L. (U.S. 1998 - C. Elliott, Swainsboro, GA).

MONIQUE PEER - Pink with White stamens and Pink and White petaloids. Medium, full peony form. Average, compact growth. L. (U.S. 1952 - McIlhenny).

MONJISU - ('California Donckelarii Variegated'). Cherry Red marbled White. Medium, rose form double. Slow, bushy growth. M. (Reported that correct name of cultivar is 'Shibori-Jusu', and also 'Mon-Jusu'). (Japan 1895 - Yokohama).

MONJISU AKA - See 'Monjisu Red'.

MONJISU RED - ('California Donckelarii Red'; 'Otome Red'; 'Shusu'; 'Monjisu Aka'). Solid Cherry Red form of 'Monjisu'.

MONSIEUR PAUGAM - ('Supresse Nobilissima').- White. Medium, loose peony form with irregular petals. Vigorous, upright growth. M. (France 1908 - Guichard).

MONSTRUOSO RUBRA - See 'Gigantea'.

MONTA HORTON - White. Medium to large, anemone form to peony form to rose form double. Average, spreading growth. E-M. (U.S. 1994 - E. and J. Atkins, Shalimar, FL).

MONTE CARLO - Light Pink. Medium, semidouble. (Sport of Japonica 'Finlandia'). (U.S. 1950 - Goletto).

MONTE CARLO SUPREME - Variegated variation of 'Monte Carlo' - Light Pink and White.

MONTEEN MOORE - Light Pink. Medium, semidouble. Average, upright growth. E-M. (U.S. 1988 - Mrs. H. Johnson, Madison, FL).

MONTELANC - White. Small, rose form double. (France Nantes Botanical Gdn. to U.S. 1971 - U.S. Dept. of Agr., Glenn Dale, MD).

MONTROSE - White. Large, rose form double. M. (Aus. 1962 - Montrose).

MOODY BOZEMAN - Light Pink dashed and striped Rose. Medium, semidouble to loose peony form. Vigorous, upright growth. M. (U.S. 1977 - W. M. Bozeman, Thunderbolt, GA).

MOODY BOZEMAN RED - Red. (Sport of Japonica 'Moody Bozeman'). (U.S. 1976 - B. F. Sapp, Garden City, GA).

MOONFLOWER - White. Large, single. M. (Aus. 1962 - Waterhouse).

MOONGLOW - White. Medium, semidouble with a few fragile stamens and petaloids. M. (U.S. Late 1800's - Magnolia).

MOONLIGHT BAY - Light Orchid Pink. Very large, semidouble. Vigorous, compact, upright growth. E-L. (U.S. 1982 - Nuccio's).

MOONLIGHT SONATA - Soft Light Pink. Medium to large, semidouble to loose peony form. Vigorous, upright growth. M-L. (U.S. 1961 - Surina's Camellia Gardens, Sepulveda, CA).

MORANGE - See 'Te Deum'.

MORGAN ELIZABETH - Pink. Small, loose peony form. Average, spreading growth. M-L. (U.S. 1998 - E. Hart, Odessa, FL).

MORGAN WHITNEY - Peach Pink. Medium to large, semidouble with irregular petals to full peony form. Vigorous, upright growth. E-M. (U.S. 1969 - Tammia).

MORNING GLOW - ('St. Mary'). White. Medium, formal double. Vigorous, compact, upright growth. E-M. (U.S. 1948 - Bradford).

MORRIS MERCURY - Red. Small, single. Open, upright, arching growth. E. (Seeds from NW South Korea - Barry Yinger, et al - before 1986). (U.S. 2011 - Morris Arboretum, Philadelphia, PA).

MORRIS MOUGHON - Light Pink moiré White. Large, rose form double. Average, open, upright growth. M-L. (Reported to be same as 'Rosea Superba Variegated'). (U.S. 1965 - G. W. Moughon, Birmingham, AL).

MOSHIO - ('Flame [Australia]'). Deep Red. Medium, semidouble. Upright, compact growth. M. (Sport of Japonica 'Oki-no-nami'). (Japan 1780 - Kantô area).

MOSS POINT RED - See 'Dolly Bowen'.

MOST PRECIOUS - Light Pink to Light Rose Pink as flower ages. Large, semidouble. Average, upright growth. M. (U.S. 1959 - E. S. Simpson, Pensacola, FL).

MOTHER OF PEARL - White with lines of Pink at base of petals. Medium, rose form double. (Sport of Japonica 'Baronne de Bleichroeder [United States]'). (Japan to U.S. 1937 - Camellia Hall).

MOUND - Red. Large, full peony form. Vigorous, upright growth. E-M. (U.S. 1959).

MOUNT SHASTA - ('Leora Hedlund'). White. Medium, full peony form. Average, compact growth. M. (U.S. 1948 - Reeves).

MOUNTAIN VIEW - White. Large, peony form. M. (Aus. 1962 - G. Waterhouse).

MR. J. D. - Dark Red. Medium to large, loose peony form. Average, open, upright growth. M. (U.S. 1997 - C. Elliott, Swainsboro, GA).

MR. WONDERFUL - Blush Pink. Medium, semidouble with irregular petals and large petaloids to full peony form. Average, upright growth. M. (U.S. 1960 - Shackelford).

MRS. ALBERT DEKKER - See 'K. Sawada'.

MRS. BALDWIN WOOD - ('Thunderhead'; 'C. N. Madsen'). White striped Phlox Pink. Medium, semidouble with irregular petals to rose form double. Average, spreading growth. M. (Variations of this cultivar include 'Thelma Dale'; 'Charlotte Bradford'; 'Leonore Weil'). (U.S. 1948 - Bradford).

MRS. BALDWIN WOOD SUPREME - Light moiré Pink with each petal bordered White. (Sport of Japonica 'Mrs. Baldwin Wood'). (U.S. 1957 - Bartlett's Nsy., Fort Valley, GA).

MRS. BENNIE FERAY - Rose Pink. Medium to large, semidouble to peony form. Average, open growth. E-M. (U.S. 1963 - Wilson).

MRS. BERTHA A. HARMS - Ivory White with faint Pink cast. Large, semidouble with wavy, crepe petals. Average, open, upright growth. M-L. (U.S. 1949 - H. H. Harms, Portland, OR).

MRS. CARL ANDERSON - Red. Large, semidouble. Vigorous, spreading growth. M. (U.S. 1958 - Carleton).

MRS. CHARLES COBB - Dark Red. Medium, semidouble to loose peony form. Vigorous, spreading growth. M. (See 'Nellie Gray' for variegated version). (U.S. Early 1900's - Magnolia).

MRS. CHARLES COBB VARIEGATED - See 'Nellie Gray'.

MRS. CHARLES JONAS - Deep Pink. Large, loose peony form. Average growth. M. (U.S. 1970 - M. A. and N. Cox, Georgetown, SC).

MRS. CHARLES SIMONS - White. Medium, semidouble to anemone form. Average, spreading growth. M-L. (For a variation of this cultivar see 'White Wings'). (U.S. 1942 - Magnolia).

MRS. CHESTER BURGESS - Rose Pink. Large, loose peony form. Bushy growth. M. (U.S. 1950 - Malbis).

MRS. CLIFF HARRIS - Light Orchid Pink veined Darker Orchid, each petal margined White with minute pin point White streaks running toward center. Large, semidouble with irregular petals to rose form double to formal double. Vigorous growth. M. (U.S. 1955 - Longview).

MRS. CLIFF HARRIS VARIEGATED - Light Orchid Pink and White variation of 'Mrs. Cliff Harris'.

MRS. CONFER - ('Uncle Sam Variegated'; 'Betsy Ross'). White flecked Rose Red. Large, rose form double. (Variegated variation of Japonica 'Uncle Sam'). (U.S. 1937 - Lindo).

MRS. D. W. DAVIS - Blush Pink. Very large, semidouble. Vigorous, compact, upright growth. M. (U.S. 1954 - D. W. Davis).

MRS. D. W. DAVIS DESCANSO - Large, full peony form. (Sport of Japonica 'Mrs. D. W. Davis'). (U.S. 1970 - Descanso).

MRS. D. W. DAVIS PEONY - Large, loose peony form. (Sport of Japonica 'Mrs. D. W. Davis'). (Note: Practically impossible to obtain by propagation). (U.S. 1959 - R. C. Brown, Sacramento, CA).

MRS. D. W. DAVIS SPECIAL - Double the number of rows of petals of original. (Sport of Japonica 'Mrs. D. W. Davis'). (U.S. 1972).

MRS. EDINGER - White striped Red to solid Red. Large, semidouble. Vigorous, compact, upright growth. M. (U.S. 1848 - Edinger).

MRS. FAIR DODD - Deep to Wine Red. Large, full peony form. Average, upright growth. M. (U.S. 1958 - Dodd).

MRS. FANNIE HENDERSON - Pale Blush Pink. Medium, peony form to anemone form with wavy outside petals and circle of petaloids and White stamens in center surrounded by five distinct whirls of stamens and petaloids. M. (U.S. 1960 - The Pines Nsy., Bath, SC).

MRS. FRANCES ROBERTS - Dark Red. Large, semidouble with upright center petals. Average growth. L. (U.S. 1980 - O. D. Roberts, Tallahassee, FL).

MRS. FRANK BISBEE - White. Large, peony form. Vigorous, spreading growth. E-M. (U.S. 1970 - F. D. Bisbee, Jacksonville, FL).

MRS. FREEMAN WEISS - Pink. Medium to large, semidouble with loose, wavy petals intermixed with stamens and petaloids. Vigorous, compact, upright growth. M. (U.S. 1944 - Magnolia).

MRS. FREEMAN WEISS VARIEGATED - Rich Pink and White variation of 'Mrs. Freeman Weiss'.

MRS. G. G. McLAURIN - Rose Pink to Dark Red. Large, semidouble to loose peony form to anemone form. Average, compact, upright growth. E-L. (U.S. 1965 - G. G. McLaurin, Dillon, SC).

MRS. GENTRY KIDD - Cerise Pink with fluorescent sheen. Very large, peony form with petals in swirls. Rapid, upright, average growth. M. (U.S. 1963 - Dr. Gilbert E. Fisher, Union Springs, AL).

MRS. GEORGE BELL - White washed and shaded Orchid Pink. Medium to large, loose peony form. Vigorous, upright growth. M. (U.S. 1979 - C. W. Thomas, San Dimas, CA).

MRS. GILBERT FISHER - Light Phlox Pink variegated White. Large, semidouble to loose peony form. Average, upright growth. M. (U.S. 1954 - Fisher).

MRS. GLEN R. JOHNSON - Pink. Medium, formal double. Average, upright growth. L. (U.S. 1975 - Dr. G. R. Johnson, Carthage, TX).

MRS. GOODWIN KNIGHT - Rose Pink. Medium to large, full peony form. Average, compact, upright growth. E. (U.S. 1958 - Huntington).

MRS. H. BOYCE - Pale Pink. Large, formal double. (Sport of Japonica 'Paolina Maggi'). (Aus. 1900 - Cremorne Nsy., Melbourne).

MRS. H. BOYCE ROSEA - ('Kallista'). Crimson. (Sport of Japonica 'Mrs. H. Boyce').

MRS. H. L. WINBIGLER - See 'Oniji'.

MRS. HARRY SINCLAIR - Pinkish white. Medium, semidouble with fluffy petals. Vigorous, upright growth. M. (U.S. - Uyematsu, Montebello, CA).

MRS. HELEN REYNOLDS - See 'Otome White'.

MRS. HOOPER CONNELL - Medium, peony form. (Sport of Japonica 'Alba Plena'). (U.S. 1950 - H. P. Connell, Baton Rouge, LA).

MRS. HOWARD ASPER - See 'Hana-Fuki'.

MRS. HUGH WHITE - White with Pink stripe on one or two petals. Large, semidouble to loose peony form. Bushy, upright growth. M-L. (U.S. 1972 - Haynie).

MRS. JIMMY DAVIS - White striped and flecked Pink. Large, anemone form with irregular shaped, notched petals and petaloids. Vigorous, open, upright growth. E-M. (U.S. 1961 - Wilson).

MRS. JIMMY DAVIS PINK - Pink. (Sport of Japonica 'Mrs. Jimmy Davis').

MRS. JOHN SUTTER - Rose Pink. Medium, single. (U.S. 1968 - Lindo).

MRS. JOSEPHINE M. HEARN - ('Delight'). Rose Pink. Medium to large, semidouble with fluted petals. Average, compact, upright growth. M. (U.S. 1934 — Hearn).

MRS. K. SAWADA - ('John Marshall'). Delicate Pink. Medium, formal double. Vigorous, compact, upright growth. M. (Plant Patent No. 481). (U.S. 1940 - Overlook).

MRS. KATHERINE M. HOWELL - Rose Red. Large, formal double. Average, spreading growth. M. (U.S. 2006 - Howell).

MRS. KENNETH PELTON - Soft Pink. Large, semidouble. Average, upright growth. M. (U.S. 1970 - Dr. J. B. Tarver, San Marino, CA).

MRS. LAWRENCE V. BRADLEY - White. Large, semidouble. Average, dense, spreading growth. M-L. (U.S. 1991 - W. Wilson, Augusta, GA).

MRS. LEROY EPPS - Pink striped White and Rose. Large, semidouble. (Sport of Japonica 'Lady Clare'). (U.S. 1970 - Mrs. Epps, Aiken, SC).

MRS. LINDSAY - Pinkish Red striped Red. Large, semidouble. Average, compact growth. M. (U.S. 1953).

MRS. LYMAN CLARKE - White washed and shaded Orchid Pink. Medium, semidouble to peony form. Average, compact growth. M-L. (U.S. 1949 - Mrs. L. Clarke, Norfolk, VA).

MRS. MAC - White. Medium, rose form double. Average, upright growth. E-M. (U.S. 2003 - Mary McLeod, Monticello, FL).

MRS. MARION MAYFIELD - White. Large, anemone form. Average, compact, upright growth. E-M. (U.S. 1977 - D. Mayfield, Baton Rouge, LA).

MRS. MARK CLARK - Soft Pink. Medium, semidouble, sometimes formal double. Vigorous, compact growth. M. (U.S. 1960 - Marbury).

MRS. MARSHALL FIELD - Soft Pink moiré White. Medium, semidouble. Average, upright growth. M. (U.S. 1960 - Fisher).

MRS. MILDRED LAMBRAKOS - Deep Pink. Medium, formal double. Average growth. M-L. (U.S. 1988 - P. C. Lambrakos, Mt. Pleasant, SC).

MRS. NANNETTE SMYRE - White. Large to very large, semidouble. Vigorous, spreading growth. M. (U.S. 1968 - H. J. Matchan, Bonneau, SC).

MRS. NELLIE EASTMAN - White striped and streaked Red. Medium, peony form to rose form double. Average, upright growth. M. (U.S. 1950 - Domoto).

MRS. PAUL GILLEY - Light Blush Pink shading Pink on edge. Large, semidouble. Average, spreading, upright growth. M. (U.S. 1973 - Gilley).

MRS. R. L. WHEELER - Light Pink with occasional Deeper Pink or Red marking, and at times sports Rose Pink and Rose Pink and White. Medium, formal double with pointed petals toward center. Average, open, upright growth. M. (U.S. 1962 - Wheeler).

MRS. R. L. WHEELER PINK - Rose Pink. (Sport of Japonica 'Mrs. R L Wheeler'). (U.S. 1962 - Wheeler).

MRS. ROSA MURRAY - Phlox Pink. Miniature, formal double. E-M. (U.S. 1961 - The Pines Nsy., Bath, SC).

MRS. SARAH SHEPHERDSON - ('Mrs. Shepherdson'). White marked Pink. Medium, anemone form. Average, compact, upright growth. M. (U.S. 1952 - Mrs. S. Shepherdson, San Bernardino, CA).

MRS. SARAH SHEPHERDSON PINK - Pink. (Sport of Japonica 'Mrs. Sarah Shepherdson').

MRS. SHEPHERDSON - See 'Mrs. Sarah Shepherdson'.

MRS. SHOWMAN - Deep Rose Pink. Medium, formal double. (U.S. 1953).

MRS. SKOTTOWE - ('Mrs. Moore's Speckled'; 'Queen Victoria's Blush'). Blush spotted with minute dots. Medium, formal double. M. (Sport of Japonica 'Jubilee'). (Aus. 1878 - Guilfoyle).

MRS. T. R. McKENZIE - See 'Vedrine'.

MRS. TINGLEY - Salmon Silver Pink. Medium, formal double. Average, compact growth. M-L. (U.S. 1949 - Tuttle Bros. Nsy., Pasadena, CA).

MRS. TSUTAKO NAKASONE - White toned Pink toward edge. Small to medium, tubular single. Narrow, upright growth. E-M. (U.S. 1985 - Nuccio's).

MRS. W. J. LYONS - Red. Medium, single. (U.S. 1953 - Rhodellia).

MRS. WALTER ALLAN - Rose Red. Medium, semidouble with irregular petals. Vigorous, compact, upright growth. M. (U.S. 1945 - Allan).

MRS. WALTER ALLAN VARIEGATED - Rose Red blotched White form of 'Mrs. Walter Allan'.

MRS. WATERS - ('Mrs. Abby Wilder Pink'). Solid Pink form of 'Mrs. Abby Wilder II'. (U.S. 1945 - Armstrong Nurseries, Ontario, CA).

MRS. WHITE - See 'Woodville Red'.

MRS. WILLIAM BECKMAN - White streaked Light Red. Medium to large, semidouble. Spreading growth. M. (U.S. 1952 - Edinger).

MRS. WOODROW HATHORN - Oxblood Red. Medium, semidouble with wavy, upright petals to loose peony form to anemone form. Vigorous, compact, upright growth. M-L. (U.S. 1979 - J. L. Carvain, Dallas, TX).

MULTITASKING - Solid Pink, solid White or variegated Pink and White with Golden anthers. Medium, anemone form. Average, upright, dense growth. E-M. (U.S. 2018 - Pat Johnson, Cairo, GA).

MURCHISON LADY - White. Large, formal double. Average, upright growth. M. (Aus. 1992 - K. Abbott, Rossmoyne, W. Aus.).

MURIEL NATHAN - Light Pink. Medium, peony form. Average, compact, upright growth. L. (U.S. 1973 - M. R. Murray, Fort Valley, GA).

MUSIC CITY - Soft Pink. Medium, formal double. Average, upright growth. E-M. (U.S. 1975 - Wilson).

MY BONNIE LASSIE - Light Blush with deeper broken Pink stripes. Large, loose peony form with clusters of stamens irregularly spaced. Average, spreading growth. M-L. (U.S. 1968 - Haynie).

MY CHOICE - Cream White delicately tinted on edge of petals. Medium to large, full peony form. Vigorous, compact, upright growth. M-L. (U.S. 1967 - Short).

MY DARLING - Light Pink. Small, single. Vigorous, compact, upright growth. M. (U.S. 1942 - Star).

MY DEBBIE - Light Red to very Dark Red. Medium, formal double form. Average, upright growth. E-M. (U.S. 2005 - Jay Ellis, Keystone Hts., FL).

MY DEBBIE VARIEGATED - Light Red to very Dark Red with variegation. Medium, formal double. Average, upright growth. E-M. (U.S. 2005 - Jay Ellis, Keystone Hts., FL).

MY FAIR LADY - Coral Pink on opening, changing to Light Pink with Deeper Pink center and outer petals. Medium, formal double. Vigorous, compact, upright growth. M. (U.S. 1953 - Short).

MY KELLEY - Pink. Large, rose form double to formal double. Average, spreading growth. E-L. (U.S. 1990 - Tammia).

MY LINDA - Soft Pink. Medium, formal double. Average, upright growth. M. (U.S. 2018 - William & Linda Nichols, Cottonwood, AL).

MY LOUISE - Coral Rose. Large, semidouble with wavy, crinkled petals. Average growth. M. (U.S. 1977 - Gilley).

MY NANCY - Pinkish Purple to Lavender mottled White with Gold anthers and White filaments. Medium, semidouble to peony form. Average, upright growth. M. (Sport of Japonica 'Mark Alan'). (U.S. 1987 - Howard. W. Ramsey, Gainesville, FL).

MY PET - Pink petals with petaloids edged Deep Pink shading to Creamy White toward base. Small, anemone form. Average, dense, upright growth. E-L. (U.S. 1994 - P. Tedesco, Felton, CA).

MY RUTH - Flame Red. Large, semidouble with large, upright, crisp petals which stand apart with a tight group of stamens. Vigorous, open, upright growth. M. (U.S. 1959 - Dr. R. T. Cale, Bessemer, AL).

MY SUE - Light Blush striped Red. Medium, formal double, with incurved petals. Vigorous, upright growth. M-L. (U.S. 1962 - F. S. Watters, Aiken, SC).

MY TRULA - Deep Pink with Yellow anthers and White filaments. Large, semidouble to peony form. Average, upright, open growth. E-M. (U.S. 2012 - N. C. Barnard, St. Elmo, AL).

MY VALENTINE - Valentine Red with the occasional White streak with Cream anthers and Cream filaments. Medium, anemone form. Average, upright, open growth. M-L. (Seedling of Japonica 'Tinsie'). (U.S. 2019 - Pat Johnson, Cairo, GA).

MYAL - Red. Large, semidouble. Slow, open, upright growth. M-L. (N.Z. 1994 - A. and R. Hannam, Putaruru).

MYNELLE HAYWARD - Blush Pink. Medium, loose peony form with irregular, fluted, upright petals. Average, compact, upright growth. E-M. (U.S. 1955 - Wheeler).

MYNELLE HAYWARD VARIEGATED - Blush Pink blotched White variation of 'Mynelle Hayward'.

MYRA D. - Blush Pink. Small, formal double with incurved petals. M. (U.S. 1977 - Haynie).

MYRA GERBING - Blush Pink. Very large, anemone form. Average, upright growth. E-L. (U.S. 1997 - Gerbing).

MYRA WADSWORTH - White striped Pink. Large, semidouble. Average, open, upright growth. E-M. (U.S. 1959 - Marbury).

MYRTIFOLIA CHINESA - Bright Pink with Lighter Pink in center. Medium, rose form double. M. (Portugal 1959 - Da Silva).

MYRTLE ANIS CANNON - White. Large, loose peony form. Average growth. M. (U.S. 1977 - M.S. Cannon, Covington, LA).

MYRTLE ICARD - Pink. Very large, semidouble. Average, dense, upright growth. M-L. (U.S. 1998 - Jernigan).

MYRTLE McLEOD - White. Large, single with cluster of bright Yellow stamens. Slow, compact growth. M. (Aus. 1956 - Cole).

MYRTLE MONROE - Pink. Large, semidouble with wavy, crinkled petals. Average, spreading growth. E-M. (U.S. 1974 - R. S. Monroe, Waycross, GA).

NADINE ESHELMAN - Shaded soft Pink. Medium, semidouble with notched petals. Average, compact growth. M. (U.S. 1958 - Ragland).

NAGASAKI - ('Mikenjaku'; 'Candida Elegantissima'; 'Tennin-Kwan'; 'S. Peter Nyce'; 'Nakasaki [Coe]'; 'Marguerita'; 'Princess Nagasaki'; 'Nagasaki Special'; 'Lonjan'). Rose Pink marbled White in varying degrees. Large, semidouble with large, outer petals and a few smaller center petals lying flat. Slow, spreading growth. M. (Japan to England 1889 - G. Waller).

NAGASAKI (COE) - See 'Nagasaki'.

NAGASAKI ROSE - Solid Rose Pink sport of 'Nagasaki'.

NAGASAKI SPECIAL - See 'Nagasaki'.

NAN CROWELL - Clear Pink fading to Blush in center. Medium, rose form double. Average, compact growth. M-L. (U.S. 1952 - Councilman).

NAN FORD - Dark Pink with Yellow anthers and Yellow filaments. Very large, semidouble to full peony to loose peony form. Vigorous, upright, dense growth. E-M. (U.S. 2013 - Howell).

NAN FORD VARIEGATED - Dark Pink and White variegated form of 'Nan Ford'. (U.S. 2013 - Howell).

NAN PICKERING - Very soft Pink. Large, formal double. Average, spreading growth. M. (Aus. 1979 - C. P. J. Pickering, Oldgate, S. Aus.).

NAN S. DODD - Light Blush shading Pink at edge. Medium, rose form double. Vigorous, compact, upright growth. M. (U.S. 1977 - Dodd).

NANA-KOMACHI - Flesh Pink streaked Rose. Medium, single. See Higo.

NANBAN-KOH - Deep Red. Medium, anemone form. Vigorous, upright growth. M. (Japan - Ancient Variety).

NANCY - Pink veined Red. Large, semidouble. (England 1951 - Caledonia).

NANCY BIRD - Light Pink. Medium, semidouble to peony form. (Sport of Japonica 'Jean Lyne'). (Aus. - Hazlewood).

NANCY COMERFORD - White with Light Pink shading. Large, semidouble. Average growth. M-L. (N.Z. 1998 - J. Reeves).

NANCY D. TOMLINSON - Pink. Large, semidouble to loose peony form. Vigorous, upright growth. M-L. (U.S. 1977 - Dodd).

NANCY D. TOMLINSON VARIEGATED - Pink blotched White variation of 'Nancy D Tomlinson'. (U.S. 1977 - Dodd).

NANCY GUNN - Light Red. Large, semidouble. Vigorous, upright growth. M. (U.S. 1975 - Haynie).

NANCY K - Pink with darker specks and streaks. Medium, semidouble. Vigorous, dense, upright growth. M. Cold hardy. (U.S. 1992 - E. and J. Atkins, Shalimar, FL).

NANCY KELLY - Red. Large, semidouble to peony form with loose petals. M. (U.S. 1962 - Mr. Kelly, Hattiesburg, MS).

NANCY LEE EDWARDS - Peach Pink. Small, rose form to formal double to peony form. Dense, upright growth. M-L. (U.S. 2002 - Marion Edwards, Jacksonville, FL).

NANCY LYNN - Rich Pink. Medium, formal double. Vigorous, dense, spreading growth. M. (U.S. 1990 - B. and A. Boll, Jacksonville, FL).

NANCY MANDARICH - White. Large to very large, anemone form to loose peony form with upright petals. Vigorous, compact, upright growth. M. (U.S. 1963 - Mandarich).

NANCY WEEMS - White. Large, semidouble with Yellow stamens and a few petaloids. (U.S. 1959 - W. B. Weems, Ellisville, MS).

NANCY'S FANCY - White. Medium, formal double. Vigorous, upright growth. E-M. (U.S. 1960 - C. G. Heflin, Marshallville, GA).

NANNETENSIS - Cherry Red. Small, formal double. Average, upright growth. M. (France 1828 - Jean Gouillon, Nantes).

NANNIE BROWN - Deep Pink. Medium to large, semidouble, sometimes with intermixed petaloids and stamens. Average, open growth. M. (U.S. 1960 - Mrs. T. S. Braswell, Monticello, FL).

NANNINE SIMMONS - Pale Pink. Medium, loose peony form with large outer petals and irregular petals in center. Average, upright growth. E. (U.S. 1950 - McIlhenny).

NAPA RED - See 'Elena Nobile'.

NAPOLEON BONAPARTE - Rose Pink. Medium, semidouble with high center. Vigorous, upright growth. M. (U.S. 1952 - Goletto).

NAPOLEON BONAPARTE VARIEGATED - Rose Pink blotched White variation of 'Napoleon Bonaparte'.

NARANJA - Bright Orange Red. Medium, semidouble. Vigorous, willowy growth. E-L. (U.S. 1956 - Tick Tock).

NARARA - White. Large, rose form double to peony form. (Aus. 1960 - Linton).

NARELLAN - White. Very large, anemone form. (Aus. 1962 - Camden Park).

NASHVILLE - Deep Red. Medium to large, semidouble. Average, upright growth. M. (U.S. 1975 - Haynie).

NATHAN HUMPHREY - Dark Red and White. Large, formal double. Average growth. M. (U.S. 1974 - Marbury).

NATIVE DANCER - Light Pink with wide, heavy stripes of Carmine. Large, semidouble. Average, compact growth. M. (U.S. 1951 - Jones).

NAUGHTY MARIETTA - Red blotched White. Large, peony form to almost formal double. Spreading growth. M. (U.S. 1961 - Monticello Nsy., Monticello, FL).

NEELIA LITTLE - Camellia Rose. Medium, semidouble with thick petals. Average, upright growth. E-M. (U.S. 1959 - E. P. Little, Handsboro, MS).

NEELY JAHNZ - Red and White. Large, semidouble. Vigorous, compact, upright growth. M. (U.S. 1959 - Mrs. E. J. Prevatt, Charleston, SC).

NEIGE D'OREE - See 'Purity'.

NEL PREVATT - Red. Large, semidouble with velvety texture. Average, open, upright growth. M. (U.S. 1969 - E. J. Prevatt, Bonneau, SC).

NEL PREVATT VARIEGATED - Red and White variation of 'Nel Prevatt'.

NELL ASHBY - White striped and blotched Pink. Medium, semidouble to loose peony form. Compact, upright growth. M. (U.S. 1958 - E. J. Prevatt, Charleston, SC).

NELL CHESTER EMBREY - White with Pink stripes. Medium, formal double. Average, spreading growth. E-M. (U.S. 1993 - G. Chester, Augusta, GA).

NELL HOOPER - Rose Red. Medium, formal double. Vigorous, dense, spreading growth. E-M. (Aus. 1973 - G. W. Hooper, Bexley North, NSW).

NELLIE ANN PHINIZY - ('Pink Star Variegated'). Rose Pink and White form of 'Pink Star'. Medium, semidouble with pointed outer petals and stamens among central petaloids. (U.S. 1948 - Fruitland).

NELLIE BLY - See 'Lady Clare'.

NELLIE GRAY - Dark Red spotted White. Medium, semidouble to loose peony form. (Variegated variation of 'Mrs. Charles Cobb'). (U.S. 1948 - Bradford).

NELLIE JONES - White. Medium, formal double. Average, upright growth. M-L. (U.S. 1988 - J. Aldrich, Brooklet, GA).

NELLIE K - Deep Pink. Large, semidouble to anemone form to peony form. Vigorous, upright growth. M-L. (U.S. 1971 - Twin Pines Way, Theodore, AL).

NELLIE McGRATH - ('Halcyon'). Rose Pink. Medium to large, semidouble to loose peony form with some folded petals. Vigorous, compact, upright growth. E-M. (U.S. 1955 - Mrs. B. J. Welp, Jr., Jacksonville, FL).

NELLIE WHITE - See 'Finlandia'.

NELSON DOUBLEDAY - Red to Rose Red. Medium, semidouble with loose, irregular petals. M. (U.S. 1950 - Middleton).

NENCINI ROSEA - Rose Pink. Miniature, semidouble. (Sport of Japonica 'Contessa Nencini'). (U.S. 1950's - Wylam).

NEW HORIZONS - Medium, rose form double to formal double of Light Rose to Dark China Rose, delicately brushed and streaked Off-White with every petal variegated Deeper Rose. (Sport of Japonica 'Uncle Sam'). (U.S. 1959 - A H Krueger and F L Ramsey, Monterey Park, CA).

NEW MOON RISING - Dark Wine Red with Golden anthers and Pink filaments. Small, single. Vigorous, upright, open growth. M-L. (Seedling of Japonica 'Fuyajo'). (U.S. 2016 - Jim Moon, Portland OR).

NEWINGTON - Scarlet. Large, anemone form. E. (Aus. 1960 - Newington College, Stanmore).

NEZ SMITHWICK - Shell Pink. Medium, full peony form. Vigorous, compact growth. E-M. (U.S. 1960 - Mrs. T. M. Smithwick, Dawson, GA).

NICK ADAMS - Dark Red. Large, semidouble with loose petals to peony form. Average, compact growth. E-M. (U.S. 1958 - Shackelford).

NICK CARTER - Dark Red. Small to medium, anemone form. Average, open, spreading growth. E-L. (N.Z. 1991 - T. Lennard, Te Puke).

NICK'S 13 - Blush Pink. Medium to large, semidouble with fluted petals. Vigorous, open growth. M. (U.S. 1965 - N. J. Adams, Albany, GA).

NICK'S 30 - Clear Light Pink. Large, semidouble. Average, upright growth. M. (U.S. 1975 - Shackelford).

NICOLE - Soft Pink striped Deep Pink. Large to very large, formal double. Upright growth. M. (Aus. 1984 - T. J. Savige, Wirlinga, NSW).

NIGHT WATCHMAN - Cardinal Red. Medium, rose form double. Average, spreading growth. M. (N.Z. 1982 - W. H. Peters, Tauranga).

NIGHTFALL - Dark Red with very Dark veins with bright Gold anthers and Pink filaments. Medium, single. Vigorous, upright growth. E-M. (Japonica 'Royal Velvet' seedling). (U.S. 2013 - Gordy).

NIKKO - Deep Pink. Small, single with flared soft Pink stamens. See Higo.

NINA ANNULETTE - Deep Rose Red with a Purple hue and White mottling with Yellow anthers and White filaments. Large, peony form. Upright growth. M-L. (U.S. 2006 - John D. Gentry, N. Augusta, SC; Propagated by John D. Henry, Jr., Richmond Hill, GA).

NINA AVERY - White washed Rose Pink with White stamens tipped Light Brown. Medium, semidouble to loose peony form with crinkled, erect center petals. Vigorous, compact, upright growth. M. (U.S. 1949 - McIlhenny).

NINA WEST - Cherry Red. Large, semidouble with wavy, crinkled petals. Average, upright growth. M. (U.S. 1981 - W. T. Shepherd, North Charleston, SC).

NINA WEST VARIEGATED - Cherry Red and White variation of 'Nina West'. (U.S. 1981 - W. T. Shepherd, North Charleston, SC).

NINA ZILKHA - Deep Pink. Medium to large, formal double with heavy petal texture. Average, upright, spreading growth. M. (Sport of Japonica 'Joy Kendrick'). (U.S. 2001 - Bob Ross, Houston, TX).

NIOI FUBUKI (FRAGRANT SNOW STORM) - White striped Rose. Medium to large, wavy single with petaloids or high crown of stamens. Vigorous, open, upright growth. M-L. Mild fragrance. (Japan 1968 - Tsugio Ôta, Kumamoto Prefecture).

NIOI FUKURIN - Light Pink bordered White with occasional Rose Pink stripe. (Sport of Japonica 'Nioi Fubuki'). See Higo.

NOB HILL - White. Large, rose form double. Average, compact, upright growth. M. (U.S. 1966 - H. S. Entriken, Sacramento, CA).

NOBILISSIMA - ('Fuji-Yama'). White with Yellow shading. Medium, full peony form. Vigorous, upright growth. E-M. (Belgium 1834 - M. Lefevre, Ghent).

NOEL - Red with White border. Medium, anemone form. Average, upright growth. E-M. (U.S. 1992 - Piet and Gaeta).

NOKOGIRIBA- TSUBAKI - Red. Small, single. (Japan 1859 - Kantô Area).

NOLA FIRTH - White. Large, formal double. Average, upright growth. E-M. (U.S. 1980 - Gilley).

NOLAN LEWIS - White shading to Pink on edge. Miniature, formal double to rose form double. Slow, upright, dense growth. E-M. (Seedling of Japonica 'China Doll'). (U.S. 2016 - Pat Johnson, Cairo, GA).

NOONIE CARROLL - Pink with Light Pink inner petals. Medium, formal double. Average, upright growth. M. (U.S. 1988 - Tammia).

NORA LAWSON - White splashed Pink. Very large, anemone form. Average, open, upright growth. E. (U.S. 1968 - Camelliana).

NORA'S CHOICE - Red with Pinky Red stamens. Large to very large, peony form. Slow, spreading growth. M-L. (N.Z. 1989 - Miss K. N. Ferguson, Uatamata).

NORMA BORLAND - White, occasionally dashed Red. Medium, full peony form with White stamens. Average, compact growth. E. (U.S. 1954 - Julington).

NORMA KNIGHT - Red. Large, peony form. Average growth. E-M. (U.S. 1964 - C. A. Knight, Beaumont, TX).

NORMAN EDWARDS - Light Pink shading to Deeper Pink. Medium, peony form. Average, compact, upright growth. M. (U.S. 1958 - McCaskill).

NORTH AUGUSTA - Cream White striped Red to Red and Red variegated White. Large, semidouble to peony form. Vigorous, upright growth. M. (U.S. 1964 - Mealing).

NORTH SHORE - Pink. Large, peony form. M. (Aus. 1966 - Miss W. Henderson, NSW).

NORTHERN LIGHT - Dark Pink. Medium, semidouble to loose peony form with narrow petals. (U.S. 1944 - Magnolia).

NORWILK - Turkey Red. Medium, semidouble to peony form. Average growth. M-L. (U.S. 1957 - Wilkinson).

NOVICK'S SEVEN - Pink. Large, anemone form to peony form with loose petals. Average, open growth. M-L. (Reported as similar to 'Elizabeth LeBey'). (U.S. 1963 - Novick).

NUCCIO'S BELLA ROSSA - Red. Large, formal double. Average, bushy, upright growth. E-L. (U.S. 2000 - Nuccio's).

NUCCIO'S BELLA ROSSA CRINKLED - Red. Medium, formal double with very wavy petals. Slow, compact, upright growth; Foliage is irregular, crinkled, Green in center with irregular Yellowish Green margin (Benten type). E-M. (Flower and foliage sport of Japonica 'Nuccio's Bella Rossa'). (U.S. 2012 - Nuccio's).

NUCCIO'S BELLA ROSSA VARIEGATED - Red blotched White variation of Nuccio's Bella Rossa. (U.S. 2001 - Nuccio's).

NUCCIO'S CAMEO - Light Pink to Coral Pink. Medium to large, formal double to rose form double. Average, compact, upright growth. E-L. (U.S. 1983 - Nuccio's).

NUCCIO'S CAMEO VARIEGATED - Light Pink to Coral Pink blotched White variation of Nuccio's Cameo. (U.S. 2014).

NUCCIO'S CAROUSEL - Soft Pink toned deeper at edge. Medium to large, semidouble of tubular form. Average, compact, upright growth. E-L. (U.S. 1988 - Nuccio's).

NUCCIO'S GEM - White. Medium to large, formal double. Vigorous, compact, upright growth. E-M. (U.S. 1970 - Nuccio's).

NUCCIO'S JEWEL - White washed and shaded Orchid Pink. Medium, full peony form. Slow, bushy growth. M. (U.S. 1977 - Nuccio's).

NUCCIO'S PEARL - White washed and shaded Orchid Pink. Medium, formal double. Vigorous, compact, upright growth. M. (U.S. 1977 - Nuccio's).

NUCCIO'S PINK LACE - Light Pink. Large, anemone form, occasional flower with rosette of center petaloids. Average, compact, upright growth. E-L. (U.S. 1987 - Nuccio's).

NYLA FRAN - Orchid Pink. Large, loose peony form with upright petals. Average, open, upright growth. E-M. (U.S. 1960 - W. F. Hutcheson, Texarkana, TX).

O. C. COTTEN - Dark Velvet Red. Medium to large, semidouble with very large petals and large crown of Pink stamens and Yellow anthers containing one to three petaloids. Vigorous, upright growth. M. (U.S. 1955 - R. B. Ching, McComb, MS).

O. C. COTTEN VARIEGATED - Dark Velvet Red blotched White variation of 'O C Cotten'.

O. K. BOWMAN - Orange Red to Orange Red blotched White. Medium to large, semidouble to anemone form with White stamens. Average, compact growth. M. (U.S. 1957 - Bowman).

OASO - Light Rose Pink variegated White. Large, single with flared White stamens which in some flowers are partially topped with Pinkish White petaloids. See Higo.

OBLIGING - White flecked Red. Large, semidouble, peony, etc. Average, upright growth. E-M. (U.S. 1956 - J. S. Gilder, San Fernando, CA).

OCTOBER AFFAIR - Light Pink with Deep Pink outer petals. Medium, formal double. Average, upright growth. E-M. (U.S. 1981 - Parks).

OCTOBER DELIGHT - See 'Marie Bracey'.

OCTOBER JOY - Deep Wine Red. Medium, loose peony form. Vigorous, upright growth. E. (U.S. 1940 - Gerbing).

ODE OF EDGEWOOD - Bright Red. Large, semidouble with wavy, crinkled petals. Average, compact, upright growth. E-M. (U.S. 1967 - Maj. R. F. Hightower, Ocala, FL).

ODORATISSIMA - ('La Graciola'). Rose Pink. Large, semidouble to peony form. Upright growth. M-L. Slightly fragrant. (For another form of this cultivar see 'Leverton's'). (Aus. 1866 - Guilfoyle).

OGI-NO-MINE - White. Medium, single with flared White stamens. See Higo.

OH BOY - Purplish Pink. Large, formal double, sometimes with cupped petals. Average, compact, upright growth. M. (U.S. 1965 - J. F. Marscher, Beaufort, SC).

OHKAN - White with Rose Red border. Medium, single with flared stamens. Slow, compact growth. M. (Sport of Japonica 'Yamato Nishiki'). See Higo.

OH-ZORA - Light Pink. Medium, single with circular White stamens. See Higo.

OKI-NO-NAMI - Pink edged White with dark Red stripes. Large, semidouble. (Japan 1710 - Kantô area).

OLD IVORY - Cream White. Medium, full peony form. (U.S. 1959 - O. H. Johnson, Hattiesburg, MS).

OLD PRINTS - Bright Red to White striped Red. Small, flat formal double with tight rows of recurring petals. Dwarf growth. E. (U.S. 1972 - Witman).

OLE MISS - Pale Pink. Medium to large, semidouble with crepe petals. Vigorous, upright growth. E-M. (U.S. 1967 - Miss R. N. Campbell, Mobile, AL).

OLGA LEACH - Pale Pink and White with Deeper Pink on outer one fourth of petals shading to almost White on inner one-third of petals. Medium, semidouble with loose petals. Vigorous, upright growth. E-M. (U.S. 1958 - Fisher).

OLIVE BARRETT - Rose Pink with Yellow anthers and Cream filaments. Medium, irregular semidouble with stamens mixed with petals. Slow, pendulous, upright growth. E-M. (U.S. 1950 - Clower).

OLIVE ELIZABETH - Carmine. Medium, loose peony form. Vigorous, compact growth. E-M. (U.S. 1950 - Clower).

OLIVE HONNOR - Crimson. Very large, anemone form. Average, upright growth. M. (N.Z. 1976 - Mrs. O. Honnor, New Plymouth).

OLIVE LEE SHEPP - White marked Deep Red. Medium, semidouble. Vigorous, upright growth. M. (Variation of this cultivar include 'Arlene Lee Shepp'; 'Raymond Beals'). (U.S. 1948 - Shepp).

OLIVIA - White. Large, semidouble with wavy, crinkled petals. Vigorous, open, upright growth. E-M. (U.S. 1969 - G. R. Howard, Charlotte, NC).

OLIVIA MARY - Red, Small, formal double with incurved petals. Average, bushy growth. M. (U.S. 2019 - Bill Lang, Fort Walton Beach, FL).

OMEGA - Blush White edged Coral. Large, semidouble. Vigorous, upright growth. M. (U.S. 1965 - Wilson).

OMEGA RED - Light Red with Red and White petaloids with heavy petal texture. Vigorous, upright growth. M. (U.S. 1994 - Jerry Hogsette, Gainesville, FL).

ONE ALONE - Blush Pink. Large, loose peony form. Vigorous, upright growth. M. (U.S. 1961 - Ashby).

ONE SECOND - Rose Red (RHS color 58c) with a slight Purplish cast with Rose Red (RHS color 58c) with a slight Purplish cast anthers and White filaments. Medium, semidouble. Average, upright growth. L. (U.S. 2018 - Auburn-Opelika Men's Camellia Club, Auburn, AL).

ONETIA HOLLAND - White. Large to very large, loose peony form. Average, compact growth. M-L. (U.S. 1954 - J. A. Holland, Upland, CA).

ONIJI - ('Lady Clare Variegated'; 'Empress Variegated'; ' Mrs. H. L. Windbigler'). Deep Pink marbled White. Large, semidouble. (Variegated variation of 'Lady Clare'). (Japan 1935 - Chugai).

OO-LA-LA! - Pink striped Red and edged White, occasionally mottled White. Medium, single to semidouble. Average, upright growth. E-L. (For a variation of this cultivar see 'Ay-Ay-Ay!'). (U.S. 1991 - Nuccio's).

OPAL HEARNE - Oriental Red. Large to very large, semidouble with irregular petals to loose peony form. (U.S. 1968 - H. C. Hearne, Ruston, LA).

OPHELIA DENT - Delicate Pink. Medium, semidouble. (U.S. 1956 - Miss M Dent, Brunswick, GA).

ORANDAKÔ (HOLLAND RED) - Deep Pink striped White. Small, formal double. Vigorous, upright growth. E-L. (Japan 1733 - Chikinshô Furoku).

ORCHID PINK - Light Pink center petals with considerable Orchid, bordered rich Pink and sometimes spotted White. Medium, semidouble. (Sport of Japonica 'Colonial Lady'). (U.S. 1939 - Carter).

OSAKAZUKI - ('Taihai'). See 'Daitairin'.

OSARAKU - Light Pink. Medium, single with flared Pale Yellow stamens which in some flowers are partially topped with soft Pink petaloids. See Higo.

OSCAR B. ELMER - Dark Velvet Red. Large, semidouble. Average, compact, upright growth. M. (U.S. 1978 - Mandarich).

OTA-HAKU - White. Small to medium, single. See Higo.

OTAHUHU BEAUTY - ('Aspasia Rosea'; 'Duke of York'; 'Paeoniaeflora Rosea'). Rose Pink. Medium, full peony form. (Sport of Japonica 'Aspasia Macarthur'). (N.Z. 1904 - Lippiatt, Otahuhu).

OTHA SHAFFER - Orchid to Deep Pink. Medium, semidouble to loose peony form. Average, spreading growth. E-L. (U.S. 1999 - Dr. Howard Smith, Gainesville, FL).

OTOME RED - See 'Monjisu Red'.

OTOME VARIEGATED - See 'Baronne De Bleichroeder (United States)'.

OTOME WHITE - ('Bleichroeder White'; 'Mrs. Helen Reynolds'). White variation of 'Baronne De Bleichroeder. M. (U.S. 1935).

OTOME-SHIBORI - See 'Baronne De Bleichroeder (United States)'.

OUR BILL - White Blush. Large, semidouble form. Average, dense, upright growth. M. (U.S. 2004 - Howard Smith, Gainesville, FL).

OUR JULIA - Deep Pink. Large, semidouble with fluted petals. Vigorous, upright growth. M. (U.S. 1964).

OUR NANCY - White with an occasional Light Pink stripe. Medium to large, semidouble form. Slow, dense, upright growth. M-L. (U.S. 1999 - Dr. Howard Smith, Gainesville, FL).

OVERLOOK WHITE - ('Late White Empress'). White. Large, semidouble with fluted petals. Vigorous, compact, upright growth. M-L. (U.S. 1961 - Overlook).

OWEN HENRY - Light Orchid Pink with Strawberry undertones. Large, anemone form. (Sport of Japonica 'Sunset Glory'). (U.S. 1964 - Short).

OYLER'S CAROLYNMARIE VARIEGATED - Red with White splotches with Gold anthers. Medium, semidouble. Slow, upright, open growth. M. (U.S. 2010 - Donald R. Oyler, Mobile, AL).

OYLER'S CHRISTINA MARIE - White. Medium, formal double. Average, upright growth. M. (U.S. 2010 - Donald R. Oyler, Mobile, AL).

OYLER'S RACHEL MARIE - Light Pink with Deeper Pink on the underside of the petals with Gold anthers. Medium, semidouble. Average, upright growth. E-M. (U.S. 2010 - Donald R. Oyler, Mobile, AL).

OYLER'S SYDNEY - Fuchsia and White with Golden anthers and Cream filaments. Medium, full peony. Slow, upright, dense growth. M-L. (U.S. 2014 - Donald R. Oyler, Mobile, AL).

OZA SHIRAH - Light Pink, feathering to White on edges of petals. Large to very large, semidouble. Vigorous, spreading and upright growth. M. (Sport of Japonica 'Borom's Gem'). (U.S. 2005 - John W. Shirah, Lakeland, FL).

OZEKI - Rose Pink. Large, single with soft Pink stamens which in some flowers are partially topped with soft Pink and White petaloids. See Higo.

PAEONIAEFLORA - See 'Aspasia Macarthur'.

PAEONIAEFLORA ROSEA - See 'Otahuhu Beauty'.

PAGAN - Light Rose Pink in center to Dark Rose Pink on outer petals and Light Pink petaloids. Large, semidouble. Average, open growth. M. (U.S. 1965 - Novick).

PAGO PAGO - White with Flesh undertone. Large, semidouble with some folded and curved petals. Average, open, upright growth. E-L. (U.S. 1973 - Haynie).

PAINTED LADY - Chalk White marked or faintly washed Pink, and sports Deep Pink and Coral Pink. Large, semidouble. Vigorous, upright growth. M. (U.S. 1959 - Braewood).

PALE PINK CLOUDS - Light Pink. Large, loose peony form. (Sport of Japonica 'Pink Clouds'). (U.S. 1956 - Fisher).

PALE PRINCESS - Pale Pink. Medium, rose form double to formal double. Spreading, upright growth. M. (U.S. 1961 - Wylam).

PALMER GILLETTE - ('Gillette's Fluffy White'). White. Medium, loose peony form. Vigorous, compact, upright growth. M. (U.S. 1946 - Huested).

PALMERSTON - See 'Cho Cho San'.

PALMYRA - Red. Large, peony form. (U.S. 1968 - N. Adams, Thomasville, GA).

PAM AMAN KIRVEN - Crimson Red with Yellow anthers and White filaments. Medium to large, full peony to loose peony form. Average, upright growth. M-L. (U.S. 2019 - Gordy).

PAMELA HARPER - Crimson. Medium to large, formal double. Vigorous, upright growth. L. (U.S. 1981 - Magnolia).

PAMELA JANE - Brilliant Red. Medium to large, peony form. Vigorous, compact, upright growth. M. (Aus. 1970 - Sebire).

PANACHE - Blended Pink and Ivory White. Medium, formal double. Vigorous, bushy growth. L. (France to U.S. [Armstrong] 1930).

PANTOMINE - Dark Rose Pink. Very large, loose peony form with ten groups of stamens interspersed with petals. Average, compact, upright growth. M. (U.S. 1965 - G. S. Clarke, Jr., Savannah, GA).

PAOLINA MAGGI - White, often with faint Pink stripe. Large, formal double. L. (For a variation of this cultivar see 'Mrs. H. Boyce'). (Italy 1855 - Maggi, Brescia).

PAPILLION - Clear Pink. Very large, semidouble with upright petaloids and soft Yellow stamens to rose form double. (U.S. 1961 - Mrs. J. P. Moon, Lake Charles, LA).

PAPOOSE - Indian Red. Miniature to small, formal double with incurved petals. Vigorous, compact, upright growth. M-L. (U.S. 1979 - McCaskill).

PARIS PINK - Silvery Rose Pink. Medium to large, formal double to rose form double. Vigorous, compact, upright growth. E-L. (U.S. 1960 - W. V. Lytle, Glendale, CA).

PARKER CONNOR - Shaded from very Palest Blush Pink at center to Pale Pink (RHS 49C) at outer edge of inner petals; outer petals shade from Pale Pink center to Deep Pink (RHS 52B) on tips. Medium, semidouble. Vigorous, upright growth. M. (U.S. 2012 - Parker Connor, Edisto Island, SC).

PARTY DRESS - Cream White shading to Pale Pink in center deepening to Lavender Pink on edge. Large, semidouble with wavy, crinkled, upright petals. Average, upright growth. M-L. (U.S. 1959 - Breschini).

PARTY GIRL - Pink. Large, semidouble. L. Distinct fragrance. (Aus. 1962 - H. K. C. Dettmann, Wahroonga).

PASHA OF PERSIA - See 'Te Deum'.

PAT BELLAMY - Dark Pink with Lavender tones on the edges with Yellow anthers and Pink filaments. Very large, single. Average, upright, dense growth. E-M. (Seedling of Japonica 'Tar Baby'). (U.S. 2019 - Pat Johnson, Cairo, GA).

PAT K - White flecked Lavender Pink shading to Lavender Pink at petal edges. Medium, rose form double. Average, open, upright growth. E-M. (U.S. 1976 - L. E. Kneipp, Shreveport, LA).

PAT LA MOTTE JONES - Glowing Pink. Large, full peony form to rose form double. M. (U.S. 1966).

PAT NIXON - Blush Pink veined Deeper Pink. Large, anemone form. (Sport of Japonica 'Richard Nixon'). (Variations of this cultivar include 'Julie Nixon' and 'Tricia'). (U.S. 1969 - Kramer).

PAT POYNER - Rose Pink. Large, anemone form. Average, open, upright growth. E-M. (U.S. 1959 - Dr. A. Mazyck, Dothan, AL).

PAT SUMMER - Dark Red. Medium, full peony form. Slow, spreading growth. M-L. (U.S. 1975 - M. R. Murray, Fort Valley, GA).

PAT'S CRUSHED VELVET - Dark Velvet Red with Yellow anthers and Yellow filaments. Large, semidouble to rose form double. Average, upright growth. M-L. (Seedling of Japonica 'Royal Velvet'). (U.S. 2016 - Pat Johnson, Cairo, GA).

PAT'S FAVORITE - Light Pink with Yellow anthers and White filaments. Medium, semidouble. Average, upright, dense growth. E-M. (U.S. 2017 - Pat Johnson, Cairo, GA).

PAT'S GARDEN - Coral Pink with Gold anthers and White filaments. Medium, anemone to loose peony. Average, upright, open growth. M-L. (Chance Japonica seedling). (U.S. 2016 - Pat Johnson, Cairo, GA).

PAT'S PRIZE - Deep Reddish Pink. Medium, formal double with incurved and notched petals. Average, upright growth. E-M. (U.S. 1997 - W. Brown, Montgomery, AL).

PAT'S WHITE - White with Gold anthers. Large, formal double to rose form double. Average, upright growth. M-L. (Chance Japonica seedling). (U.S. 2016 - Pat Johnson, Cairo, GA).

PATIENCE - Light Pink. Medium, full peony form. Upright growth. M. (U.S. 1959 - Woodlawn).

PATRICE MUNSEL - Red. Medium, semidouble with three rows of petals that open out and curl back slightly. Upright growth. M. (U.S. 1955 - Golletta).

PATRICIA ANN - Soft Pink. Large, semidouble with flaring stamens. Average, compact, upright growth. M. (U.S. 1980 - Asper).

PATRICIA HEMINGWAY - Medium Pink with Red stripes with interspersed Golden anthers and White filaments. Large, full peony form. Average, spreading growth. M-L. (U.S. 2019 - William Caldwell, Woodville. TX).

PATRICIA KOONEY - Pink freckled with White highlights. Large, semidouble to loose peony form with star shaped crown. Average, spreading growth. M. (U.S. 1987 - Tammia).

PATRICIA MARY - Pink. Large, semidouble to loose peony form. Vigorous, open growth. (N.Z. 1972 - Mrs. R. Woodrow, Gisborne).

PATRICIAN - Plum color. Large, single with loose, irregular petals. Compact, upright growth. M. (U.S. 1947 - McCaskill).

PATSY O'NEAL - Clear Pink. Medium, formal double. Average, upright growth. M-L. (U.S. 1974 - Haynie).

PATSY RISH - Pink with Deeper Pink overtone. Large to very large, loose peony form. (U.S. 1967 - W. H. Rish, Winnsboro, SC).

PATSY SMITH - Blood Red. Medium, semidouble. Average, upright growth. E-M. (U.S. 1987 - W. L. Smith, Tylertown, MS).

127

PATTI LOU - Blush white with Golden anthers. Medium, formal double to rose form double. Average, bushy growth. E-M. (U.S. 2019 - Hank Boudolf, Fort. Walton Beach, FL).

PATTI PERKINS - Rose Red with White. Small, loose peony to rose form double. Average, upright growth. (U.S. 2006 - Hyman Norsworthy, Beaumont, TX. Propagated by Read Nursery, Lucedale, MS).

PATTIE ANN VORCE - Light Pink. Medium to large, rose form double. Vigorous, open, upright growth. E-M. (U.S. 1963 - Marshall).

PATTY BENGTSON - White. Medium, formal double. Average, compact, upright growth. M. (U.S. 1965 - L. W. Strohmeyer, San Gabriel, CA).

PATTY SKINNER - Bright Pink. Large, peony form. Average growth. M. (U.S. 1966 - Julington).

PAUL HASKEE - Red. Very large, anemone form to peony form. Vigorous, dense, upright growth. E-L. (U.S. 1995 - Mandarich).

PAUL HOWARD'S WHITE - White. Medium, formal double to rose form double. Vigorous, upright growth. M. (U.S. 1945 - P. J. Howard, Los Angeles, CA).

PAUL JONES - Pale Pink penciled Pink. Large, single to semidouble. M. (For a variation of this cultivar see 'Roberta'). (Aus. 1949 - Rookwood Cemetery, NSW).

PAUL JONES SUPREME - Blush White striped Carmine. Large, flat semidouble. (Aus. 1968 - Waterhouse).

PAUL SHERRINGTON - White. Large, semidouble. Slow, dense growth. E-L. (Aus. 1995 - C. Sherrington, North Balwyn, Vic.).

PAULA DEEN - Soft Red with Yellow anthers and White filaments. Medium, semidouble to anemone. Slow, upright growth. M-L. (U.S. 2014 - Gordy).

PAULA JOHNSON - Rose Pink. Large, anemone form. Bushy, upright growth. M. (U.S. 1975 - Dr. G. R. Johnson, Carthage, TX).

PAULA SMYTH - Maroon. Miniature to small, semidouble with White stamens tipped Yellow. Average, upright growth. M-L. (N.Z. 1984 - Mrs. I. Berg, Whakatane).

PAULETTE GODDARD - Dark Red. Medium, semidouble to loose peony form to anemone form. Vigorous, upright growth. M-L. Cold hardy. (U.S. 1945 - Middleton).

PAULETTE GODDARD VARIEGATED - Dark Red blotched White form of 'Paulette Goddard'.

PAULINA - See 'Mathotiana Variegated'.

PAULINE NIELSON - Rose Pink. Miniature, semidouble with White stamens. Average growth. M-L. (U.S. 1961 - Dr. C. S. Nielson, Tallahassee, FL).

PAULINE WETZLER - Light Pink in center shading to Deep Pink on outer edge. Small, single of cupped form. Loose, pendulous growth. L. (U.S. 1957 - Miss P. Wetzler, Portland, OR).

PAULINE WINCHESTER - White marked Pink. Large, semidouble to peony form with loose petals. Average, compact growth. M. (U.S. 1958 - R. Winchester, Altadena, CA).

PAX - ('Snow Doll'; 'Yuki-Daruma'; 'White Laurel Leaf'). White. Medium to large, formal double. Average, compact, upright growth. M-L. (France to U.S. 1930 - Youtz).

PAYNE'S RED - See 'Vedrine'.

PEACE - White. Medium, semidouble. (U.S. 1956 - Tait).

PEACH BLOSSOM - ('Magnoliaeflora [England]'; 'Fleur De Peche'; 'Fleur. De Pecher'). Light Pink. Medium, semidouble. Average, compact growth. M. (England 1920 - Caledonia).

PEACH BLUSH - Pale to Light Peach Pink with very Pale Peach Pink guard petals. Medium, anemone form. Average, upright growth. M. (Aus. 1998 - Bernice Joy West, Carrum Downs, Vic.).

PEACHY PINK - Light Pink with Yellow anthers and Pink filaments. Large, semidouble to rose form double. Average, spreading, open growth. E-M. (U.S. 2019 - Pat Johnson, Cairo, GA).

PEARL BURSON - Red and White. Small, formal double. Vigorous, compact, upright growth. E-L. (U.S. 1969 - M. J. Burson, Long Beach, MS).

PEARL HARBOR - Dark Red. Medium, semidouble with irregular petals. Vigorous, compact, upright growth. L. (U.S. 1945 - Middleton).

PEARL ISOBEL - Pale Blush Pink. Medium, rose form double. Average, open, upright growth. M-L. (Aus. 1998 - B. Flanagan, Eagle Heights, Qld.).

PEARL MAXWELL - Soft Shell Pink. Medium, formal double. Vigorous, compact growth. M-L. (For a variation of this cultivar see 'Blanche Maxwell'). (U.S. 1950 - Mrs. C. O. Maxwell, Reno, GA).

PEARL SCRUGGS - White. Large, rose form double. Vigorous, upright growth. M. (U.S. 1967 - W. Littleton, Hahira, GA).

PEARL'S PET - Rose Red. Miniature, anemone form. Vigorous, compact, upright growth. E-M. (U.S. 1959 - Mrs. P. Chicco, Charleston, SC).

PEARLE COOPER - Deep Pink and White. Large, semidouble with wavy, crinkled petals. Vigorous growth. M-L. (U.S. 1968 - Gerbing).

PEARLY GATES - Shell Pink with Pearl colored bud in center. Medium, formal double to rose form double. (U.S. 1953 - Fruitland).

PEBBLE HILL PEPPERMINT - Pink with Red veins (RHS color 52c) and has Red stripes (RHS color 50a). Small, formal double. Average, upright growth. L. (U.S. 2018 - Tom Corley, Auburn AL).

PEE WEE - Red. Miniature, anemone form. Vigorous, open, upright growth. M-L. (U.S. 1959 - Wylam).

PEG O' MY HEART - White washed and shaded Orchid Pink. Medium, full peony form. Vigorous, compact growth. M. (U.S. 1960 - Shackelford).

PEGGY MILLER - Light Pink. Medium to large, formal double. Slow, spreading, open growth. E-M. (U.S. 2013 - Howell).

PEGGY STEWART - Clear Red. Small, full peony form. Average, open growth. M-L. (U.S. 1956 - J. S. Gilder, San Fernando, CA).

PEGGY'S BLUSH - White with Peach Blush. Small to medium, formal double. Vigorous, dense, upright growth. M-L. (U.S. 1991 - D. Applegate, Pensacola, FL).

PENNY PALMER - White. Medium, full peony form. (U.S. 1955 - Miss L. Palmer, Shreveport, LA).

PENNY SMITH - Deep Red. Large, full peony form. Average, upright growth. E-M. (U.S. 1987 - W. L. Smith, Tylertown, MS).

PENSACOLA BELLE - Rose Pink. Medium, full peony form. Average, open, spreading growth. E-L. (U.S. 1957 - Mrs. C. D. Boggett, Pensacola, FL).

PENSACOLA RED - Dark Red. Large, peony form to anemone form with Red stamens. Vigorous, upright growth. M. (U.S. 1958 - Bowman).

PEPPERMINT CANDY - White with Red stripes and flecks. Medium, semidouble. Average compact growth. M-L. (U.S. 2008 - CamelliaShop, Savannah, GA).

PEPPERMINT FRECKLES - Pale Pink with Pink stripes and Pink freckles with Gold anthers. Medium, loose peony to full peony. Vigorous, upright, dense growth. M-L. (Chance Japonica seedling). (U.S. 2016 - Pat Johnson, Cairo, GA).

PEPPERMINT PATTY - White striped Red and blotched White. Medium, rose form double. Average, upright growth. M-L. (U.S. 1987 - Ackerman).

PERLA - Light Pink. Large, semidouble with very thick petals. Average, spreading, upright growth. E-L. (U.S. 1967 - C. E. Blanchard, III, Carthage, TX).

PERSONALITY - Pink. Medium, anemone form. Vigorous, compact, upright growth. E-L. (Aus. 1988 - Mrs. E. M. Patridge, Macksville, NSW).

PERT - See 'Finlandia Red'.

PETE SCOTT - Bright Red. Large, semidouble to peony form. Average, compact, upright growth. M-L. (U.S. 1987 - Elizabeth R. Scott, Aiken, SC).

PETE'S FRAGRANT PINK - Pink with slight sheen shading to Darker Pink edges. Large, loose peony form. Average, upright growth. E-L. Fragrant. (U.S. 1994 - P. Tedesco, Felton, CA).

PETER COTTONTAIL - White with Yellow anthers and White filaments. Medium, anemone form. Average, upright, dense growth. E-M. (U.S. 2019 - Gordy).

PETER PAN - Cream White at base shading through Blush Pink to Cerise Pink at edges, with definite Orchid overtone. Medium, semidouble to full peony form. Average, compact growth. M-L. (U.S. 1950 - W. J. Robinson and C. J. Hayes, Norfolk, VA).

PETER REID - Red. Small, anemone form with deeply notched outer petals. Average, open, upright growth. E-L. (N.Z. 1976 - Mrs. I. Berg, Whakatane).

PETER WOODROOF - Deep Red. Large, semidouble with folded, upright center petals. Vigorous, compact, upright growth. M. (U.S. 1978 - W. E. Woodroof, Sherman Oaks, CA).

PETITE - Red with Red petaloids, each with White stripe down center. Small, anemone form. (U.S. 1958 - S. W. Miller, El Cajon, CA).

PETITE ROSINE - Blush Pink. Miniature, formal double. Vigorous, upright growth. M. (U.S. 1972 - Witman).

PHILIP TAYLOR - Vivid Red with Yellow anthers and White filaments. Medium to large, semidouble to loose peony form. Average, upright growth. M-L. (Sport of Japonica 'Philip Taylor' Peppermint'). (U.S. 2011 - Christine T. Collins, Quitman, GA).

PHILIP TAYLOR PEPPERMINT - Blush Pink with vivid Red stripes with Yellow anthers and White filaments. Medium to large, semidouble to loose peony form. Average, upright growth. M-L. (Japonica 'Horkan' x unknown pollen parent). (U.S. 2011 - Christine T. Collins, Quitman, GA).

PHILIPPA IFOULD - Soft Pink. Medium to large, formal double. M-L. (Aus. 1968 - W. Ifould, Turramurra, NSW).

PHILLIP'S CHOICE - Dark Red with Yellow anthers and Pale Pink filaments. Medium, full peony to anemone form. Slow, upright, dense growth. E-M. (U.S. 2018 - Gordy).

PHOTENIA P - Pink, sometimes variegated White. Large, semidouble. Average, bushy growth. M. (U.S. 1952 - B. Johnston, Jacksonville, FL).

PHRYNE - Delicate Pink to Silvery Pink. Large, semidouble. Vigorous, open, upright growth. E-L. (Aus. 1978 - A. Spragg, Sutherland, NSW).

PICCADILLY - Light Blush Pink splashed and flecked bright Pink. Large, semidouble to loose peony form. Average, open, upright growth. M-L. (U.S. 1969 - Haynie).

PIED PIPER - Red blotched and irregularly streaked White. Medium to large, semidouble. Vigorous, compact, upright growth. M. (U.S. 1959 - Short).

PIERATE'S PRIDE - Velvet Red. Medium to large, semidouble to anemone form. Vigorous, spreading growth. M. (U.S. 1953 - Pierates Cruz Gardens, Mt. Pleasant, SC).

PIERCE LATHROP - Rose Pink. Large, anemone form. Vigorous, upright growth. M-L. (U.S. 1983 - Feathers).

PINCUSHION - Bright Red. Small to medium, semidouble with some upright petals. Average, compact, upright growth. M. (U.S. 1988 - G. A. Stewart, Sacramento, CA).

PINE CONE - See 'Matsu-Kasa'.

PINE CONE WHITE - See 'Kagira'.

PINK BALL - Soft Pink. Medium, full peony form. Vigorous, compact, upright growth. M. (Japan to U.S. [Domoto] 1935).

PINK BALLET - Three blended shades of Pink. Large, semidouble to loose peony form with ruffled petals and petaloids. Upright growth. E. (U.S. 1959 - Braewood).

PINK BEAUTY - See 'Mathotiana Rosea'.

PINK BOUQUET - Rose Pink. Medium, rose form double. Average, compact, upright growth. M-L. (U.S. 1973 - Hudson).

PINK CHAMPAGNE - ('Camellian'). Soft Pink. Large, semidouble with irregular petals. Vigorous, open growth. L. (U.S. 1952 - Illges).

PINK CHAMPAGNE VARIEGATED - Soft Pink blotched White variation of 'Pink Champagne'.

PINK CHIFFON - Clear Pink. Medium, formal double form. Slow, dense, upright growth. M. (U.S. 2005 - Gordy).

PINK CLOUDS - Cream Pink and marked Deeper Pink changing to Light Lavender Pink as flower ages. Large, loose peony form. Vigorous, compact, upright growth. M. (Variations of this cultivar include 'Deep Pink Clouds'; 'Pale Pink Clouds'). (U.S. 1953 - Short).

PINK DAVIS - Soft Pink with Yellow stamens. Large, semidouble to peony form. E-M. (Graft-mutation or chimera of Japonica 'Mrs. D. W. Davis' and Japonica 'J. C. Williams' on Japonica 'Colonel Firey'). (U.S. 1962 - O. D. Edge, Columbus, GA).

PINK DAVIS PEONY - Large, peony form. (Sport of 'Pink Davis').

PINK DAWN - Deep Pink. Medium, formal double. Vigorous, compact, upright growth. M. (U.S. 1934 - Heam).

PINK DIDDY - Pink. Medium, rose form double to formal double to peony form. (Sport of Japonica 'Diddy Mealing'). (U.S. 1950 - Mealing).

PINK DOLL - Light Salmon Pink. Small, formal double. Average, open growth. M. (U.S. 1971 - Alfter).

PINK DREAM - Light Purplish Pink. Medium, anemone form with White stamens. Vigorous, open, upright growth. E-M. (U.S. 1959 - Truesdale Nsy., West Columbia, SC).

PINK ELEPHANT - Clear Pink with Orchid undertones. Large to very large, semidouble with velvet textured, crinkled petals and upright, folded center petals. Average, upright growth. E-L. (U.S. 1967 - Haynie).

PINK EXPLORER - Rose to Orchid Pink with some petaloids variegated and some White. Large, anemone form, with some uneven outer petals. Average, spreading growth. E-M. (U.S. 1958 - Mrs. G. Shealy, Leesville, SC).

PINK FIMBRIATA - See 'Daitairin'.

PINK FROST - Silvery Pink with White border on all petals. Medium to large, formal double. (Sport of Japonica 'Pink Pagoda'). (U.S. 1970 - S E Foster, El Cajon, CA).

PINK GOLD - Pink with Gold tipped center filaments. Large, semidouble. Vigorous, upright growth. E-L. (U.S. 1970 - E. Pieri, San Gabriel, CA).

PINK HERME - See 'Herme Pink'.

PINK ICE - Soft Lavender Pink. Medium, single with Golden stamens. Vigorous, upright growth. M-L. (U.S. 1957 - Short).

PINK IMURA - Light Rose Pink. Large, semidouble. Vigorous, upright growth. E-M. (U.S. 1953).

PINK JADE - Blush Pink. Large, semidouble. Average, upright growth. M-L. (U.S. 1980 - H. L. Paige, Lafayette, CA).

PINK JEWEL - Rose Pink to Rose Pink and White. Medium to large, formal double with cupped and pointed petals, sometimes swirled. Vigorous, upright growth. M-L. (U.S. 1972 - Alfter).

PINK JORDAN'S PRIDE - See 'Herme Pink'.

PINK KAGURA - See 'Daikagura Red'.

PINK LACE - See Hishi-Karaito'.

PINK LADY (CALIFORNIA) - See 'Lady Loch'.

PINK MAGIC - Rose Pink. Medium to large, loose peony form with silk sheen. Vigorous, upright growth. M. (U.S. 1964 - Hyde Park Nsy., Jacksonville, FL).

PINK MERMAID (KINGYO-TSUBAKI) - Spinel Pink with Golden anthers and White filaments. Medium, single with six somewhat irregular petals; most leaves narrow down then flare out to three points giving a fishtail (kingyo) appearance. M-L. Fragrant. (This plant is a sub-species of japonica - quercifolia; sometimes called Camellia japonica var. quercifolia 'Pink Mermaid'). (Canada 1994 - Introduced into North America from Japan by Piroche Plants, Pitt Meadows, British Columbia).

PINK PAGODA - Rose Pink. Medium to large, formal double. Vigorous, compact, upright growth. (For a variation of this cultivar see 'Pink Frost'). (U.S. 1963 - R. D. Moore, Los Gatos, CA).

PINK PARADE - Pink. Large, semidouble. Average, upright growth. M. (U.S. 1972 - Hudson).

PINK PARFAIT - Soft Pink. Medium to large, semidouble of water lily form. Compact, upright growth. M. (U.S. 1960 - Hudson).

PINK PASSION - Pink with Orchid overcast. Medium to large, semidouble with irregular petals. Vigorous, upright growth. E-M. (U.S. 1959 - Weisner).

PINK PEARL - ('Burgdorf Beauty'; 'Badgen's Beauty'). Light Pink with high, pointed Ivory center. Small, formal double. (Sport of Japonica 'Pink Perfection'). (Japan to Aus. 1895).

PINK PERFECTION - ('Frau Minna Seidel'; 'Usu-Otome'). Shell Pink. Small, formal double. Vigorous, upright growth. E-L. Cold hardy. (For a variation of this cultivar see 'Pink Pearl'). (Japan to U.S. 1890's - Domato).

PINK PERFUME - Watermelon Pink. Small to medium, semidouble. Average growth. M. (U.S. 1976 - Parks).

PINK POODLE - Pale delicate Pink with Gold anthers and White filaments. Large, loose peony to anemone form. Average, upright, open growth. M-L. (Seedling of Japonica 'Snow Lady'). (U.S. 2018 - Pat Johnson, Cairo, GA).

PINK POPPY - Soft Pink. Small to medium, single to semidouble with rosette of stamens in center. Slow, upright growth. M. (U.S. 1941 - Gerbing).

PINK PURITY - See 'General George Patton'.

PINK RADIANCE - Clear Pink. Large, full peony form. Average, bushy growth. M-L. (U.S. 1961 - Short).

PINK RIBBON - Pink with minor variegation. Medium to large, formal double. Average, upright, dense growth. M-L. The plant is very cold hardy. (U.S. 2013 - Howell).

PINK SATIN - Pink. Large, semidouble to rose form double. Vigorous, open, upright growth. M. (U.S. 1960 - Hudson).

PINK SHADOWS - Deep Salmon Pink with deeper shadows of Pink. Medium, semidouble with fimbriated inner petals. Average, upright, compact growth. E-M. (U.S. 1950 - Short).

PINK SHELL - See 'Lady St. Clair'.

PINK SMOKE - Light Lavender Pink. Miniature, loose anemone form. M. (U.S. 1965 - Feathers).

PINK STAR - Rose Pink. Medium, semidouble with pointed outer petals and stamens among central petaloids. Slow, compact, upright growth. M. Cold hardy. (Japan to U.S. [Domoto] 1935).

PINK STAR VARIEGATED - See 'Nellie Ann Phinizy'.

PINK SUNSET - Light Pink. Large, semidouble to loose peony form with fluffy petals. M. (U.S. 1961 - McDonald Camellia Nsy., Beach Island, SC).

PINK SUPERLATIVE - Light Pink. Medium, formal double. Vigorous, upright growth. E-L. (U.S. 1961 - T. L. Sellers, Bolivia, NC).

PINK VELVET - Velvety Pink. Medium to large, semidouble with irregular petals to loose peony form. (U.S. 1961 - H. Mura, Augusta, GA).

PINK VELVET VARIEGATED - Velvety Pink and White variation of 'Pink Velvet.'

PINK WHIRLPOOL - Pink. Small, formal double. Vigorous, open, upright growth. E-M. (U.S. 1959 - Dr. A. Mazyck, Dothan, AL).

PINK WINGS - Soft Pink. Medium to large, irregular semidouble with rabbit ears. Average, dense, upright growth. M-L. (U.S. 1993 - Nuccio's).

PINK-A-BOO - White, turning to Blush Pink and finally a Blush of Yellow with Yellow anthers and Yellow filaments. Medium, anemone form. Average, spreading growth. E-M. (U.S. 2009 - John L. Spencer, Lakeland, FL).

PINNACLE - Glowing Coral Red. Large to very large, peony form. Average, upright growth. M-L. (U.S. 1965 - Short).

PIQUANT - Cream White with Cinnamon Pink edging. Medium, semidouble. Vigorous, compact, upright growth. M-L. (U.S. 1985 - H. Hall).

PIRATE'S GOLD - Dark Red. Large, semidouble to loose peony form. Average, spreading growth. M-L. (U.S. 1969 - Haynie).

PIRATE'S GOLD MOIRED - Moired variegation. (Sport of Japonica 'Pirate's Gold'). (U.S. 1990 - V. Stone, Baton Rouge, LA).

PIRATE'S GOLD VARIEGATED - Dark Red and White variation of 'Pirate's Gold'. (U.S. 1975).

PIROUETTE - Soft Pink deepening to edge. Large, semidouble. Average, bushy, upright growth. M-L. (U.S. 1975 - W. F. Harrison, Berkeley, CA).

PIXIE - Bright Red veined White. Small, semidouble. M-L. (U.S. Late 1800's - Magnolia).

PLUM PURTY - Mauve Pink. Medium, formal double. Low, spreading growth. M-L. (U.S. 1956 - Wylam).

PLUMFIELD WHITE - White. Medium, semidouble with wavy petals. Vigorous, compact growth. M. Slightly fragrant. (U.S. 1948 - Illges).

POCAHONTAS - Rose Pink, deeper at edge. Large, rose form double. Average, open, upright growth. M-L. (U.S. 1969 - Haynie).

POD MATE - Deep Pink. Medium, rose form double to formal double. Vigorous, upright growth. M. (U.S. 1956 - D. W. Davis).

POINT PERFECTION - Vivid Red marked White. Medium, formal double with deep petals. Vigorous, compact, upright growth. E-M. (U.S. 1959 - Short).

POLAR BEAR - Chalk White. Large, semidouble. (Aus. 1957 - Waterhouse).

POLLY MITCHELL - White. Large, semidouble with upright inner petals. Slow, open growth. E. (U.S. 1958 - Miss H. Brandon, Thomasville, GA).

POP ALLEN - Dark Pink with Darker Pink flashes, petals occasionally cupped. Medium, formal double. Vigorous, upright growth. M. (U.S. 2001 - Carl Allen, Mt. Pleasant, SC).

POP'S PERFECTION - Medium Pink flecked and streaked with Darker Burgundy to Deep Coral Pink at the center of petals. Small, formal double. Slow, spreading, open growth. M-L. (U.S. 2009 - John M. Davy, Milton, FL).

POP'S PERFECTION PEPPERMINT - Burgundy stripes on a Pink background; tendency to sport one colored flower. Small, formal double. Very slow growth. M-L. (U.S. - John M. Davy, Milton, FL).

POPCORN - White. Large, semidouble with high petaloid center. (U.S. 1971 - Wilson).

POPE JOHN XXIII - White. Medium to large, formal double with heavy, velvet textured petals. Vigorous, compact, upright growth. M. (U.S. 1967 - Maitland).

POPE PIUS IX - See 'Prince Eugene Napoleon'. (Not same as cultivar listed in old literature, which is 'Pie IX').

POPPY SANS - Orange Pink. Miniature, semidouble with occasional center petaloids and upright petals. Average, upright growth. M-L. (U.S. 1956 - Metcalf).

PORCELAIN DOLL - Blush Pink. Miniature, formal double. Slow growth. L. (U.S. 1997 - Domoto).

PORTUENSE - Red. Small, peony form with variegated foliage. (Portugal 1958 - Da Silva).

PORTUGESE PINK - See 'Augusto L'Gouveia Pinto'.

POST TIME - Pink fading to Light Pink at edge. Large, semidouble. Average, open, upright growth. E-M. (U.S. 1966 - Ashby).

POTENTATE - Rose Red. Small, formal double. (Possibly a Japonica ' Reverend John G. Drayton' seedling). (Europe to U.S. 1840's - Magnolia Plantation & Gardens, Charleston, SC).

POTOMAC PILLAR - White. Medium to large, semidouble form. Average, upright growth. M-L. Cold hardy. (U.S. 1999 - Dr. Arthur A. Maryott, Gaithersburg, MD).

POUF - Cream White with one Red petal. Small, full peony form. Slow, compact, upright growth. M. (U.S. 1963 - Novick).

POWDER PUFF - White. Small to medium, peony form. Average growth. M. (U.S. 1960 - Hartman).

POWELL'S PINK - See 'Herme Pink'.

PRAIRIE FIRES - Oriental Red. Medium to large, formal double to anemone form. Average, compact growth. E-L. (U.S. 1967 - Short).

PRAIRIE JEFFERSON - Rose. Medium, formal double. Average, upright growth. M. (U.S. 1964 - Mrs. W. M. Nolan, Oak Ridge, LA).

PREACHER'S ELLA - Mass of White incurved petals shading to Orchid Pink at edge. Medium, formal double to rose form double. (Sport of Japonica 'Ella Ward Parsons'). (U.S. 1980 - J. Austin, Four Oaks, NC).

PRELUDE - Clear Turkey Red. Medium, semidouble to anemone form. Vigorous, compact, upright growth. E-M. (U.S. 1950 - E. W. Miller, Escondido, CA).

PRELUDE VARIEGATED - Turkey Red blotched White variation of 'Prelude'.

PREMIER - Clear Rose Red. Large, full peony form. Vigorous, upright growth. M-L. (U.S. 1965 - Short).

PREMIER VARIEGATED - Clear Rose Red blotched White variation of 'Premier'. (U.S. 1973 - L Baskerville, San Diego, CA).

PRESIDENT LINCOLN - Red. Medium, anemone form. Vigorous, upright growth. L. (U.S. 1955 - Goletto).

PRETTY IN PINK - Pink, with Lighter Pink center. Miniature, formal double. Average growth. M-L. (U.S. 1987 - D. Bergamini, Martinez, CA).

PRETTY LADY - See 'Gordy's Pretty Lady'.

PRETTY ONE - Coral Pink shading to White in center. Medium, semidouble to loose peony form. Vigorous, upright growth. E-L. (U.S. 1975 - Novick).

PRETTY PANTALETTES - Soft Pink with White band. Medium, semidouble. Average, upright growth. M. (U.S. 1957 - McCaskill).

PRETTY PEACH - Peach Pink. Medium, peony form. Vigorous, dense, upright growth. M-L. (U.S. 1999 - William R. Blackman, Easley, SC).

PRETTY PEGGY - Dark Red with Black veining and White moiré variegation with Yellow anthers and Pink filaments. Medium, full peony. Average, spreading and open growth. E-M. (U.S. 2016 - Ed Powers, Wilmington, NC).

PRETTY PENNY - Shell Pink, lighter at edge. Medium, formal double with pointed petals standing apart of cone form. Vigorous, upright growth. M. (U.S. 1964 - R. W. Wilder, Fairhope, AL).

PRETTY THING - Light Pink. Medium to large, semidouble. Vigorous, compact, upright growth. M. (U.S. 1971 - B. Leeton, Gulfport, MS).

PRIDE OF CALIFORNIA - Orange Pink. Miniature, formal double. Slow growth. M. (U.S. 1977 - W. L. Gilmore, Conroe, TX).

PRIDE OF GREENVILLE - ('Steven's Pink'; 'Red Dale'). Bright Red. Medium to large, full peony form. Vigorous, upright growth. M-L. (U.S. 1897 - Greenville, AL).

PRIDE OF GULFPORT - Bright Red. Large, semidouble to peony form. (U.S. 1948 — Clower).

PRIDE OF PORTLAND - See 'Lady de Saumarez'.

PRIDE OF ROSEBUD FARM - See 'Lady de Saumarez'.

PRIDE OF THE EMPEROR'S GARDEN - See 'Elegans [Chandler] Variegated'.

PRIMA BALLERINA - White washed and shaded Orchid Pink. Medium to large, semidouble with fluted petals. Average, compact growth. M-L. (U.S. 1983 - Nuccio's).

PRIMA DONNA - Bright Pink. Medium, semidouble. Vigorous, bushy growth. L. (Not the cultivar listed in old literature, which was star shaped semidouble of Pink margined White and veined Pink). (Europe to U.S. [Tea Gardens] 1890).

PRIMA DONNA VARIEGATED - Bright Pink marbled White form of 'Prima Donna'.

PRIMAVERA - White. Medium, formal double. Vigorous, upright growth. M-L. (U.S. 1950 - Nuccio's).

PRIME FRAGRANCE - Deep Red. Medium, peony form. Average, upright growth. M-L. Fragrant. (N.Z. 1994 - J. Finlay).

PRINCE CHARLIE - Velvet Red. Medium, semidouble. Slow, compact, upright growth. M-L. (U.S. 1950 - L. A. Walker, Summerville, SC).

PRINCE CHARMING - Deep Rose-Pink. Medium, anemone form with small petaloids and large petals. Vigorous, compact growth. E-M. (U.S. 1948 - John S. Armstrong, Ontario, CA).

PRINCE EUGENE NAPOLEON - ('Pope Pius IX'; 'Imbricata Rubra Plena'; 'Ladiner's Red'). Cherry Red. Medium, formal double with many small, rounded petals which are progressively smaller toward center. Average, compact, upright growth. M. (Belgium 1859 - De Coster, Melle).

PRINCE FREDERICK WILLIAM - Light Pink. Medium, formal double. Upright, open growth. M. (For a variation of this cultivar see 'Lady Hope'). (Aus. 1875 - Sheather).

PRINCE MURAT - Rose Red. Very large, rose form double. Vigorous growth. M. (U.S. 1952 - Rosa).

PRINCE OF ORANGE - ('Crusader'). Deep Orange Red. Large, loose to full peony form to anemone form. Vigorous, compact, upright growth. M. (For a variation of this cultivar see 'Governor William Bradford'). (U.S. 1950 - Clower).

PRINCE OF ORANGE VARIEGATED - See 'Governor William Bradford'.

PRINCE-N-RED - Dark Red. Small, formal double. Average, upright, dense growth. M-L. (Seedling of Japonica 'Royal Velvet'). (U.S. 2019 - Pat Johnson, Cairo, GA).

PRINCESS ANNE - See 'Rubenceus Major Variegated'.

PRINCESS BACIOCCHI - Carmine. Medium, semidouble to peony form. Vigorous, bushy growth. M. (For original cultivar see 'Princesse Baciocchi'). (U.S. 1930 - Armstrong).

PRINCESS IRENE - Rose Pink. Medium, semidouble to peony form with bell shaped petaloids among petals. Slow, upright growth. E. (Europe to U.S. [Magnolia] 1840's).

PRINCESS IRENE VARIEGATED - Rose Pink marbled White form of 'Princess Irene'.

PRINCESS LAVENDER - Lavender Pink. Large, semidouble. Vigorous, compact growth. M. (U.S. 1950 - Wilkinson).

PRINCESS LEAR - Coral Pink faintly streaked Deeper Pink. Medium, full peony form. Vigorous, open, upright growth. M. (U.S. 1958 - Ragland).

PRINCESS LUCILLE - See 'Beauty of Holland'.

PRINCESS MASAKO - White with a Red border and small and large stripes. Medium to large, lotus form semidouble to peony form. Vigorous, initially upright, later spreading growth. M-L. (Sport of Japonica 'Ikari-shibori'). (Japan 1989 - Sôshin Hirai, Saitama Prefecture).

PRINCESS MURAT - Solid Deep Rose Pink. Medium, anemone form to loose peony form with petals notched, cup-shaped and slightly crêped. Vigorous, bushy growth. M. (U.S. 1949 - Rosa).

PRINCESS NAGASAKI - See 'Nagasaki'.

PRINCESSE BACIOCCHI - Crimson with White radial bars. Medium, formal double. Slow, compact growth. M-L. (Italy 1850 - Boffi).

PRINCESS-N-PINK - Light Pink with Yellow anthers and Cream filaments. Medium, anemone. Average, upright, dense growth. E-M. (U.S. 2017 - Pat Johnson, Cairo, GA).

PRINCESS-N-WHITE - White with Yellow anthers and Creamy yellow filaments. Medium to large, anemone form. Average, upright, open growth. E-L. (U.S. 2019 - Pat Johnson, Cairo, GA).

PRISSIE MISS - Pink. Medium to large, formal double to rose form double. Vigorous, upright growth. M-L. (U.S. 1975 - Novick).

PRISTINE FRAGRANCE - Rose Pink. Medium, anemone form. Average, open, upright growth. E-L. Fragrant. (N.Z. 1993 - J. Finlay).

PRIVATE SECRETARY - Red. Medium, semidouble. Average, upright growth. M-L. (U.S. 1962).

PROFESSOR CHARLES S. SARGENT - Dark Red. Medium, full peony to anemone form. Vigorous, compact, upright growth. M. (For a variation of this cultivar see 'Woody Estes'). (U.S. 1925 - Magnolia).

PROFESSOR CHARLES S. SARGENT VARIEGATED - ('Red Shadow'). Dark Red mottled White variation of 'Professor Charles S Sargent'.

PROFESSOR FRANK HUBERT - Deep Red. Large, formal double with upright center petals. Vigorous growth. M. (U.S. 1959 - B. Smith, Orange, TX).

PROFESSORE GIOVANNI SANTARELLI - White blotched and striped dark Pink to Crimson. Medium, rose form double. Upright, bushy growth. M-L. (Italy 1860 - Santarelli).

PUCK - Deep Red. Small, single. Vigorous, bushy, spreading growth. M. (Aus. 1965 - G. Waterhouse).

PUKEKURA - White. Large, semidouble to peony form with large, rounded, outer petals and central stamens tipped with Golden anthers surrounded by folded petals. (N.Z. 1952 - Pukekura Park, New Plymouth).

PURITAN LASS - White. Small, formal double. Vigorous, bushy growth. M. (U.S. 1953 - Short).

PURITY - ('Neige d'Oree'; 'Shiragiku'; 'Harriet I. Laub'; 'Refinement'). White. Medium, rose form double to formal double. Vigorous, upright growth. L. Cold hardy. (Japan to U.S. 1887 - Domoto).

PURPLE DAWN - See 'Mathotiana'.

PURPLE EMPEROR - See 'Mathotiana'.

PURPLE GIRL - Pink with Purple cast. Medium, semidouble with loose petals. M. (U.S. 1960 - Malbis).

PURPLE PASSION - Reddish Purple center to Deep Purple outer petals with Dark Purple radial veining; Purple coloration holds true through most of the bloom season but extremely late blooms lose some of the Blue pigment. Medium, formal double. Average, upright, dense growth. M-L. (U.S. 2013 - Richard Dodd, Marshallville, GA).

PURPLE PINE CONE - Purple Rose. Medium, semidouble of pine cone form. (U.S. 1950 - Pfingstl).

PURPLE PRINCE - See 'Mathotiana'.

PURPLE SWIRL - Ashes of Roses turning to Rosy Purple. Small to medium, formal double with five complete swirls of petals radiating from center. Vigorous, upright growth. M-L. (U.S. 1960 - Tammia).

Q BALL - Deep Rose with Yellow anthers. Very large, peony form. Vigorous, upright, dense growth. E-L. (U.S. 2010 - Eleanor Grant, Dothan, AL).

QUAINTANCE - Soft Pink lightly striped Darker Pink. Medium, semidouble. (Sport of Japonica 'Herme'). (U.S. 1950 - McCaskill).

QUAKER LADY - Salmon Pink. Large, semidouble. (Sport of Japonica 'Carter's Carnival'). (U.S. 1959 - Carter).

QUE SERA SERA - Salmon Pink. Large to very large, variform; regular semidouble to semidouble with petaloids intermixed with stamens to anemone form. Vigorous, compact, upright growth. E-M. (U.S. 1982 - Nuccio's).

QUEEN BESSIE - White flushed Pink at center. Medium, semidouble with wavy petals. Vigorous, compact, upright growth. L. (U.S. 1935 - Overlook).

QUEEN DIANA - Pink shading to Pale Pink in outer petals. Medium, formal double. Vigorous, spreading, open growth. E-L. (N.Z. 1985 - J. C. Lesnie, Wanukau).

QUEEN JULIANA - See 'Southern Charm'.

QUEEN OF ENGLAND - Cherry Red striped White on inner petals. Medium, formal double. (England 1851 - Fiedler).

QUEEN OF HEARTS - Bright Dark Red with Purple shading on edges with Yellow anthers and Pink filaments. Large, semidouble. Average, upright, open growth. M-L. (Seedling of Japonica 'Ville de Nantes'). (U.S. 2019 - Pat Johnson, Cairo, GA).

QUEEN OF THE ACRES - White to Pale Pink with Pink to Red streaks. Medium, formal double. (Sport of Japonica 'Rose Queen'). (U.S. 1951 - Councilman).

QUEEN OF THE SOUTH - Blush Pink. Medium, full peony form. Compact, upright growth. E. (U.S. 1954 - Shackelford).

QUEEN OF TOMORROW - Heavy textured, lightly crinkled, fluted, edged petals and thick, leathery foliage. Large to very large, semidouble. (Sport of Japonica 'Tomorrow Variegated'). (U.S. 1971 - Charmwood Nsy., Milbrook, AL).

QUEEN TUT - White. Medium, peony form. Average, upright growth. M-L. (U.S. 1991 - J. Aldrich, Brooklet, GA).

QUEEN VICTORIA'S BLUSH (SOUTH) - See 'Souv. de Bahuaud Litou'.

QUEEN'S COURT - White. Large, semidouble with heavy petals. M. (U.S. 1973 - Haynie).

QUEEN'S ESCORT - Rose Pink with Silver sheen around edge of petals. Medium, semidouble. Vigorous, compact, upright growth. M. (U.S. 1959 - Dr. A Mazyck, Dothan, AL).

R. B. ZACHRY - Dark Red veined Darker Red. Medium to large, semidouble to loose peony form. Average growth. E-M. (U.S. 1959 - R. B. Zachry, Waycross, GA).

R. L. BRENT - White. Large, formal double of tiered form. (U.S. 1958 - Woodland).

R. L. WHEELER - Rose Pink. Very large, semidouble to anemone form with heavy outer petals and solid circle of stamens. Vigorous, upright growth. E-M. Cold hardy. (U.S. 1949 - Wheeler).

R. L. WHEELER VARIEGATED - Rose Pink and White variation of 'R L Wheeler'.

R. O. RUBEL - Variegated variation of 'Augusta Equen' - Light Rose Pink and White. (U.S. 1955 - Longview).

R. W. JONES VARIEGATED - Red and White. Large, semidouble. Average, open growth. E-M. (U.S. 2005 - H. Finley Jones, Lake Charles, LA).

RABBI PEISER - White. Medium, formal double of occasional dahlia form. Average, open, upright growth. M. (U.S. 1986 - Stone).

RACHAEL STANLEY - Dark Pink to Red with White stripe in center of petals. Medium, formal double with star shape. Average, dense, upright growth. E-M. (U.S. 1995 - E. Atkins, Shalimar, FL).

RACHEL CLAIRE - Light Pink with Golden anthers and Pinkish-White filaments. Medium to large, loose peony form, stacked with undulating petals. Average, full growth. E-M. (U.S. 2019 - Tommy Weeks, Conroe, TX).

RACHEL TARPY - White shading to Blush Pink with occasional Red lines or dashes. Medium to large, anemone form with wavy, concave, ruffled outer petals. Average growth. E-M. (U.S. 1981 - G. F. Abendroth, Shreveport, LA).

RACHEL TARPY RED - Red. (Sport of Japonica 'Rachel Tarpy'). (U.S. 1986 - G. F. Abendroth, Shreveport, LA).

RACHEL WILKES - White. Large, semidouble with stamens in circle of petals. Average, upright growth. E-M. (U.S. 1979 - Mrs. H. Johnson, Madison, FL).

RADIANT GLOW - See 'Herme Pink'.

RAGGED ROBIN - Red. Medium, semidouble with large petaloids in center. Average, compact growth. M. (U.S. 1953 - Shackelford).

RAGGEDY ANN - Dark Red. Large, full peony form. Vigorous, upright growth. E-M. (U.S. 1959 - Braewood).

RAGLAND SUPREME - Milk White. Medium, formal double. Average, spreading growth. M. (U.S. 1968 - Ragland).

RAGTIME - Pink striped Red. Medium, semidouble. Vigorous, compact, upright growth. M-L. (N.Z. 1989 - W. L. Ragg, Christchurch).

RAINSBOW END - Pink. Large, semidouble. M. (U.S. 1955 - Pat Poyner, Dothan, AL).

RALPH SNYDER - Deep Rose Pink. Medium, rose form double. Average, open growth. E-M. (U.S. 1969 - Mrs. R. A. Snyder, Orlando, FL).

RAM'S CHOICE - Tiffany Pink. Large, rose form double to formal double. Average, dense, upright growth. M. (U.S. 1992 - Mandarich).

RAMONA - Light Pink. Medium, formal double. Vigorous, bushy, upright growth. E-M. (U.S. 1979).

RAMPEY E. THOMAS - White. Medium to large, semidouble form. Average, upright growth. M. Cold hardy. (U.S. 1999 - L. Baxter, Seneca, SC).

RANGERETTE - See 'Liberty Variegated'.

RASEN-ZOME - ('Printed Woolen'). Light Rose Pink, sometimes mottled White. Medium, semidouble to peony form. Vigorous, compact growth. M-L. (Japan to U.S. [Star] 1915).

RASPBERRY ICE - Light Rose Pink with wide White petal edges and streaks of Raspberry on each petal. Medium, semidouble. (Sport of Japonica 'Cinderella'). (U.S. 1987 - Monrovia Nsy. Co., Azusa, CA).

RASPBERRY PARFAIT - Raspberry Red with touches of Creamy White. Miniature, formal double. Average, upright growth. L. (U.S. 1973 - Witman).

RASPBERRY RIPPLE - White with Pink stripes. Very large, semidouble. Average growth. E-L. (N.Z. 1989 - R. MacDonald, Waiuku).

RASPBERRY RIPPLE PICOTEE - White, with a defined Pink edge, which sometimes bleeds back into the White with Yellow anthers and Cream filaments. Very large, semidouble. Average growth. E-L. (Sport of Japonica 'Raspberry Ripple'). (N.Z. 1996 - Haydon).

RASPBERRY SHERBET - Light Fuchsia with Yellow anthers and White filaments. Large, semidouble. M-L. (U.S. 2003 - Gordon E. Eade, Pensacola, FL).

RAY BAILEY - Rose Pink. Large, peony form. Average, upright growth. M. (U.S. 1972 - Burgess).

RAY LANGE - Dark Red. Large, semidouble with wavy, crinkled petals. Vigorous, spreading, upright growth. E-M. (U.S. 1971 - W. L. Poe, Birmingham, AL).

RAYMOND BEALS - Dark Pink sport of 'Olive Lee Shepp'. Medium, semidouble. (U.S. 1950 - Shepp).

RAYMOND ZAGONE - Blush Pink. Small, rose form double to formal double. Average, spreading growth. (U.S. 1955 - A. Zagone, Lafayette, LA).

RAYNA SIMONE - Coral Rose with Yellow anthers and White filaments. Miniature, anemone. Average, upright growth. E-L. (U.S. 2017 - Don Bergamini, Martinez, CA).

RAZZLE-DAZZLE - Red with Pink and White stripes. Medium, anemone form. Average, upright growth. M-L. (U.S. 1992 - Piet and Gaeta, CA).

REBECCA RENEE - Chinese Red. Medium, semidouble. Average, upright growth. M. (U.S. 1987 - W. L. Smith, Tylertown, MS).

REBECCA SCOBEE - Pink. Medium, formal double. Vigorous, upright growth. M-L. (U.S. 2008 - CamelliaShop, Savannah, GA).

REBECCA WILSON - Pale Pink. Large, single to semidouble. Slow, spreading growth. M-L. (Aus. 1987 - E. Wilkins, Heidelberg Heights, Vic.).

REBEL VINEY - Brilliant Red. Medium, semidouble. Loose, upright growth. M. (U.S. 1951 - Mrs. W. Viney, Covina, CA).

REBEL YELL - White striped, speckled and moired Red. Large, semidouble to peony form with twisted, curled, and crepe petals. Average, upright growth. M. (U.S. 1961 - Wheeler).

REBEL YELL BLUSH - Blush Pink. (Sport of Japonica 'Rebel Yell').

REBEL YELL BLUSH VARIEGATED - Blush Pink blotched White variation of 'Rebel Yell Blush'.

REBEL YELL PINK - Pink. (Sport of Japonica 'Rebel Yell').

REBEL YELL PINK VARIEGATED - Pink blotched White variation of 'Rebel Yell Pink'.

REBEL YELL RED - Red. (Sport of Japonica 'Rebel Yell').

REBEL YELL RED VARIEGATED - Red blotched White variation of 'Rebel Yell Red'.

REBEL YELL WHITE - White. (Sport of Japonica 'Rebel Yell').

RED APRIL - Deep Red. Large, semidouble. L. (U.S. 1953 - Councilman).

RED AURORA - Rich Red with a hint of Pink. Large, semidouble to rose form. M. Cold hardy. (U.S. - Parks).

RED BALL - Dark Red. Medium, full peony form. Compact growth. E. (U.S. 1953 - Clower).

RED BIRD - Dark Red veined darker. Medium, formal double with some swirled and incurved petals. Compact, upright growth. M-L. (U.S. 1973 - Haynie).

RED BLOSSOM - Red. Large, peony form. Average growth. E-M. (U.S. 1986 - Gilley).

RED BUGLE - Red. Large, loose peony form with upright petaloids around central stamens. Vigorous, spreading growth. M. (U.S. 1963 - Novick).

RED BUTTON - Deep Red. Miniature, anemone form. Average, upright, compact growth. M. (U.S. 1960 - J. Andrey, San Fernando, CA).

RED CANDLES - Ruby Red. Medium, single of cupped form with pointed petals. Vigorous, upright growth. M. (U.S. 1959 - Short).

RED CAP - Rose Pink to Red. Medium, formal double with half folded, pointed petals shaped like six pointed star. Average growth. E-L. (U.S. 1962 - Wheeler).

RED CAP VARIEGATED - Rose Pink blotched White variation of 'Red Cap'.

RED CHIEF - Dark Red. Large, semidouble. Bushy, upright growth. M-L. (U.S. 1975 - Haynie).

RED CORAL - Bight Coral Red at the edges fading to Deep Rose Pink towards the center with darker veining with bright Yellow anthers and Light Pink fading to White filaments. Large, semidouble to loose peony. Vigorous, upright, dense growth. M-L. (U.S. 2017 - Jerry Hogsette, Gainesville, FL).

RED DAHLIA - Scarlet Red. Small to medium, loose peony form with wavy petals. Bushy growth. M-L. (U.S. 1980 - Kramer).

RED DANDY - Brilliant Orange Red. Large, semidouble with irregular petals. Vigorous, compact, upright growth. M-L. (U.S. 1975 - Nuccio's).

RED DEVIL - Red. Small to medium, semidouble. Average, upright, somewhat columnar growth. M-L. (U.S. 2009 - Nuccio's).

RED DEVIL VARIEGATED - Red variegated White variation of 'Red Devil'.

RED DOUGLAS - See 'Tricolor (Siebold) Red'.

RED ELEPHANT - See 'King Size'.

RED ENSIGN - Crimson. Large, single to semi double with a few petaloids. (Aus. 1955 - Linton).

RED GARNET - Garnet Red. Small, formal double to rose form double. Bushy growth. M-L. (U.S. 1980 - Kramer).

RED GARNET VARIEGATED - Garnet Red and White variation of 'Red Garnet'. (U.S. 1983 - Kramer).

RED GIANT - ('Apache'). Red. Large, loose peony form with many large petaloids. Average, upright growth. M. (U.S. 1954 - Shackelford).

RED HERME - See 'Herme Pink'.

RED HOT - Bright Red occasionally with one or two small White petals in center. Large, full peony form. Upright, compact growth. M. (U.S. 1959 - Hudson).

RED HOT FLARE - Satin Sheen Red with Gold anthers and Pink filaments. Miniature, single. Average, upright, open growth. E-L. (Seedling of Japonica 'Tinsie'). (U.S. 2016 - Pat Johnson, Cairo, GA).

RED HOTS - Brilliant Red. Small to medium, tubular semidouble with pointed petals. Average, upright growth. E-M. (U.S. 1992 - Nuccio's).

RED JADE (PARKS) - Light Red. Small to medium, semidouble. M-L. Cold hardy to -9°. (U.S. - Parks).

RED JORDAN'S PRIDE - See 'Herme Pink'.

RED LION - Red. Large to very large, peony form. Vigorous, upright growth. M. (U.S. 1971 - Shackelford).

RED LUSTRE - Crimson with darker sheen. Medium, anemone form. Average, open, upright growth. E-L. (U.S. 1948 - McCaskill).

RED MOON - Deep Rose Red. Large, flat semidouble with center petaloids. Vigorous, compact growth. M. (Aus. 1965 - Waterhouse).

RED MOUNTAIN - Dark Red with Yellow Anthers and White filaments. Small, full peony. Average, upright growth. E-M. (Japonica 'Man Size' seedling). (U.S. 2013 - James and Elaine Smelley, Moss Point, MS).

RED PLANET - Deep Velvety Pillar Box Red with darker veining. Medium, semidouble. Average, upright growth. M-L. (N.Z. 2004 - Haydon).

RED RED ROSE - Bright Red. Medium to large, formal double with high center like a rose. Vigorous, bushy, upright growth. (U.S. 1969 - McCaskill).

RED RHYTHM - Clear Red. Medium, formal double. Vigorous, open, upright growth. M. (U.S. 1955 - Short).

RED ROBIN - Dark Red. Large, rose form double. Average, upright growth. M-L. (U.S. 1959 - Hartman).

RED ROGUE - Deep Red to Maroon. Large, anemone form to loose peony form. Vigorous, compact, upright growth. M-L. (U.S. 1962 - Short).

RED SATIN - Satin Red with Gold anthers and Pale Pink filaments. Very large, single. Slow, upright, dense growth. E-M. (Seedling of Japonica 'Elegans Miniata'). (U.S. 2019 - Pat Johnson, Cairo, GA).

RED SHADOW - See 'Professor Charles S. Sargent Variegated'.

RED SHIFT - Very Deep Red with Yellow anthers and Golden filaments. Medium, semidouble to loose peony to full peony form Average, compact, bushy growth. M. (U.S. 2019 - Gordon Rabalais, Arnaudville, LA).

RED TULIP - Dark Red. Medium, single with pointed petals and very tubular shape. Fast, open, upright yet somewhat spreading growth. M. (U.S. 2007 - Nuccio's Nurseries).

RED VIOLA - Unusual Red with lighter and darker veining. Small to medium, single form. Vigorous, upright growth. E-L. (U.S. 2002 - John L. Spencer, Lakeland, FL).

RED WARATAH - See 'Mariana'.

RED WINE - Deep Red. Medium to large, semidouble with two rows of very broad petals surrounding crowd of Yellow stamens with a few folded petaloids. Average, spreading growth. M. (U.S. 1958 - Dr. M. B. Wine, Thomasville, GA).

RED WINGS - Dark Red. Medium, semidouble with upright petals. Average, compact growth. M. (U.S. 1953 - Shackelford).

RED WONDER - ('Island Echo'). Deep Red. Large, semidouble to rose form double with two or three rows of flat, outer petals and center of long, folded and curled inner petals. (Sport of Japonica 'Mathotiana'). (U.S. 1948 - Armstrong).

RED WONDER VARIEGATED - Dark Red blotched White variation of 'Red Wonder'.

REDA SCOTT - White. Medium, formal double. Vigorous, compact, upright growth. M-L. (U.S. 1987 - Elizabeth R. Scott, Aiken, SC).

REDBUD - Deep Red. Miniature, full peony form. Average, upright growth. M. (U.S. 1973 - A. W. Garner, Glendale, CA).

REEVES SWEETHEART - Light Pink. Medium, formal double. Vigorous, open, upright growth. M. (U.S. 1959 - Reeves).

REFINEMENT - See 'Purity'.

REG RAGLAND - Red. Large to very large, semidouble with smaller, upright center petals surrounding mass of Yellow stamens. Average, compact growth. E-L. (U.S. 1954 - W. E. Woodroof, Sherman Oaks, CA).

REG RAGLAND SUPREME - Large to very large, anemone form to peony form. (Sport of 'Reg Ragland'). (U.S. 1967 - Charmwood Nsy., Millbrook, AL).

REG RAGLAND VARIEGATED - Red blotched White variation of 'Reg Ragland'.

REGAL ROSE - Bright clear Pink. Large, rose form double with wide undulating petals and crinkly center petals around White stamens. Vigorous, upright growth. M-L. (U.S. 1963 - Ragland).

REGAL SPLENDOR - Deep Pink. Large, peony form. Average, compact, upright growth. M. (U.S. 1966 - L. W. Strohmeyer, San Gabriel, CA).

REGINA DEI GIGANTI - ('Hall Townes'; 'Gloriosa'; 'Rosalie [South]'; 'W. H. Hastie'; 'Pink Silk Satin'). Bright Pink. Medium to large, semidouble with fluted petals. Average, compact, upright growth. M-L. (Possibly not same as cultivar listed in old literature). (Italy 1855 - Luzzati).

REIHO - Snow White. Large, single. (Sport of Japonica 'Oaso'). See Higo.

REINE MARIE HENRIETTE - Rose Pink striped White to Rose Pink variegated White. Medium, formal double. Average, compact growth. M. (France 1908 - Guichard).

RELAND WESTGATE - Pink to Dark Pink. Large, loose peony form. Vigorous, upright growth. M-L. Cold hardy. (U.S. 1993 - G. Chester, Augusta, GA).

REMEMBER - Blush Pink. Medium, semidouble. (U.S. 1960 - Shackelford).

REMEY - Deep Red. Miniature, formal double. Vigorous, upright, dense growth. E-L. (U.S. 2016 - Howell).

RENA CAMPBELL - Variable: Rose to solid Red, White, White with Red stripes, and medium Pink with stripes and flecks of Deeper Pink. Medium, loose peony form. Vigorous, upright, bushy growth. M-L. (Seed parent of 'Mrs. F. L. Gibson' and seed grandparent of 'Betty Sheffield'). (U.S. 1890-1900 - Loui Lauraine Campbell, Quitman, GA).

RENA SWICK - Bright Pink veined darker. Large, semidouble with large, heavy textured petals standing apart. Average growth. M. (U.S. 1960 - Julington).

RENA SWICK VARIEGATED - Bright Pink and White variation of 'Rena Swick'.

RENA TRAVIS - Red. Medium, rose form double. Vigorous, open, upright growth. M. (U.S. 1950 - Mrs. R. B. Travis, Savannah, GA).

REUBENA HELMS - Red. Medium, rose form double to peony form. M. (U.S. 1952 - Feathers).

REUEL ADAMS - Rose variegated White. Large, semidouble with wavy, crinkled petals. Vigorous, open, upright growth. M. (U.S. 1969 - R. T. Adams, Jacksonville, FL).

REVELATION - Pink and White. Medium, semidouble to peony form. (U.S. 1942 - Magnolia).

REVEREND CLAUDE FULLERTON - Coral Pink. Large, anemone form. Average, spreading growth. M. (U.S. 1998 - J. Fowler, Smithville, GA).

REVEREND CONNIE JOHNSON - Bright Tomato Red. Large, peony form. Vigorous, open, upright growth. E-M. (U.S. 1964 - Julington).

REVEREND JOHN BENNETT - Salmon Pink. Medium, semidouble with veined petals and occasional petaloids. Slow, spreading growth. M-L. (Europe to U.S. [Magnolia] 1840's).

REVEREND JOHN BOWMAN - Shell Pink. Medium, loose peony form. Vigorous, compact, upright growth. M. (U.S. 1958 - Fisher).

REVEREND JOHN BOWMAN VARIEGATED - Shell Pink and White variation of 'Reverend John Bowman'.

REVEREND JOHN BRYANT - White turning to delicate Light Orchid. Large, formal double. Vigorous, upright growth. M. (U.S. 1966 - J. R. Bryant, Shreveport, LA).

REVEREND JOHN G. DRAYTON - ('Mary E. M.'). Light Pink. Medium, semidouble to loose peony form. Vigorous, compact, upright growth. M-L. Cold hardy. (U.S. Late 1800's -Magnolia).

REVEREND LAWRENCE V. BRADLEY - Soft Pink. Medium, formal double. Average growth. M-L. (U.S. 1988 - W. A. Wilson, Augusta, GA).

REVERE'S BABY PINK - Light Pink shading to Rose Pink at edge. Small, semidouble. Average, upright growth. E-L. (U.S. 1956 - Mrs. F. Revere, Theodore, AL).

RHODA GONZALEZ - White. Medium, full peony form. Vigorous, open growth. E. (U.S. 1952 - Mrs. C. F. Gonzalez, Pensacola, FL).

RHODELLIA KING - See 'Gosho-Garuma'.

RHYSA JOHNSON - White, Pink and Red streaks. Large, loose peony to full peony. Average, upright, spreading growth. E-L. (Chance Japonica seedling). (U.S. 2016 - Pat Johnson, Cairo, GA).

RICHARD GORDY - Deep Red with bright Gold anthers and Pink filaments. Medium, semidouble; the petals often have a waxy look. Average, upright, dense growth. M-L. (U.S. 2013 - Gordy).

RICHARD GORHAM - Red. Very large, semidouble. Vigorous, compact, upright growth. M-L. (U.S. 1959 - Mrs. R. S. Gorham, Rocky Mount, NC).

RICHARD NIXON - White shaded Pink and striped Rose Pink. Large, anemone form with outer row of upright, crinkled petals. Compact growth. E-L. (For a variation of this cultivar see 'Pat Nixon'). (U.S. 1954 - U. B. Stair, Whittier, CA).

RICHARD NIXON PINK - Rose Pink. (Sport of Japonica 'Richard Nixon').

RICHARD TURNER - Bright Red. Large, semidouble to peony form. Vigorous, upright growth. M. (U.S. 1954 - Turner).

RICHARD WARD - Blush Pink to Dark Pink edge. Small, formal double to rose form double. Average, upright growth. (U.S. 1978 - Tammia).

RICHFIELD - Rose. Large, semidouble of flat form. Vigorous, compact, upright growth. M. (U.S. 1962 - McCaskill).

RILYN BOUERES - Lavender variegated White with bright Yellow anthers and White filaments. Medium to large, semidouble. Vigorous, upright, dense growth. M-L. (U.S. 2013 - Howard and Mary Rhodes, Tallahassee, FL).

RIO RITA - Dark Red. Medium, semidouble. (Sport of Japonica 'Anita'). (U.S. 1947 - Armstrong).

RIO RITA (MAGNOLIA GARDENS) - Dark Red. Medium, semidouble. Average, compact growth. M. (U.S. 1950 - Magnolia).

RIPTIDE - See 'Judge Marvin Mann'.

RITA BLYTHE - White. Large, anemone form. Slow, bushy growth. M. (Aus. 1996 - D. Blythe, Kojonup, W. Aus.).

RIVER FARM BEAUTY - Bright Crimson Red. Large, rose form to formal double. M-L. Cold hardy to -5°F. (U.S. - Ackerman).

RIVERS YERGER - White occasionally striped Rose Pink to Red. Medium to large, full peony form. Average, compact, upright growth. M. (U.S. 1955 - Wheeler).

RIVERS YERGER PINK - Rose Pink. (Sport of Japonica 'Rivers Yerger').

RIVERS YERGER PINK VARIEGATED - Rose Pink blotched White variation of 'Rivers Yerger Pink'.

ROBBIE ANNE - Old Rose blotched and spotted White. Large, semidouble with Yellow stamens occasionally mixed with inner petals and petaloids. M-L. (U.S. 1961).

ROBERT CASAMAJOR - Turkey Red. Medium, semidouble. Average, compact growth. M-L. (U.S. 1945 - Huntington).

ROBERT CASAMAJOR VARIEGATED - Turkey Red blotched White form of 'Robert Casamajor'.

ROBERT DUNN - Rose Pink to Rose Red with silky satin sheen. Large, loose peony form. (U.S. 1962 - McDonald Camellia Nsy., Beech Island, SC).

ROBERT E. LEE - Dark Red veined darker Red with Red stamens. Medium, semidouble with loose, irregular petals and a few petaloids. Vigorous, compact growth. M. (U.S. Early 1900's - Magnolia).

ROBERT HENDRICK - Rose Pink with petaloids lighter shade of Rose. Large, peony form to anemone form. Average, open growth. M-L. (U.S. 1950 - R. Hendrick, Greenville, AL).

ROBERT HENTY - White with Pink stripes and markings. Large, semidouble to loose peony form. (Sport of Japonica 'Charles Henty'). (Aus. 1975 - Henty).

ROBERT HILLS - Dark Pink splotched White. Medium, semidouble and formal double with some imbricated petals. Average, upright growth. M. (U.S. 1980 - Tammia).

ROBERT LOWELL COOPER - Deep Red. Medium, formal double. Slow, average growth. M. (U.S. 1986 - Stone).

ROBERT McNEESE - Soft Pink. Small, anemone form to rose form double to formal double. Average, compact growth. M. (U.S. 1981 - R. McNeese, Bogalusa, LA).

ROBERT TRAIN - Dark Red. Large, semidouble with upright petals. Average, upright growth. E-M. (U.S. 1966 - Wheeler).

ROBERT TRAIN VARIEGATED - Dark Red and White variation of 'Robert Train'.

ROBERT WALKER WILDER - Light Red. Large, anemone form with large, loose, incurved petals. Average, open growth. M. (U.S. 1964 - R. W. Wilder, Fairhope, AL).

ROBERTA - Light Pink. Large, single to semidouble. (Sport of Japonica 'Paul Jones'). (Aus. 1952 - Waterhouse).

ROBERTA HARDISON - Deep Rose Pink with Purple overcast. Large, formal double. Average, upright growth. M. (U.S. 1992 - D. Hardison, Tallahassee, FL).

ROBERTA RAGLAND - Cameo Pink. Large, semidouble with folded petals and small petals inter-mingled with mass of Cream stamens. Vigorous, open, upright growth. E-M. (U.S. 1959 - Ragland).

ROBIN - Delicate Pink in center fading to Palest Pink at outer edge. Medium, anemone form to loose peony form with slightly waved petals. Vigorous, upright growth. M-L. (U.S. 1955 - J. T. Langston, Jr., Darlington, SC).

ROBIN (AUSTRALIA) - Cherry Red. Medium, single. (Aus. 1952 - Waterhouse).

ROBIN ANN CROSS - Medium Pink with Yellow anthers and White filaments. Large, semidouble to rose form double. Vigorous, upright, dense growth. M. (U.S. 2016 - Gordy).

ROBIN HOOD I - See 'Tricolor (Siebold) Red'.

ROBIN RUTH RAY - White at center blending to Pink at petal edges. Medium, semidouble. Average, open growth. M. (U.S. 1998 - W. and M. A. Ray, Fresno, CA).

ROBIN'S CANDY - Pink with Red stripes. Medium, formal double. Average, upright growth. E-L. (Sport of Japonica 'Candy Cane'). (U.S. 1990 - W. and M.A. Ray, Fresno, CA).

ROCHELLE - Pink with Red stripes. Medium, semidouble to rose form double. Average, upright growth. E-L. (U.S. 2003 - Robert E. Ehrhart, Walnut Creek, CA).

ROCHELLE MARRINAN - White center shading to Pink stripes with Gold anthers and Yellow filaments. Medium, semidouble to loose peony form. Average, spreading, open growth. E-L. (Seedling of Japonica ' China Doll'). (U.S. 2018 - Pat Johnson, Cairo, GA).

ROGER HALL - Clear Red. Medium, formal double. Vigorous, compact, upright growth. E-L. (Aus. 1979 - R. H. Hall, S. Aus.).

ROI LEOPOLD - Bright Rose Red splashed White. Medium, formal double. Compact, upright growth. M. (Belgium 1851 - Emile Defresne, Liege).

ROLL-IN' TOOMER - White with Yellow anthers and Yellow filaments. Very large, semidouble. Average, upright growth. E. (Japonica 'Moonlight Bay' x Japonica 'Joshua Youtz'). (U.S. 2017 - Kenneth Rogers, Auburn, AL).

ROMA RISORTA - Pale Pink streaked and flecked Rose Pink. Medium, rose form double. Compact, upright growth. M. (Italy 1866 - Delgrande).

ROMA RISORTA ROSEA - Pink veined Rose Pink. (Sport of Japonica 'Roma Risorta').

ROMAN SOLDIER - ('War Eagle'). Bright Red. Large, full peony form. Average, upright growth. M. (U.S. 1959 - Shackelford).

ROMAN SOLDIER VARIEGATED - Bright Red blotched White variation of 'Roman Soldier'.

ROMANY - ('Belgium Red'). Rose Red. Medium, formal double. Vigorous, upright growth. M. (Said to be the same as 'Roi Leopold'). (U.S. 1937 - Coolidge).

RONCHARBAR - Cream White. Medium, semidouble with irregular petals to rose form double. Average, open growth. M. (U.S. 1956 - Miss E. W. Boorman, Temple City, CA).

ROOSEVELT BLUES - (Frankie Bray'). Purplish Red. Medium, semidouble to peony form. Vigorous, compact, upright growth. M. (U.S. 1944 - Longview).

ROOSEVELT BLUES VARIEGATED - Purplish Red blotched White form of 'Roosevelt Blues'.

ROSA MUNDI - Red blotched White. Medium, formal double. M. (Two other cultivars are listed under this name in old literature, one a rose form double of pale Pink streaked deep Cerise Pink and the other a rose form double of Pink streaked White). (England 1832 - Press).

ROSA PANELLA - Pale Pink and Red. Large, anemone form. Vigorous, open, upright growth. L. (U.S. - Mrs. E. G. Boggs, Fayetteville, NC).

ROSALEE BELL - Soft Pink. Medium, formal double. Vigorous, compact, upright growth. M. (U.S. 1950 - Katz).

ROSALIE (CALIFORNIA) - See 'Uncle Sam'.

ROSALIE DENEEN FENDIG - Shell Pink margined White. Large, semidouble. (Sport of Japonica 'Gladys Fendig'). (U.S. 1957 - A. Fendig, Sea Island, GA).

ROSALYNN CARTER - Pink shading to Lighter Pink edges with Yellow anthers and White filaments. Large, rose form double to loose peony form; rarely formal double. Average, upright, dense growth. M. (First Lady of Georgia Series). (U.S. 2017 - Gordy).

ROSARY - ('Pink Glory'). Light Rose Pink. Medium, semidouble with loose, long, narrow petals. Average, open, upright growth. M. (Formerly named 'Finlandia F. N.'). (U.S. 1938 - Fruitland).

ROSARY VARIEGATED - ('Pink Glory Variegated'). Light Rose Pink and White form of 'Rosary'.

ROSE 'N BLOOM - Coral Rose. Large, rose form double with deep petals. Average, bushy growth. M. (U.S. 1959 - Short).

ROSE 'N BLOOM VARIEGATED - Coral Rose marked White variation of 'Rose 'n Bloom'.

ROSE AND SNOW - ('Emma Ladd'). Rose Pink spotted White. Medium, semidouble with petaloids in center. Vigorous, compact, upright growth. M-L. (U.S. 1942 - Middleton).

ROSE ANN - Delicate Pink with Pale Lavender tinge at tips of petals. Medium, full peony form. Slow, upright growth. M. (U.S. 1951 - J. L. Kahn, Pensacola, FL).

ROSE BROOKS - Radiant Pink. Medium, semidouble. Average, compact, upright growth. E-M. (U.S. 1953 - Mrs. E. R. Harlan, McComb, MS).

ROSE DAWN (DAVIS) - Deep Rose Pink. Medium, formal double to rose form double. Vigorous, spreading growth. M. (U.S. 1944 — Davis).

ROSE EIDSON - Rose Pink. Large, peony form. (Sport of Japonica 'Frank Eidson'). (U.S. 1962 - Thomasville).

ROSE GISH - Soft Light Pink. Medium to large, semidouble. Average, compact growth. M. (U.S. 1957 - McCaskill).

ROSE MAHAN - Bright Rose Pink. Large, semidouble to full peony form. Average, upright growth. M-L. (U.S. 1964 - J. R. Murdock, Monticello, FL).

ROSE MALLOW - Soft Pink with darker veins. Medium, semidouble. Slow, open growth. L. (U.S. 1944 - Overlook).

ROSE OF DAWN - See 'Magnoliaeflora'.

ROSE OF KASTELLORIZO - White. Small, formal double. Average, dense, upright growth. M-L. (Aus. 1998 - F. Abbott, Rossmoyne, W. Aus.).

ROSE QUEEN - ('Busch Garden Red'). Rose Pink. Medium, formal double. Vigorous, bushy growth. M. (For a variation of this cultivar see 'Queen of the Acres'). (U.S. 1930 - Busch Gardens, Pasadena, CA).

ROSE QUEEN VARIEGATED - Rose Pink spotted White variation of 'Rose Queen'.

ROSE SHEPHERD - Rose Pink. Large, semidouble. Average growth. E-L. (U.S. 1960 - G. W. Shepherd, Orlando, FL).

ROSEA MUNDI - Deep Pink. Medium, semidouble with irregular, wavy petals. Average, compact growth. M-L. (Not cultivar listed in old literature, which was formal double of White striped Pink). (U.S. 1946 - Magnolia).

ROSEA PLENA - Rose Pink with dark veins. Medium, formal double. Vigorous, compact, upright growth. M. (Europe to U.S. 1840's - Magnolia).

ROSEA SUPERBA - ('Ada Wilson'; 'Laura Dasher'). Rose Pink. Large to very large, rose form double to formal double. (Sport of Japonica 'Mathotiana'). (For a variation of this cultivar see 'Brooksie's Rosea'). (Europe to U.S. 1890 - Tea Gardens).

ROSEA SUPERBA VARIEGATED - ('Margaret Sandusky'). Deep Rose Pink spotted White variation of 'Rosea Superba'.

ROSELLE BELL - White. Large, anemone form. Average, open, upright growth. E-M. (U.S. 1965 - Mrs. R. A. Bell, Cairo, GA).

ROSEMARIE OSTBERG - Very Dark Pink with Gold anthers and White filaments. Medium, semidouble to anemone. Average, upright growth. M. (U.S. 2013 - Gordy).

ROSEMARY ELSOM - Shell Pink. Medium, rose form double. Spreading, upright growth. M. (Aus. 1955 - Cole).

ROSEMARY JEAN - Dusty Pink, with Lavender shading at outside edges and marked veining. Medium, formal double; petals are incurved and almost circular in shape. Average, dense, upright growth. M-L. (N.Z. 2002 - S. and J. Levy).

ROSEMARY KINZER - Light Pink. Medium to large, semidouble with occasional erect center petal. Average, compact growth. M. (U.S. 1954 - Shepp).

ROSEMARY KINZER VARIEGATED - Pale Pink blotched White variation of 'Rosemary Kinser'.

ROSENLEE - White with tiny Pink markings on some of the petals. Large, formal double. Vigorous, compact, upright growth. L. (U.S. 1955 - L. Smith, Altadena, CA).

ROSIE O'GRADY - Deep Pink. Large, semidouble. Average, spreading growth. M-L. (U.S. 1968 - Haynie).

ROSIE O'GRADY VARIEGATED - Deep Pink heavily moired White variation of 'Rosie O'Grady'. (U.S. 1968 - Haynie).

ROSULARIS - White blotched Rose Pink. Large, peony form. (Reported to be the same as - 'Marchioness of Exeter Variegated'). (U.S. 1941 - McIlhenny).

ROSY DAWN - See 'Herme Pink'.

ROSY POSY - Bright Pink. Miniature, semidouble similar to a fir cone. Average, compact, upright growth. M. (U.S. 1959 - McCaskill).

ROUGE - Rose Red. Small to medium, formal double. Vigorous, upright growth. L. (U.S. 1937 - Armstrong).

ROUGE VARIEGATED - Rose Red and White form of 'Rouge'.

ROUSE'S BIG RED - Red (RHS 46B) with Yellow anthers and White with Red base filaments. Large to very large, semidouble. Average, upright, spreading, open growth. L. (U.S. 2013 - Dennis Rouse, Auburn, AL).

ROWENA CRAIG - White with one petal having Carmine stripe or flecks. Large, single of tulip shape opening to cup shape. Vigorous, open, upright growth. E-M. (Aus. 1983 - E. Craig, Warrawee, NSW).

ROWENA HOOKS - Pink, Medium, semidouble with fluted and curled petals. (U.S. 1959 - J. R. Hooks, Fayetteville, NC).

ROX COWLEY - White to Cream suffused with Pink specks or small blotches. Medium, full peony form. Vigorous, compact growth. M. (U.S. 1952 - Wilkinson).

ROXANNE - White. Large, peony form with heavy China-like petals and Blonde stamens. Average, compact growth. M. (U.S. 1953 - Pierates Cruz Gardens, Mt. Pleasant, SC).

ROY ILES - Deep Pink. Medium to large, semidouble. Vigorous, upright, dense growth. E-L. (N.Z. 2001 - A. V. Iles).

ROY WHITEHEAD - Salmon Pink. Large, semidouble with petals standing apart. Vigorous, upright growth. M. (U.S. 1963 - Mrs. R. B. Whitehead, Valdosta, GA).

ROYAL COACHMAN - Coral Red. Large, semidouble. Average, upright growth. E-M. (U.S. 1968 - T. E. Croson, Simi, CA).

ROYAL FLUSH - Venetian Pink. Large, semidouble with heavy petals. Vigorous, compact, upright growth. M. (U.S. 1956 - Hudson).

ROYAL LADY - Coral Rose. Medium to large, semidouble with loose petals and petaloids in center. Average, compact growth. M. (U.S. 1968).

ROYAL TRUMPETEER - White opening from Blush Pink bud. Medium, semidouble with center three petals forming a trumpet. Average, compact growth. M-L. (U.S. 1955 - Marshall).

ROYAL VELVET - Dark Velvet Red. Large, semidouble. Vigorous, compact, upright growth. M. (U.S. 1987 - Nuccio's).

ROYAL VELVET VARIEGATED - Dark Velvet Red variegated White variation of 'Royal Velvet'.

ROYAL WHITE - White. Medium, semidouble, rose form double to formal double. Spreading growth. L. (U.S. 1944 - Overlook).

ROYSTON - Off White. Large, rose form double. Compact, bushy growth. E-M. (Aus. 2007 - Roy H. Campbell, Maddington).

RUBAIYAT - Ruby Red with Blue veining. Large, formal double with heavy, waxy, large rounded petals. Vigorous, upright growth. M-L. (U.S. 1969 - Julington).

RUBESCENS MAJOR - Rose Red veined Crimson. Large, formal double. Compact growth. M. (France 1895 - Guichard).

RUBESCENS MAJOR VARIEGATED - ('Princess Anne').- Red and White variation of 'Rubescens Major'). (Aus. 1962).

RUBRA VIRGINALIS - ('Jeanerette Pink'). Light Pink. Medium, full peony form. Average, upright growth. L. (U.S. 1937 - McIlhenny).

RUBY ANNIVERSARY - Ruby Red with darker veining and some White stripes. Medium to large, formal double. M-L. (N.Z. 1997 - R. Young).

RUBY GLOW - See 'Vedrine'.

RUBY IRENE - Dark Red with Yellow anthers and White filaments. Large, semidouble. Average, upright, dense growth. M. (U.S. 2019 - Gordy).

RUBY MATHEWS - Dark Ruby Red shaded Lighter Red on inside of petals. Small, formal double with incurved petals. Average, compact growth. M. (U.S. 1956 - Julington).

RUBY VELVET - Deep Red, petal edges have a Purplish tinge. Medium, peony form. Average, open, spreading growth. M-L. (N.Z. 2005 - M. and L. Mangos, Tauranga).

RUCHI RHODES - Bright Red and White with Yellow anthers and White filaments. Large, semidouble. Vigorous, upright, dense growth. M. (U.S. 2013 - Howard and Mary Rhodes, Tallahassee, FL).

RUDOLPH - Deep Red. Medium, full peony form to anemone form. Average, upright growth. E-M. (U.S. 1981 - Nuccio's).

RUDOLPH VARIEGATED - Deep Red mottled White variation of 'Rudolph'. (U.S. 1995 - Nuccio's).

RUDY'S MAGNOLIAEFLORA - Deep Pink. Medium, semidouble. (Sport of Japonica 'Magnoliaeflora'). (U.S. 1988 - F. Moore, West Covina, CA).

RUFFIAN - White with Yellowish tinge. Large, semidouble with irregular petals to peony form. Average, compact, upright growth. M-L. (U.S. 1978 - Homeyer).

RUFFLED BEAUTY - Rose Pink. Medium, loose peony form with wavy, crepe petals. M-L. (U.S. 1944 - Tea Gardens).

RUFFLED PRINCESS - Pink. Medium, semidouble to anemone form with ruffled petals. Vigorous, compact, upright growth. M. (U.S. 1958 - Shackelford).

RUFFLED PRINCESS VARIEGATED - Pink blotched White variation of 'Ruffled Princess'.

RUFFLES - White. Large, loose peony form with undulated petals. Vigorous, bushy growth. M. (U.S. 1960 - Marshall).

RULONA HOLLAND - White. Large, semidouble to loose peony form. Vigorous, upright growth. M-L. (U.S. 1975 - Haynie).

RUNT - Light Pink. Miniature, full peony form. Vigorous, compact, upright growth. M. (U.S. 1962 - Wheeler).

RUPIE - White with stripes or spots of Dark Pink sometimes producing a flower Pink on one half and White on the other half with Gold anthers and Yellow filaments. Medium to large, semidouble to loose peony. Average, upright growth. M. (U.S. 2013 - Rupert E. Drews, Charleston, SC).

RUPIE'S CHARLESTON - Pink variegated White. M. (Sport of Japonica 'Miss Charleston Variegated'). (U.S. 2004 - Rupert E. Drews, Charleston, SC).

RUSSELL CATES - Rose Red. Large, anemone form. Vigorous, upright growth. E-M. (U.S. 1958 - Mrs. R. Cates, Albany, GA).

RUSSIAN SNOW - White with small, Red flecks. Large, formal double. (U.S. 1952 - Carleton).

RUSSIAN WHITE - White with Cream center. Large, peony form. Average, compact, upright growth. M. (N.Z. 1973 - Mrs. I. Berg, Whakatane).

RUTH ANDERSON - White. Large, semidouble with alternate rows of sweet pea shaped petals forming flared cup-shaped bloom with loose center of White stamens and petaloids. Vigorous, open, upright growth. M. (U.S. 1964 - Julington).

RUTH BELL GRAHAM - Soft, Light Pink. Large, frilled formal double. Slow, upright, compact growth, E-L. (Seedling of Japonica 'Magnoliaeflora'). (U.S. 1990's - Tom Dodd, Jr., Semmes, Alabama).

RUTH BLACKWELL - Brilliant Red. Medium, semidouble with fluted petals. Average, compact growth. M. (U.S. 1959 - Gerbing).

RUTH BROOKS - Rose with Snowy White center. Medium, formal double. M. (U.S. 1973 - Haynie).

RUTH C. McNAIR - White with bright Yellow anthers with White filaments in the middle. Large, peony form having 3 to 4 rows of large, broad, layered outer petals which are slightly down curved; inner petals are upward and fluted and sometimes crinkled and irregular, mixed with many petaloids. Average, spreading, dense growth. M-L. (U.S. 2009 - John M. Davy, Pace, FL).

RUTH GOFF - Rose Pink. Large, semidouble. Vigorous, spreading growth. E-M. (U.S. 1964 - Q. C. Roberts, Ocean Springs, MS).

RUTH HIGHTOWER - Carmine Rose Pink. Large, semidouble. Average, open growth. M. (U.S. 1992 - W. Hightower, Thomaston, GA).

RUTH KEMP - Light Rose Pink. Medium, semidouble with notched petals. Upright, spreading growth. M. (Aus. 1941 - Hunter).

RUTH LANE - Pink. Large, semidouble of cupped form. (U.S. 1953 - Thomasville).

RUTH NORMAN - Brilliant Red. Large, semidouble to peony form. Average, upright growth. E-M. (U.S. 1981 - G. C. Norman, Tallahassee, FL).

RUTH R. DUNN - Pink. Medium, semidouble. Vigorous, upright growth. M-L. (U.S. 1983 - J. R. Dunn, Sumter, SC).

RUTH ROYER - ('Thelma Sanford'). Pink with various amounts of White variegation. Large, semidouble. (Sport of Japonica 'Duchess of Sutherland'). (U.S. 1949 - Flowerwood).

RUTH SEIBELS - White. Large, semidouble. Average, open, upright growth. M. (U.S. 1975 - Haynie).

RUTH STEWART - Rose. Large, full peony form. Average, compact, upright growth. M. (U.S. 1967 - R. Stewart, Minden, LA).

RUTH TINKLE - Red with faint White streaks on innermost petals and White anthers. Medium, semidouble to rose form double. Average, upright growth. M-L. (U.S. 2010 - Oscar Tinkle, Portland, OR).

RUTH VAUGHN - Porcelain White. Large, peony form to rose form double. Vigorous, open, willowy, upright growth. E-L. (U.S. 1965 - Dr. J. W. Vaughn, Lakeland, FL).

RUTH VICKERS FULWOOD - Deep Rose Red with Gold anthers and Cream filaments. Large, semidouble, sometimes displaying ruffled petals. Average, upright, dense growth. M-L. (U.S. 2015 - Gordy).

RUTHIE POPE - Bright Pink and White. Large, loose peony form. Average, open growth. E-M. (U.S. 1981 - C. R. Pope, Lafayette, LA).

RUTHIE POPE SOLID - Rose Pink. (Sport of Japonica 'Ruthie Pope'). (U.S. 1982 - C. R. Pope, Lafayette, LA).

RUTHIE THE GREAT - Light Pink with darker edges with Yellow anthers. Large, semidouble with a few petaloids. Average, upright growth. E-M. (U.S. 2015 - Robert Ehrhart, Walnut Creek, CA).

RUTLEDGE MINNIX - Bright Red. Medium, semidouble. E-L. (U.S. 1959 - Minnix Nsy., Columbus, GA).

RYAN GAINEY - Pale to Blush Pink on the center petals progressing to Deep Pink on the outer petals with Yellow anthers and White filaments. Large, semidouble; the bloom has pointed petals in the center and outer petals are notched. Average, upright growth. M-L. (Japonica 'Magnoliaeflora' seedling). (U.S. 2014 - Ryan Gainey, Decatur, GA).

RYAN'S ARGYLE - Dark Pink. Miniature, single to semidouble. Slow, upright growth. M. (U.S. 1996 - P. Eleazer, Dawson, GA).

RYE HERIOT - Deep Rose Pink. Medium, semidouble with loose petals. Vigorous, compact growth. M. (U.S. 1951 - Allan).

S. PETER NYCE - See 'Nagasaki'.

SABRINA - Light Coral Pink with few Red stripes and each petal bordered White. Medium, formal double. M-L. (U.S. 1980 - Gentry).

SACCO - ('Sacco Nova'; 'Sacco Vera'). Rose Pink to Rose Pink spotted White to deep Red. Medium, formal double. Slow growth. E. (Spelled 'Saccoi' in certain old literature). (Italy 1851 - Sacco, Milan).

SACCO NOVA - See 'Sacco'.

SACCO VERA - See 'Sacco'.

SADAHARU OH - White to Blush with Pink veining and Red highlights with Golden anthers and White filaments. Medium to large, rose form to anemone to peony form. Vigorous, upright, semi-weeping growth. E-M. (Seedling of Japonica 'Tama-no-ura'; named for Japanese baseball hero known as "The Babe Ruth of Japan"). (U.S. 2004 - Bobby Green, Green Nurseries, Fairhope, AL).

SADIE - Deep Rose Pink. Large, formal double with very symmetrical incurved petals. Vigorous, upright growth. L. (U.S. 1995 - E. Aycock, Smithfield, NC).

SADIE MANCILL - Pale Pink striped and splotched Rose. Large, semidouble to peony form with clusters of stamens intermingled with large, crinkly petaloids. Vigorous, upright, open growth. M. (U.S. 1956 - E. N. Mancill, Lafayette, LA).

SADIE MANCILL DAWN - Deep soft Pink veined Rose and edged White. (Sport of Japonica 'Sadie Mancill'). (U.S. 1964 - K. G. Durio, Jr., Opelousas, LA).

SADIE MANCILL PINK - Pink. (Sport of Japonica 'Sadie Mancill').

SAINTY'S SPECIAL - White. Large, peony form. M. (Aus. 1962 - Pymble, NSW).

SAKURABA-TSUBAKI CHERRY LEAF CAMELLIA) - ('Cherry Blossom'). Pale Pink with a few pale Red markings sometimes sporting pale Pink. Medium, semidouble with foliage resembling that of a Cherry. M. (Known in United States as 'Cherry Blossom' and exhibited as Japonica or Hybrid). (Japan 1867).

SAKURA-GARI - Light Pink. Medium, single with flared Pale Yellow stamens. See Higo.

SALLIE LILES - Rose Pink. Medium, anemone form. Average, upright growth. M-L. (U.S. 1977 - B. S. Liles, Badin, NC).

SALLIE MAYES - Light Peach Pink with slight Orchid tint. Medium, semidouble to loose peony form. Vigorous, upright growth. M. (U.S. 1956 - Wheeler).

SALLY ANACLERIO - Deep bright Red. Medium to large, semidouble to peony form; petals stand erect around Deep Yellow stamens. Average, spreading growth. L. (U.S. 1999 - Elizabeth R. Scott, Aiken, SC).

SALLY ANN - Shell Pink. Large, semidouble with occasional petaloids. Vigorous, compact, upright growth. E-M. (Aus. 1983 - P. Levick, Wahroonga, NSW).

SALLY FISHER - Pale Pink shading to Deeper Pink at edge. Medium, semidouble. Vigorous, pendulous growth. E-M. (U.S. 1986 - Feathers).

SALLY HARRELL - White. Medium, full peony form. Compact growth. E-M. (U.S. 1956 - E. H. Harrell, Thomasville, GA).

SALLY KENNEDY - Light Salmon Pink. Medium, semidouble with whirl of larger, outer petals and a few smaller petals or petaloids intermingled with stamens in center. Vigorous, open, upright growth. E-M. (U.S. 1954 - Turner).

SALMON BEAUTY - Salmon Pink. Medium, semidouble. (U.S. 1947 - Fruitland).

SALMON PRINCESS - Salmon Pink. Large, semidouble. Average, upright growth. M. (U.S. 1975 - Shackelford).

SALMON QUEEN - Salmon Pink. Medium, formal double to peony form. Vigorous, compact, upright growth. M. (U.S. 1945 - Doty and Doemer).

SAM BARRANCO - White dashed clear Pink. Small, formal double. Slow growth. E. (U.S. 1952 - S. Barranco, Beaumont, TX).

SAM BARRANCO BLUSH - Blush Pink. (Sport of Japonica 'Sam Barranco').

SAM BARRANCO PINK - Deep Pink sometimes flecked White. (Sport of Japonica 'Sam Barranco'). (U.S. 1959 - F. Barranco, Beaumont, TX).

SAM HARN - Cherry Red with White stamens. Medium, anemone form. Compact, upright growth. E-M. (U.S. 1956 - Julington).

SAM SIMPSON - Rose Red. Large, semidouble with one or two twisted, upright petals. Average, open, upright growth. M. (U.S. 1959 - E. S. Simpson, Pensacola, FL).

SAM ZERKOWSKY - Soft Pink with Pink and White center petaloids. Large, anemone form. Bushy growth. M. (U.S. 1975 - Tammia).

SAMANTHA NICOLE - Purplish Red. Medium, rose form double. Average, spreading growth. M. (U.S. 2018 - Camellia Heaven - John Grimm, Bush, LA).

SAMARKAND - Coral Rose Red blotched White. Large, semidouble with folded petals and large, irregular petaloids. Average, upright growth. M. (U.S. 1962 - McCaskill).

SAN DIMAS - Dark Red. Medium to large, semidouble with irregular petals. Average, compact growth. E-M. (U.S. 1971 - Nuccio's).

SAN DIMAS VARIEGATED - Dark Red blotched White variation of 'San Dimas'. (U.S. 1971 - Nuccio's).

SAN JACINTO - White. Medium to large, anemone to full peony form. Vigorous, compact, upright growth. M-L. (U.S. 1953 - Short).

SANDEE KHOURY - White with Yellow anthers and Cream filaments. Large, semidouble. Average, upright, open growth. E-M. (U.S. 2019 - Pat Johnson, Cairo, GA).

SANDRA DEAL - White with Gold anthers and Cream filaments. Large, rose form double. Average, upright, spreading growth. E-M. (First Lady of Georgia Series). (U.S. 2015 - Gordy).

SANDRA WILLIAMS - Dark Pink to medium Red with variegation. Small, peony form. Vigorous, dense, upright growth. E-M. (U.S. 2005 - Jay Ellis, Keystone Hts., FL).

SANDY - Bright Rose Red. Large, loose peony form. Average growth. E-M. (U.S. 1969 - S. G. Holtsclaw, Greer, SC).

SANDY SUE - White. Large, loose peony form with heavy textured wavy petals. Average, compact, upright growth. M. (U.S. 1971 - C. W. Pitkin, San Marino, CA).

SANDY WALKER - Rose Pink with slight Orange cast. Medium, semidouble. Vigorous, upright growth. E. (U.S. 1950 - W. T. Wood, Macon, GA).

SANDY WALTERS - White streaked Red. Large, semidouble with loose petals. Average, upright growth. M. (U.S. 1976 - Haynie).

SANKO-NISHIKI (BRIGHT BROCADE) - ('Sanko-Tsubaki'). Rose Pink with some petals lightly lined White. Small, semidouble with incurved petals. L. (Japan 1935 - Chugai).

SARA C. HASTIE - See 'Debutante'.

SARAH ALICE RUFFIN - White. Large to very large, semidouble with wavy crinkled petals. Average, upright growth. M-L. (U.S. 1978 - Belle Fontaine Nsy., Theodore, AL).

SARAH ANN GAVIN - Soft Rose Pink. Large, semidouble. Vigorous, upright growth. M-L. (N.Z. 1992 - D. Cameron-Gavin, Auckland).

SARAH BELLAMY - Light Pink. Large, semidouble. Vigorous, upright growth. M. (U.S. 1964 - Marbury).

SARAH BERNHARDT - White striped Pink with Yellow anthers and Yellow filaments. Medium, semidouble with stamens and petals intermixed. (U.S. Early 1900's - Magnolia Plantation & Gardens, Charleston, SC).

SARAH BETTES - Bright Pink with Silver tinged petals and petaloid tips. Large, semidouble with crinkled, folded petals and petaloids. Average, upright growth. M-L. (U.S. 1971 - Haynie).

SARAH CATHERINE - Pale Pink. Medium, semidouble. E-L. Cold hardy. (U.S. - Parks).

144

SARAH DEAN - White. Large, semidouble. Vigorous, open growth. M-L. (U.S. 1966 - Bray).

SARAH EHRLICH - Deep Pink. Large, anemone form. E-M. (U.S. 1959 - Mrs. Ehrlich, Bainbridge, GA).

SARAH ELIZABETH - Light Pink with Dark Pink stripes. Medium, formal double to rose form double. Vigorous, compact, upright growth. M-L. (Sport of Japonica 'In the Pink'). (U.S. 2001 - Miles Beach, Mt. Pleasant, SC).

SARAH FROST - ('Clark's Red'; 'Owl Face'). Crimson varying to deep Rose Pink. Medium, formal double. Vigorous, compact, upright growth. M-L. (U.S. 1841 - Ritchie and Dick. Philadelphia, PA).

SARAH HALL - Pink mixed with White. Small, full peony form. Average, upright growth. E-M. (U.S. 1980 - B. Hall, Jackson, MS).

SARAH JEAN TOLAND - Cerise (Pinky Red) with Yellow anthers and White filaments. Small, semidouble. Average, upright growth. M. (U.S. 2013 - James R. S. Toland, Sacramento, CA).

SARAH LEE - Creamy White with Pink outer petals. Miniature, formal double. Slow, open growth. M. (U.S. 1992 - Dr. O. Lewis, Picayune, MS).

SARAH LEE CANNON - White. Medium, anemone form. Vigorous, upright growth. M-L. (U.S. 1977 - M. S. Cannon, Covington, LA).

SARAH R - ('Dr. George Bunch'). Light Pink to Blush Pink with White border. Large to very large, semidouble to loose peony form. (Sport of Japonica 'Big Beauty'). (Reported to be same as 'Tillie Wirth'). (U.S. 1961 - L W Ruffin, Ellisville, MS).

SARA-HENRI S. MAYER - Blush Pink. Large, semidouble with wavy, crinkled petals and White stamens. Average, compact, upright growth. M. (U.S. 1961 - Solomon).

SARASA (SAWADA) - ('Sawada'). Flesh Pink dotted and striped darker Pink. Medium to large, semidouble. Vigorous, open, upright growth. M. (U.S. 1939 - Overlook).

SARGE FREEMAN - Bright Red. Large, semidouble. Average, spreading growth. E-M. (U.S. 1996 - Elizabeth R. Scott, Aiken, SC).

SASSAFRAS ZOE - Pink, occasionally striped Deeper Pink, fading to a White edge. Medium, single. Average, dense, bushy growth. M-L. (Aus. 2003 - Katherine Shaw, Sassafras, Victoria).

SASU - Soft Pink. Medium to large, semidouble with irregular petals. Vigorous growth. M. (U.S. 1957 - E. F. Heard, Hampton, VA).

SATELLITE - Red. Large, full peony form. Average, compact, upright growth. E-M. (U.S. 1960 - Breschini).

SATELLITE VARIEGATED - Red and White variegation of 'Satellite'.

SATIN DOLL - White with some petals edged Pink. Medium to large, semidouble to formal double form. Vigorous, upright growth. M-L. (U.S. 1999 - Bond Nursery Corp., Dallas, TX).

SATIN SHEEN - Red with Yellow anthers and Pink filaments. Large, semidouble; petals are crinkled with a satin sheen. Average, upright growth. M-L. (Seedling of Japonica 'Lipstick'). (U.S. 2018 - Pat Johnson, Cairo, GA).

SATSUMA - White. Medium to large, formal double with incurved petals. Vigorous, dense, upright growth. M-L. (Japan 1979 - originator unknown, Kagoshima).

SATSUMA KURENAI - Brilliant Orange Red. Medium to large, rose form double. Vigorous, upright, rather columnar growth. M-L. (Japan).

SAUDADE DE MARTINS BRANCO - Bright Red blotched White. Large, semidouble to anemone form. M. (Portugal 1920 - Da Silva).

SAUL HABAS - Brilliant Red. Large to very large, semidouble to peony form. Average, open, upright growth. M. (U.S. 1983 - Tammia).

SAVANNAH GIRL - Light Pink. Medium, semidouble. Average, compact growth. M. (U.S. 1959).

SAWADA NUMBER 25 - Ivory White. Medium, formal double. Slow, open growth. M. (U.S. 1965 - Overlook).

SAWADA'S DREAM - White with one-third outer petals shaded delicate Flesh Pink. Medium, formal double. Average growth. E-M. (U.S. 1958 - Overlook).

SAWADA'S MAHOGANY - Dark Red with Red and White petaloids. Medium to large, peony form. Vigorous, upright growth. E-L. (U.S. 1971 - K. Sawada, Mobile, AL. Propagated by Bobby Green, Fairhope, AL).

SCARLET BALLERINA - Red. Small to medium, hose-in-hose type semidouble. Average, upright growth. M. (N.Z. 1991 - Jury).

SCARLET BUOY - Scarlet. Small, single. Average, upright growth. E-L. (N.Z. 1981 - Jury).

SCARLET GLORY - Scarlet. Large to very large, semidouble. Average, compact, upright growth. M. (U.S. 1984 - Nuccio's).

SCARLET O'HARA - Dark Red spotted White. Medium, formal double. (Variegated variation of Japonica 'C. M. Hovey'). (U.S. 1940's - Flowerwood).

SCARLET RIBBONS - Vibrant Red with Gold anthers and Cream filaments. Medium, loose peony to rose form double. Average, spreading, open growth. E-L. (Japonica 'Jean Clere' seedling). (U.S. 2013 - Gordy).

SCENTASIA - Bright Red. Large, peony form. M. Fragrant. (N.Z. 1997 - J. Finlay).

SCENTED FIREGLOW - Bright Orange Red. Medium, semidouble. Average, upright growth. M-L. Fragrant. (N.Z. 1994 - J. Finlay).

145

SCENTED TREASURE - Rose Red to Wine Red. Medium, full peony form. Average, compact growth. M. Fragrant. (U.S. 1950 - Short).

SCENTIMENTAL - Bright Red. Large, peony form. E. Fragrant. (N.Z. 1997 - J. Finlay).

SCENTSATION - Silvery Pink. Medium to large, peony form. Average, compact, upright growth. M. Fragrant. (U.S. 1967 - Nuccio's).

SCHEHERAZADE - Coral Rose with Gold anthers and White filaments. Medium to large, semidouble to anemone form. Average, compact, upright growth. M. (U.S. 1957 - McCaskill).

SCHEHERAZADE VARIEGATED - Coral Rose blotched White variation of 'Scheherazade'.

SCOTTY FORBES - Light Pink. Large, peony form. Average growth. M. (U.S. 1972 - Burgess).

SCUDDAY ROUSSEL - Deep Pink. Medium to large, formal double with vein in center of each petal. Average, upright growth. E. (U.S. 1966 - J. S. Roussel, Shreveport, LA).

SEA FOAM - White. Medium to large, formal double. Upright growth. L. (U.S. 1959 - Weisner).

SEA PEARL - Shell Pink. Large, semidouble with five fascicles of stamens. Vigorous, open growth. M. (Aus. 1971 - Tuckfield).

SEA WITCH - Rose Pink with darker veining and lighter petal edges. Miniature to small, rose form double to formal double. Average, dense growth. M-L. (N.Z. 1990 - Originator unknown).

SEARS SPECIAL - Pink. Large, formal double of flat form with slightly curved petal edges. M-L. (U.S. 1959).

SELINA LOUISE - White with a definite Yellow center. Large, rose form double. Vigorous, upright growth. M-L. (U.S. 1952 - C. Grischow, Portland, OR).

SELMA SHELANDER - White shading to Blush Pink. Large, semidouble. Average, compact growth. E-M. (U.S. 1955 - Mrs. A. N. Shelander, Brunswick, GA).

SEMIDOUBLE BLUSH - Blush Pink with Yellow stamens. Medium, semidouble. Slow, upright growth. M. (France to U.S 1933 - Kiyono Nurseries, Crichton, AL).

SEMINOLE CHIEF - Deep Red tinged Purple. Medium, semidouble with fluted, upright petals intermingled with petaloids. Average, compact growth. E-M. (U.S. 1962 - R. A. Snyder, Orlando, FL).

SENATOR DUNCAN U. FLETCHER - Rose Red to dark Red. Medium, semidouble to peony form. Slow, upright growth. M-L. (U.S. 1943 - Gerbing).

SENTINEL STAR - White striped Red. Large, semidouble with fluted, crinkled petals and whirl of center petaloids intermingled with stamens in center. Average, spreading, upright growth. M. (U.S. 1961 - Saulando Springs Nsy., Orlando, FL).

SEPTEMBER MORN (SHIRABYÔSH) - White with Yellow anthers. Large, loose peony. E. (Japan 1859 - Kantô Area).

SERENA - White. Medium, semidouble. Average, upright growth. M. (N.Z. 1993 - Mrs. S. Blackie, Putaruru).

SERENADE - Cream White. Medium, peony form. Average, compact, upright growth. L. Fragrant. (U.S. 1957 - A. E. Johnson, Beaverton, OR).

SERGEANT BARRIOS - Rose Red with Golden anthers and White filaments. Large, semidouble. Vigorous, compact, upright growth. M. (U.S. 1940 - Semmes Nursery, Semmes, AL).

SEVENTH HEAVEN - Light Rose Pink. Large, semidouble with wide petals and small petaloids in center. Vigorous, open, upright growth. M. (U.S. 1955 - Short).

SEVENTH HEAVEN VARIEGATED - Light Rose Pink and White variation of 'Seventh Heaven'.

SEVILLE SQUARE - Dark Red. Large, semidouble to peony form. Slow, open, pendulous growth. E-M. (U.S. 1978 - Miss I. Meriwether, Pensacola, FL).

SHADOW PLAY - Neyron Rose 623 fading to 623/1 with Light Yellow anthers and White filaments. Large, semidouble with twisted petals. Vigorous, upright, free flowering growth. (U.S. 1953 - Short).

SHAH OF PERSIA - See 'Te Deum'.

SHALA'S BABY - White with Creamy center. Small, anemone form. Vigorous, upright growth. E-L. (U.S. 1985 - R. C. McNeil, Ramona, CA).

SHALIMAR - Light Pink. Medium, semidouble with loose petals. Vigorous, bushy growth. M. (U.S. 1941 - Coolidge).

SHALIMAR SUNSET - Dark Red. Medium to large, rose form double to formal double. Average, compact growth. M. (U.S. 1988 - E. and J. Atkins, Shalimar, FL).

SHANE'S CHOICE - Deep Pink. Medium to large, anemone form. Average, bushy growth. M. (Aus. 1996 - S. Wenke, Walla Walla, NSW).

SHANGRI-LA - See 'Daikagura Red'.

SHANNON NELSON - Dark Rose Pink. Large, semidouble with fluted, upright petals to loose peony form. Average growth. E-M. (U.S. 1966 - Bray).

SHARI THOMPSON - Blush Pink edged Pale Pink and spotted Deeper Pink. Medium, formal double. Average, upright growth. M. (U.S. 1988 - J. Aldrich, Brooklet, GA).

SHARON ANN WYLIE - White. Medium, peony form. Vigorous, compact, upright growth. M. (Aus. 1965 - P. A. Wylie, Dundas).

SHARON LEE - Rose. Medium, full peony form. Average, compact growth. M-L. (U.S. 1951 - Riverbank).

SHARON RAYE PEARSON - Pink. (Sport of Japonica 'Feasti'). (U.S. 1948 - Shepp).

SHARON ROSE - Red. Large, rose form double with very large, almost square outer petals. Slow, open growth. M. (U.S. 1950 - C. R. Allen, Milton, FL).

SHARON SHUMAN - Pale Pink. Medium, formal double form. Average, open growth. M-L. (U.S. 2002 - G. Stuart Watson, Albany, GA).

SHARON SMITH - Light Rose Pink. Medium, rose form double. Average, open, upright growth. E. (U.S. 1986 - W. L. Smith, Tylertown, MS).

SHARON WILSON - Light Pink and Darker Pink sections with Yellow anthers and White filaments. Medium, rose form double to semidouble. Vigorous, upright, open growth. M. (U.S. 2019 – Randolph Maphis, Tallahassee, FL).

SHARYN'S BLUSH - Rose to Red. Large, formal double. Open, upright growth. M-L. (Aus. 1984 - Pierson).

SHEATHERI - Pink shading to Silvery Pink in center. Medium, formal double. Spreading growth. M. (Aus. 1879 - Sheather).

SHEILA - Light Orchid Pink. Large, semidouble with wavy, crinkled petals. Average, upright growth. E-M. (U.S. 1973 - Gilley).

SHELBY BROTHERS - Rose Pink. Large, semidouble. Average growth. M. (U.S. 1964 - S. L. Brothers, Gainesville, FL).

SHELLIE RAE - Blush Pink. Small, formal double. Average, upright growth. M-L. (U.S. 1984 - Gentry).

SHELLYE FARBER - Cherry Red. Medium to large, semidouble with irregular petals and collarette of Red stamens around petals and Red stamens. Average, compact growth. E-M. (U.S. 1963 - J. E. Miller, New Orleans, LA).

SHEPHERDESS - Rose Coral. Large, semidouble to formal double. (Sport of Japonica 'Augusto L'Gouveia Pinto'). (U.S. 1956 - McCaskill).

SHEPP'S BOUTONNIERE - White striped Red and Pink. Small, formal double showing small tufted center when fully open. Average, compact, upright growth. M-L. (U.S. 1962 - Shepp).

SHEPP'S BOUTONNIERE BLUSH - Pink edged White. (Sport of Japonica 'Shepp's Boutonniere'). (U.S. 1962 - Shepp).

SHEPP'S BOUTONNIERE RED - Red. (Sport of Japonica 'Shepp's Boutonniere'). (U.S. 1962 - Shepp).

SHERBROOKE - See 'Kumasaka'.

SHERIDAN - Rose Red veined Blush. Medium, single of trumpet shape. Compact, columnar growth. M. (Aus. 1965 - Ballarat, Vic.).

SHERIDAN WILSON - White striped Red. Large, semidouble. Average, spreading, upright growth. M. (U.S. 1989 - W. Wilson, Augusta, GA).

SHERRIE N - White. Very large, anemone form. Average, upright growth. E-M. (U.S. 1998 - Jernigan).

SHERRY LYNN - Blush Pink. Medium, formal double with upturned and pointed petals. Average, dense, upright growth. M-L. (U.S. 1993 - Jernigan).

SHIBORI-OTOME - White striped Pink. Medium, formal double. (Japan 1800's - Kantô Area).

SHIKIBU - Rose Red. Miniature, anemone form with Rose Red petaloids edged White. Upright growth. M-L. (Japan to U.S. 1981 - Nuccio's).

SHIMMER - Brilliant Orange Red. Medium to large, semidouble with irregular petals to anemone form. Average, compact, upright growth. M-L. (U.S. 1989 - Longdon Nsy., Sebastopol, CA).

SHIN-AKEBONO (NEW DAWN) - See 'Akebono'.

SHIN-HAGOROMA - Red. Medium, single with flared soft Pink stamens that in some flowers are fully topped with White and Pink petaloids. See Higo.

SHINING HOUR - Clear delicate Pink. Medium, full peony form. Average, compact growth. E-L. (U.S. 1967 - Short).

SHINONOME - (Dawn). Scarlet streaks on pink with rose-pink filaments in a central burst. Medium, single. M. (Sport of Japonica 'Yamato-nishiki'). (Japan 1956). See Higo.

SHIN-SHIOKO - Clear Pink shaded deeper Pink. Small, semidouble. Medium, compact growth. M. (Reported that correct spelling is 'Shun-Shioko'). (Japan 1938 - Chugai).

SHIN-TSUKASA - Pink. (Sport of Japonica 'Shin-tsukasa-nishiki'). See Higo.

SHIN-TSUKASA-NISHIKI - Deep Pink striped Rose. Medium, single with flared White stamens that in some flowers are fully topped with Pink and White petaloids. See Higo.

SHIRA SAGI - White. Large, single. See Higo.

SHIRA YUKI - White with flared White stamens. Medium, single. See Higo.

SHIRABYÔSH - See 'September Morn'

SHIRAGIKU - See 'Purity'. ('Shiragiku' is reported as priority name for this cultivar but as 'Purity' [U.S. 1933 - Armstrong] has been in such common use in the U.S. we do not believe a change is necessary or warranted). (Japan 1935 - Chugai).

147

SHIRANUI (FISHING LIGHTS ON THE SEA) - Scarlet with rare White marks, with Golden anthers and White filaments in a ring. Very large, single. (Japan 1912 - Tamehachi Yoshimura, Kumamoto Prefecture). See Higo.

SHIRA-OGI - White. Medium, single with flared Pale Yellow stamens which in some flowers are partially topped with White petaloids. See Higo.

SHIRA-TAMA (WHITE BEAD) - ('Egret'). White. Medium, rose form double to formal double. Vigorous, open, upright growth. M. (Japan 1907).

SHIRLEY ANNE - Light Pink. Medium, semidouble form. Average, bushy, upright growth. M-L. (Aus. 2002 - Leslie Arnold Round, Geilston Bay, Tasmania).

SHIRLEY J. STIMSON - Bright Red. Very large, single. Slow, spreading, semi-weeping growth. E-M. (Aus. 1990 - W. Stimson, Kenthurst, NSW).

SHIRLEY MENEICE - Deep Magenta Pink with Lighter Pink flashes on inside petals. Medium, semidouble form with heart shaped petals. Average, open, spreading growth. M-L. (U.S. 2004 - Richard E. Dodd, Marshallville, GA).

SHIRLEY MILLER - Dark Orchid Pink with Lavender overtones with Yellow anthers and Pink filaments. Large, semidouble with waxy petals. Slow, spreading growth. M. (First Lady of Georgia Series). (U.S. 2018 - Gordy).

SHIRLEY NORUP - Pale Pink. Medium, formal double form. Average, compact growth. M-L. (Aus. 2003 - John Butler, Cabarlah, Qld.).

SHIRLEY'S OWN - Soft Pale Pink. Large, rose form double. Slow, spreading growth. M-L. (Aus. 1995 - K. Brown, Mitcham, Vic.).

SHIRLEY'S SURPRISE - Bright Rose Red edged Darker Gray-Purple. Medium, single. Average growth. E-M. (N.Z. 2007 - Shirley Munroe).

SHIRO CHAN - White with Light Basal Pink when first opening and generally with Pink stripe. Large to very large, anemone form. (Sport of Japonica 'C M Wilson'). (For a variation of this cultivar see 'Snow Chan'). (U.S. 1953 - Domoto).

SHIRO-BOTAN (SHIROBOTAN) - White with Yellow anthers and White filaments. Medium, semidouble to loose peony form. Vigorous growth. M. (Japan to U.S. 1931 - K. Sawada, Overlook Nurseries, Crichton, AL).

SHIRO-HAGOROMO (WHITE HAGOROMO) - White. Medium, semidouble; lotus form - hose-in-hose. Average, compact growth. M-L. (Japonica 'Magnoliaeflora' seedling). (Japan 1975 - Shigeichi Yagi, Ehime).

SHIROKINGYOBA-TSUBAKI (WHITE GOLDFISH CAMELLIA) - White with Brownish-Yellow anthers and White filaments. Medium, single with 6-7 petals; leaves 'fishtail' shaped. (Japan 1957 - Chûbu Area).

SHIRO-WAKANOURA - See 'Leucantha'.

SHIVEL DUNCAN - Red. Medium, semidouble to loose peony form. Upright growth. M. (U.S. 1957 - Mrs. W. S. Duncan, Pensacola, FL).

SHOKKÔ-NISHIKI (LIGHT OF SECHUAN BROCADE) - Dark Pink virus variegated White with Higo-like large Yellow stamens. Large, single. Very slow, upright growth. M-L. (Japan 1841 - Yashiro, Kansai Area).

SHORTY - Red variegated White. Medium, semidouble. Average growth. L. (U.S. 1980 - Habel).

SHOW TIME - Clear Light Pink. Very large, semidouble with fluted petals. Vigorous, upright growth. M. (U.S. 1978 - Nuccio's).

SHOWA-NO-HIKARI - Pink striped Rose. Medium, single with extremely flared stamens. Medium, upright growth. M-L. (Sport of Japonica 'Yamato-nishiki'). See Higo.

SHOWFIRE - Brilliant Red. Medium, single. Vigorous, open, upright growth. E-M. (Aus. 1989 - D. Coe, Glenroy, Albury, NSW).

SHUCHUKA - White with narrow picotee edge of Red. Miniature to small, semidouble to peony form. L. (Japan 1879 - Chin-Ka-Shu).

SHUSU - See 'Monjisu Red'.

SIENA ELIZABETH - Lavender Pink with Darker Pink and Lavender markings with Yellow anthers and White filaments. Small, semidouble to anemone. Average, upright growth. M-L. (chance seedling of Japonica 'Tinker Bell'). (U.S. 2017 - Don Bergamini, Martinez, CA).

SIERRA BELLE - White. Large, single to semidouble. M. (U.S. 1952 - East Lawn Nsy., Sacramento, CA).

SIERRA MADRE - White. Large, semidouble with irregular petals to loose peony form. Vigorous, compact, upright growth. M. (U.S. 1954 - Star).

SIERRA SPRING - ('Mme. Hahn Variegated'). Bright Pink and White form of 'Madame Hahn'. Medium, semidouble. (U.S. 1948 - C. Marshall, Sierra Madre, CA).

SIESTA TIME - Light Rose Pink. Large, semidouble with loose petals. Average, open, upright growth. M-L. (U.S. 1970 - Haynie).

SIEUR DE BIENVILLE - Deep Rose Pink. Medium to large, formal double to rose form double. (Sport of Japonica 'Florence Stratton'). (U.S. 1946 - McIlhenny).

SILLAY'S TARR SEEDLING - Watermelon Red. Large, rose form double with upright petals. Average, upright growth. E-M. (U.S. 1978 - W. Tarr, Orange Park, FL).

SILVER ANNIVERSARY - White. Large, semidouble with irregular petals intermixed with Golden stamens. Vigorous, compact, upright growth. E-M. (U.S. 1960 - Nuccio's).

SILVER CHALICE - White. Medium to large, full peony form. Vigorous, compact, upright growth. M. (U.S. 1963 - Nuccio's).

SILVER CLOUD - White. Very large, loose peony form. Vigorous, compact, upright growth. E-L. (U.S. 1980 - Nuccio's).

SILVER CREST - Cream White. Large, peony form to anemone form. Vigorous, bushy growth. M-L. (U.S. 1953 - Short).

SILVER ETCHING - Light Pink bordered Silver. Large, irregular semidouble with fluted and upright petals. Average, open, upright growth. M. (U.S. 1966 - S. A. Willsey, Lockhart, FL).

SILVER LACE - White. Large to very large, semidouble with irregular, lacy petals. Vigorous, compact, upright growth. E-M. (U.S. 1985 - Nuccio's).

SILVER LINING - White. Large, formal double. Vigorous growth. M. (U.S. 1958 - Shackelford).

SILVER MOON - See 'K. Sawada'.

SILVER PLUME - Soft Peach Pink. Medium to large, loose peony form. Upright growth. M-L. (U.S. 1958 - Short).

SILVER RUFFLES - White. Large to very large, loose semidouble with ruffled petals. Vigorous, slightly open, upright growth. M. (U.S. 1965 - Nuccio's).

SILVER STAR - Blush Pink. Medium, anemone form to loose peony form. Vigorous, spreading growth. (U.S. 1975 - Novick).

SILVER TOWER - White. Medium, semidouble with narrow petals. Vigorous, columnar, upright growth. M. (U.S. 1988 - Nuccio's).

SILVER TRIUMPH - White. Large to very large, semidouble. Vigorous, upright growth. E-M. (U.S. 1973 - Nuccio's).

SILVER WAVES - White. Large to very large, semidouble with wavy petals. Vigorous, bushy, upright growth. E-M. (U.S. 1969 - Nuccio's).

SILVERADO - White with faint Rose border. Medium, single. Fairly slow, upright growth. E. (U.S. 1995 - Nuccio's).

SIMEON - Pink. Large, semidouble to loose peony form with large petals. Vigorous, upright growth. E-M. (U.S. 1949 - Clower).

SIMMONS GYPSY - Rose Pink. Medium, semidouble. Average, upright growth. M-L. (N.Z. 1990 - A. Simmons, Te Puke).

SIMMONS MAGIC - Bright Red. Medium, anemone form. Vigorous, upright, dense growth. M-L. (N.Z. 1999 - A. R. and G. A. Simmons).

SIMONS LUCAS - Deep Rose Red. Large, peony form. Vigorous, upright growth. E. (U.S. 1950 - Dr. S. R. Lucas, Florence, SC).

SINCERELY - Purplish Red. Large, anemone form with many trumpet shaped petaloids. Average growth. M. (U.S. 1965 - J. F. Marscher, Beaufort, SC).

SINGING WATERS - Clear Pink. Medium to large, loose peony form. Vigorous, compact, upright growth. M. (U.S. 1960 - Shackelford).

SIR GALLAHAD - Red. Large, loose peony form. Average, compact growth. M. (U.S. 1964 - Shackelford).

SIR VICTOR DAVIES - Cardinal Red veined darker to Violet Purple. Small to medium, peony form to formal double. Average growth. M-L. (N.Z. 1991 - Jury).

SIR WINSTON CHURCHILL - White. Large to very large, semidouble with wavy, crinkled petals. Average, open growth. M-L. (U.S. 1969 - Haynie).

SISSY LACKEY - Light Rose Pink. Large, loose peony form. Average, upright growth. M. (U.S. 1958 - Middleton).

SISSY LACKEY VARIEGATED - Light Rose Pink blotched White variation of 'Sissy Lackey'.

SKIP - Deep Rose. Large, semidouble with veined, heavy textured petals and White stamens. Average, spreading growth. E-M. (U.S. 1962 - Mrs. O. Heyer, Covington, LA).

SKYLARK - Light Lavender Pink. Medium, semidouble of trumpet form. Average, bushy growth. M. (U.S. 1959 - Short).

SKYROCKET - White with flecks and/or stripes of Deep Pink. Large, anemone form. Average growth. E-L. (U.S. 1996 - H. Hall).

SLEIGH BELLS - White. Medium, semidouble. Average, bushy growth. M-L. (Aus. 1961 - J. R. Williams, Turramurra).

SLIDELL CENTENNIAL - Dark Rose Pink. Large, full peony form to rose form double to formal double. Average, open, upright growth. E-M. (U.S. 1987 - Tammia).

SMALL SLAM - Red with Red and White petaloids. Miniature to small, anemone form. Average, upright growth. M. (U.S. 1999 - Northern California Camellia Research Committee, Martinez, CA).

SMALL WONDER - Purple Red. Small, formal double with incurved petals. Slow, bushy growth. M. (U.S. 1962 - McCaskill).

SMALL WUN - Rose Pink. Miniature, anemone form. Vigorous, spreading growth. M. (U.S. 1975 - Novick).

SMILE - Rose Red. Medium, semidouble. Average, compact growth. M. (U.S. 1964 - Mrs. R. H. Brodie, Biloxi, MS).

SMITTY - Deep Rosy Red. Large, formal double to rose form double. Average, dense, upright growth. E-L. (U.S. 1995 - A. Fendig and J. Ledbetter, St. Simons Island, GA).

SMOKE RING - Light Red with Violet tinge, to a pure Light Violet, occasionally to Darker Violet shades. Medium, semidouble. Average, upright growth. M-L. (Sport of Japonica 'Dona Herzila de Freitas Magalhaes'). (N.Z. 2005 - R. and V. Bieleski, Manukau City).

149

SNELLS BLUSH - Light Blush Pink. Large, formal double. Slow, bushy growth. M-L. (Aus. 1998 - ACRS W. A. Branch).

SNOOTY BEAUTY - Glowing Rose Pink. Large, semidouble with White tipped petaloids intermixed with Golden stamens. (U.S. 1961 - H. Mura, Augusta, GA).

SNOW BABY - White. Miniature, anemone form. Average, compact, upright growth. M. (U.S. 1965 - McCaskill).

SNOW BELL - White with Dark Yellow anthers and Creamy filaments. Large, semidouble with petals firm, broad-ovate, inner crêped, apices notched, sometimes fluted. Average, spreading dense growth. M. (Japan to U.S. [Huntington Gardens]).

SNOW CHAN - ('White Elegans').- Pure White. Large to very large, anemone form. (Sport of Japonica 'Shiro Chan'). (U.S. 1957 - Nuccio's).

SNOW CLOUD - White. Large, semidouble to loose peony form with fluted petals. Average, compact growth. M. (U.S. 1953 - Jones).

SNOW CONE - White. Medium, formal double with wide, heavy petals. Bushy, upright growth. M. (U.S. 1973 - T. E. Croson, Paso Robles, CA).

SNOW DOLL - See 'Pax'.

SNOW FAIRY - White. Small, formal double to rose form double. Average, compact growth. M. (U.S. 1963 - McCaskill).

SNOW FLAME - White. Medium to large, formal double. Average, compact, upright growth. L. (U.S. 1963 - Short).

SNOW LADY - Pure White. Large, loose peony form to rose form double. Vigorous, open, upright growth. E-L. Cold hardy. (U.S. 1995 - A. Chastain, Thomasville, GA).

SNOW MAIDEN - White. Small, semidouble. Vigorous, upright, open growth. M. (U.S. 1937 - Coolidge).

SNOW MITT - White. Large, formal double. Compact, upright growth. M-L. (Aus. 1979 - J. G. Baxter, Dorchester East, Vic.).

SNOW NYMPH - White. Small, full peony form, occasionally showing stamens. Average, compact growth. E-M. (U.S. 1958 - Mrs. W. E. Milligan, Thomasville, GA).

SNOW PALACE - White. Large, peony form to anemone form with large, undulated outer guard petals. Average, compact growth. M. (U.S. 1958 - Short).

SNOW PRINCESS - White. Medium, formal double. Vigorous, compact, upright growth. L. (U.S. 1953 - Shackelford).

SNOW SWIRL - Pure White. Large, formal double with lightly ruffled petals at times. (U.S. 2005 - Gordy).

SNOW TULIP - White. Medium, single to semidouble. Vigorous, upright growth. M. (U.S. 1945 - Carter).

SNOW WHITE (ROSEDALE) - See 'Thomas D. Pitts'.

SNOW WHITE (STAR) - White. Large, semidouble with central mass of Golden stamens and occasional petaloids. M. (U.S. 1959 - Star).

SNOWDRIFT - White with Gold anthers and White filaments. Medium, semidouble. Slow, upright growth. M. (Japan to U.S. 1932 - Toichi Domoto, Hayward, CA).

SNOWIE - White with some flowers Pale Blush. Miniature, rose form double. Average, compact, upright growth. M. (U.S. 1971 - M. A. and N. Cox, Georgetown, SC).

SNOWMAN - White. Large, semidouble with curled and twisted inner petals and notched and incurved outer petals. Vigorous, spreading, upright growth. M. (U.S. 1964 - W. Stewart, Savannah, GA).

SNOWMIST - White. Miniature, single. Slow, dense growth. E-M. (U.S. 1997 - Domoto).

SNOWY EGRETS - White. Medium to large, semidouble with long, narrow, twisted, fluted petals, a loose bunch of stamens, and very narrow petaloids. Average, pendulous growth. M-L. (U.S. 1972 - Witman).

SODE-GAKUSHI - See 'Lotus'. ('Sode-Gakushi' is reported as priority name for this cultivar but as 'Lotus' has been in such common use in the U.S. we do not believe a change is necessary or warranted). (Japan 1879 - K. Ito).

SOLARIS - See 'C. M. Hovey'.

SOLITAIRE - White. Medium, formal double. Average, bushy growth. M-L. (U.S. 1953 - Short).

SOLOMAN'S PINK - ('Haynsworth's Pink').- Deep Pink. Large, formal double to rose form double. Vigorous, upright growth. M. (U.S. 1955 - A. A. Solomans, Sumter, SC).

SOMEGAWA - Red striped Pink. Medium, formal double. Vigorous, upright, open growth. L. (Japan 1895 - Yokohama).

SOMERSBY - Ruby Red edged Deeper Red. Medium, rose form double to peony form. M. (Aus. 1945 - Camellia Grove).

SOMETHING BEAUTIFUL - Pale Pink edged Burgundy Red. Small, formal double. Vigorous, compact, upright growth. M. (U.S. 1983 - E. L. Atkins, Shalimar, FL).

SON HACKNEY - Blush Pink. Large, semidouble to loose peony form with twisted petals. (U.S. 1963).

SONATA - Rose Pink. Large, full peony form. Average, pendulous growth. M. (U.S. 1955 - W. E. Schmidt, Palo Alto, CA).

SONG OF PARIS - Clear warm Pink. Medium to large, rose form double with inner petals cupped and pointed. Vigorous, bushy, upright growth. M-L. (U.S. 1969 - McCaskill).

SONGHUAPIAN (PINE CONE SCALES) - Faintest Blush Pink with a few Yellow stamens. Unknown size, rose form double opening with petals layered and apart like an opened pine cone. (China 1985 - Shanghai Botanic Garden, Shanghai).

SONORA - Rose Pink. Medium, formal double. Vigorous, upright growth. M-L. (U.S. 1951 - Riverbank).

SOSHI-ARAI (WASHED OUT WRITING) - Light Pink blotched and spotted Reddish Pink. Medium, semidouble. Vigorous, compact, upright growth. M. (Japan to U.S. [Star] 1930).

SOTAN - See 'Kamo-Hon-Ami'.

SOUND OF MUSIC - Light Pink. Very large, semidouble to peony form. Vigorous, spreading growth. M-L. (U.S. 1978 - C. E. Jones, Elizabeth City, NC).

SOUTHEASTERN FLOWER SHOW - Medium Pink (RHS 54A) with Yellow anthers and Light Yellow filaments. Very large, semidouble to anemone form. Average, upright, open growth. E-L. (U.S. 2011 - Richard "Dick" Dodd, Marshallville, GA).

SOUTHERN CHARM - ('Queen Juliana').- White. Large, semidouble. Average, upright growth. M. (U.S. 1955 - Fisher).

SOUTHERN CROSS - Crimson Red. Medium, peony form. Upright growth. M. (Aus. 1952 - Camellia Grove).

SOUTHERN SECRET - Deep Coral Pink outer petals shading to Lighter Coral Pink center. Large to very large, semidouble. Vigorous, upright growth. E-L. (U.S. 2012 - Jill Read, Lucedale, MS).

SOUTHERN SNOWBALL - White. Medium, anemone (with 12 guard petals) to full peony form. Vigorous, dense, upright growth. E-M. (U.S. 2012 - Jill Read, Lucedale, MS).

SOUTHERN STAR - Deep Rose Pink. Large, single to semidouble with star-like arrangement of petals. Vigorous, bushy growth. M. (Aus. 1965 - G. Waterhouse).

SOUTHERN TEMPTATION - White with Cream Yellow center bud. Medium to large, formal double. Vigorous, upright, dense growth. M-L. (U.S. 2016 - Jill Read, Lucedale, MS).

SOUTHLAND - Light Pink. Large, semidouble to anemone form. Pendulous growth. M-L. (U.S. 1962 - Wheeler).

SOUV. D'HENRI GUICHARD - See 'Herme'.

SOUV. DE BAHUAUD LITOU - ('Lady Frances'; 'Carole Lombard'; 'Queen Victoria's Blush [South]'). Light Pink. Large, formal double. (Sport of Japonica 'Mathotiana Alba'). (France 1908 - Bahuaud-Litou).

SPANISH BALLERINA - Burgundy Red. Small, anemone. Vigorous, upright, open growth. M-L. (Seedling of Japonica 'Tinsie'). (U.S. 2016 - Pat Johnson, Cairo, GA).

SPECIAL DELIVERY - White. Large, semidouble with wide, sweeping Golden stamens interspersed with clusters of petaloids and upright center petals. Vigorous, open, upright growth. M-L. (U.S. 1962 - D. B. Brockman, Greer, SC).

SPECIAL TRIBUTE - Salmon Pink. Medium to large, formal double to rose form double. Average, open growth. M-L. (U.S. 1956 - Short).

SPECKLES - See 'Finlandia Variegated'.

SPECTACULAR - Red. Large, anemone form. Slow, upright growth. M. (U.S. 1965 - H. Cawood, Americus, GA).

SPELLBOUND - See 'Marie Bracey'.

SPENCER HILL - Deep Rose Pink. Medium, semidouble. L. (U.S. 1953 - Fruitland).

SPENCER'S PINK - Light Pink with Pink filaments. Large, single with wavy petals. Upright growth. E. (Aus. 1940 - Mrs. G. A. Weymouth, Melbourne).

SPINDRIFT - White with Light Pink stripes. Miniature, semidouble. Average, dense growth. M-L. (U.S. 1992 - H. Hall).

SPLASH OF PINK - White with splash of Pink. Medium, peony form. Average, upright growth. M. (U.S. 1977 - Kramer).

SPLASH-O-WHITE - Red splotched White on several petals. Small to medium, semidouble. Slow growth. E-L. (U.S. 1960 - E. Pieri, San Gabriel, CA).

SPORTING CLASS - White with flecks, streaks and petals of Dark Coral Pink with White Yellow tinted anthers and Yellow filaments. Medium, peony form. Average, upright, spreading, dense growth. E. (U.S. 2008 - John M. Davy, Pace, FL).

SPOTLIGHT - Light Red. Large, semidouble. (U.S. 1961 - J. C. Robinson, La Cañada, CA).

SPRING CALL - White. Large, formal double. Vigorous, open, upright growth. M. (U.S. 1953 - Short).

SPRING DEB - Pink. Medium, full peony form. Vigorous, compact, upright growth. M-L. (U.S. 1956 - Nuccio's).

SPRING FEVER - Rose Pink. Very large, full peony form. Vigorous, compact, upright growth. M. (U.S. 1967 - Nuccio's).

SPRING FLING - Red. Medium, formal double. Average, dense, upright growth. L. (U.S. 1992 - Nuccio's).

SPRING FORMAL - Deep Pink. Medium, formal double with dahlia form. Vigorous, compact, upright growth. L. (U.S. 1986 - Nuccio's).

SPRING HILL - Pink. Large, semidouble to anemone form. Bushy, upright growth. M-L. (U.S. 1976 - Haynie).

151

SPRING SONNET - Pale Pink with Deeper Pink margin. Medium, semidouble. (Sport of Japonica 'Colonial Lady'). (U.S. 1952 - McCaskill).

SPRING TRIUMPH - Deep Coral Pink. Large, loose peony form with large center petaloids. Average, open growth. M. Cold hardy. (U.S. 1953 - Short).

SPRING'S PROMISE - Rose Red. Small, single. Average, dense growth. E-M. Cold hardy. (U.S. 1990 - Parks).

SPRINGHEAD GEM - Light Pink deeper at petal edges. Small, formal double with swirled petals. Slow, spreading growth. M-L. (U.S. 1995 - F. Wilson, Leslie, GA).

SPRINGTIDE - Soft Pink. Medium, rose form double. Vigorous, compact growth. M-L. (U.S. 1947 - Coolidge).

SPUTNIK - Dark Red. Medium, semidouble with large, upright petals. Compact growth. M-L. (U.S. 1959 - Hillcrest Nsy., Kinston, NC).

SQUADRON LEADER ASTIN - White. Miniature, semidouble. Vigorous, dense, upright growth. L. Cold hardy. (U.S. 1997 - P. Astin, Carrollton, GA).

ST. ANDRE - ('Rose Hill Rubra'). Bright Red. Medium to large, semidouble to anemone form. Average, upright growth. M. (England to U.S. [McIlhenny] 1931).

ST. IVES - White dotted and spotted Carmine. Large, loose peony form. M. (Aus. 1962 - Waterhouse).

STACKED DECK - Rose Red. Large, formal double. Vigorous, compact, upright growth. M-L. (U.S. 1981 - Alfter).

STACY SUSAN - Blush dashed Pink. Miniature, formal double. Average, upright growth. M-L. (U.S. 1976 - Haynie).

STANGATE RUBY - Dark Red with darker veining and White markings. Small, formal double. Vigorous, compact growth. M-L. (Aus. 1996 - Aldgate, S. Aus.).

STAR BRIGHT - Brilliant Rose Pink. Small to medium, semidouble with fimbriated petals. Average, bushy growth. M. (U.S. 1953 - Short).

STAR BURST - Red. Large, rose form double of star shape. Slow, spreading growth. L. (U.S. 1974 - F. Sturch, Fair Oaks, CA).

STAR FIRE - Orange Red. Medium, semidouble to peony form. Average, upright growth. M. (U.S. 1960 - Shackelford).

STAR OF DAVID - Light Red. Large, semidouble. Spreading, upright growth. E-M. (Aus. 1980 - T. J. Savige, Wirlinga, NSW).

STAR RUBY - Blood Red. Large, formal double to rose form double with four to six rows of petals. Average, upright growth. M-L. (U.S. 1962 - F. Griffin, Sr., Columbia, SC).

STAR SHADOW - Brilliant Rose Pink. Medium, semidouble. Slow, low, bushy growth. M. (U.S. 1953 - Short).

STAR SONG - Pink. Medium, anemone form to loose peony form. Vigorous, upright growth. M. (U.S. 1975 - Novick).

STARDUST - ('Duc d'Orleans Pink'; 'Mme. Adele'; 'Marguerite Gouillon Pink'). Bright Pink form of 'Marguerite Gouillon'. Medium, full peony form. (U.S. 1934 - Azalea Glen).

STARLET - Light Rose Pink. Miniature to small, formal double of star form. Vigorous, upright growth. E-M. (U.S. 1958 - F. V. Eidson, Thomasville, GA).

STARS AND BARS - Blood Red with Cream White bar down center of each petal and tipped White. Miniature, formal double with petals pinched at top. Slow, open, willowy growth. M. (U.S. 1963 - Mrs. J. V. Knapp, Tallahassee, FL).

STELLA SEWELL - White with Creamy overcast. Large, semidouble to loose peony form. Average, compact growth. M. (U.S. 1954 - Julington).

STELLAN - Vivid Red. Medium, semidouble with notched petals. Average, dense growth. M-L. (Aus. 1995 - K. Brown, Mitcham, Vic.).

STELLAR SUNRISE - Pink. Small to medium, formal double often with incurved petals. Vigorous, upright growth. M-L. Cold hardy. (U.S. 2008 - Parks).

STEPHANIE - White with Cream center. Medium, formal double. E-M. (U.S. 1954 - Mrs. F. W. Fitzpatrick, San Diego, CA).

STEPHANIE CASSAGNE GRIMM - Mauve Pink with Yellow anthers and White filaments. Medium, irregular semidouble form with interspersed stamens. Slow, upright, wispy growth. M. (U.S. 2019 - R. J. Despeaux, Covington, LA).

STEPHANIE CASSAGNE GRIMM VARIEGATED - Mauve Pink blotched white with Yellow anthers and White filaments. Medium, irregular semidouble form with interspersed stamens. Slow, upright, wispy growth. M. (U.S. 2019 - Camellia Heaven - John Grimm, Bush, LA).

STEPHANIE STANLEY - Dark Pink with White spots. Large to very large, semidouble with ruffled petals. Vigorous, open, spreading growth. M. (U.S. 1995 - E. Atkins, Shalimar, FL).

STEPHANIE'S CRIMSON STAR - Crimson. Small, formal double with pointed petals. Average, compact, bushy growth. M. (U.S. 2019 - Bobby Green, Green Nurseries, Fairhope, AL).

STEPHANIE'S HEAVENLY STAR - Lavender. Small, formal double; some petals have an occasional vegetative stripe that forms a unique star shape. Average, upright growth. L. (U.S. 2017 - Camellia Heaven - John Grimm, Metairie, LA).

STEPHEN GORDY - Deep Pink with bright Gold anthers and Pink filaments. Medium, semidouble. Vigorous, upright growth. E-M. (U.S. 2013 - Gordy).

STEPHENS GARDEN - Pink shading to Darker Pink. Small, formal double. Vigorous, upright growth. M-L. (U.S. 2008 - Bobby Green, Green Nurseries, Fairhope, AL).

STEVE BLOUNT - Light Red. Large, semidouble with fluted, curled, and twisted petals. Average, spreading, upright growth. E. (U.S. 1974 - Homeyer).

STEVE PRESTON - Pink. Large, anemone form. Vigorous, compact growth. M. (U.S. 1982 - L. C. Preston, Walnut Creek, CA).

STEVEN SAWADA - Red with Rose cast. Medium to large, semidouble. Vigorous, bushy, rounded growth. E-L. (Solid sport of Japonica 'Tricolor Superba'). (U.S. 2007 - Bobby Green, Green Nurseries, Fairhope, AL).

STEVENS PLANT - See 'Emperor of Russia'.

STEVIE COCKRELL - White heavily flecked and dashed bright Red. Small, semidouble with rounded petals, small White stamens and a few small petaloids. Average, compact growth. M. (U.S. 1958 - Julington).

STEWART'S WHITE SUPREME - White. Large, semidouble to loose peony form with upright petals. Vigorous, compact, upright growth. E-M. (U.S. 1960 - W. Stewart, Savannah, GA).

STILL HOPE - White with Pink cast. Miniature, semidouble to anemone form. Average, upright growth. M-L. (U.S. 1961 - Metcalf).

STOKE'S PINK - Pink. Large, semidouble of flat lily form with rounded petals. (U.S. 1955).

STONE GATES - Deep Rose to Blush Rose Pink. Medium, anemone form. Average, upright growth. M. (U.S. 1988 - V. Stone and T. Gates, Baton Rouge, LA).

STOP! - Red with White petaloids with Gold anthers and White filaments. Large, anemone form. Vigorous, upright, open growth. M-L. (U.S. 2018 - Nuccio's).

STOPLIGHT - Dark Red. Medium, semidouble with center petals semi-erect. Spreading growth. M-L. (U.S. 1957 - C. E. Maston, Whittier, CA).

STORM - Deep Purple Red. Medium, semidouble. (U.S. 1950 - Rosa).

STORMY WEATHER - Dark velvet Red. Medium to large, semidouble with swirled and fluted petals. Vigorous, upright growth. M-L. (U.S. 1957 - Short).

STRAWBERRY BLONDE - Light Salmon Pink lightly speckled Deep Pink. Medium, full peony form. (Sport of Japonica 'Aspasia Macarthur'). (For a variation of this cultivar see 'Glamour Girl'). (U.S. 1949 - Carter).

STRAWBERRY CREAM - Light Blush Pink to Darker Pink at edges. Large, semidouble to rose form double. Vigorous, spreading, upright growth. M-L. (U.S. 1999 - Bond Nursery Corp., Dallas, TX).

STRAWBERRY PARFAIT - China Rose Pink striped Crimson. Medium to large, semidouble to loose peony form. Average, dense, upright growth. M. (N.Z. 1991 - Jury).

STRAWBERRY SODA - Light Pink and White. Large, anemone form. Vigorous, upright growth. E. (U.S. 1966 - A. Leger, Handsboro, MS).

STRAWBERRY SWIRL - Soft Pink margined White with occasional Rose Stripe. Medium to large, peony form. Average, upright growth. E-M. (N.Z. 1989 - Jury).

STRAWBERRY VANILLA - White with Strawberry Pink stripes with Yellow anthers and Creamy Yellow filaments. Medium to large, semidouble. Average, upright, open growth. E-L. (U.S. 2018 - Pat Johnson, Cairo, GA).

STREAMLINER - White, finely striped Deep Pink. Large, semidouble. Vigorous, upright growth. L. (U.S. 1959 - Short).

STROTHER'SCHOICE - Pink. Large, loose peony form. Average, upright growth. M. (U.S. 1957 - Davis).

SUCYN - Ruby Red. Large, semidouble to loose peony form with wide petals and long, heavy textured, upright petals. Average, upright growth. E-M. (U.S. 1959 - J. E. Miller, New Orleans, LA).

SUDIE BLANCHARD - Chalk White. Large, semidouble. Average, compact growth. M. (U.S. 1989 - J. K. Blanchard, Wallace, NC).

SUE ANN MOUTON - Lighter colored pink. Very large, semidouble. (Sport of Japonica 'Mathotiana Supreme'). (U.S. 1960 - Broussard, LA).

SUE GREEN - White shading to Pink. Medium to large, anemone form. Vigorous, upright growth. E-M. (U.S. 1997 - Habel).

SUE GWATHMEY - Light Rose Pink. Large, semidouble to loose peony form. Average, bushy growth. M. (U.S. 1958 - Davis).

SUE KENDALL - Medium Pink. Miniature, formal double. Vigorous, open, upright growth. E-L. (U.S. 1998 - D. Kendall, Modesto, CA).

SUE KENDALL VARIEGATED - Medium Pink variegated White variation of 'Sue Kendall'.

SUE LAURENT - Salmon Pink. Large, peony form. Average, upright growth. M-L. (N.Z. 1993 - J. Rivett, Whakatane).

SUE SEELEY - Light Rose Pink. Large, loose peony form. Upright growth. M. (U.S. 1959).

SUE WILDER - Pink. Large, anemone form with large, loose, slightly wavy petals. Average growth. M. (U.S. 1964 - R. W. Wilder, Fairhope, AL).

SUG EDWARDS - Pink. Large, semidouble with wavy, crinkled petals. Average growth. M. (U.S. 1977 - Mrs. S. G. Edwards, Savannah, GA).

SUGAR BABE - Dark Pink to Red. Miniature, formal double. Slow growth. M. (U.S. 1959 - Hartman).

SUGAR DADDY - Pink. Large, semidouble. Vigorous, upright, spreading growth. M. (U.S. 1968 - W. H. Fleetwood, Savannah, GA).

SUGAR PLUM FAIRY - Medium Pink with Light Pink frosting toward the center of each petal. Miniature, formal double with incurved petals. Average, upright, dense growth. L. (Seedling of Japonica 'Tar Baby'). (U.S. 2018 - Pat Johnson, Cairo, GA).

SULPHUROUS - Rosy Salmon Pink edged darker Pink with occasional White stripe. Medium, formal double. Bushy growth. M-L. (Aus. 1880 - Shepherd).

SULTANA - Scarlet. Large to very large, semidouble to peony form. (Sport of Japonica 'Mathotiana'). (U.S. 1955 - McCaskill).

SUMMER PEARL - Very Light Pink with Red or Pink stripes with Yellow anthers and White filaments. Small to medium, semidouble to loose peony to rose form double. Vigorous, upright, spreading growth. E-L. (U.S. 2013 - James and Elaine Smelley).

SUMMER SUNSET - Orchid to Salmon Pink. Large, loose peony form. Vigorous, upright growth. M. (U.S. 1959 - Fisher).

SUN DIAL - Creamy White at base to Flesh Pink striped Red. Medium, anemone form. Slow, compact growth. M. (U.S. 1950 - Short).

SUN KISSED - Soft Pink with two outer petals and one center petal marked White. Medium, anemone form. M-L. (U.S. 1965 - Mrs. M. M. Hitchcock, Little Rock, AR).

SUN STORM - Dark Red with Blackish veining. Miniature, single form. Slow, dense growth. E-L. (N.Z. 2005 - R. J. MacDonald, Waiuku).

SUNBURST - Red. Medium, semidouble with sunburst of stamens showing through fluffy petals. Vigorous, upright growth. M. (U.S. 1957 - W. G. Parker, Montgomery, AL).

SUNDAE - Crimson with mass of Creamy White petaloids overlaid with Light Carmine. Miniature, anemone form. Average, upright growth. M. (N.Z. 1989 - Jury).

SUNDANCE - Dark Red with veining. Medium, semidouble with notched petals. Average, upright growth. M-L. (U.S. 1995 - M. Sherman, Albany, GA).

SUNDAY MORNING - Light Rose Pink. Large, semidouble. Average, upright growth. E-M. (U.S. 1959 - Dr. R. H. Segrest, Bonifay, FL).

SUNDOWNER - Deep Wine Red. Very large, rose form double. Vigorous, upright growth. M-L. (U.S. 1988 - H. Hall).

SUNNY JIM - White with peppermint candy stripes. Large, semidouble with irregular stamens. (U.S. 1953 - Fruitland).

SUNNY SIDE - White at center blending to Pink at edge. Small to medium, single. Average, compact, upright growth. E-M. (U.S. 1990 - Nuccio's).

SUN-RAY - Rose Red. Medium, semidouble. Vigorous, compact, upright growth. M. (U.S. 1959 - Dalraida Nsy., Montgomery, AL).

SUNSET GLORY - Coral Pink. Large, anemone form with long guard petals. Vigorous, open, upright growth. E-L. (For a variation of this cultivar see 'Owen Henry'). (U.S. 1951 - Short).

SUNSET GLORY VARIEGATED - Coral Pink blotched White variation of 'Sunset Glory'.

SUNSET OAKS - Pale Pink edged Deep Pink. Medium, semidouble. (Sport of Japonica 'Finlandia'). (U.S. 1965 - Kramer).

SUN-UP - Coral Pink. Large, loose peony form. Average, upright growth. E. (U.S. 1955 - Short).

SUN-UP VARIEGATED - Coral Pink blotched White variation of 'Sun-Up'.

SURPRISE - Pale Pink striped deeper Pink. Medium, rose form double. Average, upright growth. M. (U.S. Early 1900's - Magnolia).

SURVIVOR - Pink. Medium, full peony form. Average, open growth. M-L. (U.S. 1986 - J. B. McFerrin, Gainesville, FL).

SUSAN CARTER - See 'Frizzle White'.

SUSAN ELSOM - Bright Scarlet. Large, semidouble to peony form. Vigorous, upright growth. M. (Aus. 1963 - A. W. Jessep, Malvern).

SUSAN JOHNSON - White. Large, semidouble. Bushy, upright growth. M. (U.S. 1975 - Dr. G. R. Johnson, Carthage, TX).

SUSAN JONES - Rose Red. Large, semidouble. Vigorous, spreading, upright growth. E-M. (U.S. 1984 - Alfter).

SUSAN LYMAN WEARN - Blush Pink. Medium, formal double. Vigorous, open, upright growth. M. (U.S. 1965 - E. J. Prevatt, Bonneau, SC).

SUSAN PAGE SKINNER - White to Light Blush Pink marked Rose. Medium, semidouble with round petals. Vigorous, compact, upright growth. M. (U.S. 1964 - Julington).

SUSAN PILGRIM - Deep Rose Pink with a few White stripes. Small, anemone form. L. Cold hardy. (U.S. 1995 - Dr. C. Minarik. West Harwich, MA).

SUSAN SHACKELFORD - Pink to Deep Pink. Large, rose form double to thick semidouble. Average, spreading growth. M-L. (U.S. 1981 - Shackelford).

SUSAN SMITH - Light Pink. Medium, formal double. Average, upright growth. E. (U.S. 1986 - W. L. Smith, Tylertown, MS).

SUSAN STACEY - Red margined Purple. Large, semidouble of cupped form. (U.S. 1957 - J. H. Stacey, Bay Minnette, AL).

SUSAN STONE - Blush Pink. Medium, formal double. Average, compact growth. M. (U.S. 1953 - Mrs. W. E. Roughton, Thomasville, GA).

SUSAN TERZIAN - Rose Coral with darker veins. Large, semidouble to loose peony form to formal double. Average, compact, upright growth. M. (U.S. 1964 - L. H. Terzian, Fresno, CA).

SUSANN - Light Red to Deep Pink shading to Lighter Pink. Miniature, rose form double with three rows of tiny petals. (U.S. 1961 - F. Griffin, Sr., Columbia, SC).

SUSANNA BEARD - White with Pink outer petal edges. Large to very large, peony form. Vigorous, dense, upright growth. E-M. (U.S. 1996 - Jernigan).

SUSIE BENTLEY - Rose Pink. Large, semidouble to loose peony form. Vigorous, upright growth. E. (U.S. 1954 - Mrs. H. G. Bentley, Columbus, GA).

SUSIE FORTSON - Blood Red. Medium, semidouble. Vigorous, slender, upright growth. E-M. (U.S. 1965 - C. D. Cothran, Upland, CA).

SUSIE Q. - Deep Pink. Medium to large, loose peony form. Average growth. E-M. (U.S. 1960 - W. M. Quattlebaum, North Charleston, SC).

SUSIE Q. VARIEGATED - Deep Pink blotched White variation of 'Susie Q'.

SUTCLIFFE'S SUNSET - Rose Pink. Large, semidouble to peony form with wavy, upright petals. M. (N.Z. 1963 - Mrs. J. D. Crisp, Tiran).

SUZIE - White. Miniature, semidouble of cupped form with White petaloids in center. Average, upright growth. M-L. (U.S. 1958 - J. Audrey, San Fernando, CA).

SUZY NEWTON - Light Pink. Large, loose peony form. Slow, upright growth. M. (U.S. 1965 - C. E. Newton, Jr., Macon, GA).

SUZY STONE - Dark Red. Large, semidouble with irregular, somewhat crepe petals. Average, compact, upright growth. M. (U.S. 1975 - Gentry).

SUZY WONG - Light to Darker Salmon Pink. Large, peony form. Average growth. M. (China 1970 - Dr. Lee Chan Wong, Hong Kong).

SWAMP BUGGY - White with Pink stripes with Golden anthers and White filaments. Large, semidouble. Average, upright growth. M. (U.S. 2017 - Gilley).

SWAN LAKE (MONROVIA) - White. Large, loose peony form to rose form double to formal double. Vigorous, compact, upright growth. M. (Name previously used for a non-reticulata Hybrid cultivar). (U.S. 1971 - Monrovia Nsy., Monrovia, CA).

SWEET AFTON - Rose Red. Large, semidouble to loose peony form with petaloids and upright petals intermixed with stamens in center. Average, spreading growth. M. (U.S. 1965 - Novick).

SWEET AND LOW - Pink. Medium, single of tulip form. Average, pendulous growth. M. (U.S. 1951 - Short).

SWEET AUBURN - RHSCC 66D, moderate Purplish Pink, with Yellow anthers and Yellow-White filaments. Very large, semidouble. Vigorous, upright growth. M-L. (U.S. 2014 - Unknown origin, Auburn, AL).

SWEET BONAIR - Cream White. Medium, semidouble. Vigorous, upright growth. M. Fragrant. (U.S. 1952 - Goletto).

SWEET CECILE - Pink. Medium, semidouble with veined petals. Average, willowy growth. E-M. (U.S. 1959).

SWEET DELIGHT - Rose Pink. Medium, semidouble to peony form. Vigorous, loose, upright growth. M. Fragrant. (U.S. 1937 - Reeves).

SWEET DREAMS - Pale Orchid Pink. Medium, formal double. Vigorous, compact, upright growth. M-L. (U.S. 1984 - Nuccio's).

SWEET LARA - Red. Medium, formal double. Average open spreading growth. E-M. Cold hardy. (U.S. 2000 - V. Stone, Baton Rouge, LA).

SWEET MARY - Blush Pink center petals darkening to Shell Pink on the outer petals. Medium, formal double having a swirled pattern about 40% of the time. Average, upright, dense growth. E-M. (U.S. 2019 - Mickey Moore, Americus, GA).

SWEET OLIVE - Pink. Small, formal double. Average, open, upright growth. M-L. (Aus. 1990 - T. Savige, Wirlinga, NSW).

SWEET SIXTEEN - Light Pink. Medium, semidouble with stamens tipped with Green anthers. Average, bushy growth. M. (U.S. 1949 - Domoto).

SWEET SUE - Red. Large, semidouble with irregular petals to full peony form. Vigorous, upright growth. M. (U.S. 1956 - Hudson).

SWEET YOUNG THING - Pale Pink with Lavender cast overlaid with Deep Rose. Medium, semidouble. Vigorous, bushy growth. M. (U.S. 1957 - McCaskill).

SWEETHEART - Soft Apricot Pink, occasionally marbled White. Medium, rose form double. (Sport of Japonica 'Bleichroeder Pink'). (U.S. 1958 - Arnesen).

SWEETIE PIE - Blush Pink with one or more Red stripes. Large to very large, semidouble with occasional rabbit ears. Vigorous, upright growth. E-M. (U.S. 1997 - D. Fitzgerald, Orlando, FL).

SWEETIE PIE RED - Mauve Red with Creamy Golden anthers and Creamy Golden filaments. Large to very large, semidouble. Rapid, upright, spreading growth. E-M. (Color sport of Japonica 'Sweetie Pie'). (U.S. 2005 - Jerry Conrad, Plymouth, FL).

SWEETII VERA - ('Lewellyn Variegated'). White and pale Pink. Medium to large, peony form. Vigorous, upright, open growth. M. (England 1832 - Sweet).

SWIRLING CLOUD - White. Large, semidouble with loose petals. Average, compact growth. M. (U.S. 1955 - Feathers).

SYLPHIDE - Pink. Medium, peony form. M. (Aus. 1962 - G. Waterhouse).

SYMPHONETTE - Bright Red. Medium, semidouble. Vigorous, upright growth. M. (U.S. 1946 - Fruitland).

T. C. PATIN - Light Red. Very large, full semidouble with irregular, large petals and spray of large stamens. Vigorous, bushy growth. M. (U.S. 1974 - T. C. Patin, Hammond, LA).

T. C. PATIN VARIEGATED - Light Red blotched and marked White variation of 'T C Patin'. (U.S. 1974 - T. C. Patin, Hammond, LA).

T. K. VARIEGATED - Light Pink edged darker Pink. Medium, semidouble. Vigorous, compact growth. M. (U.S. 1937 - Kiyono).

T. P. BOWEN - White with Blush Pink iridescent undertone. Miniature, formal double. Bushy growth. M. (U.S. 1977 - Haynie).

T. S. CLOWER, JR. - White with narrow Pink stripe. Medium, formal double. Vigorous, slender, open growth. M. (U.S. 1950 - Clower).

TABBS - Crimson marbled and blotched White. Medium to large, full peony form. (Sport of Japonica 'Helenor'). (Aus. 1856 - Guilfoyle).

TABITHA - Light Pink flushed Rose; sports White streaked Deep Rose or Red, Fuchsia, and Fuchsia with one White petal. Large, semidouble. Spreading, upright growth. L. (U.S. 1963 - Mrs. K. H. McEachern, Wilmington, NC).

TADA MEIBI - Rose overcast Salmon. Miniature, formal double with incurved center petals. Slow growth. E-M. (U.S. 1986 - Stone).

TAFFETA TUTU - Apricot Pink with Pink petal edges blending to Lemon Yellow at center. Large, semidouble to loose peony form with upright petals. Vigorous, upright growth. M. Fragrant. (U.S. 1959 - Dr. L. W. Fawns, Fresno, CA).

TAFUKU-BENTEN (HAPPY GODDESS) - ('Benten-Tsubaki'; 'Otafuku-Benten'). Pink blotched and edged White. Medium, single. Vigorous, spreading growth. M. (Japan 1956 - E. Satomi, Tokyo).

TAHITI - Bright Red. Medium, single with splayed stamens. Vigorous, upright growth. M. Fragrant. (Aus. 1959 - G. Waterhouse).

TAIHAI - See 'Osakazuki'.

TAI-HEI-RAKU - Pink. Medium to large, single with flared White stamens. See Higo.

TAI-TAI - Pink. Medium to large, formal double. Vigorous, spreading growth. E-M. (U.S. 1966 - J. P. Woo, Fresno, CA).

TAKANE-NO-YUKI - Soft Pink petals, veined Deeper Pink with wide, White center, with Gold anthers and White filaments. Medium, single with crinkled edges. (Japan 1931 - Tôbei Yoshida, Kiso River, Chûbu).

TAKANINI - Deep Purplish Red. Small to medium, semidouble, anemone form centered. Vigorous, upright growth. E-L. (N.Z. 1989 - Haydon).

TALLAHASSEE GIRL - Blush Pink. Medium, semidouble to peony form. Upright growth. M. (U.S. 1948 - Rosa).

TALMONT - White. Large, formal double. Average, spreading, upright growth. E-M. (U.S. 1967 - Mrs. W. P. Bevis, Tallahassee, FL).

TAM O'SHANTER - Deep Rose outer petals and dainty Pink center petals. Medium to large, rose form double. Average, compact, upright growth. M-L. (U.S. 1967 - Haynie).

TAMA AMERICANA - Rose Red with broad White border. Medium, semidouble with occasional petaloids. Average, open, upright growth. E-M. (U.S. 1993 - Nuccio's).

TAMA BAMBINO - Rose Pink bordered White. Miniature to small, peony form with narrow, pointed petals. Average, upright growth. E-M. (U.S. 1993 - Nuccio's).

TAMA BEAUTY - Rose Pink bordered White. Medium to large, loose peony form. Average, dense growth. E-M. (U.S. 1993 - Nuccio's).

TAMA BELL - White with Red at base of petals. Miniature to small, bell-shaped single. Vigorous, loose, upright growth. E-M. (U.S. 1993 - Nuccio's).

TAMA CAROUSEL - Pink with a White border. Medium, semidouble with center petals that standup and occasional petaloids. Medium, upright, bushy growth. E-M. (Japonica 'Tama-no-ura' X Japonica 'Nuccio's Carousel'). (U.S. 2014 - Bradford King, Arcadia, CA).

TAMA ELECTRA - Brilliant Dark Red bordered White. Small to medium, single. Vigorous, compact, upright growth. E-M. (U.S. 1993 - Nuccio's).

TAMA GLITTERS - Red bordered White. Medium to large, semidouble to loose peony form. Average, spreading, upright growth. E-M. (U.S. 1993 - Nuccio's).

TAMA LOCH LAUREL - Red with White border around petals with Yellow anthers and White filaments. Medium, loose peony to semidouble with petals in center of flower are narrow, similar to petaloids. Average, upright growth. M. (Japonica 'Tama Electra' seedling). (U.S. 2016 - Mark Crawford, Valdosta, GA).

TAMA PEACOCK - Maroonish Red washing to a White border. Small to medium, semidouble form. Upright, pendulous growth. M-L. (U.S. 2000 - Nuccio's).

TAMA VELVET - Dark Red with a White border of varying width with Yellow anthers and White filaments. Medium, semidouble. Average, upright, spreading growth. E-M. (Seedling of Japonica 'Tama-no-ura'). (U.S. 2018 - Nuccio's).

TAMA VINO - Wine Red washing to broad White border. Small to medium, semidouble with long, narrow petals. Average, upright growth. E-M. (U.S. 1993 - Nuccio's).

TAMA-IKARI - Light Pink. Medium, single with circular Pale Yellow stamens. See Higo.

TAMA-NO-URA - Red bordered White. Small to medium, single. Vigorous, upright growth. M. (Japan 1973 to U.S. 1978 - Nuccio's).

TAMIE FRASER - Pale Pink center shading to Deeper Pink on outer petal edges. Large, anemone form to peony form. Average, dense, upright growth. M-L. (Aus. 1989 - M. Fraser, Nareen, Vic.).

TAMLIN FORTNER - Dark Red with Yellow anthers and Red filaments. Large to very large, semidouble. Average, upright, open growth. M-L. (Seedling of Japonica 'Scarlet Glory'). (U.S. 2017 - Pat Johnson, Cairo, GA).

TAMMIA - White with Pink center and border. Miniature to small, formal double with incurved geometric petals. Average, compact, upright growth. M-L. (U.S. 1971 - Tammia).

TAMMIA BLUSH - Blush Pink center with Darker Pink border. (Sport of Japonica 'Tammia'). (U.S. 1977 - Tammia).

TAMMIA FIRE OPAL - White flecked and streaked radiant Scarlet. (Sport of Japonica 'Tammia'). (U.S. 1978 - J L Carvain, Dallas, TX).

TAMMIA SPECKLED - White with sunken center and border, with Red speckles. Miniature to small, formal double with incurved geometric petals. Average, compact, upright growth. M-L. (Sport of Japonica 'Tammia').

TAMMY - Bright Pink. Large, formal double. Vigorous, upright, dense growth. E-M. (U.S. 2013 - Howell).

TANCHO - White streaked Crimson. Medium, single. See Higo.

TAR BABY - Blood Red. Medium, anemone form. Average, upright growth. M. (U.S. 1985 - Dr. M. B. Wine, Thomasville, GA).

TARO-AN (NAME GIVEN TO JAPANESE TEA HOUSE) - Soft Pink. Medium, single with large, round petals and heavy stamens of magnolia form. Vigorous growth. E-M. (Japan 1936 - Chugai).

TASASAGO - Pale Pink. Medium, single with flared Pale Yellow stamens. See Higo.

TATA - White. Large to very large, semidouble. Vigorous, spreading, upright growth. M-L. (U.S. 1991 - Nuccio's).

TE DEUM - ('Dr. Shepherd'; 'Firegold'; 'Moragne'; 'Pasha of Persia'; 'Shah of Persia'). Dark Red. Large, semidouble to formal double. Slow, open growth. M-L. (Probably same as cultivar 'Grand Sultan' which would have priority but, as 'Te Deum' has been in such common use in the US, we do not believe a change is necessary or warranted). (Europe to U.S. 1890 - Tea Gardens).

TEA GARDEN 45 - Dark Red. Medium, semidouble of cupped form. Vigorous, compact growth. L. (U.S. 1942 - Tea Gardens).

TECKLA - Coral Pink. Medium, semidouble with crepe petals. Average, upright growth. M-L. (U.S. 1958 - E. L. Stelling, Augusta, GA).

TECKLA VARIEGATED - Deep Pink and White variation of 'Teckla'.

TED KOHL - Rose Red. Large, full semidouble. Average, compact growth. (U.S. 1958 - J. W. Bradford, San Diego, CA).

TED KOHL VARIEGATED - Rose Red heavily blotched White variation of 'Ted Kohl.'

TEDD GILLEY - Dark Red. Large, loose peony form. Average, spreading, upright growth. M. (U.S. 1973 - Gilley).

TEDDIE ULMER - Deep Red. Medium to large, semidouble. Average, upright growth. M. (U.S. 1972 - Mealing).

TEDDY, JR. - Fuchsia Pink. Small, semidouble to rose form double with small upright petaloids with lily-like tops. (U.S. 1961 - F. Griffin, Sr., Columbia, SC).

TEE BIRD - Pink with red stripes and flecks. Small, formal double; the bloom has a large center bud. Average, upright, dense growth. L. (U.S. 2016 - Howell).

TEEN AGE QUEEN - Blush Pink usually with one small Pink stripe. Large, thick semidouble. Compact, upright growth. M. (U.S. 1969 - Shackelford).

TEN BELOW - Bright Red. Large, semidouble. M. Cold hardy. (U.S. 1960 - Ashby).

TENJU - Blush Pink. Medium to large, wavy petaled single with flared Pale Yellow stamens. See Higo.

TENNIN-KWAN - See 'Nagasaki'.

157

TERESA RAGLAND - Deep Coral Pink with White stamens. Large, semidouble with six separated fascicles of stamens in a circle spreading over petals and small, folded, swirled petals in center of incurved stamens. Average, open growth. M. (U.S. 1959 - Ragland).

TERINGA - Crimson. Large, single. Vigorous, upright growth. E-M. (Aus. 1955 - Turnbull).

TERRY CLAYTON NEWELL - Light Pink. Large, semidouble to peony form. Vigorous, upright growth. E-L. (U.S. 1966 - Bray).

TERRY GILLEY - Brilliant Red with Yellow anthers and Cream filaments. Large, semidouble with wavy, crinkled petals. Vigorous, upright growth. E-M. (Japonica 'Dr. W. G. Lee' x Japonica 'Tomorrow's Dawn'). (U.S. 1974 - Gilley).

TERRYE ELLER - Light Blush Pink with Darker Pink margins and suffused Darker Pink. Small, rose form double. Average growth. E-M. (U.S. 1960 - J. E. Miller, New Orleans, LA).

THANKSGIVING - Turkey Red. Large, semidouble. Vigorous, open growth. E-M. (U.S. 1959 - H. Larson, Orange, CA).

THE BRIDE - Blush Pink. Medium, formal double. Vigorous growth. M. (U.S. 1958 - Shackelford).

THE CZAR - Light Crimson. Large, semidouble. Slow, sturdy growth. M. (For another form of this cultivar see 'Hugh Kennedy'). (Aus. 1913 - N. Breslin, Melbourne).

THE CZAR VARIEGATED - Light Crimson blotched White variation of 'The Czar'.

THE DAFFODIL - Deep Rose. Medium, semidouble resembling a deep cup daffodil. (U.S. 1953 - Fruitland).

THE ELF - Light Pink. Medium to large, semidouble. Slow, compact, dwarf growth. M. (U.S. 1984 - Alfter).

THE FLIRT - Blush Pink. Large, semidouble with undulating, notched petals and two or three large petaloids interspersed with White stamens. Average, upright growth. M. (U.S. 1961 - Ragland).

THE MIKADO - Rose Pink with narrow, White border. Medium, semidouble. (Sport of Japonica 'Herme'). (Japan to England 1889 - G. Waller).

THE PILGRIM - Cream White. Large, full peony form. Average, upright growth. M. (U.S. 1956 - Short).

THE REAL McCOY - White. Large, semidouble with irregular petals. Vigorous, upright growth. M. (U.S. 1959 - F. McCoy, Fairhope, AL).

THE SAM STALLINGS - Cream White. Large, semidouble with stamens intermixed with petals. (U.S. 1961 - S. H. Stallings, Smithfield, NC).

THELMA DALE - Phlox Pink form of 'Mrs. Baldwin Wood'. Medium, semidouble. (U.S. 1948 - Bradford).

THELMA DALE BLUSH - Blush Pink. (Sport of Japonica 'Thelma Dale'). (U.S. 1963 - E F Wilkerson, Biloxi, MS).

THELMA SANFORD - See 'Ruth Royer'.

THEME SONG - Red. Medium to large, semidouble with stamen cluster. Slow, compact, upright growth. M. (U.S. 1975 - Novick).

THEO DE TULLIO - Light tinted Blush Pink. Large, semidouble with three alternate rows of sweet pea shaped, curved petals and narrower, curved center petals. Average, open, upright growth. M. (U.S. 1965 - Julington).

THEO'S MINI - Rose Pink. Miniature, anemone form. Average growth. M. (U.S. 1981 - Stone).

THEOLA CLARK - Rose Red. Large, peony form with White stamens. Vigorous, compact growth. M-L. (U.S. 1962 - Dr. Parker, Lucedale, MS).

THERESA BURNHAM - Dark Red. Medium, formal double. Average, upright, dense growth. E-M. (Japonica 'Marc Eleven' x unknown pollen parent). (U.S. 2013 - Walter Creighton, Semmes, AL).

THERESA MARIE - White spotted Pink and Red. Medium, rose form double to peony form. Vigorous growth. (U.S. 1951 - Malbis Nursery, Daphne, AL).

THIRTY DROPS - Delicate Pink. Miniature, anemone form. Vigorous, upright growth. M. (U.S. 1971 - D. C. Strother, Fort Valley, GA).

THOMAS CORNELIUS COLE - Bright Rose Pink. Large to very large, semidouble. Upright growth. M-L. (Aus. 1956 - Cole).

THOMAS D. PITTS - ('Snow White' [Rosedale Nursery]). White. Medium, formal double. Vigorous, compact, upright growth. M-L. (U.S. 1954 - Nuccio's).

THOMAS PLANT - See 'Frau Geheimrat Oldevig'.

THOMAS TRESEDER - Salmon Rose veined Rose. Medium, rose form double to peony form. Compact, upright growth. M. (Aus. 1949 - Hazelwood).

THOMAS WALTER SAVIGE - Red. Large, rose form double to peony form. Vigorous, spreading growth. M-L. (Aus. 1995 - T. Savige, Wirlinga, NSW).

THOMASVILLE BEAUTY - Soft Pink. Large, anemone form with some White, Pink and fimbriated petaloids. Average, spreading growth. E-M. (U.S. 1969 - Dr. M. B. Wine, Thomasville, GA).

THOMPSONII - White flecked and penciled Pink; sports Light Pink to Pink. Medium, full peony form. Vigorous, open, upright growth. E-M. (England. 1838 - Thompson).

THUMBELLINA - Rose Red sometimes edged darker. Small to medium, formal double. (Sport of Japonica 'Tom Thumb'). (U.S. 1977 - A. Krueger, Monterey Park, CA).

THUNDERBOLT - See 'Glen 40 Variegated'.

THUNDERHEAD - See 'Mrs. Baldwin Wood.'

TIARA - Orange Red. Medium, semidouble to formal double. Vigorous, compact, upright growth. M. (U.S. Early 1900's - Magnolia).

TIARA VARIEGATED - Orange Red and White form of 'Tiara'.

TICK TOCK - White striped and flecked Cherry Red. Large, full peony form. Vigorous, upright growth. E-M. (U.S. 1955 - Tick Tock).

TICK TOCK BLUSH - Blush Pink. (Sport of Japonica 'Tick Tock'). (U.S. 1962 - Tammia).

TICK TOCK RED - Red. (Sport of Japonica 'Tick Tock').

TICK TOCK RED VARIEGATED - Red marked White variation of 'Tick Tock Red'.

TICK TOCK SPECKLED - White speckled and marked Cherry Red. (Sport of Japonica 'Tick Tock'). (U.S. 1965 - Tick Tock).

TICKLED PINK - Fluorescent Pink. Medium to large, loose peony form with fluffy, outer petals. Vigorous, upright growth. E-M. (U.S. 1959 - Tammia).

TICKLED PINK VARIEGATED - Pink blotched White variation of 'Tickled Pink.'

TIDDLYWINKS - Light Pink striped Dark Pink. Miniature, formal double. Average, upright growth. L. (U.S. 1981 - J. A. Lynch, Franklinton, LA).

TIFFANY - Light Orchid Pink to Deeper Pink at edge. Large to very large, loose peony form to anemone form. Vigorous, upright growth. M. (U.S. 1962 - Dr. J. H. Urabec, La Cañada, CA).

TIFFANY'S DAWN - Pale Pink. Medium, semidouble to anemone form. Slow, upright growth. M-L. (Aus. 2002 - Jim Scott, Howrah, Tasmania).

TIFFY J - Blush Pink. Very large, loose peony form to rose form double. Average, spreading, upright growth. M. (U.S. 1991 - O. Jacobson, Jacksonville Beach, FL).

TIKI - Rosy Salmon with petaloids streaked White and edged Rosy Salmon. Small, anemone form. Vigorous, compact, upright growth. M. (U.S. 1962 - McCaskill).

TIL ANDIA - White. Large, semidouble. (U.S. 1955 - Domoto).

TILLIE RICE - See 'Claudia Phelps'.

TILLIE WIRTH - Pink and White. Large to very large, semidouble to loose peony form. (Sport of Japonica 'Big Beauty'). (U.S. 1954 - H. G. Fritchie, Slidell, LA).

TIM CROCKER'S PINK - Medium Pink. Small to medium, formal double, star form. Average, upright growth. M-L. (U.S. 2001 - Eileen C. Hart, Odessa, FL).

TIMOTHY GILLEY - Rose Pink. Large, semidouble with wavy, crinkled petals. Average growth. M. (U.S. 1982 - Gilley).

TINA - White. Large, formal double. Average, compact, upright growth. E. (U.S. 1977 - Gilley).

TINA GILLIARD - Pink. Medium, semidouble with wavy petals. Vigorous, compact, upright growth. M. (U.S. Early 1900's - Magnolia).

TINKER BELL - White striped Pink and Rose Red. Small, anemone form. Vigorous, upright growth. E-M. (For another form of this cultivar see 'Jingle Bells'). (U.S. 1958 - Nuccio's).

TINKER TOY - White speckled and striped Rose Red. Miniature, anemone form. Average, compact growth. M. (U.S. 1981 - Nuccio's).

TINKY LEE - Soft Rose Pink. Medium, formal double to rose form double. Vigorous, upright growth. E-M. (U.S. 1947 - Lee).

TINKY LEE VARIEGATED - Soft Rose Pink and White form of 'Tinky Lee'.

TINSIE - ('Bokuhan'). Red outer guard petals and White center. Miniature, anemone form. Vigorous, upright growth. E-M. (Japan to U.S. 1930 - Star).

TINSIE GOLD - Red outer guard petals and White center. Miniature, anemone form. Average, dense, upright growth. E-M. (Genetic leaf sport of Japonica 'Tinsie'; leaves having a wide Yellow border.). (Aus. 1992 - Dr. G. Downe, Endeavor Hills, Vic.).

TINSIE TWO - Deep Rose Red outer guard petals with Pink stamens and petaloids. Small, anemone form. Average, compact, upright growth. E-M. (U.S. 1959 - Short).

TINSLEY SMITH - Cherry Red to Dark Rose Red veined Dark Red. Large, semidouble with wavy petals and five groups of stamens flaring in star-like formation. Average, spreading growth. M. (U.S. 1952 - Miss R. Loman, Wilmington, NC).

TINSLEY SMITH VARIEGATED - Dark Rose Red and White variation of 'Tinsley Smith'.

TINY BELL - Salmon Pink. Small, semidouble to loose anemone form. Average, compact growth. M-L. (U.S. 1966 - Domoto).

TINY BUD - Clear Pink. Small, peony form. M-L. (U.S. 1955 - Mrs. C. Grischow, Portland, OR).

TINY ME - Light Pink with light to heavy variegation. Miniature, anemone form. Average, open, upright growth. M-L. (U.S. 1969 - Haynie).

TINY ROSE - Rose Pink. Miniature, semidouble. Average, upright growth. M. (U.S. 1997 - Domoto).

TINY TOT - White with occasional Pink streak. Miniature, formal double. Average, open, upright growth. M-L. (U.S. 1961 - Short).

TIP TIPTON - Pink. Medium to large, semidouble with irregular petals to peony form. Average growth. E. (U.S. 1963 - A. L. Tipton, Albany, GA).

TIP TOP - White with occasional Pink stripe. Miniature, formal double. Slow, upright growth. M-L. (U.S. 1980 - Mealing).

TOBY - Red. Large, semidouble. Vigorous, upright growth. M-L. (U.S. 1998 - P. Gilley, Grand Ridge, FL).

TODD GILLEY - Bright Dark Red. Large, peony form with velvet texture. Average, spreading, upright growth. M. (U.S. 1974 - Gilley).

TOICHI DOMOTO - Rose Pink with Deep Rose Pink stripes. Medium, formal double to rose form double. Slow, upright, compact growth. E-M. (U.S. 2006 - Nuccio's).

TOKAYAMA - White. Medium, formal double. Average, bushy growth. M. (Japan 1956 - Satomi).

TOKI-NO-HAGASANE (FEATHER OF WILD GOOSE) - ('Bessie Morse Bellingrath'; 'Ubane'; 'Kent Deigaard'; 'Betty Hopfer'). White blushed Pink with deeper Pink under petals. Medium, semidouble. Slow, Compact growth. L. (Japan 1934 - Chugai).

TOM CAT - Light Rose Pink. Large, semidouble with irregular, fluted petals. Average, open, upright growth. M-L. (U.S. 1964 - Dr. A. C. Tuck, Thomasville, GA).

TOM CAT VARIEGATED - Light Rose Pink blotched White variation of 'Tom Cat'.

TOM CLOWER - Phlox Pink. Medium, formal double. Vigorous, open growth. L. (U.S. 1950 - Clower).

TOM EAGLESON - Bright Red. Medium to large, rose form double. Vigorous, compact, upright growth. M. (U.S. 1973 - T. Eagleson, Port Arthur, TX).

TOM HATLEY - Vivid Deep Red with Yellow anthers and White to Pink filaments. Medium to large, classic semidouble to sometimes irregular semidouble. Average, upright, open growth. M. (U.S. 2011 - M. Thomas Hatley, Charlotte, NC).

TOM HERRIN - White marked Red, occasionally sporting Red. Large, semidouble to peony form. Vigorous, upright growth. M. (U.S. 1962 - Herrin).

TOM HERRIN RED - Red. (Sport of Japonica 'Tom Herrin').

TOM HOWE - Whit striped Pink. Large, single to anemone form. Upright growth. E-M. (U.S. 1959 - Azalea Glen).

TOM KNUDSEN - Dark Red with darker veining. Medium, formal double to rose form double to full peony form. Vigorous, compact, upright growth. E-M. (U.S. 1965 - Maitland).

TOM THUMB - Pink with each petal edged White. Small to medium, formal double. Average, upright growth. M. (For another form of this cultivar see 'Thumbellina'). (U.S. 1957 - A. Krueger, Monterey Park, CA).

TOM THUMB BLUSH - Blush Pink. (Sport of Japonica 'Tom Thumb'). (U.S. 1999 - V. Stone, Baton Rouge, LA).

TOMMIE BOWMAN - Red with Purple tint. Medium, anemone form. Average, dense, upright growth. E-M. Cold hardy. (U.S. 2000 - Elizabeth R. Scott, Aiken, SC).

TOMO-CHI-CHI - Dark Red. Large, semidouble to loose peony form. M. (U.S. 1959 - A. Funk, Savannah, GA).

TOMORROW - ('Ed Anderson'). Strawberry Red. Large to very large, semidouble with irregular petals and large petaloids to full peony form. Vigorous, open, slightly pendulous growth. E-M. (U.S. 1953 - Tick Tock).

TOMORROW CROWN JEWEL - White brushed Red in throat with occasional streak of Red on one or more petals. Large to very large, semidouble to full peony form. (Sport of Japonica 'Tomorrow'). (U.S. 1967 - Tick Tock).

TOMORROW PARK HILL - Light soft Pink generally deepening toward edge with some White variegation. Large to very large, semidouble to full peony form. (Sport of Japonica 'Tomorrow Variegated'). (U.S. 1964 - Peer).

TOMORROW PARK HILL BLUSH - Soft Light Pink. Large to very large, semidouble to full peony form. (Sport of Japonica 'Tomorrow Park Hill'). (U.S. 1979 - R. S. Magee, Bogalusa, LA).

TOMORROW PARK HILL FIMBRIATED - Soft Pink similar to 'Tomorrow Park Hill' with Yellow anthers and Yellow filaments. Large, semidouble to full peony form; the fimbriation is reliable, but varies from light to medium extending from center of bloom outward. Vigorous, upright, spreading growth. E-M. (Sport of Japonica 'Tomorrow Park Hill'). (U.S. 2016 - Jim Pinkerton, Lugoff, SC and Herbert Racoff, Columbia, SC).

TOMORROW PARK HILL PINK - Large to very large, semidouble to loose peony form. (Sport of Japonica 'Tomorrow Park Hill' without White variegation).

TOMORROW PEONY VARIEGATED - Strawberry Red. Large to very large, full peony form. (Sport of Japonica 'Tomorrow Variegated'). (U.S. 1966 - R E Ward, Jr., Birmingham, AL).

TOMORROW SUPREME - See 'Tomorrow Variegated'.

TOMORROW TUXEDO - See 'Tomorrow Variegated'.

TOMORROW VARIEGATED - ('Maverick'; 'Tomorrow Supreme'; 'Tomorrow Tuxedo'). Strawberry Red blotched White variation of 'Tomorrow'. Large to very large, semidouble to full peony form. (For another variation of this cultivar see 'Queen of Tomorrow').

TOMORROW WHITE - White. Large to very large, semidouble to full peony form. (Sport of Japonica 'Tomorrow'). (U.S. 1984 - J. Movich, La Verne, CA).

TOMORROW, LEANNE'S - Coral Rose. Large to very large, semidouble to full peony form. (Sport of Japonica 'Tomorrow'). (U.S. 1964 - L Ming, Natchez, MS).

TOMORROW, MARBURY'S LIGHT PINK - Light Pink edged Lighter Pink to White. Large to very large, semidouble to full peony form. (Sport of Japonica 'Tomorrow'). (U.S. 1977 - Marbury).

TOMORROW'S DAWN - Deep soft Pink to Light Pink shading to White at edge with some White petaloids and one or more petals having streak of Red. Large to very large, semidouble to full peony form. (Sport of Japonica 'Tomorrow'). (For a variation of this cultivar see 'Tomorrow, Leanne's'). (U.S. 1960 - L Ruffin and R Allums, Ellisville, MS).

TOMORROW'S DAWN BESSIE - Same as parent except wide border of White. Large to very large, semidouble to full peony form. (Sport of Japonica 'Tomorrow's Dawn'). (U.S. 1979 - B. Waters, Kilgore, TX).

TOMORROW'S DAWN BLUSH - Blush Pink with White border. Large to very large, semidouble to full peony form. (Sport of Japonica 'Tomorrow's Dawn'). (U.S. 1982 - C. Copeland, MS).

TOMORROW'S DELIGHT - Soft Creamy White with a few flecks and streaks of Red. Large to very large, semidouble to full peony form. (Sport of Japonica 'Tomorrow'). (U.S. 1971 - J. Fuller, Montgomery, AL).

TOMORROW'S LISA - Blush White with Red flakes and few streaks of Pink turning Red. Large to very large, semidouble to full peony form. (Sport of Japonica 'Tomorrow Park Hill'). (U.S. 1977 - A. P. Fatherree, Jackson, MS).

TOMORROW'S SWEET IMAGE - Pale Orchid Pink heavily variegated White. Large to very large, semidouble to full peony form. (Sport of Japonica 'Tomorrow Park Hill'). (Reported as similar to 'Tomorrow Park Hill'). (U.S. 1972 - J L Carvain, Fort Worth, TX).

TOMORROW'S TROPIC DAWN - White with occasional Red line or dash, fading to Blush as flower ages. Large to very large, semidouble to full peony form. (Sport of Japonica 'Tomorrow's Dawn'). (U.S. 1967 - R M Merino, Fresno, CA).

TONNIE LECHE - See 'Alba Superba'.

TONYA - Brilliant Red. Large, semidouble with wavy, crinkled petals. Vigorous, compact, upright growth. E-M. (U.S. 1976 - Gilley).

TOOEY - Soft Pink. Large, loose peony form with incurved petals covering stamens. Slow, open, upright growth. M. (U.S. 1965 - Ashby).

TOOTIE - Pink. Large to very large, semidouble. Average, upright growth. E-M. (U.S. 1982 - M. McLeod, Monticello, FL).

TOOTSIE - Chalk White. Miniature, formal double, sometimes in form of five pointed star. Slow, open, spreading growth. M-L. (U.S. 1967 - R. E. Ward, Jr., Birmingham, AL).

TOP O' THE MORN - Pink striped and blended Red. Large, semidouble. Vigorous, compact growth. M-L. (U.S. 1957 - Hearn).

TORI-NO-KO (CHICKEN) - Pinkish White slightly striped darker Pink. Large, semidouble of lotus form. Slow, compact growth. M-L. (Japan 1956 - E. Satomi, Tokyo).

TOTTS - White to Creamy Yellow. Very large, peony form. Vigorous, dense, upright growth. M-L. (U.S. 1993 - R. Ehrhart, Walnut Creek, CA).

TOUCH OF PINK - Blush Pink to Deeper Pink tipped edges. Large to very large, semidouble with irregular petals to anemone form. Vigorous, open, upright growth. E-M. (U.S. 1977 - Nuccio's).

TOUCHDOWN - Deep Rose Pink. Large to very large, loose peony form. (Sport of Japonica 'Kick Off'). (For another form of this cultivar see 'Cheerleader'). (U.S. 1962 - Nuccio's).

TOUCHDOWN BLUSH - Blush Pink. (Sport of Japonica 'Touchdown'). (U.S. 1975 - G. Stewart, Sacramento, CA).

TOY TRUMPET - Rose Pink. Miniature, semidouble. Vigorous, open, upright growth. M. (U.S. 1963 - Dr. L. E. Chow, Bakersfield, CA).

TREASURE ISLE - Clear Rose Pink. Large, full peony form. Vigorous, upright growth. M-L. (U.S. 1967 - Short).

TREV'S TINSIE - Rose Pink with Pink striped Cream petaloids. Small, anemone form. Slow, open, spreading growth. M-L. (N.Z. 1984 - T. Lennard, Te Puke).

TRICIA - Light Pink. Large, anemone form. (Sport of Japonica 'Pat Nixon'). (U.S. 1974 - Kramer).

TRICOLOR (SIEBOLD) - ('Wakanoura Variegated'). Waxy White streaked Carmine. Medium, semidouble of slightly cupped form. Vigorous, compact, upright growth. M. Cold hardy. (Variations of this cultivar include 'Dainty [California]'; 'Fred Sander'; 'Jewel Bowden'; 'Blush Tricolor'; 'Chalk Pink'). (Japan to Germany 1832 - Siebold).

TRICOLOR (SIEBOLD) FOLKI - See 'Lady de Saumarez'.

TRICOLOR (SIEBOLD) RED - ('Red Douglas'; 'Robin Hood'; 'Wakanoura Red'; 'Wakanoura-Aka'). Cold hardy. (Solid Red variation of 'Tricolor [Siebold]').

TRICOLOR (SIEBOLD) WHITE - See 'Leucantha'.

TRICOLOR CALIFORNIA - ('Crichton'). White striped Pink to solid color. Medium, semidouble. Average, compact growth. L. (For other forms of this cultivar, see 'Annie Laurie' and 'Lois Hill'). (U.S. 1928 - Armstrong).

TRICOLOR PINK - Pink with Rose color stripes with Yellow anthers and White filaments. Medium, semidouble of slightly cupped form. Vigorous, compact, upright growth. M. (Sport of Japonica 'Tricolor'). (U.S. 1937 - E. A. McIlhenny (Jungle Gardens), Avery Island, LA).

TRICOLOR SUPERBA - Variable colors from nearly White to Solid Red, but majority White striped Red or Light Pink margined white with Golden anthers and White filaments. Large, semidouble. M. (Seedling of Japonica 'Tricolor'). (U.S. 1945 - K. Sawada, Overlook Nurseries, Crichton, AL).

TRINKET - Soft Pink with shaded Pink center. Miniature to small, anemone form. Vigorous, bushy, upright growth. M. (U.S. 1973 - McCaskill).

TRIUMPH - Dark Red with Golden anthers and White filaments. Small, single. (U.S. 1942 - Magnolia Plantation & Gardens, Charleston, SC).

TRIUMPHANS - ('Triomphant'; 'Lady Parker Peony'; 'Allen's Pink'; 'Harmony'). Rose Pink splotched White. Large, peony form. Upright, open growth. M. (Belgium 1834).

TRIXEY - Bright Pink shading to White at center. Large, formal double. Slow, compact growth. L. (N.Z. 1998 - F. Upson, Kaponga).

TROJAN HORSE - Deep Pink. Large, semidouble to loose peony form. Average, upright growth. M. (U.S. 1968 - Wilkes Nsy., Moultrie, GA).

TROUBADOUR - Salmon Pink. Medium, semidouble of pine cone form. Average, compact, upright growth. M. (For another form of this cultivar, see 'Jessie Katz'). (Europe to U.S. [Magnolia] 1840's).

TRUDA JEAN - Pale Pink. Small to medium, single. Average, upright growth. E. (Aus. 1995 - Eryldene Trust, Gordon, NSW).

TRUDY - Red with Red stamens. Miniature, single with five petals. Vigorous, upright growth. M. (U.S. 1952 - F. F. Baker, Macon, GA).

TRUDY GEORGE - Pink with stripes as in 'Ben George' with Higo type stamen clusters; it has Yellow anthers and lighter colored filaments. Very large, single to semidouble. Vigorous, upright growth. M. (Sport of Japonica 'Ben George'). (U.S. 2008 - Hulyn Smith).

TRUE ECHOLS - Rose Red. Large, peony form. Average, upright growth. E-M. (U.S. 1980 - Gilley).

TRUE LOVE - Chalk White with faint dash of Pink on some petals. Large, semidouble to peony form shaped like six-pointed star. (U.S. 1959 - True's Camellias, Columbia, SC).

TSUBAKI'S BONA BELLA - Rose Pink with White marks on the center of the petals. Medium to large, formal double. Vigorous, upright growth. M-L. (Japonica 'Steve Blount' seedling). (U.S. 2013 - Tsubaki Camellias, Savannah, GA).

TSUKASA-NISHIKI - Pink mottled White. Medium, single. See Higo.

TUBBY HABEL - Dark Mahogany Red with dark veining. Medium to large, semidouble to anemone form. Average, spreading growth. L. (U.S. 1997 - Habel).

TUDOR BABY - Dark Red with petals edged Black. Small, formal double. Vigorous, upright growth. M. (U.S. 2001 - Hulyn Smith).

TUDOR BABY VARIEGATED - Dark Red, blotched White variation of 'Tudor Baby'. (U.S. 2001 - Hulyn Smith).

TUESDAY'S CHILD - Coral Red with Silver margined petals veined Red. Large, semidouble. Vigorous, upright growth. M. (U.S. 1960 - Camelliana).

TUFFET - Bright Red. Miniature, full peony form. Vigorous, upright growth. E-L. (U.S. 1963 - Mrs. B. Lindsey, San Diego, CA).

TURANDOT - Medium Red. Large, peony form. M-L. (U.S. - Parks).

TURNER DAVIS - White. Medium, formal double with incurved petals. Vigorous, compact, upright growth. M-L. (U.S. 1980 - J. Hintermister, Gainesville, FL).

TURNER'S CAMP - Dark Red. Large, semidouble with irregular petals. Average, compact growth. M. (U.S. 1954 - Turner).

TWILIGHT - Light Blush Pink. Medium to large, formal double. Vigorous, compact, upright growth. M. (U.S. 1964 - Nuccio's).

TWINKLE - White, occasionally dashed Pink. Miniature, semidouble. Average, upright growth. L. (U.S. 1958).

TYLER NATION - Coral Red. Large, semidouble with four rows of petals and inner petals wavy and fluted. Open, upright growth. E-M. (U.S. 1958 - H. E. Nation, Montgomery, AL).

UME-GAKI - (Screen of Apricot Blossoms). Pink. Large, single. See 'Higo'.

UNCLE JOHN - Purple Red. Large, full peony form. (U.S. 1955 - Malbis).

UNCLE SAM - ('Rosalie [California]'; 'Henry Barnett'). Rose Red. Large, rose form double. Vigorous, bushy growth. M. (For a variation of this cultivar see 'New Horizons'). (U.S. 1921 - Lindo).

UNCLE SAM VARIEGATED - See 'Mrs. Confer'.

UNCLE TOM - Light Purplish Pink with Yellow anthers and Pinkish filaments. Medium, full peony form. Vigorous, bushy growth. M. (U.S. 1948 - Malbis Nursery, Daphne, AL).

UNDAUNTED - Carmine Rose Pink. Medium, full peony form. Average, compact growth. L. (U.S. 1952 - Councilman).

UNFORGETTABLE - Light Pink. Large, anemone form to peony form. Vigorous, upright growth. E-L. (U.S. 1987 - M. Talia, Santa Clara, CA).

UNFORGETTABLE WHITE - White with Yellow anthers and Light Yellow filaments. Large, anemone form to peony form. Vigorous, upright growth. E-L. (Sport of Japonica 'Unforgettable').

UNRYU - Deep Pink. Small, single. Average, upright growth; each leaf is part of an unusual zigzag pattern. (Japan 1967 - Kyoto Garden Club).

USU-OTOME - See 'Pink Perfection'. ('Usu-Otome' is reported as priority name for this cultivar but, as 'Pink Perfection' [U.S. 1890's - Domoto] has been in such common use in the U.S., we do not believe a change is necessary or warranted). (Japan 1892 - Yokohama).

VAGABOND - Cardinal Red. Medium, single. Average growth. M. (Aus. 1971 - Tuckfield).

VAL PARKER - Deep Red. Large, semidouble, generally with small narrow petals standing upright and with surrounding stamens. Vigorous, compact, upright growth. M. (U.S. 1971 - Haynie).

VALE BEAUTY - White shading Pink in outer petals. Medium, formal double. Vigorous, compact upright growth. M. (Aus. 1977 - Camellia Vale Nsy., Bexley North, NSW).

VALE SUNSET - Dark Red. Medium, rose form double to peony form. Average, dense, spreading growth. M. (Aus. 1977 - Camellia Vale Nsy., Bexley North, NSW).

VALERIE - Metallic Red. Medium, semidouble. Vigorous, upright growth. E. (U.S. 1959 - Wells).

VALLEY DEE - White, sometimes streaked faint, soft Pink. Medium, loose peony form. Average, upright growth. M. (U.S. 1959 - Brodies Nsy., Biloxi, MS).

VALLEY DEE BLUSH - Very Light Purple with darker veining and White patches on some petals with Light Yellow anthers. Medium, loose peony form. Average, upright growth. M. (Sport of Japonica 'Valley Dee').

VALTEVAREDA - Pink shading to deeper Pink on outer petals. Medium, formal double of cupped form. Vigorous, compact, upright growth. L. (Italy 1853 - Rossi).

VALTEVAREDA VARIEGATED - Pink blotched White form of 'Valtevareda'.

VAN HARDEE - Red. Medium, full peony form. Average, compact growth. E-M. (U.S. 1959 - Van Hardee, Madison, FL).

VANDA - Pale Crimson. Small, formal double. Average, open upright growth. M. (Aus. 1969 - A. E. Campbell, St. Ives, NSW).

VARIEGATA - Deep Rose Pink mottled White. Medium, semidouble. Spreading growth. M. (China to England [Chandler] 1792).

VARIETY Z - Dark Pink (RHS 62A); the petaloids are Light Pink (RHS 62C) with Creamy White anthers and White filaments. Medium, rose form double to formal double. Average, upright growth. M. (U.S. 2009 - P. W. Zimmerman and Boyce Thompson, Yonkers, NY).

VASHTI - White splotched and striped Pink with occasional Red flowers. Medium, rose form double. Average, compact growth. M-L. (U.S. 1945 - F. L. Gibson, Thomasville, GA).

VAUGHN DRINKARD - Light Salmon to Dark Rose and White. (Variegated variation of Japonica 'Dona Julia'). (U.S. 1955 - Longview).

VEDRINE - ('Ruby Glow'; 'Margaret Lawrence'; 'Bolen's Pride'; 'Cleo Wittie'; 'Mrs. T. R. McKenzie'; 'Mehl's Red'; 'Payne's Red'; 'Lewis Red Peony'). Ruby Red. Medium to large, anemone to loose peony form. Vigorous, upright, spreading growth. E-M. (For a variation of this cultivar see 'Dr. Robert E. Schwartz'). (U.S. Early 1900's - Mary Swords Debaillon, Lafayette, LA).

VEILED BEAUTY - Clear Rose to Light Pink center petals. Large, rose form double to loose peony form. Average, spreading growth. M-L. (U.S. 1968 - Haynie).

VELMA GRANTHAM - White to Blush Pink with Pink flecks and stripes, sporting Blush, Dark Pink, White striped Pink and Blush bordered Deep Rose. Medium to large, semidouble with upright petals. Average, upright growth. M. (U.S. 1962 - A. Grantham, Bogalusa, LA).

VELMA GRANTHAM BLUSH - Blush Pink sometimes with Deeper Blush border. (Sport of Japonica 'Velma Grantham').

VELMA GRANTHAM PINK - Pink. (Sport of Japonica 'Velma Grantham').

VELMA GRANTHAM VARIEGATED - Pink flecked, blotched and moired White variation of 'Velma Grantham'.

VELVET GLOW - White. Large, anemone form. Vigorous, upright growth. M. (U.S. 1961 - R. W. Wilder, Fairhope, AL).

VERA CURRY - Light Pink with Darker Pink stripes. Miniature, formal double. Average, upright growth. M. (Seedling of Japonica 'Lady Laura'). (U.S. 2019 - Jim Smelley, Moss Point, MS).

VERA HARPER - Pastel Pink, petals darker to the edges and have a few Red stripes. Medium, formal double. Vigorous, spreading growth. E. (U.S. 2005 - John W. Shirah, Lakeland, FL).

VERGINE DI COLLE BEATO - ('Virgine Calubini'; 'Virgin of the Blessed Hill'). White. Medium, formal double with six to seven geometric swirls in either clockwise or counter clockwise formation. M-L. (Belgium [Versch] from Italy 1857; to U.S. from Sevesi - mid 1960's).

VERNA HALBERT - Flesh Pink. Large, semidouble with irregular petals. Average, upright growth. M. (U.S. 1971 - Haynie).

VERNICE ANN - Rose Pink. Large, peony form. Average, open, spreading growth. M. Fragrant. (U.S. 1975 - V. A. Meskell, San Marino, CA).

VERNIE KOEGLER - Rose Red. Large, semidouble to anemone form. Vigorous, upright growth. E-M. (U.S. 1985 - Alfter).

VERNON E. HOWELL - Red. Large, semidouble to full peony form. Vigorous, dense, upright growth. E-L. (U.S. 2003 - Dudley Boudreaux, Port Neches, TX).

VERNON MAYO - Rose Opal with Silver overcast. Large, anemone form. Vigorous, upright growth. M. (U.S. 1965 - Tammia).

VERY CHERRY - Very Dark Red. Large, anemone form to peony form. Average, compact, upright growth. M-L. (U.S. 1979 - W. Harmsen, Claremont, CA).

VICKI MARIE - Very Pale Pink. Large, peony form. Average, open, upright growth. M. (N.Z. 1992 - C. Treadwell, Wanganui).

VICTOR EMMANUEL - See 'Blood of China'.

VICTOR JOHNSON - Bright Red. Medium, formal double. Upright, compact growth. M-L. (U.S. 1951 - Riverbank).

VICTORIA DOWLING BEASLEY - Light Pink. Medium, semidouble with five rows of petals and top row of petals pointed. Average, upright growth. M. (U.S. 1964 - Beasley).

VICTORIA MARTIN - Pink with flecks of Red. Medium to large, rose form double. Average, spreading growth. M-L. (U.S. 2000 - T. E. Lundy, Milton, FL).

VICTORIA VANIS - Light Blush Pink. Medium, formal double. Vigorous, upright growth. M. (Japonica 'April Remembered' x unknown pollen parent). (U.S. 2009 - Hal Vanis, Henderson, TX).

VICTORIAN POSY - Bright Rose Pink. Medium, anemone form. Average, upright growth. M. (N.Z. 1972 - D. G. O'Toole, Ohope).

VICTORY - Rose Red. Large, semidouble to full peony form. Vigorous, upright growth. M. (U.S. 1942 - Youtz).

VICTORY WHITE - White. Medium, semidouble to loose peony form. Vigorous, open, upright growth. M. (U.S. 1939 - Overlook).

VIDA DAVIS - White washed Blush Pink. Large, semidouble with large petals and prominent bunched Ochre tipped stamens. (U.S. 1959).

VILLE DE NANTES - Dark Red blotched White. Medium to large, semidouble with upright, fimbriated petals. M-L. (Sport of Japonica 'Donckelarii'). (For a variation of this cultivar see 'Lady Kay'). (France 1910 - Heurtin, Nantes).

VILLE DE NANTES RED - Solid Red variation of 'Ville de Nantes'.

VIOLA SIMMONS - Rose Pink. Medium to large, semidouble to loose peony form with fluffy petals. Average, compact growth. M. (U.S. 1957 - Gerbing).

VIOLET BOUQUET - Violet Purple. Medium, anemone form. Vigorous, open, spreading growth. E-M. (U.S. 1969 - Mrs. W. H. Gates, Baton Rouge, LA).

VIRGIE'S EDEN - Baby ribbon Pink with Yellow anthers and Cream filaments. Medium, rose form double with incurved petals. Vigorous, upright growth. M-L. (U.S. 2014 - Manson Markette, Americus, GA).

VIRGIN OF THE BLESSED HILL - See 'Vergine Di Colle Beato'.

VIRGIN'S DREAM - Pink. Medium, rose form double. (U.S. 1959).

VIRGINAL - Greenish White. Medium, semidouble to anemone form. Open, upright growth. M. (Aus. 1945 - Linton).

VIRGINE CALUBINI - See 'Vergine Di Colle Beato'.

VIRGINIA ALFTER - Bright Red. Medium to large, anemone form to loose peony form. Vigorous, upright growth. E-M. (U.S. 1984 - Alfter).

VIRGINIA ALFTER VARIEGATED - Bright Red center petals and petaloids and White outer guard petals variation of 'Virginia Alfter'. (U.S. 1984 - Alfter).

VIRGINIA CAGLE - Blush Pink. Medium, semidouble with three rows of large petals and three very large, upright, wavy petals in cluster of delicate stamens forming a trumpet. E. (U.S. 1960 - Rester).

VIRGINIA CARLYON - Crimson. Medium, semidouble. Vigorous, bushy growth. (England 1972 - Carlyon).

VIRGINIA DARDEN - Red. Large, semidouble with crepe, irregular petals to anemone form. Average, upright growth. E-M. (U.S. 1966 - W. A. Fickling, Sr., Macon, GA).

VIRGINIA DAVIS - White. Medium, formal double. Vigorous, upright growth. M. (U.S. 1948 - H. Davis, El Monte, CA).

VIRGINIA EYLER - Light Pink. Medium, formal double with veined petals. Vigorous, upright growth. M. (U.S. 1953 - H. B. Stanton, Savannah, GA).

VIRGINIA FRANCO - White blushed Rose and streaked and spotted deeper Rose. Small, formal double. Upright, open, willowy growth. M. (For another form of this cultivar, see 'General Cialdini'). (Italy 1856 - Santarelli, Florence).

VIRGINIA FRANCO ROSEA - Sport of' Virginia Franco' - Light Pink veined deeper Pink and edged White.

VIRGINIA J - Pink. Large, semidouble. Average growth. E-M. (U.S. 1959 - J. H. Johnson, Andalusia, AL).

VIRGINIA LYNN - Pink. Medium to large, formal double. Average, upright growth. E-M. (U.S. 2017 - William & Linda Nichols. Cottonwood, AL).

VIRGINIA MADDOX - Rose Pink with Yellow anthers and Pale Yellow filaments. Large, single. Average, spreading growth. E-M. (First Lady of Georgia Series). (U.S. 2018 - Gordy).

VIRGINIA McCOWEN - White shading to Light Pink at edge. Large, semidouble with wavy, crinkled petals. Average, upright growth. M-L. (U.S. 1977 - Dodd).

VIRGINIA NALLE - White. Small, formal double. Average, open, upright growth. E-M. (U.S. 1989 - S. and V. Faircloth, Mobile, AL).

VIRGINIA NOEL - Red with Yellow anthers. Medium, semidouble to single - cupped shape. Average growth. E-M. (U.S.).

VIRGINIA PARRISH - Red. Medium to large, loose peony form with interspersed stamens. Vigorous, upright growth. M. (U.S. 1963 - Dr. A. C. Tuck, Thomasville, GA).

VIRGINIA RICH - Cream center to White to Light Pink to Orchid on edge. Small, rose form double with large, round petals on outer edge, becoming smaller toward center. Average, upright growth. M-L. (U.S. 1958 - Wheeler).

VIRGINIA ROBINSON - Light Orchid Pink. Large, semidouble. Vigorous, compact, upright growth. M-L. (U.S. 1957 - Nuccio's).

VIRGINIA ROBINSON VARIEGATED - Light Orchid Pink blotched White variation of 'Virginia Robinson'.

VIRGINIA SMITH - Deep Rose Pink. Medium, peony form. Average, upright growth. E. (U.S. 1986 - W. L. Smith, Tylertown, MS).

VIRGINIA SUNRISE - Red blotched White with Yellow anthers and Pink filaments. Medium to large, semidouble to anemone form. Vigorous, upright growth. M. (U.S. 2012 - Habel).

VIRGIN'S BLUSH - White flushed faintest Pink with Yellow anthers and Yellow filaments. Medium, semidouble to peony form. Vigorous, upright growth. M. (Seedling of Japonica 'Orandagasa'). (U.S. 1944 - E. A. McIlhenny [Jungle Gardens], Avery Island, LA).

VIVA - Red. Large, single. (U.S. 1959 - Nuccio's).

VIVIAN JONES - Light Red and White in varying degrees. Medium, formal double. Average growth. M-L. (U.S. 1959 - C. S. Jones, Elizabeth City, NC).

VIVIAN OEHLMAN - White. Medium, semidouble. Average, upright growth. M. (U.S. 1984 - Mrs. H. Johnson, Madison, FL).

VOGTHORSTAR - Deep Magenta Red to Deep Purple fading to Gray as the bloom ages from the edges out. Small to medium, formal double. Average, upright growth. E. (U.S. 2015 - Carrie Lee Pierson Schwartz).

VOLCANO - Scarlet Red. Large, anemone form. Vigorous, open, upright growth. M-L. (N.Z. 1992 - Haydon).

VOLUNTEER - Bright Strawberry Pink with a darker center, edged with Pale Pink at petal and petaloids' border. Medium, anemone form. Slow, dense, upright growth. E-L. (N.Z. 2003 - Mark Jury).

VOSPER'S ROSE - Soft Pink shading to petal edges. Medium, semidouble with upright center petals and petaloids in center. Vigorous, compact growth. M. (N.Z. 1959 - Mrs. J. Vosper, Tirau).

VOYANT - Blood Red. Large, semidouble to loose peony form. (U.S. 1957 - G. Willis, Thomasville, GA).

VULCAN - Deep Fiery Red. Large to very large, semidouble to peony form with irregular petals to formal double. Vigorous, upright growth. E-M. (U.S. 1958 - Wilson).

VULCAN VARIEGATED - Red dotted and blotch-White variation of 'Vulcan'.

W. H. BARNSLEY - Light Pink variegated Blush Pink. Medium to large, formal double. (U.S. 1958 - W. H. Barnsley, Apopka, FL).

W. H. RISH - Coral Pink. Large, semidouble with irregular petals and interspersed stamens. Vigorous, compact, upright growth. M. (U.S. 1970 - W. H. Rish, Winnsboro, SC).

W. L. SMITH - White striped Red to Dark Red to Pink striped Red and edged White. Large, semidouble to peony form. Average, upright growth. M-L. (U.S. 1987 - W. L. Smith, Tylertown, MS).

WAIWHETU BEAUTY - Light Pink. Medium, semidouble with loose petals. Vigorous, upright growth. M. (N.Z. 1949).

WAKAMURASAKI - Blush Pink. Small, single. Average, upright, bushy growth. M. (Japan 1970's - Sado Island, Niigata Prefecture).

WAKANOURA RED - See 'Tricolor (Siebold) Red'.

WAKANOURA VARIEGATED - See 'Tricolor (Siebold).'

WAKANOURA WHITE - See 'Leucantha'.

WAKANOURA-AKA - See 'Tricolor (Siebold) Red'.

WAKANOURA-SHIRO - See 'Leucantha'.

WALKER LEWIS - Dark Pink with White picotee edges with White anthers and White filaments. Medium, semidouble to peony form. Vigorous, upright growth. E-M. (U.S. 2010 - Pat Johnson, Cairo, GA).

WALKER'S PINK - Pink. Miniature, formal double. Upright growth. M. (U.S. 1960's - F. Hamilton, Santa Maria, CA).

WALLY B - Deep Red. Medium, anemone. Average, upright, dense growth. M. (U.S. 2017 - Gordy).

WALTER A. WILSON - White. Large, formal double. Average, open, upright growth. L. (U.S. 1980 - W. A. Wilson, Augusta, GA).

WALTER D. BELLINGRATH - Light Pink changing to Rose Pink. Large, loose peony form to anemone form. Vigorous, spreading growth. M-L. (U.S. 1955 - Longview).

WALTER D. BELLINGRATH VARIEGATED - Light Pink changing to Rose Pink blotched White variation of 'Walter D Bellingrath'.

WALTER HAZLEWOOD - Deep Red blotched White. Medium, rose form double. Average, compact, upright growth. E-L. (Aus. 1973 - Hazlewood).

WALTER'S PRETTY ONE - Light to Dark Pink. Large, formal double. Average, upright, open growth. E. (U.S. 2017 - Walter Hedges, Columbia, SC).

WAMBERAL PINK - Pink. Large, single. Low, compact growth. E-M. (Aus. 1963 - Mrs. F. V. Ward, Wamberal).

WAR CRY - Velvet Red heavily veined. Medium, loose peony form with upright petals and petaloids interspersed with fifteen groups of stamens. Average, compact, upright growth. (U.S. 1965 - G. S. Clarke, Jr., Savannah, GA).

WAR EAGLE - See 'Roman Soldier'.

WARM HEART - Coral Rose. Medium to large, semidouble with White stamens and twisted petals. Vigorous, spreading, willowy growth. M. (U.S. 1959 - Breschini).

WARRATAH - See 'Anemonaeflora'.

WARREN THOMPSON - Deep Pink with Yellow anthers and Yellow filaments. Large, semidouble. average, spreading growth. M. (U.S. 2014 - Marvin Jernigan, Warner Robbins, GA).

WARRIOR - Brilliant Red. Medium to large, semidouble to full peony form. Compact, upright growth. E-M. (U.S. 1960 - Nuccio's).

WART - Pale Pink at base shading to Deeper Pink at edge with reverse side Flesh Pink. Miniature, semidouble. Slow growth. L. (U.S. 1962 - Wheeler).

WARWICK - See 'Mathotiana Rosea'.

WATERLOO - ('Ethlington White'). White. Medium, semidouble. Vigorous, compact, upright growth. M. (U.S. 1938 - Kiyono).

WAUCISSA - Pale Blush Pink. Medium, semidouble. (U.S. 1952 - Rosa).

WEBB STANLEY - Dark Red. Medium, semidouble. Average, upright growth. M. (U.S. 1979 - H. E. Jernigan, Greenville, AL).

WEBB'S WHITE - White with Yellowish center. Medium, formal double. Average, upright, dense growth. (U.S. 1985 - Webb Hart, Slidell, LA).

WEDDING BELLS - Shaded light and Dark Blush Pink. Medium, semidouble of bell form with heavy substance. Vigorous, pendulous growth. M. (U.S. 1959 - Short).

WEDDING CAKE - Soft Pink. Large, peony form. Spreading, upright growth. E-L. (U.S. 1980 - Mandarich).

WEDDING RING - White. Medium to large, single with slender petaloids and ring of Golden stamens. Vigorous, upright growth. E-M. (U.S. 1957 - Short).

WEE WUN - Red. Small, loose peony form. Vigorous, upright growth. M. (U.S. 1974 - Novick).

WEELAUNEE - Deep Red. Medium, semidouble. (U.S. 1948 - Rosa).

WELLS CRANFORD - Red and White. Large, peony form. Average, upright growth. M-L. (U.S. 1979 - W. Cranford, Salisbury, NC).

WENDELL'S DREAM - Pink with Rose Pink streaks and flecks. Large, formal double. Vigorous, upright growth. M-L. (U.S. 2013 - Wendell Graves, Savannah, GA).

WENDY - Dark Red variegated White. Large, semidouble. Average, open, upright growth. E-L. (U.S. 1976 - Gilley).

WENDY BROWN KING - Pale Blush Pink. Medium to large, peony form. Slow, dense, upright growth. E-M. (U.S. 1997 - Wilbur B. Brown, Wilmington, NC).

WENDY GAYE - Bright Red with White striped petaloids. Large, anemone form. Vigorous, open, upright growth. M. (Aus. 1970 - Sebire).

WENDY RED - Dark Red. Large, semidouble. Average, upright, open growth. E-L. (Red form of Japonica 'Wendy'). (U.S. 1976 - Gilley).

WEST WIND - Coral Red. Large to very large, semidouble. Average, compact growth. M-L. (U.S. 1959 - Short).

WESTLAKE FRAGRANT LOTUS - (Xizi Xianghe - Chinese name). Light Pink with Yellow anthers. Small to medium, rose form double. Average, upright, spreading growth with many lateral limbs. E-M. Fragrant. [(Japonica 'Tama-Ikari' x Japonica 'Black Pearl') x Japonica 'Tiffany']. (U.S. 1997 - John Wang, Orinda, CA).

WHEEL OF FORTUNE - White striped Coral Pink. Medium to large, semidouble with cluster of stamens sometimes surrounded with erect petals. Vigorous, compact, upright growth. M. (U.S. 1959 - McCaskill).

WHITE ANGEL - See 'Laura Schafer'.

WHITE ANITA - White. Medium, semidouble. (Sport of Japonica 'Anita'). (U.S. 1958 - Tammia).

WHITE BOUQUET - White. Medium to large, semidouble. Vigorous, upright, somewhat loose growth. M. (U.S. 2006 - Nuccio's).

WHITE BUTTONS - White. Miniature, formal double. (U.S. 1960 - Domoto).

WHITE BY THE GATE - White. Medium, formal double. Vigorous, upright growth. M. (U.S. 1955 - Hyman's Nsy., Lafayette, LA).

WHITE CAPS - White. Medium, semidouble. M-L. (U.S. 1955 - Feathers).

WHITE DAIKAGURA - See 'Joshua E. Youtz'.

WHITE DEB - White. Medium, full peony form. Vigorous, bushy growth. E-M. (U.S. 1965 - Maitland).

WHITE DRAGON - White. Large, single with some petals fimbriated and crimped at margin. Average growth. L. (U.S. 1986 - Ackerman).

WHITE DREAM - White. Large, full peony form. Average, upright growth. M. (U.S. 1975 - Shackelford).

WHITE ELEGANS - See 'Snow Chan'.

WHITE EMPRESS - White. Large, semidouble with fluted petals. Vigorous, compact, upright growth. E-M. Cold hardy. (U.S. 1939 - Overlook).

WHITE FAIRY - White. Medium, semidouble. (U.S. 1957).

WHITE FOAM - White. Large, semidouble with loose petals. Upright growth. M. (U.S. 1959).

WHITE GIANT - White. Large, semidouble. Vigorous, compact, upright growth. M. (U.S. 1944 - Overlook).

WHITE GOLD - White with Golden line. Medium, anemone form. M-L. (U.S. 1959 - Baker).

WHITE HIBISCUS - White. Medium, semidouble with long, narrow petals. Average, upright growth. E. (U.S. 1940 - Overlook).

WHITE HIGH HAT - See 'Conrad Hilton'.

WHITE JEWEL - White. Miniature to small, formal double. Vigorous, open, upright growth. L. (U.S. 1996 - E. R. Bond, Dallas, TX).

WHITE JORDAN'S PRIDE - See 'Colonial Lady'.

WHITE KING - White. Medium, semidouble with large, thick petals. Upright growth. M. (U.S. 1938 - Overlook).

WHITE KNIGHT - White. Medium, formal double. Vigorous, upright growth. E-M. (U.S. 1953 - Knight's Nsy., Gainesville, FL).

WHITE LAUREL LEAF - See 'Pax'.

WHITE LILY - White. Medium, semidouble. M. (Aus. 1962 - Waterhouse).

WHITE MELBOURNE - White. Medium, single of bell form. (Aus. 1953 - Dr. C. R. Merrillees, Melbourne).

WHITE MERMAID - White with Golden anthers and White filaments. Medium, single with six somewhat irregular petals; most leaves narrow down then flare out to three points giving a fishtail [kingyo] appearance. M-L. Fragrant. (Sport of Japonica 'Pink Mermaid' [Kingyo-tsubaki]; this plant is a sub-species of japonica - quercifolia; sometimes called Camellia japonica var. quercifolia 'White Mermaid'). (Canada 1994 - Introduced into North America from Japan by Piroche Plants, Pitt Meadows, British Columbia).

WHITE NUN - White. Very large, semidouble. Vigorous, upright growth. M. (U.S. 1959 - McCaskill).

WHITE PAGODA - White, Medium, formal double. Average, upright growth. M. (U.S. from Formosa/Taiwan 1945 - Peer).

WHITE PEARL - White. Large, semidouble with wavy, crinkled petals. Average growth. M-L. (U.S. 1975 - Mrs. L. S. Carswell, Waycross, GA).

WHITE PEONY - White. Medium, full peony form. Vigorous, compact, upright growth. M-L. (U.S. 1938 - Gerbing).

WHITE PERFECTION - White. Small, formal double. Vigorous, compact growth. M. (U.S. 1939 - Jannoch).

WHITE PIN CUSHION - White. Medium, semidouble with stamens standing out like pins in pin cushion. M. (U.S. 1958 - Baker).

WHITE POM POM - White with Cream White petaloids. Large, loose semidouble to anemone form. (U.S. 1953).

WHITE PORCELAIN - White. Large, formal double. Average, upright, open growth. E-M. (U.S. 2006 - Howell).

WHITE PRINCESS - ('Lady of the Lourdes'). Cream White. Medium, peony form. Vigorous, upright growth. M. (Japan to U.S. [Jannoch] 1945).

WHITE QUEEN - White. Medium, semidouble with petals somewhat small and pointed at tips. Vigorous, compact, upright growth. M-L. Cold hardy. (U.S. 1943 - Overlook).

WHITE STAR - White. Small to medium, semidouble. Slow, dense growth. M-L. Ed. (Note: Not same cultivar which is listed in NOMENCLATURE SUPPLEMENT as synonym for 'Candidissima'). (Aus. 1995 - K. Brown, Mitcham, Vic.).

WHITE SUPERLATIVE - White. Large, high centered peony form. Vigorous, upright growth. M. (U.S. 1969 - Shackelford).

WHITE SURPRISE - Ivory White, Medium, semidouble. (Sport of Japonica 'Look-Away'). (U.S. 1975 - Mealing).

WHITE SWAN (McILHENNY) - White with Gold anthers and Yellow filaments. Small to medium, loose peony form with central petals interspersed with a few stamens. L. (U.S. 1945 - E. A. McIlhenny - Jungle Gardens, Avery Island, LA).

WHITE THRONE - White. Large, semidouble with wide petals. Vigorous, upright growth. M. (U.S. 1953 - Short).

WHITE TULIP - White. Medium, single of cupped form with oval petals. Open, spreading growth. M. (Aus. 1952 - Cheeseman, Melbourne).

WHITE VELVET - White. Medium to large, rose form double with wavy, velvet textured petals overlaid in alternate rows graduated in size giving a tiered effect. Average growth. M. (U.S. 1960 - Julington).

WHITE WINGS - White. Large, semidouble with wide, wavy petals. Average, spreading growth. L. (Sport of Japonica 'Mrs. Charles Simons'). (U.S. 1963 - O. D. Edge, Columbus, GA).

WHITNEY GAETA - Light Pink deepening to Coral Pink at margin. Small to medium, formal double. Compact, upright growth. E-M. (U.S. 1989 - Piet and Gaeta).

WHOOPEE - Pink Veined Red with White margin. Small to medium, semidouble. Average, upright growth. E-M. (U.S. 2000 - Frank A. Wilson III, Leslie, GA).

WHOOPEE RED - Purplish Red. (Sport of Japonica 'Whoopee'). (U.S. 2011 - Charles Ritter, Melrose, FL).

WICKE - Pink, White, Red and variegated flowers on same plant. Small, semidouble. M. (U.S. 1950 - H. H. Harms, Portland, OR).

WIDDLE WUN - Rose Pink. Miniature, anemone form. Average, upright growth. M. (U.S. 1975 - Novick).

WIDE AWAKE - Bright Red. Medium, single with crimped, flat petals. Vigorous, compact, upright growth. M. (N.Z. 1970 - B. J. Rayner, Stratford).

WILAMINA - Clear soft Pink with Darker Pink edge and White tipped center. Small, formal double with incurved petals. Average, compact growth. M. (U.S. 1951 - C. H. Peterson, Downey, CA).

WILDER - Light Pink shading to Cream White in center. Large, formal double of flat form. M. (U.S. 1959).

WILDFIRE - Orange Red. Medium, semidouble. Vigorous, upright growth. E-M. (U.S. 1963 - Nuccio's).

WILDWOOD - Light Pink. Large, semidouble to loose peony form with very thin petals. Upright, compact growth. M-L. (U.S. 1953 - W. R. Marvin, Walterboro, SC).

WILDWOOD VARIEGATED - Light Pink and White variation of 'Wildwood.'

WILL REHDER - Rose Pink. Large, peony form. Average, spreading growth. E. (U.S. 1963 - N. B. Rehder, Wilmington, NC).

WILL SARGENT - Red with Yellow anthers and Yellow filaments. Small to medium, semidouble. Slow, upright, dense growth. M-L. (U.S. 2018 - Joseph Louis & Joanne Raska, Deland, FL).

WILL SUMMERSETT - Soft Pink. Large, semidouble. Average, spreading growth. M-L. (U.S. 1964 - W. B. Summersett, Columbia, SC).

WILLARD SCOTT - Pale Pink edged Deeper Pink. Medium, formal double to full peony form. Vigorous, open, upright growth. E-M. (U.S. 1986 - Stone).

WILLIAM BARTLETT - Pale Pink profusely flecked Deeper Pink. Large, formal double. (Aus. 1958 - Hazlewood).

WILLIAM BULL - Rose Pink shading to Pink in center. Medium, formal double. Upright growth. M. (Variations of this cultivar include 'Kayel' and 'Wrightii'). (Aus. 1878 - Shepherd).

WILLIAM C. CROMLEY - Light Red. Medium, loose peony form. Average growth. M-L. (U.S. 1991 - J. Aldrich, Brooklet, GA).

WILLIAM C. NOELL - Delicate Pink shading to Deeper Pink outer petals with White center. Miniature to small, formal double. Average, compact, upright growth. (U.S. 1972 - J. S. Howard, Salemburg, NC).

WILLIAM E. COLBY - Blood Red. Large, semidouble. Bushy, spreading growth. M-L. (U.S. 1957 - Feathers).

WILLIAM FORREST BRAY - Dark Red with darker veins and Purple border. Large, formal double. Vigorous, compact growth. M-L. (U.S. 1966 - Bray).

WILLIAM FORREST BRAY VARIEGATED - Dark Red blotched White variation of 'William Forrest Bray'. (U.S. 1966 - Bray).

WILLIAM GEORGE BEAVIS - Soft Rose Pink. Medium, semidouble. Average, compact growth. M. (Aus. 1968 - Mrs. W. G. Beavis, Doncaster, Vic.).

WILLIAM H. CUTTER - Rose. Medium to large, semidouble with small petaloids in center. Vigorous, compact, upright growth. M. (U.S. 1955 - W. H. Cutter, Macon, GA).

WILLIAM H. CUTTER VARIEGATED - Rose blotched White variation of 'William H Cutter'.

WILLIAM HONEY - White striped Carmine, sporting Carmine. Medium, anemone form with stamens inclined to occur in bunches interspersed with large, upright petaloids. Vigorous, bushy, slightly pendulous growth. M-L. (Aus. 1955 - A. W. Jessep, Melbourne).

WILLIAM JACKSON - Red with Fuschia overlays. Large to very large, loose to full peony form or semidouble. Vigorous, compact, upright growth. E-L. (U.S. 1972 - W. B. Jackson, Tyler, TX).

WILLIAM JACKSON PINK - Dark Pink with Yellow anthers, Large to very Large, loose to full peony form or semidouble. Vigorous, compact, upright growth. E-L. (Sport of Japonica 'William Jackson'). (U.S. 2019 - Tommy Weeks, Conroe, TX).

WILLIAM PAULK - Red striped White. Large, semidouble. Vigorous, spreading, upright growth. M. (U.S. 1989 - E. Paulk, Ocala, FL).

WILLIAM PAULK LAVENDER - Deep Lavender with Gold anthers and Pink filaments. Medium, semidouble. M-L. (Sport of Japonica 'William Paulk'. (U.S. 2007 - Gordy).

WILLIAM PENN - ('Bell Camp'; 'Purple Peony'). Dark Purple Red marbled White. Small to medium, full peony form. Vigorous, slender, willowy growth. M. (Not the cultivar listed in old literature). (U.S. 1854 - Ritchie and Dick, Philadelphia, PA).

WILLIAM R. BLANCHARD - Deep Pink to Light Red. Medium, semidouble. (U.S. 1953 - Thomasville, GA).

WILLIAM ROSA - Salmon Pink. Medium, semidouble. Compact, upright growth. M. (U.S. 1954 - Rosa).

WILLIAM S. HASTIE - See 'Mathotiana'.

WILLIAM S. HASTIE (MISSISSIPPI) - See 'C. M. Hovey'.

WILLIAM SPRAGG - Deep Red marbled and flecked White. Large, semidouble. Average, compact, upright growth. M-L. (Aus. 1975 - Mrs. A. Spragg, Sutherland, NSW).

WILLIAMINA SOPER - Pale Pink striped Deeper Pink. Medium, formal double. M. (Aus. 1980 - Oke's Gdn. Nsy., Bomaderry, NSW).

WILLIAMS MIDDLETON - Dark Red veined lighter Red. Large, semidouble. Vigorous, upright growth. M-L. (U.S. 1941 - Middleton).

WILLIE HITE - Light Pink shading to Deeper Pink at petal edges. Medium, semidouble with heart-shaped petal edges and crinkled center petals. Vigorous, compact, upright growth. E-M. (U.S. 1956 - W. M. Hite, Marion, SC).

WILLIE MOORE - Red with darker stripes. Large, semidouble. Average, compact growth. M. (U.S. 1950 - Tick Tock).

WILLIE MOORE VARIEGATED - Red and White variation of 'Willie Moore'.

WILLIE'S CHILD - Deep Rose Pink. Medium, peony form. Vigorous, compact, upright growth. M. (U.S. 1956 - Tick Tock).

WILLIE'S CHILD VARIEGATED - Deep Rose Pink blotched White variation of 'Willie's Child'.

WILLMETTA - Apple Blossom Pink. Small, single resembling an apple blossom. Slow, open, willowy growth. (U.S. 1950 - Will and Metta. Jensen, Kent, WA.).

WILMA SHEFFIELD - Dark Cerise Pink. Large, semidouble with upright petals and occasional intermingled stamens and petaloids. Average, spreading growth. M. (U.S. 1962 - H. G. Sheffield, Silsbee, TX).

WILMER STEWART - Brilliant Pink blotched White. Large, semidouble. Average, upright growth. E-M. (U.S. 1979 - W. Stewart, Savannah, GA).

WIND SONG - Deep Pink. Large, loose peony form with segments of Golden stamens interspersed among petals. (U.S. 1960 - Camelliana).

WINGED VICTORY - White. Large, semidouble to peony form. (Aus. 1966 - G. Waterhouse).

WINGS - See 'Herme Pink'.

WINGS OF SONG - Clear White. Medium to large, loose peony form with large petaloids. (U.S. 1960 - Shackelford).

WINIFRED BALDWIN - Pink and White bordered White. Large, semidouble. Average, upright growth. M. (U.S. 1989 - Mrs. D. Baldwin, Charleston, SC).

WINIFRED HAFELE - Cherry Red with Light Red tipped Light Gold stamens. Large, loose peony form with large, wavy petals and two sets of stamens. Average growth. L. (U.S. 1960 - Julington).

WINIFRED WOMACK - ('Bobby Guillot'). Blush Pink. Medium, semidouble. Vigorous, slightly pendulous growth. M. (U.S. 1955 - A. Davis, Coden, AL).

WINIFRED YOUNG - Pink. Medium, semidouble. Open, spreading growth. M-L. (N.Z. 1989 - K. Brushfield).

WINKIE - Dark Rose Pink. Large, rose form double with crinkled, upright petals. Vigorous, open, upright growth. E-L. (Similar to 'Tomorrow'). (U.S. 1969 - Dunn's Camellia Gdns., Mobile, AL).

WINNIE DAVIS II - See 'Donckelarii'.

WINTER CARNIVAL - White. Medium, formal double. Average, compact growth. M. (U.S. 1953 - Short).

WINTER CHEER - Crimson with lighter center. Medium, semidouble with irregular petals. Bushy growth. M-L. (Aus. 1945 - A. O. Ellison, Sydney).

WINTER MORN - White. Large, semidouble to anemone form. Vigorous, upright growth. M. (U.S. 1955 - E. W. Miller, Escondido, CA).

WINTER TREASURE - White, sometimes with small dash of Rose-Red. Large, semidouble with slightly wavy, notched petals. Vigorous, slightly pendulous, upright growth. E-M. (U.S. 1952 - Miss R. Loman, Wilmington, NC).

WISHING STAR - Light Pink. Medium to large, semidouble to anemone form with star-shaped outer petals. Vigorous, compact, upright growth. M. (U.S. 1958 - McCaskill).

WITCH DOCTOR - Rose Red. Large, semidouble to rose form double. Average, compact growth. E-M. (U.S. 1960 - G. Demetropolis, Mobile, AL).

WITMAN YELLOW - White tinged Yellow. Medium, semidouble. Average, upright growth. M. (U.S. 1963 - Homeyer).

WOBBY BOY - White, flecked and blotched Light Pink, shading to Darker Pink. Medium, semidouble. Average, compact, upright growth. M-L. (U.S. 1983 - W Herbert, Ruston, LA).

WONDER CHILD - See 'Betty Sheffield Blush'.

WONDER OF WHITE - White. Medium, formal double. Vigorous, upright growth. E-M. (U.S. 2002 - Gordon E. Eade, Pensacola, FL).

WONDERLAND - Brilliant, Deep Rose. Large, semidouble to peony form. Vigorous, open growth. M-L. (U.S. 1960 - Short).

WOOD SPRITE - Blush Pink. Small, semidouble. Vigorous, bushy, upright growth. M. (U.S. 1959 - McCaskill).

WOODLAND GLEN - Rose Red with touch of White on last row of petals. Large, semidouble. Average, open, upright growth. M. (U.S. 1965 - Novick).

WOODLAND MANOR - Vibrant Red. Very large, semidouble. Average, upright, spreading growth. M-L. (Seedling of Japonica 'Royal Velvet'). (U.S. 2016 - Pat Johnson, Cairo, GA).

WOODLANDS BEAUTY - Red. Large, anemone form. Average, bushy growth. E-L. (N.Z. 1975 - Mrs. R. J. Clarke, Auckland).

WOODROW JOHNSON - Rose Pink. Large, peony form. Vigorous, upright growth. M. (U.S. 1949 - Katz).

WOODVILLE RED - ('Mrs. White'; 'Martin Roberts'; 'Kollock'; 'Gruenwald Red'; 'Henri Bry'). Deep Strawberry Red. Large, peony form. Slow, upright growth. M. (For variations of this cultivar see Japonica 'Early Woodville Red Blush' and 'Woodville Red Blush'). (Europe to U.S. 1822 - Woodville, MS).

WOODVILLE RED BLUSH - Blush Pink fading to White. (Sport of Japonica 'Woodville Red'). (U.S. 1961 - L G Thomas, Mobile, AL).

WOODY ESTES - Light Pink speckled and striped Red. Medium, full peony to anemone form. (Sport of Japonica 'Professor Charles S. Sargent'). (U.S. 1956 - C. Estes, Sea Island, GA).

WRONG - Deep Rose Pink. Large, anemone form with notched outer petals surrounding petaloids in bunches surrounding wavy petals, stamens and petaloids. Average, upright growth. E-M. (U.S. 1963 - Ashby).

WRONG VARIEGATED - Deep Rose Pink blotched White variation of 'Wrong'.

WROUGHTII - See 'Amenonaeflora Alba'

WYLMER POOL - White to Blush with Pink petals, solid Pink and Pink and White. Large, semidouble to peony form to formal double. Vigorous, compact, upright growth. E-M. (U.S. 1973 - Tammia).

WYN CARTER - Dark Purplish Red veined Darker Red. Medium, rose form double. Average, open, upright growth. M-L. (N.Z. 1991 - T. Lennard, Te Puke).

WYN HAWKES - White. Large, single. Vigorous, upright growth. E. (Aus. 1985 - R. Hawkes, Woodside, S. Aus.).

WYNELLE GREENWAY - Medium Pink with Yellow anthers and White filaments. Medium, semidouble to rose form double. Average, upright, open growth. M-L. (U.S. 2018 - Pat Johnson, Cairo, GA).

WYNYARD - Pink. Medium, peony form. M. (Aus. 1962 - Wynyard, Tasmania).

WYTE BYDA TWAYLA - White. Medium to large, formal double. Average, upright growth. M. (U.S. 2019 - Camellia Heaven - John Grimm, Bush, LA).

XIZI XIANGHE - See 'Westlake Fragrant Lotus'

X-TRA PINK - Deep to Light Rose Pink, at times with Bluish sheen or Bluish undertones and veining. Large, semidouble to anemone form to peony form. Average, upright growth. M. (U.S. 1998 - P. Gilley, Grand Ridge, FL).

YAMATO-NISHIKI - White variegated Pink and Red. Medium, single with full flared stamens. Slow, compact growth. M. (For other forms of this cultivar see below and 'Ohkan' and 'Showa-no-Hikari'). See Higo.

YAMATO-NISHIKI ROSE - Pink. (Sport of Japonica 'Yamato-Nishiki').

YEAMANS HALL - Shell Pink with Darker Pink striping. Medium, formal double. E-L. (U.S. 2006 - Sam Borom. Propagated by Coastal Carolina Camellia Society. Mt. Merrillees, Vic.).

YIRGELLA - White. Medium, formal double with Green leaves which are Yellow toward edge. (Foliage sport of Japonica 'Isabel'). (For another form of this cultivar see 'Geoff Hamilton'). (Aus. 1975 - S. Compton, Gosford, NSW).

YOBUKO-DORI - Pale Pink. Small, single. M. (For other variations of this cultivar see 'Aka-Yobuko-Dori'; 'Shiro-Yobuko-Dori'). (Japan 1956 - Satomi).

YOHEI-HAKU - White to Pale Pink. Medium, semidouble to peony for to anemone form. Average, compact growth. E. (Japan 1936 - Chugai).

YONA P. DOWDLE - Pink veined Deep Pink. Large, semidouble with very large, wavy, upright petals. Vigorous, upright growth. E-L. (U.S. 1970 - C. L. Dowdle, Gulfport, MS).

YOSEMITE - Rose Red. Medium, semidouble. Average, compact growth. M. (U.S. 1950 - A. A. Baugh, Oakland, CA).

YOURS TRULY - ('Lady Vansittart Shell'). Pink streaked Deep Pink and bordered White. Medium, semidouble. (Sport of Japonica 'Lady Vansittart'). (U.S. 1949 - J. S. Tormey, Temple City, CA).

YOUTZ WILD ROSE - Rose Pink. Medium, semidouble. Average, compact growth. M. (U.S. 1950 - Youtz).

YUKI-BOTAN (SNOWISH PEONY) - ('Pride of Descanso'). White. Large, semidouble to loose peony form with irregular petals. Vigorous, upright growth. M. (Japan 1895 - Yokohama).

YUKI-DARUMA - See 'Pax'.

YUKI-KOMACHI - Rose Pink. Medium, single with flared Pale Yellow stamens. See Higo.

YUKIMI-GURUMA   (SNOW-VIEWING CARRIAGE) - White with Golden anthers and Light Yellow filaments. Large, single. Upright growth. M. (Japan 1859).

YUKI-SUGATA - White. Medium, single. See Higo.

YURI-SHIBHORI (LILY VARIEGATED) - White with Crimson stripes with Golden anthers and White filaments. Small, single. (Japan 1976 - Kan Utsugi, Osaka).

YUYAKE-FUJI - Deep Pink veined deeper, fading to White margins. Small, single - 5-6 petals. (Sport of Japonica 'Yuri-shibori'). (Japan 1988).

YVONNE TYSON - Phlox Pink with Salmon undertone. Medium, anemone form. Average, compact growth. M. (U.S. 1950 - W. V. Tyson, Savannah, GA).

YVONNE TYSON VARIEGATED - Phlox Pink and White variation of 'Yvonne Tyson'.

ZAC CHAFFIN - Red and White streaked. Large, semidouble. Vigorous, spreading, upright growth. M-L. (U.S. 1994 - Dr. O. Lewis, Picayune, MS).

ZAMBO - Crimson veined Darker Red. Medium, formal double. M. (Aus. 1874 - Dr. R. C. Merrillees, Vic.).

ZEBULON - Soft White petals very lightly tinted with soft Amaranth, chopped and streaked with Vermillion with Yellow anthers and Yellow filaments. Large, semidouble to full peony. Average, upright and spreading growth. M. (U.S. 2014 - Waters, England, imported from Nantes, France).

ZELDA FITZGERALD - Blush Pink with darker ruffled border and stamen boss a blend of Pinks with Dark Yellow anthers. Medium, anemone form. Average, compact, upright growth. M. (U.S. 2008 - Bobby Green, Green Nurseries, Fairhope, AL).

ZELMA CROCKETT - Red and Pink. Medium to large, anemone form. Average, open, upright growth. M. (U.S. 2003 - Jack Midgett, Virginia Beach, VA).

ZENOBIA - Oriental Red. Very large, peony form with clusters of Gold stamens between petal layers and rabbit ears in center. Average, open, upright growth. E-L. (U.S. 1994 - Z. Kendig, Lutherville, MD).

ZEPHYR - Fire Red. Large, peony form with Golden stamens interspersed with curving petaloids. (U.S. 1965 - Wilson).

ZILPHA SLAUENWHITE - Rose Pink. Small, semidouble with upright petals intermingled with stamens. Average, upright growth. M. (U.S. 1965 - Mrs. E. Cain, Mullins, SC).

ZINA MARIE - Pale Pink center deepening to Rich Pink at edges. Medium, formal double. Slow, bushy growth. M. (U.S. 1980 - Feathers).

ZING - Rose Red. Miniature, formal double. Vigorous, bushy upright growth. M. (U.S. 1973 - McCaskill).

ZOE ELIZABETH - Blood Red. Medium, formal double. Upright growth. M-L. (Aus. 1985 - R. Keightley, Wattlepark, S. Aus.).

ZORINA - Deep Red. Large, formal double to rose form double. L. (U.S. 1969 - Armstrong).

ZUIKO-NISHIKI - White splashed Red. Medium, single. See Higo.

Species Reticulata and Hybrids
With Reticulata Parentage

The predominant opinion is that Reticulata is not a distinct species, but is a hybrid of other species, probably largely Pitardii (which also is believed to be a hybrid) fractionally combined with Japonica.

The Yunnan Reticulatas, which were imported into the United States from China in 1948 by Ralph S. Peer of Hollywood, California, and Descanso Gardens of La Canada, generally have been listed as Reticulata and their seedlings listed as Reticulata Hybrids. It is the opinion of many that such cultivars represent garden forms of Reticulata, some Pitardii Variety Yunnanica, and some hybrid crosses of both. Many such cultivars are over three hundred years old.

Therefore it is believed advisable to list Reticulatas and Hybrids with Reticulata Parentage in this same section. Cultivars imported directly to the United States from China during the 40's, 50's, 60's and 80's have been marked with an asterisk (*).

A. P. FATHERREE - Deep Red veined deeper. Large to very large, semidouble. Vigorous, upright, open growth. M-L. (Reticulata 'Cornelian' seedling). (U.S. 1980 - Pursel).

ADA EMILY - Scarlet. Large, semidouble to peony form. Spreading, open growth. M-L. (Reticulata hybrid 'Balderdash' seedling). (Aus. 1984 - Pierson).

ADA SEBIRE - Deep Rose. Very large, peony form. Vigorous, upright growth. M. (Reticulata 'Tali Queen' seedling). (Aus. 1977 - Sebire).

ADDIE BLACK - Red. Very large, semidouble. Vigorous, upright growth. E-M. (Reticulata hybrid 'Wild Form' seedling). (N.Z. 1972 - Miss A. Black, Whakatane).

ADORING PURE - ('Chongjie' - Chinese Name). Very light Purple when opening, becoming almost Pure White when fully open. Large, semidouble; it has 19 petals and 2-3 whorls; inner petals are incurved and in a "v" shape and lighter color at the outer petals. M. (Reticulata hybrid 'Suzanne Withers' x Japonica 'Kona'). (U.S. 2007 - John Wang, Orinda, CA).

ADRENE WHEELER - Medium Pink with frosted edges with Yellow anthers and White filaments. Very large, semidouble. Vigorous, upright, dense growth. L. (Reticulata hybrid 'Suzanne Withers' x Reticulata hybrid 'Annabelle Fetterman'). (U.S. 2013 - Hulyn Smith).

ADRIENNE BOUERES - Dark Pink with bright Yellow anthers and White filaments. Medium to large, rose form double. Average, spreading growth. M-L. (Reticulata hybrid 'Frank Houser' seedling). (U.S. 2013 - Howard and Mary Rhodes, Tallahassee, FL).

AL GUNN - Rich Pink. Very large, semidouble with curled, incurved petals. Vigorous, upright spreading growth. M. (Reticulata seedling). (U.S. 1979 - A. Gunn and W. Goertz, San Marino, CA).

ALASKAN QUEEN - Blush Pink fading to White. Very large, semidouble. Vigorous, upright growth. M. (Reticulata hybrid 'LASCA Beauty' seedling). (Aus. 1986 - B. Hooper, Bexley North, NSW).

ALFONS - Flame to Ruby Red. Very large, semidouble to peony form. Average, upright, open growth. E-L. (Reticulata hybrid 'Yvonne Amizonica' x Japonica 'San Dimas'). (N.Z. 1992 - A. Gamlin, Manaia).

ALFUS JOHNSON - Deep Red. Large to very large, semidouble. Average growth. M-L. (Reticulata 'Crimson Robe' x Reticulata hybrid 'Jean Pursel'). (U.S. 1982 - Pursel).

ALI HUNT - Pink with Darker Pink veining throughout each petal with bright Yellow anthers and White filaments. Medium to large, semidouble. Vigorous, upright growth. M-L. (U.S. 2013 - Hulyn Smith).

ALICE COLLINS - Deep Rose to Fuchsia. Large, semidouble to peony form. Vigorous, upright, open growth. M-L. (Reticulata hybrid 'Buddha' x Reticulata 'Tali Queen'). (U.S. 1979 - Homeyer).

ALICE McCOUGHTRY - Deep Coral Rose. Very large, full peony form. Open, spreading growth. M-L. (Reticulata hybrid 'Buddha' x Reticulata 'Cornelian'). (Aus. 1982 - T. E. Pierson, Hurstville, NSW).

ALICE SPRAGG - Deep Pink shading to soft Pink. Very large, semidouble to peony form. Dwarf growth. M. (Hybrid 'Charles Colbert' x Reticulata 'Cornelian'). (Aus. 1977 - A. Spragg, Sutherland, NSW).

ALISA - Salmon Pink. Medium, semidouble. Average growth. M. (Reticulata seedling). (U.S. 1982 - Feathers).

ALISON LENNARD - Carmine. Very large, loose peony form. Vigorous, spreading growth. E-M. (Saluenensis x Reticulata 'Crimson Robe'). (N.Z. 1982 - Mrs. I. Berg, Whakatane).

ALISON SEBIRE - Light Pink. Very large, semidouble. Vigorous, upright, compact growth. M. (Reticulata 'Willow Wand' seedling). (Aus. 1976 - Sebire).

ALLAN RAPER - Pale Pink, fading to White. Very large, rose form double. Vigorous, upright, open growth. E-M. (Reticulata hybrid 'Suzanne Withers' x Reticulata hybrid 'Arcadia'). (Aus. 1998 - Dr. R. M. Withers, Donvale, Vic.).

ALLAN WALTON - Rose veined Red. Very large, formal double. Upright, open growth. M-L. (Reticulata hybrid 'Samantha' seedling). (Aus. 1984 - Pierson).

ALMA WOOD - Vivid Red. Large, semidouble. Vigorous, upright, compact growth. M. (Reticulata hybrid 'Crimson Robe' x Reticulata hybrid 'Nuccio's Ruby'). (U.S. 1982 - Piet and Gaeta).

AMANDA LISA - Bright Deep Red. Very large, peony form. Average, upright, compact growth. M. (Reticulata hybrid x Japonica). (N.Z. 1984 - Clark).

AMANDA MANDARICH - Roseine Purple. Large to very large, semidouble. Average, upright, open growth. M. (Reticulata hybrid 'Carl Tourje' x Reticulata hybrid 'Lilette Witman'). (U.S. 1997 - Mandarich).

AMARIE - Pink with Golden anthers and Pink filaments. Very large, semidouble. Vigorous, upright growth. M. (Reticulata hybrid 'Buddy Bills' x Reticulata hybrid 'Arcadia'). (U.S. 2002 - Hulyn Smith).

AMAZING GRACE ABBOTT - Soft Pink. Large, semidouble. Average, upright growth. M. (Reticulata hybrid 'LASCA Beauty' seedling). (Aus. 2007 - Keith Abbott, Rossmoyne).

AMY PEARSON - Bright Red lighter at edge. Very large, semidouble. Vigorous, upright, compact growth. M. Reticulata 'Cornelian' seedling). (Aus. 1974 - Tuckfield).

ANGELIA DEAN - Deep Dark Black Red. Large to very large, rose form double to formal double. Average, upright, dense growth. M-L. (Reticulata hybrid 'Silver Mist' x Reticulata hybrid 'Nuccio's Ruby'). (U.S. 1996 - Jernigan).

ANN DAY - Light Orchid Pink to Deeper Pink. Very large, semidouble with large petaloids. Vigorous, upright growth. M-L. (Reticulata 'Crimson Robe' x Japonica 'Tiffany'). (U.S. 1973 - W. E. Sellers, Mobile, AL).

ANN ENGLISH - Deep Pink with Purple cast. Very large, semidouble form with high rabbit ears. Average, spreading growth. M-L. (U.S. 1999 - Jernigan).

ANN'S DELIGHT - Deep Pink. Very large, peony form. Average, upright, spreading growth. M. (Aus. 2003 - H. L. Lane, Melville, W. Aus.).

ANNABELLE FETTERMAN - Pale Pink. Large to very large, semidouble. Vigorous, upright growth. M. (Reticulata 'Cornelian' x Reticulata 'Crimson Robe'). (U.S. 1984 - Pursel).

ANNALISA - Soft Pink. Large, semidouble. Open growth. M-L. (Reticulata seedling). (U.S. 1977 - Kramer).

ANNE HIGHTOWER - Medium Pink with frosting with Yellow anthers and White filaments. Very large, semidouble. Vigorous, spreading growth. M. (Reticulata hybrid 'Suzanne Withers' x Reticulata hybrid 'Jean Pursel'). (U.S. 2015 - Hulyn Smith).

ANNE LOUISE HOWARD - Rich Pink. Very large, semidouble. Upright, open growth. M. (Reticulata hybrid 'Glowing Embers' seedling). (N.Z. 2007 - Harvey Howard).

ANNE McCULLOCH HILL - Intense Cerise Pink. Medium, rose form double. Average, upright growth. E. (Sasanqua 'Crimson King' x Reticulata 'Lion Head'). (U.S. 1977 - Parks).

ANZAC - Deep Rose. Medium, formal double. (Reticulata hybrid 'Barbara Clark' x Japonica 'Somersby'). (N.Z. 1966 - Clark).

APPLAUSE - Salmon Pink. Large, loose peony form. Vigorous, upright growth. M. (Reticulata 'Moutancha' x Reticulata hybrid 'Elizabeth Johnstone'). (U.S. 1980 - Nuccio's).

ARBUTUS GUM - Light to Deep Rose Pink. Large, semidouble with upright petals. Average, upright growth. M. (Reticulata x Japonica). (U.S. 1971 - Maitland).

ARCADIA - Salmon Pink. Very large, semidouble to loose peony form. Vigorous, upright, open growth. M-L. (Reticulata hybrid 'Mouchang' x Sasanqua 'Bonanza'). (U.S. 1979 - Piet).

ARCH OF TRIUMPH - Deep Pink to Wine Red. Very large, loose peony form. Vigorous, upright, bushy growth. E-M. (Reticulata hybrid 'Wild Form' seedling). (U.S. 1970 - Feathers).

ARNOLD'S PRIDE - Pink. Very large, peony form. Average, upright, open growth. M-L. (Aus. 2003 - John Paddison, Burradoo, NSW).

ARTHUR KNIGHT - White. Large, peony form. Upright, open growth. M-L. (Reticulata seedling). (Aus. 1981 - A. Knight, Heathfield, S. Aus.).

ASTRA - Rose Pink with White inner petals. Large, rose form double. Average, upright, compact growth. M-L. (Reticulata seedling). (U.S. 1979 - H. H. Smith, Yuba City, CA).

AURORA'S BLUEBIRD - Rose Pink. Large, anemone form. Spreading, open growth. M-L. (Reticulata hybrid 'Balderdash' seedling). (Aus. 1984 - Pierson).

AVALON SUNRISE - Medium Pink with Gold stamens. Small to medium, single; profuse bloomer. Compact growth; flower sheds by itself. M. [(Pitardii var. 'Yunnanica' x Reticulata 'Purple Gown') x (Reticulata hybrid 'Buddha' x Fraterna hybrid 'Tiny Princess')]. (U.S. 1988 - Charvet).

AZTEC - Deep Rose Red. Very large, semidouble with irregular petals to loose peony form. Average, upright, open growth. E-L. (Reticulata 'Crimson Robe' x Japonica 'Lotus'). (Similar to 'Howard Asper'). (U.S. 1971 - Asper).

*BABY FACE - ('Tongzimian' - Chinese Name). White, usually shaded Pink. Medium to large, semidouble to formal double. Average growth. (Yunnan Reticulata). (China to U.S. 1980 - U. C. Bot. Gdn, CA).

BAGBY HALL - Red. Large to very large, semidouble. Average, upright growth. L. (Reticulata 'Crimson Robe' x Reticulata/Japonica hybrid). (U.S. 1981 - Pursel).

BALDERDASH - Red. Very large, semidouble with folded crepe petals and notched petal edges. Vigorous growth. M. (Reticulata hybrid 'Wild Form' x Reticulata 'Crimson Robe'). (N.Z. 1967 - Dr. Jane Crisp, Tirau).

BAOSHIHUA - See 'Jewel Flower'.

BAOYUHONG - See 'Red Jewel'.

BAOZHU CHA - See 'Nobel Pearl'.

BARBARA BUTLER - Bright Coral Pink. Very large, semidouble. Vigorous, upright, open growth. L. (U.S. 2013 - Hulyn Smith).

BARBARA CLARK - Rose Pink. Medium, semidouble. Vigorous, compact, upright growth. E-L. (Saluenensis x Reticulata 'Captain Rawes'). (N.Z. 1958 - Doak).

BARBARA GOFF - Soft Pink (RHS 68B) with Yellow anthers and Yellow filaments. Very large, semidouble to rose form double to formal double. Average, upright growth. E-L. (U.S. 2009 - Gordon Goff, Lafayette, CA).

BARBARA SEBIRE - Salmon Pink. Very large, peony form. Open, upright growth. M. (Reticulata seedling). (Aus. 1985 - Sebire).

BEAUTIFUL DAY - White with Blush on outer petals. Medium, irregular formal double. Strong, upright, open growth. M. {(Pitardii var. 'Yunnanica' x Reticulata Hybrid 'Forty-Niner') x [Reticulata 'Crimson Robe' x (Reticulata 'Crimson Robe' x Fraterna)]}. (U.S. 2007 - Charvet).

BEN FATHERREE - Rose. Large to very large, semidouble. Vigorous, open, upright growth. M-L. (Reticulata hybrid 'Arch of Triumph' x Reticulata/ Japonica hybrid). (U.S. 1980 - Pursel).

BERG'S FLAME - Flame Red with Rose Pink stamens. Very large, single with crinkled petals. Average, upright growth. E. (Saluenensis/Reticulata hybrid x Japonica 'Mahogany Glow'). (N.Z. 1983 - Mrs. J. Berg, Whakatane).

BERNADETTE KARSTEN - Carmine Pink. Very large, semidouble. Vigorous, upright growth. M-L. (Reticulata x Japonica). (U.S. 1967 - Maitland).

BERYL'S CHOICE - Soft Salmon Pink. Large, peony form. Spreading, upright growth. M-L. (Reticulata 'Tali Queen' seedling). (Aus. 1980 - Sebire).

BETH DEAN - Red. Very large, semidouble. Vigorous, upright growth. M-L. (Reticulata 'Crimson Robe' seedling). (U.S. 1994 - Pursel).

BETHANY FATHERREE - Rose Pink. Very large, semidouble. Vigorous, upright growth. M-L. (Reticulata 'Crimson Robe seedling x Reticulata/Japonica hybrid). (U.S. 1980 - Pursel).

BETTE DURRANT - Rose. Medium, semidouble. Compact, upright growth. M-L. (Saluenensis x Reticulata 'Captain Rawes'). (N.Z. 1961 - Doak).

BETTE JEAN DAUGHARTY - Light or clear Pink with Golden Yellow anthers and Yellow filaments. Very large, semidouble. Vigorous, upright growth. M-L. (Reticulata 'Suzanne Withers' x Reticulata 'Nita McRae'). (U.S. 2009 - Hulyn Smith).

BETTY'S DELIGHT - Coral Pink. Small, formal double. Slow, compact, bushy growth. M-L. (Reticulata hybrid 'Brian' seedling). (Aus. 1990 - Mildorrie Camellias, Jasper's Brush, NSW).

BEULAH HENNLY - Light Pink with Yellow anthers and White filaments. Large, semidouble. Vigorous, upright, open growth. L. (U.S. 2013 - Hulyn Smith).

BEV PIET - Very Dark Red. Medium, semidouble. Vigorous, compact growth. M-L. (Reticulata hybrid 'Fire Chief' x Reticulata hybrid 'Nuccio's Ruby'). (U.S. 1986 - Piet and Gaeta).

BEV PIET VARIEGATED - Very Dark Red and White variation of 'Bev Piet'. (U.S. 1986 - Piet and Gaeta).

BIG APPLE - Dark Red. Large to very large, semidouble to peony form. Average growth. M-L. (Reticulata 'Crimson Robe' x Reticulata hybrid 'Jean Pursel'). (U.S. 1984 - Pursel).

BIG DIPPER - Carmine Pink. Very large, semidouble. Vigorous, upright, spreading growth. E. (Reticulata 'Tali Queen' seedling). (U.S. 1987 - Hall).

BIGG AL'S - Red. Very large, semidouble to loose peony. Vigorous, upright, dense growth. E-M. (U.S. 1999 - Albert Biggs, Sacramento, CA).

174

BILL FICKLING - Medium Pink with Golden anthers and White filaments. Medium, semidouble. Vigorous, upright growth. M-L. (U.S. 2015 - Hulyn Smith).

BILL GOERTZ - Red. Large, semidouble with upright, heavily notched petals and flared stamens. Average, upright, compact growth. M-L. (Reticulata hybrid 'William Hertrich' x Japonica 'Clark Hubbs'). (U.S. 1985 - W. F. Goertz, Duarte, CA).

BILL JOHNSTON - Red. Very large, semidouble to loose peony form. Average, upright, spreading growth. E-M. (Reticulata 'Tali Queen' x Reticulata hybrid 'Buddha'). (U.S. 1981 - Homeyer).

BILL LA ROSE - Burgundy Red. Large to very large, semidouble. Average, upright growth. M-L. (Reticulata 'Crimson Robe' x Reticulata/Japonica hybrid). (U.S. 1981 - Pursel).

BILL WOODROOF - Scarlet, occasionally toned lighter. Very large, semidouble to loose peony form. Vigorous, upright, compact growth. M. (Reticulata hybrid). (U.S. 1989 - Nuccio's).

BILL'S PINK - Light Pink. Large, peony form. Vigorous, open, spreading growth. M-L. (Reticulata hybrid 'Trewithen Pink' seedling). (N.Z. 1984 - E. W. E. Butcher, Hamilton).

BILLY HARDWICK - Flame Red. Very large, semidouble with ruffled petal edges. Vigorous, upright growth. M-L. (Reticulata 'Tali Queen' seedling). (U.S. 1996 - Jernigan).

BILLY MANN - Dark Pink. Large, semidouble. Vigorous, upright, open growth. M. (Reticulata seedling). (U.S. 1975 - Kramer).

BLACK LACE - Dark Velvet Red. Medium, rose form double to formal double with incurved petals. Upright, compact growth. M-L. (Hybrid 'Donation' x Reticulata 'Crimson Robe'). (U.S. 1968 - L. W. Ruffin, Ellisville, MS).

BLACK LACE PEONY - Dark Velvet Red. Medium, full peony form. (Sport of Reticulata hybrid 'Black Lace'). (U.S. 1982 - R L Wines, Ocala, FL).

BLAIR BROWN - Dark Pink. Large to very large, semidouble to peony form. Vigorous, upright growth. M-L. (Reticulata 'Crimson Robe' x Reticulata hybrid 'Jean Pursel'). (U.S. 1985 - Pursel).

BLOOMFIELD - Velvety Red. Large to very large, rose form double. Vigorous, upright, open growth. M-L. [Reticulata' Crimson Robe ' x (Reticulata 'Cornelian' x Japonica 'Finlandia')]. (U.S. 1985 - Charvet).

BLOSSOM TIME - Pink. Very large, peony form. Vigorous, upright growth. M. (Reticulata hybrid 'Buddha' seedling). (Aus. 1974 - Sebire).

BLUE TWILIGHT - Bluish Pink with Yellow anthers and Pinkish filaments. Large, semidouble with ruffled petals. Vigorous, open growth. M. (C. x williamsii 'William's Lavender' x Reticulata 'Cornelian'). (U.S. 1965 - Parks).

BOB SANSING - Red. Large to very large, semidouble. Vigorous, upright growth. M-L. (Reticulata 'Crimson Robe' seedling). (U.S. 1981 - Pursel).

BRAVO - Scarlet Red, often toned lighter toward center. Large to very large, irregular semidouble with crinkled petals. Vigorous, upright growth. M. (Reticulata seedling). (U.S. 1990 - Nuccio's).

BRAXTON BRAGG - Bright Orchid Pink. Large, peony form. Strong, very compact growth. E-M. [(Pitardii var. 'Yunnanica' x Reticulata hybrid 'Forty- Niner') x (Reticulata hybrid 'Buddha' x Reticulata hybrid 'Forty-Niner')]. (U.S. 2005 - Charvet).

BRIAN - Dark Pink with Silvery cast. Medium, semidouble. Upright, compact growth. M-L. (Saluenensis x Reticulata 'Captain Rawes'). (N.Z. 1958 - Doak).

BRIAN BOHRU - Red. Medium, semidouble. Slow, dense, spreading growth. M-L. (Reticulata hybrid 'Brian Variegated' seedling). (Aus. 1991 - Mildorrie Camellias, Jasper's Brush, NSW).

BRIAN GAETA - Bright Pink speckled White. Large to very large, semidouble with wavy petals. Vigorous, spreading growth. E-M. (Reticulata hybrid 'Pink Sparkle' x Granthamiana). (U.S. 1989 - Piet and Gaeta).

BRIGHT BEAUTY - Light Red. Very large, semidouble to anemone form. Upright, open growth. M. (Aus. 1984 - Sebire).

*BRIGHT LEAF PINK - ('Liangye Yinhong' - Chinese Name). Veined Pink. Medium to large, semidouble with wavy petals. M. (Yunnan Reticulata). (China to U.S. 1980 - U. C. Bot. Gdn, CA).

*BRIGHT RED GOWN - ('Dahongpao' - Chinese Name). Crimson. Large to very large, semidouble with wavy petals. E. (Yunnan Reticulata). (China to U.S. 1980 - U. C. Bot. Gdn, CA).

BRILLIANT BUTTERFLY - Rose Red. Large, semidouble with open rows of thickly textured petals with crimped and wavy margins. Average, bushy growth. M-L. (Reticulata hybrid 'Wild Form' x Reticulata 'Butterfly Wings'). (N.Z. 1969 - Dr. Jane Crisp, Tirau).

*BROCADE GOWN RED - ('Jinpaohong' - Chinese Name). Deep Crimson. Large to very large, rose form double. M. (Yunnan Reticulata). (China to U.S. 1980 - U. C. Bot. Gdn, CA).

BROOKE MAPHIS - Pink with Golden anthers and White filaments. Large, semidouble to rose form double. Average, upright growth. M-L. (U.S. 2008 - Homeyer).

BROOKE-LYN - Lavender Pink. Large, formal double. Dense, spreading growth. M-L. (Reticulata hybrid 'Grand Jury' x Japonica 'Cho-Cho-San'). (Aus. 1983 - B. Hooper, Bexley North, NSW).

BRYANT WHITE - Flame to Dark Red with Yellow anthers and Pink to White filaments. Large, semidouble. Slow, open growth. L. (U.S. 2013 - Hulyn Smith).

BUBBLES - Red. Large, semidouble. Average, upright, open growth. E. (Saluenensis seedling x Reticulata 'Crimson Robe'). (N.Z. 1973 - Mrs. I. Berg, Whakatane).

BUBBLES RIVETT - Glowing Red. Very large, peony form with rabbit ears. Average, open, spreading growth. M-L. (Reticulata seedling). (N.Z. 1993 - J. Rivett, Whakatane).

BUDDHA - Rose Pink. Very large, semidouble with irregular, upright, wavy petals. Vigorous, upright growth. M. (Reticulata x Pitardii Variety Yunnanica). (China to U.S. 1950 - Descanso).

BUDDHA'S CHILD - Phlox Pink. Large, semidouble. Average, upright, compact growth. E-M. (Reticulata hybrid 'Buddha' x Sasanqua/Reticulata hybrid). (U.S. 1981 - Parks).

BUDDY BILLS - Rose Pink. Large to very large, semidouble to loose peony form. Vigorous, upright, spreading growth. M-L. (Reticulata 'Cornelian' x Japonica 'Mrs. D. W. Davis'). (U.S. 1981 - Pursel).

BUDDY ENGLISH - Deep Pink. Very large, semidouble. Average, upright growth. M-L. (Reticulata hybrid 'Jean Pursel' seedling). (U.S. 1998 - Jernigan).

BUDDY GARRETT - Light Pink. Medium to large, rose form double. Average, spreading growth. M-L. (Reticulata 'Crimson Robe' x Reticulata hybrid 'Jean Pursel'). (U.S. 1983 - Pursel).

BUMBLE BEE - Fluorescent Pink. Large, anemone form to loose peony form. Vigorous, upright, open growth. E-M. (Japonica 'Debutante' x Reticulata 'Crimson Robe'). (U.S. 1972 - G. Priest, Bakersfield, CA).

BUMBLE BEE VARIEGATED - Fluorescent Pink blotched White variation of 'Bumble Bee'. (U.S. 1982 - Alfter).

BUNNY GIRL - Pale Pink. Large, loose peony form. Average, upright, open growth. E. (Reticulata hybrid 'Dream Girl' x Oleifera 'Jaune'). (N.Z. 1984 - O. Blumhardt, Whangarei).

BURGUNDY QUEEN - Deep Red. Very large, semidouble. Vigorous, upright growth. M. (Reticulata 'Tali Queen' seedling). (Aus. 1970 - Sebire).

BUSTER BUSH - Pink veined Dark Pink to Light Red. Very large, semidouble to loose peony form. Average, upright, open growth. M. (Reticulata hybrid 'Buddha' x Reticulata hybrid 'Trewithin Pink'). (U.S. 1990 - Homeyer).

BUTTERFLY GIRL - Pale Pink, fading to Lighter Pink at center. Very large, semidouble to peony form. Vigorous, upright growth. M. (Reticulata hybrid 'Suzanne Withers' x Reticulata hybrid 'Jean Pursel'). (Aus. 2000 - Dr. R. M. Withers, Donvale, Vic.).

*BUTTERFLY PINK - ('Fenhudie' - Chinese Name). Veined Pink. Medium to large, semidouble with irregular, wavy petals. M. (Yunnan Reticulata). (China to U.S. 1980 - U. C. Bot. Gdn, CA).

BUTTERFLY SPRING - ('Fu Dei Qiuan' - Chinese Name). Medium Pink. Large, formal double with inner petals incurved and outer petals reflexed. Vigorous, well-branched growth. [(Reticulata hybrid Suzanne Withers' x Reticulata hybrid 'White Retic') x Reticulata hybrid 'Ruta Hagmann']. (U.S. 2012 - John Wang, Orinda, CA).

*BUTTERFLY WINGS - ('Houye Diechi' - Chinese Name). Rose Pink. Very large, semidouble with irregular, broad, wavy petals resembling wings of butterfly. Slender, open growth. M. (Yunnan Reticulata). (China to U.S. 1948 - Descanso and Peer).

CAITLIN OLIVIA - Mid Pink. Very large, semidouble form. Open, upright, spreading growth. M. (Reticulata hybrid 'LASCA Beauty' seedling). (Aus. 2005 - John Butler, Cabarlah, Qld.).

CALEDO - Light Orchid Pink. Very large, semidouble. Vigorous growth. E-M. (Reticulata hybrid 'Confucius' x Reticulata 'Willow Wand'). (Aus. 1968 - Tuckfield).

CALIFORNIA DAWN - Light Pink. Large, semidouble to loose peony form with crinkled petals. Vigorous, upright, compact growth. E-M. (Sasanqua x Reticulata). (U.S. 1987 - Nuccio's).

CALIFORNIA FANTASY - Glowing Pink. Very large, semidouble to loose peony form. Vigorous, open, upright growth. M. (Reticulata hybrid 'Carl Tourje' seedling). (U.S. 1992 - Hall).

CALIFORNIA SUNRISE - Blush Pink. Medium to large, semidouble with upright petals. Vigorous, upright, open growth. E. (Sasanqua x Reticulata hybrid). (U.S. 1988 - Nuccio's).

CALIFORNIA SUNSET - Deep Rose Pink. Large, semidouble with flared Golden stamens and wavy petals. Average, open growth. E. (Sasanqua x Reticulata). (U.S. 1988 - Nuccio's).

CAMBRIA - Rose Red. Very large, semidouble to loose peony form. Vigorous growth. E-M. (Reticulata seedling). (N.Z. 1978 - Clark).

CAMELLIA CITY - Rose Red. Very large, semidouble. Average, upright growth. L. (Reticulata 'Crimson Robe' x Reticulata hybrid 'Jean Pursel'). (U.S. 1981 - Pursel).

CAMELOT - Rose Pink. Large, semidouble. Vigorous, upright, open growth. M. (Reticulata hybrid 'Buddha' seedling). (Aus. 1976 - Sebire).

CAMERON COOPER - Vivid Pink. Large to very large, rose form double to peony form. Vigorous, upright, compact growth. E-L. (Reticulata 'Cornelian' x Japonica 'Mrs. D. W. Davis.'). (U.S. 1976 - Pursel).

CANADIAN CAPERS - Light Mauve Pink. Medium, semidouble. Vigorous, upright growth. M-L. (Reticulata seedling). (U.S. 1977 - V. Shuey, Temple City, CA).

CAPITAN - Light Crimson. Large, semidouble with upright petals. Vigorous, upright growth. M-L. (Reticulata seedling). (U.S. 1975 - Kramer).

CAPRICIOUS - Rose Bengal. Very large, semidouble to loose peony form. Vigorous, upright, spreading growth. M. (Reticulata 'Crimson Robe' x Japonica 'Ville De Nantes.'). (U.S. 1974 - Homeyer).

***CAPTAIN RAWES** - ('Guixia' - Chinese Name). Carmine Rose Pink. Very large, semidouble with irregular petals. Average, open growth. L. (China [Canton] to England 1820).

CARL TOURJE - Soft Pink with shadings of Deeper Pink. Large, semidouble with wavy petals. Vigorous, upright, open growth. M. (Pitardii Variety Yunnanica x Reticulata 'Cornelian'). (U.S. 1960 - Huntington).

CAROL HOLLAND - Purple Red. Large, semidouble. Average, upright growth. E-M. (Reticulata hybrid 'Buddha' seedling). (U.S. 1988 - R. E. Ehrhart, Walnut Creek, CA).

CAROLYN PHILLIPS - Dark Rose Pink. Very large, semidouble to loose peony. Vigorous upright growth. L. (Reticulata hybrid 'Valley Knudsen' x Reticulata hybrid 'Jean Pursel'). (U.S. 2008 - CamelliaShop, Savannah, GA).

CAROLYN SNOWDON - Rose Red. Large, semidouble with Yellow stamens. Vigorous, upright growth. E. (Reticulata hybrid 'Buddha' x Japonica 'Ville de Nantes'). (England 1986 - Dr. J. A. Smart, Barnstable, N. Devon).

CEZANNE - Rose Pink. Large, semidouble of hose-in-hose form. Average, upright, open growth. M. (Reticulata 'Tali Queen' seedling). (Aus. 1971 - Tuckfield).

CHANCES ARE - Magenta Rose. Very large, semidouble. Vigorous, upright growth. E-M. (Reticulata hybrid 'Pink Sparkle' seedling). (U.S. 1996 - Hall).

***CHANG'S TEMPLE** - ('Zhangjia Cha' - Chinese Name). China Rose. Very large, semidouble; large, open center with some petaloids, up to 20 petals in 4 or 5 rows; petals are deeply notched, some with multiple markings. Vigorous, compact growth with very large leaves. M-L. (Yunnan Reticulata). (China to N.Z. 1964 - Durrant).

CHARLES R. BUTLER - Cerise Pink. Large to very large, semidouble with upright, crinkled petals. Average, open growth. M. (Reticulata seedling). (U.S. 1984 - Belle Fontaine Nsy., Theodore, AL).

CHARLIE BUSH - Pink shading to Light Pink at petal edges. Very large, peony form with fluted petals. Slow, upright, dense growth. M-L. (Reticulata hybrid 'Arch of Triumph' x Reticulata hybrid 'LASCA Beauty'). (Aus. 1995 - J. Hunt, Montrose, Vic.).

CHARLOTTE JONES - Medium Pink with Yellow anthers and White filaments. Large, semidouble to rose form double. Average, upright, spreading growth. M-L. (U.S. 2018 - Frank Pursel & Hulyn Smith).

CHEAP FRILLS - Light Pink. Medium, semidouble to peony form with very wavy petal edges. Strong, compact growth. M-L. (Pitardii var. 'Yunnanica' x Reticulata hybrid 'Forty-Niner') x {Pitardii var. 'Yunnanica' x [(Reticulata 'Purple Gown' x Reticulata 'Crimson Robe') x (Reticulata 'Crimson Robe' x Fraterna)]}). (U.S. 2007 - Charvet).

CHERRY GLOW - Glowing Red. Very large, loose peony form. Vigorous, upright, open growth. M. (Reticulata 'Crimson Robe' seedling). (Aus. 1970 - Sebire).

CHERRY RIPE - Cerise. Very large, single with veined and slightly crinkled petals. Average, open growth. M. (Reticulata seedling). (U.S. 1971 - Asper).

CHINA GIRL - Deep Pink. Large, semidouble. Average, upright, open growth. E-M. (Oleifera 'Narumi-Gata' x Reticulata 'Cornelian'). (U.S. 1981 - Parks).

CHINA LADY - Rich Orchid Pink. Very large, semidouble with irregular petals. Vigorous, upright growth. E-L. (Reticulata hybrid 'Buddha' x Granthamiana). (U.S. 1968 - Nuccio's).

CHITTAGONG - Sweet pea Red. Large to very large, semidouble with wavy, crinkled petals. Average, spreading growth. M. (Reticulata seedling). (U.S. 1970 - Peer).

CHONGJEI - See 'Adoring Pure'.

CHOO CHOO - Red. Large to very large, semidouble. Average, upright, open growth. M-L. (Reticulata hybrid 'Buddha' seedling). (U.S. 1972 - Alfter).

CHRISSIE'S RETIC - White in center shading to Pale Pink at edge. Very large, peony form. Average, upright, compact growth. M. (Reticulata hybrid). (N.Z. 1987 - Haydon).

CHRISTINE GONOS - Pink. Large to very large, semidouble to anemone form. Average, upright, open, spreading growth. M-L. (Reticulata hybrid 'Mouchang' x Japonica 'Mrs. D. W. Davis' x Japonica 'Estella d'Ancona'). (U.S. 1994 - Mandarich).

CHRISTMAS EVE - Bright Pink. Large, semidouble with occasional rabbit ears. Vigorous growth. (Oleifera x Reticulata 'Cornelian'). (U.S. - Parks).

CHRISTOPHER HOLMAN - Clear Red. Large, semidouble to peony form. Vigorous, upright growth. M-L. (Reticulata hybrid 'Pharaoh' seedling). (U.S. 1983 - Gilley).

*CHRYSANTHEMUM PETAL - ('Juban' - Chinese Name). Light Carmine Pink. Medium, rose form double to formal double with fluted petals. Slender, open growth. E. (Yunnan Reticulata). (China to U.S. 1948 - Descanso and Peer).

CHUCK RITTER - Medium Pink to Darker Pink with Golden anthers and White filaments. Large, semidouble to full peony; flower form and color varies on the same bush; the placement and number of stamens varies with each bloom; may have petaloids mixed with stamens. Average, upright, open growth. L. (U.S. 2015 - Hulyn Smith).

*CHUXIONG GOLD - ('Chuxiongjin' - Chinese Name). Deep Pink with soft Light Purple tone, gradually becoming Lighter Pink towards the edges. Very large, peony form. Vigorous, spreading growth. E. (Collected in Yunnan, China). (Aus. - Bob Cherry, Paradise Plants, Kulnura).

*CHUXIONGJIN - See 'Chuxiong Gold'.

CINDY KENDRICK - Soft Pink. Very large, semidouble. L. (Reticulata hybrid 'Valley Knudsen' x Reticulata hybrid 'Jean Pursel'). (U.S. 2008 - CamelliaShop, Savannah, GA).

CITY OF NEWBERG - Medium Pink fading at the petal edges with Bright Yellow anthers and Pale Yellow filaments. Very large, semidouble. Vigorous, upright, open growth. E-M. [(Pitardii var.yun. x Reticulata hybrid 'Purple Gown') x (Pitardii var.yun. x Japonica 'Guilio Nuccio')] x Sasanqua 'Narumigata'. (U.S. 2018 - Dan Charvet, Fort Bragg, CA).

CLAIRE MAXWELL - Pink. Medium to large, semidouble to rose form double. Average, spreading growth. M-L. (Reticulata 'Crimson Robe' x Reticulata hybrid 'Jean Pursel'). (U.S. 1983 - Pursel).

COACH TOM OSBORNE - Red. Very large, semidouble. Average, upright, open growth. E-M. (Reticulata seedling). (U.S. 1997 - A. Buchholz, Cupertino, CA).

COLIN J GARRETT - Soft Pink, fading to very Pale Pink at center. Large, semidouble form. Upright, open, spreading growth. M-L. (Aus. 2005 - John Butler, Cabarlah, Qld.).

COLLEEN SHERRINGTON - Light Pink. Medium, rose form double with veined and notched petals. Vigorous, dense, spreading growth. E-M. (Hybrid 'Donation' x Reticulata hybrid 'Valley Knudsen'). (Aus. 1994 - C. Sherrington, Balwyn, Vic.).

COMBER'S PRIDE - Deep Red. Very large, semidouble to peony form. Average, upright growth. M. (Reticulata hybrid 'Craig Clark' x Reticulata hybrid 'Jean Pursel'). (U.S. 1995 - Homeyer).

*CONFUCIUS - Orchid Pink. Large, semidouble with high center and intermingled petaloids and stamens in center. Average, upright, compact growth. M. (Reticulata x Pitardii Variety Yunnanica). (China to U.S. 1950 - Descanso).

CONGRATULATIONS - Pale Orchid Pink. Very large, formal double with wavy petals. M. (Reticulata seedling). (N.Z. 1997 - Cambrian Nsy.).

CORINNE SEBIRE - Rose Opal. Very large, semidouble. Vigorous, open, upright growth. M. (Reticulata hybrid 'Buddha' seedling). (Aus. 1976 - Sebire).

*CORNELIAN - (Damanao' - Chinese Name). Turkey Red to Deep Rose Pink marbled White. Large to very large, semidouble to peony form with irregular, wavy, crinkled, spiraled petals and a few petaloids in center. Vigorous, compact growth. M. (Variegated form of Reticulata 'Lion Head'). (Yunnan Reticulata). (China to U.S. 1948 - Descanso and Peer).

*CORNELIAN CHRYSANTHEMUM PETAL - ('Manao Juban' - (Chinese Name). Pink shaded White. Medium, rose form double. E. (Yunnan Reticulata). (China to U.S. 1980 - U. C. Bot. Gdn, CA).

*CORNELIAN PURPLE GOWN - ('Manao Zipao' - Chinese Name). Turkey Red marked White. Large to very large, semidouble with irregular, twisted, upright petals. M. (Yunnan Reticulata). (China to U.S. 1980 - U. C. Bot. Gdn, CA).

CORRY VAN GASTEREN - Deep Pink. Large to very large, semidouble. Average, upright growth. M-L. (Reticulata 'Cornelian' x Japonica). (U.S. 1974 - A. N. Funari, Santa Clara, CA).

COTTAGE QUEEN - White with Deeper Rose colored base petals. Medium, single to semidouble. Strong, upright, open growth. M. {(Pitardii var. 'Yunnanica' x Reticulata hybrid 'Forty-Niner') x [(Pitardii var. 'Yunnanica' x Reticulata 'Purple Gown') x (Saluenensis x Transnokoensis)]}. (U.S. 2007 - Charvet).

CRAIG CLARK - Deep Carmine. Very large, semidouble. Vigorous, upright growth. M. (Reticulata 'Cornelian' seedling). (N.Z. 1967 - Clark).

*CRANE CREST - ('Heding Cha' - Chinese Name). Turkey Red. Large to very large, rose form double. M-L. (Yunnan Reticulata). (China to U.S. 1980 - U. C. Bot. Gdn, CA).

CREIGHTON DELIGHT - Pink with White frosting with Yellow anthers and White filaments. Very large, semidouble. Slow, upright, open growth. L. (Seedling of Reticulata hybrid 'Suzanne Withers'). (U.S. 2016 - Walter Creighton, Semmes, AL).

CRESTA BLANCA - White. Very large, semidouble. Vigorous, upright growth. M-L. (Japonica x Reticulata 'Crimson Robe'). (U.S. 1961 - Feathers).

CRIMSON CANDLES - Bright Rose Red. Small, single. Vigorous, upright growth. L. Cold hardy. (Reticulata x Fraterna seedling). (U.S. 1995 - Parks).

CRIMSON CROWN - Crimson. Large, single. Vigorous, open growth. M-L. (Japonica 'Christine Lee' x Reticulata 'Crimson Robe'). (U.S. 1965 - Hilsman).

*CRIMSON ROBE - ('Dataohong' - Chinese Name). Carmine Red. Very large, semidouble with wavy, crinkled, crepe textured petals. Vigorous, spreading growth. M. (Yunnan Reticulata). (China to U.S. 1948 - Descanso and Peer).

CRINOLINE - Salmon Pink. Large to very large, semidouble to rose form double with wavy petals. Open, upright growth. M. (Reticulata hybrid 'LASCA Beauty' seedling). (Aus. 1985 - Sebire).

CRYSTAL CITY - Bright Pink with iridescent petals. Large to very large, semidouble to loose peony form. Upright, pendulous growth. M-L. (Reticulata 'Cornelian' x Japonica seedling). (U.S. 1974 - A. N. Funari, Santa Clara, CA).

CULLEN W. COATES - Red with Purple cast. Large, semidouble to peony form. Vigorous, upright growth. M. (U.S. 1999 - Barbara C. Tuffli, Atherton, CA).

CURTAIN CALL - Deep Coral Rose. Very large, semidouble with irregular petals. Vigorous, open growth. M-L. (Reticulata seedling). (U.S. 1979 - Nuccio's).

DA QIO - See 'Zhanqun Lady'.

DAGUIYE - See 'Large Osmanthus Leaf'.

DAHONGPAO - See 'Bright Red Gown'.

*DALI BUTTERFLY WING - ('Dali Diechi' - Chinese Name). Carmine. Large to very large, semidouble with irregular upright petals. (Yunnan Reticulata). (China to U.S. 1980 - U. C. Bot. Gdn, CA).

DALI CHA - See 'Tali Queen'.

DALI DIECHI - See 'Dali Butterfly Wing'.

DALLAS - Orchid Pink. Large, semidouble to loose peony form. Open growth. M-L. (Reticulata seedling). (U.S. 1977 - Kramer).

DALLAS PRICE - Dark Red. Medium to large, semidouble to rose form double. Vigorous, upright growth. M-L. (Reticulata 'Crimson Robe' x Reticulata hybrid 'Arch of Triumph'). (U.S. 1984 - Pursel).

DAMANAO - See 'Cornelian'.

DANA HOMEYER - Dark Ruby Red. Large to very large, semidouble to peony form. Vigorous, upright, open growth. E-M. (Reticulata/Japonica x Reticulata 'Crimson Robe'/Granthamiana). (U.S. 1989 - Homeyer).

DANDAHONG - See 'Pale Bright Red'.

DARK JEWEL - Very Dark Red. Large, peony form. Upright, open growth. M. (Reticulata 'Cornelian' seedling). (Aus. 1985 - Sebire).

DATAOHONG - See 'Crimson Robe'.

DAVID BELLAMY - Bright Pink with Gold anthers and Creamy White filaments. Large to very large, semidouble. Slow, upright growth. M-L. (Seedling of Reticulata hybrid 'Frank Houser Var.'). (U.S. 2018 - Pat Johnson, Cairo, GA).

DAVID FEATHERS - Pink. Large to very large, semidouble form. Average, upright growth. E-M. (U.S. 2003 - Northern CA Camellia Research Committee).

DAYINHONG - See 'Shot Silk'.

DE LANCEY - Dark Red. Very large, semidouble. Upright, open growth. M. (Reticulata hybrid 'William Hertrich' seedling). (Aus. 1979 - Sebire).

DEBBIE ANDERTON - Cardinal Red. Large, full peony form. Average, upright, compact growth. E. (Reticulata hybrid 'William Hertrich' seedling). (N.Z. 1984 - T. Lennard, Te Puke).

DEBBIE ODOM - Pink with fluorescent sheen. Large, semidouble. Vigorous, upright, open growth. M-L. (Reticulata hybrid 'Trewithen Pink'/'Tali Queen' x Reticulata hybrid 'Lilette Witman'). (U.S. 2008 - Jernigan).

DEBRET - Salmon Pink. Large, full peony form. Average, compact growth. L. (Japonica 'Debutante' seedling x Reticulata 'Crimson Robe'). (U.S. - 1983 - Feathers).

DEBUT - China Rose. Very large, loose peony form. Vigorous, upright, compact growth. M. (Reticulata x Japonica). (U.S. 1977 - Nuccio's).

DELTA DAWN - Rose Pink. Very large, semidouble with upright petals. Average, spreading growth. M-L. (Reticulata/Japonica hybrid x Reticulata 'Cornelian'). (U.S. 1980 - Pursel).

DEN BURTON - Bright Scarlet Red. Very large, peony form. Average, upright, dense growth. M-L. (Reticulata x Japonica seedling). (N.Z. 1999 - Haydon).

DESCANSO MIST - Red with iridescent petals. Large, formal double to peony form. Average, upright growth. M. (Reticulata x Japonica). (U.S. 1970 - Maitland).

DESERT MOON - Light Pink marked Deeper Pink toward edge. Large to very large, semidouble with irregular upright petals. Vigorous, upright compact growth. M. (Reticulata hybrid 'LASCA Beauty' seedling). (U.S. 1989 - Longdon Nsy., Sebastopol, CA).

DIAMOND HEAD - Red. Large, semidouble with crinkled petals. Open growth. M. (Japonica 'Lady Vansittart Red' x Reticulata 'Crimson Robe'). (U.S. 1961 - Feathers).

DIANNE CLARK - Phlox Pink. Large, semidouble. Vigorous, upright growth. M. (N.Z. 1984 - Dr. B. W. Goa).

DICK GOODSON - Dark Red. Large to very large, semidouble. Average, upright growth. M-L. (Reticulata 'Cornelian' x Japonica 'Mrs. D. W. Davis'). (U.S. 1979 - Pursel).

DICK PARKER - Lavender Pink. Large, semidouble. Vigorous, upright, open growth. M-L. (Reticulata seedling). (U.S. 1975 - Kramer).

DINGXIANGHONG - See 'Lilac Red'.

DOBRO - Red. Very large, rose form double to formal double. Vigorous, upright, dense growth. E-L. (Reticulata hybrid 'Hulyn Smith' x Reticulata hybrid 'Harold L. Paige'). (U.S. 1992 - Mandarich).

DOLLY WEST - Salmon Pink with White cast. Very large, semidouble to anemone form. Vigorous, upright growth. E-L. (Reticulata hybrid 'Wild Form' seedling). (Aus. 1981 - T. E. Pierson, Hurstville, NSW).

DOLORES HOPE - Light Rose Pink veined Orchid with some center petals shaded White. Very large, semidouble with irregular petals. Vigorous, upright, open growth. M. (Reticulata x Japonica). (U.S. 1971 - Peer).

DONNA BLAIR - Bright Pink to Rose Red. Very large, semidouble with upright petals. Vigorous, upright growth. M-L. (Reticulata 'Butterfly Wings' x Japonica 'All-American'). (U.S. 1981 - Alfter).

DONNA LOUISE TIMMINS - Silver Rose with heavy Silver overtones. Large, anemone form. Upright, open growth. E-L. (Reticulata hybrid 'Tranquility' seedling). (Aus. 1984 - Pierson).

DORA ELISE - Deep Pink. Large, semidouble. Average, upright growth. M-L. (Reticulata 'Crimson Robe' seedling). (N.Z. 1974 - Mrs. E. D. Clark, Matamata).

DORA LEE - Bright Pink. Very large, semidouble to loose peony form. Vigorous, upright growth. L. (Reticulata hybrid 'Valley Knudsen' x Reticulata hybrid 'Jean Pursel'). (U.S. 2008 - CamelliaShop, Savannah, GA).

DORIS FOWLER - Red. Large, semidouble. Vigorous, upright, open growth. M-L. (Reticulata 'Crimson Robe' x Reticulata hybrid 'Jean Pursel'). (U.S. 1984 - Pursel).

DORIS MAE - Orchid Pink with Yellow anthers and White filaments. Medium, loose peony to full peony form. Vigorous, upright, dense growth. M-L. (Seedling of Reticulata hybrid 'Frank Houser'). (U.S. 2016 - Al and Doris Lefebvre, Gulfport, MS).

DOROTHEE ROGERS - Deep Rose Pink heavily moired Darker Pink. Very large, peony form. M-L. (Reticulata hybrid 'Three Dreams' seedling). (Aus. 1984 - Pierson).

DOROTHY JEAN - Orange Red. Very large, anemone form. Vigorous, upright, open growth. M. (Reticulata seedling). (Aus. 1987 - Dr. J. I. Luke).

DORRIE HIGGINS - Rich Plum Red with Silver sheen. Very large, loose peony form. Upright, open growth. E. (Reticulata 'Crimson Robe' x Reticulata hybrid 'William Hertrich'). (Aus. 1982 - T. E. Pierson, Hurstville, NSW).

DOT SPENGLER - Spiraea Red. Small, semidouble to loose peony form. Average, spreading growth. E. (Sasanqua 'Crimson King' x Reticulata 'Lion Head'). (U.S. 1977 - Parks).

*DOUBLE BOWL - ('Lianrui' - Chinese Name). Light Pink. Medium to large, semidouble. M. (Yunnan Reticulata). (China to U.S. 1980 - U. C. Bot. Gdn, CA).

DR. ALVIN JOHNSON - Red. Large, semidouble. Average, upright growth. E-L. (Reticulata 'Crimson Robe' x Reticulata/Japonica hybrid). (U.S. 1982 - Pursel).

DR. ANNETTE THOMAS - Dark Pink with frosting at times with Golden anthers and White filaments. Very large, semidouble. Vigorous, upright growth. L. (U.S. 2015 - Hulyn Smith).

DR. BOB WITHERS - Pink at the tips of the petals, fading to Pale Pink at the base. Very large, peony form. Vigorous, upright growth. M. (Reticulata hybrid 'Suzanne Withers' x Reticulata hybrid 'Jean Pursel'). (Aus. 2000 - Dr. R. M. Withers, Donvale, Vic.).

DR. BOB WOMACK - Light Red with Yellow anthers. Very large, semidouble. Average, upright growth. M. (Japonica 'Letitia Schrader' x Reticulata hybrid 'Buddha'). (U.S. 1973 - R. K. Womack, Shreveport, LA).

DR. BRIAN DOAK - Deep Pink with darker veining and petal edges almost White. Very large, full peony form. Average, upright growth. M. (Reticulata 'Tali Queen' seedling). (N.Z. 1974 - Durrant).

DR. CLIFFORD PARKS - Red with Orange cast. Very large, semidouble to anemone form to loose or full peony form. Vigorous growth. M. (Reticulata 'Crimson Robe' x Japonica 'Kramer's Supreme'). (U.S. 1971 - Los Angeles State and County Arboretum [Dr. Clifford R. Parks], Arcadia, CA).

DR. DAN NATHAN - Deep Red. Large to very large, semidouble. Vigorous, upright growth. M-L. (Reticulata 'Crimson Robe' x Lutchuensis). (U.S. 1981 - Pursel).

DR. DAN NATHAN SUPREME - Pink with fluorescent sheen. Large to very large, semidouble. Vigorous, upright, open growth. M-L. [(Reticulata hybrid 'Trewithen Pink' x Reticulata 'Tali Queen') x Reticulata hybrid 'Lilette Witman']. (U.S. 1991 - Jernigan).

DR. DAVE - Dark Red with frosted sheen. Very large, semidouble. Vigorous, upright growth. M-L. (Reticulata 'Crimson Robe' x Lutchuensis). (U.S. 1992 - Pursel).

DR. DOREEN CLARK - Rose Pink, deepens at center. Very large, full semidouble to loose peony form. Vigorous, upright growth. E-L. (Reticulata hybrid 'Ellie Rubensohn' seedling). (Aus. 2002 - Patrick Clark, Pymble, NSW).

DR. EMIL CARROLL - Burgundy Red. Large to very large, loose peony form to semidouble. Average, upright growth. M-L. (Reticulata 'Crimson Robe' x Reticulata/Japonica hybrid). (U.S. 1983 - Pursel).

DR. FRED E. HEITMAN - Deep bright Red with fluorescent sheen. Very large, semidouble to rose form double. Average, upright, dense growth. M. (Reticulata hybrid 'Nuccio's Ruby' x Reticulata hybrid 'Lilette Whitman'). (U.S. 1995 - Mandarich).

DR. GORDON RICHMOND - Salmon Pink. Large, full semidouble to rose form double. Vigorous, upright, compact growth. M. (Reticulata 'Cornelian' x Japonica 'Mrs. D. W. Davis). (U.S. 1983 - Parks).

DR. HARRY MOORE - Cerise Red with sheen. Large, semidouble to loose peony form. Vigorous, upright, spreading growth. M-L. (Reticulata x Japonica). (U.S. 1980 - Kramer).

DR. JACK DAVIS - Rose Red. Large to very large, semidouble. Average, upright growth. M. (Reticulata 'Crimson Robe' x Reticulata/Japonica hybrid). (U.S. 1981 - Pursel).

DR. JAMES W. FRICK - Clear Pink washed Silver. Very large, semidouble. Vigorous, upright, open growth. L. (Reticulata hybrid 'Buddha' x Reticulata hybrid 'William Hertrich'). (U.S. 1981 - M. O'Malley, Woodside, CA).

DR. JANE CRISP - Silver Pink with darker veining and Silver edges. Very large, loose peony form. Upright growth. E-L. (Pitardii/Reticulata hybrid x Reticulata 'Willow Wand'). (N.Z. 1977 - Durrant).

DR. JOHN D. LAWSON - Purplish Pink edged with thin White line. Large, semidouble. Average, upright growth. M. (Reticulata hybrid 'Fluted Orchid' x Japonica 'Marjorie Magnificent'). (U.S. 1970 - Dr. J. D. Lawson, Antioch, CA).

DR. JON BAILEY - Light Pink with Gold anthers and Yellow filaments. Large, semidouble. Vigorous, upright growth. M-L. (U.S. 2017 - Frank Pursel, Oakland, CA & Hulyn Smith, Valdosta, GA).

DR. LESLEY - Phlox Pink with Lavender cast. Large, semidouble with crinkled petals. Upright, compact growth. M-L. (Saluenensis x Reticulata 'Captain Rawes'). (N.Z. 1961 - Doak).

DR. LOUIS POLIZZI - White washed and shaded Orchid Pink. Medium, semidouble with upright, fluffy petals to full peony form. Vigorous, upright compact growth. E-M. (Saluenensis x Reticulata 'Captain Rawes'). (U.S. 1969 - Tammia).

DR. R. P. McDONALD - Burgundy Red. Large, semidouble to peony form with crinkled petals. M-L. (Reticulata 'Crimson Robe' x Reticulata/Japonica hybrid). (U.S. 1981 - Pursel).

DR. REEVES WELLS - Dark Red. Large, semidouble. Vigorous, upright growth. M-L. (Non-Reticulata hybrid x Reticulata/Japonica hybrid). (U.S. 1983 - Pursel).

DR. T. E. PIERSON - Deep Rich Pink. Very large, loosely imbricated formal double. Upright, open growth. M-L. (Reticulata hybrid 'Samantha' seedling). (Aus. 1982 - T. E. Pierson, Hurstville, NSW).

DR. WILLIAM D. BATTLE - Soft Pastel Pink. Large, semidouble. Average, upright growth. E-M. (Reticulata hybrid 'Buddha' x Fraterna). (U.S. 1984 - B. Butler, Modesto, CA).

DREAM BABY - Bright Pink. Miniature, semidouble. Average growth. M. (Hybrid 'Dream Girl' x Reticulata hybrid 'Buddha'/Fraterna seedling). (N.Z. 1986 - O. Blumhardt, Whangarei).

DREAM CASTLE - Silver Pink. Very large, semidouble with fluted, upright petals. Vigorous, upright, open growth. M. (Reticulata 'Crimson Robe' x Japonica 'Coronation'). (U.S. 1972 - Nuccio's).

DREAM GIRL - Salmon Pink. Large to very large, semidouble with fluted, upright petals. Vigorous, upright growth. (Oleifera 'Naruma-Gata' x Reticulata hybrid 'Buddha'). (U.S. 1965 - Asper).

DUXIN DIECHI - See 'Single Heart Butterfly'.

DYNASTY - Deep Pink. Very large, full peony form. Vigorous, upright growth. M. (Reticulata hybrid 'Buddha' seedling). (U.S. 1985 - Hall).

EALON MAGEE - Red. Large, semidouble with high center. Average, upright growth. M-L. (Reticulata 'Crimson Robe' x Reticulata/Japonica hybrid). (U.S. 1982 - Pursel).

*EARLY CRIMSON - ('Zaotaohong' - Chinese Name). Large to very large, semidouble with irregular, upright petals. E. (Yunnan Reticulata). (China to N.Z. 1964 - Durrant; China to U.S. 1980 - U. C. Bot. Gdn, CA).

EARLY GIRLY - Red, some Pinkish petals and a hint of Orange. Very large, rose form double with wavy petals. Average, upright, spreading growth. E-L. (Reticulata hybrid 'Nuccio's Ruby' x Reticulata hybrid 'Emma Gaeta'). (U.S. 1996 - T. Lee, Carmichael, CA).

*EARLY PEONY - ('Zaomudan' - Chinese Name). China Rose. Large, semidouble with upright, folded center petals with notched margins. Vigorous growth. M. (Yunnan Reticulata). (China to N.Z. 1964 - Durrant).

EASY VIRTUE - Bright Red veined Dark Red. Very large, single. Vigorous, upright, spreading growth. E-M. (Reticulata 'Crimson Robe'/Granthamiana x Reticulata hybrid 'Mouchang'). (U.S. 1988 - Homeyer).

ED ATKINS - Reddish Pink. Large to very large, semidouble. Average, spreading growth. M-L. (Reticulata 'Crimson Robe' x Reticulata hybrid 'Jean Pursel'). (U.S. 1983 - Pursel).

ED LAURENT - Deep Burgundy Red. Large to very large, semidouble. Average, upright growth. M-L. (Reticulata 'Crimson Robe' x Reticulata hybrid 'Jean Pursel'). (U.S. 1982 - Pursel).

ED'S RED - Light Red with Reddish sheen. Large to very large, semidouble to rose form double. Average, upright, spreading growth. M-L. (Reticulata hybrid 'Hulyn Smith' seedling). (U.S. 1995 - E. Atkins, Shalimar, FL).

EDEN QUEEN - Red. Very large, semidouble. Average, upright, open growth. M. (Reticulata 'Cornelian' seedling). (N.Z. 1973 - Clark).

EDEN ROC - Light crepe Pink. Large, semidouble with irregular petals and narrow column of stamens. Vigorous, upright growth. M. (Reticulata hybrid 'Wild Form' seedling). (U.S. 1973 - Feathers).

EDITH MAZZEI - Rose Pink with Deeper Pink veining. Large to very large, rose form double to semidouble. Average, upright, open growth. M-L. (Reticulata 'Crimson Robe' x Reticulata hybrid 'Jean Pursel'). (U.S. 1982 - Pursel).

EDNA HANNAN - Glowing Red. Very large, semidouble. Average, upright growth. M. (Reticulata seedling). (N.Z. 1990 - N. Hannan, Te Puke).

EDWARD'S DREAM - Deep Pink. Large, semidouble to rose form double. Vigorous, upright growth. E-M. (Reticulata seedling). (Aus. 1998 - R. Cherry, Kulnura, NSW).

EIGHTEEN YEAR-OLD MAIDEN - ('Se Ba Bian' - Chinese Name;'18 Years Young Lady'). White with small patches of Pink to Red on the outer petals. Large, loose peony form. (Reticulata hybrid 'Wang WW#8' x Reticulata hybrid 'Ruta Hagmann'). (U.S. 2012 - John Wang, Orinda, CA).

EILEEN SEBIRE - Deep Cyclamen Pink. Very large, peony form. Vigorous, upright, compact growth. M-L. (Reticulata 'Cornelian' seedling). (Aus. 1987 - Sebire).

EL GRECO - Currant Red. Large, semidouble. Vigorous, upright growth. M. (Reticulata 'Crimson Robe' seedling). (Aus. 1971 - Tuckfield).

ELAINE - Medium Pink with bright Yellow anthers and White filaments. Very large, semidouble; the petals are fluted. Vigorous, upright, spreading growth. M-L. (Reticulata hybrid 'Curtain Call' x Reticulata hybrid 'Pleasant Memories'). (U.S. 2013 - James and Elaine Smelley).

ELISE WINTER - Rose Pink fading at center. Large, rose form double. Vigorous, upright, open growth. M-L. (Reticulata 'Crimson Robe' x Reticulata/ Japonica hybrid). (U.S. 1980 - Pursel).

ELIZABETH ASTLES - Bright Pink. Very large, semidouble to loose peony form. Vigorous, upright growth. M. (Reticulata hybrid 'Buddha' seedling). (Aus. 1976 - Sebire).

ELIZABETH B. HUNT - Pink with Golden anthers and White filaments. Medium to large, semidouble to rose form double. Vigorous, upright, spreading growth. E-L. (Reticulata hybrid 'Suzanne Withers' x Reticulata hybrid 'Delta Dawn'). (U.S. 2007 - Hulyn Smith).

ELIZABETH JOHNSTONE - Bright Rose. Large, single. (Reticulata hybrid 'Wild Form' seedling). (England 1957).

ELLIE RUBENSOHN - Rosy Crimson. Very large, semidouble to loose peony form with undulating petals. Average, upright, spreading growth. M. (Reticulata 'Crimson Robe' x Reticulata 'Purple Gown'). (Aus. 1963 - S. Rubensohn, Dural, NSW).

ELSIE DRYDEN - Delicate Light Pink with Lavender cast. Large, semidouble. Average growth. M. (Reticulata 'Confucius' x Japonica). (U.S. 1969 - H. E. Dryden, San Marino, CA).

ELSIE HUGHES - Pink. Very large, formal double to rose form double. Average, spreading growth. M. (Reticulata 'Crimson Robe' x Reticulata hybrid 'Cameron Cooper'). (U.S. 1985 - Pursel).

ELSIE MAY - Salmon Pink. Very large, semidouble to anemone form. Upright, open growth. M-L. (Reticulata 'Cornelian' x Reticulata hybrid 'Buddha'). (Aus. 1984 - Pierson).

ELSIE ROSS - Light Pink. Very large, semidouble to peony form with notched petals. Vigorous, upright, open growth. M. (Reticulata hybrid 'Suzanne Withers' x Reticulata hybrid 'Jean Pursel'). (Aus. 1996 - Dr. R. Withers, Donvale, Vic.).

ELSPETH BERG - Red. Large, semidouble with some upright petals. Average, upright, open growth. E-M. (Saluenensis x Reticulata 'Crimson Robe'). (N.Z. 1975 - Mrs. I. Berg, Whakatane).

EMILY J. BOX - Wine Red with Silver cast. Large, rose form double to formal double. Average, upright, open growth. M. (Reticulata hybrid 'Wild Form' seedling). (Aus. 1970 - F. U. Spencer, Cheltenham, Vic.).

EMILY KATE CAPLE - Red. Large, semidouble to loose peony form. Average, upright growth. M. (Pitardii x Reticulata). (N.Z. 1973 - Mrs. A. B. Durrant, Rotorua).

EMMA GAETA - Deep Rose Pink. Very large, semidouble with folded, upright, center petals. Vigorous, upright, open growth. E-L. (Reticulata 'Cornelian' x Reticulata hybrid 'Mouchang'). (U.S. 1979 - Piet).

EMMA GAETA VARIEGATED - Deep Rose Pink heavily blotched White form of 'Emma Gaeta'. (U.S. 1980 - Piet).

EMMA L - Dark Pink with deeper veining. Large, peony form. Average, upright, open growth. E. (Reticulata hybrid 'Dream Girl' seedling). (N.Z. 1993 - T. Lennard, Te Puke).

*EMPTY MOUTH - ('Qingkou' - Chinese Name). Crimson. Small, single of trumpet form. M. (Yunnan Reticulata). (China to U.S. 1980 - U. C. Bot. Gdn, CA).

*ENVYING SKY'S HEIGHT - ('Hentiangao' - Chinese Name). Light Carmine with margin of petals shaded White. Medium, semidouble to rose form double. Very slow growth. L. (Yunnan Reticulata). (China to N.Z. 1964 - Durrant; China to U.S. 1980 - U. C. Bot. Gdn, CA).

ERHAI ZHENZU - See 'Lake Erhai Pearl'.

ERICA WOMERSLEY - Deep Pink faintly edged Mauve. Large, semidouble with notched petals. Vigorous, upright, compact growth. M-L. (Hybrid 'Charles Colbert' x Reticulata 'Cornelian'). (Aus. 1975 - Mrs. A. Spragg, Sutherland, NSW).

ERIN LILY - Scarlet Red. Small, single. Slow, open, spreading growth. E-M. (Reticulata hybrid 'Brian Variegated' seedling). (Aus. 1990 - Mildorrie Camellias, Jasper's Brush, NSW).

ERNEST AYCOCK - Deep Pink. Very large, semidouble. Vigorous, upright growth. M. (Reticulata hybrid 'LASCA Beauty' x Reticulata hybrid 'Mildred Pitkin'). (U.S. 1988 - J. Austin, Four Oaks, NC).

ERNEST McDONALD - Red. Large to very large, full semidouble. Average, upright growth. M-L. (Reticulata 'Crimson Robe' x Reticulata/Japonica hybrid. (U.S. 1981 - Pursel).

ESPAÑA - Deep China Rose with White central petaloids. Very large, rose form double. Average, upright, compact growth. M-L. (Reticulata hybrid 'Nuccio's Ruby' seedling). (U.S. 1987 - H. S. Hall, San Anselmo, CA).

EUGENE STOCKMAN - Deep Red with deeper veining. Large to very large, semidouble. Vigorous, upright growth. M-L. (Reticulata 'Cornelian' x Japonica 'Mrs. D. W. Davis'). (U.S. 1979 - Pursel).

EVELYN C. BELLAMY - Pink with Dark Pink stripes with Yellow anthers and Yellow filaments. Large, semidouble. Vigorous, upright, open growth. M-L. (Seedling of Reticulata hybrid 'Valley Knudsen'). (U.S. 2016 - Pat Johnson, Cairo, GA).

EVELYN KILSBY - Deep Red. Very large, semidouble with rabbit ears. Vigorous, upright, open growth. M-L. (Reticulata seedling). (U.S. 1993 - Pursel).

EVENING GLOW PEARL - ('Ye Ming Zu' - Chinese Name). White washed with light Pink with Golden stamens. Large to very large, loose peony form with a mixed center of petaloids and stamens. Vigorous, upright, well-branched growth. L. (Reticulata hybrid 'Suzanne Withers' x Japonica 'Kona'). (U.S. 2012 - John Wang, Orinda, CA).

FAIR LASS - Persian Rose shading to White at center. Large, semidouble. Vigorous, upright, compact growth. E-L. (Saluenensis x Reticulata 'Captain Rawes'). (N.Z. 1961 - Doak).

FAIRY WINGS - White. Medium, semidouble with undulating petals and stamens in broad cylinder. Upright, columnar growth. E-M. (Japonica x Reticulata 'Crimson Robe'). (U.S. 1955 - Feathers).

RETICULATA

D-F

FANCY PANTS - White to Blush Pink to Lavender edge. Large, semidouble. Average, upright growth. M. (Reticulata 'Crimson Robe' x Granthamiana seedling). (U.S. 1989 - Homeyer).

FANNIE LOUISE MAPHIS - Pink with Golden anthers and White filaments. Very large, semidouble to rose form double. Vigorous, upright, spreading growth. M. (Reticulata hybrid 'Suzanne Withers' x Reticulata hybrid 'Delta Dawn'). (U.S. 1997 - Hulyn Smith).

FATHER L. - Bright Cerise Pink. Large to very large, semidouble. Average, spreading growth. M. (Reticulata hybrid). (U.S. 1973 - Kramer).

FENEJIAO - See 'Pretty Pink'.

*FENGSHAN CAMELLIA - ('Fengshan Cha' - Chinese Name). Carmine. Large to very large, rose form double with wavy petals. (Yunnan Reticulata). (China to U.S. 1980 - U. C. Bot. Gdn, CA).

FENGSHAN CHA - See 'Fengshan Camellia'.

FENHUDIE - See 'Butterfly Pink'.

FIESTA GRANDE - Light Lavender Pink. Medium, semidouble to loose peony form. Vigorous, upright, compact growth. E-L. (Japonica x Reticulata hybrid 'Flower Girl'). (U.S. 1986 - Piet and Gaeta).

FIESTA GRANDE VARIEGATED - Light Lavender Pink and White variation of 'Fiesta Grande'. (U.S. 1990 - Piet and Gaeta).

FIGHT ON - Dark Red with Red stamens tipped with Golden anthers. Medium, semidouble. Average, upright, compact growth. L. (Reticulata hybrid 'Flower Girl' x Reticulata 'Crimson Robe'). (U.S. 1982 - Piet and Gaeta).

FILOLI RED - Brilliant Red. Very large, semidouble. Vigorous, upright growth. M-L. (Reticulata seedling). (U.S. 1996 - Hall).

FINE PURE - ('Miaojie' - Chinese Name). Light Pink petals with Darker Pink edges, sometimes frosted White with Yellow anthers and White filaments. Very large, semidouble; petals in about three whorls, the inner incurved, the outer flat with emarginated apex. Vigorous, upright growth. M-L. (Reticulata hybrid 'Suzanne Withers' x Japonica 'Kona'). (U.S. 2007 - John Wang, Orinda, CA).

FIRE CHIEF - Deep Red. Large, semidouble to peony form. Average, upright, spreading growth. L. (Japonica 'Donckelarii' x Reticulata 'Cornelian'). (U.S. 1963 - Asper).

FIRE CHIEF VARIEGATED - Deep Red moired White variation of 'Fire Chief'.

*FIRST CLASS RED - ('Yipinhong' - Chinese Name). Light Red. Large to very large, semidouble with irregular center petals. L. (Yunnan Reticulata). (China to U.S. 1980 - U. C. Bot. Gdn, CA).

FIVE-O - Pink. Large, semidouble. Vigorous, upright, open growth. M. (Reticulata seedling). (U.S. 1975 - Kramer).

FLAMING YOUTH - Light Red. Large, single. Vigorous, open growth. E-M. (Reticulata hybrid 'Wild Form' seedling). (U.S. 1977 - Feathers).

FLAMINGO PRINCESS - Light Hot Pink with Yellow anthers and Cream filaments. Large, semidouble. Average, upright, open growth. M-L. (U.S. 2019 - Pat Johnson, Cairo, GA).

*FLAT DALI CAMELLIA - ('Pingban Dali Cha' - Chinese Name). Carmine. Large to very large, semidouble with wavy petals. E. (Yunnan Reticulata). (China to U.S. 1980 - U. C. Bot. Gdn, CA).

FLORRIE BURKE - Light Salmon Pink. Medium to large, semidouble. Average, upright growth. M. (Reticulata 'Crimson Robe' x Saluenensis). (N.Z. 1984 - Mrs. F. E. Burke, Whakatane).

FLORRIE'S THEME - Deep Salmon Pink. Large, formal double. Upright, open growth. M. (Reticulata hybrid 'Florrie Burke' seedling). (N.Z. 1987 - M. Burke, Whakatane).

FLOWER BOY - Mauve Pink. Medium, rose form double. Open, spreading growth. M-L. (Reticulata hybrid 'Flower Girl' seedling). (Aus. 1982 - Sebire).

FLOWER GIRL - Pink. Large to very large, semidouble to peony form. Vigorous, upright growth. (Oleifera 'Narumi-Gata' x Reticulata 'Cornelian'). (U.S. 1965 - Asper).

FLUTED ORCHID - Pale Orchid Pink. Medium, semidouble with fluted petals and central trumpet-shaped collection of petaloids and stamens. (Saluenensis x Reticulata 'Crimson Robe'). (U.S. 1960 - Feathers).

FLUTED SILK - Pink with center petaloids tinged White. Very large, semidouble with irregular, wavy petals. Vigorous, upright growth. M. (Reticulata 'Shot Silk' seedling). (U.S. 1988 - Hall).

FLY FLY - ('Pian Pian' - Chinese Name). White center with outer petals pink with white picotee edges and sometimes petal veining can be observed. Large to very large, semidouble. Very bushy growth. M-L. (Reticulata hybrid 'Suzanne Withers' x Japonica 'Kona'). (U.S. 2012 - John Wang, Orinda, CA).

FORTIETH ANNIVERSARY - Ruby Red. Large to very large, semidouble with upright petals. Vigorous, upright, spreading growth. E. (Reticulata 'Crimson Robe' x Reticulata hybrid). (U.S. 1985 - Pursel).

FORTUNA - Rose Red. Very large, semidouble. Average, upright growth. E-M. (Reticulata hybrid 'Buddha' x Hybrid 'Donation'). (N.Z. 1980 - P. R. McNab, Levin).

FORTY-NINER - Brilliant Red. Medium to large, full peony form. Vigorous, spreading growth. E-M. (Reticulata 'Butterfly Wings' x Japonica 'Indian Summer'). (U.S. 1969 - Asper).

FOUR WINDS - Orchid Pink. Large to very large, semidouble. M. (Reticulata 'Crimson Robe' x Japonica 'Tiffany'). (U.S. 1971 - Asper).

FRANCIE L. - Rose Pink. Large to very large, semidouble with irregular, upright, wavy petals. (Saluenensis 'Apple Blossom' x Reticulata hybrid 'Buddha'). (U.S. 1964 - Nuccio's).

FRANCIE L. SURPRISE - Rose Pink variegated White. Large to very large, peony form. (Sport of Reticulata hybrid 'Francie L'). (U.S. 1980 - C. X. Copeland, Jackson, MS).

FRANCIE L. VARIEGATED - Rose Pink and blotched White form of 'Francie L.'. (U.S. 1970).

FRANCIE L. WHITE - White. Large to very large, semidouble. M-L. (Sport of Reticulata hybrid 'Francie L'.). (U.S. 1998 - Dr. Dan Nathan, Fort Valley, GA).

FRANK HOUSER - Red. Very large, semidouble to peony form. Vigorous, upright, spreading, open growth. E-M. (Reticulata hybrid 'Buddha' x Japonica 'Steve Blount'). (U.S. 1989 - Homeyer).

FRANK HOUSER VARIEGATED - Red and White form of 'Frank Houser'. (U.S. 1990 - Jernigan).

FRANK PURSEL - Red. Very large, heavy semidouble to peony form. Vigorous, upright growth. M-L. (Reticulata/Japonica hybrid x Reticulata 'Cornelian'). (U.S. 1987 - Pursel).

FRED LEE - Red. Large to very large, heavy semidouble to peony form. Vigorous, upright growth. M. (Reticulata seedling). (U.S. 1985 - Pursel).

FRED PARKES - Deep Pink. Very large, semidouble to loose peony form with fluted petals. Average, upright, spreading growth. M. (Reticulata hybrid 'William Hertrich' x Reticulata hybrid 'Mouchang'). (Aus. 1992 - E. Parkes, East Brighton, Vic.).

FRED S. TUCKFIELD - Rose Pink with deeper veining. Large, formal double to rose form double. Average, very bushy growth. L. (Reticulata 'Confucius' seedling). (Aus. 1968 - Tuckfield).

FRED SPENCER - Dark Red. Very large, semidouble. Upright, compact growth. M. (Reticulata 'Crimson Robe' seedling). (Aus. 1980 - F. N. Spencer, Cheltenham, Vic.).

FREGEO - Pink, notched petals with Deeper Pink Stripes. Large, semidouble. Vigorous, upright, bushy growth. M-L. (Reticulata hybrid 'Phyl Doak' seedling). (Aus. 1998 - ACRS W. A. Branch).

FRIENDLY SKIES - Rose Pink with slightly lighter margination. Large, semidouble. Average, upright growth. E. (Reticulata hybrid). (U.S. 1980 - Feathers).

FU DEI QIUAN - See 'Butterfly Spring'.

FUCHSIA - Fuchsia with Gold anthers and Pinkish filaments. Medium, single. Average, upright, spreading growth. M-L. (Seedling of Reticulata hybrid 'Mark Cannon'). (U.S. 2016 - Pat Johnson, Cairo, GA).

GAEL'S DREAM - Soft Rose Pink shading to Carmine. Very large, semidouble. Vigorous, upright growth. E. (Reticulata hybrid 'Dream Girl' x Reticulata). (N.Z. 1987 - T. Lennard, Te Puke).

GAINSBOROUGH - Red. Very large, loose peony form. Average, open growth. M. (Reticulata 'Confucius' seedling). (Aus. 1971 - Tuckfield).

GENE KING - Deep Red. Large to very large, semidouble. Average, upright growth. M-L. (Reticulata 'Crimson Robe' x Reticulata hybrid 'Jean Pursel'). (U.S. 1982 - Pursel).

GEOFFREY DAVIS - Pink. Large, peony form. Slow, open, spreading growth. M-L. (Reticulata seedling). (Aus. 1996 - E. Parkes, East Brighton, Vic.).

GEORGE FIRTH - Dark Red. Large, peony form. Average growth. M. (Reticulata hybrid 'Maude Sugg' seedling). (U.S. 1984 - Gilley).

GEORGE GERBING - Pink. Very large, semidouble. Vigorous, upright, open growth. M-L. (Reticulata hybrid 'Patricia Coull' x Japonica 'Ville de Nantes'). (U.S. 1993 - Jernigan)).

GEORGE SPENCER - Rose. Large to very large, formal double. Slow, upright growth. M. (Reticulata hybrid 'Frank Houser' x unknown pollen parent). (U.S. 2009 - John L. Spencer, Lakeland, FL).

GEORGIE GIRL - Orchid Pink fading to Silvery Pink edged petals. Very large, semidouble with heavily veined petals. Upright, compact growth. M-L. (Reticulata 'Crimson Robe' seedling). (Aus. 1980 - Sebire).

GILFORD - Bright Red. Very large, semidouble. Vigorous, upright, open growth. M. (Reticulata hybrid 'Wild Form' seedling). (Aus. 1970 - F. N. Spencer, Cheltenham, Vic.).

GILLEY'S FOREVER - Dark Pink with Golden anthers and White filaments. Large, semidouble. Average, upright, spreading growth. M-L. (Seedling of Reticulata hybrid 'Valley Knudsen'). (U.S. 2016 - Gilley).

GILLIAM HAWKE - Deep Red. Very large, peony form. Slow, upright growth. M-L. (Reticulata seedling). (Aus. 1995 - J. Hawke, Carrara, Qld.).

GIORGIO'S PRIDE - Dark Red. Large to very large, semidouble. Average growth. M-L. (Reticulata 'Crimson Robe' x Reticulata hybrid 'Mary Stringfellow'). (U.S. 1984 - Pursel).

GLADYS HERBERT - Light Pink. Large to very large, semidouble. Average, spreading growth. M. (Reticulata hybrid). (U.S. 1973 - Kramer).

GLADYS PARKS - Rose Pink. Large, full semidouble to rose form double. Average, upright growth. (Reticulata 'Crimson Robe' x Japonica 'Kramer's Supreme'). (U.S. 1983 - Parks).

GLADYS WALKER - Dark Red. Very large, peony form to rose form double. Average, upright, open growth. L. (Reticulata 'Crimson Robe' x Reticulata hybrid 'Jean Pursel'). (U.S. 1992 - Homeyer).

GLOWING EMBERS - Red. Very large, semidouble to loose peony form. Average, upright, open growth. E. (Reticulata 'Crimson Robe' x Reticulata 'Lion Head'). (N.Z. 1976 - A. M. Burwell, Inglewood).

GOLDEN GLIMMER - White with the faintest Pink Blush and light shading of Yellow at base of petals. Very large, semidouble form. Average, upright, spreading growth. M. (Reticulata hybrid 'Wild Form' x Reticulata hybrid 'Suzanne Withers' x Nitidissima). (Aus. 2003 - Mr. Geoffrey and Mrs. Colleen Sherrington, Balwyn North, Vic.).

*GOLDEN HEART PEARL - ('Jinxin Baozhu' - Chinese Name). Carmine. Very large, semidouble with wavy petals. E. (Yunnan Reticulata). (China to U.S. 1980 - U. C. Bot. Gdn, CA).

*GOLDEN STAMEN HIBISCUS - ('Jinrui Furong' - Chinese Name). Light Pink shaded deeper in center. Large, semidouble. E. (Yunnan Reticulata). (China to U.S. 1980 - U. C. Bot. Gdn, CA).

GORDON HOWELL - Rose Red. Large, semidouble. Average, upright growth. M-L. (Reticulata 'Crimson Robe' x Reticulata hybrid 'Jean Pursel'). (U.S. 1982 - Pursel).

GRACE ROGERS - Rose to Red. Large, semidouble to anemone form. Spreading growth. M-L. (Reticulata 'Cornelian' x Reticulata hybrid 'Buddha'). (Aus. 1984 - Pierson).

GRAEM YATES - Pink to bright Red. Very large, peony form. Vigorous, compact growth. E-M. (Reticulata hybrid 'Francie L.' x Japonica 'Jonathan'). (U.S. 1988 - G. Yates, Charlotte, NC).

GRAEM YATES VARIEGATED - Pink blotched White form of 'Graem Yates'. (U.S. 1989).

GRAND JURY - Salmon Pink. Large, semidouble to peony form. Open, spreading growth. M. (Saluenensis x Reticulata hybrid 'Salutation'). (N.Z. 1962 - Jury).

GRANDANDY - Red with distinctive White frosting with Yellow anthers and White filaments. Very large, semidouble. Average, upright growth. L. [(Reticulata 'Crimson Robe' x Lutchuensis) x Reticulata hybrid 'Lilette Witman']. (U.S. 2013 - Hulyn Smith).

GREAT PEACH BLOSSOM - Soft medium Pink. Medium, semidouble. Strong, upright, open growth. M. [(Pitardii var. 'Yunnanica' x Reticulata 'Purple Gown') x Nitidissima 'Golden Glow']. (U.S. 2008 - Charvet).

GREYSTONE - Soft Pink shading lighter to edge. Large, loose peony form. Vigorous, upright, open growth. M. (Reticulata hybrid 'Buddha' x Reticulata x Saluenensis). (N.Z. 1971 - R. F. Shaw, Henderson).

GUALALA GLOW - Glowing Coral Pink. Very large, semidouble. Compact growth. M. [(Pitardii var. 'Yunnanica' x Reticulata hybrid 'Forty-Niner') x (Reticulata hybrid 'Buddha' x Hybrid 'Coral Delight')]. (U.S. 2002 - Charvet).

GUIXIA - See 'Captain Rawes'.

GUIYEY ANGHONG - See 'Osmanthus Leaf Carmine'.

GUY RICE - Pink. Large to very large, semidouble. Vigorous, upright growth. M-L. (Reticulata 'Crimson Robe' x Reticulata hybrid 'Jean Pursel'). (U.S. 1981 - Pursel).

GWEN WASHBOURNE - Reddish Pink. Very large, semidouble to loose peony form. Average growth. M. (Reticulata seedling). (N.Z. 1974 - Mrs. G. Washbourne, Morrinsville).

GWYNETH SCOTT - Deep glowing Red. Very large, semidouble to loose peony form. Average, upright growth. M-L. (Reticulata hybrid 'Nuccio's Ruby' seedling). (N.Z. 1990 - J. Hansen, Waikanae).

GYPSY LIGHTS - White with Pink Blush. Small, single. Strong, upright, well-branched growth; flower sheds by itself. M. {Pitardii var. 'Yunnanica' x [Reticulata 'Crimson Robe' x (Reticulata 'Crimson Robe' x Fraterna)]}. (U.S. 1999 - Charvet).

H. C. RAMBATH - Bright Deep Red. Very large, semidouble to loose peony form. Vigorous, upright, open growth. E-L. (Reticulata hybrid 'Nuccio's Ruby' x Reticulata 'Crimson Robe'). (U.S. 1992 - Mandarich).

HALL'S PRIDE - Salmon Pink. Very large, semidouble. Vigorous, upright, open growth. M-L. (Reticulata 'Cornelian' seedling). (U.S. 1985 - H. S. Hall, San Anselmo, CA).

HALL'S PRIDE VARIEGATED - Salmon Pink heavily blotched White variation of 'Hall's Pride'.

HANK STONE - Dark Rose Pink outer petals shading to soft Pink center petals. Large, rose form double. Average, upright growth. M-L. (Reticulata 'Crimson Robe' x Reticulata hybrid 'Arch of Triumph'). (U.S. 1986 - Pursel).

HAPPINESS - Red. Large, semidouble with deeply notched and folded petals. Average, upright, pendulous growth. E. (Pitardii/Yunnanensis hybrid x Reticulata 'Willow Wand'). (N.Z. 1976 - Durrant).

HAPPY DAYS - Rose Pink. Medium to large, rose form double. Vigorous, upright, compact growth. M. (Reticulata 'Cornelian' x Hybrid 'Brigadoon' seedling). (U.S. 1979 - Pursel).

HARBINGER - Dark Red. Large, semidouble. Vigorous, upright, compact growth. E. (Reticulata 'Crimson Robe' seedling). (Aus. 1971 - Sebire).

HARKAWAY - Currant Red. Medium, semidouble with crimped, irregular petals. Average, upright, open growth. M. (Reticulata 'Crimson Robe' seedling). (Aus. 1971 - Tuckfield).

HAROLD AUSTIN - Rose Red. Very large, semidouble. Average, spreading growth. M. (Reticulata 'Crimson Robe' seedling). (N.Z. 1983 - H. G. Austin, New Plymouth).

HAROLD L. PAIGE - Bright Red. Very large, rose form double to peony form. Vigorous, spreading growth. L. (Japonica 'Adolph Audusson' x Reticulata 'Crimson Robe'). (U.S. 1972 - J. Osegueda, Oakland, CA).

HAROLD MURPHY - Glowing Coral Pink. Medium, peony form. Strong, upright, well-branched growth. M-L. {[(Pitardii var. 'Yunnanica' x Reticulata 'Purple Gown') x (Reticulata hybrid 'Buddha' x Fraterna hybrid 'Tiny Princess')] x Reticulata hybrid 'Harold L. Paige'}. (U.S. 2008 - Charvet).

HARRIET SALMON - Rose to Dark Red. Very large, semidouble with upright petals. Vigorous, upright, open growth. M. (Reticulata hybrid 'Buddha' x Japonica 'All American'). (U.S. 1981 - Alfter).

HARRY M. BLOOM - Salmon Red. Large, semidouble with wavy, crinkled petals. Vigorous, upright, compact growth. E-L. (Saluenensis 'Apple Blossom' x Reticulata 'Crimson Robe'). (U.S. 1982 - Feathers).

HAZEL GROSSO - Light Red. Very large, semidouble with irregular petals. Average, upright growth. M. (Reticulata seedling). (U.S. 1983 - R. F. Roggia, San Jose, CA).

HAZEL LENNARD - Rose Pink. Very large, peony form. Vigorous, upright growth. E-M. (Reticulata seedling). (N.Z. 1985 - T. Lennard, Te Puke).

HEARTWOOD BOLERO - Medium Pink. Large, formal double to rose form double with ruffled petal edges. Strong, upright growth; bud set up and down the stem. M. (Pitardii var. 'Yunnanica' x Reticulata 'Purple Gown'). (U.S. 1981 - Charvet).

HEARTWOOD FANDANGO - Bright Pink. Medium, semidouble to irregular double form with very wavy petal margins. Strong, upright, open growth. E. {(Pitardii var. 'Yunnanica' x Reticulata 'Purple Gown') x [(Pitardii var. 'Yunnanica' x (Reticulata 'Purple Gown' x Forrestii)]}. (U.S. 2011 - Charvet).

HEDING CHA - See 'Crane Crest'.

HELEN DOGGETT - Deep Pink. Very large, semidouble with upright petals. Vigorous, upright growth. M-L. (Reticulata seedling). (U.S. 1983 - B. Butler, Modesto, CA).

HENRY'S SURPRISE - Deep Red. Very large, semidouble. Vigorous, upright, open growth. M-L. (Reticulata 'Chang's Temple' seedling). (N.Z. 1999 - H. B. McCounel).

HENTIANGAO - See 'Envying Sky's Height'.

HERALDINGS - Flesh Pink. Large, formal double. Vigorous, spreading growth. M-L. (Reticulata hybrid x Japonica 'Mark Alan Variegated'). (U.S. 1984 - Mrs. M. O'Malley, Woodside, CA).

HIGH FEVER - Deep Rose Pink. Very large, loose peony form with rabbit ears. Vigorous, upright, open growth. M. (Reticulata 'Cornelian' seedling). (U.S. 1996 - Hall).

HIGH ROLLER - Rose Pink veined Red. Large to very large, semidouble. Vigorous, upright growth. E-L. (Reticulata 'Crimson Robe' x Reticulata hybrid 'Jean Pursel'). (U.S. 1980 - Pursel).

HIGH SIERRA - Spiraea Red. Very large, semidouble to loose peony form. Vigorous, upright, spreading growth. M-L. (Reticulata hybrid 'Lilette Witman' seedling). (U.S. 1996 - Hall).

HIGH SKY - Pink. Very large, semidouble with irregular, wavy petals. Vigorous, upright growth. M. (Reticulata hybrid 'Mouchang' seedling). (U.S. 1988 - Hall).

HIGHLAND GEM - Deep Pink. Very large, peony form. Average, upright, open growth. M-L. (Aus. 2003 - John Paddison, Burradoo, NSW).

HIGHLIGHT - Brilliant Red. Large, semidouble with wavy petals. Vigorous, open growth. M. (Reticulata 'Purple Gown' x Saluenensis). (N.Z. 1969 - Jury).

HILLARY TRAMONTE - Dark Pink, shading deeper at edge of petals. Very large, peony form. Average, upright, open growth. M. (Aus. 2003 - Mrs. Hilary Tramonte, Kew, Vic.).

HODY WILSON - Dark Red. Very large, semidouble with irregular petals to rose form double. Vigorous, upright, compact growth. M-L. (Reticulata 'Crimson Robe' x Reticulata hybrid 'Kohinor'). (U.S. 1979 - Piet).

HOLY PURE (SHENGJIE) - ('Sheng Jie'). Inner two whorls White lightly tinged Pink, outer whorls slightly Darker Pink with Light Purple margins, sometimes frosted White with Yellow anthers and White filaments. Large to very large, rose form double to semidouble. Vigorous, upright growth. M-L. (Reticulata hybrid 'Suzanne Withers' x Japonica 'Kona'). (U.S. 2007 - John Wang, Orinda, CA).

HONGWAN CHA - See 'Red Bowl'.

HONGXIA - See 'Red Cloud'.

HOUYE DIECHI - See 'Butterfly Wings'.

HOWARD ASPER - Salmon Pink. Very large, peony form with loose, upright petals. Vigorous, upright, spreading growth with very large, heavy foliage. M-L. (Reticulata 'Cornelian' x Japonica 'Coronation'). (U.S. 1963 - Asper).

HOWARD BURNETTE - Currant Red. Very large, semidouble to loose peony form. Average, upright, dense, spreading growth. E-L. (Reticulata 'Crimson Robe' x Reticulata hybrid 'Nuccio's Ruby'). (U.S. 1997 - Mandarich).

HOWARD CAPLE - Red. Large, semidouble. Pyramidal growth. E-M. (Reticulata hybrid 'Wild Form' x Reticulata 'Shot Silk'). (N.Z. 1972 - Dr. J. Crisp, Tirau).

HOWARD DUMAS - Currant Red. Very large, semidouble with upright petals to peony form. Average, upright, open growth. M. (Japonica 'Elizabeth Boardman' x Reticulata). (U.S. 1983 - Homeyer).

HOWARD RHODES - Dark Red with Yellow anthers and Yellow filaments. Large, peony form. Vigorous, upright growth. M. (Reticulata hybrid 'Buddy Bills' x Reticulata hybrid 'Jean Pursel'). (U.S. 2010 - Hulyn Smith).

HUIA - Deep Rose Pink. Very large, semidouble. Vigorous, upright, compact growth. M. (Reticulata 'Cornelian' seedling). (N.Z. 1984 - Clark).

HULYN SMITH - Soft Pink. Large, semidouble. Average, upright growth. M-L. (Reticulata 'Cornelian' x Japonica 'Mrs. D. W. Davis'). (U.S. 1979 - Pursel).

HULYN'S MEADOWBROOK - Medium Pink, sometimes frosted White with Gold anthers and White filaments; the bloom is often fluorescent. Very large, semidouble to full peony. Vigorous, upright, spreading growth. M-L. (Reticulata hybrid 'Suzanne Withers' x Reticulata hybrid 'Frank Houser'). (U.S. 2014 - Hulyn Smith).

HULYN'S SWEET EMILY - Dark Pink with White anthers and Red filaments. Very large, peony form. Average, dense growth. M. (Reticulata hybrid 'Hulyn Smith' x Reticulata hybrid 'Delta Dawn'). (U.S. 2010 - Hulyn Smith).

HY-BALL - Wine Red. Medium, peony form of ball type with petaloid center. Upright, columnar growth. M-L. (Hybrid 'Williams Lavender' x Reticulata 'Crimson Robe'). (U.S. 1955 - Feathers).

HYMAN'S RETIC - Orchid Pink. Very large, loose peony to semidouble form. Vigorous, upright growth. M-L. (U.S. 1999 - Hyman R. Norsworthy, Beaumont, TX).

IDA BERG - Red. Very large, semidouble. Vigorous, upright growth. M. (Reticulata seedling x Reticulata 'Purple Gown'). (N.Z. 1973 - L. Berg, Whakatane).

IDA COSSOM - Rose Pink. Very large, semidouble to peony form. Upright, open growth. M. (Reticulata hybrid 'LASCA Beauty' seedling). (Aus. 1984 - Sebire).

IDA GREEN - Rose Pink shaded Orange. Large, rose form double. Average, upright growth. E. (Saluenensis x Reticulata 'Crimson Robe'). (N.Z. 1983 - Mrs. I. Berg, Whakatane).

IDA'S JOY - Glowing Red. Large, peony form. Average, upright growth. M-L. (Reticulata seedling). (N.Z. 1989 - Mrs. I. Berg, Whakatane).

ILAM CHERRY - Bright Cherry Red. Very large, semidouble. Vigorous, upright growth. M. (Reticulata seedling). (N.Z. 1977 - Mrs. A. M. Coker, Christchurch).

ILAM MIST - Pink with darker veining. Large, semidouble. Average, upright, compact growth. E-L. (Reticulata seedling). (N.Z. 1973 - Mrs. A. M. Coker, Christchurch).

IN LOVING MEMORY - Light Pink. Large to very large, semidouble to loose peony form. Rapid, average form growth. M-L. (Reticulata hybrid 'Gael's Dream' x. Sasanqua). (N.Z. 2007 - Haydon).

INAMORATA - Rose Pink. Medium, single. Slow, open growth. (Saluenensis x Reticulata hybrid 'Wild Form'). (England 1950 - Hanger).

INNOVATION - Wine Red with Lavender overtones. Large, peony form with twisted fluted petals. Vigorous, slightly open growth. E-L. (Hybrid 'Williams Lavender' x Reticulata 'Crimson Robe'). (U.S. 1965 - Feathers).

INSPIRATION - Phlox Pink. Medium, semidouble. (Reticulata x Saluenensis). (England 1954 - Hanger).

INTERVAL - Salmon Pink. Large to very large, single with high narrow cone of stamens. Bushy growth. M. (Japonica x Reticulata). (U.S. 1975 - Feathers).

*INTOXICATINGLY BEAUTIFUL RED - ('Zuijiaohong' - Chinese Name). Carmine. Very large, semidouble with wavy petals. E. (Yunnan Reticulata). (China to U.S. 1980 - U. C. Bot. Gdn, CA).

IRENE BERGAMINI - Vibrant medium Pink with Yellow anthers and White filaments. Medium to large, semidouble. Average, upright, spreading growth. M. (U.S. 2015 - Don Bergamini, Martinez, CA).

IRIS LAUGHEAD - Orchid Pink shaded Lavender. Large to very large, semidouble. Average, spreading growth. M. (Reticulata hybrid). (U.S. 1973 - Kramer).

IVAN MITCHELL - Dark Red. Large, rose form double to formal double. Average, upright growth. M-L. (Reticulata hybrid). (U.S. 1986 - Pursel).

J. D. DEAN - Pink. Very large, rose form double. Vigorous, upright growth. M. (Reticulata hybrid 'Buddy Bills' x Reticulata hybrid 'Dr. Emil Carroll'). (U.S. 1991 - Pursel).

J. W. ROGERS - Rose Red. Medium, semidouble to rose form double. Vigorous, upright growth. M-L. (Reticulata 'Crimson Robe' x Reticulata hybrid 'Jean Pursel'). (U.S. 1986 - Pursel).

JACK GRIMM - Pink with White filaments and Yellow anthers, Very large, semidouble. Average, upright growth. L. (U.S. 2019 - Camellia Heaven - John Grimm, Bush, LA).

JACK MANDARICH - Spiraea Red. Medium to large, formal double to rose form double with undulating petals. Average, upright, spreading growth. E-L. (Reticulata hybrid 'Lilette Witman' x Reticulata hybrid 'Hulyn Smith'). (U.S. 1995 - Mandarich).

*JADE STRIPED RED - ('Yudaihong' - Chinese Name). White veined Crimson. Large to very large, semidouble with irregular petals. E. (Yunnan Reticulata). (China to U.S. 1980 - U. C. Bot. Gdn, CA).

JAMES McCOY - Deep Burgundy Red. Large to very large, semidouble. Vigorous, upright growth. M-L. (Reticulata 'Crimson Robe' x Reticulata/Saluenensis hybrid). (U.S. 1980 - Pursel).

JAN DETRICK - Medium Pink. Large, semidouble. Strong, upright, open growth. M. {Pitardii var. 'Yunnanica' x [Reticulata 'Crimson Robe' x (Reticulata 'Crimson Robe' x Fraterna)]}. (U.S. 1999 - Charvet).

JAN HUGHES - Purplish Pink. Large, semidouble with wavy petals. Upright growth. M. (Saluenensis/ Reticulata hybrid x Reticulata 'Willow Wand'). (N.Z. 1977 - Mrs. I. Berg, Whakatane).

JANET - Pink. Very large, semidouble to peony form. Vigorous, upright growth. M. (Reticulata hybrid 'Buddy Bills' x Reticulata 'Cornelian'). (U.S. 1995 - Pursel).

JANET CLARK - Light Crimson. Large, semidouble with wavy, crimped, heavily textured outer petals. Vigorous, upright, open growth. M. (Reticulata 'Cornelian' seedling). (N.Z. 1967 - Clark).

JANET COWAN - Red. Large, semidouble to loose peony form. Average, open, spreading growth. E-L. (Saluenensis x Reticulata 'Crimson Robe'). (N.Z. 1975 - Mrs. I. Berg, Whakatane).

JANET SMITH - Rich Pink. Large to very large, semidouble. Vigorous, upright growth. M. (Reticulata 'Cornelian' x Japonica 'Mrs. D. W. Davis'). (U.S. 1979 - Pursel).

JANUS - Deep Red to Lighter Red with White center petals. Very large, rose form double to semidouble. Upright growth. M. (Reticulata 'Crimson Robe' seedling). (Aus. 1968 - Tuckfield).

JEAN ANDERTON - Crimson. Small, single. Vigorous, open, spreading growth. M-L. (Reticulata seedling). (N.Z. 1984 - T. Lennard, Te Puke).

JEAN B. SAXBY - Rose Red. Very large, peony form. Vigorous, upright, open growth. M-L. (Reticulata 'Crimson Robe' x Japonica). (U.S. 1980 - J. Osagueda, Oakland, CA).

JEAN COMBER - Clear Pink. Large to very large, semidouble. Average, upright, compact growth. M-L. (Reticulata 'Crimson Robe' x Reticulata 'Cornelian'). (U.S. 1984 - Pursel).

JEAN PURSEL - Light Purplish Pink. Very large, peony form. Vigorous, upright growth. M-L. (Reticulata 'Crimson Robe' x Reticulata/Japonica hybrid). (U.S. 1975 - Pursel).

JEAN PURSEL BLUSH - Pink Blush. (Sport of Reticulata hybrid 'Jean Pursel'). (U.S. 1985 - Gentry).

JEAN TOLAND - Deep Rose Red. Large to very large, semidouble. Average growth. M-L. (Reticulata 'Crimson Robe' x Reticulata/Japonica hybrid). (U.S. 1981 - Pursel).

JEANNIE RUTH - Light to medium Red with Golden anthers and White filaments. Medium, semidouble. Average, upright, open growth. L. (U.S. 2015 - Hulyn Smith).

JEFF WHITE - Dark Red with Golden anthers and White filaments. Large, semidouble to loose peony form. Vigorous, upright, spreading growth. L. (U.S. 2016 - Frank Pursel and Hulyn Smith).

JENIFER MARGARET - White. Medium, semidouble, hose-in-hose form. Slow, upright, dense growth. E-M. (Reticulata hybrid 'Brian Variegated' seedling). (Aus. 1990 - Mildorrie Camellias, Jasper's Brush, NSW).

JENNY MAPHIS - Very Light Pink, nearly White, with Darker Pink at edges - almost translucent with Golden anthers and White filaments. Medium, rose form double. Vigorous, upright, spreading growth. M-L. (U.S. 2015 - Frank Pursel and Hulyn Smith).

JESSE J. GILLEY - Rose Pink. Large, semidouble to loose peony form. Average, upright growth. M-L. (Reticulata hybrid 'Craig Clark' seedling). (U.S. 1983 - Gilley).

JESSICA WILSON - Cyclamen Pink, color deepens at petal edges. Large, formal double. Vigorous, upright, open growth. M-L. (Reticulata hybrid 'Buddha' seedling). (Aus. 2005 - J. and P. Wilson, Figtree, NSW).

*JEWEL FLOWER - ('Baoshihua' - Chinese Name). Crimson. Large, semidouble with wavy petals. E. (Yunnan Reticulata). (China to U.S. 1980 - U. C. Bot. Gdn, CA).

JIANYE YINHONG - See 'Pointed Leaf Crimson'.

JILL RIVETT - Lavender Pink. Very large, peony form. Average, spreading growth. E-L. (Reticulata seedling). (N.Z. 1993 - J. Rivett, Whakatane).

JILL TUCKFIELD - Pink. Large, semidouble. (Reticulata 'Crimson Robe' seedling). (Aus. 1976 - Tuckfield).

JIM BERG - Red. Very large, semidouble to loose peony form. Average, upright, open growth. M. (Reticulata 'Cornelian' seedling). (N.Z. 1975 - Mrs. I. Berg, Whakatane).

JIM HANSEN - Bold pillar-box Red. Very large, loose to full peony form. Average, upright, open growth. M. (Reticulata seedling). (N.Z. 1997 - D. Hansen).

JIM MILLAR - Soft Pink. Very large, semidouble to open peony form. Upright, open growth. M. (Pitardii x Yunnanensis/Reticulata seedling). (N.Z. 1980 - Mrs. A. B. Durrant, Rotorua).

JIM PINKERTON - Rose Red. Very large, peony form. Vigorous, upright growth. M-L. (Reticulata hybrid 'Buddha x [Reticulata hybrid 'Crimson Robe' x Lutchuensis]). (U.S. 1998 - Pursel).

JIM RIVETT - Pink with darker veins and Paler margins. Large, formal double to rose form double with large petaloids streaked with White. Upright, open growth. M-L. (Saluenensis x Reticulata 'Crimson Robe'). (N.Z. 1980 - Mrs. L. Berg, Whakatane).

JIM SMELLEY - Dark Pink with bright Yellow anthers and White filaments. Very large, semidouble. Vigorous, upright, open growth. M-L. (Reticulata hybrid 'Curtain Call' x Reticulata hybrid 'Pleasant Memories'). (U.S. 2013 - James and Elaine Smelley, Moss Point, MS).

JING JING - See 'Shining Jade'.

*JINGAN CAMELLIA - ('Jingan Cha' - Chinese Name). Scarlet. Very large, loose peony form. L. (Yunnan Reticulata). (China to U.S. 1980 - U. C. Bot. Gdn, CA).

JINGAN CHA - See 'Jingan Camellia.'

JINPAOHONG - See 'Brocade Gown Red'.

JINRUI FURONG - See 'Golden Stamen Hisbiscus'.

JINXIN BOAZHU - See 'Golden Heart Pearl'.

JOANNE DIBBLE - Rose. Large, semidouble with wide, thick, upright petals. Average, upright growth. M. (Japonica 'Elizabeth Boardman' x Reticulata hybrid 'Trewithen Pink'). (U.S. 1971 - Witman).

JOANNE'S OWN - Deep Pink shading to Pink at petal edges. Large, rose form double with notched, folded and fluted petals. Vigorous, upright growth. M-L. (Reticulata hybrid 'Brilliant Butterfly' seedling). (Aus. 1995 - K. Brown, Mitcham, Vic.).

JOCELYN MOORE - Lavender Pink. Medium, rose form double. Average, upright growth. L. (Reticulata seedling). (N.Z. 1993 - Mrs. K. Campbell, Wanganui).

JOHN ANSON FORD - Deep Rose Pink. Large, semidouble with wavy, crinkled petals. Slow, upright, compact growth. M-L. (Hybrid 'Williams Lavender' seedling x Reticulata 'Purple Gown'). (U.S. 1971 - L. A. State and County Arboretum, Arcadia, CA).

JOHN BELL - Deep Red. Large, semidouble. Average, upright growth. M-L. (Reticulata 'Crimson Robe' x Reticulata/Japonica hybrid). (U.S. 1982 - Pursel).

JOHN COMBER - Pink. Large to very large, semidouble. Average, upright growth. M-L. (Reticulata 'Crimson Robe' x Reticulata hybrid 'Jean Pursel'). (U.S. 1982 - Pursel).

JOHN DRUECKER - Clear Dark Red with Golden stamens. Very large, single; flower sheds by itself. M. (Reticulata 'Crimson Robe' x Japonica 'Ville de Nantes'). (U.S. 1981 - Charvet).

JOHN HALL - Apricot Pink. Very large, semidouble with upright petals. Vigorous, upright spreading growth. M-L. (Reticulata hybrid 'Mouchang' seedling). (U.S. 1986 - Hall).

JOHN HUNT - Pink. Very large, semidouble to loose peony form to rose form double with veined and occasionally notched petals. Vigorous, upright, open growth. M-L. (Reticulata hybrid 'Arch of Triumph' x Reticulata hybrid 'LASCA Beauty'). (Aus. 1988 - J. Hunt, Boronia, Vic.).

JOHN MOVICH - Dark Red. Very large, semidouble with circle of upright petals. Vigorous, upright, spreading growth. M-L. (Reticulata seedling). (U.S. 1983 - J. Movich, La Verne, CA).

JOHN NEWSOME - Red. Large, semidouble. Average, spreading growth. M-L. (Reticulata 'Crimson Robe' x Reticulata hybrid). (U.S. 1983 - Pursel).

JOHN TAYLOR - Dark Red. Very large, semidouble with irregular petals. Vigorous, spreading growth. M. (Reticulata x Japonica). (U.S. 1967 - Maitland).

JO-JO - Raspberry Red. Miniature, semidouble. Average, upright, open growth. E-L. (Reticulata 'Shot Silk' seedling). (U.S. 1981 - J. Movich, La Verne, CA).

JOY - Blush Pink edged Red. Medium, semidouble with upright crepe petals. Vigorous, upright growth. M-L. (Reticulata hybrid 'Carl Tourje' seedling). (U.S. 1973 - T. Pearce, Shreveport, LA).

JOYCE ADELE BROOKS - Orchid Pink veined Deeper Pink. Very large, semidouble to formal double. Upright, open growth. M. (Reticulata seedling). (Aus. 1979 - Mrs. M. Tuckfield, Monbulk, Vic.).

JOYCE CONNELL - Lavender Rose. Very large, semidouble. Vigorous, spreading growth. E-L. (Reticulata hybrid 'Buddha' seedling). (U.S. 1977 - Feathers).

JOYCE LA ROSE - Red. Large to very large, semidouble. Average, upright growth. M-L. (Reticulata 'Crimson Robe' x Reticulata/Japonica hybrid). (U.S. 1981 - Pursel).

JUANITA WALKER - Pink veined Darker Pink. Large to very large, semidouble. Average, upright growth. L. (Reticulata 'Cornelian' x Reticulata 'Crimson Robe'). (U.S. 1980 - Pursel).

JUBAN - See 'Chrysanthemum Petal'.

JUDGE JACKSON - Deep Pink to Red. Large to very large, semidouble. Average, upright, compact growth. M-L. (Reticulata 'Crimson Robe' x Lutchuensis). (U.S. 1980 - Pursel).

JUDITH TOOMAJIAN - Pink. Large to very large, semidouble to rose form double. Average, upright, spreading growth. M-L. (Reticulata 'Crimson Robe' x Reticulata hybrid 'Jean Pursel'). (U.S. 1982 - Pursel).

JUDY NORDAN - Pink. Large, semidouble with large, upright petals. Average, upright, compact growth. M-L. (Reticulata 'Shot Silk' seedling). (U.S. 1968 - M. Nordan, Hueytown, AL).

JULIE BALLARD - Deep Pink. Medium, anemone form to peony form. Vigorous, upright growth. E-M. (Reticulata hybrid 'Show Girl' seedling). (Aus. 1989 - K. Ballard, Mt. Waverly, Vic.).

JULIE KATE - Deep Salmon Pink. Large, loose peony form to rose form double. Average, upright, open growth. M-L. (Reticulata seedling). (N.Z. 1990 - J. Hansen, Waikanae).

JUNE CURRY - Light Pink with Yellow anthers and White filaments. Medium, semidouble. Vigorous, upright, open growth. L. (Reticulata hybrid 'Suzanne Withers' x Reticulata hybrid 'Annabelle Fetterman'). (U.S. 2013 - Hulyn Smith).

JUNE NORMAN - Dark Rose Pink to Rose Red. Medium to large, formal double with curled and swirled center petals. Average growth. M-L. (Reticulata hybrid 'Diamond Head' seedling). (U.S. 1989 - J. Norman, Keystone Hts., FL).

JUNE TOMLINSON - Medium Pink with Golden anthers and White filaments. Large, semidouble to rose form double. Vigorous, upright growth. M-L. (U.S. 2015 - Hulyn Smith).

K. O. HESTER - Orchid Pink. Large to very large, semidouble with irregular, upright petals. Vigorous, upright, open growth. M. (Reticulata 'Tali Queen' seedling). (U.S. 1972 - K. O. Hester, Laguna Hills, CA).

KAI MEI'S CHOICE - Brilliant Pink. Large, semidouble. Upright, narrow growth. E. ([Sasanqua x Sasanqua] x Reticulata). (U.S. 1995 - Parks).

KALIMNA - Bright Red. Very large, semidouble to loose peony form. Vigorous, upright, open growth. M. (Reticulata 'Crimson Robe' seedling). (Aus. 1970 - Sebire).

KARRIE ARMIJO - Salmon Pink with light veining. Large to very large, semidouble to peony form. Vigorous, upright, open growth. E-L. (Reticulata hybrid 'Mandalay Queen' seedling). (U.S. 1989 - Piet and Gaeta).

KATHY REID - Bright Cerise Pink. Large, peony form. Average, upright, compact growth. M. (Saluenensis x Reticulata 'Crimson Robe'). (N.Z. 1983 - Mrs. I. Berg, Whakatane).

KATIE SHIPLEY - Bright Red. Large to very large, peony form. Average, upright, open growth. M-L. (Reticulata hybrid 'Craig Clark' x Reticulata hybrid 'Jean Pursel'). (U.S. 1996 - Homeyer).

KAY HALLSTONE - Light Pink washed (veined) White. Very large, semidouble. Vigorous, upright, open, spreading growth. M-L. (Reticulata hybrid 'Mouchang Variegated' x Hybrid 'Brigadoon'). (U.S. 1992 - Hall).

KAY THOMERSON - Light Pink with Dark Pink picotee edges with Yellow anthers and White filaments. Large, peony to semidouble. Vigorous, upright growth. M. (Reticulata hybrid 'Suzanne Withers' x Reticulata hybrid 'Annabelle Fetterman'). (U.S. 2010 - Hulyn Smith).

KAYE FULLER - Rose Pink shaded Cyclamen. Large, anemone form. Average, upright growth. M. (Reticulata 'Chang's Temple'). (Aus. 1982 - J. Hunt, South Croydon, Vic.).

KEITH BALLARD - Pale Pink at center shading to Deep Pink on outer petals. Large, peony form to rose form double. Vigorous, upright, open growth. M. (Reticulata hybrid 'Suzanne Withers' x Japonica 'Mrs. Bertha A. Harms'). (Aus. 1992 - Dr. R. Withers, Donvale, Vic.).

KELLY ABBOTT - Dark Red with Gold stamens. Large, peony form. Vigorous, upright growth. M. (Reticulata hybrid 'Mouchang' seedling). (Aus. 2007 - Keith Abbott, Rossmoyne).

KEN SPRAGG - Pink with some petals streaked White. Very large, semidouble with upright, notched inner petals. Upright, spreading growth. M-L. (Reticulata seedling). (Aus. 1980 - A. Spragg, Sutherland, NSW).

KERN COUNTY - Dark Rich Red. Large, semidouble to loose peony form. Vigorous, upright growth. M. (Reticulata hybrid 'Buddha' seedling). (U.S. 1968 - Alfter).

KETCAM BURCH - Rose Pink. Very large, semidouble. Vigorous, upright growth. M. (Reticulata hybrid 'Buddha' seedling). (Aus. 1972 - Sebire).

KI-NO-MOTO#92 - Light Yellow. Medium, cup-shaped single. Slow spreading growth. M-L. (Japonica, Nitidissima, Reticulata in background). (U.S. - Nuccio's Hybridizer Kazuo Yoshikawa, Japan).

KI-NO-MOTO#95 - Light Yellow. Large, semidouble. Slow, upright growth. M-L. (Reticulata hybrid 'LASCA Beauty' x Japonica). (U.S. - Nuccio's Hybridizer Kazuo Yoshikawa, Japan).

KIRI TE KANAWA - Fuchsia Pink. Medium, semidouble. Average, compact, upright growth. E-L. (Pitardii x Reticulata hybrid 'Buddha'). (N.Z. 1972).

KIRSTY RIVETT - Salmon Pink. Very large, peony form. Average, spreading growth. M. (Saluenensis x Reticulata 'Crimson Robe' x Reticulata seedling). (N.Z. - 1983 - Mrs. I. Berg, Whakatane).

KIWI TRIUMPH - China Rose. Very large, heavy petaled semidouble with irregular, inner petals. Vigorous, compact, upright growth. M. (Reticulata 'Cornelian' seedling). (N.Z. 1970 - Clark).

KOGANE-YURI - Light Yellow. Small, single tubular form. Medium, upright, slender growth. M. (Saluenensis-Reticulata hybrid 'Barbara Clark' x Nitidissima). (U.S. - Nuccio's Hybridizer Kazuo Yoshikawa, Japan).

KOHINOR - Orchid Pink. Large to very large, semidouble with irregular, upright petals. Vigorous, upright growth. M. (Reticulata hybrid 'Buddha' seedling). (U.S. 1968 - Peer).

KRISTIE WILSON - Vibrant Deep Pink shading to White at center. Very large, rose form double. Average, dense, upright growth. M-L. (Reticulata 'Cornelian' seedling). (Aus. 1998 - J. and P. Wilson, Figtree, NSW).

*KUNMING SPRING - ('Kunmingchun' - Chinese Name). Deep Orchid Pink. Large, semidouble with irregular, upright petals. E. (Yunnan Reticulata). (China to U.S. 1980 - U. C. Bot. Gdn, CA).

KUNMINGCHUN - See 'Kunming Spring'.

KWAN YUEN - Coral Rose. Very large, semidouble to rose form double. Strong, upright, compact growth. M. (Reticulata hybrid 'Buddha' x Hybrid 'Coral Delight'). (U.S. 1981 - Charvet).

KWAN YUEN SPECIAL - Coral Rose variegated White. Very large, semidouble to rose form double. Strong, upright, compact growth. M. (Reticulata hybrid 'Buddha' x Hybrid 'Coral Delight'). (U.S. 2009 - Charvet).

L. H. PAUL - Dark Pink with Lighter Pink at edges with Golden anthers and White filaments. Very large, semidouble to peony form. M-L. (Reticulata hybrid 'Suzanne Withers' x Reticulata hybrid 'Jean Pursel'). (U.S. 1996 - Hulyn Smith).

LA PETITE - Pink shaded Cyclamen. Miniature, semidouble to peony form. Spreading, upright growth. M. (Reticulata hybrid 'Janet Clark' x Fraterna). (Aus. 1981 - Camellia Lodge Nsy., Noble Park, Vic.).

LACY LOVE - Light Purplish Pink. Large to very large, semidouble. Vigorous, upright growth. M-L. (Reticulata 'Crimson Robe' x Reticulata hybrid 'Jean Pursel'). (U.S. 1980 - Pursel).

LADY GLENCORA - Pink. Very large, semidouble to peony form. Average growth. E-L. (N.Z. 1981 - A. H. Burwell, Inglewood).

LADY LOVE - Light Pink. Medium to large, formal double. Average, dense growth. M. (Hybrid 'Coral Delight' x Reticulata hybrid 'Royalty'). (U.S. 1995 - T. Croson, Powers, OR).

LADY PAMELA - White shading from Light Pink to Darker Pink at outer petal edges. Large, semidouble with high rabbit ears. Vigorous, open, upright growth. M. (Reticulata hybrid 'Suzanne Withers' x Reticulata hybrid 'Arcadia'). (Aus. 1996 - Dr. R. Withers, Donvale, Vic.).

LADY RUTH RITTER - Dark Red with Golden Yellow anthers and Yellow filaments. Medium, semidouble. Slow, dense growth. M-L. (Previously called 'Lady Ruth Red'). (U.S. 2009 - Hulyn Smith).

LAFAYETTE BEAUTY - Silvery Pink. Very large, semidouble with wavy, crinkled petals. Vigorous, upright growth. M. (Reticulata hybrid 'LASCA Beauty' seedling). (U.S. 1983 - Feathers).

LAKE ERHAI PEARL - ('Erhai Zenzu' - Chinese Name; 'Er Lake Pearl'). Picotee coloring, White center and Pink margins; color changes with opening flower to a Light Purple shade. Medium, formal double with petals slightly incurved, tight upright bud center; 55-60 imbricated petals. M-L. [(Reticulata hybrid 'Suzanne Withers' x 'Nitidissima hybrid 'Honeymoon') x Japonica 'Elaine's Betty']. (U.S. 2015 - John Wang, Orinda, CA).

*LARGE OSMANTHUS LEAF - ('Daguiye' - Chinese Name). Deep Carmine. Large, semidouble to peony form. M-L. (Yunnan Reticulata). (China to U.S. 1980 - U. C. Bot. Gdn, CA).

LARRY DAVIS - Mauve Pink. Large, peony form. Average, upright growth. M. (Reticulata 'Crimson Robe' seedling). (N.Z. 1984 - Mrs. I. Berg, Whakatane).

LARRY PIET - Rich Dark Red. Large to very large, rose form double to peony form. Vigorous, compact growth. E-L. (Reticulata hybrid 'Pharaoh' x Reticulata hybrid 'Harold L. Paige'). (U.S. 1989 - Piet and Gaeta).

LASCA BEAUTY - Soft Pink. Very large, semidouble with heavy textured thick petals. Vigorous, open, upright growth. M. (Reticulata 'Cornelian' x Japonica 'Mrs. D. W. Davis'). (U.S. 1973 - Dr. Clifford R. Parks, Los Angeles State and County Arboretum, Arcadia, CA).

LAURETTA FEATHERS - Blush White edged Pink. Large to very large, semidouble with crepe petals. Vigorous, compact, upright growth. E. (Reticulata hybrid 'LASCA Beauty' seedling). (U.S. 1983 - Feathers).

LEE GAETA - Dark Red. Large to very large, semidouble with upright petals. Vigorous, open, upright growth. E-L. (Reticulata hybrid 'Emma Gaeta' x Reticulata hybrid 'Arcadia'). (U.S. 1989 - Piet and Gaeta).

LEE ROY SMITH - Pink highly frosted with Golden anthers and White filaments. Very large, semidouble. Vigorous, upright growth. M. (Reticulata hybrid 'Suzanne Withers' x Reticulata hybrid 'Delta Dawn'). (U.S. 1992 - Originated by Jack Mandarich and propagated by Hulyn Smith).

LEGACY - Purplish to Deep Red. Large, semidouble. Vigorous, open, upright growth. (Reticulata 'Crimson Robe' x Reticulata 'Tali Queen'). (U.S. 1974 - C. W. Lattin, Lauderdale, MS).

LEN BRAY - Pink with Fuchsia tinge. Large, formal double. Compact, upright growth. M-L. (Reticulata hybrid 'Barbara Clark' seedling). (Aus. 1980 - T. J. Savige, Wirlinga, NSW).

LEONARD MESSEL - Rose. Large, semidouble. (Reticulata hybrid 'Wild Form' x Williamsii 'Mary Christian'). (England 1958 - Mrs. L C R Messel, Nymans Garden, Sussex).

LES BERG - Red. Large, loose peony form. Vigorous, upright growth. M. (Reticulata seedling). (N.Z. 1972 - Mr. and Mrs. L. Berg, Whakatane).

LES ROSE - Mid Pink. Very large, semidouble form. Open, spreading, upright growth. M-L. (Reticulata hybrid 'LASCA Beauty' seedling). (Aus. 2003 - John Butler, Cabarlah, Qld).

LESLIE RIVETT - Bright Scarlet. Very large, peony form. Average, upright growth. M-L. (Reticulata 'Crimson Robe' x Japonica 'Dixie Knight'). (N.Z. 1984 - Mrs. I. Berg, Whakatane).

LETITIA MAC - Rose Pink. Large, semidouble. Average, open, upright growth. M. (Saluenensis x Reticulata hybrid 'Buddha'). (N.Z. 1972 - Clark).

LEW FETTERMAN - Red. Very large, semidouble form. Average, upright, open growth. M-L. (U.S. 2001 - Jernigan).

LIANGYE YINHONG - See 'Bright Leaf Pink'.

LIANRUI - See 'Double Bowl'.

LILA AKEL - Dark Salmon Rose. Very large, semidouble to peony form. Average, upright growth. M. (Reticulata seedling x Saluenensis). (N.Z. 1986 - Mrs. I. Berg, Whakatane).

LILA NAFF - Silver Pink. Large, semidouble with wide petals. Vigorous, compact, upright growth. M. (Reticulata 'Butterfly Wings' seedling). (U.S. 1967 - Tammia).

*LILAC RED - ('Dingxianghong' - Chinese Name). Carmine. Large to very large, semidouble with wavy petals. L. (Yunnan Reticulata). (China to U.S. 1980 - U. C. Bot. Gdn, CA).

LILETTE WITMAN - Rose Pink with delicate Silver Blush. Very large, loose peony form. Vigorous, open, upright growth. E-M. (Reticulata hybrid 'Buddha' x Reticulata 'Cornelian'). (U.S. 1973 - Homeyer).

LILLIAN A. - Deep Pink to Lighter Pink at edge. Very large, loose peony form. Vigorous growth. E. (Reticulata hybrid 'Buddha' seedling). (U.S. 1982 - L. G. McKeever, Orinda, CA).

LILLY MARIE NICHOLS - Dark Pink with Yellow anthers and White filaments. Very large, semidouble to loose peony form. Average, upright, spreading growth. L. The bloom is fragrant. (U.S. 2016 - Hulyn Smith).

LIME LIGHT - Rose Pink. Large, semidouble with notched, folded, upright center petals. Vigorous, upright growth. M. (Reticulata hybrid 'Wild Form' x Reticulata 'Shot Silk'). (N.Z. 1971 - D. O'Toole, Ohope).

LINDA CAROL - Light Pink. Very large, semidouble. Vigorous, open, upright growth. E-M. (Reticulata 'Cornelian' x Japonica 'Mrs. D. W. Davis'). (U.S. 1995 - Pursel).

LINDA GILMORE - White heavily striped Crimson. Medium, formal double. Average, compact, upright growth. M-L. (Japonica 'Lady Vansittart' x Reticulata 'Crimson Robe'). (U.S. 1977 - Feathers).

LINDA GRIFFIN - Light Pink with bright Yellow anthers and White filaments. Very large, semidouble. Vigorous, upright, open growth. M-L. (Reticulata hybrid 'Curtain Call' x Reticulata hybrid 'Pleasant Memories'). (U.S. 2013 - James and Elaine Smelley, Moss Point, MS).

LINDA LEE EHRHART - Silvery Pink with Yellow anthers and White filaments. Large, semidouble. Average, upright, spreading growth. E-L. (Reticulata hybrid 'Lauretta Feathers' seedling). (U.S. 2013 - Robert E. Ehrhart, Walnut Creek, CA).

LINLEY REID - Soft Pink. Large, peony form. Average, upright growth. M. (Reticulata seedling). (N.Z. 1986 - Mrs. I. Berg, Whakatane).

LINTON BAGGS - Red with luminous petals. Large, semidouble to loose peony form. Average, upright growth. M-L. (Reticulata seedling). (U.S. 1977 - L. D. Baggs, Jr., Macon, GA).

*LION HEAD - ('Shizitou' - Chinese Name). Deep Turkey Red. Large to very large, peony form with irregular, heavy, crinkled petals near base, arching over and covering center as flower develops. Vigorous, compact growth. M. (Yunnan Reticulata). (China to U.S. 1948 - Descanso and Peer).

LISA GAEL - Rose Pink. Large, rose form double. Compact, upright growth. M. (Reticulata 'Purple Gown' seedling). (N.Z. 1967 - Clark).

LIUYE YINHONG - See 'Willow Wand'.

LOIS BOUDREAUX - Dark Rose Pink. Medium, semidouble to loose peony. Average, dense, upright growth. M. (U.S. 2003 - Hyman R. Norsworthy, Beaumont, TX).

LOIS JEAN - Medium Pink with Golden anthers and White filaments. Very large, semidouble. Vigorous, upright growth. L. (U.S. 2016 - Hulyn Smith).

LOIS SHINAULT - Orchid Pink shading lighter in center. Very large, semidouble with irregular petals ruffled on edges and upright center petals. Average, spreading growth. E-M. (Reticulata 'Crimson Robe' x Granthamiana). (U.S. 1973 - L. H. Shinault, Northridge, CA).

LOLOMA - Pink. Very large, semidouble. Vigorous, open, upright growth. M. (Reticulata seedling). (Aus. 1971 - Sebire).

LOUISE GERBING - Red. Very large, semidouble with upright petals. Vigorous, open, upright growth. E-M. (Reticulata seedling). (U.S. 1994 - Jernigan).

LOVELY LADY - Soft Pink with Salmon cast. Large, formal double with ruffled petals. Compact, upright growth. M. (Reticulata hybrid 'Pink Sparkle' seedling). (Aus. 1981 - Sebire).

LOWANNA - Red. Very large, peony form. Vigorous, open, upright growth. (Reticulata 'Crimson Robe' seedling). (Aus. 1979 - Sebire).

LUANYE YINHONG - See 'Ovate Leaf Pink'.

LUCILLE HARKEY - Dark Pink. Large to very large, semidouble. Average, upright growth. M. (Reticulata hybrid x Reticulata 'Crimson Robe'). (U.S. 1980 - Pursel).

LUCKY STRIKE - Cerise Pink. Very large, peony form. Vigorous, open, upright growth. M. (Reticulata hybrid 'Mouchang' seedling). (U.S. 1992 - Hall).

LUMINOUS - Neyron Rose with White moiré. Very large, semidouble. Vigorous, spreading, upright growth. E-M. (Reticulata hybrid 'Carl Tourje' seedling). (U.S. 1996 - Hall).

LUPE - Rose Pink. Large, semidouble with irregular petals. Average, open, upright growth. M-L. (U.S. 1979 - H. H. Smith, Yuba City, CA).

LYNETTE HOOPER - Deep Red shading to very Dark Red at petal edges. Very large, semidouble to peony form. Spreading growth. M. (Reticulata 'Cornelian' x Japonica 'Ville de Nantes'). (Aus. 1981 - Camellia Vale Nsy., Bexley North, NSW).

MACKENZIE GREEN - Rose Pink with Golden anthers and White filaments. Very large, semidouble to rose form double. Average, upright growth. M. (Reticulata hybrid 'Arc of Triumph' x Reticulata hybrid 'Jean Pursel'). (U.S. 2007 - Jack Mandarich, Garner, NC).

MAGGIE BUSH - Orchid Pink. Large to very large, semidouble with upright petals to anemone form. Average growth. M. (Reticulata 'Cornelian' x Reticulata hybrid 'Jean Pursel'). (U.S. 1985 - Pursel).

*MAGNOLIA CAMELLIA - ('Yulan Cha' - Chinese Name). Crimson. Small, single of magnolia form. M. (Yunnan Reticulata). (China to U.S. 1980 - U. C. Bot. Gdn, CA).

MAI TAI - Soft Baby Pink washed White. Small, semidouble with three tiers of crinkled, crepe and wavy petals. Average, compact, upright growth. M-L. (Reticulata hybrid 'Nuccio's Ruby' seedling). (U.S. 1988 - Hall).

MAISE CHETTLE - Deep Pink. Large, loose peony form. Open, upright growth. M-L. (Reticulata hybrid 'Buddha' x Reticulata 'Cornelian'). (Aus. 1982 - T. E. Pierson, Hurstville, NSW).

MALCOLM BURKE - Cyclamen Pink with darker veining. Large, semidouble. Vigorous, open, upright growth. M-L. (Reticulata hybrid 'Florrie Burke' seedling). (N.Z. 1991 - F. Burke, Whakatane).

MANAO JUBAN - See 'Cornelian Chrysanthemum Petal'.

MANAO ZIPAO - See 'Cornelian Purple Gown'.

MANDALAY QUEEN - Rose Pink. Very large, semidouble with fluted petals. Vigorous, open, upright growth. M-L. (Reticulata 'Tali Queen' seedling). (U.S. 1966 - Shade and Shadow Nsy., Mountain View, CA).

MANDY SMITH - Red with frosted sheen. Large to very large, peony form. Vigorous, upright growth. M. (Reticulata 'Cornelian' x Reticulata hybrid 'Jean Pursel'). (U.S. 1991 - Pursel).

MARGARET BERNHARDT - Rose Red. Medium, formal double. Average, upright growth. M-L. (Reticulata 'Crimson Robe' x Reticulata hybrid 'Jean Pursel'). (U.S. 1982 - Pursel).

MARGARET G. GILL - Orchid picotee shaded darker toward edges with Golden anthers and White filaments. Medium, semidouble. Average, upright open growth. E-M. {(Pitardii var. 'Yunnanica' x Reticulata 'Purple Gown') x [(Pitardii var. 'Yunnanica' x Fraterna) x Japonica 'Tom Knudsen']}. (U.S. 2009 - Charvet).

MARGARET HILFORD - Deep Red. Large to very large, semidouble. Vigorous, open, upright growth. E-M. (Reticulata seedling). (N.Z. 1980 - J. N. Rolfe, Hamilton).

MARGARET NIELSEN - Fuchsia Pink. Large, semidouble. Average, upright growth. E-L. (Reticulata seedling). (N.Z. 1991 - A. Gamlin, Manaia).

MARGARET VICKERY - Deep to Blush Pink. Large, semidouble to peony form. Vigorous, open, upright growth. M. (Reticulata hybrid 'Pink Sparkle' x Reticulata hybrid 'Jean Pursel'). (U.S. 1989 - Homeyer).

MARGARET WELLS CHOICE - Deep rich Salmon Pink. Large to very large, semidouble. Vigorous, upright growth. M. (Reticulata 'Cornelian' x Reticulata hybrid 'Arcadia'). (U.S. 1983 - Piet and Gaeta).

MARGARET'S SIX - Turkey Red. Very large, semidouble to peony form. Open, upright growth. E-L. (Reticulata 'Cornelian' x Reticulata hybrid 'Buddha'). (Aus. 1981 - T. E. Pierson, Hurtsville, NSW).

MARIE HANSEN - Deep Rose Pink. Very large, semidouble to loose peony form. Average, open, upright growth. E-M. (Reticulata seedling). (N.Z. 1990 - J. Hansen, Waikanae).

MARIEL - Soft Pink. Large, semidouble. Strong, upright growth. (Aus. 2006 - Audrey O'Ferrall, NSW).

MARILYN EVANS - Deep Red. Medium to large, rose form double with notched and fluted petals. Vigorous, open growth. M-L. (Reticulata seedling). (Aus. 1995 - J. Hawke, Carrara, Qld.).

MARILYN MAPHIS - Pink highly frosted with Golden anthers and White filaments. Very large, semidouble. Vigorous, upright open growth. M. (Reticulata hybrid 'Lilette Witman' x Reticulata hybrid 'Hulyn Smith'). (U.S. 2007 - Jack Mandarich, Garner, NC).

MARION EDWARDS - Bright Red. Large to very large, semidouble. Vigorous, upright growth. M-L. (Reticulata 'Crimson Robe' x Reticulata hybrid 'Arch of Triumph'). (U.S. 1984 - Pursel).

MARJORIE O'MALLEY - Rose Red. Large to very large, semidouble to loose peony form. M-L. (Reticulata 'Crimson Robe' x Reticulata hybrid 'Jean Pursel'). (U.S. 1982 - Pursel).

MARK CANNON - Rich Orchid Pink. Large, semidouble. Average, upright growth. M-L. (Reticulata hybrid 'Arch of Triumph' seedling). (U.S. 1983 - Gilley).

MARK'S SURPRISE - Deep Pink. Very large, peony form. Average growth. E-M. (Reticulata hybrid 'Francie L.' seedling). (Aus. 1984 - Sebire).

MARVIN SOWELL - Light Crimson. Large, semidouble to loose peony form. Vigorous, upright growth. M-L. (Reticulata seedling). (U.S. 1979 - Kramer).

MARY A. BERGAMINI - Hot Pink. Large, peony form. Average, spreading growth. M-L. (Reticulata hybrid 'Arch of Triumph' seedling). (U.S. 2006 - Don Bergamini, Martinez, CA).

MARY BAINE - Pink variegated White. Medium, rose form double. Average, open, upright growth. M-L. (Reticulata hybrid 'Pink Sparkle' x Japonica 'Julie Nixon'). (U.S. 1989 - R. B. Gramling, Tallahassee, FL).

MARY CAROL - Medium pink with Yellow anthers and White filaments. Large, semidouble. Average, upright, open growth. M-L. (Reticulata hybrid 'Cloisonné' x Reticulata hybrid 'Pleasant Memories'). (U.S. 2019 - Gordy).

MARY CATHERINE CAPE - Medium Pink frosted White with Yellow anthers and White filaments. Medium, semidouble. Average, upright, open growth. L. (Reticulata hybrid 'Suzanne Withers' x Reticulata hybrid 'Annabelle Fetterman'). (U.S. 2013 - Hulyn Smith).

MARY ELIZABETH DOWDEN - Pink, heavily veined, Silver sheen. Medium to large, semidouble form. Average, open, spreading growth. M. (U.S. 2006 - Robert A. Stroud and Charles C. Bush, Slidell, LA).

MARY EVANS FERGUSON - Bright Red. Large to very large, semidouble to peony form. Vigorous, spreading, upright growth. M. (Reticulata 'Crimson Robe' seedling x Reticulata hybrid 'Jean Pursel'). (U.S. 1989 - Homeyer).

MARY GIBBONS - Mid Pink. Large, semidouble. Upright, Average, open growth. M. (Reticulata hybrid 'Glowing Embers' seedling). (N.Z. 2007 - Harvey Howard).

MARY GOLOMBIEWSKI - Purplish Red. Large, peony form. Average, open, upright growth. M. (Reticulata 'Crimson Robe' x Reticulata hybrid 'Buddha'). (U.S. 1974 - Homeyer).

MARY JACQUELYN - Rose Pink with Lavender hues. Large, semidouble. Vigorous, upright growth. M-L. (Reticulata hybrid 'Valley Knudsen' seedling). (U.S. 2007 - Marvin Brown, Savannah, GA).

MARY KAY - Pink. Large, formal double to semidouble to loose peony form. Average, spreading, upright growth. M-L. (Reticulata 'Crimson Robe' x Reticulata hybrid 'Jean Pursel'). (U.S. 1982 - Pursel).

MARY LOU WATFORD - Pink with Yellow anthers and Yellow filaments. Very large, semidouble. Average, upright, dense growth. L. (U.S. 2009 - Hulyn Smith).

MARY MAUD SHARPE - Medium to Dark Pink with Yellow anthers and White filaments. Medium, semidouble to loose peony; the bloom is sometimes frosted and is fluorescent. Vigorous, upright, dense growth. M-L. (Reticulata hybrid 'Suzanne Withers' x Reticulata hybrid 'Annabelle Fetterman'). (U.S. 2014 - Hulyn Smith).

MARY MOVICH - Deep Pink. Very large, semidouble. Vigorous, open, upright growth. M-L. (Reticulata seedling). (U.S. 1981 - J. Movich, La Verne, CA).

MARY MUSANTE - Red. Large, rose form double to formal double. Average, upright growth. M. (Reticulata hybrid 'Arch of Triumph' x Reticulata hybrid 'Jean Pursel'). (U.S. 1996 - Mandarich).

MARY O'DONNELL - Orchid Pink. Medium to large, peony form to rose form double to formal double. Vigorous, dense, spreading, upright growth. E-L. (Reticulata hybrid 'Lilette Whitman' x Reticulata hybrid 'Hulyn Smith'). (U.S. 1992 - Mandarich).

MARY RHODES - Light Pink shading to White with Yellow anthers and White filaments. Large, semidouble. Vigorous, upright, spreading growth. L. (Reticulata hybrid 'Suzanne Withers' x Reticulata hybrid 'Annabelle Fetterman'). (U.S. 2013 - Hulyn Smith).

MARY STRINGFELLOW - Bright Pink veined Red. Large to very large, semidouble. Vigorous, upright growth. M-L. (Reticulata 'Cornelian' x Japonica 'Mrs. D. W. Davis'). (U.S. 1980 - Pursel).

MARY WILLIAMS - Crimson to Rose. Large, single. (Reticulata hybrid 'Wild Form' seedling).

MASSEE LANE - Pink. Large, anemone form. Vigorous, spreading, upright growth. M. (Reticulata hybrid 'Phyl Doak' seedling). (U.S. 1972 - M. E. Rowell, Fresno, CA).

MAUDE SUGG - Light Pink. Large, semidouble. Vigorous, open, upright growth. M-L. (Reticulata seedling). (U.S. 1975 - Kramer).

MAUREEN SCHLOSS - Dark Pink with Yellow anthers and White filaments. Large, semidouble to peony form. Vigorous, upright growth. M-L. (Reticulata hybrid 'Hulyn Smith' x Reticulata hybrid 'Jean Pursel'). (U.S. 2010 - Hulyn Smith).

MAY WESTBROOK - Red. Very large, semidouble. Vigorous, open, upright growth. M. (Reticulata 'Crimson Robe' seedling). (Aus. 1976 - Sebire).

MAYE TAOHONG - See 'Reticulate Leaf Crimson'.

MAYE YINHONG - See 'Reticulate Leaf Pink'.

MAYHILLS - Bright Red. Large, semidouble with fluted, notched petals. Vigorous, upright growth. E-M. (Reticulata 'Shot Silk' x Reticulata 'Crimson Robe'). (N.Z. 1970 - Dr. J. Crisp, Tirau).

MAYOR TALIA - Pink to Light Lavender. Medium to large, semidouble with rabbit ears. Average, open, upright growth. E-M. (Reticulata seedling). (U.S. 1992 - A. Buchholz, Cupertino, CA).

MEIHONG GUIYE - See 'Rosy Osmanthus Leaf'.

MEME - Pink fading to Pale Pink in center. Medium, formal double. Vigorous, spreading growth. E-M. (Reticulata hybrid 'Diamond Head' x unknown pollen parent). (U.S. 1982 - T. E. Lundy, Pensacola, FL).

MEMORY LANE - Shell Pink with Darker Pink edges with Yellow anthers and White filaments. Medium, rose form double. Average, upright, spreading growth. L. (Reticulata hybrid 'Lady Pamela' x Reticulata hybrid 'In Loving Memory'). (N.Z. 2015 - Haydon).

MEREDITH GREEN - Rose Pink with Golden anthers and White filaments. Very large, rose form double to semidouble. Average, upright, spreading growth. M. (Reticulata hybrid 'Royalty' x Reticulata hybrid 'Jean Pursel'). (U.S. 2008 - Hulyn Smith).

MIAOJIE - See 'Fine Pure'.

MILDRED PITKIN - Deep Pink. Large, semidouble with wavy, crinkled petals. Average, open, upright growth. M. (Reticulata x Japonica). (U.S. 1976 - Maitland).

MILES BEACH - Red frosted with Golden anthers and Red filaments. Large to very large, semidouble form. Vigorous, upright growth. E-L. (Reticulata 'Crimson Robe' x Reticulata hybrid 'Woodford Harrison'). (U.S. 2002 - Pursel).

MILO ROWELL - Deep rich Pink. Very large, semidouble with irregular petals to loose peony form. Vigorous, compact, upright growth. M. (Reticulata 'Crimson Robe' x Japonica 'Tiffany'). (U.S. 1968 - Asper).

MILTON H. BROWN - Brownish Red. Very large, semidouble with upright petals. Vigorous growth. M-L. (Reticulata seedling). (U.S. 1989 - Feathers).

MING TEMPLE - Silvery Pink. Large, semidouble to loose peony form with crepe petals. Strong, columnar, compact growth. M-L. (Reticulata 'Cornelian' seedling). (U.S. 1972 - Feathers).

MIRIAM HOMEYER - Lavender Pink to Deeper Pink center to Lighter Pink picotee border. Large to very large, semidouble to peony form. Vigorous, open, upright growth. M. (Reticulata 'Crimson Robe' x Reticulata hybrid 'Trewithen Pink'). (U.S. 1975 - Homeyer).

MISS DALLAS - Pink. Large to very large, semidouble. Average, open, upright growth. M-L. (Reticulata 'Crimson Robe' x Reticulata hybrid 'Jean Pursel'). (U.S. 1982 - Pursel).

MISS HOUSTON - Pink. Large to very large, semidouble. Average, compact, upright growth. M-L. (Reticulata 'Crimson Robe' x Reticulata hybrid 'Jean Pursel'). (U.S. 1982 - Pursel).

MISS REBECCA - Red. Very large, rose form double. Average, upright growth. M-L. (Reticulata 'Purple Gown' seedling). (Aus. 1983 - E. Kettle, Cheltenham, Vic.).

MISS SALLY - Red with fluted petals. Very large, semidouble. Average, spreading growth. M. (Reticulata seedling). (U.S. 2004 - Douglas M. Simon, Norfolk, VA).

MISS SANTA CLARA - Pink tinged Lavender. Large to very large, semidouble. Vigorous, upright growth. M-L. (Reticulata seedling). (U.S. 1980 - M. Talia, Santa Clara, CA).

MISS TULARE - Bright Red to Rose Red. Large to very large, full peony form to rose form double to formal double. Vigorous, upright growth. E-M. (Reticulata 'Crimson Robe' seedling). (U.S. 1975 - M. W. Abramson, Tulare, CA).

MISS TULARE VARIEGATED - Bright Red to Rose Red blotched White form of 'Miss Tulare'. (U.S. 1977 - M W Abramson, Tulare, CA).

MOLLY O'TOOLE - Vivid Cherry Red. Large, semidouble. Average, upright growth. M. (Reticulata 'Cornelian' x Reticulata 'Crimson Robe'). (N.Z. 1972 - D. G. O'Toole, Ohope).

MOON FESTIVAL - Medium Pink. Very large, single. M. (Sasanqua x {Sasanqua x Reticulata hybrid}). (U.S. - Parks).

MOONRISE - White to Blush Pink, Pale Yellow at base. Very large, semidouble. Vigorous, upright, open growth. E-L. (Reticulata/Granthamiana hybrid). (U.S. 2000 - Nuccio's).

MOUCHANG - Salmon Pink. Very large, single to semidouble. Vigorous, upright growth. M. (Reticulata 'Cornelian' x Reticulata 'Moutancha'). (U.S. 1966 - Asper).

*MOUTANCHA - ('Mudan Cha' - Chinese Name). Bright Pink veined White and striped White on inner petals. Large to very large, full peony with wavy, crinkled, crepe-like petals. Average growth. L. (Yunnan Reticulata). (China to U.S. 1948 - Descanso and Peer).

MRS. DAN NATHAN - Pink with heavy sheen. Very large, semidouble with high rabbit ears. Average, open, upright growth. E-L. (Reticulata hybrid 'Pink Sparkle' x Reticulata hybrid 'Nuccio's Ruby'). (U.S. 1994 - Jernigan).

MRS. H. C. RAMBATH - Rose Red. Very large, semidouble to loose peony form. Vigorous, open, upright growth. M-L. (Reticulata hybrid 'Mouchang' x Reticulata 'Crimson Robe'). (U.S. 1997 - Mandarich).

MUDAN CHA - See 'Moutancha'.

MURILLO - Bright Pink veined deeper. Very large, semidouble to loose peony form. Average, open growth. M. (Reticulata 'Crimson Robe' seedling). (Aus. 1968 - Tuckfield).

MURRAY SHORES - Burgundy Red. Large, semidouble. Average, upright growth. M-L. (Reticulata 'Crimson Robe' x Japonica/Reticulata hybrid). (U.S. 1983 - Pursel).

MY ERNESTINE - Rose Pink. Large, peony form. Average, spreading, upright growth. M. (Japonica 'Dr. W. G. Lee' x Reticulata hybrid 'Mouchang'). (U.S. 1977 - Gilley).

MYRA PRICE - Orchid Pink; flag petaloids with Pinkish White filaments into a one White base. Large, anemone form. Vigorous, open and spreading, upright growth. M-L. (Sport of Reticulata hybrid 'Mouchang'). (N.Z. 2003 - Haydon).

NANCY CALLAWAY - Dark Red with Light Purple cast. Very large, rose form double. Average, upright, open growth. M-L. (U.S. 1999 - Jernigan).

NANCY REAGAN - Rose Pink. Very large, semidouble with irregular, upright, wavy petals. Average, upright growth. M. (Reticulata seedling). (U.S. 1981 - W. F. Goertz, San Marino, CA).

NANSHAN PURPLE JADE - ('Nanshan Ziyu' - Chinese Name; 'South Mountain Lavender Jade'; 'Nan Shan Zi Yu'). Pink with Lavender Purple undertones with Yellow anthers and White filaments. Medium, rose form double to formal double imbricated with apices of petals inward curved. Average, upright growth. M-L. (Reticulata hybrid 'Suzanne Withers' x Japonica 'Nuccio's Jewel'). (U.S. 2009 - John Wang, Orinda, CA).

NANSHAN ZIYU - See 'Nanshan Purple Jade'.

*NARROW OSMANTHUS LEAF - ('Xiguiye' - Chinese Name). Deep Crimson. Large to very large, semidouble with irregular, upright petals. L. (Yunnan Reticulata). (China to U.S. 1980 - U. C. Bot. Gdn, CA).

NEDRA ANN MATHIS - Light Pink with Golden anthers and White filaments. Large to very large, semidouble to peony form. Vigorous, upright, spreading growth. M-L. (Reticulata hybrid 'Suzanne Withers' x Reticulata hybrid 'Jean Pursel'). (U.S. 1996 - Hulyn Smith).

NEIL ARMSTRONG - Dull Pink with Bluish cast. Medium to large, semidouble. Slow, spreading growth. M-L. (Japonica `Debutante' x Reticulata). (U.S. 1971 - Dr. R. K. Womack, Shreveport, LA).

NELL WATSON - Light Pink. Large to very large, semidouble. Average, upright growth. M-L. (Reticulata 'Crimson Robe' x Reticulata hybrid 'Jean Pursel'). (U.S. 1981 - Pursel).

NEON TETRA - Lavender Violet. Large, single with crinkled petal edges. Average, open, upright growth. M-L. (Reticulata 'Crimson Robe' x Saluenensis). (U.S. 1986 - Ackerman).

NEW YEAR - Crimson. Very large, semidouble. Average, upright growth. E-L. (Reticulata seedling). (N.Z. 1972 - Clark).

NICKY RHODES - Re d. Medium, semidouble. Average, compact, upright growth. M. (Japonica 'Mahogany Glow' x Saluenensis/Reticulata hybrid). (N.Z. 1975 - Mrs. I. Berg, Whakatane).

NIJINSKI - Pale Pink. Medium, semidouble. Open, upright growth. (Reticulata hybrid 'Salutation' seedling). (England 1972 - Carlyon).

NITA McRAE - Orchid Pink. Large, peony form. Vigorous, upright growth. M. (U.S. 2001 - Hulyn Smith).

NO REGRETS - Light Orchid Pink. Medium, loose peony form; many petals are upright and folded with wavy margins. Slow, strong, upright growth. M. {(Pitardii var. 'Yunnanica' x Reticulata hybrid 'Forty- Niner') x [(Pitardii var. 'Yunnanica' x Reticulata 'Purple Gown') x (Saluenensis x Trasnokoensis)]}. (U.S. 2006 - Charvet).

*NOBLE PEARL - ('Baozhu Cha' - Chinese Name). Oriental Red. Large to very large, semidouble with large, heavily textured, outer petals, and crinkled inner petals. Compact growth. L. (Yunnan Reticulata). (China to U.S. 1980 - U. C. Bot. Gdn, CA).

NORA KATE - Bright Pink with Yellow anthers and White filaments. Very large, semidouble. Average, upright, spreading growth. M. (U.S. 2018 - Don Bergamini, Martinez, CA).

NORTH BAY - White with Orchid Blush. Medium, semidouble with fluted petals. Vigorous, upright, open growth. E-M. {Pitardii var. 'Yunnanica' x. [Reticulata 'Crimson Robe' x. (Reticulata 'Crimson Robe' x Fraterna)]}. (U.S. 1999 - Charvet).

NOTRE DAME - Pink washed Silver. Very large, loose peony form. Vigorous, upright growth. M-L. (Reticulata seedling). (U.S. 1977 - Mrs. M. O'Malley, Woodside, CA).

NOYO PRINCESS - Pink. Medium, peony form. Strong, upright, well-branched growth. E-M. (Pitardii var. 'Yunnanica' x Reticulata 'Purple Gown'). (U.S. 1981 - Charvet).

NUCCIO'S RUBY - Very Dark Rich Red. Large to very large, semidouble with irregular, ruffled petals. Average, compact, upright growth. M. (Reticulata seedling). (U.S. 1974 - Nuccio's).

ORIENTAL ECHO - Clear Pink with misty Silver overcast and center petals moired and edged White. Medium to large, formal double to rose form double with petals rounded at edge, slightly notched and waved, and small, upright center petals. Upright, pendulous growth. M. (Reticulata 'Crimson Robe' seedling). (U.S. 1968 - C. W. Lattin, Lauderdale, MS).

*OSMANTHUS LEAF CARMINE - ('Guiye Yanghong' - Chinese Name). Carmine. Large to very large, semidouble with wavy, upright petals. E. (Yunnan Reticulata). (China to U.S. 1980 - U. C. Bot. Gdn, CA).

OTARA ROSE - Phlox Pink. Very large, semidouble. Compact, upright growth. M-L. (Saluenensis x Reticulata 'Captain Rawes'). (N.Z. 1958 - Doak).

OTTO HOPFER - Light Red. Large to very large, semidouble with irregular petals. Vigorous, upright growth. M. (Reticulata 'Crimson Robe' x Japonica 'Lotus'). (U.S. 1970 - D. Hopfer, San Francisco, CA).

OUR GRANDDAUGHTERS - Raspberry Pink, shading deeper on the petals' edges. Very large, semidouble form. Open, upright growth. E-L. (Reticulata hybrid 'Wild Form' x Reticulata hybrid 'Suzanne Withers' x Nitidissima). (Aus. 2005 - Colleen Sherrington, Balwyn North, Vic.).

OUR KERRY - Deep veined Red. Large to very large, semidouble. Vigorous, open, upright growth. M-L. (Reticulata 'Crimson Robe' x Reticulata hybrid 'Jean Pursel'). (U.S. 1980 - Pursel).

OUR KIM - Pink to Neyron Rose. Large, peony form. Vigorous, open, upright growth. M. (Reticulata hybrid 'Suzanne Withers' x Reticulata hybrid 'Jean Pursel'). (Aus. 1996 - Dr. R. Withers, Donvale, Vic.).

OUR SELECTION - Dark Pink to Red. Very large, peony form. Open, upright growth. M-L. (Reticulata 'Lion Head' seedling). (Aus. 1984 - Sebire).

*OVATE LEAF PINK - ('Luanye Yinhong' - Chinese Name). Light Pink shaded deeper in center. Large to very large, semidouble. E. (Yunnan Reticulata). (China to U.S. 1980 - U. C. Bot. Gdn, CA).

OVATION - Mauve Pink. Large, semidouble. Rapid, bushy, compact, upright growth. M. (Reticulata hybrid 'Overture' seedling). (Aus. 2006 - Norm Prentice, Garfield, Vic.).

OVER NAVARRO - Silvery Light Pink. Large, semidouble to rose form double. Strong, well-branched growth. M. [(Pitardii var. 'Yunnanica' x Reticulata hybrid 'Forty-Niner') x Hybrid 'Coral Delight']. (U.S. 2009 - Charvet).

OVERTURE - Bright Red. Very large, semidouble with upright petals. Vigorous, compact, upright growth. M. (Reticulata 'Crimson Robe' seedling). (Aus. 1971 - Tuckfield).

PACIFIC CORAL - Coral Pink. Small, peony form. Slow, upright, very compact growth. E-M. {[(Pitardii var. 'Yunnanica' x Reticulata 'Purple Gown) x (Reticulata hybrid 'Buddha' x Fraterna hybrid 'Tiny Princess')] x (Reticulata hybrid Buddha' x Reticulata hybrid 'Forty-Niner')}. (U.S. 2009 - Charvet).

PACIFIC STAR - Medium Pink. Miniature, single with star shaped petals; the plant has the appearance of a small peach tree. M. {Reticulata 'Crimson Robe' x [Fraterna x (Open Pollination or selfed)]}. (U.S. 1992 - Charvet).

PAGODA - ('Songzilin' - Chinese Name). Deep Scarlet. Large, deep formal double to rose form double. Compact growth. M. (Yunnan Reticulata). (China to England 1857).

*PALE BRIGHT RED - (Dandahong' - Chinese Name). Pale Crimson. Large to very large, semidouble with wavy, upright petals. M. (Yunnan Reticulata). (China to U.S. 1980 - U. C. Bot. Gdn, CA).

PAPRIKA - Spiraea Red with Silver fluorescence on all petals. Very large, semidouble. Vigorous, dense, spreading, upright growth. E-L. (Reticulata hybrid 'Lilette Witman' x Reticulata hybrid 'Nuccio's Ruby'). (U.S. 1997 - Mandarich).

PARKES RED GLOW - Dark Red. Very large, semidouble. Open, upright growth. L. (Reticulata 'Cornelian' seedling). (Aus. 1980 - E. Parkes, East Brighton, Vic.).

PAT B. JOHNSON - Bright Red with Yellow anthers and Yellow filaments. Large, semidouble. Vigorous, upright, spreading growth. M-L. (Seedling of Reticulata hybrid 'Mark Cannon'). (U.S. 2016 - Pat Johnson, Cairo, GA).

PAT GURNSEY - Red to Deep Pink with Pale almost White edges. Very large, semidouble. Average, compact, upright growth. M. (Reticulata 'Tali Queen' seedling). (N.Z. 1973 - Mrs. A. B. Durrant, Rotorua).

PAT PINKERTON - Dark Red. Large to very large, semidouble. Slow, open, upright growth. M-L. (Reticulata hybrid 'Arch of Triumph' x {Reticulata 'Crimson Robe' x Lutchuensis}). (U.S. 1997 - Pursel).

PAT'S ROSE - Dark Red Rose with Yellow anthers and White filaments. Medium, semidouble to rose form double. Slow, upright, dense growth. M-L. (Seedling of Reticulata hybrid 'Mark Cannon'). (U.S. 2017 - Pat Johnson, Cairo, GA).

PATRICIA COULL - Soft Pink. Very large, semidouble. Vigorous, open, upright growth. M. (Reticulata hybrid 'Buddha' x Japonica). (N.Z. 1970 - B. J. Rayner, Stratford, N.Z).

PATRICIA HASKEE - Pink. Large to very large, semidouble to rose form double with very high upright petals. Average, spreading, upright growth. E-M. (Reticulata hybrid 'Lilette Whitman' x Reticulata hybrid 'Hulyn Smith'). (U.S. 1995 - Mandarich).

PATSY CLINE - Clear Pink. Large to very large, semidouble to peony form. Average growth. M-L. (Reticulata 'Crimson Robe' x Reticulata hybrid 'Jean Pursel'). (U.S. 1984 - Pursel).

PAUL HARKEY - Dark Red with heavy veins and flecked White in center. Large to very large, semidouble. M-L. (Reticulata 'Crimson Robe' x Reticulata/Japonica hybrid). (U.S. 1982 - Pursel).

PAUL HARVEY - Orchid Pink shaded Lavender. Large, semidouble. Vigorous, open, upright growth. M-L. (Reticulata seedling). (U.S. 1975 - Kramer).

PAVLOVA - Clear bright Red. Very large, semidouble. Vigorous, spreading, upright growth. M-L. (Reticulata seedling). (Aus. 1978 - L. Hobbs, Doncaster East, Vic.).

PEARL S. BUCK - Dark Red frosted White. Very large, semidouble. Average, upright growth. M-L. (Reticulata 'Cornelian' x Reticulata hybrid 'James McCoy'). (U.S. 1991 - Pursel).

PEARL TERRY - Rose Pink with veining. Large to very large, rose form double to formal double. Vigorous, upright growth. E-L. (Reticulata hybrid 'Buddy Bills' x Reticulata hybrid 'Jean Pursel'). (U.S. 1992 - Pursel).

PEKING - Deep Red. Large to very large, semidouble with irregular petals to loose or full peony form. Vigorous, upright growth. (Reticulata seedling). (U.S. 1975 - Peer).

PETE GALLI - Cardinal Red. Large to very large, semidouble. Average, dense, spreading, upright growth. E-L. (Reticulata 'Crimson Robe' x Reticulata hybrid 'Mouchang'). (U.S. 1997 - Mandarich).

PHARAOH - Old Rose. Very large, semidouble with wavy petals to full peony form. Average, upright growth. M. (Reticulata 'Cornelian' seedling). (U.S. 1971 - Asper).

PHILLIP MANDARICH - Pink. Very large, semidouble. Vigorous, dense, spreading, upright growth. M-L. (Reticulata hybrid 'Arch of Triumph' x Reticulata hybrid 'Jean Pursel'). (U.S. 1992 - Mandarich).

PHILLIPA LENNARD - Deep Red. Large, loose peony form. Average, open, spreading growth. E. (Reticulata hybrid 'Flower Girl' x Reticulata hybrid 'Nuccio's Ruby'). (N.Z. 1991 - T. Lennard, Te Puke).

PHYL DOAK - Rose Bengal. Large to very large, semidouble. Compact, upright growth. E-L. (Saluenensis x Reticulata 'Captain Rawes'). (N.Z. 1958 - Doak).

PHYLLIS - Old Rose. Large, semidouble with irregular, crinkled petals. Average, compact, upright growth. M-L. (U.S. 1979 - H. H. Smith, Yuba City, CA).

PHYLLIS CLELAND - Coral Red. Very large, semidouble. Vigorous, open, upright growth. L. (Reticulata seedling). (N.Z. 1992 - R. Cleland, Stratford).

PHYLLIS HUNT - Edged Deep Pink, shading from Light Pink to White at center. Large, rose form double. Slow, open, spreading growth. L. (Reticulata hybrid 'Suzanne Withers' x Japonica 'Mrs. D. W. Davis Special'). (Aus. 1998 - John Hunt, Boronia, Vic.).

PIAN PIAN - See 'Fly Fly'.

PIKES PEAK - Rose Red. Large to very large, semidouble with upright center petals. Average, upright growth. M-L. (Reticulata 'Crimson Robe' x Reticulata hybrid 'Jean Pursel'). (U.S. 1980 - Pursel).

*PINE SHELL - ('Songzike' - Chinese Name). Deep Scarlet. Large, formal double to rose form double. (Yunnan Reticulata). (Similar to 'Pagoda' but smaller petals). (China to U.S. 1980 - U. C. Bot. Gdn, CA).

PINGBAN DALI CHA - See 'Flat Dali Camellia'.

PINK ACE - Deep Pink. Large, peony form. Rapid, upright, open growth. M. (Aus. 2007 - Norm Prentice, Garfield, Vic.).

*PINK BUTTERFLY WING - ('Yinhong Diechi' - Chinese Name). Light Orchid Pink. Very large, semidouble with irregular, twisted center petals. M. (Yunnan Reticulata). (China to U.S. 1980 - U. C. Bot. Gdn, CA).

PINK CHABLIS - Light Rose Pink. Very large, semidouble with heart shaped, wavy, crinkled petals. Vigorous, open, upright growth. M. (Japonica x Reticulata hybrid 'Buddha'). (U.S. 1977 - A. B. Parker, Sebastopol, CA).

PINK CREPE DE CHINE - Light Rose Pink with a White effervescence. Very large, semidouble with crepe, crinkled and upright center petals. Vigorous, open growth. M. (Reticulata 'Shot Silk' seedling). (U.S. 1988 - Hall).

PINK DELIGHT - Deep Pink. Large, peony form. Vigorous, open, upright growth. E. (Reticulata 'Willow Wand' seedling). (Aus. 1971 - Sebire).

PINK SPARKLE - Light Pink with iridescent petals. Large to very large, semidouble with irregular petals. Vigorous, upright growth. M. (Reticulata x Japonica). (U.S. 1967 - Maitland).

PIXIE DUST - Dark Intense Pink with flared light Yellow Anthers and light Yellow filaments. Medium, single. Vigorous, upright growth; blooms don't shatter. E. Cold hardy to -4 degrees. (Sasanqua 'Mikunika' x Reticulata hybrid 'Kurenai'). (U.S. 2016 - Parks).

PLEASANT MEMORIES - Pink. Very large, semidouble with irregular petals. Average, compact, upright growth. M-L. (Reticulata seedling). (U.S. 1983 - M. Gum, San Gabriel, CA).

*POINTED LEAF CRIMSON - ('Jianye Yinhong' - Chinese Name). Veined Light Pink. Large, semidouble. M. (Yunnan Reticulata). (China to U.S. 1980 - U. C. Bot. Gdn, CA).

POP GEE - Deep Rose Pink. Very large, semidouble with heavy cluster of stamens. Vigorous, open, upright growth. E-M. (Reticulata 'Crimson Robe' x Granthamiana). (U.S. 1974 - Homeyer).

POP HOMEYER - Deep Rose Pink and White and Pink center radial stripes. Large to very large, semidouble to anemone form to peony form. Vigorous, spreading, upright growth. E-L. (Reticulata 'Crimson Robe' x 'Granthamiana'). (U.S. 1978 - Homeyer).

POWDERED BEAUTY - Red with Silver fluorescence. Very large, loose peony form. Average, upright, spreading growth. E-L. (U.S. 2000 - Edith Mazzei, Clayton, CA).

PRETTY LADY - Pink. Large, formal double to rose form double. Vigorous, open, upright growth. M-L. (Reticulata hybrid 'Suzanne Withers' x Reticulata hybrid 'Jean Pursel'). (Aus. 1998 - Dr. R. Withers, Donvale, Vic.).

PRETTY PINK - ('Fenejiao' - Chinese Name). Spinel Pink. Medium, semidouble with outer petals slightly undulate, inner whorls curved, erect. E. (China 1981 - Kunming Botanical Garden).

PRIME TIME - Deep Red. Large to very large, semidouble. Average, upright growth. M-L. (Reticulata 'Crimson Robe' x Reticulata/Japonica hybrid). (U.S. 1980 - Pursel).

PROFESSOR JAMES MAY - Spinel Pink. Medium to large, peony form. Vigorous, open, upright growth. M-L. (Aus. 1984 - M. E. Greentree, Kingsgrove, NSW).

PROFESSOR JOHN L. SPENCER - Red with Yellow anthers and Rose filaments. Medium, rose form double. Vigorous, upright, spreading, open growth. (U.S. 2006 - John L Spencer, Lakeland, FL).

***PROFESSOR TSAI** - ('Maye Taohong' - Chinese Name; 'Reticulate Leaf Crimson'). Delicate Rose Pink often fading to Silver-Pink at center. Medium, semidouble with open tiers of waved petals surrounding center of petaloids with a few stamens. Average growth. M-L. (China - there is an old tree at the Panlong Temple estimated to be over 600 years old - Kunming, Yunnan).

PROMISES - Rose Red. Large, semidouble with occasional upright petals. Vigorous, open, upright growth. E-M. (Reticulata 'Crimson Robe' x Granthamiana). (U.S. 1975 - Homeyer).

***PURPLE GOWN** - ('Zipao' - Chinese Name). Dark Purple Red with pin stripes of White to Wine Red. Large to very large, formal double to peony form with wavy petals. Compact growth. M. (Yunnan Reticulata). (China to U.S. 1948 - Descanso and Peer).

PURPLE PETAL - ('Zi Pian' - Chinese Name). Purple/Pink with Yellow stamens. Medium, semidouble with raised fluted petals. Leggy, upright growth. (Reticulata hybrid 'W. P. Gilley' x Lapidea). (U.S. 2012 - John Wang, Orinda, CA).

PURPLETTE - Deep Purplish Red with veining. Miniature, semidouble. Average, spreading growth. M-L. (Japonica x Reticulata). (U.S. 1983 - Feathers).

PUTUO PURPLE LIGHT - ('Putuo Ziguang' and 'Pu Tuo Zi Guan' - Chinese Names). Light Purple, paler when fully open, slightly Yellowish white in the middle with a White radial stripe in the center of each petal. Medium, semidouble. Vigorous, upright growth. (Reticulata hybrid 'Suzanne Withers' x Nitidissima hybrid 'Honeymoon'). (U.S. 2005 - John Wang, Orinda, CA).

PUTUO ZIGUANG - See Putuo Purple Light'.

QINGKOU - See 'Empty Mouth'.

QUEEN BEE - Soft Pink. Very large, irregular semidouble. Vigorous, upright growth. M-L. (Reticulata seedling). (U.S. 1993 - Nuccio's).

R. L. BRENT - Rose Red. Large to very large, semidouble. Vigorous, upright growth. M-L. (Reticulata 'Crimson Robe' x Reticulata hybrid). (U.S. 1982 - Pursel).

RAGGED DRAGON - Orange Red. Large, semidouble. Average, dense growth. M. (Hybrid 'Coral Delight' x Reticulata hybrid 'Royalty'). (U.S. 1995 - T. Croson, Powers, OR).

RANDOLPH MAPHIS - Red frosted with Golden anthers and Red filaments. Large to very large, semidouble to peony form. Vigorous, upright growth. M. (U.S. 2008 - Hulyn Smith).

RASPBERRY GLOW - Crimson Red with an unusual lightness at the base of the petals. Very large, semidouble. Average, upright growth. M. (Reticulata 'Crimson Robe' seedling). (N.Z. 1989 - H. and V. Cave, Wanganui).

RAY GENTRY - Red with Golden anthers and Golden filaments. Very large, semidouble to peony form. Vigorous, upright growth. M-L. (U.S. 2004 - Hulyn Smith).

RAY WATSON - Dark Red. Large to very large, semidouble. Average, upright growth. M-L. (Reticulata 'Cornelian' x Reticulata/Japonica hybrid). (U.S. 1982 - Pursel).

REBECCA MARGARET - Dark Pink with Golden Yellow anthers and Yellow filaments. Medium, semidouble. Vigorous, spreading, dense growth. M-L. (Reticulata hybrid 'Suzanne Withers' x Reticulata hybrid 'Annabelle Fetterman'). (U.S. 2009 - Hulyn Smith).

REBEL LADY - Deep Red. Large to very large, semidouble with upright center petals. Average, upright growth. E-L. (Reticulata hybrid 'Arch of Triumph' x Reticulata/Japonica hybrid). (U.S. 1980 - Pursel).

***RED BOWL** - ('Hongwan Cha' - Chinese Name). Crimson. Large, single of cupped form. E. (Yunnan Reticulata). (China to U.S. 1980 - U. C. Bot. Gdn, CA).

R
E
T
I
C
U
L
A
T
A

P-R

RED CHINA - Crimson to Carmine Red with Yellow stamens. Very large, semidouble. Vigorous, upright, open growth; very floriferous. E. (Reticulata hybrid 'Trewithen Pink' x Reticulata 'Cornelian'). (N.Z. 1971 - F. Jury, Waitara, N.Z).

*RED CLOUD - ('Hongxia' - Chinese Name). Deep Crimson. Very large, semidouble with wavy, twisted, upright petals. M. (Yunnan Reticulata). (China to U.S. 1980 - U. C. Bot. Gdn, CA).

RED CRYSTAL - Scarlet with Pink stamens tipped Yellow. Very large, single to semidouble. Average, open growth. M. (Reticulata 'Crimson Robe' x Japonica 'Wildfire'). (N.Z. 1984 - O. Blumhardt, Whangarei).

RED EMPEROR - Deep Red. Very large, semidouble with irregular petals. Average, compact growth. M-L. (Reticulata 'Crimson Robe' x Reticulata 'Cornelian'). (U.S. 1970 - Asper).

*RED JEWEL - ('Baoyuhong' - Chinese Name). Deep Pink. Large, semidouble with wavy petals and a few center petaloids. E. (Yunnan Reticulata). (China to U.S. 1980 - U. C. Bot. Gdn, CA).

REDWOOD CITY - Red. Large to very large, semidouble to anemone form. Vigorous, spreading growth. M-L. (Reticulata 'Cornelian' x Japonica/ Reticulata hybrid). (U.S. 1979 - Pursel).

RENA BERGAMINI - Red. Medium, rose form double to formal double. Vigorous, spreading, upright growth. E-M. (Reticulata hybrid 'Bernadette Karsten' x Japonica 'Eleanor Martin'). (U.S. 1993 - Mandarich).

RENEE LAND - Pink. Very large, semidouble. Vigorous, upright growth. M-L. (Reticulata 'Crimson Robe' x Reticulata hybrid 'Jean Pursel'). (U.S. 1994 - Pursel).

RENEGADE - Deep Purple Red. Large, semidouble to anemone form. Vigorous, open, upright growth. M-L. (Reticulata 'Crimson Robe' x Reticulata hybrid 'Jean Pursel'). (U.S. 1989 - Homeyer).

*RETICULATE LEAF CRIMSON - ('Maye Taohong' - Chinese Name; 'Professor Tsai'). Delicate Rose Pink, often fading to Silver-Pink at center. Medium, semidouble with open tiers of waved petals surrounding center of petaloids with a few stamens. Average growth. M-L. (China - there is an old tree at the Panlong Temple estimated to be over 600 years old - Kunming, Yunnan).

*RETICULATE LEAF PINK - ('Maye Yinhong' - Chinese Name). Bright Spinel Pink with Red veins. Medium, semidouble with irregular, loose petals. Vigorous, bushy growth. M. (Yunnan Reticulata). (China to N.Z. 1964 - Durrant).

RHONDA KERRI - China Rose. Large, semidouble. Vigorous, compact, upright growth. M. (Reticulata 'Cornelian' seedling). (N.Z. 1967 - Clark).

RICHARD CARTER - Silvery Pink. Large, semidouble. Average, upright growth. M-L. (Reticulata 'Crimson Robe' x Reticulata hybrid 'Jean Pursel'). (U.S. 1976 - Pursel).

RICHARD MIMS - Light Pink with Yellow anthers and White filaments. Large, semidouble to loose peony form. Average, upright, spreading growth. M-L. (U.S. 2016 - Hulyn Smith).

RICK WOOD - Rose Pink. Large, semidouble. Average, upright growth. E-L. (Reticulata hybrid 'Arch of Triumph' x Reticulata/Japonica hybrid). (U.S. 1980 - Pursel).

RITA THORNTON - Pink. Very large, peony form. Vigorous, upright growth. E-M. (Reticulata hybrid 'Buddha' seedling). (Aus. 1976 - Sebire).

ROB ROY - Pale Pink to Deeper Pink edge. Medium to large, semidouble with irregular petals. Average, upright, bushy growth. (Reticulata 'Shot Silk' x Hybrid 'J. C. Williams'). (U.S. 1970 - T E Croson, Simi, CA).

ROBERT EHRHART - Dark Pink. Very large, full peony to loose peony. Average, upright growth. M-L. (U.S. 2016 - Robert Ehrhart, Walnut Creek, CA).

ROBERT FORTUNE - See 'Pagoda'.

ROBERT FOWLER - Red. Large to very large, semidouble. Average, compact, upright growth. M-L. (Reticulata 'Crimson Robe' x Reticulata hybrid 'Jean Pursel'). (U.S. 1982 - Pursel).

ROBERTS JEWEL - Rose. Large to very large, semidouble. Vigorous, compact, upright growth. M. (Reticulata 'Crimson Robe' x Reticulata hybrid 'Arch of Triumph'). (U.S. 1979 - Pursel).

ROBYN JAY - Bright Pink with Yellow anthers and Yellow filaments. Large, rose form double. Average, upright growth. L. (U.S. 2012 - Donald Lesmeister, Carmichael, CA).

ROCCO - Red. Very large, semidouble to loose peony form. Average, open, upright growth. M-L. (Reticulata hybrid 'Mouchang' x Reticulata 'Purple Gown'). (U.S. 1992 - Mandarich).

ROSCOE DEAN - Deep Rose Pink with Pink sheen. Very large, semidouble to peony form. Vigorous, open, spreading, upright growth. M-L. (Reticulata hybrid 'Mouchang' x Reticulata hybrid 'Pharaoh'). (U.S. 1996 - Jernigan).

ROSE GEM - Coral Pink. Very large, semidouble. Average, open, upright growth. E. (Reticulata seedling). (Aus. 1971 - Sebire).

ROSE TWILIGHT - Neon Pink. Large, single. Very open growth. (Williamsii 'William Lavender' x Reticulata). (U.S.).

ROSS CLARK - Tyrian Pink. Very large, semidouble. Upright growth. M. (Saluenensis x Reticulata hybrid 'Buddha'). (N.Z. 1967 - Clark).

*ROSY OSMANTHUS LEAF - ('Meihong Guiye' - Chinese Name). Deep Pink. Large to very large, semidouble with occasional wavy petals. Average growth. (Yunnan Reticulata). (China to U.S. 1980 - U. C. Bot. Gdn, CA).

ROY STRINGFELLOW - Red. Large to very large, semidouble. Vigorous, upright growth. L. (Reticulata 'Crimson Robe' x Reticulata hybrid 'Jean Pursel'). (U.S. 1981 - Pursel).

ROYAL ROBE - Red. Medium, semidouble to peony form with irregular, upright petals. (Japonica x Reticulata 'Crimson Robe'). (U.S. 1960 - Feathers).

ROYALTY - Bright Pink deeper in center. Very large, semidouble with wavy, crinkled petals. Average, upright growth. M. (Japonica 'Clarise Carleton' x Reticulata 'Cornelian'). (U.S. 1968 - T. E. Croson, Simi, CA).

ROYALTY VARIEGATED - Bright Pink and White form of 'Royalty'. (U.S. 1974).

RUBY GIRL - Salmon Rose, with Pink overcast and iridescent color. Very large, semidouble form. Average, compact, upright growth. E-M. (Reticulata hybrid 'Nuccio's Ruby' x Japonica 'Drama Girl'). (Aus. 2005 - Donal R. Coe, Albury, NSW).

RUBY QUEEN - Vibrant Red. Very large, semidouble. Vigorous, upright growth. M. (Reticulata 'Crimson Robe' x Reticulata 'Purple Gown'). (N.Z. 1984 - O. Blumhardt, Whangarei).

RUBY WOODROFFE - Clear Pink. Very large, semidouble to peony form. Vigorous, upright growth. E-M. (Reticulata 'Confucius' seedling). (N.Z. 1981 - Mrs. A. B. Durrant, Rotorua).

RUDY TATUM - Red. Large to very large, semidouble. Average, upright growth. L. (Reticulata 'Crimson Robe' x Reticulata/Japonica hybrid). (U.S. 1981 - Pursel).

RUTA HAGMANN - Light Blush Coral Pink. Very large, peony form. Average, open, spreading, upright growth. M-L. (Reticulata hybrid 'Curtain Call' seedling). (U.S. 1992 - D. Hagmann, Orinda, CA).

RUTH JERNIGAN - Red with frosted sheen. Very large, semidouble with high petals. Vigorous, upright growth. E-M. (Reticulata hybrid 'Harbinger' x Reticulata 'Crimson Robe'). (U.S. 1991 - Jernigan).

RUTH LAURENT - Red. Large, semidouble. Average, upright growth. M-L. (Reticulata 'Crimson Robe' x Reticulata hybrid 'Jean Pursel'). (U.S. 1982 - Pursel).

RUTH LENNON - Bright Orchid Pink. Large, semidouble. Average, dense growth. M. (Reticulata hybrid 'Valley Knudsen' seedling). (U.S. 1991 - L. and B. Baxter, Seneca, SC).

RUTHIE K. - Vivid Rose Pink. Very large, semidouble with irregular upright petals. Average, open, upright growth. M. (Reticulata seedling). (U.S. 1975 - H. Foust, Orange County, CA).

S. P. DUNN - Red. Very large, semidouble. Vigorous, upright growth. M-L. (Reticulata 'Crimson Robe' x Reticulata/Japonica hybrid). (U.S. 1981 - Pursel).

SAIJUBAN - See 'Superior Chrysanthemum Petal'.

SAIMUDAN - See 'Superior Peony'.

SAITAOHONG - See 'Superior Crimson'.

SALLY CHRISTINE - Pale Pink. Very large, semidouble with notched and fluted petals. Vigorous, open, upright growth. M. (Reticulata hybrid 'Suzanne Withers' x Reticulata hybrid 'LASCA Beauty'). (Aus. 1996 - Dr. R. Withers, Donvale, Vic.).

SALMA WALKER - Deep Rose Pink. Very large, peony form. Open, upright growth. E-M. (Reticulata 'Cornelian' x Reticulata hybrid 'Buddha'). (Aus. 1980 - T. E. Pierson, Hurstville, NSW).

SALUTATION - Delicate Pale Pink. Large, single to semidouble. Vigorous, open, upright growth. M. (Saluenensis x Reticulata 'Captain Rawes'). (England: 1936 - Clarke).

SAM WELLBORN - Medium Pink with Golden anthers and White filaments. Very large, rose form double to semidouble. Vigorous, upright, dense growth. E-L. (Seedling of Reticulata hybrid 'Frank Houser'). (U.S. 2018 - James Smelley, Moss Point, Mississippi).

SAMANTHA - China Pink. Very large, semidouble to loose peony form with upright petals. (Reticulata 'Cornelian' seedling). (Aus. 1967 - Tuckfield).

SAN MARINO - Dark Red. Large, semidouble with heavy textured petals. Average, spreading, upright growth. M. (Reticulata seedling). (U.S. 1975 - W. F. Goertz, San Marino, CA).

SANDRA GAETA - Pink. Large, semidouble with upright, twisted petals. Average, open, spreading growth. E-L. (Reticulata hybrid 'Arcadia' x Nitidissima 'Olympic Gold'). (U.S. 1989 - Piet and Gaeta).

SANDY CLARK - Soft Pink. Large, semidouble. Vigorous, upright growth. M. (Reticulata hybrid 'Buddha' x Saluenensis). (N.Z. 1970 - Clark).

SARA DUNHAM - Rose Pink veined Red. Medium to large, semidouble to rose form double. Vigorous, upright growth. M-L. (Reticulata 'Cornelian' x Reticulata hybrid 'Jean Pursel'). (U.S. 1983 - Pursel).

SARA OLIVER - Deep Salmon Pink. Large to very large, loose peony form. Vigorous, spreading, upright growth. M. (Reticulata seedling). (U.S. 1977 - Kramer).

SARA PAUL - Medium Pink with Gold anthers and White filaments. Very large, semidouble to rose form double. Vigorous, upright, spreading growth. (Reticulata hybrid 'Suzanne Withers' x Reticulata hybrid 'Delta Dawn'). (U.S. 2007 - Hulyn Smith).

SARAH FOULDS - China Rose with Purplish overtones toward center. Medium to large, semidouble to rose form double with wavy petals. Average growth. M. (Reticulata hybrid 'Arbutus Gum' seedling). (Aus. 1995 - J. Powell, Helensburgh, NSW).

SARAH JANE - Pale Pink. Very large, formal double to rose form double with fluted petals Silver veined at center. Compact, upright growth. M. (Reticulata hybrid). (Aus. 1987 - K. Strudwick, S. Aus.).

SARAH KATHERINE - Silvery Pink. Large, peony form. Open, upright growth. M-L. (Reticulata seedling). (Aus. 1984 - Mrs. J. Wood, Oyster Bay, NSW).

SATAN'S ROBE - Oriental Red. Large, semidouble. Vigorous, upright growth. M. (Hybrid 'Satan's Satin' x Reticulata 'Crimson Robe'). (U.S. 1965 - Feathers).

SCARLET TEMPTATION - Bright Rose Red with bright Yellow stamens. Large, single with ruffled petals. Erect, branching growth. M. Cold hardy. (Hybrid 'William's Lavender' x Reticulata 'Purple Gown'). (U.S. 2008 - Parks).

SCOTT LEWIS - Light Pink with Yellow anthers and Pink filaments. Very large, loose peony to rose form double. Average, upright, open growth. L. (Seedling of Reticulata hybrid 'Curtain Call'). (U.S. 2016 - Pat Johnson, Cairo, GA).

SCOTT MAPHIS - Bright Red with heavy frosting with Golden anthers and White filaments. Very large, semidouble. Average, upright growth. M-L. (U.S. 2015 - Frank Pursel and Hulyn Smith).

SE BA BIAN - See 'Eighteen Year-Old Maiden'.

SEAN ARMIJO - Brilliant Pink speckled White. Large to very large, semidouble with upright petals. E-M. (Reticulata 'Crimson Robe' x Granthamiana). (U.S. 1989 - Piet and Gaeta).

SHAMAN - Crimson. Very large, peony form. Vigorous, upright growth. L. (Japonica 'Hi-no-maru' x Reticulata hybrid 'Buddha'). (Japan 1987 - Y. Andoh, Kobe).

SHANGHAI LADY - Light Orchid Pink. Very large, semidouble with irregular petals. Vigorous, spreading, upright growth. E-M. (Reticulata hybrid 'China Lady' x Reticulata hybrid 'Buddha'). (U.S. 1981 - Nuccio's).

SHARILYN GREEN - Medium Pink with some frosting with Golden anthers and White filaments. Large, semidouble. Vigorous, upright growth. E-M. (U.S. 2015 - Hulyn Smith).

SHAY DEAN - Pink. Very large, rose form double. Vigorous, open, upright growth. E-L. (Reticulata hybrid 'Craig Clark' x Reticulata hybrid 'Nuccio's Ruby'). (U.S. 1995 - Jernigan).

SHELTER COVE - Bright Medium Pink imbued with a very warm undertone. Large, rose form to formal double. Strong, upright, open growth. M. [(Pitardii var. 'Yunnanica' x Reticulata 'Purple Gown') x (Open Pollination or selfed)]. (U.S. 2005 - Charvet).

SHENGJIE - See 'Holy Pure'.

SHERRIDA CRAWFORD - Light Pink with White anthers and White filaments. Medium to large, semidouble to rose form double. Vigorous, upright growth. M-L. (Reticulata hybrid 'Suzanne Withers' x Reticulata hybrid 'Jean Pursel'). (U.S. 2010 - Hulyn Smith).

SHINING JADE - ('Jing Jing - Chinese Name). Light Pink and White. Medium, rose form double. [(Reticulata hybrid 'Suzanne Withers' x 'Nitidissima hybrid 'Honeymoon') x Tunganica]. (U.S. 2012 - John Wang, Orinda, CA).

SHIZITOU - See 'Lion Head'.

SHOALHAVEN - Rose Pink. Very large, single to semidouble. Spreading, upright growth. M-L. Reticulata hybrid 'Balderdash' seedling). (Aus. 1984 - Pierson).

*SHOT SILK - ('Dayinhong' - Chinese Name). Brilliant Spinel Pink. Large, semidouble with loose, wavy petals. Vigorous growth. E. (Yunnan Reticulata). (China to U.S. 1948 - Descanso and Peer).

SHOW GIRL - Pink. Large to very large, semidouble to peony form. Vigorous, open, upright growth. M. (Oleifera 'Narumi-Gata' x Reticulata 'Cornelian'). (U.S. 1965 - Asper).

SILK ROAD - Medium Pink silk-like. Medium, single. Strong, upright, well-branched growth. E-M. {(Pitardii var. 'Yunnanica' x Reticulata hybrid 'Forty-Niner') x [(Pitardii var. 'Yunnanica' x Fraterna hybrid 'Tiny Princess') x Japonica 'Tom Knudsen']}. (U.S. 2009 - Charvet).

SILVER MIST - Pale Pink with iridescent petals. Large to very large, semidouble with irregular petals. Average, compact growth. M. (Reticulata x Japonica). (U.S. 1967 - Maitland).

SILVER SHADOW - Silvery White and Pink moiré. Very large, rose form double with imbricated and incurved petals in tiers. Average, open, upright growth. M-L. (Reticulata hybrid 'Carl Tourje' seedling). (U.S. 1987 - Hall).

SIMPATICA - Pink. Very large, formal double. Open, upright growth. M-L. (Reticulata seedling). (Aus. 1980 - T. J. Savige, Wirlinga, NSW).

SINGAPORE SAL - Deep Magenta Red. Very large, semidouble. Vigorous, open, upright growth. E-M. (Reticulata hybrid 'Mary Williams' seedling). (U.S. 1976 - Mr. and Mrs. H. S. Putnam, Long Beach, CA; McCaskill).

***SINGLE HEART BUTTERFLY** - ('Duxin Diechi' - (Chinese Name). Veined Light Pink. Very large, semidouble with irregular, twisted, upright petals. M. (Yunnan Reticulata). (China to U.S. 1980 - U. C. Bot. Gdn, CA).

SIR ERIC PEARCE - Light Pink, darker toward center. Very large, peony form to formal double. Open, upright growth. M-L. (Reticulata hybrid 'Buddha' seedling). (Aus. 1984 - K. Ballard, Waverley, Vic.).

SIR ROBERT MULDOON - Glowing Pink. Large, peony form. Average, upright growth. E. (Reticulata seedling). (N.Z. 1991 - A. Gamlin, Manaia).

SISTER MARY LEO - Deep Rose. Large, semidouble. Average, open, upright growth. M. (Reticulata x Saluenensis). (N.Z. 1972 - Clark).

SKIP'S CHOICE - Pale Pink with Yellow anthers and White filaments. Medium, semidouble. Average, spreading, open growth. L. (Reticulata hybrid 'Phyllis Hunt' seedling). (U.S. 2013 - James and Elaine Smelley, Moss Point, MS).

SLEEPING BEAUTY - Medium Pink, shading to near White inside. Large, single or semidouble. Average, open, spreading growth. M. (Reticulata x Reticulata x Japonica 'False Howard Asper'). (N.Z. 2003 - O. Blumhardt).

***SMALL LEAF PEONY** - ('Xiaoye Mudan' - Chinese Name). Crimson. Large to very large, loose peony form. M-L. (Yunnan Reticulata). (China to U.S. 1980 - U. C. Bot. Gdn, CA).

***SMALL MAGNOLIA** - ('Xiaoyulan' (Chinese Name). Crimson. Small, single of magnolia form. M. (Yunnan Reticulata). (China to U.S. 1980 - U. C. Bot. Gdn, CA).

***SMALL OSMANTHUS LEAF** - ('Xiaoguiye' - Chinese Name). Orchid Pink. Medium, rose form double. Vigorous, slender, open growth. M-L. (Yunnan Reticulata). (China to N.Z. 1964 - Durrant).

SOFTGLOW - Soft Pink. Very large, semidouble with broad, rounded, wavy petals. Average, compact, upright growth. E-M. (Reticulata hybrid 'LASCA Beauty' seedling). (Aus. 1993 - D. Coe, Albury, NSW).

SONGSIKE - See 'Pine Shell'.

SONGZILIN - See 'Pagoda'.

SOUTH PACIFIC - China Rose. Very large, semidouble. Average, open, upright growth. M. (Saluenensis x Reticulata hybrid 'Buddha'). (N.Z. 1972 - Clark).

SOUTH PORT - Deep Red. Large to very large, semidouble with upright center petals. Average, upright growth. E-L. (Reticulata hybrid 'Arch of Triumph' x Reticulata/Japonica hybrid). (U.S. 1980 - Pursel).

SPARKLER - Iridescent Light Pink. Very large, loose peony form. Vigorous open, upright growth. M. (Reticulata hybrid 'Pink Sparkle' seedling). (U.S. 1985 - H. S. Hall, San Anselmo, CA).

SPENCER SMILEY - Soft Pink. Very large, semidouble with irregular, wavy petals. Vigorous, upright growth. M-L. (Reticulata 'Cornelian' seedling). (U.S. 1986 - Hall).

SPENCER WALDEN - Red. Large to very large, semidouble. Average, upright growth. M-L. (Reticulata hybrid 'Arch of Triumph' x Reticulata/Japonica hybrid). (U.S. 1981 - Pursel).

***SPINEL PINK PEONY** - ('Yinfen Mudan' - Chinese Name). Clear Pink. Large to very large, loose peony form. E. (Yunnan Reticulata). (China to U.S. 1980 - U. C. Bot. Gdn, CA).

SPRINGTIME - Pale Rose. Very large, semidouble. Vigorous, compact, upright growth. E-M. (Reticulata hybrid 'Buddha' seedling). (Aus. 1976 - Sebire).

ST. PATRICK - Light Red. Very large, rose form double. Vigorous, open, upright growth. M. (Reticulata hybrid 'Mouchang' seedling). (Aus. 1998 - Dr. R. Withers, Donvale, Vic.).

STANDING OVATION - Deep Red. Very large, semidouble with upright petals. Vigorous, upright growth. M. (Reticulata seedling). (U.S. 1984 - Nuccio's).

STAR IS BORN - Light Pink. Very large, semidouble. Average, compact growth. M. (Reticulata x Japonica). (U.S. 1986 - Nuccio's).

STAR OF INDIA - Oriental Red. Large, semidouble with fluted hose-in-hose petals. Vigorous, upright growth. M. (Reticulata 'Crimson Robe' seedling). (Aus. 1971 - Tuckfield).

STAR OF TOOWOOMBA - Pink, central petals streaked Pale Pink. Very large, rose form double. Open, spreading, upright growth. M-L. (Reticulata hybrid 'Mouchang' seedling). (Aus. 2003 - John Butler, Cabarlah, Qld.).

STEPHEN BULLOCK - Deep Red. Very large, peony form to rose form double. Vigorous, compact growth. M. (Reticulata hybrid 'Janet Clark' seedling). (Aus. 1986 - A.J.S. Bullock, Bentleigh, Vic.).

STRIKE IT RICH - Clear Pink with Yellow anthers. Very large, semidouble with 60 to 70 petals and a few petaloids. Rapid growth. M. (U.S. 1972 - Richard F. Roggia, San Jose, CA).

RETICULATA S-S

STUART WATSON - Red. Large to very large, semidouble. Vigorous, upright growth. M-L. (Reticulata 'Crimson Robe' x Reticulata/Japonica hybrid). (U.S. 1981 - Pursel).

SUE RHODES - Rich Pink. Very large, semidouble to peony form with fluted petals. Upright growth. E-M. (Reticulata 'Crimson Robe' seedling). (N.Z. 1978 - Mrs. I. Berg, Whakatane).

SUGAR DREAM - Pink. Medium, anemone form. Average, open, upright growth, E. (Reticulata hybrid 'Dream Girl' x Oleifera 'Jaune'). (N.Z. 1984 - O. Blumhardt, Whangarei).

SUNNINGHILL - Rose Pink. Large, semidouble with irregular petals. Vigorous, upright growth. M. (Saluenensis x Reticulata). (N.Z. 1968 - Clark).

SUNSET - Orange Red. Large to very large, semidouble with irregular petals. Average, upright growth. M-L. (Reticulata x Japonica). (U.S. 1971 - Maitland).

SUPERBA - Rich Carmine. Large, single to semidouble. (Reticulata hybrid 'Wild Form' seedling).

*SUPERIOR CHRYSANTHEMUM PETAL - ('Saijuban' - Chinese Name). Crimson. Large, semidouble with wavy petals. L. (Yunnan Reticulata). (China to U.S. 1980 - U. C. Bot. Gdn, CA).

*SUPERIOR CRIMSON - ('Saitaohong' - Chinese Name). Crimson. Large, semidouble with irregular, wavy, upright petals. E. (Yunnan Reticulata). (China to U.S. 1980 - U. C. Bot. Gdn, CA).

*SUPERIOR PEONY - ('Saimudan' - Chinese Name). Crimson. Very large, loose peony form. E. (Yunnan Reticulata). (China to U.S. 1980 - U. C. Bot. Gdn, CA).

SUSAN GOLOMBIEWSKI - Deep glowing Red. Very large, semidouble. Vigorous, spreading, upright growth. M. (Reticulata 'Crimson Robe' seedling x Reticulata hybrid 'Jean Pursel'). (U.S. 1989 - Homeyer).

SUSIE B - Lavender Pink. Medium, formal double to rose form double. Open, upright growth. M-L. (Reticulata hybrid 'Carl Tourje' seedling). (Aus. 1982 - T. E. Pierson, Hurstville, NSW).

SUSIE O'NEILL - Pale to medium Pink. Very large, anemone to loose peony form. Vigorous, open and upright growth. M-L. (Reticulata hybrid 'Suzanne Withers' x Reticulata hybrid 'Jean Pursel'). (Aus. 2002 - Dr. R. M. Withers, Donvale, Vic.).

SUTHERLAND ROTARY - Deep Salmon Rose Pink edged paler. Very large, semidouble to loose peony form with upright, heavily ruffled petals. Open, spreading growth. M-L. (Reticulata hybrid 'Buddha' x Reticulata 'Cornelian'). (Aus. 1982 - S. Rotary, Jannah, NSW).

SUZANNE WITHERS - White deepening to Orchid Pink from center to edge. Large, semidouble to peony form with crepe petals. Open, upright growth. M. (Reticulata seedling). (Aus. 1979 - E. D. Kettle, Cheltenham, Vic.).

SWEET WILLIAM - Bright Pink. Medium, semidouble. Vigorous, upright, spreading growth. E-M. (Reticulata hybrid 'Dream Girl' seedling). (U.S. 2008 - CamelliaShop, Savannah, GA).

SYDNEY WOODROFFE - Deep Pink. Large, semidouble. Vigorous, upright growth. E-M. (Reticulata hybrid 'Buddha' seedling). (N.Z. 1981 - Mrs. A. B. Durrant and Mrs. D. Johnson, Rotorua).

T'ANG - Lavender Pink. Large, semidouble with irregular, upright, wavy petals. Vigorous, open, upright growth. M. (Reticulata hybrid 'Buddha' seedling). (U.S. 1966 - E. Rideout, Laguna Hills, CA).

TAKUEIYEH - See 'Large Osmanthus Leaf'.

*TALI QUEEN - ('Dali Cha' - Chinese Name). Turkey Red to Deep Pink. Very large, semidouble with irregular petals and with very large, heavily textured outer petals and wavy inner petals interspersed with clusters of stamens. Average, upright growth. M. (Yunnan Reticulata). (China to U.S. 1948 - Descanso and Peer).

TANGO - Black Red Crimson. Large to very large, formal double. Average, dense, spreading, upright growth. E-M. (Reticulata hybrid 'Carl Tourje' x Reticulata hybrid 'Craig Clark'). (U.S. 1996 - Hall).

TARANTELLA - Vibrant Red with Bright Yellow anthers and Cream filaments. Medium, peony form. Vigorous, upright, average density growth. E-M. [(Sasanqua x Reticulata hybrid 'Gael's Dream') x Japonica 'Takanini']. (New Zealand, 2008 - Neville Hayden, Takanini).

TED CRAIG - Red. Very large, semidouble. Average, spreading, upright growth. M-L. (Reticulata hybrid 'William Hertrich' x Japonica 'Drama Girl'). (Aus. 1993 - T. Craig, N. Bondi, NSW).

TEMPLE BOWEN - Deep Red. Large to very large, semidouble. Vigorous, upright growth. M-L. (Reticulata 'Crimson Robe' x Reticulata/Non-Reticulata hybrid). (U.S. 1981 - Pursel).

TEMPLE FESTIVAL - Red. Very large, semidouble. Average, open growth. M. (Reticulata hybrid 'Buddha' x Reticulata 'Crimson Robe'). (N.Z. 1972 - D. G. O'Toole, Ohope).

TEMPLE GARDEN - Deep Pink. Very large, peony form with fluted and wavy petals. Vigorous, open growth. M. (Reticulata hybrid 'Lila Naff' seedling). (Aus. 1986 - B. Hooper, Bexley North, NSW).

TEMPLE MIST - Rose Pink with iridescent petals. Large to very large, semidouble with irregular petals. Average, upright growth. M. (Reticulata x Japonica). (U.S. 1967 - Maitland).

TEN PLUS - Pink with mottled Whitish Pink center petals. Large to very large, semidouble. Average, upright growth. M-L. (Reticulata 'Crimson Robe' x Reticulata/Japonica hybrid). (U.S. 1980 - Pursel).

TERRELL WEAVER - Flame to Dark Red. Large to very large, semidouble to loose peony form with thick fluted and twisted petals. Vigorous, spreading, upright growth. M. (Reticulata 'Crimson Robe' x Japonica 'Ville De Nantes'). (U.S. 1974 - Homeyer).

THAI SILK - Salmon Pink. Medium, single with crepe and crinkled petals. Slow, dwarf, bushy growth. E-M. (Reticulata seedling). (U.S. 1992 - Nuccio's).

THOMAS E. GILLEY - Bright Pink. Large, semidouble with crinkled petals. Average, upright growth. M-L. (Reticulata hybrid 'Mouchang' seedling). (U.S. 1983 - Gilley).

THREE DREAMS - Deep Rose Pink. Large to very large, semidouble with wavy, crinkled petals. M. (Reticulata hybrid 'Buddha' seedling). (U.S. 1970 - Peer).

TINY GIRL - Salmon Pink. Small, formal double. Vigorous, open growth. M-L. (Sasanqua/Reticulata seedling). (U.S. 1981 - E. P. Akin, Shreveport, La).

TITIRANGI - China Rose. Large, semidouble. Average, open, upright growth. E-L. (Saluenensis x Reticulata hybrid 'Buddha'). (N.Z. 1972 - Clark).

TITLETOWN USA - Light Pink with Golden Yellow anthers and Yellow filaments. Medium to large, semidouble. Average, upright growth. M-L. (Reticulata hybrid 'Suzanne Withers' x Reticulata hybrid 'Hulyn Smith). (U.S. 2009 - Hulyn Smith).

TOM DURRANT - Crimson. Large, peony form. Average, bushy, upright growth. M-L. (Reticulata hybrid 'Wild Form' x Reticulata 'Shot Silk'). (N.Z. 1966 - Dr. Jane Crisp, Tirau).

TOM HOFFMAN - Red. Large to very large, semidouble. Average, compact, upright growth. M-L. (Reticulata 'Crimson Robe' x Reticulata/Japonica hybrid). (U.S. 1982 - Pursel).

TOMMY LAND - Dark Red. Very large, semidouble. Average, upright growth. M. (Reticulata 'Crimson Robe' x Lutchuensis). (U.S. 1991 - Pursel).

TOMMY WEEKS - Dark Red. Large, semidouble. Average, spreading growth. M-L. (Reticulata 'Crimson Robe' x Reticulata hybrid 'Jean Pursel'). (U.S. 1983 - Pursel).

TONGZIMIAN - See 'Baby Face'.

TONY HUNT - Pink. Very large, semidouble to loose peony form. Vigorous, upright growth. M. (Reticulata hybrid 'Overture' x Reticulata hybrid 'LASCA Beauty'). (Aus. 1991 - J. Hunt, Boronia, Vic.).

TONY PINHEIRO - Red. Very large, semidouble. Vigorous, upright, dense growth. E-L. (Reticulata hybrid 'Four Winds' x Reticulata hybrid 'Lillette Witman'). (U.S. 2000 - Mary Jo Pinheiro, Modesto, CA).

TONY'S JOY - Bright Red. Large to very large, semidouble. Vigorous, upright growth. M. (Reticulata x Japonica). (U.S. 1975 - A. Funari, Santa Clara, CA).

TRACEY SPENCER - Rose Pink. Very large, semidouble with crimped, fluted petals. Vigorous, upright growth. E. (Reticulata hybrid 'Wild Form' seedling). (Aus. 1970 - F. N. Spencer, Cheltenham, Vic.).

TRANQUILLITY - Rose Pink. Large, semidouble to loose peony form. Vigorous, open, upright growth. M. (Reticulata 'Cornelian' seedling). (Aus. 1969 - H. A. Pederson, Collaroy Plateau, NSW).

TREVOR LENNARD - Deep Pink. Large, peony form. Average, open, spreading growth. E-M. (Reticulata hybrid 'Flower Girl' x Reticulata hybrid 'Carl Tourje'). (N.Z. 1991 - T. Lennard, Te Puke).

TREWITHEN PINK - Deep Rose. Large, semidouble. L. (Reticulata hybrid 'Wild Form' seedling). (Aus. 1947 - Waterhouse).

TRISTREM CARLYON - Rose Pink. Medium, peony form. Vigorous, upright growth. (Japonica 'Rosea Simplex' x Reticulata hybrid 'Salutation'). (England 1972 - Carlyon).

TROPHY - Orchid Pink. Large, irregular rose form double. Vigorous, compact, upright growth; outstanding with gibberellic treatment. L. (Japonica 'Mrs. D. W. Davis Descanso' x Reticulata hybrid 'Nuccio's Ruby'). (U.S. 1988 - Nuccio's).

TRUDY SMITH - Dark Red. Large to very large, semidouble to full peony form. Average growth. M-L. (Reticulata 'Crimson Robe' x Reticulata/Japonica hybrid). (U.S. 1982 - Pursel).

TRUMPET FANFARE - Pillar Box Red. Medium, semidouble form, trumpet shaped. Average, dense, upright growth; petals are long, narrow and recurved. E. (Saluenensis x Japonica 'Ruby Bells' x Japonica x Reticulata hybrid 'Diamond Head'). (N.Z. 2003 - O. Blumhardt).

TUI SONG - Rose Pink. Large, semidouble. Upright growth. M. (Reticulata 'Cornelian' seedling). (N.Z. 1967 - Clark).

VAL BIELESKI - Salmon Pink fading to Lighter Pink. Very large, semidouble. Vigorous, spreading growth. M-L. (Sport of Reticulata hybrid 'Valentine Day'). (N.Z. 2000 - Haydon).

VALE QUEEN - Iridescent Pink. Very large, semidouble with irregular petals. Average, open, upright growth. M-L. (Reticulata 'Willow Wand' x Reticulata 'Crimson Robe'). (Aus. 1977 - Camellia Vale Nsy., Bexley North, NSW).

VALENTINE DAY - Salmon Pink. Large to very large, formal double with Rosebud center. Vigorous, upright growth. M. (Reticulata 'Crimson Robe' x Japonica 'Tiffany'). (U.S. 1969 - Asper).

VALENTINE DAY VARIEGATED - Salmon Pink and White form of 'Valentine Day'. (U.S. 1975).

VALLEY KNUDSEN - Deep Orchid Pink. Medium to large, semidouble to loose peony form. Vigorous, compact, upright growth. M-L. (Saluenensis x Reticulata hybrid 'Buddha'). (U.S. 1958 - Asper).

VANNATE - Oriental Red. Medium to large, single with heavy textured petals. Slow, bushy growth. M. (Japonica 'Lady Vansittart' x Reticulata 'Crimson Robe'). (U.S. 1968 - Feathers).

VANNINE - White to White striped Pink to Pink. Medium to large, semidouble. Vigorous, bushy growth. M. (Japonica 'Lady Vansittart' x Reticulata 'Crimson Robe'). (U.S. 1968 - Feathers).

*VERMILLION PURPLE GOWN - ('Zhusha Zipao'- Chinese Name). Oriental Red. Very large, loose peony form. M. (Yunnan Reticulata). (China To U.S. 1980 - U. C. Bot. Gdn, CA).

VI HENDERSON - Red. Very large, semidouble to peony form. Average, open, upright growth. M. (Reticulata 'Crimson Robe' seedling). (Aus. 1976 - Sebire).

VI STONE - Deep bright Pink veined Red and edged White. Large, formal double to rose form double. Vigorous, upright growth. M-L. (Reticulata 'Cornelian' x Reticulata hybrid 'Jean Pursel'). (U.S. 1980 - Pursel).

VICTOR CORKILL - Rose Red veined darker. Very large, semidouble. Compact, upright growth. M-L. (Reticulata hybrid 'William Hertrich' seedling). (N.Z. 1982 - A. Gamlin, Manaia).

VICTORIA WHIDDON - Light Pink with Golden Yellow anthers and Yellow filaments. Large to very large, semidouble. Vigorous, upright growth. M-L. (Reticulata hybrid 'Suzanne Withers' x Reticulata hybrid 'Annabelle Fetterman'). (U.S. 2009 - Hulyn Smith).

VINCE DOOLEY - Scarlet Red with Pink stamens and anthers. Very large, single form. Vigorous, upright growth. M. (Reticulata hybrid 'Red Crystal' x Japonica 'Silver Lace'). (U.S. 2004 - Homeyer).

VIOLET BOON - Red. Large, semidouble to loose peony form. Average, open, upright growth. E-L. (Reticulata seedling). (N.Z. 1975 - Mrs. I. Berg, Whakatane).

VIOLETTE ROSE - Lavender. Large, semidouble. Vigorous, open growth, E-M. (Reticulata hybrid 'Buddha' seedling). (U.S. 1970 - Feathers).

VIRGINIA MATHIS - Veined soft Pink becoming lighter at edge. Very large, semidouble to peony form. Vigorous, upright growth. M. (Reticulata 'Crimson Robe' x Reticulata hybrid 'Jean Pursel'). (U.S. 1985 - Pursel).

W. M. JERNIGAN - Pink with veining. Very large, semidouble. Average, upright, open growth. M-L. (Reticulata hybrid 'Nuccio's Ruby' seedling). (U.S. 1998 - Jernigan).

W. P. GILLEY - Bright Pink. Large, semidouble with irregular petals. Average, upright growth. M-L. (Reticulata hybrid 'Mouchang' seedling). (U.S. 1983 - Gilley).

W. P. GILLEY VARIEGATED - Bright Pink heavily blotched White variation of 'W P Gilley'.

WAIRERE - Pink. Very large, semidouble to peony form. Upright, compact growth. (Reticulata seedling). (N.Z. 1980 - H. K. Clark, Matamata).

WALLY FRESHWATER - Deep Red. Large to very large, semidouble. Average, upright growth. M-L. (Reticulata 'Crimson Robe' x Reticulata/Japonica hybrid). (U.S. 1982 - Pursel).

WALTER DUNN - Burgundy Red. Medium to large, rose form double. Average, spreading growth. M-L. (Reticulata 'Crimson Robe' x Reticulata hybrid 'Jean Pursel'). (U.S. 1978 - Pursel).

WALTER HOMEYER - Red with heavy frosting with Gold anthers and Gold filaments. Very large, semidouble to peony form. Average, upright, open growth. M-L. (U.S. 2004 - Hulyn Smith).

WANDIN SEBIRE - Deep Orchid Pink. Very large, semidouble. Average, upright, compact growth. M-L. (Reticulata 'Crimson Robe' seedling). (Aus. 1977 - Sebire).

WARWICK BERG - Clear bright Red. Very large, formal double. Upright growth. M. (Saluenensis x Reticulata 'Crimson Robe'). (N.Z. 1978 - Mrs. I. Berg, Whakatane).

WAYNE REID - Glowing bright Pink, shaded lighter. Large, peony form. Average, upright, open growth. M-L. (Reticulata seedling). (N.Z. 1993 - J. Rivett, Whakatane).

*WELCOMING SPRING RED - ('Yingchunhong' - Chinese Name). Crimson shaded White. Large, semidouble with wavy petals. E. (Yunnan Reticulata). (China to U.S. 1980 - U. C. Bot. Gdn, CA).

WESTFIELD - Dark Pink. Very large, semidouble. Upright growth. M. (Reticulata seedling). (Aus. 1979 - E. Kettle, Cheltenham, Vic.).

WHITE RETIC - White with Blush Pink under petals. Large, semidouble. Vigorous, upright, open growth. M-L. (Reticulata seedling). (U.S. 1977 - H. Fish, Santa Cruz, CA).

WILD FORM - Shades of Pink, ranging from Lavender to Light Salmon Pink. Medium to large, single. Vigorous, upright, compact growth. L. (From seed [China] with parentage unknown). (England 1932 - G. Forrest).

WILD SILK - China Rose. Large, semidouble with upright petals. Vigorous, bushy growth. M-L. (Reticulata hybrid 'Wild Form' x Reticulata 'Shot Silk'). (N.Z. 1969 - Durrant).

WILLIAM HERTRICH - Deep Cherry Red. Very large, semidouble with heavy irregular petals, folded and intermixed with stamens. Vigorous, bushy growth. M. (Reticulata 'Cornelian' seedling). (U.S. 1962 - Asper).

WILLIAM SELLERS - Deep Crimson. Very large, semidouble with very large folding petals. Slow, spreading growth. M-L. (Reticulata 'Tali Queen' x Reticulata 'Cornelian'). (U.S. 1976 - W. E. Sellers, Mobile, AL).

*WILLOW WAND - ('Liuye Yinhung' - Chinese Name). Light Orchid Pink. Large, rose form double to semidouble with irregular, wavy petals of silky, velvety texture. Vigorous, upright growth. M. (Yunnan Reticulata). (China to U.S. 1948 - Descanso and Peer).

WIN HOULDEN - Dark Rose. Large, peony form. Average, spreading growth. M. (Reticulata 'Crimson Robe' x Saluenensis). (N.Z. 1982 - Mrs. I. Berg, Whakatane).

WINDALE - Bright Red. Large to very large, semidouble with crinkled petals. Average, upright growth. M-L. (Reticulata 'Crimson Robe' x Japonica 'Reg Ragland'). (U.S. 1975 - G. Stewart, Sacramento, CA).

WINIFRED SEBIRE - Deep Rose Pink. Very large, semidouble to peony form. Vigorous, open, upright growth. M. (Reticulata 'Tali Queen' seedling). (Aus. 1972 - Sebire).

WINNER'S CIRCLE - Salmon Pink. Very large, semidouble to loose peony form. Vigorous, upright, compact growth. M. (Reticulata seedling). (U.S. 1984 - Nuccio's).

WINTER SUN - Deep Pink. Large, loose peony form. Vigorous, open, spreading growth. E-M. (Reticulata 'Crimson Robe' seedling). (Aus. 1970 - Tuckfield).

WINTER'S OWN - Pink. Large to very large, semidouble to peony form. Vigorous, upright growth. E-M. (Reticulata hybrid 'LASCA Beauty' x Reticulata hybrid 'Arbutus Gum'). (Aus. 1985 - M. Greentree, Kingsgrove, NSW).

WINTER'S OWN VARIEGATED - Pale Pink marbled and moired White variation of 'Winter's Own'. (Aus. 1989 - M Greentree, Kingsgrove, NSW).

WOODFORD HARRISON - Deep Rose Red veined red. Very large, semidouble. Vigorous, upright, spreading growth. M-L. (Reticulata 'Crimson Robe' x Reticulata/Japonica hybrid). (U.S. 1980 - Pursel).

XIAOGUIYE - See 'Small Osmanthus Leaf'.
XIAOYE MUDAN - See 'Small Leaf Peony'.
XIAOYULAN - See 'Small Magnolia'.
XIGUIYE - See 'Narrow Osmanthus Leaf'.

YE MING ZU - See 'Evening Glow Pearl'.
YELLOW AND PURPLE - ('Yiao Huang Wei Zi' - Chinese Name; 'Tinges of Yellow and Purple'). Light Pink with Light Purple/Lavender undertones and a small amount of Yellow at the base of the central petals. Medium, formal double with slightly waved petals. Average, open growth. [(Reticulata hybrid 'Suzanne Withers' x 'Nitidissima hybrid 'Honeymoon') x Japonica Elaine's Betty']. (U.S. 2012 - John Wang, Orinda, CA).

YIAO HUANG WEI ZI - See 'Yellow and Purple'
YIFEN MUDAN - See 'Spinel Pink Peony'.
YINGCHUN HONG - See 'Welcoming Spring Red'.
YINHONG DIECHI - See 'Pink Butterfly Wing'.
YIPINHONG - See 'First Class Red'.
YOSHIAKI ANDOH - Dark Red. Medium to large, single with flared Golden stamens. Vigorous, upright, compact growth. M-L. (Reticulata 'Cornelian' x Japonica 'Mrs. D. W. Davis'). (U.S. 1986 - Piet and Gaeta).
YUDAIHONG - See 'Jade Striped Red'.
YULAN CHA - See 'Magnolia Camellia'.

YVONNE AMIZONICA - Dark Ruby Red. Large, semidouble to peony form. Average, dense, spreading growth. E-L. (Reticulata seedling). (N.Z. 1991 - H. Burwell, Inglewood).

YVONNE ROLFE - Light Crimson Pink. Very large, loose peony form. Open, upright growth. M-L. (Reticulata hybrid 'Arch of Triumph' seedling). (Aus. 1983 - B. Hooper, Bexley North, NSW).

ZAOMUDAN - See 'Early Peony'.
ZAOTAOHONG - See 'Early Crimson'.
ZELL BOYCE - Orchid Pink. Large to very large, semidouble to loose peony form. M-L. (Reticulata seedling). (U.S. 1975 - Gentry).

ZHANGJIA CHA - See 'Chang's Temple'.
ZHANQUN LADY - ('Da Qio' - Chinese Name). Very Light Pink with slightly Deeper Pink on petal outer rim. Large to very large, rose form double to formal double with upstanding, separated, and mainly fluted petals. Vigorous growth. L. [(Reticulata hybrid 'Suzanne Withers' x 'Nitidissima hybrid 'Honeymoon') x Japonica 'Kona']. (U.S. 2012 - John Wang, Orinda, CA).
ZHUSHA ZIPAO - See 'Vermillion Purple Gown'.
ZI PIAN - See 'Purple Petal'.
ZIPAO - See 'Purple Gown'.
ZUIJIAOHONG - See 'Intoxicatingly Beautiful Red'.

Hybrids With Other Than Reticulata Parentage (Non-Reticulata Hybrids)

Hybrids with Reticulata parentage previously have been listed in the section entitled 'Species Reticulata and Hybrids with Reticulata Parentage. The following are cultivars of hybrids with parentage other than Reticulata. Many of these hybrids are Saluenensis x Japonica which generally are known as Williamsii Hybrids.

ABBOTT'S FOLLY - Light Lavender Pink. Small, formal double. Average, compact growth. M-L. (Hybrid 'Margaret Waterhouse' x Hiemalis 'Kanjiro'). (Aus. 1998 - K. Abbott, Rossmayne, W. Aus.).

ACK-SCENT - Shell Pink. Medium, full peony form. Average, upright growth. M-L. Deep spicy fragrance. (Japonica 'Kramer's Supreme' x Hybrid 'Fragrant Pink'). (U.S. 1978 - Ackerman).

ACK-SCENT SPICE - Deep Rose Red. Medium, anemone form to peony form. Average, dense, spreading growth. M-L. Lemon to spicy fragrance. (Japonica 'Fragrant Star' x Lutchuensis). (U.S. 1995 - Ackerman).

ADMIRATION (MARCHANT) - Cherry Red. Small, single. (Saluenensis x Japonica). (England. 1956 - Marchant, Keepers Hill Nursery).

ADORABLE - Bright Pink. Small to medium, formal double. Upright, compact growth. M-L. (Pitardii seedling). (Aus. 1979 - Sebire).

ADRIANNE ILA - Light Pink to Pale Pink. Miniature, single with notched petals. Slow, weeping growth. E. Fragrant. (Hybrid 'Snow Drop' seedling). (Aus. 1995 - M. Baker, Macleod, Vic.).

AFTERWARDS - Pale Pink, lighter toward center. Very large, rose form double. M-L. (Japonica 'Bertha Harmes' x. Oleifera 'Plain Jane). (U.S. 2007 - Ackerman).

AILSA JAMES - Rose Pink veined deeper. Very large, peony form. Average, open, spreading growth. M. (N.Z. 1984 - T. Lennard, Te Puke).

ALEXANDRA ROSE - Deep Pink to White. Miniature, single. Slow, open, spreading growth. M-L. (Rosaeflora x Lutchuensis). (Aus. 1992 - A. Spragg, Sutherland, NSW).

ALICE B. DUPONT - Light Yellow. Small, semidouble. Very slow, compact growth. M-L. (Nitidissima x Hybrid 'Golden Glow'). (U.S. 2008 - CamelliaShop, Savannah, GA).

ALICE EVELYN - White shading to Pale Pink at the edge. Miniature, single cup-shaped flower. Slow, dwarf, dense growth. M-L. (Aus. 2006 - Marjorie Baker, Vic.).

ALICE K. CUTTER - Pink. Large, anemone form. Vigorous, spreading growth. M. (Japonica 'Mrs. Bertha Harms' x Hybrid Parks 69-2 (Japonica 'Reg Ragland' x Lutchuensis). (U.S. 1972 - Dr. R. K. Cutter, Berkeley, CA).

ALICE MAUD - Pink. Medium, peony form. Average, upright growth. L. (Hybrid 'Elegant Beauty' seedling). (N.Z. 1995 - B. Simmons, Blenheim).

ALLURE - Pink variegated White. Medium, semidouble to peony form. Vigorous, spreading growth. M. Fragrant. (Japonica 'Reg Ragland' x Lutchuensis x Japonica 'Mrs. Bertha A. Harms'). (U.S. 1998 - W. and M. A. Ray, Fresno, CA).

ALPEN GLOW - Two shades of Pink. Miniature, single to semidouble. Open, upright growth. M. (Hybrid 'Snow Drop' seedling). (Aus. 1985 - Sebire).

ANGEL WINGS - White washed and shaded Orchid Pink. Medium, semidouble with narrow, upright petals. Average, compact growth. M. (Japonica 'Dr. Tinsley' x Saluenensis). (U.S. 1970 - Kramer).

ANGEL WINGS VARIEGATED - Orchid Pink and White variation of 'Angel Wings'. (U.S. 1979 - Kramer).

ANNE HAZELWOOD - Red. Large, semidouble. Slow, compact growth. M-L. (Hybrid 'Donation' seedling). (Aus. 1967 - Hazlewood).

ANNE MICHELLE - Light Pink shading to soft Pink at center. Medium, semidouble to peony form. Slow, open growth. M. (Pitardii seedling). (Aus. 1990 - K. Brown, Mitcham, Vic.).

ANNE'S MEMORIAL - White. Large, semidouble to rose form double with slightly notched petals. Vigorous, upright growth. E-M. (Hybrid 'Bowen Bryant' seedling). (Aus. 1994 - A. Truran, Hornsby, NSW).

ANNETTE CAROL - Pale Pink. Small, peony form. Spreading, open growth. M-L. (Pitardii seedling). (Aus. 1981 - Sebire).

ANTICIPATION - Deep Rose. Large, peony form. Upright growth. M. (Saluenensis x Japonica 'Leviathan'). (N.Z. 1962 - Jury).

ANTICIPATION VARIEGATED - Deep Rose and White form of 'Anticipation'. (N.Z. 1978 - Jury).

NON-RETIC

H
Y
B
R
I
D

A-A

ANTIQUE CHARM - Soft Pink with paler edges. Medium, rose form double. Very slow, dense, upright growth. M. (Hybrid seedling). (N.Z. 1993 - Jury).

APPLE BLOSSOM - Pink and White. Medium, single. Vigorous, upright growth. M-L. (Saluenensis x Japonica; origin unknown).

ARALUEN STAR - Pale to Light Pink. Medium, semidouble form. Average growth. M-L. (Hybrid 'Prudence' seedling). (Aus. 2003 - R. H. Campbell, Maddington, W. Aus.).

ARCTIC DAWN - Neon Coral Pink. Medium, loose peony form. Open, slightly pendulous growth. L. Cold hardy to -5°F. (Hybrid 'November Pink' x Oleifera 'Lu Shan Snow'). (U.S. 2005 - Ackerman).

ARCTIC SNOW - White with hints of Pink at petal tips. Large, single. Vigorous, spreading growth. E. (U.S. - Ackerman).

ARIELS SONG - White. Miniature, single. Average, open, upright growth. M-L. (Fraterna x Tsaii). (N.Z. 1989 - Mrs. A. Durrant, Rotorua).

ARMSTRONG'S SUPREME - Currant Red. Medium to large, semidouble with wavy margins and occasional folded, upright petals. Average, spreading, upright growth. M. (Japonica 'Ville de Nantes' x Hybrid 'J. C. Williams'). (U.S. 1970 - Armstrong).

AROMATICA - Variegated Pale Pink petals, with Deep Flesh-Pink radial stripes. Large, semidouble to peony form. Slow, open growth. E-M. Fragrant. (Hybrid 'Scented Sun' x Japonica 'Kramer's Supreme'). (N.Z. 2002 - J. Finlay).

ASHTON'S BALLET - Two tone Pink. Medium, rose form double. Average, upright growth. E-L. Cold hardy to -10°F. (Japonica x Oleifera). (U.S. 2000 - Ackerman).

ASHTON'S CAMEO - Deep Lavender Pink. Medium, semidouble to loose peony form. Spreading, compact growth. M. Cold hardy to - 10°F. (Hybrid 'Winter's Charm x Oleifera 'Plain Jane'). (U.S. 2004 - Ackerman).

ASHTON'S FRAGRANT JEWEL - Baby Pink. Miniature, single. Rounded compact growth with small leaves. Very early, fragrant and floriferous with a long blooming season. (Lutchuensis x Japonica). (U.S. 2013 - Ackerman).

ASHTON'S HIGH RISE - Medium Pinkish Red with Creamy White anthers. Medium, rose form double. Upright growth. M. Cold hardy. (Japonica 'Billie McCaskill' x Japonica variety Z). (U.S. 2007 - Ackerman).

ASHTON'S PINK - Lavender Pink. Medium, semidouble. Average, spreading growth. E-M. Cold hardy to -10°F. (Japonica x Oleifera). (U.S. 2000 - Ackerman).

ASHTON'S PINK CLOUD - Medium Light Pink. Miniature to small, peony form. Average, rounded growth. Cold hardy to -15°F. Very floriferous (Oleifera 'Plain Jane' x Japonica). (U.S. 2013 - Ackerman).

ASHTON'S PRELUDE - Shell Pink. Medium, anemone form. Average to slow, dense growth. E. Cold hardy to -10°F. (Oleifera 'Plain Jane' x Sasanqua 'Setsusan'). (U.S. 2003 - Ackerman).

ASHTON'S PRIDE - Lavender Pink. Medium, single. Average, dense, spreading growth. E. Cold hardy to -15°F. (Oleifera x Sasanqua). (U.S. 1995 - Ackerman).

ASHTON'S RED BELL - Fire engine Red. Medium, single bell shape. Average, medium growth, wider than it is tall; profuse bloomer with long lasting with thick petals. E-M. Cold hardy to -15°F. (Oleifera 'Plain Jane' x Japonica). (U.S. 2013 - Ackerman).

ASHTON'S SHOOTING STAR - Bright Red (RHS 54A) stripes over White background with Golden Yellow anthers and Creamy White filaments. Large, single. Average, spreading, dense growth. M. (Japonica 'Mrs. Bertha A. Harris' x Oleifera 'Plain Jane'). (U.S. 2010 - Ackerman).

ASHTON'S SNOW - White. Medium, single to semidouble form. Average, dense, spreading growth. E-L. Cold hardy to -15°F. (Japonica 'Billie McCaskill' x Oleifera 'Plain Jane'). (U.S. 2002 - Ackerman).

ASHTON'S SUPREME - Bright Lavender Pink. Small, anemone to peony form. Average, dense, upright growth. E-M. Very cold hardy. [(Hiemalis 'Bill Wylam' x Oleifera 'Plain Jane') x Oleifera 'Narumi-Gata' x Oleifera 'Plain Jane')]. (U.S. 2003 - Ackerman).

AUTUMN FRAGRANCE - Light Pink. Medium, single form. Average, open, upright growth. E-M. Honeycomb fragrance. (Hybrid 'Fragrant One' x Japonica 'Scentasia'). (N.Z. 2002 - J. Finlay).

AUTUMN GLORY - White flushed Pink toward edge. Large, single. (Japonica 'Spencer's Pink' x Granthamiana). (Aus. 1967 - Mrs. E McMinn, Noble Park, Vic.).

AUTUMN HERALD - Soft Pink shading to White at base. Small, single. Average, dense, spreading growth. E-L. (Pitardii Variety Yunnanica x Pitardii). (N.Z. 1995 - Haydon).

AUTUMN JEWEL - Salmon Pink. Medium, formal double. Vigorous, spreading, bushy growth. E-L. (Saluenensis seedling). (U.S. 2000 - Nuccio's).

AUTUMN PINK ICICLE - Deep Pink. Medium, semidouble. Vigorous, upright, dense growth. E-M. Very cold hardy. (U.S. 1998 - Bond Nursery Corp., Dallas, TX).

AUTUMN SPIRIT - Bright Deep Pink. Small to medium, peony form. Moderately vigorous, bushy growth. Cold hardy. (Oleifera x Sasanqua). (U.S. 2008 - Parks).

AVALANCHE - Creamy White. Medium, semidouble. Average, dense, spreading, weeping growth. M. (Hybrid 'Fantastic' x Hybrid 'Daintiness'). (N.Z. 1991 - Jury).

AVALON - Rose Pink overlaid with Cerise. Large, semidouble with notched and irregular petals. (Hybrid 'Williams Lavender' x Japonica). (U.S. 1962 - McCaskill).

BABY BEAR - Light Pink to White. Miniature, single. Dwarf, compact growth. M. (Rosaeflora x Tsaii). (N.Z. 1976 - Haydon).

BABY BROTHER - White. Miniature, single. Slow, dense, rounded, dwarf growth. M-L. (Rosaeflora x Tsaii). (N.Z. 1990 - Haydon).

BABY FACE - Blush Pink to Deeper Pink edges. Small, rose form double. M-L. (Saluenensis hybrid). (U.S. 1977 - H. Fish, Santa Cruz, CA).

BABY RHODO - White with Orchid Pink fringes with bright Yellow anthers and White filaments. Miniature, peony form. Slow, low growth. M-L. (N.Z. 1987 - Haydon).

BABY WILLOW - White. Miniature, single. Average, dwarf, weeping growth. M. (Rosaeflora x Tsaii Hybrid). (N.Z. 1983 - Haydon).

BALLET IN PINK - Orchid Pink. Large, peony form. Upright growth; profuse bloomer. (Saluenensis x Japonica 'Kramer's Supreme'). (U.S. 2008 - Parks).

BALLET QUEEN - Salmon Pink. Large, peony form. Average growth. M-L. (Saluenensis x Japonica 'Leviathan'). (N.Z. 1975 - Jury).

BARBARA ANNE - Rose Pink. Large, semidouble. Vigorous, dense, upright growth. E-L. (Saluenensis seedling). (Aus. 1990 - A. Raper, The Patch, Vic.).

BARBARA RATLIFF - Orchid Pink. Large, semidouble. Compact, upright growth. M-L. (Hybrid 'Holland Orchid' x Japonica 'Angel'). (U.S. 1981 - Alfter).

BARBARA RATLIFF VARIEGATED - Light Pink with Orchid Pink overtone blotched White variation of 'Barbara Ratliff'. (U.S. 1982 - Alfter).

BARBARA'S OWN - White. Miniature, single with notched and wrinkled petals. Average, open, spreading growth. E-M. (Pitardii seedling). (Aus. 1993 - K. Brown, Mitcham, Vic.).

BARTLEY PINK - Bright Cherry Pink. Small, single. (Saluenensis x Japonica). (England 1955 - Dalrymple, Bartley, Southhampton).

BE MINE - Light Pink shading to Dark Pink with Yellow anthers and Cream filaments. Large, semidouble. Average, upright, open growth. M-L. (U.S. 2019 - Pat Johnson, Cairo, GA).

BEATRICE MICHAEL - Pale Pink. Medium, semidouble with occasional petaloids. Spreading growth. (Saluenensis x Japonica). (England 1954 - Williams).

BELINDA CARLYON - Red. Medium, single. Compact growth. (Japonica x Heterophylla 'Barbara Hillier'). (England 1972 - Carlyon).

BELLBIRD - Rose Pink. Small, single of bell-shape. Vigorous, spreading growth. M. (Hybrid 'Cornish Snow' seedling). (Aus. 1970 - Tuckfield).

BELLE PRINCESS - Pink to Pale Pink with Yellow anthers and Light Yellow filaments. Miniature, semidouble. Average, upright growth. E-M. (Japonica 'Kuro-tsubaki' x species from Section Theopsis). (China 2009 - Jian-Guo Fei, Yong-hong Hu and Ya-li Zhang, Shanghai Botanical Garden of Shanghai, China).

BELLS - Mauve Pink. Medium, single. Vigorous, bushy growth. M. (Hybrid Williamsii seedling). (Aus. 1965 - Eagle Heights).

BELLS OF ERIN - Deep Rose Pink. Medium, anemone form of trumpet or bell shape when opening. (U.S. 1961 - James).

BEST WISHES - Pale Pink, shading to an almost White at the center and Darker Pink at the edges. Small, rose form double to peony form with petals broad and ruffled. Slow to average, dense growth. M-L. (Pitardii seedling). (N.Z. 2004 - Neville Haydon).

BETTS SUPREME - Soft Pink. Large to very large, semidouble with Yellow anthers tipped White. Average, spreading growth. E-L. (N.Z. 1986 - P. A. Betts, Te Awamutu).

BETTY BOSWELL - Red with White edges. Medium, peony form. Average, upright growth. E-M. (Japonica 'Tama-No-Ura' x Henryamina). (N.Z. 2006 - Jim Finlay, Whangarei).

BETTY RIDLEY - Pink. Medium to large, formal double. Slow, open, upright growth. M-L. (Japonica 'Marie Bracey' x Hybrid 'Felice Harris'). (U.S. 1973 - Homeyer).

BETTY RIDLEY VARIEGATED - Pink and White variation of 'Betty Ridley'. (U.S. 1978).

BEVERLY L. BAYLIES - Light Pink deeper at edge. Medium, semidouble. Vigorous, upright growth. E-L. (Saluenensis seedling). (U.S. 1986 - Huntington Botanical Gardens).

BIG MO - Soft Pink. Medium, semidouble with Golden stamens. Vigorous, spreading growth. E. (Oleifera x Hiemalis 'Showa-No-Sakae'). (U.S. 1960 - R. Carr, Tulare, CA).

BLACK KNIGHT - Black Red. Large, rose form double. Average, compact, upright growth. M-L. (Hybrid 'Phillipa Forwood' x Japonica 'Kuro-Tsubaki'). (U.S. 1965 - McCaskill).

BLACK OPAL - Black Red. Small to medium, semidouble. Slow, compact growth. L. (Hybrid 'Ruby Bells' x Japonica 'Kuro Tsubaki'). (N.Z. 1985 - O. Blumhardt, Whangarei).

BLISSFUL DAWN - White shaded Pink toward edge. Large to very large, semidouble. Average growth. M. (Hybrid 'Donation' seedling). (N.Z. 1982 - O. Blumhardt, Whangarei).

BLONDY - White. Miniature, anemone form. Open, upright growth. E-M. (Hybrid 'Snowdrop' seedling). (Aus. 1986 - Sebire).

BLUE BIRD - Deep Pink with Blue cast. Medium, semidouble. Open, upright growth. E-M. (Saluenensis x Japonica). (N.Z. 1977 - Mrs. I. Berg, Whakatane).

BLUE DANUBE - Rose Lavender. Medium, peony form. Vigorous, compact, upright growth. M. (Hybrid Williamsii x Japonica). (U.S. 1960 - McCaskill).

BLUEBLOOD - Rose Pink with Blue overtones. Medium, peony form. Vigorous, bushy, upright growth. M. (Hybrid 'Phillipa Forwood' x Japonica). (U.S. 1969 - McCaskill).

BLUSHING FOUNTAINS - Light Pink. Small, single. Moderate, upright growth with arching branches. L. (Japonica x Tsaii). (U.S. 2014 - Camellia Forest, Chapel Hill, NC).

BOGONG SNOW - White slightly flushed Pink. Miniature, anemone form. Spreading, weeping growth. E-M. (Hybrid 'Tiny Princess' x Fraterna). (Aus. 1985 - T. J. Savige, Wirlinga, NSW).

BONNIE LASSIE - Pale Orchid Pink. Large, semidouble. (Hybrid 'Sylvia May' seedling). (U.S. 1957 - James).

BONNIE MARIE - Phlox Pink. Large, semidouble to anemone form with fluted petals. Vigorous, compact, upright growth. E-L. (Hybrid 'Robbie' x Japonica 'Charlotte Bradford'). (For a variation of this cultivar see 'FBI'). (U.S. 1959 - James).

BOOZIE B - Very Light Orchid Pink, darker at the edges, with Magenta Rose stripes. Medium to large, loose semidouble to rose form double. Vigorous, open, spreading, upright growth. M. (Hybrid 'Creation' seedling). (U.S. 1993 - F. Becker, Brookhaven, MS).

BOW BELLS - Rose Pink, deeper at base and in veins. Small, semidouble of funnel form. M-L. Fragrant. (Saluenensis x Japonica). (England. 1954 - Marchant, Keepers Hill Nursery).

BOWEN BRYANT - Deep Pink. Large, semidouble. Vigorous, open, upright growth. M. (Saluenensis x Japonica). (Aus. 1960 - Waterhouse).

BOWEN BRYANT VARIEGATED - Deep Pink blotched White variation of 'Bowen Bryant'. (Aus. 1966 - Hazlewood).

BRANDON'S BEAUTY - Deep Red with Yellow anthers and Yellow filaments. Small to medium, semidouble to single; the petals are often notched on outer edges. Slow, upright, dense growth. E. (Japonica 'Lady Clare' x unknown Sasanqua). (U.S. 2016 - Thomas Sellers, Bolivia, NC).

BRIDAL FRAGRANCE - White. Large, peony form. Vigorous growth. M-L. Fragrant. (Hybrid 'Scented Sun' x Hybrid 'High Fragrance'). (N.Z. 1995 - J. Finlay).

BRIE - Medium Pink with White anthers and White filaments. Small, semidouble. Compact, upright growth. E. (Seedling of Hybrid 'Yume'). (U.S. 2016 - Tsubaki Camellias, Savannah, GA).

BRIGADOON - Rose Pink. Medium, semidouble. Compact, upright growth. M. (Saluenensis x Japonica 'Princess Bacciocchi'). (U.S. 1960 - Armstrong).

BRIGHT EYES - Deep Pink. Medium, semidouble. Slow, bushy, spreading growth. E-L. (Pitardii seedling). (Aus. 1989 - E. Sebire, Wandin North, Vic.).

BUNNY EARS - Pink. Miniature to small, semidouble with rabbit ears. Vigorous, bushy, upright growth. M-L. (Roseaflora Hybrid). (U.S. 1999 - Nuccio's).

BURMA BABY - White washed and veined Pink. Small, single. Vigorous, open growth. E. (Japonica x Irrawadiensis). (U.S. 1965 - Hilsman).

BURMA BEATNIK - Red. Medium, anemone form. Vigorous, open growth. E-M. (Japonica x Irrawadiensis). (U.S. 1965 - Hilsman).

BUTTERMINT - Very Creamy White to Pale Yellow. Miniature, formal double to rose form double to occasionally peony form. Average, upright growth. E-L. (Kissi seedling). (U.S. 1997 - Nuccio's).

BUTTONS 'N BOWS - Light Pink shading deeper at edge. Small, formal double. Average, compact growth. E-M. (Saluenensis hybrid). (U.S. 1985 - Nuccio's).

BUZZ ALDRIN - Light Pink. Large, anemone form. Average growth. E. (Japonica 'Reg Ragland' x Granthamiana). (U.S. 1971 - Dr. R. K. Womack, Shreveport, LA).

C. F. COATES - Deep Rose. Medium, single with fishtail foliage. Open, upright growth. M. (Saluenensis x Japonica 'Quercifolia'). (England 1935 - Kew Gardens, London).

CAERHAYS - Rose. Medium, semidouble of flat form with three rows of rounded petals and some petaloids mixed with stamens. Spreading, pendulous growth. (Saluenensis x Japonica 'Lady Clare'). (England 1948 - Williams).

CALIFORNIA SNOW - White. Small, single. M. (Hybrid 'Sylvia May' seedling). (U.S. 1958 - Feathers).

CAMEO ROSE - China Rose Pink. Medium, rose form double. Average, semi-dwarf growth. (Hybrid 'Fantastic' x Hybrid 'Elsie Jury'). (N.Z. 1991 - Jury).

CAMPFIRE - Orange Red with Golden anthers and Golden filaments. Small, single - flat. Average, bushy, upright growth. E-M. (U.S. 2007 - Nuccio's Nurseries, Altadena, CA).

CANDLE GLOW - White with Light Pink center. Medium, single. Average, compact growth. E-M. (Cuspidata x Japonica). (U.S. 1980 - Nuccio's).

CAPTURED ENRICHES - Pastel Pinkish White. Miniature, semidouble with flowers clustered on branches. Average, compact, upright growth. M. (Rosaeflora x Fraterna). (U.S. 1983 - A. H. Krueger, Monterey Park, CA).

CAROLINA MOONMIST - Salmon Pink. Medium, single. Average, dense, spreading, upright growth. E. Cold hardy. (Oleifera x Sasanqua). (U.S. 1997 - J. Raulston, Raleigh, NC).

CAROLYN ADAMS - Soft Pink. Medium, formal double. Vigorous, upright growth. E-L. (Saluenensis x Japonica 'Lotus'). (U.S. 1975 - Tammia).

CAROLYN LOUISE - Soft Pink fading to White at base of petals. Medium, semidouble with notched petals. Vigorous, open, upright growth. E-M. (Saluenensis seedling). (Aus. 1993 - A. Raper, The Patch, Vic.).

CAROUSEL - Pale Pink striped Orchid. Medium, semidouble. (Hybrid 'Sylvia May' seedling). (U.S. 1957 - James).

CASCADING WHITE - White. Miniature to small, semidouble to peony form. Average, pendulous, upright growth. E-L. (Hybrid 'Wirlinga Princess' seedling). (Aus. 1989 - K. Brown, Mitcham, Vic.).

CELEBRATION - Light Orchid Pink. Medium, semidouble. Upright growth. M. (Saluenensis x Japonica). (England 1962 - R. Veitch, Exeter).

CHARLEAN - Pink with faint Orchid overtone. Large, semidouble with Pink filaments and Lemon Yellow anthers and scattered stamens. Vigorous, spreading, upright growth. M-L. (Japonica 'Donckelarii' x Hybrid 'Donation'). (U.S. 1963 - W. Stewart, Savannah, GA).

CHARLES COLBERT - Amaranth Rose. Medium, semidouble with incurved petals. (Saluenensis x Japonica). (Aus. 1959 - Waterhouse).

CHARLES MICHAEL - Pale Pink. Large, semidouble with long petals. (Saluenensis x Japonica). (England 1951 - Williams).

CHARSY - Rose Pink. Small to medium, semidouble to peony. Average, upright, open growth. M-L. (Sport of Hybrid 'Mary Phoebe Taylor'). (U.S. 2015 - Chuck Ritter, Melrose, FL).

CHILD OF GRACE - Pink, lighter on outer petals, darker in center. Small, formal double with slightly cupped and bi-lobed petals. Average, dense growth. M-L. (Hybrid 'Nicky Crisp' seedling). (N.Z. 1999 - Haydon).

CHIMES - Deep Rose Red. Small, single of bell form. M-L. (Saluenensis x Japonica). (England. 1955 - Marchant, Keepers Hill Nursery).

CHINA CLAY - White. Medium, semidouble. Open growth. (Saluenensis x Japonica 'Marjorie Magnificent'). (England 1972 - Carlyon).

CHIPMUNK - Rose Pink. Medium, semidouble with Golden stamens and petaloids intermixed. Vigorous, bushy growth. M. (Hybrid 'J. C. Williams' seedling). (U.S. 1960 - R. Carr, Tulare, CA).

CHOICE FRAGRANCE - Bright Pink. Medium, anemone form. Average, upright growth. E-M. Fragrant. {Japonica 'Mrs. Bertha A. Harms' seedling x Hybrid 'Salab'} x Japonica 'Erin Farmer'}. (N.Z. 2002 - J. Finlay).

CHRISTMAS DAFFODIL - White tinged Blush Pink at petal tips. Small, anemone form. Vigorous, compact growth. E-M. (Japonica 'Elizabeth Boardman' x Hybrid 'Tiny Princess'). (U.S. 1971 - Witman).

CHRISTMAS ROSE - Rose Pink to Light Red. Unknown size, rose form double. M. (Williamsii x Sasanqua). (U.S. 1988 - Parks).

CILE MITCHELL - Light Orchid Pink. Large, rose form double to formal double. Vigorous, dense, upright growth. E-M. (Saluenensis x Japonica). (U.S. 1992 - Hulyn Smith).

CINNAMON CINDY - Rose Pink with White center petaloids. Miniature, peony form, Deep cinnamon fragrance. E-M. (Japonica 'Kenyo-Tai' x Lutchuensis). (U.S. 1973 - Ackerman).

CINNAMON SCENTSATION - Rose Pink to White. Small, single. Average, open, spreading growth. M-L. Highly fragrant. (Sport of Hybrid 'Cinnamon Cindy'). (U.S. 1995 - Ackerman).

CITATION - ('Williamsii Semidouble'). Silver Blush Pink. Large, semidouble with irregular petals. Vigorous, open, upright growth. M. (Saluenensis x Japonica). (England 1950 - Lord Aberconway, Bodnant, North Wales).

CLAIRE BULL - Light Pink with White flecks. Large, formal double. Average, dense, upright growth. M-L. (Hybrid seedling). (N.Z. 1990 - D. Bull, Auckland).

CLAIRVOYANT - Pale Pink with slightly deeper shading toward edge. Large, loose peony form. Average, spreading growth. M-L. (Saluenensis x Japonica 'Betty Sheffield Supreme'). (N.Z. 1986 - C. Spicer, Feilding).

CLARRIE FAWCETT - Rose. Large, semidouble. Open, upright growth. M. (Saluenensis x Japonica). (Aus. 1960 - Waterhouse).

COL. R. D. HICKS - Red. Medium, anemone form. Average, upright growth. M-L. (Hybrid 'Salut' x Japonica 'Kramer's Supreme'). (U.S. 1982 - Pursel).

COMMANDER EDWARD FREDRICKSON - Pale Yellow with Yellow anthers and Yellow filaments. Miniature, semidouble. Average, upright, open growth. E-L. (U.S. 2013 - Gena Owens Fredrickson, Wilmington, NC).

CONTEMPLATION - Lavender Pink. Medium, semidouble with occasional petaloids. Slow, compact growth. M-L. (Pitardii x Japonica). (N.Z. 1985 - Mrs. A. B. Durrant, Rotarua).

COPPELIA - Carmine Rose. Medium, single. (Saluenensis x Japonica). (England 1950 - Hanger).

COPPELIA ALBA - White. Medium, single. Upright growth. M. (Saluenensis x Japonica). (England 1955).

CORAL BOUQUET - Rich Coral Pink, toned lighter near center. Medium to large, single form with wavy petals. Average, bushy, columnar growth. M. (U.S. 2006 - Nuccio's).

CORAL DELIGHT - Deep Coral Pink. Small to medium, semidouble. Slow, compact, bushy growth. M. (Saluenensis x Japonica 'Dr. Tinsley'). (U.S. 1975 - Kramer).

CORAL DELIGHT VARIEGATED - Coral Pink and blotched White variation of 'Coral Delight'. (U.S. 1975 - Kramer).

CORAL MAE - Rich Pink. Large, semidouble; petals are long, thin, notched, fluted and curled back. Average, upright, spreading growth. E-L. (Hybrid 'Prudence' seedling). (Aus. 1998 - Mrs. M. Baker, Macleod, Vic.).

CORIN - Clear Pink. Large, semidouble. Compact growth. M. (Saluenensis seedling). (N.Z. 1981 - Miss I. Corbett and Mrs. P. Austin, Taranaki).

CORINNE DAWN - Soft Pink. Medium, formal double. Vigorous, compact, upright growth. M. (Hybrid 'Donation' seedling). (Aus. 1969 - Sebire).

CORNISH SNOW - White with occasional Pink Blush. Small, single. Open, upright growth. M. (Saluenensis x Cuspidata). (England 1950 - Williams).

CORNISH SPRING - Pink. Small, single. Vigorous, upright growth. (Japonica 'Rosea Simplex' x Cuspidata). (England 1972 - Carlyon).

CREATION - ('Hybrid 203'). Luminous soft Pink. Large, semidouble to anemone form. Slow, bushy growth. M. (Japonica 'Elegans [Chandler]' x Hybrid 'Apple Blossom'). (U.S. 1958 - McCaskill).

CREATION BLUSH - Light Pink with each petal bordered. (Sport of Hybrid 'Creation'). (U.S. 1959 - McCaskill).

CREATION VARIEGATED - White with occasional Pink spot variation of 'Creation'. (U.S. 1959 - McCaskill).

CRINKLES - Rose. Large, semidouble with crinkled petals. Bushy, upright growth. (Saluenensis x Japonica). (Aus. 1955 - Waterhouse).

CUPCAKE - Coral Pink, lighter toward middle, occasional Deeper Coral Pink stripes. Small, single form. Average, bushy, compact and upright growth. M-L. (U.S. 2006 - Nuccio's).

CYCLAMEN - Deep Pink flushed and veined toward base with warmer color approaching Scarlet. Small to medium, single. (Saluenensis x Japonica). (England. 1956 - Marchant, Keepers Hill Nursery).

DAINTINESS - Salmon Pink. Large, semidouble. Average, open growth. M. (Saluenensis x Japonica 'Magnoliaeflora'). (U.S. 1975 - Jury).

DAINTY DALE - Shaded soft Orchid Pink. Large, peony form. Vigorous, compact, upright growth. M-L. (Hybrid 'Robbie' x Japonica 'Dr. Tinsley'). (U.S. 1961 - James).

DAME SILVIA - Bright Scarlet Pink. Medium, semidouble to anemone form. Average, upright growth. M-L. Floral, rose-like fragrance. (Hybrid 'Fragrant One' x Japonica 'Tama-no-ura'). (N.Z. 2002 - J. Finlay).

DANCING BLAZE - Dark Red with Yellow anthers and Red filaments. Medium, semidouble. Slow, spreading growth. M. (Hybrid 'Peggy Burton' x Japonica 'Black Magic'). (N.Z. 2010 - Haydon).

DARK NITE - Crimson. Medium, peony form. Average, open, upright growth. M-L. (Japonica 'Australis' x Hybrid 'Joyful Bells'). (N.Z. 1981 - Jury).

DARLEEN STONER - Cranberry-Coral with a splash of White on centermost petals. Medium to large, semidouble to peony form. Vigorous, upright growth. E-L. (Hybrid 'Coral Delight' x Japonica 'Kramer's Supreme'). (U.S. 2006 - Martin F. Stoner, Pomona, CA).

DAUGHTER'S RED - ('Nü'erhong' - Chinese Name; 'Daughter's Red Rice Wine'). Dark Pink with Yellow anthers and White filaments, Large, semidouble with veined petals. M. Very fragrant. (Hybrid 'D3[4]' x Hybrid 'Superscent'). (U.S. 2008 - John Wang, Orinda, CA).

DAVE'S WEEPER - Lilac White. Miniature, single. Average, spreading growth. M-L. (Fraterna x Japonica). (U.S. 1996 - Feathers).

DAWN OF CREATION - Bright Rose. Large, semidouble. Rounded, well-branched growth. E-M. [(Pitardii var. 'Yunnanica' x. Yunnanensis) x Japonica 'Scentsation']. (U.S. 2011 - Charvet).

DEBBIE - Clear Spinel Pink. Medium, peony form. (Saluenensis x Japonica 'Debutante'). (N.Z. 1965 - Jury).

DEBBIE'S CARNATION - Bright Carmine Pink. Medium, peony form. Compact, spreading, upright growth. E-L. (Saluenensis x Japonica 'Debutante'). (N.Z. 1984 - F. Jury, Tikorangi).

DEBO - Bright Red. Medium, single. Vigorous, dense, spreading growth. E-M. Fragrant. (Japonica x Vernalis). (U.S. 1998 - R. Bond, Dallas, TX).

DELORES EDWARDS - Light Orchid Pink. Large, semidouble to anemone form to peony form. Compact, spreading, upright growth. E-M. (Saluenensis x Japonica). (U.S. 1989 - Hulyn Smith).

DEMURE - Pale Pink with deeper edges. Small, single. Average, spreading growth. E-M. (Saluenensis x Japonica). (U.S. 1955 - Feathers).

DIANA LENNARD - Deep Pink shaded to Light Pink. Medium, formal double. Average, open, upright growth. M-L. (Hybrid 'Elegant Beauty' seedling). (N.Z. 1982 - T. Lennard, Te Puke).

DIEGO ARMIJO - Light Orchid Pink. Medium, semidouble with long, notched petals. Vigorous growth. E-L. (Hybrid 'Gay Time' x Hybrid 'Angel Wings'). (U.S. 1989 - Piet and Gaeta).

DON ESTES - Creamy White. Medium, formal double. Average, upright, open growth. M-L. (Seedling of Non-reticulata hybrid 'Jury's Yellow'). (U.S. 2018 - Shirley Estes, Brookhaven, MS).

DONATION - Orchid Pink. Medium to large, semidouble. Vigorous, compact, upright growth. M. (Saluenensis x Japonica 'Donckelarii'). (England 1941 - Clarke).

DONATION VARIEGATED - Orchid Pink blotched White variation of 'Donation'. (England 1950 - Clarke).

DONNA RITA - Light Red. Small, peony form. Slow, dense, upright growth. E-L. (Hybrid 'Mary Phoebe Taylor' seedling). (Aus. 1993 - Sebire).

DONROSE PENDANT - Deep Pink. Large, semidouble opening with pointed Rosebud center. M-L. (Saluenensis x Japonica). (England 1955).

DOROTHY AIMEE - Light Pink. Miniature, single form and trumpet shaped. Slow, dense and spreading growth. M-L. (Rosaeflora seedling). (N.Z. 2004 - Dorothy Hansen).

DOROTHY JAMES - White at base shading to Pale Flesh Pink with one-quarter inch Rose band on petals. Medium, formal double. Slow, compact, upright growth. M. (Hybrid 'Robbie' x Japonica 'Dr. Tinsley'). (U.S. 1960 - James).

DOROTHY JOHNSON - Soft Pink with Silver cast and petal edges. Medium, semidouble with pointed petals. M-L. (Hybrid 'Donation' seedling). (N.Z. 1970 - Mrs. A. B. Durrant, Tirau).

DOUGLAS DEANE HALL - Deep Rose Pink to Red. Small, rose form double to formal double. Average growth. E-M. (Rusticana 'Yoshida' x Japonica 'White Butterfly'). (U.S. 1987 - Ackerman).

DR. COLIN CRISP - White. Medium, semidouble. Slow, spreading, dense growth. M-L. (Hybrid 'Nicky Crisp' seedling). (N.Z. 1999 - Haydon).

DR. JANE NORWOOD - White shaded Orchid Pink. Medium, peony form. Vigorous, open, upright growth. M-L. (Hybrid 'J. C. Williams' seedling). (U.S. 1980 - A. R. Parler, Eloree, MS).

DR. RALPH WATKINS - Phlox Pink. Medium, loose peony form. Vigorous, compact, upright growth. L. (Saluenensis x Japonica 'Princess Lavender'). (U.S. 1977 - Parks).

DR. ROBERT K. CUTTER - Red veined. Large, anemone form. Average, upright growth. M-L. Fragrant. (Japonica/Saluenensis hybrid x unnamed Hybrid). (U.S. 1983 - Dr. R. K. Cutter, Berkeley, CA).

DR. ZHIVAGO - Orchid with Pink overtone. Medium, peony form. Average, open, upright growth. M-L. (Hybrid 'William's Lavender' seedling). (U.S. 1980 - T. Sellers, Salemberg, NC).

DRAGON FIREBALL - ('Longhuozhu' - Chinese name). Red with White margins with Yellow anthers and Light Yellow filaments. Small to medium, anemone. Vigorous, upright growth. M. (Japonica 'Merry Christmas' x Hybrid 'Virginia W. Cutter'). (U.S. 2008 - John Wang, Orinda CA).

DREAM ANGEL - Blend of soft Pinks marbled White with Light Yellow anthers and Light Yellow filaments. Small, semidouble. Average, compact, rounded growth. E-L. (Hybrid 'Yume' x Sasanqua). (U.S. 2013 - Bobby Green, Green Nurseries, Fairhope, AL).

DREAM BOAT - Bright Pink with Lavender cast. Medium to large, formal double with incurved petals. Average, open, upright growth. M. (Saluenensis x Japonica 'K. Sawada'). (N.Z. 1976 - Jury).

DREAM QUILT - White heavily dappled Bright Pink with Yellow anthers and Yellow filaments. Medium, single. Average, low, spreading, bushy growth. E-L. (Hybrid 'Yume' x Sasanqua). (U.S. 2013 - Bobby Green, Green Nurseries, Fairhope, AL).

DREAM TEAM - Strong Rose Pink and White with Yellow anthers and Light Yellow filaments. Medium, semidouble. Average, bushy growth. E-L. (Hybrid 'Yume' x Sasanqua). (U.S. 2012 - Bobby Green, Green Nurseries, Fairhope, AL).

DREAM WEAVER - Blush with Rose marbling. Medium to large, semidouble to rose form double. Extremely Vigorous, Upright, bushy growth E-L. (Hybrid 'Yume' x Sasanqua). (U.S. 2015 - Bobby Green, Green Nurseries, Fairhope, AL).

DRESDEN CHINA - Pale Pink. Large, peony form. Slow, spreading, upright growth. M-L. (Saluenensis x Japonica 'Joshua E. Youtz'). (N.Z. 1980 - F. Jury, Waitara).

DRIFTING SCENT - Pink. Large, peony form. Average, upright growth. M-L. Fragrant. (Japonica 'Mrs. Bertha A. Harms' x Hybrid 'Salab' x Japonica 'Look-Away'). (N.Z. 1993 - J. Finlay).

E. G. WATERHOUSE - Light Pink. Medium, formal double. Vigorous, upright growth. M-L. (Saluenensis x Japonica). (Aus. 1954 - Waterhouse).

E. G. WATERHOUSE VARIEGATED - Light Pink blotched White variation of Hybrid 'E G Waterhouse'. (Aus. 1960 - Waterhouse).

E. LLOYD ANSELL - Light Pink. Large, peony form. Vigorous, upright growth. E-M. (Aus. 1980 - K. M. Knuckey, Mt. Evelyn, Vic.).

E. T. R. CARLYON - Candid White. Medium, semidouble to rose form double. Vigorous, upright growth. L. (Hybrid 'J C Williams' x Japonica 'Adolphe Audusson'). (England 1972 - Carlyon).

EDNA RALEY - White washed Flesh Pink. Large, semidouble to peony form. Compact, upright growth. E-M. (Hybrid 'Robbie' x Japonica 'Charlotte Bradford'). (U.S. 1960 - James).

EDWARD CARLYON - Salmon Pink. Medium, rose form double. Spreading growth. M. (Saluenensis x Japonica 'Adolphe Audusson'). (England 1981 - Carlyon).

EDWARD MARSHALL BOEHM - Rose Pink. Large, semidouble. Vigorous, upright growth. E. (Saluenensis x Japonica 'Cecile Brunazzi'). (England 1978 - J. J. Gallagher, Dorset).

EL DORADO - Light Pink. Large, full peony form. Average, spreading growth. M. (Pitardii x Japonica 'Tiffany'). (U.S. 1967 - Asper).

ELAINE LEE - White. Medium, semidouble. Average, upright growth. E-M. Flower and plant cold hardy to -10°F. (U.S. 1999 - Ackerman).

ELEGANT BEAUTY - Deep Rose. Large, anemone form. Open, upright growth. M. (Saluenensis x Japonica 'Elegans [Chandler]'). (N.Z. 1962 - Jury).

ELIZA LOCKLEY - Pink. Large, semidouble. Slow, dense, weeping growth. E-L. Slight vanilla fragrance. (Hybrid 'Margaret Waterhouse' seedling). (Aus. 1990 - C. Davidson, Wahroonga, NSW).

ELIZABETH ROTHSCHILD - Rose Pink. Medium, semidouble. M-L. (Saluenensis x Japonica). (England 1950 - Hanger).

ELLA GAMLIN - Deep Pink. Medium, single with flaring stamens. Average, open growth. E-M. (Saluenensis x Japonica). (N.Z. 1972 - B. G. Rayner, Stratford).

ELLAMINE - Pink. Large, single. (Saluenensis x Japonica). (Aus. 1955 - Waterhouse).

ELSAKI - Rose Pink. Large, peony form. L. (Saluenensis x Japonica). (England 1957).

ELSIE JURY - Clear Pink with shaded Orchid undertone. Medium to large, full peony form. Average, open, spreading growth. M-L. (Saluenensis x Japonica 'Pukekura White'). (For another form of this cultivar see 'Fair Jury'). (N.Z. 1964 - Jury).

EMMA JANE - White. Medium to large, semidouble. Average, open, spreading growth. M-L. (Saluenensis seedling). (N.Z. 1992 - P. Matthews, Auckland).

EMMA LENNARD - Salmon Pink. Miniature, semidouble. Average, open growth. E. (Rosaeflora seedling). (N.Z. 1981 - T. Lennard, Te Puke).

EMPIRE ROSE - Crimson Red. Small to medium, peony form to rose form double. Average growth. M. (Hybrid 'Rendezvous' seedling). (N.Z. 1991 - Jury).

ERYLDENE EXCELSIS - Pink with Bluish tinge. Large, semidouble. Spreading growth. M. (Saluenensis 'Sunnybrook' x Japonica 'Waiwhetu Beauty'). (N.Z. 1981 - Jury).

ESME SPENCE - Soft Pink. Medium, anemone form. Average, compact growth. E-M. Fragrant. (Fraterna x Japonica). (N.Z. 1977 - Mrs. E. G. Spence, Tirau).

ETHEL McMILLAN - Dark Pink with paler Pink center. Large, loose peony form. Average, open growth. (N.Z. 1987 - T. Lennard, Te Puke).

ETOWAH PINK - Medium Pink to Cream Pink. Small to medium, semidouble with slightly cupped petals. Average, upright growth. E-M. (Hybrid 'Winter's Charm' seedling). (U.S. - 2015 - Grady Stokes, Marshallville, GA).

218

ETSU-BOTAN - Peach Pink. Large to very large, loose peony form; stamens dispersed among petals. Vigorous, upright growth; leaves large, oblong. E-M. (Amplexicaulis x Japonica 'Tama Americana'). (Japan 2005 - Shunsuke and Yukie Hisatomi, Fukuoka Prefecture).

EXUBERANCE - Pink. Large, semidouble. Vigorous, compact, upright growth. M. (Saluenensis seedling). (Aus. 1971 - E. L. Ansell, Lilydale, Vic.).

EYE BRIGHT - Deep Pink. Small, anemone form. Average, open, upright growth. M. (Japonica 'Tinsie' x Pitardii). (N.Z. 1998 - O. Blumhardt, Whangarei).

FAIR JURY - White with flecks and stripes of Mauve Pink. Large, full peony form. (Sport of Hybrid 'Elsie Jury'). (N.Z. 1982 - O. Blumhardt, Whangarei).

FAIRWEATHER FAVORITE - White with Pink underside. Small to medium, semidouble form. Average, upright, dense growth. E-M. Cold hardy to -15°F. (U.S. 1998 - Ackerman).

FAIRY BLUSH - Apple blossom with bright Pink buds. Miniature, single. Vigorous, open, upright growth. E-L. Fragrant. (Lutchuensis seedling). (N.Z. 1993 - M. Jury, North Taranaki).

FAIRY BOUQUET - Light Pink. Medium, peony form. Average, compact, upright growth. M-L. (Pitardii seedling). (Aus. 1977 - Sebire).

FAIRY FLOSS - Pale Mauve Pink. Miniature, anemone form with notched petals. Low, spreading growth. M-L. (Hybrid 'Sprite' seedling). (Aus. 1994 - E. Sebire, Wandin North, Vic.).

FAIRY WAND - Bright Rose Red. Miniature, semidouble. Average, open, upright growth. M. (Saluenensis x Japonica 'Fuyajo'). (N.Z. 1982 - Blumhardt, Whangare).

FALLEN ANGEL - Lavender with Yellow pigments. Medium, semidouble to anemone to peony form. Average, spreading, upright growth. E-M. (Japonica x Granthamiana). (U.S. 1974 - Homeyer).

FANTASTIC - Pink. Large, single. Average, spreading growth. E-L. (Saluenensis x Japonica 'Pukekura'). (N.Z. 1981 - Jury).

FARFALLA - Pink. Medium, single. M. (Saluenensis x Japonica). (Aus. 1962 - Waterhouse).

FBI - Light Lavender. Miniature, anemone form. (Sport of Hybrid 'Bonnie Marie').

FELICE HARRIS - Pale Orchid Pink. Large, semidouble with fluted petals. Vigorous, upright, compact growth. M. (Saluenensis x Japonica). (U.S. 1960 - Asper).

FELICE HARRIS VARIEGATED - Pale Orchid Pink variegated form of 'Felice Harris'. (U.S. 1963 - Mark S. Cannon, Dothan, AL).

FESTIVAL OF LIGHTS - Pale Pink with some petals having Deep Pink stripes. Miniature, single. Average, columnar growth. M-L. (Pitardii seedling). (N.Z. 2001 - Haydon).

FIMBRIATED FRAGRANCE - Tomato Red. Medium, rose form double with no obvious petaloids and stamens with bright Yellow anthers. Average, upright and dense growth. E-M. Light fragrance. (Hybrid 'Scented Sun' x Japonica 'Kramer's Supreme'). (N.Z. 1999 - J. Finlay).

FIRE 'N ICE - Bright Red. Medium to large, semidouble to rose form double. Average, dense, upright growth. L. Cold hardy to -10°F. (Japonica 'Tricolor [Siebold]' x Oleifera). (U.S. 1992 - Ackerman).

FIRE FROST - Center Soft Frosted Pink with White overtones blending to Dark to Medium Pink edges with Yellow Anthers and White filaments. Small, loose peony form. Vigorous, upright, dense growth. M-L. (U.S. 2019 - Jill & Glenn Read, Lucedale, MS).

FIRST BLUSH - Blush Pink edged Pink. Medium, formal double to rose form double. Average, compact, upright growth. M. (U.S. 1989 - Kramer).

FIRST FLUSH - Blush Pink. Small, single. Vigorous, erect growth. E. (Probably C.x williamsii). (England to U.S. 1948 - Marchant, Keeper's Hill Nursery).

FIRST FORMAL - Baby Pink. Medium, formal double. (Hybrid 'Sylvia May' seedling). (U.S. 1957 - James).

FLAMENCO DANCER - Deep Coral Rose shaded to Light Pink. Small to medium, semidouble with some upright, furled petals. Slow, compact growth. M. (Saluenensis seedling). (U.S. 1980 - Kramer).

FLIRTATION - Silvery Pink. Medium, single. Compact, upright growth. E-M. (Japonica 'Lady Vansittart' x Saluenensis). (U.S. 1961 - Armstrong).

FORTUNE'S SMILE - Deep, veined Rose. Medium, single with six petals. Slow, dense, spreading growth. (Saluenensis x Japonica 'Hassaku'). (N.Z. 1962 - Jury).

FRAGRANCE OF SLEEVE - Pale Pink veined Darker Pink. Miniature, single. Average, open, upright growth. E-M. Fragrant. (Japonica x Kissi). (U.S. 1983 - Ackerman).

FRAGRANT ASIA - Bright Pink. Medium, single form. Average, upright growth. E-M. Strong fragrance. (Hybrid 'Fragrant One' x Japonica 'Scentasia'). (N.Z. 2002 - J. Finlay).

FRAGRANT BURGUNDY - Dark Rose Red. Medium, peony form. Average density, upright growth. M-L. Rose and clove fragrance. (Hybrid 'Fragrant One' x Yuhsienensis'). (N.Z. 2002 - J. Finlay).

FRAGRANT CASCADE - Pale Pink. Medium, single. Average, dense, weeping growth. E-L. Fragrant. (Japonica 'Mrs. Bertha A. Harms' x 'King's Ransom' x Hybrid 'Scentuous'). (N.Z. 1993 - J. Finlay).

FRAGRANT CONCUBINE - Dark Pink with Yellow anthers. Medium, loose peony to semidouble. Vigorous, upright growth, E-M. Fragrance resembling woman's face power. (Hybrid 'Salab' x Japonica 'Tiffany'). (U.S. 1999 - John Wang, Orinda, CA).

FRAGRANT DREAM - Soft Pink. Miniature to small, single. Vigorous, willowy, upright growth. E-M. Fragrant. (Hybrid 'Tiny Princess' x Lutchuensis). (Aus. 1989 - G. Hooper, Bexley North, NSW).

FRAGRANT DRIFT - China Rose Pink. Medium, peony form. Slow, dense, upright growth. M-L. Fragrant. (Hybrid 'Scentuous' seedling). (N.Z. 1993 - J. Finlay).

FRAGRANT FAIRIES - Pale Blush Pink tinged Blush Mauve with an occasional stripe. Miniature, single with crepe and notched petals. Vigorous, upright growth. E-L. Fragrant. (Hybrid 'Snow Drop' seedling). (Aus. 1994 - M. Baker, Macleod, Vic.).

FRAGRANT GENESIS - Bright Light Red. Medium, anemone to peony form. Average, upright growth. M. Light honeycomb fragrance. [(Japonica 'Mrs. Bertha A. Harms' x Hybrid 'Salab') x Japonica 'Tama-Ikari'] x Japonica 'Kramer's Supreme'). (N.Z. 1999 - J. Finlay).

FRAGRANT JEWEL - Glowing bright Pink. Medium, rose form double to peony form. Average, upright growth. E-M. Strong carnation and clove fragrance. (Hybrid 'Fragrant One' x Japonica 'Kramer's Supreme'). (N.Z. 2002 - J. Finlay).

FRAGRANT JOY - Dark Lavender Pink. Miniature, rose form double. Average, upright growth. E-M. Fragrant. (Rusticana x Lutchuensis). (U.S. 1983 - Ackerman).

FRAGRANT LADY - Ivory White with Pink flush on outer petals. Large, semidouble. M-L. Fragrant. (Japonica 'Mrs. Bertha A. Harms' x Hybrid 'Salab' x Japonica 'Erin Farmer'). (N.Z. 1996 - J. Finlay).

FRAGRANT LEGEND - Bright Red. Large, peony form. Slow and spreading growth. E-M. Fragrant. (Hybrid 'Fragrant One' x Japonica 'Kramer's Supreme'). (N.Z. 2002 - J. Finlay).

FRAGRANT ONE - Light Pink with Darker Pink petal tips shading to White in center. Large, single. Average, open, spreading growth. E-L. Fragrant. ([Japonica 'Mrs. Bertha A. Harms' x Hybrid 'Salab'] x Japonica Tamaikari'). (N.Z. 1998 - J. Finlay).

FRAGRANT PATHFINDER - Deep Pink. Large, single. Average, spreading, open growth. E-M. Hay-like fragrance. (Hybrid 'Scented Sun' x Japonica 'Kramer's Supreme'). (N.Z. 1999 - J. Finlay).

FRAGRANT PINK - Deep Pink. Miniature, peony form. Average, spreading growth. E-L. Fragrant. (Rusticana x Lutchuensis). (U.S. 1968 - Ackerman).

FRAGRANT PINK IMPROVED - Fragrant flowered polyploid variation of 'Fragrant Pink' produced by colchicine treatment. (U.S. 1975 - Ackerman).

FRAGRANT PIXIES - Pale Pink shading to Deep Pink at outer edges. Miniature, single with notched petals. Slow, weeping growth. E. Fragrant. (Hybrid seedling). (Aus. 1995 - M. Baker, Macleod, Vic.).

FRAGRANT RIPPLE - White to very Light Pink, marked with Light Pink stripes and Darker Pink stripes. Medium, anemone form. Average, upright growth. M. Very light gardenia fragrance. [(Japonica 'Mrs. Bertha A. Harms' x Hybrid 'Salab') x Japonica 'Tama-Ikari'] x Japonica 'Kramer's Supreme'. (N.Z. 1999 - J. Finlay).

FRAGRANT RUBY - Red, darkening as flower matures. Large, peony form. Average, upright growth. E-M. Fragrant. (Hybrid 'Fragrant One' x Japonica 'Tama Glitters'). (N.Z. 2005 - J. Finlay).

FRANCES UPSON - Silver Pink. Very large, semidouble. Average, open, upright growth. E-L. (Japonica Hybrid). (N.Z. 1981 - F. V. Upson, Kaponga).

FRANCIS HANGER - White. Medium, single with blooms up and down stems. Upright growth. (Saluenensis x Japonica). (England 1953 - Hanger).

FRANK WAGHORN - Deep Pink. Miniature, single trumpet form with notched petals. Slow, open growth. E-L. (Pitardii seedling). (Aus. 1995 - K. Brown, Mitcham, Vic.).

FREEDOM BELL - Bright Red. Small, bell shaped semidouble. Vigorous, upright, compact growth. E-M. (U.S. 1965 - Nuccio's).

FROLIC - White with touch of Pink. Miniature, single. Slow, spreading growth. E-L. (Rosaeflora seedling). (N.Z. 1990 - P. Austin).

FROST PRINCE - Deep Pink. Medium, single. Average, upright growth. E. (Hiemalis 'Shishi-Gashira' x Oleifera). (U.S. 1978 - Ackerman).

FROST PRINCESS - Lavender Pink. Medium, semidouble. Average growth. E. (Hiemalis 'Bill Wylam' x Oleifera). (U.S. 1981 - Ackerman).

FROTH - Pink. Medium, semidouble to peony form. Slow growth. M. (Hybrid 'Elegant Beauty' x Hybrid 'Donation'). (N.Z. 1980 - P. R. McNab, Levin).

GALAXIE - White striped Reddish Pink. Medium, semidouble sometimes with cupped o r twisted upright petals. Average, upright growth. M-L. (Saluenensis x Japonica 'Finlandia Variegated'). (U.S. 1963 - Metcalf).

GARDEN GLORY - Rich Orchid Pink. Medium, rose form double to formal double. Vigorous, upright growth. E-L. (Saluenensis x Japonica). (U.S. 1974 - Nuccio's).

GARNET GLEAM - Vivid Garnet Red. Small to medium, trumpet shaped single with Pink filaments and Golden stamens. Slow, spreading growth. E-L. (Pitardii x Pitardii/Japonica seedling). (N.Z. 1980 - Mrs. A. B. Durrant, Rotorua).

GAY BABY - Deep Orchid Pink. Miniature, semidouble. Open, upright growth. M. (Saluenensis/ Japonica hybrid x Hybrid 'Tiny Princess'). (N.Z. 1978 - O. Blumhardt, Whangarei).

GAY BUTTONS - Cerise Pink. Miniature, single form. Average, open and upright growth. E-M. (Japonica 'Tinsie' {Bokuhan} x Pitardii). (N.Z. 2003 - Mark Jury).

GAY MAGNOLIA - White with Pinkish Lavender throat; sports solid Pink. Small, semidouble. Bushy growth. M. (Aus. 1968 - Hawthorne, Vic.).

GAY PIXIE - Light Orchid Pink with Darker Pink stripes. Large, peony form. Open, upright growth. M-L. (Pitardii seedling). (Aus. 1979 - Sebire).

GAY TIME - White washed and shaded Orchid Pink. Medium, semidouble to formal double. Average, upright growth. M. (Saluenensis x Japonica 'Mathotiana'). (N.Z. 1970 - Jury).

GAYLE'S MONA - White with Pink undertones looking like a watermark with Darker Pink veins with Yellow anthers and White filaments. Large, semidouble to loose peony form. Slow, upright, spreading growth. L. (Sport of Non-reticulata hybrid 'Mona Jury'). (U.S. 2019 - Steve & Gayle Lawrence, Tallahassee, FL).

GEORGE BLANDFORD - Carmine Rose. Large, semidouble to anemone form. Vigorous, spreading growth. M. (Saluenensis x Japonica 'Lady Clare'). (England 1958 - Williams).

GLAD RAGS - Soft Pink. Large, semidouble with irregular, upright petals. Vigorous, pendulous, upright growth. E-M. (Japonica 'Party Girl' x Saluenensis). (Aus. 1969 - H. Dettman, Wahroonga, NSW).

GLENN'S ORBIT - Deep Orchid Pink. Medium, semidouble to loose peony form. Vigorous, upright growth. M. (Hybrid 'Donation' seedling). (England 1967 - G. H. Johnstone, Cornwall).

GLORY OF CANTERBURY - Deep Lavender. Medium, semidouble with upright petals. Slow, compact growth. L. (Saluenensis x Japonica). (U.S. 1964 - Metcalf).

GLORY OF ISIS - Bright medium Pink. Very large, peony form. Strong, upright, very well-branched growth. M-L. [(Pitardii var. 'Yunnanica' x Yunnanensis) x Hybrid 'Utsukushi Asahe']. (U.S. 2011 - Charvet).

GOLDEN FLEECE - White with Golden anthers and Light Yellow filaments. Large, loose peony form. Average, compact growth. M-L. (Japonica 'Frank Gibson' x C.x williamsii 'Feathers Red Peony'). (U.S. 1970 - David L. Feathers, Lafayette, CA).

GOLDEN GLOW - Creamy White deepening to Light Yellow at base with edge and back of petals slightly toned Pink. Medium, semidouble. Average, dense, upright growth. L. ([Japonica 'Guilio Nuccio' x Pitardii] x Chrysantha). (U.S. 1994 - Nuccio's).

GOLDEN SPANGLES - Variegated leaf of 'Mary Christian'. (England 1957).

GOOD FRAGRANCE - Dark Orange, Red edge to a Pink center. Medium to large, semidouble form. Average growth. Fragrance suggestive of honeysuckle or raspberry. ('Fragrant One' x Yuhsienensis). (N.Z. 2001 - J. Finlay).

GRACE CAPLE - Faint Blush Pink fading to White. Large, semidouble to peony form. Slow, compact growth. E-L. (Pitardii x Japonica). (N.Z. 1974 - Durrant).

GRACE GAMLIN - Deep Pink. Large, anemone form. Average, upright growth. M. (Saluenensis seedling). (N.Z. 1979 - A. P. Gamlin, Manaia).

GRAND FRAGRANCE - Bright Deep Pink to Red. Medium to large, semidouble with a large compact central core of stamens. Average growth. M-L. Light fragrance. ([(Japonica 'Mrs. Bertha A. Harms' x Hybrid 'Salab') x Hybrid 'Scentuous'] x Japonica 'Nioi-Fubuki'). (N.Z. 1999 - J. Finlay).

GRANNIE - Light Pink. Medium, single. Average, open, upright growth. E-L. (Saluenensis x Granthamiana). (N.Z. 1975 - Jury).

GWAVAS - Dusty Pink. Medium, semidouble. Vigorous, upright growth. L. (Hybrid 'J C Williams' x Japonica 'The Mikado'). (England 1972 - Carlyon).

HALLSTONE SPICY - Bright Pink. Small, peony. Upright growth. M. Spicy fragrance. (U.S. 2008 - Ken Hallstone, Lafayette, CA).

NON-RETIC

HYBRID

F-H

221

HAREM - Dark Pink shading lighter in center. Medium, semidouble of hose-in-hose form. Average, open growth. M. (Hybrid 'Lady Gowrie' seedling). (Aus. 1971 - Tuckfield).

HARI WITHERS - Deep Pink fading to Pale Pink at edge. Medium, formal double. Vigorous, spreading, upright growth. M. (Saluenensis seedling). (Aus. 1985 - Dr. R. M. Withers, Hawthorne, Vic.).

HARRY SWAN - Fushine Pink. Large, semidouble. Open, upright growth. M. (Saluenensis seedling). (N.Z. 1984 - R. H. Swan).

HARRY SWINBURN - Clear Rose Pink. Large, peony form. Average, open, upright growth. E-L. (Saluenensis seedling). (N.Z. 1981 - A. P. Gamblin, Manaia).

HARU-GASUMI - Rose Pink. Miniature, semidouble. E-M. (Japonica x Lutchuensis). (U.S. 1981 - Parks).

HEARTWOOD SALUTE - White to Blush Pink. Miniature to small, unknown form. Strong, upright, open, weeping growth. E-M. Fragrant. (Saluenensis x Lutchuensis). (U.S. 1981 - Charvet).

HELEN B. - Bright Pink with Yellow anthers and White filaments. Miniature, rose form double. Vigorous, open, upright growth. M-L. (Lutchuensis x Japonica). (U.S. 1985 - Jernigan).

HELEN O'CONNOR - Bright Pink with Yellow anthers and Yellow filaments. Medium, semidouble. Vigorous, upright growth. L. Cold hardy. (Oleifera 'Plain Jane' x Japonica). (U.S. 2013 - Ackerman).

HIDE 'N SEEK - Pale Mauve Pink. Miniature, single with crepe and notched petals. Slow, dense, weeping growth. E-M. (Fraterna seedling). (Aus. 1994 - M. Baker, Vic.).

HIGH FRAGRANCE - Pale Ivory Pink with Deeper Pink shading at edge. Medium, peony form. Vigorous, open growth. M. Fragrant. (Japonica 'Mrs. Bertha A. Harms' x [Hybrid 'Scentuous' x Hybrid 'Salab']). (N.Z. 1986 - J. Finlay).

HILDA JAGGS - Soft Pink with Darker Pink petal edges. Large, semidouble. Vigorous, dense, upright growth. M-L. (Pitardii Variety Yunnanica x Pitardii). (N.Z. 1995 - Haydon).

HIRAETHLYN - Pink shading to Darker Pink. Medium, single of funnel form. Vigorous, compact, upright growth. Fragrant. (Saluenensis x Japonica). (England 1950 - Lord Aberconway, Bodnant, So. Wales).

HOLLAND ORCHID - Orchid Pink. Medium, single of trumpet form. Compact, upright to compact, low growth. M. (Saluenensis x Japonica). (U.S. 1961 - J. A. Holland, Upland, CA).

HONEYMOON - Coral Pink bud opening to a very Creamy White with Yellow petals at the base. Medium to large, semidouble. Vigorous, open, upright growth. L. (Japonica 'Guilio Nuccio' x Pitardii x Chrysantha). (U.S. 1992 - Nuccio's).

HOT PINK - Hot Pink. Medium, semidouble of tulip form. Vigorous, spreading, upright growth. E-L. (Hybrid seedling). (U.S. 1987 - R. E. Ehrhart, Walnut Creek, CA).

HOT STUFF - Very Bluish Deep Pink. Medium, semidouble form. Average, open, upright growth. M-L. (U.S. 2006 - Nuccio's).

HUNTSMAN - Bright Red. Large, peony form. Average, open, upright growth. E-L. (Saluenensis x Japonica 'Arajishi'). (N.Z. 1975 - Jury).

HYPERSCENT - Bright Scarlet. Medium, rose form double. Slow, dense growth. E-L. Fragrant. (Japonica 'Mrs. Bertha A. Harms' x Hybrid 'Scentuous'). (N.Z. 1993 - J. Finlay).

I AM FRAGRANT - Pale Pink petals with curled Deeper Pink petaloids. Large, anemone form. Average growth. E-M. Light fragrance. (Hybrid 'Fragrant One' x Japonica 'Kramer's Supreme'). (N.Z. 2002 - J. Finlay).

ICE CREAM SMOOTHIE - Deep Pink, shading from a near White center through Pale Pink. Medium, peony form. Slow, dense and spreading growth. M-L. (Pitardii seedling). (N.Z. 2004 - Haydon).

ICE FOLLIES - Bright Pink. Large, semidouble. Average, dense, upright growth. L. Cold hardy to -5°F. (Hybrid 'November Pink' x Oleifera 'Lu Shan Snow'). (U.S. 1992 - Ackerman).

ICE MELTED - Light Pink with lighter center. Medium, semidouble. Vigorous, upright growth. M. Fragrant. (Hybrid 'Scentuous' seedling). (N.Z. 1991 - J. Finlay).

INTOSCENT - Pink, shading from bright Pink tips to a Lighter Pink at center. Large, peony form. Vigorous, upright growth. M-L. Fragrant. (Hybrid 'Fragrant One' x Japonica 'Scentasia'). (N.Z. 2002 - J. Finlay).

ISABEL CORDELIA - Medium Pink and White with White anthers and White filaments. Miniature, single. Vigorous, upright growth. E. (Seedling of Hybrid 'Yume'). (U.S. 2016 - Tsubaki Camellias, Savannah, GA).

ISABEL'S SURPRISE - White to Light Pink with Darker Pink streaks. Miniature, bell shaped single. Average, open, spreading, upright growth. E-M. (Hybrid seedling). (N.Z. 1992 - J. White, Whakatane).

ISARIBI - Rose Pink. Miniature, semidouble. Vigorous, compact, upright growth. M-L. (Japonica 'Berenice Boddy' x other species). (U.S. 1981 - Parks).

ISLAND SUNSET - Rich Coral Pink, lighter at center. Medium to large, semidouble form. Average, bushy, upright growth. M-L. (U.S. 2006 - Nuccio's).

ITTY BIT - Soft Pink. Miniature, anemone form. Slow, spreading growth. M. (Saluenensis x Hybrid 'Tiny Princess'). (N.Z. 1984 - F. E. Jury).

J. C. WILLIAMS - Phlox Pink. Medium, single. Vigorous, upright, pendulous growth. E-L. (Saluenensis x Japonica). (England 1940 - Williams).

J. MALCOLM GILLIES - Pink with Darker Pink shading on outer petals. Large, peony form. Vigorous, upright growth. L. (Aus. 1980 - E. L. Ansell, Lilydale, Vic.).

JACKPOT - Coral Pink. Miniature to small, flat and round shaped semidouble form; profuse bloomer. Average, bushy, compact and upright growth. M-L. (U.S. 2006 - Nuccio's).

JACOB GAETA - Light Pink speckled White with light streak of Yellow in center of petals. Medium, semidouble. E-L. (Hybrid 'Gay Time' x Hybrid 'Angel Wings' x Nitidissima 'Olympic Gold'). (U.S. 1989 - Piet and Gaeta).

JAMES S. REEVE - Rose Red. Very large, semidouble. Average, upright, spreading growth. M. (Saluenensis x Japonica). (U.S. 1999 - Hall).

JAMIE - Vivid Red. Medium, semidouble of hose-in-hose form. (Hybrid Williamsii seedling). (Aus. 1968 - Waterhouse).

JANE STEPTOE - Bright Pink. Medium, semidouble. Average, dense growth. E-L. (Hybrid seedling). (N.Z. 1990 - W. Rolston, Levin).

JANNINE POWELL - Pale Pink shading to Deep Pink at petal edges. Miniature, semidouble. Vigorous, bushy growth. E-M. (Hybrid 'Alpen Glo' x Sasanqua). (Aus. 1995 - J. Powell, Helensburgh, NSW).

JAPANESE FANTASY - White shading to Pink at tip of petals. Miniature, single. Vigorous, dense, upright growth. E. (Japonica 'Berenice Boddy' x Saluenensis/Rosaeflora). (U.S. 1990 - Parks).

JEAN CLARIS - Bright Rose Pink. Large, formal double with slightly incurved petals and notched outer petals. Average growth. M. (Saluenensis x Japonica 'K. Sawada'). (N.Z. 1984 - O. Blumhardt, Whangarei).

JENEFER CARLYON - Silvery Pink. Large, semidouble. Spreading growth. (Saluenensis x Japonica 'C M Wilson'). (England 1972 - Carlyon).

JESSICA CHRISTINA - Red. Medium, formal double. Slow, open, upright growth. L. (Hybrid seedling). (N.Z. 1990 - J. Judge, Tauranga).

JILL'S JEWEL - White with Yellow Anthers and White filaments. Miniature, semidouble. Slow, spreading, dense, dwarf form growth. M-L. (U.S. 2019 - Jill & Glenn Read, Lucedale, MS).

JIM TAYLOR - Light Rose with deeper overcast. Medium, rose form double to formal double. Average, compact, upright growth. M. (Saluenensis seedling). (N.Z. 1975 - J. Taylor, Alton).

JIMMY JAMES - Flesh Pink. Large, semidouble to peony form with ruffled petals interspersed among Golden stamens. Compact, upright growth. E-L. (Hybrid 'Robbie' x Japonica 'Charlotte Bradford'). (U.S. 1960 - James).

JINHUA'S JADE TRAY - ('Yupan Jinhua' - Chinese name). White to Light Pink or Yellowish with Green tone, edged with Pink with Yellow anthers and Yellow filaments. Large to very large, anemone to peony form; petals broad and wrinkled or serrated at the edges and waved; a large number of petaloids mixed with stamens forming a central raised ball. Vigorous, upright growth. E-L. Sweetly fragrant. (Williamsii x fragrant cultivar). (U.S. 2007 - John Wang, Orinda, CA).

JOAN TREHANE - Rose Pink. Medium, rose form double to formal double. Spreading growth. (Saluenensis x Japonica 'Herme.'). (England 1980 - D. Trehane and Son).

JOANNE GAETA - Pink. Large, full peony form. Average, open, spreading growth. E-L. (Japonica 'Charlie Bettes' x Hybrid 'Elsie Jury'). (U.S. 1989 - Piet and Gaeta).

JOE NUCCIO - Orchid Pink with incurved tips of petals toned Deeper Pink. Medium, formal double. Average, dense, upright growth. E-L. (Hybrid 'Garden Glory' seedling). (U.S. 1991 - Nuccio's).

JOHN PICKTHORN - Deep Phlox Pink. Medium, single. Upright growth. E-M. (Saluenensis x Japonica). (England 1961 - Williams).

JOYFUL BELLS - Wine Red. Small, single with six petals. Vigorous growth. M. (Saluenensis x Japonica 'Fuyajo'). (N.Z. 1962 - Jury).

JUBILATION - Pink with occasional Deeper Pink fleck. Large to very large, rose form double. Upright growth. M-L. (Unnamed Hybrid x Japonica 'Betty Sheffield Supreme'). (N.Z. 1978 - Jury).

JUDY ANN MORRIS - Rose Pink fading to Gray White on edge. Small, peony form to rose form double. Compact, upright growth. M-L. (Hybrid 'Donation' seedling). (Aus. 1986 - E. Bramley, Croydon, Vic.).

JULIA - Lavender Pink and White. Medium to large, rose form double to formal double. Average, up right growth. M. (Hybrid seedling). (U.S. 1983 - E. Atkins, Shalimar, FL).

JULIA HAMITER - Delicate Blush Pink to White. Medium, semidouble to rose form double to formal double. Average, compact growth. M. (Hybrid 'Donation' seedling). (U.S. 1964 - F. Hamiter, Shreveport, LA).

JULIA PINK - Lavender Pink. (Sport of Hybrid 'Julia'). (U.S. 1987 - D. Lesmeister, Carmichael, CA).

JULIE - Salmon Pink to Peach Pink. Medium to large, peony form to rose form double. Average, dense, upright growth. M. (Hybrid 'Robbie' x Japonica 'Dr. Tinsley'). (U.S. 1961 - V. James, Aptos, CA).

JULIE FELIX - Soft Pink to very Pale Pink in center. Very large, rose form double. Slow, open growth. M-L. (Saluenensis x Japonica 'Joshua E. Youtz'). (N.Z. 1983 - F. Jury, Waitara).

JULIE VARIEGATED - Salmon Pink to Peach Pink and White variation of 'Julie'. (U.S. 1981, - D. Bergamini, Martinez, CA).

JULIE'S OWN - Light Pink with White tipped petals. Miniature, semidouble with notched and folded petals. Average, spreading growth. E-M. Fragrant. (Hybrid 'Wirlinga Princess' seedling). (Aus. 1993 - K. Brown, Mitcham, Vic.).

JULIET SPENCER - Deep Pink. Large, semidouble to peony form. Average, open growth. M-L. (Saluenensis x Japonica 'Daikagura'). (N.Z. 1975 - Jury).

JUNIE GIRL - White in center shading out to very Pale Pink. Medium to large, loose peony form. Vigorous, open, upright growth. E-L. (Saluenensis x Japonica 'Betty Sheffield Supreme'). (N.Z. 1985 - C. Spicer, Feilding).

JURY'S APPLE BLOSSOM SUN - Mid Pink tips to a Light Pink base. Medium, semidouble form. Slow, dense and average growth. E-M. (Pitardii seedling). (N.Z. 2003 - Mark Jury).

JURY'S CHARITY - Deep Rose Pink. Medium, semidouble. Average, bushy growth. E-L. (Saluenensis x Japonica 'Waiwhetu Beauty'). (N.Z. 1975 - Jury).

JURY'S MOON MOTH - Pale Pink. Large, semidouble form. Average growth. M. (Pitardii var. Pitardii x Japonica 'K. Sawada'). (N.Z. 2003 - Mark Jury).

JURY'S PEARL - Pale Pink at the outside, shading to a Creamy Pink at the center. Large, rose form double. Average, dense and upright growth. M. (Pitardii var. Pitardii x Japonica 'Tomorrow'). (N.Z. 2003 - Mark Jury).

JURY'S SUNGLOW - Crimson. Small to medium, anemone form to peony form. Average, compact, upright growth. M. (Japonica 'Kimberley' x Hybrid 'Dark Night'). (N.Z. 1989 - Jury).

JURY'S YELLOW - White with Cream-Yellow petaloids. Medium, anemone form. Average, compact, upright growth. E-L. (Saluenensis/Japonica hybrid x Japonica 'Gwenneth Morey'). (N.Z. 1976 - Jury).

JUST PEACHY - Peach Pink to Cream with Yellow anthers and White filaments. Medium, anemone form. E-L. Fragrant. (Hybrid 'Salab' seedling). (U.S. 1998 - Don Bergamini, Martinez, CA).

KAGIROHI (FIRST LIGHT OF DAWN) - Pale Yellow. Small to medium, formal double. Upright growth. L. (Nitidissima x Japonica 'Silver Chalice'). (Japan 1996 - Kazuo Yoshikawa, Ishikawa).

KATIE LEE - Light Pink deepening at edge. Small, single. Slow, open growth. M-L. (Japonica 'Tiffany' x Lutchuensis). (N.Z. 1988 - J. R. Finlay).

KENBARANNE - Soft Pink edge shading to White at center. Miniature, semidouble to loose peony form. Average, weeping, spreading growth. E-L. (Hybrid 'Snow Drop' seedling). (Aus. 1989 - K. Brown, Mitcham, Vic.).

KERRY ANNE FRASER - Red shading to Rose in center. Large, rose form double to formal double. Average, spreading, open growth. M-L. (N.Z. 1985 - T. Lennard, Te Puke).

KERRY ELIZABETH - Very Pale Pink. Large, anemone form. Slow, spreading growth. M-L. Flower is weakly fragrant. (Hybrid 'Scented Sun' x Japonica 'Kramer's Supreme'). (N.Z. 2002 - J. Finlay).

KIA ORA - Phlox Pink. Large, semidouble. Dense, spreading growth. M. (Saluenensis x Japonica 'Lotus'). (N.Z. 1962 - Jury).

KICHO - Pale Yellow. Small, tubular single. Vigorous, upright growth. (Japonica 'Hatsu-Arashi' x Nitidissima). (U.S. 1990 - Nuccio's hybridizer Tadao Yamaguchi, Japan).

KIHO - Light Yellow. Small to medium, single with tubular, wavy petals. Vigorous, upright growth. E-M. (U.S. 1990 - Nuccio's hybridizer Tadao Yamaguchi, Japan).

KI-NO-GOZEN - Light Yellow. Small to medium, single cup-shaped with thick petals. Vigorous, upright growth. (Japonica 'Jomanji' x Nitidissima). (U.S. 1990 - Nuccio's hybridizer Tadao Yamaguchi, Japan).

KI-NO-JÔMAN(JI). (YELLOW JÔMAN TEMPLE) - Unusual shade of Salmon Pink. Small, single form. Upright, bushy growth. M-L. (Japonica 'Jômanji' x Nitidissima). (Japan 2007 - Tadao Yamaguchi, Ishikawa).

KI-NO-SENRITSU (YELLOW MELODY). - Soft Light Yellow. Small to medium, peony to loose peony form. Moderate, upright, open growth. M. (Japan 1998 - Tadao Yamaguchi, Ishikawa).

KOGANE NISHIKI - Pale Yellow with slender stripes of Red. Small, trumpet shaped single. Vigorous, upright growth. M-L. (U.S. 1993 - Nuccio's hybridizer Tadao Yamaguchi, Japan).

KOTO-NO-KAORI - Rose Pink. Small, single. Average, upright, lacy growth. E-M. Fragrant. (Japonica Tôkai x Lutchuensis). (Japan 1977 - Kaoru Hagiya, Niigata Prefecture).

KRAMER'S FLUTED CORAL - Coral to Darker Coral at edge. Medium, semidouble with fluted petals. (U.S. 1983 - Kramer).

KRAMER'S FLUTED CORAL VARIEGATED - Coral and White variation of 'Kramer's Fluted Coral'. (U.S. 1989 - Kramer).

LADY CUTLER - Bright Pink. Large, semidouble. Vigorous, spreading, upright growth. (Saluenensis x Japonica 'Ville De Nantes'). (N.Z. 1971 - Jury).

LADY GOWRIE - Pink. Large, semidouble. Vigorous, compact, upright growth. M. (Saluenensis x Japonica). (Aus. 1954 - Waterhouse).

LADY LEE - Salmon Pink. Medium, rose form double to formal double with four tiers of petals. E-L. (Saluenensis x Japonica 'Debutante'). (U.S. 1966 - Feathers).

LADY'S MAID - Light Orchid Pink. Medium, semidouble. Vigorous, compact, upright growth. M. (Saluenensis x Japonica). (Aus. 1960 - Waterhouse).

LAMMERTSII - White. Small, single. Vigorous, compact, upright growth. M. (U.S. 1952 - Dr. W. E. Lammerts, Livermore, CA).

LAVENDER GIRL - Burgundy Red with Lavender edge with Yellow anthers and White filaments. Medium, semidouble to anemone. Slow, upright, dense growth. M-L. (Seedling of Hybrid 'Super Star'). (U.S. 2016 - Pat Johnson, Cairo, GA).

LAVENDER PRINCE II - Rose Orchid Pink. Large, semidouble. Vigorous, open, upright growth. M-L. (Japonica 'Princess Lavender' x Hybrid 'William's Lavender'). (U.S. 1981 - Parks).

LAVENDER SWIRL - Soft Lavender Pink becoming Darker Pink in center. Large to very large, formal double. Average, upright growth. M. (Saluenensis x Japonica 'K. Sawada'). (N.Z. 1998 - O. Blumhardt, Whangarei).

LEAH GAY - Blush Pink to Pink at edges. Small to medium, formal double. Average, open growth. E-M. (Japonica 'Mrs. D. W. Davis' x Hybrid 'Gay Time'). (U.S. 1990 - Taylor's Nsy., Lecompte, LA).

LEMON TWIST - Off White to Pale Yellow, deeper at center. Medium, semidouble. Vigorous, somewhat open, upright growth. L. (Japonica 'Guilio Nuccio' x Pitardii x Nitidissima). (U.S. 1996 - Nuccio's).

LES JURY - Red. Medium to large, peony form to formal double. Vigorous, upright growth. M. (Hybrid 'Rendezvous' seedling). (N.Z. 1991 - Jury).

LIDDYBOW - Soft Pink with deeper veining, and pale edges. Miniature, single. Average, spreading, upright growth. E-M. Fragrant. (Fraterna seedling). (N.Z. 1991 - J. Hansen, Waikanae).

LILAC TIME - Mauve Pink. Medium, rose form double to formal double. Slow growth. M. (Hybrid 'Elegant Beauty' x Hybrid 'Donation'). (N.Z. 1980 - P. R. McNab, Levin).

LISA BEASLEY - Pink. Miniature, rose form double. Average, spreading, upright growth. L. Fragrant. (Fraterna x Japonica). (U.S. 1993 - Jernigan).

LITTLE ANN - Pink to Deeper Pink at outer edges. Miniature, semidouble to anemone form. Slow, dwarf growth. E-M. (Wabisuke 'Fuiri-Kocho-Wabisuke' x Hiemalis 'Kanjiro'). (Aus. 1990 - K. Abbott, Rossmoyne, W. Aus.).

LITTLE LAVENDER - Lavender Pink. Miniature, anemone form. Vigorous, compact, upright growth. M. (Hybrid 'Phillipa Forwood' x Japonica). (U.S. 1965 - McCaskill).

LITTLE LISA LEIGH - Pink fading to soft Pink on outer edges. Miniature, single with notched petals. Slow, spreading, weeping growth. E-L. Fragrant. (Hybrid 'Snowdrop' seedling). (Aus. 1993 - M. Baker, MacLeod, Vic.).

LOLLYPOP - Pale Pink stippled deeper. Miniature, rose form double. Average, open growth. E-M. (Hybrid 'Cornish Snow' seedling). (Aus. 1971 - Tuckffield).

LONDONTOWNE - Deep Red Pink. Unknown size, semidouble to loose peony. Cold hardy to -5°F. (Japonica 'Mrs. Bertha A. Harms' x. Oleifera 'Plain Jane'). (U.S. 2009 - Ackerman).

LONDONTOWNE BLUSH - Pale Pink. Medium, single to semidouble. Average, upright growth. L. Cold hardy to -10°F. (Oleifera 'Plain Jane' x Sasanqua). (U.S. 2002 - Ackerman).

LONGHUOZHU - See 'Dragon Fireball'.

LOUISE DOWD - Cerise. Miniature, semidouble with notched petals. Average, spreading, upright growth. L. (Wabisuke 'Sukiya' x Japonica). (U.S. 1981 - J. E. Rose, Gaithersburg, MD).

NON-RETIC

H
Y
B
R
I
D

J-L

LUCKY STAR - Rich Pink. Medium, semidouble. Average, dense, upright growth. M-L. (Saluenensis x Japonica '#9156'). (U.S. 1995 - Nuccio's).

MADISON - White, small, semidouble. Vigorous upright growth. E. (Hybrid 'Snow Flurry' seedling). (U.S. 2008 - CamelliaShop, Savannah, GA).

MANDY - Pale Pink. Miniature, semidouble. Open, weeping growth. M-L. Fragrant. (Rosaeflora seedling). (Aus. 1984 - Sebire).

MARBLE COLUMN - Pink at the outer edge shading to near White at center. Miniature, single. Vigorous, slender, upright growth. E-L. (Sasanqua x Fraterna). (N.Z. 1999 - Haydon).

MARGARET WATERHOUSE - Light Pink. Medium, semidouble. Vigorous, upright growth. E. (Saluenensis x Japonica). (Aus. 1955 - Waterhouse).

MARGIE SELBY THOMAS - Lavender Pink. Medium to large, semidouble. Vigorous, open, upright growth. M-L. (Japonica x Wabisuke). (U.S. 2000 - Kala T. Corcoran, Slidell, LA).

MARJORIE WALDEGRAVE - Rose Pink. Medium, semidouble. Vigorous growth. (Saluenensis x Japonica 'Marjorie Magnificent'). (England 1972 - Carlyon).

MARJORIE'S DREAM - White. Miniature, loose peony form with notched petals. Slow, spreading, weeping growth. E-M. Fragrant. (Hybrid 'Snow Drop' seedling). (Aus. 1993 - M. Baker, Macleod, Vic.).

MARJORY RAMSEY - Deep Rose. Medium, peony form to anemone form. Average, open, upright growth. M. (Hybrid 'Elegant Beauty' seedling). (N.Z. 1972 - P. D. Ramsey, Hawera).

MARNA - Bright Pink shading to Darker Pink. Medium, semidouble. Average, upright growth. E-M. Fragrant. (Japonica 'Mrs. Bertha Harms' x Hybrid 'Salut'). (U.S. 1984 - W. F. Harrison, Berkeley, CA).

MAROON MIST - Dark Maroon Red. Large, single to semidouble with Deep Orange anthers. L. Cold hardy to -5°F. (Japonica 'Tricolor [Siebold] Red' x. Oleifera 'Plain Jane'). (U.S. - Ackerman).

MARSHALL - Light Pink with Darker Pink stripes and flecks. Small, single. Vigorous, upright growth. E. (Hybrid 'Yume' seedling). (U.S. 2008 - CamelliaShop, Savannah, GA).

MARY CHRISTIAN - Phlox Pink. Small, single. Open, upright growth. (Saluenensis x Japonica). (England 1942 - Williams).

MARY JOBSON - Rose Pink. Medium, single. Upright growth. E-M. (Saluenensis x Japonica). (England 1961 - Williams).

MARY PHOEBE TAYLOR - Light Rose Pink. Very large, peony form. Average, open, upright growth. E-M. (Saluenensis seedling). (N.Z. 1975 - J. Taylor, Alton).

MASON FARM - White tinged with Pink. Large, unknown form. Vigorous growth; leaves are large, thick and leathery. VE. Cold hardy. (Oleifera x Sasanqua). (U.S. 1995 - Parks).

MASTERSCENT - Coral Red. Large, peony form. Average, open, upright growth. E-L. Fragrant. (Japonica 'Mrs. Bertha A. Harms' x Hybrid 'Scentuous'). (N.Z. 1993 - J. Finlay).

MAXISCENT - Light Pink. Medium, semidouble to loose peony form. Average growth. E-M. Strong fragrance. ([Japonica 'Mrs. Bertha A. Harms' x 'Hybrid 'Salab'] x Japonica 'Kramer's Supreme'). (N.Z. 2005 - J. Finlay).

MAYOR WEBB HART - Fuchsia Pink. Large, semidouble. Spreading, upright growth. M. (Hybrid 'Donation' seedling). (U.S. 1980 - Tammia).

MENDOCINO BELLE - Blush Pink. Medium, single bell-shaped. Upright, open growth. M. (Pitardii var. 'Yunnanica' x Rosaeflora 'Wirlinga Bell'). (U.S. 2009 - Charvet).

MIA ELIZAVETA - Light Pink center shading to Darker Pink at petal edges with White blotches with gold anthers and pinkish-white filaments. Small to medium, rose form double. Average, with thin branches and twiggy growth. M-L. (Japonica 'Fran Mathis' x Non-reticulata hybrid 'Spring Daze'). (U.S. 2019 - Tommy Weeks, Conroe, TX).

MICHAEL - Blush Pink. Medium, single. (Saluenensis x Japonica). (England 1950 - Williams).

MIEKO TANAKA - True Red. Small, single. Average, well branched growth. E-L. (Vernalis 'Gaisen' x Japonica). (Japan - Dr. Tanaka).

MILDRED VEITCH - Orchid Pink. Large, semidouble to anemone form with loose center. Compact, upright growth. M. (Saluenensis x Japonica 'Elegans Chandler'). (England 1962 - R. Veitch, Exeter).

MILKY WAY - White. Small, single. Slow, compact growth. (Cuspidata x Fraterna). (U.S. 1965 - Hilsman).

MIMOSA JURY - Soft Pink. Medium, formal double. Average, upright growth. E-L. (Saluenensis x Japonica 'K. Sawada'). (N.Z. 1993 - M. Jury, North Taranaki).

MINATO-NO-AKEBONO - Light Pink toned Deep Pink. Miniature, single. Average, upright somewhat loose growth. E-M. Fragrant. (Japan 1981 - Masaomi Murata).

MINATO-NO-HARU (HARBOR IN SPRING) - Deep Peach Pink. Miniature, single. Average, upright, floriferous, slightly loose growth. M-L. Fragrant. (Japonica 'Kon-wabisuke' x Lutchuensis). (Japan 1987 - Masaome Murata, Kanagawa).

MINI MINT - White heavily striped Pink. Small, formal double with high bud center. Slow, bushy growth. M. (Hybrid 'Donation' seedling). (U.S. 1970 - Feathers).

MIRAGE - Bright Rose Red. Large, semidouble. Average growth. E-L. (Saluenensis x Japonica 'Moshio'). (N.Z. 1975 - Jury).

MISS ADELINE - White striped Pale Pink. Medium, semidouble with wavy, crinkled petals. Average, open, upright growth. M. (Hybrid 'Donation' x Japonica). (U.S. 1977 - F. F. Becker, Brookhaven, MS).

MISS BESS - Light Pink. Medium, anemone form to semidouble. Average growth. M-L. (Hybrid 'Donation' x Japonica 'J. J. Pringle Smith'). (U.S. 1970 - Alfter).

MISS JENNIE - Peach Pink outer petals to almost White in center. Large, rose form double. Vigorous, spreading growth. E-M. (Hybrid 'Brigadoon' x Hybrid 'El Dorado'). (U.S. 1982 - T. E. Lundy, Pensacola, FL).

MISS TINYTOT PRINCESS - Light Pink. Miniature, formal double. M. (Saluenensis seedling). (U.S. 1979 - Kramer).

MISS WESTERN HILLS - Medium Pink in the outer part, to a Light Creamy Pink at the center. Large, peony to anemone form. Vigorous, upright growth. M-L. Lightly fragrant. (Hybrid 'Fragrant On e' x Japonica 'Tama-no-ura'). (N.Z. 2002 - J. Finlay).

MISTY - White. Medium, semidouble. Spreading, upright growth. M. (Hybrid 'Wynne Rayner' seedling). (Aus. 1986 - B. Hooper, Bexley North, NSW).

MONA JURY - Apricot Pink. Large, peony form. Average, open growth. E-L. (Saluenensis/Japonica hybrid x Japonica 'Betty Sheffield Supreme'). (U.S. 1976 - Jury).

MONAH JOHNSTONE - Light Pastel Pink. Large, semidouble. Open, upright growth. M-L. (Saluenensis x Japonica 'Princess Lavender'). (U.S. 1980 - Parks).

MONTEREY SUNSET - Rose Red. Large, peony form with flat outer petals and swirled and twisted inner petals interspersed with stamens. Vigorous, compact, upright growth. M. (Hybrid 'Robbie' seedling). (U.S. 1960 - James).

MONTICELLO - Rich Pink. Large, peony form with loose petals. M-L. (Hybrid 'Sylvia May' seedling). (U.S. 1957 - Feathers).

MOONBEAM - Soft Pink. Large, rose form double with notched petals. Vigorous, open, upright growth. M-L. (Pitardii seedling). (Aus. 1988 - Sebire).

MOONSONG - Coral Red. Medium, formal double. Average, open, upright growth. E-L. (Hybrid 'Taylor Maid' seedling). (N.Z. 1992 - Haydon).

MOONSTRUCK - White toned Pink at center and at outer edges. Medium, single. Average, upright growth. M-L. (Japonica x Cuspidata). (U.S. 1996 - Nuccio's).

MOPSY - Pale Pink. Miniature, single to semidouble with fluted petals. Dwarf, compact growth. E-M. (Pitardii seedling). (Aus. 1987 - Sebire).

MRS. WALTER A. WILSON - Lavender Rose Pink. Large, formal double. Slow, upright growth. E-L. (Hybrid 'Donation' seedling). (U.S. 1989 - W. Wilson, Augusta, GA).

MS MO - Rich Orchid Pink. Large, semidouble to full peony form. Upright, well-branched growth. E-M. (Pitardii var. 'Yunnanica' x Japonica 'Tom Knudsen'). (U.S. 2005 - Charvet).

MULTIFLORA - Pink. Medium, semidouble. Vigorous, slightly spreading growth. M. (Saluenensis hybrid seedling). (Aus. 1971 - E. L. Ansell, Lilydale, Vic.).

MURIEL TUCKFIELD - Ivory White. Medium, semidouble. Vigorous, compact, upright growth. M-L. (Hybrid 'Cornish Snow' seedling). (Aus. 1974 - Tuckfield).

MY DIANE - Deep Pink. Large, peony form. Average, spreading, upright growth. M-L. (Saluenensis x Japonica 'Daikagura'). (N.Z. 1975 - Jury).

NANTEN PINK - Soft Pink. Large, semidouble. Average, open growth. M. (Saluenensis x Japonica). (England 1956 - K. M. White, Devon).

NARIDA - Deep Pink. Large, semidouble. Average, bushy growth. E-L. (Saluenensis x Japonica 'Waiwhetu Beauty'). (N.Z. 1975 - Jury).

NATALIE CAROL - Pink. Medium, rose form double. Average, dense, upright growth. M-L. (Hybrid seedling). (N.Z. 1998 - M. Hurley).

NEISHA GAMLIN - Rose Pink edged Ruby. Large, peony form. Open, spreading growth. M. (Saluenensis seedling). (N.Z. 1980 - A. P. Gamlin, Manaia).

NELL REID - White to Off-White center, merging to Light Pink and edged Darker Pink. Large, semidouble. Open, upright growth. M. (Hybrid 'Lady Gowrie' seedling). (Aus. 1983 - J. B. Reid, Castle Hill, NSW).

NICE FRAGRANCE - Bright Pink shading to Deeper Pink in center. Medium to large, peony form to rose form double. Slow growth. E-M. Fragrant. ([Japonica 'Mrs. Bertha A. Harms' x Hybrid 'Salab'] x Hybrid 'Scentuous'). (N.Z. 1998 - J. Finlay).

NICKY CRISP - Pale Lavender Pink. Small to medium, semidouble. Slow, compact growth. E-L. (Pitardii x Pitardii/Japonica seedling). (N.Z. 1980 - Mrs. A. B. Durrant, Rotorua).

NIGHT RIDER - Very Dark Black Red. Miniature to small, semidouble. Average, upright growth. M-L. (Hybrid 'Ruby Bells' x Japonica 'Kuro Tsubaki'). (N.Z. 1985 - O. Blumhardt, Whangarei).

NONIE HAYDON - Pink. Large, peony form. Average growth. M-L. (Yunnanica x Pitardii). (N.Z. 1990 - Haydon).

NORINA - Fuchsia Pink, becoming lighter at center. Miniature, semidouble to anemone form. Average, upright growth. M-L. (Hybrid 'Alpen Glo' seedling). (N.Z. 1999 - Haydon).

NOVEMBER PINK - Phlox Pink. Medium, single. E. (Saluenensis x Japonica). (England 1951 - Williams).

NÜ'ERHONG - See 'Daughter's Red'.

NYMPH - Pale Pink flushed Ivory. Miniature, semidouble. Vigorous, spreading growth. E-L. Fragrant. (Lutchuensis x Japonica 'Helen Metson'). (N.Z. 1982 - D. G. O'Toole, Christchurch).

OLÉ - Pink. Small, rose form double. Compact growth. L. (Saluenensis hybrid). (U.S. 1977 - H. Fish, Santa Cruz, CA).

OLGUITA - Pink shading to White on the petals in varying degrees with Gold anthers and Yellow filaments. Small, semidouble. Average, upright, dense growth. E-L. (Non-reticulata hybrid 'Yume' x Sasanqua) x (unknown Sasanqua). (U.S. 2018 - Bobby Green, Fairhope, AL).

OMIGOROMO (BEAUTIFUL KIMONO) - Soft Pink toned slightly lighter near center with Dark Yellow anthers and Light Yellow filaments.. Small to medium, single, slightly cupped. Average, upright, somewhat arching growth.

OPAL PRINCESS - Blush Pink. Medium, formal double. Average, dense, upright growth. M-L. (Japonica 'Berenice Boddy' x Hybrid 'Mona Jury'). (N.Z. 1991 - Jury).

OPTICAL ILLUSION - Yellow with Pink overtones. Medium, formal double with strap-like petals that can be arranged in a somewhat spiral pattern. (Flava x Japonica). (U.S. 2015 - Parks).

ORCHID BEAUTY - Light Orchid Pink, edged Deeper Pink. Medium to large, formal double form. Average, open and upright growth. (U.S. 2002 - Nuccio's).

ORCHID PRINCESS - Pale Orchid Pink. Large, semidouble. Vigorous, compact, upright growth. M-L. (Saluenensis seedling). (U.S. 1987 - Nuccio's).

OUR BETTY - Light Pink. Medium to large, tulip form semidouble with two distinct rows of long slim petals. Upright growth. M. (U.S. 1982 - Kramer).

OUR BETTY VARIEGATED - Light Pink and White variation of 'Our Betty'. (N.Z. 1988).

OUR MELISSA - Pink. Small, anemone form. Vigorous, weeping growth. E-L. (Pitardii seedling). (Aus. 1986 - Sebire).

PACIFIC BEAUTY - Pink. Large, rose form double to formal double with occasional star formation of petals. Average, compact, upright growth. M. (Japonica 'Waiwhetu Beauty' x Hybrid 'Elsie Jury'). (N.Z. 1989 - Jury).

PADDY'S PERFUMED - Pink. Small, anemone form. Average, open, spreading growth. M. Fragrant. (Japonica 'Tama-Ikari' x Hybrid 'Esme Spence'). (N.Z. 1991 - J. Finlay).

PAIGE CAMELLIA - Bright Pink. Medium, formal double. Vigorous, upright, open growth. E-L. (Hybrid 'Julia' x unknown pollen parent). (U.S. 2013 - Walter Creighton, Semmes, AL).

PALE OPAL - White at center, shading from Pale Pink to Red at tips. Medium, loose peony form. M. (Pitardii seedling). (Aus. 1993 - Sebire).

PALM SUNDAY - Orchid Pink. Large, peony form. Average, upright growth. M. (Hybrid 'Donation' seedling). (U.S. 1967 - W. B. Brown, Wilmington, NC).

PAPER DOLLS - Light Pink toning deeper toward edges. Small, formal double. Vigorous, upright, somewhat columnar growth. E-M. (Irrawadiensis seedling). (U.S. 1997 - Nuccio's).

PAPERCHASE - Rose Pink. Medium, formal double. Vigorous, upright growth. M. (Saluenensis x Japonica). (N.Z. 1982 - B. J. Rayner, Stratford).

PARADISE LITTLE JEN - Pale Pink edged Darker Pink. Miniature to small, rose form double. Moderate, compact, weeping growth. E-M. (Rosaeflora seedling). (Aus. 1998 - M. Cherry, Kulnura, NSW).

PARISIENNE - Cherry Red. Medium to large, semidouble. Average, upright growth. M. (Hybrid 'Grannie' x Hybrid 'Jury's Yellow'). (N.Z. 1991 - Jury).

PARKSIDE - Clear Pink. Medium, semidouble. (Saluenensis x Japonica). (England 1955).

PAT NELSON - Pink to Mauve. Medium to large, peony to anemone form. Average, upright growth. M. (N.Z. 2004 - Ian Wills).

PATRICIA M. BATES - Deep Red with darker veining. Small to medium, semidouble to peony form. Average, dense, upright growth. M-L. (Hybrid seedling). (N.Z. 1990 - P. Bates).

PAT'S PINK - Bright Pink with Yellow anthers and Whitish filaments. Medium, semidouble to loose peony form. Vigorous, upright, spreading growth. E-L. (Seedling of Hybrid 'Taylor's Perfection'). (U.S. 2016 - Pat Johnson, Cairo, GA).

PATTI SUE - Light Pink, darkening at center. Miniature, deep trumpet shaped single form. Average growth. M-L. (Pitardii x Hybrid 'Prudence'). (N.Z. 2004 - Kathlyn Craig).

PEARLY CASCADE - Bright Pink. Small, semidouble form. Slow, open and spreading growth; a mass of cascading, deep shaped flowers grow in a ground cover type of growth. M. (Pitardii seedling). (N.Z. 2003 - Mark Jury).

PEARLY SHELLS - Pearly Pink. Large, formal double. Average, open, upright growth. M-L. (Saluenensis x Japonica 'K. Sawada'). (N.Z. 1984 - F. Jury, Tikorangi).

PEEKABOO - Bright Pink. Small, formal double. Average, dense, spreading growth. M-L. (Hybrid 'Fairy Bouquet' seedling). (N.Z. 1995 - Haydon).

PEGGY BURTON - Pink shading to a Lighter Pink at center. Medium, semidouble. Slow, dense, spreading growth. M-L. (Hybrid 'Nicky Crisp' seedling). (N.Z. 1999 - Haydon).

PERFUMED PEARL - Pink, lighter at petal base, Lighter Pink petaloids. Medium, anemone form. Average, upright growth. E-M. Light honeycomb fragrance. (Hybrid 'Scented Sun' x Japonica 'Kramer's Supreme'). (N.Z. 1999 - J. Finlay).

PERQUISITE - Soft Pink. Large to very large, semidouble with heavy textured petals. Average, spreading growth. M-L. (Hybrid 'Donation' seedling). (N.Z. 1986 - C. Spicer, Feilding).

PERSUASION - Purplish Red. Miniature, single of trumpet shape with Golden stamens. Slow, spreading growth. E-L. (Pitardii x Japonica 'Fuyajo'). (N.Z. 1983 - Mrs. A. Durrant, Rotorua).

PHIL PIET - Pink and White. Large to very large, semidouble. Vigorous, dense growth. E-M. (Granthamiana x Hybrid 'Elsie Jury'). (U.S. 1992 - Piet and Gaeta).

PHIL PIET PINK - Solid Pink. Large to very large, semidouble. Vigorous, dense growth. E-M. (Sport of Hybrid 'Phil Piet'). (U.S. 2001 - Chuck Ritter, Melrose, FL).

PHILIPPA FORWOOD - Dawn Pink. Medium, single. Vigorous, upright growth. M-L. (Saluenensis x Japonica). (Confused with true 'J. C. Williams'). (England 1940 - Williams).

PHYL SHEPHERD - Pale Pink shading to White. Miniature, semidouble to anemone form. Spreading growth. E-M. (Cuspidata x Hybrid 'Cinnamon Cindy'). (Aus. 1985 - M. Harmon, East Burwood, Vic.).

PHYLLIS AUSTIN - Deep Pink. Medium, formal double. Average, open growth. M. (Saluenensis x Japonica). (N.Z. 1972 - B. J. Rayner, Stratford).

PINK BOUNTY - Pink, fading to base of petals. Very large, semidouble form. Vigorous, bushy and upright growth; in full bloom, plant displays a weeping form. E-L. (Hybrid 'Donation' seedling). (Aus. 2005 - Neil D. Saltmarsh, Warragul, Vic.).

PINK BOUQUET (MONROVIA) - Light Rose Pink fluorescent petals. Medium to large, semidouble. Vigorous, compact, upright growth. M. (Japonica 'Pink Parfait' x Saluenensis). (U.S. 1975 - Monrovia Nsy., Azusa, CA).

PINK CAMEO - Pink overcast Silver. Medium, peony form. Average, compact, upright growth. M-L. (Pitardii seedling). (Aus. 1977 - Sebire).

PINK CASCADE - Pale Pink. Miniature, single with six petals. Weeping growth. M. (Saluenensis x Japonica 'Spencer's Pink'). (N.Z. 1965 - B. J. Rayner, Stratford).

PINK CREPE - Pale Pink with slightly darker shading at outer edges. Miniature, single with crepe and notched petals. Slow, weeping growth. E-M. Fragrant. (Hybrid 'Snow Drop' seedling). (Aus. 1994 - M. Baker, Macleod, Vic.).

PINK DAHLIA - Lavender Pink. Medium, dahlia shaped formal double with slender, pointed petals. M-L. (Saluenensis seedling). (U.S. 1980 - Kramer).

PINK DAHLIA VARIEGATED - Lavender Pink and White variation of 'Pink Dahlia'. (U.S. 1983 - Kramer).

PINK ICICLE - Shell Pink. Large, peony form. Average, compact, upright growth. M. Cold hardy to -5°F. (Hybrid 'November Pink' x Oleifera 'Lu Shan Snow'). (U.S. 1986 - Ackerman).

PINK POSY - Pale Pink. Miniature to small, semidouble. Average, dense, upright growth. M. Fragrant. (Hybrid 'Tiny Princess' seedling). (Aus. 1995 - D. Waldon, Woodonga, Vic.).

PINK RUFFLES - Light Pink. Medium, semidouble. M-L. (Pitardii seedling). (Aus. 1983 - Sebire).

PINK SERENADE - Bright Pink, Medium, single. (U.S. 2008 - Parks).

PINK SPIDER - Light Fuschia Pink with Yellow anthers and Pink filaments. Medium, semidouble. Slow, upright, dense growth. M-L. (Seedling of Non-reticulata hybrid 'Bonnie Marie'). (U.S. 2019 - Pat Johnson, Cairo, GA).

PINK TULIP - Pink. Medium, single. M. (Hybrid 'J. C. Williams' seedling). (Aus. 1962).

PINK WAVE - Pale Pink. Medium, single with prominent stamens. (Saluenensis x Japonica). (England 1960 - Williams).

POLAR ICE - White. Medium, anemone form. Average, spreading growth. E. Cold hardy to -10°F. ('Frost Princess' x Oleifera). (U.S. 1987 - Ackerman).

POLARIS - Radiant Pink. Large, semidouble to loose peony form with long, narrow, separated petals scalloped at ends. Vigorous, spreading, upright growth. M. (Japonica 'Hishi-Karaito' x Hybrid 'J. C. Williams'). (U.S. 1964 - J. L. Sparkman, Jacksonville, FL).

POLKA DOT - White to Blush Pink. Miniature, single. Slow, open, spreading growth. M-L. (Rosaeflora seedling). (N.Z. 1995 - D. Hansen, Waikanae).

POLLY HEATON - Deep Fuchsine Pink with Bluish undertone. Large, semidouble. Vigorous, pendulous growth. E-L. (Hybrid 'J C Williams' x Japonica 'Blood of China'). (U.S. 1976 - Hall).

POLLY TRAPNELL DORSEY - White. Miniature to small, single form. Slow, upright growth. M. (Hybrid seedling). (U.S. 2005 - John Thornton Hilleary, Baltimore, MD).

POLYANNA - Rose Pink with deeper veining. Medium, rose form double to formal double. Average, dense, upright growth. M. (Hybrid seedling). (N.Z. 1991 - Jury).

POMO MOUND - White. Small, single. Neat, compact growth. E-M. Slightly fragrant. (Grijsii x unknown pollen parent). (U.S. 1998 - Charvet).

POPSY - White. Miniature, single. Dwarf growth. M. (Pitardii seedling). (Aus. 1985 - Sebire).

PRINCESS DI - White. Miniature, single; petals wavy and notched. Slow, upright growth. M-L. (Aus. 1998 - Mr. and Mrs. G. Waldon, Wodonga, Vic.).

PRUDENCE - Rich Pink. Miniature, semidouble. Dwarf, upright growth. M. (Pitardii seedling). (N.Z. 1971 - Mrs. A. B. Durrant, Rotorua).

PUMPHREY'S PRIDE - Medium Pink shading to Lighter Pink at center with Yellow anthers. Medium, rose form double. Average, spreading, dense growth. M. Cold hardy. (Japonica 'Tricolor Red' x Oleifera 'Plain Jane'). (U.S. 2007 - Ackerman).

PUNKIN - Rose Pink outer petals shading to Lighter Pink at center. Small, formal double with incurved petals. Vigorous growth. M. (U.S. 1966 - Novick).

PURPLE FIRE - Bright, Deep Rose Purple. Medium, single form. Average to slow growth. E-L. (Pitardii seedling). (N.Z. 2004 - Haydon).

QUINTESSENCE - White with Yellow anthers and White filaments. Miniature, single. Slow, spreading growth. E-M. Fragrant. (Lutchuensis hybrid). (N.Z. 1985 - J. C. Lesnie, Wanakau).

R. M. COODE - Pink. Medium, semidouble. Open, upright growth. L. (Saluenensis x Japonica 'Adolphe Audusson'). (England 1972 - Carlyon).

RADIATING FRAGRANCE - Very Light Pink, with very Dark Pink sectors. Large, rose form double, variegated. Average, dense growth. M-L. Fruity fragrance. (Hybrid 'Fragrant One' x Japonica 'Scentasia'). (N.Z. 2002 - J. Finlay).

RAG DOLL - Deep Pink. Small, peony form. Average, open, upright growth. M. (Japonica 'Tinsie' x Lutchuensis). (N.Z. 1998 - O. Blumhardt, Whangarei).

RASPBERRY DELIGHT - Raspberry Rose. Large, semidouble with large, fluted petals. Vigorous, open, upright growth. M-L. (Hybrid 'William's Lavender' x Japonica). (U.S. 1973 - McCaskill).

RASPBERRY FLAMBE - Rose color. Medium, formal double. Average, upright growth. M. (U.S. 2006 - Kramer).

REBECCA RICHARDSON - Pink. Large, semidouble. Average, compact, upright growth. E-M. (Hybrid 'Donation' x Japonica). (U.S. 1978 - Tammia).

RED DRAGON - Deep Cherry Red. Medium, semidouble. Average, open growth. E. (Saluenensis x Japonica). (N.Z. 1982 - G. B. Greenfield, Whangarei).

RED FELLOW - Bright Red. Large, semidouble. Average, spreading growth. L. Cold hardy to -5°F. (Japonica 'Tricolor Red [Siebold].' x Oleifera 'Plain Jane'). (U.S. 2000 - Ackerman).

RED QUEEN - Deep Cherry Red. Medium, single. (Saluenensis x Japonica 'Apollo'). (England 1960 - R. Veitch, Exeter).

REESE JOHNSON, JR. - Medium Red. Medium, formal double to rose form double. Average, upright, dense growth. M-L. (Seedling of Hybrid 'Super Star'). (U.S. 2016 - Pat Johnson, Cairo, GA).

RENDEZVOUS - Scarlet Crimson. Medium, semidouble. Average growth. M. (Hybrid 'Joyful Bells' x Japonica 'Australis'). (N.Z. 1976 - Jury).

RHONDA ELIZABETH - Red. Medium, semidouble. Compact, upright growth. M. (Pitardii seedling). (Aus. 1985 - Sebire).

RICHARD H. CLERE - Soft Pink. Medium to large, peony form. Average, spreading growth. M. (Saluenensis x Japonica). (N.Z. 1970 - B. J. Rayner, Stratford).

ROBBIE - Deep Orchid Pink. Very large, semidouble. Slow, compact, upright growth. M. (Hybrid 'Sylvia May' seedling). (U.S. 1958 - James).

ROBIN RISE - Salmon Pink. Medium, semidouble. Vigorous, open, upright growth. E-M. (Hybrid 'Margaret Waterhouse' seedling). (Aus. 1982 - Tuckfield).

ROBYN McMINN - Soft clear Pink. Medium, formal double. Vigorous compact, upright growth. E-L. (Hybrid 'Donation' seedling). (Aus. 1970 - Mrs. N. R. McMinn, Noble Park, Vic.).

ROSABELLE - Rose Pink. Miniature, semidouble. Open, spreading growth. M. (Rosaeflora seedling). (Aus. 1981 - Sebire).

ROSE BOUQUET - Rose. Large, rose form double. Spreading growth. M. (Saluenensis x Japonica 'Tiffany'). (N.Z. 1980 - F. M. Jury, Waitara).

ROSE HOLLARD - Rose Pink. Large, rose form double. Average, open growth. M-L. (Saluenensis seedling). (N.Z. 1972 - B. J. Rayner, Stratford).

ROSE PARADE - Deep Rose Pink. Medium, formal double. Vigorous, compact, upright growth. E-L. (Hybrid 'Donation' x Japonica). (U.S. 1969 - Nuccio's).

ROSEMARY SAWLE - Warm Pink. Medium, single. Compact growth. (Heterophylla 'Barbara Hillier' seedling). (England 1972 - Carlyon).

ROSEMARY WILLIAMS - Rose Pink. Medium, single blooming down stem. Compact, upright growth. (Saluenensis x Japonica). (England 1961 - Williams).

ROSINA SOBECK - Light Pink, slightly darker at margins, with Yellow anthers and White filaments. Medium, semidouble - cup-shaped with loosely arranged stamens and occasional small twisted central petals. Average, spreading growth. M-L. (U.S. 1967 - John E. Sobeck, California).

ROSY PILLAR - Rose Pink. Medium, single. Average, upright, columnar growth. (U.S. 2007 - Nuccio's).

ROYAL INTRIGUE - Bright Orchid Red. Very large, semidouble. Vigorous, strong growth. L. (Japonica 'Princess Lavender' x Hybrid 'William's Lavender'). (U.S. 1995 - Parks).

RUBY BELLS - Dark Red. Miniature, single. Open, spreading growth. E-M. (Saluenensis x Japonica 'Fuyajo'). (N.Z. 1987 - O. Blumhardt, Whangarei).

RUBY WEDDING - Currant Red. Medium, anemone form to peony form. Average, dense, upright growth. M. (Hybrid 'Dark Nite' seedling). (N.Z. 1991 - Jury).

RUTH SMITH - Pale Pink edged Deep Pink. Medium, peony form. Vigorous, open, upright growth. M. (Hybrid 'Donation' x Hybrid 'Anticipation'). (U.S. 1989 - Jernigan).

SALAB - Pink. Medium, single. Vigorous, dense, compact growth. Musky fragrance. (Sasanqua 'Apple Blossom' x Saluenensis). (U.S. 1971 - Feathers).

SALAMANDER - Bright Red. Medium, single. Open, upright growth. E-L. (Saluenensis x Japonica 'Flame'). (N.Z. 1960 - Jury).

SALLY J. SAVAGE - Pink shaded Lilac. Miniature to small, formal double. Upright growth. M-L. (Hybrid 'Debbie' seedling). (Aus. 1981 - C. A. Newman, Bayswater, W. Aus.).

SALUT - Orchid Pink. Miniature, single. Vigorous, spreading growth. M. Fragrant. (Saluenensis x Lutchuensis). (U.S. 1981 - Stone).

SANDRA ANN - Soft Pink. Large, semidouble with long oval notched petals. Slow, upright growth. E. (Pitardii seedling). (N.Z. 1996 - E. Hansen).

SANTA CRUZ - Deep Pink. Medium, rose form double to formal double. Fragrant. (Hybrid 'Sylvia May' seedling). (U.S. 1957 - James).

SARA RITTER - Pink. Small, semidouble with wavy, crinkled petals. Slow, spreading growth. M-L. (Pitardii x Japonica). (U.S. 1972 C. D. Cothren, Pomona, CA).

SATAN'S SATIN - Brilliant Red with sheen. Medium, single. E-M. (Hybrid seedling). (U.S. 1960 - Feathers).

SATIN GOWN - Satin Pink. Large, semidouble. Average growth. M-L. (Saluenensis x Japonica 'Waiwhetu Beauty'). (N.Z. 1975 - Jury).

SAYONARA - Pink. Medium, semidouble. Bushy growth. M. (Saluenensis x Japonica). (Aus. 1965 - Waterhouse).

SCENTED GEM - Fuchsia Pink with White petaloids. Miniature, semidouble. Open, upright growth. E-M. Fragrant. (Lutchuensis x Japonica 'Tinsie'). (U.S. 1983 - Domoto).

SCENTED SNOW - White. Large, anemone. Rapid, upright growth. E. Especially sweet fragrance. (Sasanqua 'Northern Lights' x Oleifera. (U.S. 2008 - Camellia Forest, Chapel Hill, NC).

SCENTED SUN - White with occasional Pink stripe; sometimes sports Rose or Blush Pink. Large to very large, semidouble with upright petals. Vigorous, upright growth. M. Fragrant. (U.S. 1985 - K. Hallstone, Lafayette, CA).

SCENTED SWIRL - Deep Pink. Large, peony form. Average, open, upright growth. M-L. Fragrant. (Hybrid 'Scentuous' x Japonica 'Kramer's Supreme'). (N.Z. 1993 - J. Finlay).

SCENTUOUS - White with Pink flush on backs of petals. Small, semidouble. Average, open growth. M-L. Fragrant. (Japonica 'Tiffany' x Lutchuensis). (N.Z. 1981 - J. Finlay).

NON-RETIC

HYBRID

P-S

SCINTILLATING FRAGRANCE - Dark Pink. Medium, rose form double to peony form. Average growth. M-L. Honey and Rose fragrance. (Hybrid 'Hyperscent' x Japonica 'Tami-Ikari'). (N.Z. 2002 - J. Finlay).

SEASPRAY - White. Miniature, single. Vigorous, upright growth. M-L. (Hybrid 'Snow Drop' seedling). (N.Z. 1995 - Haydon).

SEMI-RAMIS - White with faint Pink cast. Small, single. Vigorous, upright growth. E. (Oleifera x Vernalis). (U.S. 1960 - R. Carr, Tulare, CA).

SENORITA - Rose Pink with deeper margins. Medium, anemone form. Average, spreading, upright growth. M-L. (Saluenensis x Japonica 'Herme'). (N.Z. 1975 - Jury).

SENRITSU-KO - Light Yellow edges toned Pink. Small to medium, formal double to rose form double. Moderate, upright, open growth. M. (Hybrid 'Kiho' x Nitidissima). (Japan 2007 - Tadao Yamaguchi, Ishikawa).

SHARLIE RAYNER - Soft Pink shading to White in center. Medium, semidouble. Average, open, upright growth. M-L. (Pitardii x Japonica). (N.Z. 1972 - B. J. Rayner, Stratford).

SHIRLEY ESTES - White. Medium, loose peony. Average, upright, dense growth. M. (Hybrid 'Jury's Yellow' x Homeyer's 257 x E. Boardman). (U.S. 2006 - Hyman Norsworthy Beaumont, TX).

SHOCK WAVE - Very brilliant Deep Bluish Pink with White filaments and Yellow anthers. Medium, single. Fast, upright, open growth. M-L. (U.S. 2017 -Nuccio's Nurseries).

SHOCKING PINK - Tyrian Rose. Medium, semidouble with petals and petaloids ruffled and intermixed with stamens. Average, compact, upright growth. M-L. (Saluenensis x Japonica). (Aus. 1955 - Waterhouse).

SHOKO - Light Yellow. Small, single with thick petals. Vigorous, open, upright growth. E-M. (U.S. 1989 - Nuccio's hybridizer Tadao Yamaguchi, Japan).

SHOWBOAT - White with Pink petal edges occasionally incurved. Large, rose form double. Vigorous, upright somewhat open growth. E-L. (U.S. 2012 - Nuccio's).

SILVER COLUMN - White. Miniature, single. Vigorous, slender, upright growth. E-L. (Sasanqua x Fraterna). (N.Z. 1999 - Haydon).

SISTER CAMILLA - Pure White. Miniature, single cup-shaped flower. Dwarf, dense, weeping growth. M-L. (Hybrid 'Snow Drop' seedling). (Aus. 2006 - Marjorie Baker, Vic.).

SLEEPING SCENT - Deep Pink a t petal edges shading Lighter Pink toward center. Medium, semidouble. Average growth. M-L. Fragrant. ([Japonica 'Mrs. Bertha A. Harms' x Hybrid 'Salab' x Japonica 'Erin Farmer'] x Japonica 'Tamaikari'). (N.Z. 1998 - J. Finlay).

SMOOTH FRAGRANCE - Deep Pink with some veining of the petals. Large, semidouble to peony form. Average, vigorous, dense growth. E-M. Light fragrance. (Hybrid 'Scented Sun' x Japonica 'Tama- Ikari'). (N.Z. 1999 - J. Finlay).

SNIPPET - Soft Pink to almost White center petals and Light Pink outer petals. Small, semidouble with long, narrow, notched petals. Dwarf, compact growth. M. (Pitardii seedling). (N.Z. 1971 - Mrs. A. B. Durrant, Rotorua).

SNOW DROP - White edged Pink. Miniature, single. Open, upright growth. E-L. (Pitardii x Fraterna). (Aus. 1979 - Sebire).

SNOW DROP CASCADE - White shading to Pink on petal edges. Miniature, single to semidouble. Spreading growth. E-M. (Hybrid 'Snow Drop' seedling). (Aus. 2005 - Steve Campbell).

SNOW FLURRY - White. Small, anemone form. Slow, spreading growth. E. Cold hardy to -10°F. (Oleifera 'Plain Jane' x Hybrid 'Frost Princess'). (U.S. 1986 - Ackerman).

SNOWSTORM - White. Miniature, single with notched petals. Vigorous, spreading, weeping growth. E-M. (Hybrid 'Snow Drop' seedling). (Aus. 1994 - A. Raper, The Patch, Vic.).

SOFTLY - Soft Lavender suffusing to Cream in center. Medium to large, formal double. Average, upright growth. M-L. (Saluenensis x Japonica 'Joshua E. Youtz'). (N.Z. 1983 - F. Jury, Waitara).

SOFTLY FRAGRANT - Pale Pink. Medium, peony form. Vigorous, upright growth. M-L. Light, spicy fragrance. (Hybrid 'Fragrant One' x Japonica 'Scentasia'). (N.Z. 2002 - J. Finlay).

SOLSTICE - Light Yellow. Medium, rose form double. Vigorous, upright growth with narrow Light Green leaves with long leaf tips. (Flava x Japonica). (U.S. 2009 - Parks).

SOPHIE DUCKER - Pink, shading to White at base of petals with Pale Pink petaloids at center. Miniature, anemone form. Slow, open growth. E. (Hybrid 'Our Melissa' seedling). (Aus. 1998 - Dr. R. Withers, Donvale, Vic.).

SOUTH SEAS - Silver Pink flushed Rose Pink on margins. Medium, semidouble to loose peony form. Vigorous, compact, upright growth. M. (Saluenensis x Japonica 'C. M. Wilson'). (N.Z. 1967 - F. Jury, Waitara, N.Z).

SOUZA'S PAVLOVA - Clear Pink. Medium, peony form. Average, open growth. M-L. Fragrant. (Japonica 'Nioi-Fubuki' x Hybrid 'Scentuous'). (N.Z. 1987 - J. Finlay).

SPANKED BABY - Baby Pink. Medium, semidouble. Slow, spreading growth. E-M. (Hybrid 'Sylvia May' seedling). (U.S. 1956 - James).

SPINDLE TOP CENTENIAL - White. Small, formal double; fully imbricated petals, with very small petaloids at center. Average, upright, dense growth. E-M. (Rusticana 'Botan-Yuki' x Japonica 'Mary Lilla Dumas'). (U.S. 1999 - H. R. Norsworthy, Beaumont, TX).

SPINK - Rose Pink. Small, single. Open, upright growth. E-M. (Hybrid 'Snow Drop' seedling). (Aus. 1986 - Sebire).

SPITFIRE - Bright Cherry Red. Large, semidouble. Rapid, upright, bushy growth. (Hybrid 'Wynne Rayner' x Japonica 'Kramer's Supreme'). (Aus. 2006 - P. G. Edwards. Vic.).

SPRING AWAKENING - Pink. Miniature, semidouble to rose form double. Vigorous, open, upright growth. E-M. (Japonica 'Donckelarii' x Saluenensis/Rosaeflora). (U.S. 1990 - Parks).

SPRING CARDINAL - Crimson Red. Miniature to small, formal double. Average, upright, dense growth. E-M. Cold hardy to -10°F. (Japonica 'Tricolor [Siebold]. Red' x Oleifera 'Plain Jane'). (U.S. 1999 - Ackerman).

SPRING CIRCUS - Bright Pink. Medium, anemone form. Average, dense, upright growth. M. Cold hardy to -10°F. (Japonica 'Tricolor [Siebold] Red' x Oleifera 'Plain Jane'). (U.S. 1995 - Ackerman).

SPRING DAZE - Blush Pink edged Coral Pink. Small to medium, formal double to rose form double. Average, compact, upright growth. M-L. (U.S. 1989 - Kramer).

SPRING FANFARE - Pink. Miniature, single. Vigorous, spreading, upright growth. L. ([Japonica 'Kuro Tsubaki' x Hybrid 'Tiny Princess'] x Tsaii). (Aus. 1998 - T. J. Savige, Wirlinga, NSW).

SPRING FESTIVAL - Pink fading to Light Pink in center. Miniature, rose form double. Narrow, upright growth. M-L. (Cuspidata seedling). (U.S. 1975 - Domoto).

SPRING FRILL - Bright, iridescent Pink. Large to very large, rose form double. Slow, spreading growth. L. Cold hardy to -10°F. (Oleifera 'Plain Jane' x Vernalis 'Egao'). (U.S. 1992 - Ackerman).

SPRING MIST - Blush Pink. Miniature, semidouble. Vigorous, spreading growth. E-M. Fragrant. (Japonica Snow Bell' x Lutchuensis). (U.S. 1982 - A. E. Longley and Parks).

SPRING SURPRISE - Deep Pink at petal edges shading to Blush Pink at center. Medium, semidouble. Slow, dense, upright growth. M. (Saluenensis seedling). (N.Z. 1998 - O. Blumhardt, Whangarei).

SPRING WIND - White tinged Pink. Miniature, single. Average, open, spreading growth. M. (Japonica x Lutchuensis). (U.S. 1983 - Ackerman).

SPRITE - Light Salmon Pink. Small, rose form double. Average, compact, upright growth. M-L. (Pitardii seedling). (Aus. 1977 - Sebire).

SPURDLE HERITAGE - Bright Scarlet Red with deeper veining. Medium to large, semidouble. Average, upright growth. M. (Hybrid 'Fantastic' x Hybrid 'Rendezvous'). (N.Z. 1991 - Jury).

ST. EWE - Rose Pink. Medium, single of cupped form. Vigorous, upright growth. M. (Saluenensis x Japonica). (England 1947 - Williams).

STANDARD BEARER - Light Pink. Miniature, anemone form. Vigorous, dense, spreading growth. M-L. (Hybrid 'Wirlinga Princess' seedling). (Aus. 1992 - Haydon).

STARS 'N STRIPES - White striped Rose Red, often with Rose Red border. Medium, single. Average, upright, spreading growth. E-M. (Hybrid 'Christmas Rose' seedling). (U.S. 1999 - Nuccio's).

STEPHANIE'S TINY STAR - Red with Yellow anthers and White filaments. Miniature, single. Average, bushy growth. E. (U.S. 2019 - Bobby Green, Green Nurseries, Fairhope, AL).

STEPHEN LOUIS CASSAGNE - Pink shading to White on edges. Small, formal double. Average, bushy growth. (U.S. 2019 - Camellia Heaven - John Grimm, Bush, LA).

STRAWBERRY MOON - Medium Pink and White with White anthers and White filaments. Small, semidouble to peony form. Vigorous, upright growth. E. (Seedling of Hybrid 'Yume'). (U.S. 2016 - Tsubaki Camellias, Savannah, GA).

STRICTLY BALLROOM - Pale Pink with Darker Pink at the edge of petal early in season. Miniature, single; petals round and slightly notched. Average, upright growth. M-L. (Hybrid' Wirlinga Belle ' seedling). (Aus. 1998 - Mr. and Mrs. G. Waldon, Wodonga, Vic.).

STRING OF PEARLS - Very Light Blush Pink. Medium, formal double. Average, upright growth. M. (Japonica 'Snowman' x Hybrid 'Charlean'). (U.S. 1979 - W. Stewart, Savannah, GA).

SUN SONG - Soft Pink. Large, formal double. Average growth. E-L. (Hybrid 'Elegant Beauty' seedling). (N.Z. 1980 - Haydon).

SUN WORSHIPER - Red. Medium, rose form double. Vigorous, upright growth. M. (Hongkongensis x Rusticana). (U.S. 1983 - Ackerman).

SUPER STAR - White. Large, semidouble with White stamens tipped Gold. Slow to average growth. E-L. (Saluenensis x Japonica). (N.Z. 1984 - Mrs. J. E. Shaw, Wairua).

SUPERSCENT - Faint Blush Pink. Large, peony form. Average, open growth. M-L. Fragrant. (Hybrid x Japonica 'Spring Source'). (N.Z. 1987 - J. Finlay).

SURVIVOR (PARKS) - White. Large, single. Upright, compact growth. Cold hardy to -9°F. (Oleifera 'Narumi-Gata x Oleifera). (U.S. 1988 - Parks).

SWAN LAKE - Snow White. Medium, semidouble of hose-in-hose form. Bushy growth. M-L. (Name subsequently used for Japonica cultivar by a commercial nursery). (Aus. 1968 - Tuckfield).

SWEET DEBORAH JANE - Outer petals are mid Pink at the edges, shading to Light Pink at center and innermost petals a Pale Creamy Pink. Large, rose form double to peony form. Average growth. M-L. Fragrant. (Hybrid 'Fragrant One' x Japonica 'Kramer's Supreme'). (N.Z. 2002 - J. Finlay).

SWEET EMILY KATE - Light Pink shading to Pale Pink in center. Small to medium, full peony form. Slow, pendulous growth. M-L. Fragrant. (Japonica x Lutchuensis). (Aus. 1987 - R. Garnett, Beaumaris, Vic.).

SWEET EMMA - White with outer petals flushed Pink. Medium to large, anemone form. E. Fragrant. (Japonica 'Tamaikari' x Japonica 'Mrs. Bertha A. Harms' x Hybrid 'Salab'). (N.Z. 1996 - J. Finlay).

SWEET GEM - Lavender Pink with Yellow anthers and Light Yellow filaments. Miniature, single. Vigorous, upright growth. E-M. (Japonica 'Kuro-tsubaki' x species from Section Theopsis). (China 2009 - Jian-Guo Fei, Yong-hong Hu and Ya-li Zhang, Shanghai Botanical Garden of Shanghai, China).

SWEET JANE - Pale Pink center shading to Deeper Pink on outer petals. Miniature, peony form to formal double. Vigorous, upright growth. M. (Japonica 'Edith Linton' x Transnokoensis). (Aus. 1992 - R. Garnett, Beaumaris, Vic.).

SWEET OCTOBER - White with Golden Yellow anthers and Cream filaments. Small to medium, single. Vigorous, upright growth. E. (Oleifera 'Lu Shan Snow' x Sasanqua 'White Queen'). (U.S. 2009 - Ackerman).

SWEET SCENTED - Bright Pink. Medium, semidouble form. Average growth. Fragrant, reminiscent of tea. (Japonica [Higo] 'Mikuni-no-homare' x Hybrid 'High Fragrance'). (N.Z. 2002 - J. Finlay).

SWEET SCENTSATION - Dark Orchid Pink edges fading to Blush Pink with White overtones with a center of a mixture of Dark Orchid Pink and Blush Pink with White overtones with Golden anthers and Golden filaments. Large, loose peony to semidouble with upright petals. Vigorous, upright, open growth. E-M. Very fragrant. (U.S. 2016 - Jill Read, Lucedale, MS).

SWEETBIRD OF YOUTH - Lavender Pink. Large, semidouble with Golden stamens and petaloids intermixed. Vigorous, compact growth. E-M. (Hybrid 'J. C. Williams' seedling). (U.S. 1960 - R. Carr, Tulare, CA).

SYLVIA MAY - Pale Pink. Medium, single with long, narrow petals. Slow, open, upright growth. M. (Cuspidata x Saluenensis). (England to U.S. 1950 - Dr. W. Wells, Oakland, CA).

SYLVIA MAY WELLS - Pale Blush shaded to Light Lavender Pink. Large, loose peony form. Average, upright growth. M-L. (U.S. 1966 - H. L. Paige, Lafayette, CA).

TAMBORINE'S JEWEL - Fuchsine Pink. Medium, semidouble; 19-20 petals in 3 tiers. Average, broad, upright growth. M-L. (Aus. 1999 - Kevin J. Coase, Tamborine Mtn., Qld.).

TAMZIN COULL - Deep Pink. Large, rose form double. Open, upright growth. M. (N.Z. 1980 - Mrs. B. J. Rayner, Stratford).

TATTERS - White. Medium, peony form. M. (Saluenensis x Japonica). (Aus. 1962 - Waterhouse).

TAYLOR MAID - Bright Pink. Large, anemone form. Average, compact, upright growth. M. (Saluenensis x Japonica). (N.Z. 1984 - J. Taylor, Alton, Taranaki).

TAYLOR'S PERFECTION - Light Pink. Large, semidouble with occasional petaloids. Average, open, upright growth. M-L. (Saluenensis seedling). (N.Z. 1975 - J. Taylor, Alton).

TAYLOR'S SUPREME - Rose Pink. Large, semidouble with some petaloids. Average, upright growth. M-L. (Saluenensis seedling). (N.Z. 1975 - J. Taylor, Alton).

THE DUCHESS OF CORNWALL - Pale Silvery Pink. Large, semidouble. Spreading growth. M. (Saluenensis x Japonica 'Adolphe Audusson'). (England 1981 - Carlyon).

THE RED BARON - Deep Red. Medium, rose form double. Vigorous, compact, upright growth. E. (Hybrid 'J. C. Williams' seedling). (U.S. 1975 - C. R. Phillips, Frederick, MD).

TIDBIT - Blush Pink with Dark Pink markings. Miniature, semidouble of pine cone form. (Hybrid seedling). (U.S. 1983 - Kramer).

TINY BIT - Soft Pink. Miniature, anemone form. Slow, spreading growth. M. (Saluenensis x Non-reticulata hybrid 'Tiny Princes'). (N.Z. 1987 - F. Jury, Tikorangi).

TINY PRINCESS - White shaded delicate Pink. Miniature, semidouble to peony form with loose petals and small petaloids. Slow growth. E-M. (Japonica 'Akebono' x Fraterna). (U.S. 1961 - Sawada).

TINY STAR - Soft Pink. Miniature, semidouble. Open, upright growth. E-M. (Japonica 'Berenice Boddy' x Hybrid 'Tiny Princess'). (N.Z. 1978 - O. Blumhardt, Whangarei).

TIPTOE - Silvery Pink deepening to Cherry Pink at edge. Medium, semidouble. Compact, upright growth. (Japonica x Williamsii 'Farfalla'). (Aus. 1965 - Camellia Grove Nsy.).

TOGETHERNESS - Pale Pink shading to Deep Pink at outer petal edges. Miniature, single, with fluted and notched petals. Slow, dense, upright growth. E-M. Fragrant. (Hybrid 'Snow Drop' seedling). (Aus. 1995 - M. Baker, Macleod, Vic.).

TOM PERKINS - Rose Red outer petals, Neyron-Rose mid petals, and blossom Pink inner petals. Large, formal double with high imbricated petals. Vigorous, upright growth. M. (Hybrid 'Creation' seedling). (U.S. 1994 - F. Becker II, Brookhaven, MS).

TONI FINLAY'S FRAGRANT - Pink. Medium, anemone form. Average growth. E-M. Fragrant. (Japonica 'Mrs. Bertha A. Harms' x Hybrid 'Salab' x Japonica 'Look-Away'). (N.Z. 1994 - J. Finlay).

TONI LEE - Pale to Deep Pink. Miniature, single. Slow, spreading growth. E-L. (Hybrid seedling). (N.Z. 1994 - K. Watson, Waikanae).

TOP FRAGRANCE - Deep Pink. Medium, anemone to peony form. Average, upright, dense growth. E-M. Light fragrance. ([(Japonica 'Mrs. Bertha A. Harms' x Hybrid 'Salab') x Japonica Tama-Ikari] x Japonica 'Kramer's Supreme'). (N.Z. 1999 - J. Finlay).

TOPIARY PINK - Clear Blush Pink. Miniature, formal double form with no stamens; dense pillar form. Slow, upright growth. M. (Pitardii seedling). (N.Z. 2003 - Mark Jury).

TRANSPINK - Soft Pink. Miniature, trumpet shaped single form. Average, dense and upright growth. M-L. Honey fragrance. (Transnokoensis seedling). (N.Z. 2004 - Haydon).

TRANSTASMAN - Pale Pink edged Deeper Pink. Miniature, single. Average, upright growth. M-L. (Pitardii Variety Pitardii x Transnokoensis). (Aus. 1998 - R. Garnett, Beaumaris, Vic.).

TREASURE TROVE - Deep Red. Medium, peony form. Slow, dwarf, dense growth. M. (Hybrid 'Fantastic' x Hybrid 'Dark Nite'). (N.Z. 1991 - Jury).

TREGREHAN - Apricot Pink. Medium, semidouble to rose form double. Vigorous, upright growth. (Saluenensis x Japonica 'Marjorie Magnificent'). (England 1972 - Carlyon).

TULIP TIME - Light Pink. Medium, single of tulip form. Vigorous, upright growth. M. (Saluenensis hybrid). (U.S. 1978 - Feathers).

TURKISH DELIGHT - Light Lavender Pink. Medium, semidouble with long, narrow, fluted, reflexed petals. Bushy growth. M. (Hybrid 'Cornish Snow' seedling). (Aus. 1968 - Tuckfield).

TU-TU - Deep Orchid Pink. Small, peony form. Average, compact, upright growth. M. (Sasanqua x Hiemalis 'Shishi-Gashira'). (U.S. 1982 - Mrs. T. K. Knight, Baton Rouge, LA).

TWILIGHT GLOW - Rose. Unknown size, single. Compact, hardy growth. Cold hardy. (Oleifera x Sasanqua). (U.S. 2008 - Parks).

TWINKLE STAR - Purplish Rose Pink. Small, rose form double to formal double. Average, open, upright growth. M. (Hybrid 'Elegant Beauty' x Japonica 'Tinsie'). (N.Z. 1989 - Jury).

TWO MARTHAS - Lavender Pink. Medium, semidouble. Vigorous, compact, upright growth. E. (Sasanqua x Kissi). (U.S. 1981 - Ackerman).

UTSUKUSHI-ASAYE - Coral. Medium, semidouble. M. (Japonica 'Dr. Tinsley' x Saluenensis). (U.S. 1979 - Kramer).

UTSUKUSHI-ASAYE VARIEGATED - Coral and White variation of 'Utsukushi-Asaye'. (U.S. 1979 - Kramer).

VANILLA MOON - Blush Pink with White anthers and White filaments. Small, single. Vigorous, upright growth. E. (Seedling of Hybrid 'Yume'). (U.S. 2016 - Tsubaki Camellias, Savannah, GA).

VERNAL BREEZE - White. Small, single. Vigorous, upright growth; the plant has long arching branches. E. Very fragrant. (Japonica x C. lutchuensis). (U.S. 2014 - Camellia Forest, Chapel Hill, NC).

VERVE - Pink in center to Deeper Pink with Red petal tips. Small, semidouble. Vigorous, open, upright growth. M-L. (Saluenensis x Japonica 'Debutante'). (U.S. 1983 - Feathers).

VICKI GALVIN - Pale Pink edged Rose Pink. Large, semidouble. Compact, upright growth. M. (Hybrid 'Margaret Waterhouse' x Japonica 'Great Eastern'). (Aus. 1980 - M. L. Galvin, Sylvania, NSW).

VILIA - Soft Lavender Pink shading deeper at edge. Large, semidouble with wavy, velvet textured petals. Vigorous, compact, upright growth. M. (Hybrid 'Williams Lavender' x Japonica 'Kuro-Tsubaki'). (U.S. 1961 - McCaskill).

VILLES DELIGHT - Crimson. Medium, semidouble. Slow growth. (Saluenensis x Japonica hybrid x Japonica 'Ville De Nantes'). (N.Z. 1981 - Jury).

NON-RETIC

H
Y
B
R
I
D

S-V

VIRGINIA R. - Pink. Small, formal double. (Saluenensis seedling). (U.S. 1983 - Kramer).

VIRGINIA R. VARIEGATED - Pink and White variation of 'Virginia R.'. (U.S. 1983 - Kramer).

VIRGINIA W. CUTTER - Red. Large, anemone form. Vigorous growth. M. (Japonica 'Mrs. Bertha A. Harms' x Lutchuensis 'Ackerman's 63-32'). (U.S. 1972 - Dr. R. K. Cutter, Berkeley CA).

VIRGINIA WOMACK - Light Pink. Medium, formal double. Average, upright growth. E. (Hybrid 'Felice Harris' x unknown pollen parent). (U.S. 1976 - Dr. R. K. Womack).

VONNIE CAVE - Pale Cream, flushed Pink on reverse side of sepals. Miniature, single or semidouble form. Average, open and spreading growth. E. (Pitardii seedling). (N.Z. 2004 - Peter Cave).

W. C. WYATT - Pink, sometimes variegated. Large, semidouble. E-M. (Japonica 'Muriel Nathan' x Hybrid 'Robbie'). (U.S. 1998 - Mandarich).

WALDON'S FOLLY - Light Pink in center fading to Pale Pink toward outer edges. Miniature, semidouble with rounded, occasionally notched petals. M-L. (Hybrid 'Rosabelle' seedling). (Aus. 1993 - D. Waldon, Wodonga, Vic.).

WALTZ DREAM - Orchid Pink. Very large, semidouble. Vigorous, open, upright growth. M. (Hybrid 'Williams Lavender' x Japonica 'Kuro-Tsubaki'). (U.S. 1961 - McCaskill).

WALTZ TIME - Lilac Pink. Medium, semidouble. Vigorous, bushy, upright growth. M. (Hybrid 'Williams Lavender' x Japonica 'Kuro-Tsubaki'). (U.S. 1960 - McCaskill).

WALTZ TIME SUPREME - Deep Rose Pink. Medium, semidouble. Average growth. (Hybrid 'Waltz Time' seedling). (U.S. 1981 - Gilley).

WALTZ TIME VARIEGATED - Lilac Pink blotched White variation of 'Waltz Time'. (U.S. 1961 - McCaskill).

WATER LILY - Lavender tinted bright Pink. Medium, formal double. Vigorous, compact, upright growth. E-M. (Saluenensis x Japonica 'K. Sawada'). (N.Z. 1967 - F. Jury, Waitara).

WENDZALEA - Glowing Ruby Red with Yellow anthers and Whitish filaments. Medium, single. Vigorous, upright growth; blooms twice; once July to November and again February to March; prefers full sun. (Japonica 'Wendy' x C. azalea). (U.S. 2009 - Hulyn Smith).

WHIMSICAL - Soft Pink flecked and streaked Deep Pink. Large, semidouble. Slow, upright growth. L. (Saluenensis/Japonica hybrid x Japonica 'Betty Sheffield Supreme'). (N.Z. 1989 - C. Spicer, Feilding).

WHITE ELF - White flushed Pink at margin. Miniature, single. Slow, compact, upright growth. E-L. (Pitardii/Fraterna seedling x Japonica 'Fragrant Star'). (U.S. 1986 - Ackerman).

WHITE LIGHTENING - White with Faint Blush Pink on back of petals. Medium to large, formal double. Bushy growth. E-L. (Saluenensis x Japonica 'Hallelujah'). (U.S. - Piet and Gaeta, Arcadia, CA).

WHITE WISH - White. Very large, semidouble. Vigorous, upright growth. M-L. (Japonica 'Silver Chalice' x Granthamiana seedling). (U.S. 1986 - Piet and Gaeta).

WHITEOUT - White. Medium, anemone form with petals and petaloids mixed together. Average, spreading, open growth. E-M. Very light fragrance. (Japonica 'Tama-Ikari' x Hybrid 'Superscent'). (N.Z. 1999 - J. Finlay).

WIL'S WONDER - Lavender Pink. Medium, semidouble, flat flower with creped texture. Medium, upright narrow growth. M-L. (Sasanqua 'Paradise Belinda' x Hybrid 'Spring Festival' x Fraterna). (Aus. 2006 - Rhodoglen Nursery, Vic.).

WILBER FOSS - Brilliant Pinkish Red. Large, full peony form. Vigorous, upright growth. E-L. (Saluenensis x Japonica 'Beau Harp'). (N.Z. 1971 - Jury).

WILLIAM CARLYON - Pink. Medium, single. Spreading growth. (Japonica 'Jupiter' x Hybrid 'Donation'). (England 1972 - Carlyon).

WILLIAM'S LAVENDER - Lavender Pink. Medium, single. Vigorous, spreading, upright growth. M. (Saluenensis x Japonica). (U.S. 1950 - Fruitland).

WILLIAMSII ALBA - White. Medium, single to semidouble with fluted and twisted petals. Vigorous, compact, bushy growth. E-M. (Hybrid 'J. C. Williams' seedling). (U.S. 1960 - R. Carr, Tulare, CA).

WILLIAMSII SEMIDOUBLE - See 'Citation'.

WINTER GEM - Cherry Red. Medium, formal double. Vigorous, compact, upright growth. E-L. (Hybrid 'Margaret Waterhouse' seedling). (Aus. 1977 - Sebire).

WINTER ROUGE - Hot Pink. Medium, semidouble with rabbit ears. Vigorous, open, spreading growth. E-M. Fragrant. Cold hardy. (Oleifera x Sasanqua). (U.S. 1997 - T. Dodd Nsy., Semmes, AL).

WINTER'S BEAUTY - Shell Pink. Small, peony form. Average, dense, upright growth. E-M. Musky fragrance. Cold hardy to -15°F. (Japonica 'Billie McCaskill' x Oleifera). (U.S. 1995 - Ackerman).

WINTER'S BEAUTY CHARTREUSE - Pink. Small, semidouble. Average, upright, dense growth. E-M. Cold hardy. (Sport of Hybrid 'Winter's Beauty'). (U.S. - Camellia Forest, Chapel Hill, NC).

WINTER'S CHARM - Lavender Pink. Medium, full peony form. Average, upright growth. E. Cold hardy to -10°F. (Sasanqua x Oleifera). (U.S. 1987 - Ackerman).

WINTER'S CUPID - White flushed Pink near apex with large central cluster of Golden anthers. Unknown size, semidouble with curved and fluted petals. L. (Oleifera 'Plain Jane' x Oleifera 'Narumi-gata' x Hiemalis 'Shishi-Gashira'. (U.S. 2008 - Ackerman).

WINTER'S DANCER - Dark Pink shading to Light Pink at margins. Unknown size, semidouble to loose peony form. Slow, spreading growth. M. (Hiemalis 'Bill Wylam' x Oleifera 'Plain Jane'). (U.S. - Ackerman).

WINTER'S DARLING - Deep Cerise Pink. Miniature, anemone form. Average, spreading growth. E. Cold hardy to -10°F. (Hiemalis 'Shishi-Gashira' x Oleifera). (U.S. 1992 - Ackerman).

WINTER'S DREAM - Pink. Medium, semidouble. Average, compact, upright growth. E. Cold hardy. (Hiemalis 'Peach Puff' x Oleifera 'Plain Jane'). (U.S. 1988 - Ackerman).

WINTER'S FANCY - Deep Pink. Unknown size, semidouble with creped petals. M. (Hiemalis 'Bill Wylam' x Hiemalis 'Shishi-Gashira' x Oleifera 'Plane Jane'). (U.S. 2009 - Ackerman).

WINTER'S FILY - White. Small to medium, anemone form to formal double. Average, upright growth. E. (Sasanqua 'Mini-No- Yuki' x Oleifera). (U.S. 1990 - Ackerman).

WINTER'S FIRE - Bright Reddish Pink. Medium, semidouble. Average, upright growth. E. Cold hardy to -10°F. (Oleifera/Sasanqua x Vernalis). (U.S. 1992 - Ackerman).

WINTER'S FIRE VARIEGATED - Bright Reddish Pink with White spots and streaks. Medium, semidouble. Average, upright growth. E. (Oleifera/Sasanqua x Vernalis). (Discovered in 2005 on 'Winter's Fire' US National Arboretum). (U.S. 2013 - Ackerman).

WINTER'S HOPE - White. Medium, semidouble. Average, spreading growth. E. Cold hardy to - 10°F. (Oleifera x Hybrid 'Frost Princess'). (U.S. 1987 - Ackerman).

WINTER'S INTERLUDE - Pink. Miniature to small, anemone form. Average, dense, upright growth. E. Cold hardy to -15°F. (Oleifera seedling). (U.S. 1990 - Ackerman).

WINTER'S JOY - Pink. Medium, semidouble with fluted petals. Average, upright growth. E. Cold hardy to -10˚F. ({Oleifera 'Narumi-Gata' x Oleifera 'Plain Jane'). (U.S. 1997 - Ackerman).

WINTER'S MOONLIGHT - White. Unknown size, single to anemone form. Average, compact growth. M-L. Cold hardy to -15°F. (Japonica 'Tricolor Red [Siebold].' x. Oleifera 'Plain Jane'). (U.S. 2009 - Ackerman).

WINTER'S PEONY - Light Pink. Small, peony to rose form double. Average, upright, dense growth. E-M. Cold hardy to -5°F. (Oleifera 'Plain Jane' x Oleifera 'Narumi-Gata' x Hiemalis 'Shishi-Gashira'). (U.S. 1999 - Ackerman).

WINTER'S RED RIDER - Lavender Pink. Miniature to small, single. Very slow, upright, dense growth. E. Cold hardy to -10°F. (Hiemalis 'Shishi-Gashira' x Oleifera 'Lu Shan Snow'). (U.S. 2000 - Ackerman).

WINTER'S ROSE - Shell Pink. Miniature, formal double. Average, spreading growth. E. Cold hardy to -15°F. (Oleifera 'Plain Jane' x Hiemalis). (U.S. 1988 - Ackerman).

WINTER'S SNOWMAN - White. Small, semidouble to anemone form. Average, upright growth. E. Cold hardy to -10°F. (Sasanqua Oleifera x Hiemalis 'Shishi-Gashira' x Oleifera 'Plain Jane'). (U.S. 1997 - Ackerman).

WINTER'S STAR - Violet Pink. Large, single. Average, compact, upright growth. E. Cold hardy to -5°F. (Oleifera 'Lu Shan Snow' x Hiemalis 'Showa-no- Sakae'). (U.S. 1988 - Ackerman).

WINTER'S STAR II - Lower growing version of 'Winter's Star'. (U.S. 1997 - Bond Nsy., Dallas, TX).

WINTER'S STAR LIGHT - White to Blush Pink with some Light Pink flecks. Medium, single. Average, dense, upright growth. E-M. Cold hardy. (Hybrid 'Frost Prince' x Hiemalis). (U.S. 1997 - Bond Nsy., Dallas, TX).

WINTER'S SUNSET - Lavender Pink. Medium, single. Average, upright growth. E. Cold hardy to -5°F. (Oleifera ' Plain Jane' x Hybrid 'Frost Princess'). (U.S. 1998 - Ackerman).

WINTER'S TOUGHIE - Lavender Pink. Unknown size, semidouble with fluted petals. Slow to moderate growth, somewhat spreading. M. (Oleifera 'Plain Jane' x Sasanqua 'Jean May'). (U.S. 2009 - Ackerman).

WINTER'S WATERLILY - White. Small to medium, anemone form to formal double. Average, upright, somewhat spreading growth. E. (Sasanqua 'Mine-no-yuki' x Oleifera). (U.S. Ackerman).

WINTON - Carmine. Small, single. (Cuspidata x Saluenensis). (England 1950 - Williams).

WIRLINGA BELLE - Soft Pink. Medium, single. Average, open growth. E-M. (Rosaeflora x Williamsii seedlings). (Aus. 1973 - T. J. Savige, Wirlinga, NSW).

WIRLINGA BRIDE - White. Miniature, single with crepe petals. Vigorous, spreading growth. E-M. (Tsaii x Cuspidata x Fraterna). (Aus. 1992 - T. J. Savige, Wirlinga, NSW).

WIRLINGA CASCADE - Pink. Miniature, single. Vigorous, open, upright growth. M. (Hybrid 'Wirlinga Belle' seedling). (Aus. 1987 - T. J. Savige, Wirlinga, NSW).

WIRLINGA GEM - Pale Pink deepening to petal edge. Miniature, single. Spreading, pendulous growth. E. (Hybrid 'Tiny Princess' x Roseaflora). (Aus. 1981 - T. J. Savige, Wirlinga, NSW).

WIRLINGA JEWEL - Pink with lightly veined Deeper Pink petals. Miniature, rose form double to formal double. Average, open growth. E. (Hybrid 'Tiny Princess' seedling). (Aus. 1998 - T. J. Savige, Wirlinga, NSW).

WIRLINGA PLUM BLOSSOM - Light Pink. Miniature, single. Vigorous, upright, open growth. E-M. (Rosaeflora x Fraterna seedling). (Aus. 1999 - T. J. Savige, Wirlinga, NSW).

WIRLINGA PRINCESS - Pale Pink fading White at center with Deeper Pink under petals. Miniature, single to semidouble with crinkled petals. Average, open, spreading growth. M. (Hybrid 'Tiny Princess' x Rosaeflora). (Aus. 1977 - T. J. Savige, Wirlinga, NSW).

WIRLINGA ROSETTE - Soft Pink. Miniature, semidouble. Average, upright growth. M. (Hybrid 'Tiny Princess' seedling). (Aus. 1996 - T. J. Savige, Wirlinga, NSW).

WIRLINGA RUFFLES - Light Pink to Pink. Miniature, semidouble; petals ruffled with filament in a center cluster. Vigorous, open growth. E-M. (Hybrid 'Tiny Princess' seedling). (Aus. 1998 - T. J. Savige, Wirlinga, NSW).

WO-HE-LO - Rose Pink. Medium, rose form double. Average, upright growth. M. (Saluenensis hybrid). (U.S. 1975 - Kramer).

WYNNE RAYNER - Lavender Pink. Medium to large, semidouble to anemone form. Vigorous, open growth. M. (Saluenensis seedling). (N.Z. 1967 - B. J. Rayner, Stratford).

YESTERDAY - Bright Pink. Large, semidouble. Vigorous, upright growth. M-L. (Saluenensis x Japonica 'Tomorrow'). (England 1981 - Carlyon).

YOI MACHI - White margined Pink and occasionally marked Pink. Miniature, single. Average, compact, upright growth. E-M. (Oleifera 'Narumi-Gata' x Fraterna). (U.S. 1981 - Parks).

YUME (DREAM) - Pink blotched White (genetic variegation). Small, single. Average, loose upright growth. M-L. (Hiemalis 'Shishi-Gashira' x Yuhsienensis). (Japan.1992 - Kaoru Hagiya, Niigata).

YUMMY FRAGRANCE - Bright Red. Medium, peony form. Average, upright growth. E-L. Fragrant. Japonica 'Mrs. Bertha A. Harms' x (Hybrid 'Salab' seedling x Japonica 'Kramer's Supreme'). (N.Z. 1994 - J. Finlay).

YUPAN JINHUA - See 'Jinhua's Jade Tray'.

YVONNE MARIE - White. Very large, peony form. Slow, spreading growth. M-L. (Saluenensis x Japonica). (N.Z. 1984 - Mrs. J. E. Shaw, Wairua).

Species Edithae

DALU JIUQU (NINE BENDS IN MAINLAND) - Deep Pink. Small to medium, formal double. Vigorous spreading growth with brown calyx. L. (China 2007 - Gao, Jiyin, Fujian Province).

DALU JIUQU VARIEGATED - Deep Pink blotched White. Small to medium, formal double. Vigorous, spreading growth. L. (Virus variegated form of Edithae 'Dalu Jiuqu'). (U.S. 2019 - County Line Nursery - Tommy Alden, Byron, GA).

HEIMUDAN (DARK PEONY) - Crimson to Purplish crimson. Medium, peony form with 4 to 5 outer rows, irregularly imbricated with brown calyx. M. (China 1989 - Gao and Zhuang, Fujian Province).

Species Granthamiana

PINK GRANTHAMIANA - Pink with Yellow Anthers and Yellow Filaments. Large, single. (Granthamiana style bloom). (U.S.1993 - Steve Campbell, CA).

Species Hiemalis

Origin unknown. There is evidence that this may not be a separate species but rather a Non-Reticulata hybrid with Japonica and Sasanqua parentage.

APHRODITE - White, edged Magenta Pink often with Peach-Pink bud center. Medium, rose form double; petals are wavy and ruffled edged.

AUTUMN GOLD - Rose Red shading to Darker Red on margins. Small, semidouble to peony form.

BENI-KAN-TSUBAKI - See 'Shishi-Gashira'.

BILL WYLAM - Deep Rose. Medium, semidouble with fluted petals.

BONSAI BABY - Deep Red. Small, rose form double to formal double.

BORDERLINE BEAUTY - White with Magenta-Pink, narrow Picotee border and wavy petals. Medium, peony form.

CHANSONETTE - Brilliant Pink. Medium, formal double with ruffled petals. (Hiemalis 'Shishi-Gashira' seedling). (Ralph S. Peer Sasanqua seedling Award of American Camellia Society - First Award Season-1959).

CHIRI-TSUBAKI - ('Pink Shishi-Gashira'). Light Pink. Small, semidouble to rose form double.

CHRISTMAS CANDLES - Bright Red. Medium, semidouble.

DAZZLER - Rose Red. Medium, semidouble.

ELFIN ROSE - Rose Pink. Small, rose form double.

FROSTED PINK - Blush Pink with frosted cast on petals. Medium, formal double. Upright spreading growth. E-M. (U.S. 2000 - A. Landry, Baton Rouge, LA).

FUJI-NO-YUKI - White, Blush on tips when beginning to bloom with Yellow anthers and Cream filaments. Large, semidouble. E. (Japan 1957 - Matasaburô Tsuda, Kumamoto Prefecture).

GIGANTEA - Red. Medium, single.

GREEN'S BLUES - Violet Purple, aging to Blue; the unique color is not dependent on cold weather. Miniature to small, rose form double. (U.S. 2004 - Bobby Green, Green Nurseries, Fairhope, AL).

HIRYÛ (AUSTRALIAN) - See 'Kanjiro'.

INTERLUDE - Light Pink. Small, rose form double to formal double.

KANJIRO - ('Hiryû [Australia']). Rose Pink shading to Rose Red on edges of petals. Small to medium, semidouble.

KAN-TSUBAKI - Crimson Pink. Small, semidouble.

KARA-GOROMO - Deep Pink. Small, semidouble.

KELLY McKNIGHT - Brilliant Red. Small, rose form double.

KIRA-SHIRO-KANTSUBAKI - White. Small, semidouble. E. (Japan 1960's - Kira Firm, Nishio City, Chiba Prefecture).

MARY JENNIFER - Pale Pink to Pink with darker margin. Medium, semidouble.

MEOTO-ZAKI - Pink touched and edged White. Small, semidouble with curled petals, producing two flowers from each bud.

MINUET - Light Pink. Small, semidouble to peony form with large petals.

MIRANDY - Rose Pink shaded with a frosty White. Small, semidouble with fluted petals.

NOELA'S PICK - Bright Pink. Medium, semidouble.

PARADISE BEVERLY - Deep Pink. Miniature, rose form double.

PARADISE CAROLINE - Deep Pink. Small, rose form double.

PARADISE JILL - White. Miniature, rose form double.

PARADISE SANDRA - Deep Pink. Medium, single.

PEACH PUFF - Soft Pink, center petaloids have Peach cast. Small, anemone form. (Hiemalis 'Showa-no-Sakae' seedling).

PEERLESS - Bright Rose Pink. Small, loose peony form.

PINK GODDESS - Pink. Very large, single cup-shaped. (U.S. - Parks).

PINK SHISHI-GASHIRA - See 'Chiri-tsubaki'.

PINK SHOWER - Light Pink. Medium, semidouble with petals shirred at edges and notched and flared stamens.

PRETTY PATSY - Light Purple, deepening at edge of petals. Miniature, semidouble form.

PURPLE HAZE - Purple (in acid soil). Small, rose form double. Slow, bushy, conical growth. E-M. (Hiemalis 'Reverend Ida' seedling). (U.S. 2012 - Bobby Green, Green Nurseries, Fairhope, AL).

REVEREND IDA - Ruby Red. Small, semidouble to rose form double. Average, low, dense, spreading growth. E-L. (Hiemalis 'Shishi-Gashira' seedling). (U.S. 1992 - Tom Dodd Nsy., Semmes, AL).

ROSE ANN - Deep Rose fading as bloom ages. Small, semidouble.

ROSE OF AUTUMN - Glowing Rose Pink. Medium, rose form double opening to many petaled semidouble.

SANDAN - Deep Pink. Unknown size, rose form double.

SANDAN-ZAKI - Rose. Small, semidouble with three flowers sometimes being produced from a single bud.

SEIKAIHA (QUIET OCEAN WAVES) - Rose-Pink. Medium, formal double to rose form double. E-M. (Japan - Kumamoto Prefecture).

SHIKISHIMA (POETIC NAME FOR JAPAN) - Medium Pink with Yellow anthers and Yellow filaments. Medium, semidouble. Dense growth. E-M. (Japan - Shishido, Yajirô, Kumamoto Prefecture).

SHISHI-GASHIRA - ('Beni-Kan-Tsubaki'; 'Shishigashira'). Red. Small, semidouble to rose form double.

SHOWA SUPREME - Soft Pink. Medium, peony form.

SHOWA-NO-SAKAE - ('Usubeni'). Soft Pink, occasionally marbled White. Small to medium, semidouble to rose form double. Cold hardy.

SOMERSET - Deep Pink with Silver cast. Medium, semidouble.

SPARKLING BURGUNDY - Ruby Rose overlaid with sheen of Lavender. Small to medium, peony form with intermingled stamens and petaloids.

SPARKLING BURGUNDY BLUSH - Light Blush Pink with Yellow anthers. Small to medium, semidouble; the bloom consists of 39 petals. Vigorous, upright, compact growth. E. (Sport of Hiemalis 'Sparkling Burgundy'). (U.S. 2019 - Camellia Heaven - John Grimm, Bush, LA).

STAN JONES - Pale Pink edged Deep Rose Pink. Medium, semidouble.

TU-TU - Orchid Pink. Medium, semidouble with tufted petals in center. Upright growth. E-M. (U.S. 1982 - Mrs. T. K. McKnight, Baton Rouge, LA).

USUBENI - See 'Showa-No-Sakae'.

WILD HEART - Pale Lavender outer petals with Light Lavender heart shading to Darker Purplish Pink center with Yellow anthers and Yellow filaments. Small to medium, semidouble. Vigorous, upright, dense growth. E-M. (Color sport of Hiemalis 'Kanjiro'). (U.S. 2016 - Glenn Read, Lucedale, MS).

WILLIAM LANIER HUNT - Dark Orchid Pink. Medium, peony form. M. (U.S. 1986 - Parks).

WINSOME - White edged Pink. Medium, semidouble to anemone form. Vigorous, bushy, spreading growth. M. (Hiemalis 'Shishi-Gashira' x Vernalis 'Tovre'). (U.S. 1955 - McCaskill).

Species Oleifera

COVINGTON - Deeper colored and twisted petaled. (Sport of Oleifera 'Narumi-gata').

JAUNE - White with large center of Yellow petaloids and a few stamens of Darker Yellow. Small, anemone form. (China to France, 1850 - Fortune's Yellow Camellia).

LU SHAN SNOW - White. Medium, single. E. Musky fragrance. Cold hardy. (U.S. 1995 - Ackerman).

NARUMI-GATA - White shaded Pink. Medium to large, single of cupped form.

PLAIN JANE - White. Small to medium, single form. Slow, dense, upright growth. E. Very cold hardy. (U.S. 2002 - Ackerman).

RISH PLANT - White. Small, single.

WILD FORM - White. Small, single.

Species Rusticana (Snow Camellia)

ABE - Rose Pink slight streaked White. Medium, rose form double.
AGA - Pinkish White. Medium, single to semidouble of magnolia form.
AI-AI-GASA - Red. Medium, peony form.
AI-NO-IZUMI - Light Pink. Small, formal double.
AMA-NO-GAWA (THE MILKY WAY) - Red with Yellow anthers. Small, loose peony. M. (Japan 1986).
ARAISO - Red. Medium, peony form.
AWA-YUKI - White. Medium, semidouble.

BANSHO - Rose Pink. Medium, rose form double.
BENI-KAGAMI - Crimson. Medium, peony form.
BENI-MARU - Deep Red. Medium, rose form double.
BENI-MAZE - Crimson. Large, peony form.
BONONRI - Pink. Medium, rose form double.
BOTAN-YUKI - Blush Pink with Yellow petaloid center. Miniature, anemone form.

FUKURIN-KKYU - White or Pale Pink, shaded Deeper Pink with a White border, or Red in various degrees up to Solid Red with Yellow anthers and White filaments. Miniature, semidouble with foliage bordered light Green. L. (Sport of Rusticana 'Komomiji'). (Japan - Kantô area to U.S. 1930 - Star Nursery, Sierra Madre, CA).

HAMON - Pink. Medium, rose form double.
HANAMI GASA - White heavily striped Rose Red. Medium to large, rose form double. Vigorous, bushy, upright growth. M-L.
HATANO - Deep Red. Medium, rose form double.
HIMATSURI - Rose Red blotched White. Miniature, loose anemone form.
HIMEGOTO - White. Medium, rose form double.
HIME-SHIRA-YUKI - White. Miniature, semidouble.

HIRAIZUMI - Red. Medium, peony form.
HONEN - Rose Pink. Medium, peony form.
HOSHI-SEKAI - Pink. Unknown size, single with variegated foliage.

ICHIRAKU - White. Miniature, bell shaped single.
IRORI-BI - Deep Red. Medium, peony form.
ITSUKAMACHI - Red. Miniature to small, semidouble.
ITSUKAMACHI VARIEGATED - Red and White variation of ' Itsukamachi'.
IZUME - Coral Pink. Medium, semidouble. Bushy, round growth. M-L.

JAKKO - White. Medium, semidouble to rose form double.

KANKO - Pink. Unknown size, single with variegated foliage.
KANOSE - Soft Pink. Large, semidouble to rose form double.
KAO-MAJIMA - Red. Miniature, rose form double.
KASUGA-YAMA - Red blotched White. Small, irregular semidouble.
KAZA HANA - White with spaced crinkled petals. Small, single. Medium, compact, upright growth. M-L.
KAZA-HANI - White. Medium, single.
KIN-SEKAI - Pink. Unknown size, single with variegated foliage.
KOSHIJI - Red. Medium, single to semidouble.
KOSHI-NO-FUBUKI (BLIZZARD OF NIIGATA) - Red. Small, tubular to campanulate single. (Mutation of a wild C. japonica var. rusticana). (Japan 1956 - Niigata Prefecture).
KOSHI-NO-OTOME - Red. Medium, rose form double.
KOTO-HAJIME - White. Miniature, anemone form.

MANGETSU - Pink. Unknown size, single with variegated foliage.
MIDARE-GAMI - Crimson. Medium, peony form.
MIZU-YOSHI - White. Small, rose form double.

NISHIKI KIRIN - Pink striped Red. Small, rose form double. Very showy, compact, shrubby, upright growth. M-L.

OSAKI - Light Pink to White. Medium, semidouble.

RAKU-JITSU - Purplish Rose Pink. Large, rose form double.
RANBU - Crimson. Medium, peony form.
REIGYOKU (BEAUTIFUL JEWEL) - Light Red with a central burst of Golden anthers and Yellow filaments. Small to medium, single of five petals of irregular length. Compact growth; glossy Green foliage with blotch of Light Yellow in center at maturity. M. (Japan to U.S. 1975).
REIZANHO (BEAUTIFUL MOUNTAIN RIDGE) - Red with Yellow anthers and Creamy filaments. Medium to small, single. (Japan 1957 - Niigata Prefecture).

SEISO - Pink to Light Pink. Medium, anemone form to peony form.
SHIMA-CHIDORI - Red spotted White. Miniature, rose form double.
SHIRO KARAKO - White. Miniature to small, anemone form. Vigorous, spreading growth. M.
SHOOTING STAR - White. Medium, semidouble.

TAIYÔ (THE SUN) - Claret Rose with Yellow anthers and Creamy filaments. Small, single. Slow, upright growth; bloom has broad, overlapping petals, emarginate and slightly creped, with a compact stamen column; this snow Camellia cultivar has Light Yellow variegation along the midrib and the major veins of the Dark Green, glossy leaves. M-L. (Japan 1966 - Niigata Prefecture).
TASHIRO - White. Medium, rose form double.
TOKAMACHI - Purplish Pink. Medium, single to semidouble.
TOTENKO - Red. Medium, peony form.
TSUGAWA - Pink fading to White at edges. Small, rose form double.
TSUKI-SEKAI - Pink. Unknown size, single with variegated foliage.
TSUZUMI-OKA - Crimson. Large, rose form double.

YAMAYA - Pink tinted Purple. Medium, single.
YOSHIDA - Red. Large, single.
YUKI OGUNI - Light Coral Pink. Small, semidouble to loose peony form. Somewhat slow, compact, spreading growth. E-M.
YUKI-FUJIN - Light Pink. Miniature, single.
YUKI-GESHIKI - Blush Pink with Creamy petaloids. Small to medium, anemone to peony form.
YUKI-KOMACHI - Light Pink. Miniature, peony.
YUKI-SHIRO - White. Medium, single.
YUMEJI - Pink. Large, peony form.

Species Saluenensis

ALBA SIMPLEX - White. Small, single.
APPLE BLOSSOM - Pink and White. Small, single.

DOGROSE - Pale Rose. Small, single. M-L.

HAYDON'S COMPACT - Light Pink petals Whitening toward the base. Miniature, single form. Vigorous, dense, spreading and low growth; genetic dwarf form.

MACROPHYLLA - Dainty Pale Rose. Small, single of bell form. L.

ROSE BOWL - Rose Pink. Small, single with crinkled petals.

Species Sasanqua

AGLAIA - Pink shading to a darker almost Wine-colored center. Medium to large, peony. Vigorous spreading growth. (U.S. 1995 - Bobby Green, Green Nurseries, Fairhope, AL).
AGNES MORRIS - Light Pink. Small, rose form double.

AGNES O. SOLOMON - Light Pink. Small to medium, loose semidouble to peony form. Cold hardy. (U.S. 1953 - Orton Plantation, Winnabow, NC).

ALABAMA BEAUTY - Red. Small, loose peony form. Vigorous, full upright growth. E. (U.S. - Tom Dodd Nursery, Semmes, Alabama).

ALBERT RAYMOND - Deep Pink toned Purple on the edges. Medium, semidouble. Upright, spreading growth. (Aus. 2006 - Albert Raymond and Gwenda Norris, Qld.).

ALBINO - White. Miniature, formal double.

ALICE C - Pink. Large, single.

ALISON SPRAGG - Rose Pink. Medium, semidouble to peony form.

ANGEL'S KISS - Pink. Medium, peony. Rapid, upright growth. E. (U.S. 2008 - Camellia Forest, Chapel Hill, NC).

APPLE BLOSSOM (COOLIDGE) - White Blushed Pink. Unknown size, single.

ARTEL - Deep Red. Medium, semidouble.

ASAHI-GAI - White in center to Pink on outside. Small, single.

ASAKURA - White shaded Pink. Medium, semidouble.

AUNT ALMA - Pink. Small, peony form.

AUTUMN CARNIVAL - White with small Pink radial stripes with Yellow anthers and Yellow filaments. Small, single. Slow, upright growth. E. (Sasanqua 'Twilight Glow' seedling). (U.S. 2014 - Camellia Forest, Chapel Hill, NC).

AUTUMN DAWN - White with edges toned Deeper Pink. Medium, loose peony.

AUTUMN DELIGHT - White with Blush Pink at edge. Medium, rose form double.

AUTUMN MOON - White. Medium, single with very thick petals.

AUTUMN ROCKET - White. Medium, anemone to rose form double.

AUTUMN SENTINEL - Pink. Miniature, peony to rose form double.

AUTUMN SUN - Rose Red. Unknown size, semidouble. Upright, very compact dense growth. E-M. (U.S. - Parks).

AUTUMN SUNRISE - White with a Red tip on each petal. Large, single - cup-shaped. Vigorous, dense and upright growth. (U.S. - Parks).

AUTUMN SURPRISE - Delicate Pink. Miniature, semidouble to peony form. Average, upright growth. E. (U.S. 1965 - A. Rester, Bogalusa, LA).

AVERY WARRINER - Medium Pink fading to Light Pink at the petal edges with Yellow anthers and Yellow filaments. Small, semidouble. Vigorous, upright growth. E-M. (U.S. 2018 - Tom Warriner, Birmingham, AL).

AVRIL CARR - White. Medium, semidouble.

AWAKE - Rosy Pink, sometimes shading lighter toward center. Medium, semidouble.

BE MY CHERIE - Deep Red merging into White at base with White based Red petaloids. Medium, anemone form.

BEATRICE EMILY - Violet Red with White petaloid center. Medium, anemone form.

BENI-ZURU (PINK CRANE) - Deep Rose Pink. Small, single with twisted petals.

BERT JONES - Silver Pink. Medium to large, semidouble.

BETH LENNARD - Phlox Pink petaloids with Fuchsia Purple outer petals. Medium, rose form double.

BETSY BAKER - Light Silver Pink. Medium, rose form double with ruffled petals.

BETTIE PATRICIA - Persian Rose. Medium, rose form double.

BETTYE JO - White. Medium, formal double with petals cleft and slightly incurved petals.

BEWITCHED - Rose Pink. Small, semidouble.

BONANZA - Deep Red. Medium, semi-peony form.

BOOM-A-LOOM - Pale Pink border shading into White. Medium, semidouble with upright petals.

BROOKSIE ANDERSON - Light Orchid Pink. Miniature, rose form double.

BUBBLE GUM - Deep Pink with Yellow anthers and White filaments. Medium, semidouble. Average, upright growth. M. (U.S. 2019 - Gordy).

BUTLER'S BEAUTY - Pink to Lavender Pink, darker at edges. Miniature to small, semidouble to rose form double. Vigorous, upright growth. (U.S. 2003 - Robert W. Butler, Hilton Head Island, SC).

CALLIOPE - White edged and suffused Pink. Miniature, loose peony to rose form double.

CAMILLIA BEASLEY - Pink with sheen. Medium to large, semidouble.

CANDY REITER - Shell Pink. Unknown size, single.

CAROLYN ANDERTON - White flushed Pink. Medium, semidouble. Fragrant.

CAVALIER'S LADY - Lavender Pink. Medium, rose form double.

CECILIA - White with Rose Pink tinges around petal's edges. Large, rose form double. Vigorous, upright growth. E.

CHEOPS - Pale Lavender Rose Pink. Medium, peony form to formal double.

CHERIE - Pale Pink. Unknown size, semidouble to rose form double.

CHERILYN - Light Pink. Medium, peony form.

CHOJI GURUMA - Light Pink turning deeper toward edge of petals and petaloids. Miniature, anemone form.

CLEOPATRA - Rose Pink. Medium, semidouble. Cold hardy.

CLEOPATRA WHITE - White. Medium, semidouble.

CLEOPATRA'S BLUSH - Blush Pink. Small, unknown form. (Sport of Sasanqua 'Cleopatra').

COCOANUT ICE - Pink striped White. Medium, single.

COLLEEN - Pink. Unknown size, single.

COOL BREEZE - White with Yellow anthers and Cream filaments. Medium, rose form double. Vigorous, upright, dense growth. E-M. (U.S. 2016 - Glenn Read, Lucedale, MS).

COOLGARDIE STAR - White. Miniature, anemone form to rose form double. Fragrant.

COTTON CANDY - ('Hyman's Semidouble Pink'). Clear Pink. Medium, semidouble with ruffled petals.

CREEK - White. Medium, single.

CRIMSON KING - Mahogany Red. Small, single.

CRIMSON TIDE - Red. Small, semidouble with ruffled petals.

DAYDAWN BELLE - Pink. Miniature, semidouble to rose form double.

DAYDREAM - White edged Deep Rose Pink. Medium, single.

DAYDREAM BELIEVER - Pure White. Medium, single. Fast, upright growth. E. Fragrant. (U.S. 2000 - Bobby Green, Green Nurseries, Fairhope, AL).

DOUBLE RAINBOW - White bordered Rose Red. Small to medium, semidouble.

DWARF ROSE - Light Pink. Small, rose form double.

DWARF SHISHI - Bright Red. Miniature, semidouble.

DWARF SHISHI WHITE - White. Miniature, semidouble.

EARLY PEARLY - White with Blush center petals. Small, rose form double.

EDNA BUTLER - Silver Pink. Medium, semidouble with crinkled petals.

ELFIN - Pink. Small, formal double.

ELSIE BRINSLEY - Soft Rose Pink. Medium, semidouble.

EMMA PEEBLES - Light Pink fading to delicate Pink. Medium, semidouble.

ENISHI - Pink. Miniature to small, rose form double.

EXQUISITE - Pale Pink. Medium, single.

FAIRY QUEEN (McCASKILL) - Light Pink. Medium, single.

FALLING STAR - Creamy White with an occasional brush of palest Pink on petal edges. Miniature, single form.

FASHION NOTE - Cream with Rose Pink border. Medium, single with occasional upright petals.

FASHION PLATE - White edged Pink to Dark Pink. Medium, single.

FAY CHARLES - Light Rose Pink. Medium, semidouble with broad petals.

FEATHERED EDGE - White to Blush gradually darkening toward the edge and having feathered streaks radiating toward the center. Medium, semidouble to loose peony. Compact, rounded growth. (U.S. 2005 - Bobby Green, Green Nurseries, Fairhope, AL).

FENYU (SHANGHAI) - White center with Pink edge with Yellow anthers and Light Yellow filaments. Small to medium, semidouble. Average, dense growth. E. (Hiemalis 'Shishi-Gashira' x Sasanqua 'Shinonome'). (China 2009 - Jian Guo Fei, Yong- hong Hu and Ya-li Zhang, Shanghai Botanical Garden of Shanghai, China).

FLORA STOUT - Rose Pink veined Lighter Pink. Medium, semidouble.

FLORITA - White with Pink on outer petals. Medium, anemone form.

FLUTED WHITE - See 'Setsugekka'.

FRAGRANT SWEET - White. Medium, single. Fragrant.

FRANK PERSONS - White. Medium, peony form.

FRENCH VANILLA - Creamy White. Large, single.

FREYDA - Light Rose Pink with some petaloids showing White. Medium, rose form double with some outside notched petals.

FRILLED WHITE - White. Medium, semidouble with frilled petals.

FROSTY - White. Medium, semidouble with irregular petals.

FUJI-NO-MINE - White. Medium, rose form double.

FUKUZUTSUMI - White shaded Rose Pink. Medium, single to semidouble.

GAY - White. Medium, single.

GAY SUE - White with Cream anthers. Medium, semidouble with frilled petals.

GEOFFREY JAMES - Light Pink. Miniature, anemone form.

GERDA'S GEM - Light Pink. Medium, semidouble.

GIN-NO-ZAI (SILVER BATON) - White edged Lavender with splayed Yellow anthers and Yellow filaments. Medium, single. E. (Japan 1789 - Kansai District).

GLENORIE - Deep Red. Small to medium, semidouble.

GOLDEN PHOENIX - White with Dark Pink edges. Unknown size, single. (U.S. - Camellia Forest Nursery, Chapel Hill, NC).

GOSSAMER WINGS - Light Pink. Small, single.

GRANDIFLORA - Pink with Yellow anthers and Yellow filaments. Large, single. Vigorous growth. (U.S. 1963 - Tingel Nursery, MD).

GREG BAKER - Dark Pink with Yellow anthers and Yellow filaments. Large, semidouble; the bloom has rabbit ears. Vigorous, upright, dense growth. E. (U.S. 2016 - Jay Ellis, Keystone Heights, FL).

GULF BREEZE - Phlox Pink to Carmine Rose. Large, single. Average, upright, dense growth, E. (U.S. 1956 - Overlook).

GWEN PIKE - Shell Pink. Small, semidouble.

GWENDA - Pale Pink with Lavender tones. Medium, loose cup-shaped peony. Medium, upright growth. M-L. (Aus. 2006 - Albert Raymond and Gwenda Norris Qld.).

HANA-DAIJIN (MINISTER OF FLOWER) - ('Hana-Otodo'). Deep Rose Pink. Medium, semidouble.

HANA-JIMAN - White edged Pink. Medium, semidouble. Cold hardy.

HANA-NANA - White bordered with intense Deep Pink. Unknown size, single. Compact growth. (Sasanqua 'Hana-Jiman' seedling). (U.S. 1996 - Bobby Green, Green Nurseries, Fairhope, AL).

HANA-NO-YUKI (SNOW ON FLOWER) - Pink flushed White. Medium, semidouble.

HARKARA-MIKAWA - See 'Mikawa-No-Tsu'.

HARRIETTE RUSTER - White tipped Pink. Medium, anemone form. Medium, spreading average density growth. E-L. (U.S. 1959 - Marvin Ruster, Pasadena, CA).

HEBE - See 'Hugh Evans'.

HINODE-GUMO - White shaded Pink. Medium, single with fluted petals.

HINODE-NO-UMI - Deep Crimson. Small, single of flat form.

HOBBS' CHOICE - Pale to Light Pink. Medium to large, single.

HOT FLASH - Red with Gold anthers and Creamy filaments. Small, semidouble. Vigorous, low, spreading growth. E.

HUGH EVANS - ('Hebe'). Pink. Small, single.

HUGH EVANS BLUSH - Very Light Blush Pink, almost White. Medium, single. Upright, somewhat lacy growth; profuse bloomer. (Sport of Sasanqua 'Hugh Evans').

HYMAN'S SEMIDOUBLE PINK - See 'Cotton Candy'.

IZMA - White with Pink on reverse side. Medium, semidouble.

JAMES HOWIESON - Deep Red. Small, rose form double with notched petals.

JANE MORGAN - White with Rose Pink edged petals. Medium, semidouble.

JANNALI - White with occasional Pink on outside of petals. Medium, single with crinkled petals.

JANOME-GASA - Deep Pink bordered Pink and striped White with White under petals. Medium, semidouble.

JARICK'S SURPRISE - Light Pink to Pink. Medium, loose peony form to rose form double. (Previously listed incorrectly as 'Jack's Surprise').

JEAN MAY - Shell Pink. Medium, rose form double. Cold hardy.

JEAN NEWMAN - White at center darkening to Red Purple at edges. Small, rose form double with notched petals.

JEANNIE GWYNNE - Carmine Pink. Medium, single to anemone form.

JENNIFER SUSAN - Pale Pink. Medium, rose form double with curled petals.

JEWEL BOX - White edged Light Pink. Small, single.

JILL PILL - White tinted Coral to Orchid Pink on tips of petals. Medium, semidouble to peony form.

JITSU-GETSU (SUN & MOON) - Red flowers and White ones, according to shoot. Small, single. E. (Sport of Japonica 'Higo-kyô-nishiki'). (Japan).

JOYFUL KNIGHT - Deep Red. Small, anemone form.

JUIL - Soft Mauve Pink to delicate Pink. Medium, semidouble with occasional petaloids.

JULIE ANNE - Deep Rosy Red with Silver streak down each petal. Medium, peony form.

JURY'S JOY - Creamy White at base deepening to soft Pink at edge. Medium, semidouble to peony form.

JUSTRITE - Intense Carmine Red with Golden anthers and Golden filaments. Medium, semidouble with creped and fluted petals with a large flair of stamens. Vigorous, upright, dense growth. M-L. (U.S. 2016 - Glenn Read, Lucedale, MS).

KAIDO-MARU - White flushed Pink, darker toward edges. Medium, semidouble with curled petals.

KAWAE - White bordered Red. Small, single.

KELLY'S EYE - Red shading to Deep Maroon Red on outer edges. Miniature, anemone form to rose form double.

KELSEY BEASLEY - Red. Medium to large, semidouble with crinkled petals.

KENKYÔ - White with a Pink cast with Golden anthers and Yellow filaments. Medium, single - inner petals curved. E. (Japan 1898).

KIRSTY ANNE - Pink Blushed White. Large, single.

KOGYOKU - See 'Ko-gyoku'.

KO-GYOKU - ('Little Gem'; 'Kogyoku'). Pink bud opening Pinkish White. Small, rose form double.

LAURA CLAIRE - Soft Pink fading to Cream Medium, formal double with incurved petals. (U.S. 2006 - Gordy).

LESLIE ANN - White tipped Reddish Lavender. Small, semidouble with irregular petals to peony form.

LIL ROSE - Brilliant Rose Red, Small, rose form double to semidouble. Average, spreading growth. M. (U.S. 2015 - Nuccio's).

LISA - Deep Pink. Small, semidouble to loose formal double. Vigorous, compact growth. E.

LITTLE GEM - See 'Ko-Gyoku'.

LITTLE PEARL - Pink buds opening pure White. Small, irregular semidouble.

LUCINDA - Pink. Medium, peony form.

LU-LU - Pink fading to Blush. Large, semidouble to peony form with loose petals.

MAIDEN'S BLUSH - Blush Pink with golden anthers and light yellow filaments. Small, single with 5 fluted petals, spreading, slender stamens. (Japan to U.S. 1909 - Sawada Overlook Nursery, Crichton, AL).

MARGUERITE BULLARD - Peony Pink. Medium, peony form.

MARIE KIRK - White with Yellow anthers and White filaments. Small, rose form double to formal double with heart-shaped petals. Vigorous, upright growth. E. (U.S. 2000 - Arthur A Kirk, Portsmouth, VA).

MARIE STEINER - Rich Pink with narrow Dark Pink edge. Miniature to small, peony form.

MARIE YOUNG - Pink. Unknown size, single to peony form with loose petals.

MARILYN DIVE - Fuchsine Pink. Medium, semidouble.

MARINA MIST - Blush buds, opening White. Medium, single form.

MARINA PEARL - White with Blush Pink edges, center and buds. Miniature, formal double form. Vigorous, open growth.

MARJORIE HOBBS - White shading to Pale Pink. Small, formal double with notched and folded petals.

MARMION - Light Pink. Medium, semidouble with wavy petals.

MARY AUSTIN - Light Pink to Pink with Lavender traces with Golden stamens. Medium, semidouble with wavy petals, occasional petaloids and short, tightly grouped.

McILHENNY'S DOUBLE WHITE - White. Medium, rose form double with incurved petals.

MERRY EDNA - Shaded Pink. Medium, single.

MIDNIGHT LOVER - Deep Burgundy Red. Small, single.

MIDNIGHT RUBY - Dark Purple Red. Miniature, rose form double to formal double.

MIGNONNE - Light Pink. Small, formal double.

MIKAWA-NO-TSU - ('Sanga-No-Tsu'; 'Harkara-Mikawa'). Crimson shaded White on petals and petaloid stamens. Small, anemone form.

MIMSIE - Pink. Small, single to semidouble.

MIN PIN - Deep Red. Miniature, anemone form.

MINE-NO-YUKI - ('Snow'; 'White Doves'). White. Small, semidouble to loose peony form.

MININA - Light Pink. Small, single.

MISS ED - Light Pink with Lavender and Deeper Pink tints. Miniature to small, peony form with wavy and notched petals.

MISS PENDERLEA - White Coral margined Pink. Medium, semidouble with ruffled petals.

MISTY MOON - Light Lavender Pink. Medium to large, irregular semidouble.

MOIRE - Rose Pink. Small, single with broad, crepe petals.

MOMOZONO (PEACH GARDEN) - Shell Pink. Small, single.

MOMOZONO-NISHIKI - Rose shaded White. Medium, semidouble with curled petals.

MONDEL - Dark Pink at center quickly shading to a Lighter Pink with Yellow anthers and Yellow filaments. Small to medium, single with seven petals. Vigorous, upright growth. M-L. Fragrant. (Sport of Vernalis 'Yuletide'). (U.S. 2011 - Monrovia Nurseries, Azusa, CA).

MOON MOTH - White. Medium, single.

MOTHERS DAY - White with a slightly uneven edging of Pink with Yellow filaments with Yellow anthers. Medium, single. (Sport of Sasanqua 'Plantation Pink').

MYKEN - White. Medium, single.

NAN WOOD - Bright Rose. Medium, semidouble.

NANETTE - Brilliant Deep Pink. Medium, rose form double.

NARUMIGATA (NARUMI BAY) - White with delicate Magenta-Pink margins with Yellow anthers and Light Yellow filaments. Small to medium, single - cup shaped. Vigorous, spreading growth. E. (Japan - Ashizawa, Kantô district).

NAVAJO - Rose Red fading to White in center. Medium, semidouble.

NICKA - Deep Rose Pink. Medium, semidouble to peony form with stamens intermixed with large petals and petaloids.

NO DOUBT - Rich Crimson Rose Red with Golden anthers and Golden filaments. Medium, loose peony to semidouble. Vigorous, upright, dense growth. E-M. (U.S. 2016 - Glenn Read, Lucedale, MS).

NODAMI-USHIRO - Rose Pink. Medium to large, single.

NORA - Rose Pink with Pink tipped Yellow stamens. Medium, semidouble.

NORTHERN EXPOSURE - White with Golden anthers. Medium, single. Upright growth. E.

NORTHERN LIGHTS - White with Pink edges. Large, single.

OCEAN SPRINGS - White with wide Red border. Small, single.

OCTOBER MAGIC BRIDE - ('Green 99-096'). White. Small to medium, loose peony. Dense, semi-dwarf conical growth. (U.S. 1999 - Bobby Green, Green Nurseries, Fairhope, AL).

OCTOBER MAGIC CARPET - ('Green 01-006'). Bright Pink with Yellow anthers and Yellow filaments. Medium, semidouble with ruffled petals. Average, dense, spreading, low growth, M. (U.S. 2001 - Bobby Green, Green Nurseries, Fairhope, AL).

OCTOBER MAGIC DAWN - ('Green 99-012'). Soft Peach Pink. Medium to large, rose form double to peony form. Dense, conical to pyramidal growth. L. (U.S. 1999 - Bobby Green, Green Nurseries, Fairhope, AL).

OCTOBER MAGIC INSPIRATION - ('Green 97-039'). White with Pinkish-Violet edges. Medium, peony form. (Sasanqua 'Mine-no-yuki' seedling). (U.S. 1997- Bobby Green, Green Nurseries, Fairhope, AL).

OCTOBER MAGIC IVORY - ('Green 99-016'). White. Medium, semidouble to loose peony form with ruffled petals. Vigorous, bushy, upright growth. M. (Sasanqua 'Mine-No-Yuki' seedling). (U.S. 1999 - Bobby Green, Green Nurseries, Fairhope, AL).

OCTOBER MAGIC ORCHID - (Green 94-035'). Varying tones of White and orchid Pink. Small to medium, semidouble. Dense, semi-dwarf growth. E-L. (U.S. 2000 - Bobby Green, Green Nurseries, Fairhope, AL).

OCTOBER MAGIC PINK PERPLEXION - ('Green 01-006'). Soft Pink. Medium, rose form double. Average, bushy, spreading, rounded growth. M. (U.S. 2001 - Bobby Green, Green Nurseries, Fairhope, AL).

OCTOBER MAGIC ROSE - ('Green 98-009'). Coral Red. Small, peony form. Columnar growth. (U.S. 1999 - Bobby Green, Green Nurseries, Fairhope, AL).

OCTOBER MAGIC RUBY - ('Green 02-003'). Red. Small to medium, peony form. Dense, semi-dwarf growth. E-L. (U.S. 2002 - Bobby Green, Green Nurseries, Fairhope, AL).

OCTOBER MAGIC SNOW - ('Green 94-010'). White, often edged in Pink and a Pink cast appearing in the center. Medium, peony form; medium rounded form. (Sasanqua 'Mine-no-yuki' seedling). (U.S. 1994 - Bobby Green, Green Nurseries, Fairhope, AL).

OKKE'S DELIGHT - Pink. Small, anemone form.

OLD FAITHFUL - Deep Pink to Pale Mauve Pink. Medium, semidouble to loose peony form.

OLD GLORY - White with dark pink edging with golden anthers and yellow filaments. Medium, wide open single to semidouble with sprayed stamens and ruffled petals. Upright growth. (U.S. 2009 - Nuccio's).

ONINSKI - White shading to Pink at edges with Gold anthers and White filaments. Small, single. E.

ORCHID MIST - Soft Orchid with soft Gold anthers and Cream filaments. Small to medium, single. Vigorous, upright growth. E. (U.S. 2013 - Gordy).

OUR LINDA - Pink. Medium, rose form double.

PAINTED DESERT - Pale Pink to near White, bordered Deep Rose Red. Large, single form. Slow, compact, stout and upright growth.

PALE MOONLIGHT - Pale Orchid Pink. Medium, semidouble with upright petals.

PAPAVER - ('Rosea Papaver'). Soft Pink. Small, single of cupped form.

PARADISE AUDREY - Light Pink shading to Pale Shell Pink. Miniature, semidouble. (Sport of Sasanqua 'Paradise Hilda').

PARADISE BABY JANE - White with Pink margins. Miniature, semidouble.

PARADISE BARBARA - White. Medium, single.

PARADISE BELINDA - Deep Pink shading to a Lighter Pink at center. Large, semidouble form.

PARADISE BLUSH - White with an outer Pink edge. Small, semidouble.

PARADISE DONNA - Pink. Medium, semidouble to rose form double.

PARADISE GILLIAN - White faintly edged Red. Medium, rose form double to formal double.

PARADISE GLOW - Deep Pink to Red on outer edge of petals, fading to a Light Pink center. Medium, single.

PARADISE HELEN - White, cup shaped with a faint Pink edge. Medium, anemone form.

PARADISE HILDA - Deep Pink. Small, anemone form.

PARADISE JENNI - White edged Pink. Medium, rose form double.

PARADISE JENNIFER - White broadly edged Deep Pink. Small, semidouble.

PARADISE JOAN - Deep Pink to Red. Small, rose form double.

PARADISE LEONIE - White with Pink edges. Medium, rose form double.

PARADISE LITTLE LIANE - White lightly edged with a Pink margin. Miniature, anemone.

PARADISE LOUISE - Light Pink. Medium, rose form double.

PARADISE ODETTE - Pink. Small, formal double to rose form double.

PARADISE PEARL - White with Light Pink petal margins. Medium, anemone to semidouble form.

PARADISE PETITE - Pale Pink. Miniature, rose form double; flower center is a combination of small petals and petaloids shading to Pink.

PARADISE SAYAKA - Pink outer edge shading to White at center. Small, single to semidouble form.

PARADISE SYLVIA - Deep Red. Miniature, single.

PARADISE VENESSA - White petals that are edged and toned Pink. Large, semidouble.

PARIS ALMOND - Blush Pink, paler inside. Medium, semidouble with turned-down petals.

PERKY - Pink. Medium, loose peony form with long, narrow twisted petals notched at end.

PETER HORENI - White with Pink outer bud petal and edge. Medium, single form with recurved petals and prominent stamens. Fragrant.

PINK ALLISON - Shell Pink. Small, formal double with eight rows of petals and two small petaloids cupping over center.

PINK BUTTERFLY - Bright Pink. Very large, unknown form. E-M. (U.S. - Parks).

PINK FLUFF - Pink shading to Light Pink toward center. Medium, semidouble with upright petals.

PINK LASSIE - Light Pink. Medium, peony form.

PINK PARASOL - Soft Pink with bright Gold anthers and Pink filaments. Medium, single. Vigorous, upright growth. E. (U.S. 2013 - Gordy).

PINK PRINCESS - Deep Rose Pink. Medium, semidouble.

PINK SERENADE - Deep Pink. Large, single. (U.S. - Parks).

PINK SNOW - Light Pink with Lavender trace. Small, semidouble.

PINK SNOW DWARF - Light Pink with Lavender trace with Yellow anthers and Yellow filaments. Small to medium, semidouble. Slow, spreading growth. E. (Sport of Sasanqua 'Pink Snow'). (U.S. 2013 - Howell).

PINK SURPRISE - Pink. Miniature, semidouble.

PLANTATION PINK - Pink. Medium to large, single.

PRATTEN'S PINK - See 'Shell Pink Special'.

PYGMY - Pink to White margined Deep Pink with back of petals Red with Purplish tint. Small, single. Dwarf growth.

QUEENSLANDER - Soft Silver Pink. Medium, rose form double opening from bud center.

RAINBOW - White with each petal bordered Red. Medium, single.

RANDELL CORBETT - White edged Pink. Medium, irregular semidouble to rose form double.

RED OCTOBER - Vibrant Neon Red with Deeper Neon Red shading at edges of petals. Small, anemone to loose peony. Vigorous, upright, dense growth. E-M. (U.S. 2016 - Glenn Read, Lucedale, MS).

RED WILLOW - Red. Small, semidouble.

REVEREND JIM JEFFREY - Deep Purple with Yellow anthers and Yellow filaments. Miniature, semidouble to loose peony form; the plant has a semi-dwarf form. Slow, upright, dense growth. E-M. (U.S. 2013 - Howell).

RIVERSIDE - White. Medium, single with crepe petals.

ROB'S PINK - Soft Pink. Small, semidouble.

ROBYN DUNNE - Soft Mauve tipped White. Medium, semidouble with notched petals.

ROSEA - Deep Rose Pink. Small, single.

ROSEA PAPAVER - See 'Papaver'.

ROSEMARY McGEOCH - Deep Pink, occasionally shading to Blush White. Large, single.

ROSETTE - Rose Pink. Miniature to small, rose form double.

ROSY MORN - Deep Rose. Small to medium, semidouble.

ROWENA GORDON - Bright Pink. Medium, semidouble with occasional petaloids.

RUBY DAVIDSON - White center, with Blush edges with deep Yellow anthers. Miniature to small, semidouble form. Average, spreading growth.

RUSSHAY - Orchid Pink shading to Deeper Pink toward center. Medium, semidouble.

SALLY JANE - White shading to Blush Shell Pink. Large, single.

SANDRA GAIL - Cyclamen Pink. Small, loose peony. Slow, bushy, dwarf growth. E-M. (Aus. 2006 - Albert Raymond and Gwenda Norris, Qld.).

SANGA-NO-TSU - See 'Mikawa-No-Tsu'.

SANTOZAKI (THREE FLOWERED) - Pink with White overtones and Darker Pink edges with Yellow anthers and Yellow filaments. Medium, single. Fast growth. E-M. (Japan).

SARITA - Purple Red shading toward center. Medium, semidouble.

SARREL - Pink with some White variegation. Small to medium, anemone form to peony form.

SASANQUA COMPACTA - White bordered Rose Red. Medium, single.

SATIN PINK - Light Pink. Small, single.

SEKIYÔ (SETTING SUN) - Bright Pink. Large, single. E. Fragrant.

SEPTEMBER SONG - Light Pink. Medium, single.

SETSUGEKKA - ('Fluted White'). White. Medium to large, semidouble. Cold hardy.

SEVEN OPALS - Shaded Pink. Medium, single.

SEVENTH DESIRE - Cerise Pink. Medium, semidouble. E-M.

SHARON ELIZABETH - Nearly identical flowers to original plant but with much larger plant. (Sport of Sasanqua 'Cleopatra').

SHELL PINK SPECIAL - ('Pratten's Pink'). Shell Pink. Medium, single.

SHELLEY MAREE - Pale Pink. Medium, peony form.

SHICHI-FUKUJIN - Rose Pink edged Mallow Pink. Medium to large, semidouble with crinkled petals.

SHIKOKU STARS - White. Unknown size, single with widely sprayed stamens. (Collected from the northern regions of Shikoku Island, Japan). (U.S. 2011 - Camellia Forest Nursery, Chapel Hill, NC).

SHINONOME - Flesh Pink. Medium to large, single.

SHIRLEY SPENCER - Light Pink. Medium, semidouble with fringed petals.

SILVER DOLLAR - White. Small, peony form.

SILVER SCREEN - Almost Pure White with a hint of Cream coloring at base. Medium, semidouble form.

SINGING RIVER - White shaded Pink. Medium, single.

SISTER ROSALIE - White with a Pink edge of some petals. Medium, semidouble to peony form.

SLIM 'N TRIM - Deep Rose Pink. Medium, single.

SNOW - See 'Mine-No-Yuki'.

SNOWFALL - White. Small, single.

SNOWFLAKE (SAWADA) - White. Medium, single.

SPREADY FREDDY - Deep Pink. Miniature, anemone. Low, spreading growth.

STEPHANIE GOLDEN - Hot Pink. Medium, semidouble.

STEPHANIE'S SOFT PINK - Pink, Small, formal double. Average, rounded, bushy growth. E. (Seedling of Sasanqua 'Stephanie Golden'). (U.S. 2019 - Bobby Green, Green Nurseries, Fairhope, AL).

STEPHANIE'S SUPER NOVA - White with Pink edges with Golden anthers and White filaments. Large, single. Average, bushy growth. E. (U.S. 2019 - Bobby Green, Green Nurseries, Fairhope, AL).

STRAWBERRY LIMEADE - Strawberry Pink with petals tipped Lime Green and a Lime Green center. Miniature, formal double. Vigorous, upright, dense growth. E-M. (U.S. 2012 - Glenn Read, Lucedale, MS).

SUNRISE SERENADE - Light Pink shading near White at the center. Medium, loose peony. Fragrant.

SUNSHINE - Cream color. Unknown size, single.

SUPER ROSEA - Rose Pink. Unknown size, single. (U.S. 1944 - Greenbrier Farms, Norfolk, VA).

SUSAN YELTON - Frosty Pink. Medium, semidouble.

SUSY DIRR - ('Green 99-031'). Bright Pink. Large, formal double. Rapid, bushy growth. (U.S. 1999 - Bobby Green, Green Nurseries, Fairhope, AL).

SWEET SHEREE - Magenta Rose. Medium, semidouble.

TAISHUHAI - White shading to Deep Red on edge. Medium to large, single.

TAKARA-AWASE (TREASURE TROVE) - Pink shaded White and bordered Pink. Unknown size, semidouble.

TANYA - Deep Rose Pink. Small, single.

TEENAGER - Rose Pink. Medium, single.

TELSTAR - White, inside Light Pink to Dark Pink with Rose border. Medium, semidouble with crinkled petals.

TEMPTATION - White Blushed Pink on petal edges. Medium, single.

THALIA - White flower with outer half suffused with Pink. Miniature, loose peony to rose form double. Dense, semi-dwarf growth. E-M. (U.S. 1996 - Bobby Green, Green Nurseries, Fairhope, AL).

THE HOBBIT - Creamy White. Small to medium, single to semidouble. Average, dense, medium growth. E. (N.Z. 2007 - Haydon).

THE SURREALIST - Glowing shade of Rose-Red. Large, unknown form. Fast, bushy, upright growth. E-L. (U.S. 2015 - Bobby Green, Green Nurseries, Fairhope, AL).

TINY PEARL - Light Pearl Pink. Miniature, semidouble.

TWINKLE TWINKLE - White, sometimes tinted Pink. Miniature, semidouble form with pointed petals, star shaped. (U.S. - Nuccio's).

VALE MIST - White. Small, semidouble.

VALE PRINCESS - Light Lavender Pink. Medium, semidouble with fluted petals.

VERITY BETTINE - Pink. Medium, single.

VIOLA SPRAGG - Rose to Red. Small, peony form.

VIOLET WEYMOUTH - Rose fading to Silvery Pink. Unknown size, semidouble.

WAVE CREST - White. Medium, single with long, fluted petals.

WEEPING MAIDEN - White fading to Bluish Pink at edge. Medium, single. Fragrant.

WEROONA - White deeply stained Rose with Deeper Rose under petals. Medium, semidouble.

WHITE CROSS - White. Medium, semidouble.

WHITE DOVES - See 'Mine-No-Yuki'.

S
P
E
C
I
E
S

WHITE FRILLS - White. Small, peony form.
WHITE QUEEN - White. Medium, single.
WHITE SATIN - White. Medium, single.
WIRLINGA GARLAND - Deep Pink. Medium, semidouble.
WIRLINGA SNOW DRIFT - White with Pink margins on the petals. Medium to large, semidouble.

YAE-ARARE - White edged Pink. Medium to large, single.
YANHONG - Deep Red to Red (RHS 53A or 53B) with Yellow anthers and Light Yellow filaments. Small, semidouble. Average, dense growth. M. (Hiemalis 'Shishi-Gashira' x Sasanqua Shinonome'). (China 2009 - Jian Guo Fei, Yonghong Hu and Ya-li Zhang, Shanghai Botanical Garden of Shanghai, China).

Species Vernalis

Origin unknown. There is evidence that this is not a separate species, but is a Non-Reticulata hybrid with Japonica and Sasanqua parentage.

BENI-SUZUME - Deep Pink shaded White. Small, rose form double.

DABNEY'S STAR - White with Pink blends. Large, semidouble. Vigorous, bushy, upright growth. M-L. (Vernalis 'Star Above Star' seedling). (U.S. 2012 - Bobby Green, Green Nurseries, Fairhope, AL).
DAWN - See 'Gin-ryu'.
DAWN SONG - Pink edged White. Small, full irregular semidouble.
DECEMBER ROSE - Rose Pink. Medium to large, semidouble. Vigorous, spreading, upright growth. E-L. (Not a Sasanqua). (U.S. 2002 - Nuccio's).

EGAO (SMILING FACE) - Deep Pink, Deeper Pink in the lower half of the petals with Yellow Stamens and Pale Yellow filaments. Medium to large, semidouble. Vigorous upright, somewhat spreading growth. M. (Not to be confused with Japonica 'Egao' - a separate variety). (Japan to U.S. 1977 - Nuccio's).
EGAO CORKSCREW - Pink. Small to medium, semidouble to loose peony form with ruffled petals. Average, spreading growth; distinctive zig-zag growth habit. M. (Sport of Vernalis 'Egao'). (Previously considered to be a non-retic hybrid). (U.S. 2000 - Nuccio's).
EGAO FORMAL PINK - Bright Pink. Medium, formal double with some blooms a spiral. Average, open, spreading growth. M-L. (Vernalis 'Egao' seedling). (U.S. 2011 - Bobby Green, Green Nurseries, Fairhope, AL).
EOS - White, lightly edged Pink. Medium to large, semidouble.

GIN-RYO - See 'Gin-ryu'.
GIN-RYU - ('Dawn'; 'Gin-ryo'). White, sometimes diffused Pink. Unknown size, semidouble.

GLAD TIDINGS - Deep Rose Pink to Red with Golden anthers and Yellow filaments. Small, semidouble. Rapid, erect, dense growth. E-L. (Seedling of Vernalis 'Yuletide'). (U.S. 1986 - Houghton S. Hall, San Anselmo, CA).
GRADY'S EGAO - Light Pink, veined, with fine White edge. Medium, semidouble.

HIMEKÔKI (PRINCESS KÔKI) - Deep Pink with Gold anthers. Medium, semidouble. M. (Japan 1974 - Tsuyoshi Muramatsu, Shimane Prefecture).
HIRYO - See 'Hiryû'.
HIRYO-NISHIKI - See 'Hiryû-Nishiki'.
HIRYÛ (FLYING DRAGON) - ('Hiryo'; 'Red Bird'). Deep Crimson Red. Small, rose form double.
HIRYÛ-NISHIKI (FLYING DRAGON BROCADE) - ('Hiryo-Nishiki'). Crimson splashed White. Unknown size, rose form double.
HOSHI-HIRYÛ - Crimson dotted White. (Sport of Vernalis 'Hiryû').

KAMAKURA-SHIBORI - Red shaded White. Small, single.
KOTSUZUMI (SMALL DRUM) - Peach red, Small, single. (Japan 1977 - Matsumura and Yatsuhiro Maeda, Inasa Town, Shizuoka Prefecture).
KYO-NISHIKI - White striped Pink. Unknown size, single.

MONDEL - See 'Pink Yuletide'.

PINK YULETIDE - Dark Pink at center quickly shading to a Lighter Pink with Yellow anthers and Yellow filaments. Small to medium, single with seven petals. Vigorous, upright growth. M-L. Fragrant. (Sport of Vernalis 'Yuletide'). (U.S. 2011 - Monrovia Nurseries, Azusa, CA).
PINK-A-BOO - See 'Pink Yuletide'.

RED BIRD - See 'Hiryû'.

RYÛKÔ (DRAGON LIGHT) - Deep Red with Yellow anthers and Yellow filaments. Small, single. Fast growth. M-L. (Japan 1972 - Katsuhiro Maeda, Hanamatsu City, Shizuoka Prefecture).

SAYOHIME (PRINCESS OF SAYO) - Pink with Yellow anthers and Yellow filaments. Small, single. (Japan 1973 - Saburô Kumazawa & Mamoru Oda, Hirado City, Nagasaki Prefecture).

SHIBORI-EGAO (VARIEGATED SMILING FACE) - Deep Rose blotched White. Medium to large, unknown form. Variegated form of 'Egao'.

SHIBORI EGAO CORKSCREW - Pink mottled White variation of Vernalis 'Egao Corkscrew'. (Previously considered to be a non-retic hybrid). (U.S. 2006 - Nuccio's).

STAR ABOVE STAR - White shading to Lavender Pink at edge. Medium, semidouble.

SUNBEAM - Rose Pink with lighter tones on the petals with Yellow anthers and Yellow filaments. Large, semidouble. Low, spreading growth . (U.S. 2010 - Nuccio's Nurseries, Altadena, CA).

WINIFRED HILLS - Purple Red. Medium, anemone.

YULETIDE - Orange Red. Small, single. Average, upright, dense growth. E. Cold hardy. (Seedling of Vernalis 'Hiryu'). (U.S. 1963 - Nuccio's Nurseries).

YULETIDE CANDLE - Brilliant waxy Red. Large, single. Vigorous, upright growth. E-M. (Vernalis 'Yuletide' seedling). (U.S. 2014 - Bobby Green, Green Nurseries, Fairhope, AL).

YULETIDE SPIRIT - Deep Coral Red. Large, single. Dense, upright, spreading growth. (Vernalis 'Yuletide' seedling). (U.S. 2000 - Bobby Green, Green Nurseries, Fairhope, AL).

Species Wabisuke

AKA-WABISUKE - See 'Beni-Wabisu'

AZUMA WABISUKE - See 'Kocho-Wabisuke'.

BENI-WABISUKE - ('Aka-Wabisuke'). Red. Small, single. E.

CAMPANULATA BICOLOR - Pink shading to Rose. Small, single. Vigorous, bushy growth. L.

CAMPANULATA SUBUVIDULA - Scarlet. Small, single. Vigorous, bushy growth. L.

CAMPANULATA WHITE - White. Small, single bell form. Vigorous, bushy growth. L.

FUIRI-KOCHO-WABISUKE - Variegated leaf form of 'Kocho-Wabisuke'.

FUKURIN WABISUKE - Light Pink bordered White. Small, single. Medium, upright growth. E-M.

HATSU-KARI - See 'Shibori-Wabisuke'.

HANA WABISUKE - Rose Pink. Small, single. Medium, upright growth. E-M. Fragrant.

ICHIKO-WABISUKE - Red with Light Yellow anthers and Whitish filaments. Small, single - campanulate. E-M. (Japan 1980's - Garden of Ueda Toshirô, Aichi-ken).

JUDITH - See 'Taro-kaja'

KOCHO-WABISUKE - ('Azuma-Wabisuke'; 'Easter Wabisuke'). Light Red. Small, single of trumpet form. Vigorous, compact growth. E-M.

LITTLE PRINCESS - White shaded Blush Pink. Small, single.

MOMOIRO-WABISUKE - ('Tokiiro-Wabisuke'). Soft Pink. Small, single of trumpet form. E-M.

OTOHIME - Rose Pink often blotched White. Small, single. Medium, upright, compact growth. E-M.

SAOTOME - Light Pink with White stamens. Small, single with fluted petals. E-M. (Cultivar currently under this name in US is 'Sukiya').

SHIBORI-WABISUKE - ('Hatsu-Kari'). Reddish Pink and White. Small, single.

SHIRO-WABISUKE - ('Wabisuke White'). White. Small, single cupped form. Slow, compact growth. E.

SHOWA WABISUKE - (Saluenensis 'Apple Blossom'). White toned Light Pink. Small, single. Medium, upright growth. Very fragrant.

SPRING SONG - Light Pink with Light Yellow anthers and Light Yellow filaments. Small, single; flowers open to a trumpet shape. E. Cold hardy. (Wabisuke 'Sukiya' seedling). (U.S. 2014 - Camellia Forest, Chapel Hill, NC).

SUKIYA - Pinkish White. Small, single. Vigorous, open growth. E-M.

SUKIYA LITTLE PRINCESS - Very Light Pink; stamens sometimes have pale anthers. Small, single. Average, upright, open growth. E-M.

TARO-KAJA - ('Judith'). Pink. Small, single bell form.

TOKIIRO-WABISUKE - See 'Momoiro-Wabisuke'

Camellia Species

The genus Camellia is endemic to Southeastern Asia. It is a large genus belonging to the tea family or theaceae. Professor Sealy (1958) comprehensively studied the 81 known species and grouped them into 12 sections. Ming (2000) followed Sealy's system placing the number of species at 199. Professor Chang (1998). worked with more plant material in his investigation. He estimated the number of species to be 280. More recently Gao, Parks and Du (2005) described 198 species in their book, Collected *Species of the Genus Camellia, An Illustrated Outline*. New species still are being discovered in remote areas of Asia, so the actual number is still in flux. Listed below are the species grown in the English-speaking world, particularly in the United States of America.

AMPLEXICAULIS - Purplish Red. Small, single. Leaves oblong-elliptical and very large. Blooms summer and autumn and can flower all year under controlled conditions.

ASSIMILIS - Flowers, White; leaves sharply Red, elliptic, 2 1/2" x 7/8"; a shrub. Hong Kong.

AZALEA WEI (Chinese Name - 'Changii Ye'). Common name Camellia Azalea. Flower bright Red. Single. Blooms summer to autumn and can bloom continuously. Leaves long and narrow.

BREVISTYLA - Flowers, White; leaves small, elliptic, 1 5/8" x 5/8". A slender tree growing to 25'. Taiwan.

CAUDATA - Flowers, White; leaves sharp pointed elliptic, 3" x 3/4". An erect shrub becoming a small tree. Northeastern India, Northern Burma, Vietnam, Island of Hainan, Taiwan.

CHEKIANGOLEOSA - Flowers, Red, large (3 1/2" - 4 1/2"). funnel shaped; leaves large serrate on upper half of margin. Small tree 7' - 10'. Southern China.

CHRYSANTHA - See C. nitidissima variety nitidissima. Southern China.

CHRYSANTHOIDES - Bright Yellow. Tiny (about 1 ½ inches in diameter), single bloom. Heavily ribbed foliage. Medium, upright, bushy upright growth. The foliage emerges with a strong Burgundy Red color and the large leaves have strongly impressed veins. Spring bloom. Southern Guangxi, China.

CHUNII - Light Salmon. Small, single. Fast, upright, open growth. M-L. (U.S. 2012 - from seeds collected in Sichuan Province, China by Richard Schulhof and Tim Thibault propagated by Nuccio's).

CONFUSA - Flowers White with 5 - 6 petals, 1 1/4" - 1 1/2" in diameter. Blooms December to February. Leaves elliptic, 2" - 2 1/4" long and 3/4" - 1 1/4" wide, Deep Green. China, Thailand, Laos and Burma.

CONNAT - Flowers, White; leaves oblong-elliptic with blunt apex, 3 1/2" x 1 1/4". A shrub becoming a small spreading tree up to 28'. Siam.

CORDIFOLIA - Tiny White bloom, slightly fragrant. Soft textured small foliage. Spreading growth. M-L.

COSTEI - White. Miniature, single with 5 petals. Average, upright, soft growth. Serrated, leathery, oblong-elliptic leaves are 2" x 3" long and 1/2" x 1/ 1/2" wide. Foliage hangs down giving the plant a weeping appearance. M. (Guangxi, Guizhou, Hubei, Hunan, Sichuan, Yunnan Provinces, China - 1500' - 4500' altitude).

CRAPNELLIANA - Flowers, White, 3" - 4" in diameter; leaves elliptic with blunt apex, edges slightly denticulated, 4" x 2". A shrub becoming a small tree up to 22'. Only one tree was found (1904). and this has now disappeared. Hong Kong.

CUSPIDATA - Flowers, White; leaves pointed and narrow-elliptic, 2 1/2" x 3/4", leathery. Grows into a tall shrub. Southern China.

DRUPIFERA - Flowers White 6 - 7 petals, 3 1/2" in diameter. Blooms November and December. Leaves oblong-elliptic 2 3/4" long and Dark Green. Cold hardy. Vietnam.

EDITHAE - Rose Red. Medium, single to formal double. Dark Green heavily ribbed leaves. Upright, bushy growth. L.

EUPHLEBIA - Flowers small, Yellow. Leaves Deep Green, elliptical, long heavily veined. A shrub 6 ft. high. Indo-China.

FLUVIATILES - Flowers White 1" in diameter, single (five or six petals). followed by small Green to Red fruit. Leaves Pale Green long and narrow. Average, erect growth. E. Guangdong, Guangxi, Hainan provinces, China, Northeast India, North Myanmar.

FORRESTII - Flowers, White, fragrant and very small; leaves pointed at both ends, elliptic, 1'' x 5/8''. A shrub or small tree. Southern China and Vietnam.

FRATERNA - Flowers, small, White or whitish lilac and fragrant; leaves pointed-elliptic, 2 1/2'' x 1 1/4'' with serrations Black tipped. Grows into a tall shrub. Central China.

FURFURACEA - Flowers, White, fragrant; leaves oblong-elliptic, 4 1/2'' x 1 5/8''. A shrub growing to 9'. Vietnam, Island of Hainan.

GAUDICHAUDI - White. Small wavy petaled, single. Thick foliage with Cinnamon color bark. Vigorous, upright growth. M-L.

GIGANTOCARPA - Flowers White, 6 - 7 petals, 4" - 4 3/4" in diameter. Blooms November to January. Leaves elliptic to oblong-elliptic, large, 3 1/2" - 6" long and 2" - 2 3/4" wide, shining Yellow-Green. Large seed capsules. Kwangsi, China.

GLABSIPETALA - White toned Pink. Medium, single to semidouble. Small reticulata-like leaves, Upright growth. E-M.

GRANTHAMIANA - Flowers, White, very large; leaves oblong-elliptic with pointed apex, leathery, shallow serrations, 4'' x 1 1/2''. The only known existing wild plant is now a small tree 10' high. Hong Kong.

GRIJSII - Flowers, White sometimes fragrant; leaves elliptic and sharply pointed, edges sharply serrulate, 3 1/4'' x 1 1/4''. A shrub up to 9'. Eastern China.

GRIJSII 'GRIJSII SELECT' - Larger flower than Grijsii with darker foliage. Fragrant. (U.S. - Nuccio's).

GRIJSII 'ZHENZHUCHA' - White. Miniature, formal double to rose form with crinkled petals. Anise-like fragrant (Nuccio's).

HANDELII - Flowers 1" - 1 1/2" in diameter, single. White. Leaves are small 1" oblong with a slight Pink/Brown look. Upright. M. Guizhou, Hunan and Jiangxi Provinces, China.

HIEMALIS - This species identified by Nakai is unknown in its wild form. It closely resembles C. sasanqua except the blossoming period is much later. It was originally imported into Japan from Shanghai. It is a shrub growing into a small tree and is presently known only in its garden forms developed in China, Japan and the United States.

HONGKONGENSIS - Flowers, large, crimson, with petals partly velvety on the back; leaves elliptic and sharply pointed, leathery, Dark Shining Green and smooth above, Bright Green below, almost smooth edge, 3 1/2'' x 1''. A shrub becoming a tree up to 33'. Hong Kong.

HOZANENSIS - Flowers Red, 5 - 6 petals, 1 1/4" - 1 1/2" in diameter. Blooms February to April. Leaves oblong-elliptic to elliptic, 2 3/4" - 3 1/8" long and 1 1/2" - 2" wide. Deep Green. Japan, Okinawa, Taiwan.

IRRAWADIENSIS - Flowers, White; leaves elliptic, 4'' x 1 1/4''. A tall openly branched shrub, growing to 22'. Burma.

JAPONICA - Flowers rosy Red, medium sized; leaves elliptic-oblong with sharp apex 3 1/4'' x 1 1/2''. A shrub growing into a tree to 50'. Japan, Liu Kiu Islands, Korean Archipelago, Eastern China.

KISSI - Flowers, White sometimes fragrant; leaves narrow elliptic, pointed, serrulate for one-quarter to two-thirds the length from the apex, 2 5/8'' x 1''. A shrub growing to a tree up to 40'. Northeast India, Nepal, Burma, Southern China, Island of Hainan, Vietnam.

LAPIDEA - Orchid Pink frosted lighter in the center. Medium, single bloom. Narrow serrated leaves. Upright growth. M-L.

LONGICARPA - Flowers White, cup shaped, very small, single with Golden stamens and waxy petals. Leaves elliptic, 2 1/3" - 2 3/4" long and 3/4" - 1 1/4" wide. Shrub grows to tree 10'. high. Yunnan and Guangxi Provinces, China.

LUTCHUENSIS - Flower, small, White; leaves small, sharp pointed, elliptic to oblong, 1 1/4'' x 1/2''. A shrub growing to 10'. Fragrant. Ryukyu Islands, Japan.

MALIFLORA - Flowers, soft Pink, tinted and margined Rose Red, small semidouble; leaves pointed elliptic, 1 7/8'' x 1''. A shrub growing into a small tree. Central China.

MEIOCARPA - White. Small, single with incurved stamens toward the flower center.

MIYAGII - Flowers, White and small; leaves medium Green, margins mostly crenate to serrate, 2 1/2'' x 1 1/2''. Fragrant. Okinawa.

NITIDISSIMA - The full botanical name is C. nitidissima variety nitidissima (formerly called C. chrysantha). Small single to semidouble, Golden Yellow with shiny, heavy textured petals. Vigorous, upright, open growth with very large, heavily ribbed, distinctive foliage. M.

NOKOENSIS - Flowers, small, White; leaves sharply pointed-elliptic, 1 1/2'' x 1/2''. A shrub growing into a small bushy tree up to 25'. Taiwan.

OBTUSIFOLIA - Flowers small, White, single. E. Develops Cinnamon colored bark with age. Jiangxi, Hubei, Zhejiang, Fujian and Guangdong Provinces, China.

OCTAPETALA - Flower, Pale Yellow, 1" - 2" across, single. Leaves large and distinctive with a glossy Light Green-Grayish cast. The Brown fruits are massive and are the size of oranges and most seeds germinate. E. Southwestern Zhejiang Province into western Fujian Province, China

OLEIFERA - Flowers, White, fragrant, elliptic, serrulate, apex pointed, 2 1/2'' x 1 1/8''. A shrub becoming a small tree up to 22'. Eastern, Central and Southern China, Hong Kong, Island of Hainan, Vietnam, Laos, Cochinchina, Burma, Northeast India, Thailand.

PARVIFLORA - Flowers, White and very small; leaves narrow-elliptic with blunt apex, edges only slightly serrulate, 2 1/4'' x 3/4''. A shrub growing to 10' tall. Island of Hainan.

PARVILIMBA - Flowers tiny White or flushed with Red, single; leaves perhaps the smallest leaves in the genus. Shrub grows to about 3' meter tall. M. Sichuan Province, China.

PITARDII - Flowers, Rose to White; leaves, elliptic and pointed, regularly serrulate, 3 1/2'' x 1 1/2''. An open branched shrub.

PITARDII VARIETY 'YUNNANICA' - Flowers Deep Pink to White, 5 - 6 petals, 2" - 2 3/4" in diameter. Flowering January to March. Leaves oblong-elliptic to narrow-elliptic, 2 1/4" - 4 1/4" long and 3/4" -1 1/4" wide.

POLYODONTA - Flowers Deep Red, 5 - 7 petals 2 3/4" - 4" in diameter. Blooms February to March. Leaves oblong-elliptic 4" - 5 1/2" long and 1 1/2" - 2 1/4" wide, shining Deep Green with pointed serration. Guangxi Province, China.

PUNICEIFLORA - Very small Pink single. Medium, upright, open growth. Older branches smooth and Gray. E-M.

PURPUREA - Small single Dark Red. Dark Green foliage. Upright, compact growth. M.

RETICULATA - Flowers Rose colored more than 3'' in diameter; leaves broad elliptic with pointed apex, edges serrulate, 4 1/2'' x 1 7/8''. A loosely branched shrub becoming a tree up to 50'. Grows in thickets and open pine forests at altitudes of 6,000' to 9,000'. Southern China.

ROSAEFLORA - Flowers, about 1 1/4'', Pinkish Rose; leaves elliptic, bluntly pointed, 2 1/4'' x 7/8''. A shrub becoming a small tree. Habitat unknown but probably China.

ROSAEFLORA 'GRANDE' - Blush Pink. Small to medium, weeping growth. Vigorous, upright, open, spreading growth. M-L. (A selected Rosaeflora seedling with larger flowers and leaves). M-L. (U.S. - Nuccio's).

RUSTICANA - Subspecies of Japonica.

SALICIFOLIA - Flowers, White with a slight perfume; leaves narrow-elliptic with a sharp apex, 3'' x 7/8''. A shrub growing into a small tree. Hong Kong and Taiwan.

SALUENENSIS - White flushed with Pink or Pale Rose Pink to Deep Rose Pink with diameters up to 2''; leaves elliptic, narrow and pointed, 2'' x 3/4''. A very compact much branched shrub growing to 15'. Southern China.

SASANQUA - Flowers, White; leaves small elliptic, pointed, thinly leathery, 1 1/4'' x 1/2''. A densely leafy shrub becoming a small tree up to 15'. Southern Japan and Liu Kiu Islands.

SEMISERRATA - Flowers, Red about 2 1/2'' in diameter; leaves elliptic-oblong, 6'' x 2 3/8''. Description of plant not given. Eastern China.

SINENSIS - Flowers, White, leaves elliptic with rounded apex, size quite variable according to the cultivar, maximum reported 5 3/4'' x 2''. These leaves constitute the tea of commerce. A shrub growing into a tree up to 53'. China, Tibet, Taiwan, Japan, Laos, Vietnam, Siam, Burma.

SINENSIS (89#3) - Small White single with elongated flower stem and soft Green reticulated leaves. Medium, upright growth. E-M.

SINENSIS 'BLACK SINENSIS' - Very Dark Maroonish Green foliage with small Maroonish Pink flowers. Rounded and compact. E-M.

SINENSIS 'MADISON TEA' - Light Pink. Miniature, single. Vigorous, compact growth. Medium crinkled leaf tea. E. (U.S. 2008 - CamelliaShop, Savannah, GA).

SINENSIS 'MOUNDY' - A sinensis seedling with a mounding and more compact growth than other sinensis species. The White flower is slightly larger than other sinensis. E-M. (U.S. - Nuccio's).

SINENSIS 'OLD SAVANNAH TEA' - White. Miniature, single. Vigorous, upright, spreading growth. Large leaf tea. E. (U.S. 2008 - CamelliaShop, Savannah, GA).

SINENSIS 'QUEEN BEES TEA' - White. Miniature, single. Vigorous, upright growth. Large leaf tea. E. (U.S. 2008 - CamelliaShop, Savannah, GA).

SUBINTEGA - Intense Rose Red small flower with narrow long foliage. Slow, very bushy growth. M-L.

SYNAPTICA - Single White flower with Golden stamens. Fragrant, strong upright bush. E.

SYNAPTICA 'MAGNOLIA MOON' - White. Very large, unknown form. Very fragrant. Vigorous, spreading growth. M. (U.S. 2008 - CamelliaShop, Savannah, GA).

TALIENSIS - Flowers, White; leaves elliptic with rounded apex 5'' x 2 1/2''. A shrub growing into a small tree about 22'. Southern China.

TENUIFLORA - Flowers White, 5 - 6 petals, very small about 1 1/4" in diameter. Blooms in October to December. Leaves elliptic to oblong elliptic 1 1/2" - 2" long and 3/4" - 1 1/4" wide. Bright shiny Green. Guangxi and Yunnan Provinces, China.

TENUIVALIS - Light Pink toned lighter. Medium, single. Leaves are Dark Green small to medium. M-L. Sichuan Province, China.

TRANSARISANENSIS - Flowers, White; leaves small and pointed but with blunt apex, 1 1/2'' x 1/2''. A shrub growing into a small tree. Taiwan.

TRANSNOKOENSIS - Flowers, White with buds tinted Red, very small; leaves narrow and tapering to a blunt apex, 1 1/2'' x 1/2''. A shrub growing into a small tree. Taiwan.

TRICHOCLADE - Flowers White with outer edges soft Pink. Five petals 5/8" - 3/4" in diameter with long stamens. Blooms March to April. Leaves oblong-ovate to ovate, 3/4" - 1 3/8" long and 3/8" - 3/4" wide. Shrub grows to a tree with spreading branches. Chekiang and Taiwan.

TRUNCATA - Flowers White, 5 petals 1 3/4" in diameter single. Leaves ovate 1/2" in length. Compact. L. Yunnan Province, China.

TSAII - Flowers, small White with prominent three pointed stigma; leaves pointed, long narrow elliptic, 2 1/2'' x 3/4''. A shrub growing into a small tree. Fragrant. Southern China, Burma, Vietnam.

TUNGHINENSIS - Pale Yellow. Small, single. Glossy, medium-size foliage. Average, upright, fairly shrubby growth. M-L. Guangxi Province, China.

VERNALIS - Origin unknown. Possibly a hybrid of C. Japonica x C. Sasanqua.

VIETNAMENSIS - Flowers, White. Small tree 16' - 26'. Vietnam.

WABISUKE - Origin unknown. Reported that it is a subspecies of Japonica.

YUNNANENSIS - Flowers, White, variable in size; leaves elliptic with sharp apex, 2 1/2'' x 1 1/4''. A shrub growing to 22'. Grows at altitudes between 5,000' and 10,000' and flowers July to November. Fragrant. Southern China.

YUSHSIENENSIS - Flowers White, 5 - 7 petals, 2" - 2 3/4" in diameter. Blooms November to January. Fragrant. Leaves elliptic to broad elliptic, 2 1/4" - 3 1/2" long and 1 1/4" - 1 1/2" wide, Yellowish Green. Hunan. Province, China.

255

Cold-Hardy Camellias

Hybridizers, Dr. William Ackerman, Dr. Clifford Parks, and Longwood Gardens have introduced many camellias that are cold-hardy, which has extended the range where camellias can be grown successfully. Following are lists of cold-hardy camellias included in this edition of Camellia Nomenclature:

Japonicas

'Amy Maryott'
'April Blues'
'April Blush'
'April Dawn'
'April Kiss'
'April Melody'
'April Pink'
'April Remembered'
'April Rose'
'April Snow'
'April Tryst'
'Aunt Jetty'
'Bebe Woodward'
'Berenice Body'
'Betty Sette'
'Blood of China'
'Bob Hope'
'C. M. Wilson'
'Carlton Maryott'
'Charles Minarik'
'Classic Pink''
'Cream Puff'
'Debutante'
'Donckelarii'
'Doris Stone'
'Dorothy Minarik'
'Dorothy's Folly'
'Dr. Tinsley'
'Eleanor Hagood'
'Elegans (Chandler)'
'Ernestine Law'
'Eyes of March'
'Flame'
'Frost Queen'
'Gail Phelan'
'Glen 40'
'Governor Mouton'
'Harbor Lights'
'Herme'
'Jarvis Red'
'Jerry Hill'
'Korean Fire'
'Korean Snow'
'Kumasaka'
'Kuro Delight'
'Lady Clare'
'Lady Vansittart'
'Lady Vansittart Red'
'Lela Ashley'
'Lelia Maryott'

'Leucantha'
'Lib Scott'
'Lil Symonds'
'Longwood Centennial'
'Longwood Valentine'
'Maiden of Great Promise'
'Marie Bracey'
'Marie Goodlett'
'Mary Allen Sargent'
'Mathotiana'
'Miss Fort Walton Beach'
'Molly Hamilton'
'Momoiro Bokuhan'
'Nancy K'
'Paulette Goddard'
'Pink Perfection'
'Pink Ribbon'
'Pink Star'
'Potomac Pillar'
'Purity'
'R. L. Wheeler'
'Rampey E. Thomas'
'Red Aurora'
'Red Jade'
'Reland Westgate'
'Reverend John G. Drayton'
'River Farm Beauty'
'Sarah Catherine'
'Snow Lady'
'Spring Triumph'
'Spring's Promise'
'Squadron Leader Astin'
'Stellar Sunrise'
'Susan Pilgrim'
'Sweet Lara'
'Ten Below'
'Tommie Bowman'
'Tricolor (Siebold)'
'Tricolor (Siebold) Red'
'White Empress'
'White Queen'

Reticulata Hybrids

'Crimson Candles'
'Pixie Dust'
'Scarlet Temptation'

Non-Reticulata Hybrids

'Arctic Dawn'
'Ashton's Ballet'
'Ashton's Cameo'
'Ashton's High Rise'
'Ashton's Pink'
'Ashton's Pink Cloud'
'Ashton's Prelude'
'Ashton's Pride'
'Ashton's Red Bell'
'Ashton's Snow'
'Ashton's Supreme'
'Autumn Pink Icicle'
'Autumn Spirit'
'Carolina Moonmist'
'Elaine Lee'
'Fairweather Favorite'
'Fire 'n Ice'
'Helen O'Connor'
'Ice Follies'
'Londontowne'
'Londontowne Blush'
'Maroon Mist'
'Mason Farm'
'Pink Icicle'
'Polar Ice'
'Pumphrey's Pride'
'Red Fellow'
'Snow Flurry'
'Spring Cardinal'
'Spring Circus'
'Spring Frill'
'Survivor'
'Twilight Glow'
'Winter Rouge'
'Winter's Beauty'
'Winter's Beauty Chartreuse'
'Winter's Charm'
'Winter's Darling'
'Winter's Dream'
'Winter's Fire'
'Winter's Hope'

'Winter's Interlude'
'Winter's Joy'
'Winter's Moonlight'
'Winter's Peony'
'Winter's Red Rider'
'Winter's Rose'
'Winter's Snowman'
'Winter's Star'
'Winter's Star Light'
'Winter's Sunset'

Sasanqua Hiemails & Vernalis

'Agners O. Solomon'
'Cleopatra'
'Hana-jiman'
'Jean May'
'Setsugekka'
'Showa-no sakae'
'Yuletide'

Species Oleifera

'Lu Shan Snow'
'Plain Jane'

Species Wabisuke

'Spring Song'

Species

C. Drupifera

Fragrant Camellias

Beginning in the early 1960's, efforts were made using *C. lutchuensis* to incorporate floral fragrance into commercially acceptable cultivars. Dr. Robert K. Cutter of Berkeley, California was a pioneer in this work. Unfortunately his untimely death curtailed his breeding program before completion. He did, however, introduce two fragrant backcross hybrids, 'Alice K. Cutter' and 'Virginia W. Cutter'. Kenneth Hallstone, of Lafayette, California took over and progressed with the work of Cutter for several years, introducing 'Scented Sun'. Toichi Domoto was another of the early U. S. pioneers, introducing 'Scented Gem' in 1983. William L. Ackerman, in his book, *Beyond the Camellia Belt* (2007, p. 130). states "I was also working along similar lines at the time. A few early introductions included 'Fragrant Pink', 'Ack-Scent' and 'Ack-Scent Spice'. My breeding goal of fragrance came to an abrupt halt in the late 1970's. A series of severe winters from 1976 through 1980 in the Washington, D. C. metropolitan area caused wide devastation of local camellia plants. An emphasis toward developing cold-hardy camellias became the full time goal of our breeding program. However, work on floral fragrance continues with J. Finley of Whangerei, New Zealand, who began breeding scented camellias in 1970 and has continued through to the present.... Others 'down under' have also been busy including M. Baker, R. Garnett, and G. Hooper of Australia."

Following are lists of fragrant camellias included in this edition of Camellia Nomenclature:

Japonicas

'Amy Maryot'
'Apricot Muffin'
'Aroma'
'Athena'
'B. C. Goodman'
'Barbara Mary'
'Bessie Dickson'
'Brian Anderton'
'Buddy'
'Candy Stripe'
'Carol's Katie'
'Colonial Lady'
'Cucamonga'
'Fragrance'
'Fragrant'
'Fragrant Boutonniere'
'Fragrant Frill'
'Fragrant Girl'
'Fragrant Jonquil'
'Fragrant Star'
'Fragrant Striped'
'Grantham's Fragrant'
'Heaven Scent'
'Heavenly Fragrance'
'High Noon'
'Iced Fragrance'
'Jim Finlay's Fragrant'
'Kramer's Beauty'
'Kramer's Delight'
'Kramer's Supreme'
'Kramer's Supreme Var.'
'Nioi Fubuki'
'Odoratissima'
'Party Girl'
'Pete's Fragrant Pink'
'Pink Mermaid'
'Plumfield White'

'Prime Fragrance'
'Pristine Fragrance'
'Scentasia'
'Scented Fireglow'
'Scented Treasure'
'Scentimental'
'Scentsation'
'Serenade'
'Sweet Bonair'
'Sweet Delight'
'Taffeta Tutu'
'Tahiti'
'Vernice Ann'
'Westlake Fragrant Lotus'
'White Mermaid'

Reticulata Hybrids

'Lilly Marie Nichols'

Non-Reticulata Hybrids

'Ack-scent'
'Ack-scent Spice'
'Adrianne Ila'
'Allure'
'Aromatica'
'Ashton's Fragrant Jewel'
'Autumn Fragrance'
'Bow Bells'
'Bridal Fragrance'
'Choice Fragrance'
'Cinnamon Cindy'
'Cinnamon Scentsation'
'Dame Silvia'
'Daughter's Red'
'Debo'

'Dr. Robert E. Cutter'
'Drifting Scent'
'Eliza Lockley'
'Esme Spence'
'Fairy Blush'
'Fimbriated Fragrance'
'Fragrance of Sleeve'
'Fragrant Asia'
'Fragrant Burgundy'
'Fragrant Cascade'
'Fragrant Concubine'
'Fragrant Dream'
'Fragrant Drift'
'Fragrant Fairies'
'Fragrant Genesis'
'Fragrant Jewel'
'Fragrant Joy'
'Fragrant Lady'
'Fragrant Legend'
'Fragrant One'
'Fragrant Pathfinder'
'Fragrant Pink'
'Fragrant Pink Improved'
'Fragrant Pixies'
'Fragrant Ripple'
'Fragrant Ruby'
'Good Fragrance'
'Grand Fragrance'
'Hallstone Spicy'
'Heartwood Salute'
'High Fragrance'
'Hiraethlyn'
'Hyperscent'
'I Am Fragrant'
'Ice Melted'
'Intoscent'
'Jinhua's Jade Tray'
'Julie's Own'
'Just Peachy'

'Kerry Elizabeth'
'Koto-No-Kaori'
'Liddybow'
'Lisa Beasley'
'Little Lisa Leigh'
'Mandy'
'Marjorie's Dream'
'Marna'
'Masterscent'
'Maxiscent'
'Minato-No-Akebono'
'Minato-No-Haru'
'Miss Western Hills'
'Nice Fragrance'
'Nymph'
'Paddy's Perfumed'
'Perfumed Pearl'
'Pink Crepe'
'Pink Posy'
'Pomo Mound'
'Quintessence'
'Radiating Fragrance'
'Salab
'Salut'
'Santa Cruz'
'Scented Gem'
'Scented Snow'
'Scented Sun'
'Scented Swirl'
'Scentuous'
'Scintillating Fragrance'
'Sleeping Scent'

'Smooth Fragrance'
'Softly Fragrant'
'Souza's Pavlova'
'Spring Mist'
'Superscent'
'Sweet Deborah Jane'
'Sweet Emily Kate'
'Sweet Emma'
'Sweet October'
'Sweet Scented'
'Sweet Scentsation'
'Togetherness'
'Toni Finlay's Fragrant'
'Top Fragrance'
'Transpink'
'Vernal Breeze'
'White Elf'
'Whiteout'
'Winter Rouge'
'Winter's Beauty'
'Yummy Fragrance

Species Oleifera
'Lu Shan Snow'

Species Sasanquas
'Carolyn Anderton'
'Coolgardie Star'
'Daydream Believer'
'Fragrant Sweet'
'Mondel'

'Peter Horeni'
'Sekiyo'
'Sunrise Serenade'
'Weeping Maiden'

Species Vernalis
'Pink Yuletide'

Species Wabisuke
'Hana Wabisuke'
'Showa Wabisuke'

Species
Cordifolia
Forrestii
Fraterna
Fukuracea
Grijsii
Grijsii 'Grijsii Select'
Grijsii 'Zhenzhucha'
Kissi
Lutchuensis
Miyagii
Oleifera
Synaptica
Synaptica 'Magnolia Moon'
Tsaii
Yunnanensis
Yushienensis